A History of
The Expansion of Christianity

Volume III
THREE CENTURIES OF ADVANCE

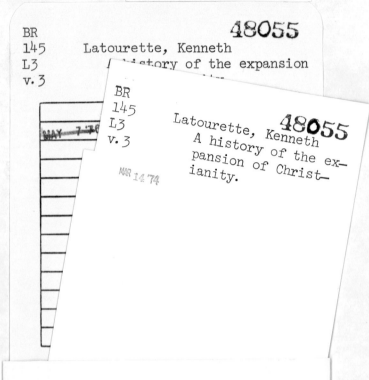

A History of
THE EXPANSION OF CHRISTIANITY
(*Volume III*)

THREE CENTURIES
OF ADVANCE
A.D. 1500-A.D. 1800

by

KENNETH SCOTT LATOURETTE

THE PATERNOSTER PRESS

ISBN: 0 85364 116 1

THREE CENTURIES OF ADVANCE

Copyright © 1939, 1967 by Harper and Row, Publishers
Published by special arrangement with Harper and Row, Publishers,
New York
Printed in the United States of America
This edition is distributed by The Paternoster Press
Paternoster House, 3 Mount Radford Crescent
Exeter, Devon, by arrangement with
The Zondervan Publishing House, Grand Rapids, Mich., U.S.A.

This Edition 1971

AUSTRALIA:
Emu Book Agencies Pty., Ltd., 511 Kent Street, Sydney, N.S.W.

SOUTH AFRICA:
Oxford University Press, P.O. Box 1141, Oxford House,
11, Buitencingle Street, Cape Town

In memory of

HARLAN PAGE BEACH

1854–1933

Contents

Chapter I

INTRODUCTORY. Movements Characterizing the New Age: the Rise of Absolute Monarchies in Europe, Scientific Discoveries, the Commercial Revolution, the Geographic Discoveries and Settlements by Europeans, the Revival in Western Christianity Expressing Itself Through the Rise of Protestantism and the Roman Catholic Reformation. THE NEW MISSIONARY MOVEMENT: FEATURES AND ORGANIZATION. I

Chapter II

EUROPE, NORTH AFRICA, AND THE NEAR EAST. 55

Chapter III

SPANISH AMERICA. General Features of the Spanish Conquest and of Spanish Missions; the West Indies; Mexico; New Mexico and Arizona; Texas; California; Florida and Georgia; Central América; Venezuela; New Granada; Negroes; Peru; Chile; Paraguay and the Argentine. 83

Chapter IV

PORTUGUESE AMERICA. 160

Chapter V

FRENCH AMERICA. Acadia, Canada; the Mississippi Valley; the West Indies; Guiana. 168

Chapter VI

PROTESTANTISM IN THE AMERICAS. The Thirteen British Colonies; The West Indies; Surinam; Greenland; Labrador. 186

Chapter VII

WEST, SOUTH, AND EAST AFRICA, AND THE NEIGHBOURING ISLANDS. 240

Chapter VIII

INDIA. The Rise and Growth of Roman Catholic Missions; the Retardment of Roman Catholic Missions; the Beginnings of Protestant Missions; the Effect of Christianity; the Effect on Christianity. 247

Chapter IX

CEYLON. 285

Chapter X

BURMA, THE MALAY PENINSULA, SIAM, AND INDO-CHINA. 293

Chapter XI

THE EAST INDIES (THE MALAY ARCHIPELAGO). 300

Chapter XII

THE PHILIPPINE ISLANDS. 307

Chapter XIII

JAPAN. 322

Chapter XIV

THE CHINESE EMPIRE: FORMOSA, TIBET, AND KOREA. 336

Chapter XV

RUSSIAN ASIA AND ALASKA. 367

Chapter XVI

THE EFFECT OF CHRISTIANITY UPON ITS ENVIRONMENT. General: on Western Europe; Religion and Morals, Political Life and Government, International Relations, Social Organization, Social Reform and Poor Relief, Economic Organization, Intellectual Life, Aesthetic Life: on Russia: on the Expansion of Europe and on the Peoples and Cultures Affected by that Expansion. 372

Chapter XVII

THE EFFECT OF THE ENVIRONMENT ON CHRISTIANITY. In Europe; on Protestantism, on Roman Catholicism, on Russian Christianity: Outside of Europe. 427

Chapter XVIII

RETROSPECT AND PROSPECT. 450

BIBLIOGRAPHY. 458

INDEX. 487

MAPS. *facing* 504

   I. Europe and the Near East.

   II. North America, Central America, and the West Indies.

   III. South America.

   IV. Africa and Adjacent Islands.

   V. Asia (Except the Near East) and Adjacent Islands.

The author wishes to express his gratitude to Dean Luther A. Weigle for helpful criticisms, particularly on Chapters II-VI, and to Mrs. Charles T. Lincoln for her careful typing of the manuscript and for suggestions as to style. He is also deeply indebted to the officers and librarians of the Congregation for the Propagation of the Faith for unfailingly courteous assistance and, as always, to the staffs of the libraries of Yale University and especially to Professor Raymond P. Morris, Librarian of the Yale University Divinity School and its Day Missions Library.

A History of
The Expansion of Christianity

Volume III
THREE CENTURIES OF ADVANCE
A.D. 1500-A.D. 1800

Chapter I

INTRODUCTORY. MOVEMENTS CHARACTERIZING THE NEW AGE: THE RISE OF ABSOLUTE MONARCHIES IN EUROPE, SCIENTIFIC DISCOVERIES, THE COMMERCIAL REVOLUTION, THE GEOGRAPHIC DISCOVERIES AND SETTLEMENTS BY EUROPEANS, THE REVIVAL IN WESTERN CHRISTIANITY EXPRESSING ITSELF THROUGH THE RISE OF PROTESTANTISM AND THE ROMAN CATHOLIC REFORMATION. THE NEW MISSIONARY MOVEMENT: FEATURES AND ORGANIZATION

IN THE fifteenth century and in the first half of the sixteenth century Christianity faced a major crisis. It was now fifteen hundred years old. The first flush of enthusiasm, characteristic of a new religion, was presumably long past. A younger rival, Islam, was continuing to supplant it in wide regions and was threatening its remaining strongholds. Cultures which professed other faiths now surpassed in area, population, and power those which called themselves Christian. No longer, as in the fourth, fifth, and sixth centuries, was Christianity the faith of the richest and most important unit of mankind. Even in the lands where it was still officially the religion of the community, Christianity was in jeopardy. The culture—that of "Medieval" Europe—which had grown up under its ægis and of which it was an integral part, was passing. A new order was coming into being. Much of that new order was indifferent or even antagonistic to Christianity or sought to control it for its own purposes. In Western Europe, where Christianity had seemed most vigorous, decay had fastened itself on the Church. Ecclesiastical leaders disregarded Christian ethics in their programmes and practices and used their positions to advance their private interests in the promotion of art, the accumulation of wealth, and the acquisition of political power for themselves and their families. At the same time a vast expansion, commercial and territorial, was beginning which by the twentieth century was to carry European peoples throughout the globe and give them dominance over the rest of mankind. Under these circumstances, could Christianity continue to spread? Could it even survive? Had it sufficient vigour to enable it to permeate the new culture of Europe and to follow European peoples to other lands, to retain their allegiance, and to win the nations

1

with whom Europeans brought it in contact? In A.D. 1500 the outlook was far from promising.

Yet Christianity not only survived. It also displayed new life. In Western and Northern Europe it revived, showed more vigour than ever before, and made an even deeper impress upon the culture of Europe than it had previously been able to do. It accompanied Europeans on their wanderings and to their new settlements. The nations of European blood which arose in the Americas, in Africa, and in the South Seas were professedly Christian, and in several, including the most powerful of them, Christianity was as active as in any land in Europe. Some non-European peoples came over almost bodily to Christianity. In others large Christian groups arose. A profound influence was exerted on non-European cultures and upon peoples who remained non-Christian. Never had any religion spread so widely. Never had any faith had so great an effect upon so large a proportion of mankind.

In a certain sense the period in the spread of Christianity which began about A.D. 1500 has continued to the present. Some of the forces which characterized it, notably the expansion of European peoples and the new burst of life in Christianity and the forms of the faith to which that gave rise, are still with us. Indeed, here and there are indications, to which we shall come in later volumes, that only in the past twenty-five years has the age reached its end.

However, the three centuries from A.D. 1500 to A.D. 1800 form a major subdivision. In them Christianity expanded chiefly through Roman Catholicism. Towards the end of the eighteenth century the Occidental world again passed into a new age. For a time in the eighteenth century Christianity appeared to be declining. In the nineteenth century, in contrast, new life again broke out in it. After A.D. 1800 Christianity displayed greater vitality than ever before. Protestantism especially showed unprecedented vigour. Both Protestantism and the Roman Catholic form of Christianity were widely propagated, but the former now made an even deeper impression upon mankind than did the latter. We must therefore treat the years from A.D. 1500 to A.D. 1800 as a distinct unit and reserve for later volumes the nineteenth and twentieth centuries.

First of all we must say something of those circumstances which were mentioned in the first paragraph and in the first half of the second paragraph. We must enumerate the movements of the years immediately before A.D. 1500 and of the centuries between A.D. 1500 and A.D. 1800 in the midst of which Christianity was set. We must also describe the fresh burst of life in Christianity and the machinery which this created for the propagation of the faith.

In A.D. 1500 the threat to Christianity, as we have suggested, came in part from the Moslems. In the fourteenth and fifteenth centuries, as will be recalled by readers of the preceding volume, Christianity suffered seemingly disastrous losses in Asia. The far-flung frontiers of the Nestorian churches in China and Central Asia were wiped out and the Christian communities either perished or were assimilated to other faiths. Roman Catholic missions and the small Christian groups gathered by them in China and Central Asia disappeared. A dwindling Nestorianism survived in Persia, Mesopotamia, and adjoining regions. In several of the cities of Central Asia and India a few Armenian Christians were found, chiefly as merchants. In India communities of Nestorians— "Syrian Christians"—remained. However, Asiatic Christianity became confined almost entirely to the extreme west of the vast continent. Even there it was threatened. In the latter half of the fifteenth century the Ottoman Turks wiped out the remnants of the Byzantine Empire—that state which for nearly a millennium had been a leader in civilization and a bulwark of Christendom against invasion from the East. The patriarchs of the Greek Church became subject to Moslem Turkish monarchs. Not content with the capture of Constantinople, the Turks carried their arms far into Europe. Divisions and jealousies between the European powers made difficult and usually impossible a united front against the invader. Pope after Pope frantically sought to rally Western Christendom, but never was the voice of Rome heeded as it had been in the summons to the Crusades of the eleventh and twelfth centuries.[1] The Papacy was no longer the political leader of the West. Islam became firmly planted in the Balkan Peninsula. Within realms ruled by Moslems—and these included the Near East and the north shore of Africa, once strongholds of Christianity—such Christian communities as persisted were either barely holding their own or were losing ground. Thus in the Sudan, where Christianity had long been the prevailing faith, in A.D. 1500 the Church was distinctly on the way to extinction, and in Egypt leakages from the Coptic fold to Islam were occurring. On the eve of the beginning of the Portuguese settlements in India and of the Spanish conquests in the Americas, the faith of Mohammed was more widely spread geographically than was that of Jesus. Its area was growing while that of Christianity was rapidly declining. Politically it was more powerful. To the hypothetical visitor from Mars, as late as 1490 it would have seemed that in the eight-centuries-old struggle between the Cross and the Crescent the latter was now on its way to final triumph. The future seemed to lie not with the Christ but with the Prophet. Except in the Iberian Peninsula

---

[1] On some of these efforts of the Popes see Pastor, *History of the Popes*, Vol. II, p. 277; Vol. III, p. 19; Vol. X, pp. 170, 179; Vol. XV, pp. xliii, xliv.

and in Sicily, wherever the two had come in conflict, the latter and not the former was winning.

Would the influence of Jesus persist or would it perish from the earth? If it were to go on and to spread it would have to be from Western and Northern Europe. Only there did Christian communities exist which were not politically subject to Islam or which were not, as in Ethiopia, on the defensive against Islam, or, as in India, encysted minorities of foreign origin surrounded by religions imbedded in the affections and institutions of highly civilized peoples. In Western and Northern Europe Christianity was the official faith of the various governments, to it the overwhelming majority of the population gave at least their nominal allegiance, and the only external threat was from Islam, on the southern and eastern borders.

The position which it held in Western and Northern Europe, however, did not ensure Christianity a large future. In A.D. 1500 the peoples and culture of that region did not enjoy the pre-eminence which came to be theirs in succeeding centuries. In more than one area were civilized folk numerically more impressive and politically more important. The Ottoman Empire in the Near East and the Ming Empire in China loomed much more prominently than did Western Christendom. Compared with them any one of the European kingdoms of the day, even the vaunted Holy Roman Empire with its proud lineage, was a petty principality.

Moreover, as we have suggested, the Christianity of Western Europe was suffering from internal weaknesses. In this, its one great remaining stronghold, Christianity was threatened and appeared to be losing ground.

In the realm of the intellect and of the æsthetic spirit Christianity seemed to be a waning influence. The Renaissance was turning the attention of many to the pre-Christian culture of the Græco-Roman world. The warm admiration for the art and literature of pagan antiquity tended to a contempt for the achievements of Medieval Europe and to an ill-concealed attitude of superiority towards the faith which had been so closely associated with the culture of the Middle Ages. A few were hostile. Many were not so much hostile as indifferent or patronizing. Moreover, the humanism which was associated with the Renaissance tended to exalt the individual at the expense of God, and to rely for the attainment of knowledge upon the power of man's mind rather than upon divine revelation.

Great discoveries were being made. In geography the Portuguese were opening up a new route to India and the Spice Islands, and Columbus and his successors were bringing to the astonished eyes of Europe the intoxicating vision of a New World.

Copernicus and, a little later, Galileo, disclosed a new heaven in a manner which for many proved disconcerting to religious faith.

Novel appliances came into use—the compass, mechanical clocks, lenses for glasses, microscopes, and telescopes—the product of man's inventive genius. Printing by moveable type made books much more numerous and so tended to popularize learning. Living became more comfortable. The foundations were laid for modern zoology and anatomy. A little later came the development of the inductive method. Mathematics registered marked progress. The inclination of the compass was discovered and the earth itself was declared to be a huge magnet. European man was beginning to use his brains to effect that mastery of his physical environment which became so marked a feature of later centuries.

Art gave less attention to Christian themes than in the Middle Ages.

The European spirit, exhilarated and made confident by a new consciousness of the powers of man's mind, tended to have less awe for God and, when it thought of Him at all, wished to use Him as a tool for the achievement of this-worldly ends. Could Christianity continue to live in this new atmosphere?

To be sure, much of this was not new. In the Middle Ages large numbers of those who called themselves Christians had sought to coerce God into the support of their private interests. Scepticism and indifference had been widespread.

Moreover, the large majority of those affected by the new spirit remained professed Christians and of these a fair proportion were earnest and convinced in their faith.

A case, too, can be made for the thesis that much of the temper of the new age and of its intellectual and geographic achievements was the fruit of Christianity. Largely as the result of the educational efforts of the Church, learning had now ceased to be the exclusive possession of the clergy, whose chief preoccupation was presumably the Christian faith, and was shared with the laity, who, like their predecessors in the Middle Ages, less frequently than the clergy made Christianity their chief concern. Even the daring and the confidence of the human spirit may have been a product of Christianity. Yet, even if he granted that the new features which characterized the age might be the result of Christianity, the neutral observer could well raise the question as to whether, by contributing to this new age, Christianity had not prepared the way for its own doom.

In the realm of government Christianity was seriously threatened. The powers of monarchs were being strengthened. Machiavelli was preaching a statecraft which exalted the prince, set forth political principles which were quite opposed to the ethics of Christianity, and either ignored religion or made it the tool of the state. A number of the kings were extending their control over the Church within their realms. This came to be notorious in lands where Protestantism prevailed. It is not always recognized that domination of Church by state was just as absolute in some countries which were enthusiastically Roman Catholic. It is true that throughout the Middle Ages strong monarchs sought, and sometimes with success, to bring the Church in their domains under their sway. However, more now went much further than had formerly been possible. In 1438 Charles VII by the Pragmatic Sanction of Bourges markedly limited the power of the Popes over the Church in France. In 1516 Francis I and Pope Leo X entered into a concordat the effect of which was to give the King the right to nominate to almost all the higher vacant ecclesiastical posts in France.[2] In Spain the power of the throne over the Church was rapidly increased. Ferdinand and Isabella, under whom the united Spanish monarchy registered extraordinary progress, professed to be loyal Roman Catholics. Isabella was especially devout. Yet they possessed through Papal grants the right of patronage over many churches and later insisted that no bishop could be appointed to serve in their domains without their approval.[3] Pope Alexander VI made large concessions to the Spanish crown. Charles V, a zealous Roman Catholic, obtained from the Pope the complete and permanent right of placing the royal candidates in all the episcopal and archiepiscopal sees of Spain, and the Spanish government enjoyed the power of conferring almost all other benefices to which revenues were attached and of controlling the military orders.[4] By the time that Philip II ascended the throne, the power of the crown over the Spanish Church was practically complete. Yet Philip II, who fought so relentlessly against heresy, still further augmented the royal control, and that in spite of the opposition of the Pope. Indeed, one of the presidents of Philip's council declared that there was no Pope in Spain.[5] In Portugal, too, since the fourteenth century, the crown had been extending its authority over the Church.[6] Even the Venetian Republic claimed the right to appoint the incumbents of all the bishoprics in its territories.[7] Could a church so dominated by the state hope to have any real life of its own? Would it not become simply an arm of the government? That certainly would seem to be the logic of the

[2] Pastor, *op. cit.*, Vol. IV, p. 321; Smith, *The Age of the Reformation*, p. 184; Lindsay, *A History of the Reformation*, Vol. I, pp. 24, 25.

[3] Mecham, *Church and State in Latin America*, pp. 6-11.

[4] Pastor, *History of the Popes*, Vol. IX, p. 213, Vol. XVI, pp. 354-356.

[5] Pastor, *op. cit.*, Vol. XVI, pp. 357-362, Vol. XVIII, pp. 1-71; Marie R. Madden in Guilday, *The Catholic Church in Contemporary Europe, 1919-1931*, pp. 294-308.

[6] Jann, *Die katholischen Missionen in Indien, China, und Japan*, pp. 3-25.

[7] Pastor, *op. cit.*, Vol. X, pp. 372, 373.

situation. Or would the Christian impulse show sufficient vitality to overcome the handicap and propagate itself at home and abroad?

In the realm of economics Christianity faced a new situation. The old feudal, manorial, and agricultural structure had long been disintegrating. The commercial classes were pushing to the fore and capitalism was in process of development. The Church had become closely integrated with the old order. Could Christianity survive the death of the old and make its impress upon the new?

The age of geographic discoveries had come. Spaniards and Portuguese were conquering much of the Americas. English, Dutch, French, and Scandinavians were to follow them and parcel out the New World. The Portuguese nosed their way around Africa to India and the East Indies and there founded trading posts. The Spaniards laid claim to the Philippines. Later, too, British, Dutch, French, and Scandinavians established themselves on the southern and eastern shores of Asia and on the adjoining islands. The Russians pushed their frontiers across Siberia and into Alaska. Would Christianity have the vigour to accompany these merchants, conquerors, and settlers, modify with its ethics the impact of the European upon the non-European peoples, hold the Europeans and their descendants to the faith of their fathers, and win converts from the peoples about them? Here was the greatest movement of peoples which the human race had ever seen. Could Christianity permeate it with the spirit of Jesus? Could Christianity through it become world-wide and mould the race as a whole?

In A.D. 1500 he would have been either a brave or a rash prophet who would have ventured his reputation on the prediction that Christianity would rise to the challenge of the new day. The Roman Catholic Church, the sole official form of Christianity in Western Europe, had suffered in prestige. In the fourteenth century the seat of the Popes had been removed to Avignon and for several decades the successors of Peter were largely subservient to France. This "Babylonian Exile" was followed by a prolonged division in the Church over rival claimants to the Fisherman's throne and by dissensions accompanying the attempt to terminate the schism and to make Church councils an effective check on Papal supremacy. Hardly had the schism ended and the conciliar movement dwindled before the successful reassertion of Papal authority, when the Papacy fell under the spell of the Renaissance and of humanism. In the fifteenth and in the early part of the sixteenth century several occupants of the Roman see were predominantly secular in spirit. They encouraged art and literature and beautified Rome, but they were often more interested in their collections of books and of art objects and in Italian politics than they were in the spiritual welfare of Western Europe. Nepotism abounded. Several of the higher members of the hierarchy were notorious for their luxurious living and their violation of the rule of clerical chastity. The heavy financial exactions on Europe made necessary by the extravagance of the Papal court aroused unrest. The scandalous state of morals of Rome helped to bring the Church and the clergy into contempt. Throughout much of Europe the clergy were derided for their ignorance, worldliness, and corruption. At the very time when America was discovered and the Portuguese reached India by way of the new sea route around Africa and when vast new territories and immense populations were opened to the propagation of the Christian faith, the most infamous of the pontiffs of this corrupt period, the handsome and able but unmoral and unscrupulous Alexander VI, occupied the Papal chair.

The corruption of the Church and the contempt felt for its leadership at the outset of the sixteenth century can easily be overemphasized. More than once in the preceding thousand years by their profligacy and their flagrant worldliness the occupants of the Papacy had given scandal to all honest men. Monks and clergy had repeatedly violated their vows and used their positions for self-aggrandizement and sordid dissipation. The sneer at the expense of the clergy had long been chronic.

Yet seldom, if ever, had the contrast between profession and practice in the leadership of the Church been so serious a menace to the future of Christianity. If it were to expand or even if it were to continue to exist Christianity had now to look to Western and Northern Europe. Europe was moving away from those Middle Ages of which the Church had been an integral part and in the new day might be tempted to discard Christianity along with other features of the era which was closing. Discovery and conquest were opening the greatest door for expansion which any religion had ever had. A corrupt and moribund Church could scarcely hope to take advantage of the situation to propagate its faith. It might well seem that the impulse from Jesus was now spent and that Christianity had entered upon a tragic decline just when it was confronted by the most challenging opportunity in its history.

Fortunately for the fate of the influence of Jesus, these delinquencies and weaknesses in the leadership of organized Christianity are not the entire story. On the eve of the new day indications were not lacking of a rising tide of life. As we have seen in the preceding volume, Christianity had penetrated Europe from the top down and in the thirteenth, fourteenth, and fifteenth centuries was stirring the emerging middle classes of the cities and the urban and rural proletariat to new religious movements. In contrast with the earlier monastic revivals, led largely by members of the aristocracy, the mendicant orders of the thirteenth century drew much of their initial leadership from the humbler classes. Peter Waldo and his Poor Men of Lyons made their chief appeal to merchants and to those who laboured with their hands. John Hus was the son of a peasant. In the preceding volume we have spoken of the German mystics and of the Brethren of the Common Life. Increasingly as the centuries passed Christianity gave rise to movements, many of them sects denounced by the official Church but some of them finding a home under the ægis of that body, which gave evidence of a pulsing and, on the whole, a growing life. In the middle classes and in humble homes there was much of simple, earnest piety which centred about Jesus and which cherished the main tenets of what had long been taught the masses as the essential features of Christianity. Many of the humanists, especially north of the Alps, were deeply religious. Much of the dissatisfaction with the clergy was due to the stirrings of a conscience which was increasingly impatient with the contradiction between the leadership of the Church and the Christian ideal. In Germany on the eve of the Reformation many churches and monasteries were being built. In Germany, too, manuals were in circulation whose purpose it was to help priests with their preaching and with their parish work. Translations of the Bible in more than one of the vernacular tongues of Western Europe had been published. The *Theologia Germanica*, a product of the mysticism of the later Middle Ages, had a profound effect upon Luther.[8]

In the sixteenth century these currents of life, greatly augmented by new movements, came to fruition in religious awakenings more extensive than any which Christianity had before known. Nor did they stop then. After a pause in the eighteenth century they broke out with even greater strength in the nineteenth and twentieth centuries.

Of all the religions which have attracted large groups of mankind and have spread beyond the bounds of one country, in the four centuries after A.D. 1500 only Christianity displayed increasing vitality and grew in power over the human race. In an earlier volume we noted that all the major religions appeared before A.D. 650—most of them between 650 B.C. and A.D. 650. Concerning all of these except Christianity it is possible to speak of the history of their rise and decline. Islam, Buddhism, Hinduism, and Confucianism seem to have less vigour and less power over men than in A.D. 1500. Occasionally, as we have seen, there have been ebbs in the onward flow of Christianity. After each ebb, however, the tide has come back and has gone on to new heights. In the main the movement has been forward. The historian can speak of the rise of Christianity, but if he views the entire sweep of its history he cannot with accuracy speak of

[8] *Theologia Germanica*, Winkworth's translation (London, Macmillan and Co., 1874, pp. lxvii, 213), p. xxi.

its decline. Beginning with the sixteenth century Christianity has been especially marked by pulsing life.

However, it is only the Christianity of Western and Northern Europe, and particularly of Western Europe and of peoples descended from emigrants from Western Europe which has displayed that life. The vigour and expansion of Christianity during the past four centuries have been closely associated with the striking vigour and phenomenal expansion of European, and particularly of Western European peoples.

Immediately the question arises as to the significance of this connexion. Is it accidental? Is one the cause of the other? Or, are both the results of some underlying but hidden cause? Is Christianity the source of the position which the European peoples have come to occupy in the past four centuries? Is the vigour manifested by Christianity a by-product of the abounding vitality of European stocks in recent times? Or are both the outcome of some other factor, such as climate? What is it which has impelled Europeans alone among all mankind to go to the ends of the earth, to climb the highest mountains, to rest ill content short of the North and South Poles, to explore the secrets of the physical universe, to seek to make all nature serve them, to master the land, the sea, and the air, to search into the secrets of the starry universe, to institute new forms of government and of industry, to create new types of Christianity, and to go as Christian missionaries to all peoples? Is it mere chance? Is it the fact that Europeans live in the portions of the earth where temperature and cyclical changes in weather stimulate the human organism to greater activity than elsewhere? Is it something in the genes or the germ plasm peculiar to European stocks? Is it the impulse given by the Greek mind? Or is it in the type of Christianity which took shape among Western Europeans?

Probably at our present stage of knowledge no one of us ought to be dogmatic in his reply. Yet the modern mind is unwilling to dismiss the problem with a vague shifting of the responsibility to chance. It seeks concrete causes. It must be pointed out, moreover, that climate alone cannot be the source, for in other areas which so far as we can see possess similar conditions the same results have not followed. Probably it is not race, for the religious awakenings, the geographic discoveries, and the intellectual activity have not been confined to any one of the many racial strains of Western Europe. Nor is it merely the heritage of Greek thought, for in some areas in which that was strong, as in those dominated by the earlier Arab culture and in the Byzantine Empire, there did not follow such a burst of energy and creativity as the past few centuries have seen among Western European peoples. Probably, too, what is called Christianity is not solely responsible, for among some peoples, who for centuries have been Christian, cultural stagnation has long prevailed.

However, it may be significant that these sterile spots in Christendom have been mostly among minorities on the defensive against Islam or Hinduism, that the places of greatest energy and cultural creativity have been Western Europe and the colonies of Western Europeans, and that through the centuries since the collapse of the Roman Empire in the West the Christian impulse has, on the whole, had freer course in these same regions and has been less subject to restraint by the state than elsewhere. A case, then, can be made for the hypothesis that the Christian impulse lies back of much of the intellectual, spiritual, and physical energy of Western Europeans of the past four or five centuries.

Whatever the answer to these questions, it must be clear that in the centuries since A.D. 1500 Christianity has profoundly modified the culture of Western Europe and the effects of its expansion. If it has been a major cause of the creativity and expansion of modern Europe, it has been only one of the factors involved. Much in the Europe and among the European peoples of the four centuries since A.D. 1500 has been quite contradictory to all for which Jesus stood. However, the impulse from Jesus which gave rise to Christianity has been one of the most powerful of the factors, has opposed some of the others, and has stamped an indelible impress upon the whole of the life and outreach of Western Europe. To this phase of our story we will return, with amplifications, in later chapters and in succeeding volumes.

Of the new life in the Christianity of Europe in the sixteenth century we must not here attempt to write in detail. Its importance and the effect it has had on the European spirit is attested by a vast literature.[9] Its story has taken its place prominently in all the accounts of the course of European history since

---

[9] Roland H. Bainton, *Bibliography of the Continental Reformation. Materials Available in English* (Chicago, The American Society of Church History, 1935, pp. 54), is by an expert in the field. Karl Schottenloher, *Bibliographie zur deutschen Geschichte im Zeitalter der Glaubensspaltung, 1517-1585* (Leipzig, K. W. Hiersmann, 3 vol., 1933-1936), is very full. Shirley Jackson Case et alii, *A Bibliographical Guide to the History of Christianity* (The University of Chicago Press, 1931, pp. ix, 265), on pp. 94-106 has a selected bibliography on the Protestant Reformation and on pp. 106-108 on the Catholic Reformation.

Standard summaries in English, both from the Protestant viewpoint, are Thomas M. Lindsay, *A History of the Reformation* (New York, Charles Scribner's Sons, 2 vols., 1906, 1907), and Preserved Smith, *The Age of the Reformation* (New York, Henry Holt and Co., 1920, pp. xii, 861).

Standard works which deal with the Catholic Reformation are Leopold von Ranke, *Die römischen Päpste, ihre Kirche und ihr Staat in 16 und 17 Jahrhundert* (3 vols., 1834-1836), of which an English translation is by E. Foster (London, Henry G. Bohn, 3 vols., 1850-1853), and Ludwig Pastor, *The History of the Popes from the Close of the Middle Ages* (St. Louis, B. Herder, 20 vols., 1902 ff). See also B. J. Kidd, *The Counter-Reformation, 1550-1600* (London, Society for Promoting Christian Knowledge, 1933, pp. 271).

the Middle Ages. It helps to mark the transition to what historians have chosen to call the modern world. All that is needed here, and, indeed, all that is consistent with the purposes of our narrative is the briefest possible summary, together with some interpretations which bear upon the on-going process of the expansion of Christianity.

The awakening, as we have said, was the most widely spread and the most stirring which Christianity had yet known. It falls into two main divisions—what are usually known as the Protestant Reformation and the Catholic Reformation.

It is important to note that even in its beginnings what is collectively designated as Protestantism was not a single stream. Protestantism is, moreover, a term which almost accidentally came into use and is really a misnomer. To focus attention upon the negative aspects of those movements which broke away from the Roman Catholic Church or which were rejected by it, is to miss their significance. Primarily these movements were not criticisms of the existing Church, although they did severely censure the features in that body which they believed to be departures from the faith and practice of Jesus and his apostles. Essentially they were the positive expressions of fresh religious experiences and of vigorous affirmations. Even the designation of Reformation is misleading. To be sure, the creators of the movements which are grouped under that name sought to "reform" the Church as they knew it, to purge it of what they conceived to be its departures from the original Christian Gospel, and to purify it of all which to them appeared contrary to the faith which had been delivered to the early Christians by Jesus through the apostles. Yet in fact what was denominated the Reformation gave rise to new bodies and to fresh expressions of religious experience which were not exact reproductions of anything which had gone before and which were not a complete return to the New Testament. The new wine gave shape to new wineskins. Even the word Evangelical, used by so many to designate themselves, is not ideal, for it implies that other Christians are not true to the Evangel, the original Christian message, and it becomes a term of division, irritating to Christians of different traditions who think of themselves as having been loyal to Jesus and to the early apostles. Nor will "non-Catholic," now employed so extensively by Roman Catholics, serve any better, for many of those outside the Roman Catholic fold believe themselves to be in the stream of œcumenical or Catholic Christianity and resent the attempt to restrict the word Catholic to any one body of Christians.

It is probably now too late to free our vocabularies from the words Protestant Reformation, Evangelical, and non-Catholic, or to coin new terms and win for them general acceptance. As we employ these standard names, however, we must always remember that we do so only for convenience and because they have the sanction of long usage. We shall take the designation Protestant as embracing all those movements which historically have developed out of Latin Christianity but which are not included in the Roman Catholic Church. Let us do so, however, with a consciousness of the limitations and inaccuracies of that word.

Protestantism is usually said to begin with Martin Luther. For it the crucial date 1517 is given because that was the year in which Luther nailed his theses to the church door in Wittenberg and so began a controversy which eventually took him out of the ecclesiastical fold of his fathers. Luther was undoubtedly the leading figure in sixteenth century Protestantism and has unquestionably left his mark upon almost all the movements which are included under the Protestant name. His theses, too, began an upheaval which has not yet subsided.

To see Protestantism as it was and to understand it through the centuries, however, we must remind ourselves that it broke out spontaneously in many different quarters and that into it entered several different currents. Humanism and the fructifying influences of the Renaissance had almost no effect on Luther, but Erasmus, who did so much to prepare the way for Protestantism, was an outstanding expression of them both. Zwingli came by way of humanism. Calvin owed to humanism and to deeply religious humanists in France much of the initial impulse which started him on his way. Luther arrived at his position through an agonizing struggle of the soul which, although it involved a wrestling of mind, issued in an experience which was primarily that of the emotions and the will. Others, among them early leaders in Socinianism, reached their convictions chiefly by way of the intellect. Many of the Anabaptists seem to go back to impulses given by medieval, pre-Lutheran sects, or at least were in a stream which bore marked likenesses to medieval movements. So, too, some of the Protestant groups in Bohemia and Moravia appear to have had their rootage in the pre-Reformation John Hus and Peter Waldo.

We must also remind ourselves that Protestantism was by no means a purely religious movement and that not all its origins can be traced to the impulse given by Jesus. Into it entered what in the nineteenth and twentieth centuries would be called nationalism—such as the resentment of Germans against ecclesiastical taxation for the benefit of Italian Rome and the particularist feelings which had long been present in England. The political trend towards absolutist monarchical states was important, the desire of each prince to control the Church and its leaders as fully as all other institutions and persons in his realm. This was a powerful factor in the separation of Scandinavia, of England, and of much of Germany from Rome and in the commitment of these regions to Protestantism. The idiosyncrasies and wishes of individual princes had their place in giving complexion to the resulting churches. As examples one need only to recall the part which Henry the Eighth's desire for an heir and his wayward passions had in the creation of the independent Church of England, the place which the status of her mother had in determining the religious affiliations of Elizabeth, and how much the inclusiveness of the Church of England owes to the determination of Elizabeth to maintain unity in her realms. Economic unrest had a share. In Germany this prepared for that Peasants' Revolt which took its inspiration in part from Luther. In some regions, too, Protestantism was particularly strong in the cities and was to a certain extent a product of urban life.

Yet when all these non-religious causes are mentioned, the fact remains that Protestantism was in its origin primarily a group of religious movements. It was religious conviction which made it possible. Fresh religious experiences lay back of it. The most stirring of these centred about Jesus. In Protestantism the impulse which came from Jesus was breaking out afresh and more vigorously than ever before.

We must also note that the series of religious awakenings which gave rise to Protestantism did not cease with the sixteenth century. In the seventeenth century came the flowering of Puritanism and the pulsing life which, joined with political and economic forces, overthrew the monarchy in England, and in the Commonwealth period expressed itself through a number of varied movements. To the seventeenth century belongs the origin of the Quakers. In the seventeenth century, too, came the beginnings of Pietism. Pietism arose partly as a protest against the low state of the life of much of Lutheranism in its day and as a reaction against the decay in morals and religion brought to Germany by the Thirty Years' War. It was an indication that in the Christianity of Germany was enough vitality to bring a renewal of life in the face of lethargy and of near despair. In Protestantism and in Roman Catholicism the eighteenth century was a time of rationalism. Christianity was openly challenged. Within many church circles enthusiasm was deplored. Yet the eighteenth century saw the beginnings of the Moravian movement—a union of Pietism with some remnants of small, persecuted, radical sects. In the eighteenth century, too, in part from contact with the Moravians, came the Wesleyan revival, the most potent which English Christianity had seen since the flowering of Puritanism. In the English colonies in America, almost contemporaneously with the Wesleyan revival and at the outset independent of it, broke out the Great Awakening. The nineteenth and twentieth centuries, as we are to see in later volumes, were the period of the greatest vigour of Protestantism, and, indeed, of Christianity as a whole.

In Protestantism Christianity became more varied than it had been at any time since its earliest centuries. The contrast in this respect between the progress of Christianity in the Græco-Roman world and among Western European peoples is striking. In the Græco-Roman world the impulse which came from Jesus almost immediately had a large number of different expressions. Then as the centuries passed most of these disappeared and the majority of Christians were included within one Catholic Church. In Western and particularly in North-western Europe, on the other hand, Christianity was propagated chiefly through one church—which called itself Catholic—although for a time Arianism attracted large numbers. Then, as the centuries passed, the Christianity of that region took on diverse forms and eventually, through Protestantism, became more multiform than at any previous time in its history. The reasons for the difference are not altogether clear. Obviously the adoption of Christianity by the Roman state and the powerful support given by the Emperors to one type of the faith (partly in the interests of political unity) was one cause of the approach to uniformity after the third century. It may be that before Constantine the need for a common front against persecution was a factor. It may be, too, that in a decaying world, such as was the Roman Empire after the second century, there was less inclination to venture on new ways and more of a trust in authority. In Western Europe one cause of the proliferation may have been that Christianity was becoming the conscious property of the masses and that an increasing number were impelled, unawed by the authority of the great church which had so long tutored the descendants of the barbarians, to think for themselves on the faith which had been handed down to them. Perhaps, too, in an age which was pulsing with new life, as was the Europe of the thirteenth and fourteenth and particularly of the fifteenth century and after, the human spirit became more venturesome and less submissive to the authority of the past. Whatever the causes, the fact is clear. In the Græco-Roman world the movement in Christianity was from diversity towards uniformity. In Western Europe it was from uniformity to diversity.

By no means all of the awakening in the Christianity of Western Europe in the sixteenth century expressed itself through Protestantism. Much of it, as we have suggested, remained within the old church and gave rise to the Catholic Reformation. Often the portion of the revival which kept to the Roman Catholic Church is denominated the Counter-Reformation. While the impetus towards the elimination of abuses within the old church was accentuated by the Protestant revolt and by the obvious alternative of reform or death, it is not in accord with the facts to speak of the new life in the old church as simply a protective reaction against Protestantism. Much of it had a common origin with Protestantism in the rising tides of life in the Christianity of Western Europe. In the two wings of the great religious awakening of the sixteenth century Western Christianity was beginning to come of age. The faith which had been accepted centuries before was now at last ploughing deeply into the European soul and was bringing forth fruit on a large scale. In the case of Protestantism the fresh ferment broke the old wineskins. In the Catholic Reformation it found the old wineskins still sufficiently flexible to retain it.

In its religious phases, Protestantism in its origin was from the humbler classes, while, in the main, the Catholic Reformation was led by aristocrats. The most powerful religious influence in early Protestantism, Martin Luther, was of peasant stock. Zwingli was born in more comfortable circumstances, but was from a village and was of peasant ancestry. Melanchthon was of artisan paternity. While Calvin was reared in aristocratic surroundings, his paternal grandfather was a manual labourer. In contrast, the most influential spiritual force in the Catholic Reformation was Ignatius Loyola, who was of the nobility of the Basque regions. A number of the other outstanding figures were of noble ancestry. Thus Gaetano di Tiene and Giovanni Pietro Caraffa (later Pope under the title of Paul IV), the founders of one of the orders, the Theatines, which brought new life to the old church, were of the Italian nobility. The Barnabites, another of the new orders, had an aristocrat as a founder.

To be sure, the lines between the two wings of the movement were not closely drawn according to classes. Many princes espoused the Protestant cause and used it for their own ends. One of the new groups in the Roman Catholic fold, the Capuchins, a fresh offshoot of the Franciscans, was largely, at least at the outset, from the humbler ranks of society.

However, the distinction seems to be real and to have significance. In Protestantism the new life came from the bottom upward. It was the product of the stirring of the soul of the common man by the faith which had been handed down from the aristocracy. Even more fully than in the Franciscan and Dominican movements and the popular heretical sects of the Middle Ages, the religion which had been adopted *en masse* centuries before was now being appropriated as their own by the lower strata of society and they were giving to it their own complexion. Moreover, in general Protestantism stood for the priesthood of all believers and the direct access of each Christian to God. Roman Catholicism, on the other hand, retained the priesthood and the hierarchy in control of the Church and as mediators between God and men in certain matters essential to salvation. An aristocracy is usually conservative, attached to old traditions, and identifies its interests with the maintenance of existing institutions. It was natural, therefore, that a movement led by members of the upper classes, as was the Catholic Reformation, should express itself in ways more in accord with the past than did Protestantism, the wing of the reform movement led by scions of the middle and lower classes, groups struggling for power and less interested in preserving the old order.

Both the Protestant and the Roman Catholic wing of the revival strove to lift the level of the masses of Christians more nearly to New Testament standards. In this they resembled the Irish missions to the Continent in the early Middle Ages, with their penitentials as a means of moral discipline for the members of the Church, and the Franciscan and Dominican movements of the thirteenth century. However, in this case the approach was much more varied and probably reached greater numbers. Earlier those who desired to live the perfect life usually felt it necessary to join a monastic group. Protestants either looked askance at monasticism or repudiated it entirely and many of the Protestant sects sought to bring all members of the Church to the ideals of the New Testament. Roman Catholicism through catechisms endeavoured to give to the laity a better education in things Christian, and through an improved training in seminaries established for that purpose for the seculars who made up the majority of the parish priests laboured to improve the character of the clergy and through them that of the laity. Loyola strove to extend piety beyond the cloisters, and in the seventeenth century Francis de Sales directed his *Introduction to the Devout Life* to those "living in the world" and not, as had been formerly customary, to those who had renounced the world for the cloistered life.[10] Determined efforts were being made by both Protestants and Roman Catholics to deepen the Christianity of the majority of Europeans and make it something more than nominal.

Moreover, both Protestantism and Roman Catholicism tended to be more activistic and less contemplative than the Christianity of the Middle Ages. As we have seen in an earlier volume, the Christianity of the West early tended to be more activistic than that of the East. After A.D. 1500 it became much more so. Protestantism made very much less of worship and contemplation than had the Mediaeval Church.[11] The great new order of the Catholic Reformation, the Society of Jesus, made much of *Spiritual Exercises* in which

[10] Kirk, *The Vision of God,* p. 405.
[11] Kirk, *op. cit.,* p. 431.

meditation had its part, but it sent its members out into the world into vigorous activity of many kinds.

From the standpoint of the expansion of Christianity, it is important to note that it was a Christianity with these emphases which chiefly spread during the succeeding centuries. It was a Christianity which endeavoured—although not always effectively—to bring all Christianity to New Testament standards of living, and one which emphasized moral transformation and activity rather than contemplation. Particularly was this true of Protestantism. Roman Catholicism departed less widely from medieval Christianity, made less effort to bring all the laity to a high level, and perpetuated more of the tradition of worship and contemplation.

As in the Protestant wing of the movement, so in the Roman Catholic, the new vigour showed itself in a variety of ways. Pulsing life could never completely follow the past nor be confined to any one mould.

As was to be expected, a number of new orders arose. Traditionally revivals in the Latin Church had expressed themselves through new sodalities, communities which took the time-honoured vows of poverty, chastity, and obedience, and fresh monastic orders. It was natural, as we have suggested, that an awakening led by aristocrats should largely conform to precedent. About 1517, the very year in which Luther nailed his theses to the door of the church at Wittenberg and set Germany afire, a group of distinguished men, noted for their learning and piety, constituted themselves into a sodality termed the Oratory of the Divine Love, whose purpose it was to reawaken the spiritual life and to restore order and due observance in the public services of the Church. Of the relatively small number who constituted the group, several were later elevated to the Cardinalate and one became Pope. One of the Oratory of Divine Love, a noble of Vicenza, founded a community of secular priests, the Theatines, largely recruited from the aristocracy, for the purpose of improving the morals of the clergy. The Theatines became a nursery of bishops who strove to carry through their dioceses the spirit of the reform movement.[12] The Camaldulians or Camaldolese, an order of reformed Benedictines, dating back to the eleventh century, were refounded, and revived the hermit life.[13] In 1532 the Paulines, or Clerks Regular of St. Paul, later known as Barnabites, were established.[14] They devoted themselves to the instruction of the young and the cure of souls and, unlike the Theatines and perhaps because they were

[12] For a brief summary with excellent bibliographical notes, see Heimbucher, *Die Orden und Kongregationen der katholischen Kirche,* Vol. III, pp. 258-269.
[13] Heimbucher, *op. cit.,* Vol. I, p. 404.
[14] For a brief summary and an excellent selected bibliography, see Heimbucher, *op. cit.,* Vol. III, pp. 270-274.

not so aristocratic in origin, held open air missions. The Brethren of Charity, begun in 1534, were for the care of the sick. Out of the work of John of Avila, known as the Apostle of Andalusia, came a community, the Hospitallers, also for the comfort of the sick. The Somaschi, with a nobleman as their founder, devoted themselves to the waifs left by the repeated wars in Italy.[15] The Congregation of the Oratory arose out of the labours of Philip Neri, who was the founder and inspiration of a centre at Rome for prayer, conference, and music which had marked effect in raising the tone of the Roman clergy.[16] In 1535 Angela Merici of Brescia founded the Ursulines for tending the sick and teaching young girls.[17] They are said to have been the first teaching order of women in the Church. A congregation of secular priests, the Oblates of St. Ambrose, were founded in 1578 by Borromeo, a reforming Bishop of Milan.[18] The list might be prolonged. It would include the Angelicalas, founded by the Countess Louise Torelli of Guastalla in 1530,[19] the Clerks Regular of the Mother of God, founded in 1583 at Lucca by the scion of a wealthy family for the instruction of poor children,[20] and a number of others.[21]

The most widely spread and powerful of the new orders was the Society of Jesus, the creation of Ignatius de Loyola. Loyola was a contemporary of Luther and like the latter had a profound religious experience. Like the latter, too, his faith centred about Jesus and the God whom he believed to have revealed himself in Jesus. However, unlike the son of the German peasant, this son of the Basque nobility remained within the ancient church. The society which he founded took the traditional monastic vows—although it differed vastly from the prototype of Western monasticism, the Benedictines—and became the chief arm of the Roman Catholic Church as the latter strove to win back the Protestants and to carry the Christian message to the new lands opened by the discoveries of the fifteenth and sixteenth centuries. Part of the change which it wrought in Roman Catholic lands is seen in the fact that the third general of the Society was a great-grandson of the infamous and luxurious Borgia Pope, Alexander VI, and had been stirred by the Society to resign his dukedom and go about with a beggar's sack to collect alms. In the contrast between the great-grandfather and the great-grandson is seen something

[15] For a brief summary and a brief selected bibliography, see Heimbucher, *op. cit.*, Vol. III, pp. 275-278.
[16] For a brief summary and an excellent brief bibliography, see Heimbucher, *op. cit.*, Vol. III, pp. 413-424.
[17] For a brief summary and selected bibliography, see Heimbucher, *op. cit.*, Vol. II, pp. 273-287.
[18] For a brief summary and a bibliography, see Heimbucher, *op. cit.*, Vol. III, pp. 411-413.
[19] Heimbucher, *op. cit.*, Vol. II, p. 287.
[20] Heimbucher, *op. cit.*, Vol. III, pp. 287-280.
[21] See brief accounts of these in Heimbucher, *op. cit.*, Vol. III.

of the alteration achieved in the Roman Catholic Church by the reform movement.[22]

As was also to be expected, improvement was made in the old orders and here and there these elder bodies put forth new shoots. Towards the close of the fifteenth century the austere and masterly Ximenez de Cisneros carried out in Spain purification of his own order, the Conventual Franciscans.[23] In Spain, also near the end of the fifteenth century, the Discalced Franciscans came into being. The Observants, who held to a strict allegiance to the original rule of Francis, were reorganized in 1517 and, rather than the lax Conventuals, were recognized as the true followers of the saint of Assisi. As we have suggested, the Capuchins came into being as a fresh branch of the Franciscan movement. They spread rapidly. By the end of their second century they numbered 31,157 in sixty-four provinces.[24] The sixteenth century outburst of Spanish Christian mysticism gave birth, through a younger contemporary of Ignatius, Theresa, and her friend, John of the Cross, to the Discalced (or Barefooted) Carmelites, an attempt to introduce a stricter life among the Carmelites.[25] In 1539 one of the leaders in the reform movement was elected the head of the Augustinians and undertook a personal inspection of all the houses of the order. Not far from the same time, by Papal order, a general visitation of the Dominican houses was made to purify them of heresy and abuses.[26] The Cistercians in Italy and Sicily were investigated, and the Humiliati, who had become rich and corrupt, were suppressed.[27] A number of new Benedictine houses were founded.[28]

Eventually, too, the new life captured the Papacy. The struggle at Rome was prolonged. The victory for the stricter party was not quickly won. Now and again a reforming Pope was succeeded by one of the other type. Yet the rising tide could not be suppressed and eventually the Papacy and the Papal Curia were constrained to conform. Before the close of the sixteenth century reform was unmistakably in the ascendant. Thus Paul IV, who was elected Pope in

---

[22] For a selected list from the huge bibliography on the Jesuits, see Heimbucher, *op. cit.*, Vol. III, pp. 2-12.

[23] One of the more recent books on Ximenes is Reginald Merton, *Cardinal Ximenes and the Making of Spain* (London, Kegan Paul, Trench, Trubner and Co., 1934, pp. xiv, 279).

[24] Rocco da Cesinale, *Storia delle Missioni dei Cappuccini* (Paris, P. Lethielleux, Rome, Tipografia Barbèra, 3 vols., 1867-1873), Vol. I, p. 21; Aurelius, *De Kapucijnen en de Missie* (Brasscheat, A de Bièvre, c. 1927, pp. 151), pp. 20-22; Heimbucher, *op. cit.*, Vol. II, pp. 387-412, which also contains an excellent selected bibliography.

[25] For a brief summary and selected bibliography, see Heimbucher, *op. cit.*, Vol. II, pp. 546-554.

[26] Pastor, *History of the Popes*, Vol. XI, pp. 510-512, 51}.

[27] Pastor, *op. cit.*, Vol. XVIII, pp. 240-248.

[28] Heimbucher, *op. cit.*, Vol. I, pp. 300-305.

1559, although he himself had had several illegitimate children before he received major orders, commanded prelates to reside in their charges. This means that pluralism was greatly reduced.[29] Under Pius V (1566-1572) the reform movement finally triumphed. This austere Dominican brought simplicity of living into the Papal court and led in many changes which tended to improve the moral and spiritual life of the clergy and of the Church.

The Council of Trent, which met at intervals from 1545 into 1563, defined Roman Catholic doctrine as against the tenets of the Protestants, and enacted measures designed to purge the Church of many of the abuses which had scandalized Europe.

For the spread of Christianity it is significant and important that the new life appeared early in Spain, the most powerful of the colonizing powers of the sixteenth century, and penetrated to the other great colonial power of the century, Portugal.

As we have suggested, Ximenez early began a purge of the Church in Spain. While still a young cleric, he threw up his benefices, joined himself to the Franciscans, and entered upon a life of extreme austerity. In 1492, the fateful year of the first voyage of Columbus, he became, against his will, the confessor of Isabella. That deeply religious queen had already begun a moral cleansing of her court. In Ximenez she found a man who fitted in with her ideals and his promotion was rapid. He became highly influential in affairs of state. In 1495 he was elevated to the see of Toledo, the most powerful in the realm. He was far from successful in making his spirit entirely prevail among the Spanish clergy, but he carried much weight. The Christian humanism of Erasmus long had a profound effect. Although later vigorous efforts were made to stamp out Erasmianism, this was not until it had had wide currency in certain circles.[30] As we have seen, the founder of the Jesuits was from Spain, and the great mystics, Theresa and John of the Cross, were of that land. Under Isabella and some of her successors the enlarged power of the crown over the Spanish Church was utilized to effect reforms in the latter. This was especially true in the reign of Philip II. Until past the middle of the sixteenth century, indeed, the Roman Catholic Reformation was chiefly confined to Spain and Italy. While only a minority of Spaniards seem to have been thoroughly committed to the movement, and some of the clergy who went to the New World represented the older corrupt traditions, numbers of those who crossed the ocean were children of the new day. Religious revival coincided with geographic discov-

[29] Pastor, *op. cit.,* Vol. XV, p. 74, Vol. XVI, pp. 78, 79.

[30] See on this and on many of the reform movements in Spain, the masterly book, Marcel Bataillon, *Érasme et l'Espagne* (Paris, Librairie, E. Droz, 1937, pp. lix, 903).

eries, political conquests, and the subjugation and exploitation of the native races of America, and profoundly affected these other movements.

In Portugal, too, the new life made itself felt, although not in any marked fashion so soon as in Spain. Very early in their career the Jesuits won the enthusiastic support of King John III. John sent one of the original members, Francis Xavier, to the Portuguese territories in the East and turned over to the Society the leading educational centre of the realm, the University of Coimbra. At Coimbra a Jesuit college was founded in 1542 as a training school for missionaries and from this school soon went out missionaries to India, Brazil, and the Congo.[31] It was from a congregation of Benedictines which had been reshaped by the reform movement through the union of a number of Benedictine and Cistercian foundations that the first Benedictine foundation in Brazil sprang.[32] In the latter half of the sixteenth century a reform of monasteries similar to that carried out in Spain was instituted in Portugal at the request of the King.[33]

As in Protestantism, so in Roman Catholicism, the new life did not cease with the sixteenth century. To be sure, in Spain and Portugal something of a decline set in, but the revival made itself felt elsewhere. It was especially noticeable in France. In that realm the Catholic Reformation was late in acquiring strength. For a time Protestantism was strong. The civil wars of the sixteenth century were discouraging to much activity in the old church. Such representatives of the Roman Catholic revival as the Capuchins and the Jesuits were slow in effecting a foothold. However, by the seventeenth century internal political unity and peace had been more nearly achieved and the situation became more favourable. The conversion of Henry IV to Roman Catholicism, although for political purposes, and the end of the wars of religion created an atmosphere in which the new life could flourish. Capuchins and Jesuits became influential. Early in the seventeenth century the Spanish Carmelites who owed so much to Theresa were introduced. In the first half of the century Francis de Sales, like so many of the leaders of the Catholic Reform, of aristocratic stock, and in part a product of Jesuit education, by his treatises gave a fresh impulse to the devotional life, especially of the laity.[34] Partly as a protest against the type of piety represented by

[31] Huonder, *Der hl. Ignatius von Loyola und der Missionsberuf der Gesellschaft Jesu*, pp. 23-26.

[32] Pastor, *History of the Popes*, Vol. XIX, pp. 115, 116; Jann, *Die katholischen Missionen in Indien, China, und Japan*, p. 115.

[33] Pastor, *op. cit.*, Vol. XVII, p. 256.

[34] On the extensive literature on Francis de Sales and by him, see Michael Müller, *St. Francis de Sales* (New York, Sheed and Ward, 1937, pp. x, 226), a series of semi-popular lectures, sympathetic, based on wide reading, by a Roman Catholic. On Francis

Francis de Sales and as a religious movement of great power but ultimately outlawed, Jansenism arose.[35] In the seventeenth century Vincent de Paul initiated the Congregation of the Priests of the Mission, better known as the Lazarists, which was designed to improve the religious life of the poor in rural regions but was soon to be very active in missions abroad. He also began the Daughters of Charity, foundling hospitals, and a hospital for galley slaves. He sent missionaries to North Africa and Madagascar.[36] In the seventeenth century, too, the Sulpicians were founded. Towards the end of the seventeenth century a revival within the Franciscan stream took the form of the Recollects. In 1643 the Eudists were founded for the purpose of raising the religious level of the masses and for the education of worthy secular priests in seminaries.[37] Also towards the end of the seventeenth century the Brothers of Christian Schools were begun, a movement for popular education.[38] This new life appeared in time to make itself felt in the colonial and commercial activities of the French in North America and India, for these did not assume impressive proportions until the seventeenth and eighteenth centuries.

In Roman Catholicism much more than in Protestantism, the eighteenth century was one of quiescence. Rationalism and the accompanying Deism undercut zeal. We shall note later how on most geographic frontiers of Roman Catholicism as the century progressed advance slowed down or stopped. We shall see, too, that, as with Protestanism, the pause was only the prelude to a fresh outburst of life. As in Protestantism, moreover, even in the eighteenth century, in Roman Catholicism there were signs of vitality. Thus the Sisters of Charity of Namur[39] came into being, the Redemptionists

de Sales and sixteenth, seventeenth, and eighteenth century religious movements in France, see Henri Bremond, *A Literary History of Religious Thought in France from the Wars of Religion down to Our Own Times,* translated by K. L. Montgomery (London, Society for Promoting Christian Knowledge, 2 vols., 1928), scholarly, warmly pro-Roman Catholic.

[35] Of the large literature on Jansenism, for our purpose only one title need here be mentioned—the recent scholarly study, Nigel Abercrombie, *The Origins of Jansenism* (Oxford, The Clarendon Press, 1936, pp. xii, 341). Abercrombie carries the story to the end of Port Royal.

[36] Pierre Coste, *The Life and Works of Saint Vincent de Paul,* translated from the French by J. Leonard (London, Burns Oates and Washbourne, 1934-1935), *passim;* Pierre Coste, *La Congrégation de la Mission dite de Saint-Lazare* (Paris, Librairie Lecoffre, J. Gabalda et Fils, 1924, pp. viii, 231), pp. 2-16, 193-196; Gurchard, *Saint Vincent de Paul* (Paris, Desclée de Brouwer et Cie, pp. 331), *passim.*

[37] Heimbucher, *op. cit.,* Vol. III, pp. 442-452.

[38] George Rigault, *Histoire Générale de l'Institut des Frères des Écoles Chrétiennes* (Paris, Librairie Plon, Vol. I, 1937), *passim.*

[39] Alfred Corman, *Annuaire des Missions Catholiques au Congo Belge . . . 1924* (Brussels, Librairie Albert Dewit, 1924, pp. 228), p. 88.

were founded for popular evangelism, and the Passionists were brought into existence.[40]

In Russia Christianity displayed new vigour, but in quite different fashion from Western Europe. After the fall of the Byzantine Empire before the Moslem Turk, Russians came to think of Moscow as the "third Rome," the successor to Rome and Constantinople as the centre of orthodox Christianity. When in the seventeenth century the Patriarch Nikon undertook, partly for the purpose of inducing the portion of the church which looked to Kiev for leadership to accept the authority of the Patriarchate of Moscow, the revision of the service books to bring them closer to those of Kiev and of the Greek Church, severe opposition broke forth. This took the form of adherence to the unamended service books and to the customary ritual. Towards the end of the seventeenth and in the eighteenth century sects of various kinds arose within the Russian Church or broke with it. Some of these seem to have been due to Protestant influence. Others were quite indigenous. Of them we are to say more later. Here we must note that none of them greatly aided in the extension of Russian Christianity.[41]

Geographic expansion of the faith arose out of the new life in the Christianity of Northern and Western Europe. In the three centuries between A.D. 1500 and A.D. 1800 all three branches of Christianity which experienced the awakenings directed part of their energy towards the propagation of their religion. All three took advantage of the geographic discoveries, the commerce, and the migrations of European peoples to spread the Christian message and to extend the borders of their particular wings of the Church.

Of these three major branches, the most active in the extension of Christianity during this period was Roman Catholicism. The majority of the missions of these first three hundred years of the expansion of European peoples were by those who looked to the Pope as the co-ordinating centre of their faith.

The reasons for this preponderance of Roman Catholics were varied.

As compared with Russian Christianity, the explorations, trade, and settlements of the period brought Roman Catholics in touch with larger numbers of non-Christian peoples. Moreover, Roman Catholicism was more activistic and less contemplative and quietistic than was Russian Orthodoxy. This had

---

[40] Élie Marie, *Aux Avant-Postes de la Chrétienté, Histoire des Instituts Religieux et Missionaires* (Paris, P. Lethlielleux, 1930, pp. xii, 343), pp. 246-253; Heimbucher, *op. cit.,* Vol. III, pp. 309-333.

[41] Vernadsky, *A History of Russia*, pp. 76-79; Frederick C. Conybeare, *Russian Dissenters, passim;* Paul Milukow, *Skizzen russischer Kulturgeschichte*, Vol. II, pp. 38-44, 75-77.

been true before A.D. 1500. As, after A.D. 1500, Roman Catholicism and especially Roman Catholic monasticism became increasingly activistic, the contrast was intensified. Because of this difference, Roman Catholics were more
aggressive as missionaries than were the Russian Orthodox. The Russian
dissenters seem to have developed little inclination to carry their interpretation
of the faith to non-Christians. Possibly this was in part because they were
minorities whose energies were expended in winning adherents from the
Orthodox or in maintaining their existence in the face of opposition, and in
part because they inherited the attitude of the Orthodox which valued worship and the inner life above activity. Yet Russian Christians, as we are to see
later, were by no means entirely lacking in efforts to win the non-Christians
on their borders.

The greater prominence of Roman Catholics as against Protestants in the
propagation of Christianity is ascribable to at least six causes.[42]

First of all, in the initial stages of the movement, Protestantism was so
engrossed in making a place for itself against Roman Catholicism, in working
out its own theological positions, in controversies among its various leaders,
and in effecting an organization, that its members had little leisure for concern for non-Christians outside of Western Europe.

In the second place, perhaps partly as an unconscious outgrowth of the latter
position, several of the early leaders of Protestantism disavowed any obligation to carry the Christian message to non-Christians. Thus Luther and
Melanchthon both believed that the end of the world was so imminent that
no time remained to spread the Gospel throughout the world. The new
Testament command to "preach the Gospel to every creature" Luther held
had been binding only upon the original Apostles, and he maintained that
the proclamation of the Christian message throughout the earth as a preliminary prophesied by the New Testament to the end of the age had long
before been accomplished.[43]

A third cause—and again this is really a subdivision of the first—was preoccupation with the wars which arose out of the separation of the Protestants
from the Roman Catholic Church. These conflicts were particularly acute in
Germany, France, and the Netherlands. Protestants were fighting for their
very existence and had little leisure for anything outside Western Europe.

A fourth reason was the comparative indifference of Protestant governments
to spreading the Christian message among non-Christians. Most of the large

[42] Some of these reasons, but bearing mostly upon German missions, are given in
Warneck, *Geschichte der protestantischen Missionen*, pp. 7-41.

[43] Warneck, *op. cit.*, pp. 8-20, in which a number of pertinent excerpts are given from
the writings of Luther.

Protestant bodies were state churches, subject to the control of the secular authorities. None of the Protestant princes was as deeply concerned that non-Christian peoples be taught the Christian faith as were a number of the monarchs of Roman Catholic Spain and Portugal. Indeed, the English East India Company, through which the government controlled British trade and possessions in India and the Far East, for a time bitterly and resolutely opposed missions.

In the fifth place, Protestants lacked the monks who for more than a thousand years had been the chief agents for propagating the faith. Even when they were interested in giving the Gospel to non-Christians, Protestants did not have ready to hand machinery for spreading it among non-Christians. Not since before the year 500 had the mass of the secular clergy and of Christians who remained "in the world" had more than the most casual interest in winning to the Christian faith non-Christians outside of the professedly Christian lands. It was chiefly from among those, clerical and lay, who had abandoned "the world" and joined monastic groups that missionaries had come. An occasional Pope had given them active support. Often princes had backed them financially, morally, or by force of arms, and had even taken the initiative in summoning them to the task of conversion. However, it was monks by whom the actual task of religious instruction was performed. In contrast, Protestants had forsworn monasticism and the Papacy, and, as we have said, very few Protestant princes have ever shown much concern for propagating the Christian faith among non-Christians.

The sixth and chief reason why in general Protestants were not active in propagating the faith among non-Christians was that until the seventeenth and eighteenth centuries they had relatively little touch with non-Christian peoples. Almost none of the Protestant churches bordered upon Moslem territory. Not until the rise of the British and Dutch sea power did Protestant peoples have much direct commercial contact with non-Christians. Of the Protestants only the Dutch and the British had substantial numbers of non-Christians under their political control in the New World and the East, and, with the exception of the Thirteen Colonies, until the rapid growth of British power in North America and India in the second half of the eighteenth century—almost at the end of the period—neither British nor Dutch colonial possessions covered much territory. In few lands where Europeans were not politically dominant were missions possible. In some of the larger non-Christian lands, as in China and Japan, they were prohibited. It is significant that wherever Protestants were in intimate touch with non-Christians missions early sprang up, and that in some instances they penetrated beyond the borders of the Protestant political control. Protestantism proved missionary wherever it had close contacts with non-Christians.

In contrast, Roman Catholicism was in a much more favourable position. As one compares its situation point by point with the factors which militated against Protestant activity in the spread of the faith overseas, the reasons for its greater missionary activity become apparent.

In some lands, as in France, Roman Catholics were too absorbed in the struggle with Protestantism to have energy or thought for foreign missions. However, in Spain and Portugal, the countries most in touch with non-Christian peoples, Protestantism was never a serious menace and such traces of it as existed were early eliminated. Under Philip II Spain expended much of her energy in attempting to stamp out Protestantism in the Netherlands, but at home she was not seriously divided religiously and abroad could act with singleness of purpose. Earnest Roman Catholics were, therefore, more at liberty than were zealous Protestants to give themselves to foreign missions.

Moreover, far from showing the indifference of the early leaders of Protestantism, several of the outstanding figures in the Catholic Reformation were thoroughly committed to foreign missions. Ignatius Loyola, the most influential single man in the Catholic Reformation, was eager to go as a missionary to the Moslems. For a time near its inception his spiritual child, the Society of Jesus, seemed inclined to devote its energies exclusively to foreign missions. Several of the Popes who championed the reform movement interested themselves in the spread of the faith.

Roman Catholics, like Protestants, engaged in what are often known as the Wars of Religion, of which the differences between the two groups were prominent causes. Italy was repeatedly torn by wars into which the religious element entered slightly if at all. Yet, with the exception of the Scandinavian countries, every land in which Protestantism was prominent was divided religiously, sometimes between Roman Catholics and Protestants, and sometimes among differing divisions of Protestants. This was true of Germany, of Switzerland, of France, of the Netherlands, of England, and even of Scotland. On the other hand, the major Roman Catholic power of the sixteenth century, Spain, was never divided by religious wars. Portugal, too, remained united religiously, and by the seventeenth century the Edict of Nantes had so solved the problem of religious division on the principle of live and let live that the presence of a strong Protestant minority did not divert the attention of French Roman Catholics from missions outside the borders of their country.

Then, too, several leading Roman Catholic monarchs, quite unlike the rulers of Protestant countries, actively supported the propagation of the faith among non-Christians in other lands. This was notably true of Philip II of Spain, but the interest of a number of other, less prominent kings of Spain and Portugal was also marked.

Moreover, Roman Catholics needed to create few new instruments for the spread of the faith. As in the years between A.D. 500 and A.D. 1500, most of the missionaries were monks, and secular rulers initiated or actively supported their efforts. Some of the orders which had been prominent in Roman Catholic missions in the Middle Ages, notably the Franciscans and Dominicans, awoke to life in the days of the Roman Catholic Reformation, and extended their labours over wider areas in non-Christian lands than they had done even in the first flush of their youth. To them was added the Society of Jesus. Never had medieval monarchs accorded more hearty support to the spread of Christianity among their subjects than the kings of Spain and Portugal gave to missions among their non-European subjects in the Americas and the East. More constantly than before the year 1500, the Papacy was active in its assistance. To be sure, after A.D. 1500 more often than in the Middle Ages, the Papacy was crowded out by the monarch from the direct supervision of missions. In the Spanish and Portuguese possessions the Papacy was permitted simply to give formal approval to the ecclesiastical appointments and decisions of the state. In India and China, as we are to see, prolonged struggles between the Papacy and the Portuguese state for control of ecclesiastical affairs handicapped the extension of the faith. Yet Rome was more constantly interested in missions than it had been before 1500. Even the jealously limited voice permitted it in Spanish and Portuguese colonial possessions was greater than the complete silence of Rome in the early stages of the conversion of Scandinavia. Rome, too, developed machinery for a more continuous supervision and co-ordination of missions than had existed in the Middle Ages.

Most important of all the reasons for the preponderance of Roman Catholicism in the expansion of Christianity in the three centuries after A.D. 1500 was the more extensive contact of Roman Catholics with non-Christian peoples. Roman Catholics led in the explorations of the fifteenth and sixteenth centuries. The territories occupied by Roman Catholic Spain, Portugal, and France in the Americas and the East were somewhat larger in area and were inhabited by much more numerous populations than were those over which the Greek Orthodox Russians extended their sway and were overwhelmingly greater both in area and in population than were those in the hands of Protestant powers before A.D. 1750. After A.D. 1750 the lands controlled by

British peoples in the New World and in India rapidly expanded, but this was only in the last half century of the period which here concerns us. Roman Catholics had access to non-Christian peoples to a much greater degree than did Protestants or Russian Orthodox. It was primarily for this reason that the new life within the Christianity of Europe in the sixteenth and seventeenth centuries made for the extension of the faith more through Roman Catholic than through either Protestant or Russian Orthodox channels.

The extensive and incredibly daring and persistent Roman Catholic missionary effort is not all the story. While Protestants were slow in becoming interested in propagating their faith among non-Christians and before A.D. 1800 the missions of Roman Catholics were far more extensive than were those of Protestants, as each century passed Protestants were progressively more energetic in spreading the Christian faith and Roman Catholic activity slowed down. Protestants were more aggressively missionary in the seventeenth than in the sixteenth century and in the eighteenth than in the seventeenth century. On the other hand, before A.D. 1800 Roman Catholic Christianity had its greatest expansion in the sixteenth century. In the seventeenth century its gains were still notable, but it suffered severe losses, particularly in Japan and at the hands of the Dutch. In the eighteenth century its advance was markedly retarded and in some areas was turned into a retreat. Not until the nineteenth century did the tide turn once more in its favour.

Moreover, although Roman Catholicism and Russian Orthodoxy spread over far larger areas before A.D. 1800 than did Protestantism, the Christian communities founded by Protestants proved to have much more inward vitality than did those established by the other two branches of the faith. The communities arising out of Roman Catholic and Russian Orthodox efforts required a continuous influx of missionaries from the mother countries to maintain their vigour and even their existence. This was true both of the descendants of Christian white settlers from Europe and of the converts from the indigenous races. The Roman Catholic and Russian Orthodox communities in the Americas and Asia in this period were never the scenes of marked religious revivals. From them went out comparatively few missionaries to the frontiers and to other lands. If European missionaries were withdrawn, most of them either abandoned the faith or deteriorated in the quality of their religious life. On the other hand, several of the Protestant communities on the Atlantic seaboard of North America displayed abounding vitality. In the first half of the eighteenth century they were the scene of a profound and extensive religious revival, the Great Awakening. Although reinforced later by Whitefield from England, in its origin and in most of its leadership the

Great Awakening sprang from the soil. It was American. Out of the Great Awakening arose a number of efforts, predominantly by American-born whites, to win the Indians to the faith. In the nineteenth and twentieth centuries, moreover, from the Protestant communities in the United States came one of the greatest missionary movements in the history of any religion. As we are to see in later volumes, this exerted itself with marked success both in winning the whites, the Indians, and the Negroes within the United States, and in missions to many other lands and peoples. In contrast, the white Roman Catholic populations in the Americas who were offspring of pre-nineteenth century immigrants sent out comparatively few missionaries to the frontiers of their own lands and to other countries. Some exceptions there were, but not numerous enough to invalidate the generalization.

The causes for this difference seem not necessarily to lie in the essential nature of Protestantism or of Roman Catholicism. Certainly in the twentieth century the Roman Catholic communities in the United States, made up of immigrants and their descendants, have been increasingly energetic in initiating and maintaining missions in other lands. The reasons for the contrast must probably be sought in part in the colonial policies of the respective powers. The Spanish regime was paternalistic. In the Americas most of the higher offices in state as well as Church were filled by Spanish-born appointees. American-born whites—Creoles—were kept in subordination. The colonies were minutely and rigorously controlled by the home government. The atmosphere was not encouraging to Creole initiative. On the other hand, considerable freedom was given to the British settlers in North America. In ecclesiastical affairs the colonists eventually enjoyed almost complete autonomy. Under such circumstances initiative was to be expected, both in the internal life of the churches and in the propagation of the faith. It may be, too, that climate is partly accountable—the more relaxing tropics on the one hand and the more stimulating temperate regions on the other. Social and economic factors may also have entered—the lazy pride of the Creole, expecting support by the subject Indians, and the energetic self-reliance of the small farmers, artisans, and merchants who made up so large a proportion of the population of the British North American colonies. In French Canada after the cession to Great Britain in 1763, the Roman Catholics constituted an enclave which emotionally was largely on the defensive and which gave little thought to other lands or peoples.

It must be noted that the Christian communities gathered from indigenous peoples by Protestants as well as by Roman Catholics and Russian Orthodox in the centuries between A.D. 1500 and A.D. 1800 proved passive and relatively

sterile in movements to propagate the faith. This was strikingly different from
the experience in Europe in the preceding period. There some of the most
noteworthy and successful efforts to carry Christianity into new areas were
by those whose forefathers only two or three generations back had been
pagans. Repeatedly the expansion of Christianity was from the recently won
frontiers of the faith.

Here the causes varied from country to country. In Spanish and Portuguese
America the native races were kept too subservient to the white man to
permit much initiative. In British and French America the Indian tribes were
too badly disintegrated by contact with the white man to build stable communities from which missionaries could go. In most of Asia persecution was
too severe to allow of much active propagation of the faith outside of territories
actually under the control of Europeans. Not until the nineteenth and twentieth centuries did Christians of non-European descent engage in much effort
to spread to others the faith which had come to them from Europeans.

Not only was Roman Catholicism the most active of the branches of Christianity in propagating the faith among non-Christians between A.D. 1500 and
A.D. 1800. It also gained ground at the expense of other divisions of Christianity. This it did even as against the two major groups which, with it, were
active in missionary efforts for non-Christians, the Protestants and the Russian
Orthodox.

A full account of the missions of one type of Christianity among the
adherents of another type is outside the scope of this work. To go into that
story with anything approaching the fulness with which we are attempting
to narrate the spread of Christianity among non-Christians or by migration
into regions previously unoccupied by the faith would extend these volumes
beyond all proper limits. However, passing mention must be made of such
efforts, although in the briefest possible summary. Of attempts to bring into
communion with Rome the non-Roman Catholic Christians in lands under the
political control of Moslems and those in Central and Southern Europe who
traced their spiritual descent to Greek Orthódoxy we are to speak in the
next chapter. Here we must say a word concerning Roman Catholic activities
among Protestants.

Roman Catholics regarded Protestantism in all its varied forms as heretical
and as a departure from the true faith and the true Church. They did not
accept the secession as final and felt it to be their duty to try to win back
their erring brethren. That they would do by persuasion if possible and by
force if necessary. The largest contributions of active missionaries in this
effort were from the major order which had arisen from the Catholic Refor-

mation, the Society of Jesus. The Capuchins, also the offspring of the Catholic Reformation, had an important share, and aid came from some of the older orders who had been galvanized into fresh life by the new currents. In some regions, the efforts against Protestantism succeeded. In others they failed.

The failure was notable in England. Here for a time under Mary the old church was restored, but under Elizabeth separation from Rome was once more effected and all the heroic zeal of missionaries could not alter the result.[44]

The areas won back included Poland, where Protestantism had been very strong, particularly among the nobility and the *intelligentsia*, Bohemia, and part of Switzerland. Protestantism, too, was all but eliminated from Italy, and by the revocation of the Edict of Nantes (1685) and the persecutions which followed was markedly reduced in France. In much of the Rhine country, in Southern Germany, and in Austria, too, Protestantism either suffered a reduction in numbers or was stamped out.

The causes of the recession of the Protestant wave were many, and varied from region to region. In some, the divisions into the several types of Protestantism brought weakness. In most of the areas where Roman Catholicism regained ground, the ruling prince or king had espoused the cause of the old church and saw in the Protestants a challenge to his authority. Often the ruthless use of force was employed to convert, expel, or kill the recalcitrants. Nearly everywhere Jesuits, with their warm religious zeal, their schools, and their diplomacy, proved effective agents. The Thirty Years' War (1618-1648) also made for Roman Catholic advance.

When, by the beginning of the eighteenth century, the territorial boundaries between Roman Catholicism and Protestantism assumed something of stability, Protestantism had become confined chiefly to the Teutonic peoples. Except for French-speaking Switzerland, for minorities in France, for the Celtic Welsh, for some of the Highland Scotch, and for enclaves in Hungary and Transylvania, Protestantism was almost entirely confined to peoples of Teutonic stock. It was chiefly by those of Teutonic lineage that the Protestant forms of Christianity were propagated by migration and conversion. Whether this means, as some would have us believe, that Protestantism is the stamp which the Teutonic genius has placed on Christianity, and its emergence the indication that the Teutonic nations had at last made their own the faith which centuries before had been accepted from the non-Teutonic South,

---

[44] From the large bibliography on this subject, a convenient semi-popular summary, from a scholarly Roman Catholic viewpoint, is David Mathew, *Catholicism in England, 1535-1935. Portrait of a Minority, Its Culture and Tradition* (London, Longmans, Green and Co., 1936, pp. xii, 304).

we must not here attempt to decide. To that we will revert later. It is clear, however, that Protestantism has spread chiefly in association with Teutonic peoples—the English, Scotch, Dutch, Germans, and Scandinavians.

From the standpoint of the expansion of Christianity, most of the gains of Roman Catholicism against Protestantism were not of great importance. With one exception, none of the lands from which Protestantism, having once constituted a large numerical element, was all but eliminated, became a major source of Roman Catholic missionaries. The most notable of the lands which were rewon, Poland and Bohemia, were not maritime powers and had no natural contacts with non-Christian peoples. The one exception was France. Even here, however, the reduction of Protestantism in strength probably did not make either for a great increase in Roman Catholic missionaries or for a restriction of the areas outside of Europe occupied by Protestantism. Indeed, the Huguenot migrations induced by persecution strengthened Protestantism in several non-French areas.

Much of the expansion of Roman Catholicism between A.D. 1500 and A.D. 1800 was, as we have said, by machinery and methods which had been tested with time. Most of the missionaries were regulars, in the monastic tradition. Some of the orders of medieval origin, notably the Franciscans and the Dominicans, were prominent in the missions of the Church. We also hear of the Mercedarians and the Hieronymites, founded in the thirteenth and fourteenth centuries respectively.[45] As previously, princes and governmental officials gave active support and often took the initiative in the propagation of the faith. The Papacy interested itself in missions. Conversions were largely *en masse,* by the natural groupings of tribes, or, in India, of castes.

However, some new instruments came into being. Of the new orders we have already spoken. Several of these, notably the Jesuits and the Capuchins, became active in carrying the faith to new frontiers. As we have said, Loyola, the founder of the Society of Jesus, committed himself and his followers to missions among non-Christians. So early did the Society fulfil his dream that he lived to see its members active in India, in the East Indies, in Japan, on the Congo, in America, in the Near East, on the coast of North Africa, and in Abyssinia.[46]

One agency of an entirely new type was the *Sacra Congregatio de Propaganda Fide,* or the Congregation for the Propagation of the Faith, usually

---

[45] Schwager, *Die katholische Heidenmission der Gegenwart,* p. 15.

[46] Huonder, *Der hl. Ignatius von Loyola und der Missionsberuf der Gesellschaft Jesu, passim.*

designated briefly as the Propaganda.[47] This arose partly out of the conviction that Rome should take a more active part in the spread of the faith. It was the outgrowth of several suggestions and experiments, some of them for the training of missionaries in Rome and some of them for greater facilities for initiating, reinforcing, and directing missions from Rome. Thus in 1568 Papal congregations had been created for the conversion of pagans and of heretics. A little later a congregation for the interests of the Church in the Near Orient came into existence. Suggestions were offered to the Papacy for the founding of seminaries for the preparation of missionaries to heretics, pagans, and Moslems. Finally, in 1622, the Propaganda was created. Out of the efforts of Vives, a Spanish prelate, arose a school for the training of missionaries. For the use of this institution, Vives gave his palace on the Piazza di Spagna (1627), and here, in 1627, Pope Urban VIII formally instituted a college, the *Collegium Urbanum de Propaganda Fide*, according to the plan of Vives, for the education of two youths from each of the nations. A few years later this college was placed directly under the Propaganda. Urban VIII also added a press to the Propaganda. In the course of time this came into the possession of type for a large number of different languages, especially of Asia, and in the second half of the eighteenth century was in some respects the outstanding printing establishment of Europe.

The Propaganda ensured a more constant interest of the Papacy in the spread of the faith. Heretofore that concern had varied with the particular pontiff who chanced to be on the throne of Peter. While an individual Pope could still quicken or retard the work of missions, henceforth, with a recognized body for the encouragement and supervision of the propagation of the faith, the predilection of the reigning Pope could not have so profound an effect. Then, too, the Propaganda permitted the accumulation of experience at Rome. It also provided a means for combating the trend to make Roman Catholic missions the tools of the imperialistic policies of the colonizing and commercial powers and tended to strengthen the religious aspects of the missionary enterprise. Almost inevitably conflicts arose between the Propaganda

[47] On the formation and early history of the Propaganda see Schmidlin, *Die Gründung der Propaganda Kongregation (1622)* in *Zeitschrift für Missionswissenschaft*, Vol. XII (1922), pp. 1-14, valuable especially for its summary and its bibliography; L. Kilger, *Die ersten fünfzig Jahre Propaganda*, in the same periodical, Vol. XII, pp. 15-30; K. Pieper, *Ein Blick in die Missionsmethodischen Erlasse der Propaganda,* in the same periodical, Vol. XII, pp. 31-51; K. Hoffmann, *Das erste päpstliche Missionsinstitut*, in the same periodical, Vol. XII, pp. 76-82; Schmidlin, *Katholische Missionsgeschichte*, pp. 207-215; Van der Essen in Descamps, *Histoire Générale Comparée des Missions*, pp. 362-367, 373-375; Schwager, *Die katholische Heidenmission der Gegenwart*, pp. 17-20; Pastor, *History of the Popes*, Vol. XVIII, p. 349.

and some of the colonial powers, notably with Portugal. These we are to describe in later chapters.

In spite of friction with some of the Roman Catholic governments, the Propaganda flourished. Through it the Papacy directed not only missions in non-Christian lands, but also many of the efforts to win back Protestant lands to the Roman Catholic fold. It was made wealthy by the gifts of Cardinals and Popes and was accorded special privileges. As early as 1649 it exercised direct supervision over forty-six missions and over more than three hundred missionaries. It sent out relatively few missionaries directly, but it trained a number of the clergy for labour in the lands over which its jurisdiction extended, and it constituted the agency through which Rome exercised much of the Papal supervision of missions. It was at once a symbol, an instrument, and a promise of a continuing interest of the Papacy in the spread of the faith, and evidence of a resolution to assert the authority of Rome over the frontiers of the Church.

Another new instrument, one which also blazed new trails in organization for the propagation of the Roman Catholic form of Christianity, was La Société des Missions Étrangères of Paris.[48] Unlike any preceding society or order in the Roman Catholic Church, this was purely for the purpose of furthering missions among non-Christian peoples. Earlier Roman Catholic bodies which had engaged in propagating the faith among non-Christians, such as the Benedictines, the Franciscans, the Dominicans, and the Jesuits, had divided their energies between this and other objectives. This Society of Foreign Missions was formally founded in 1663. The leading spirit in calling it into existence was François Pallu. Pallu, himself a missionary to the Far East, was deeply convinced of the importance of raising up an indigenous secular clergy for the infant Christian communities in Eastern and Southern Asia. Only thus, he and his colleagues believed, could these communities enjoy a healthy life and become energetic centres for the spread of the faith in these regions. Regulars, priests who were members of religious orders, and especially orders manned chiefly by Europeans and directed from Europe, could not, they maintained, provide satisfactory leadership for the Church

---

[48] Adrien Launay, a member of the Society, utilized the manuscript archives in preparing a number of volumes on the history of the organization, its general course of development, and its record in separate regions. For the founding of the Society the best account is in the first volume of his *Histoire Générale de la Société des Missions-Étrangères* (Paris, Pierre Téqui, 3 vols., 1894). A briefer semi-popular account is in his *La Société des Missions-Étrangères* (Paris, Pierre Téqui, 1919, pp. 211).

See also Schwager, *Die katholische Heidenmission der Gegenwart*, p. 40, and François Pallu, *Relation Abregée des Missions et des Voyages des Evesques François envoyez aux Royaumes de la Chine, Cochinchine, Tonquin, et Siam* (Paris, Denys Bechet, 1668, pp. 148).

in Asia. If the Church were to be really rooted in non-European lands, the bulk of its parish clergy must, as in Europe, be seculars, of native stocks and under native bishops. These, Pallu and his associates held, could best be recruited and trained by seculars. Regulars, when they had native seculars in their missions, kept them in subordination to the orders. Under the domination of the regulars, the secular clergy could never have come to its normal place of leadership. The Foreign Missionary Society of Paris, therefore, had as its purpose the sending out of secular priests to help initiate the work of conversion and to raise up a native secular clergy. Its organization, like that of most vigorous movements, developed gradually. It centred about a seminary in Paris. In 1665 a union was effected with a seminary in Quebec, founded by Montmorency Laval, the first Bishop of Quebec, and so Canada was added to its fields. Control rested largely in the directors of the Paris seminary, men chosen from among those with long missionary experience. By A.D. 1700 the society had recruited one hundred and nineteen priests, and by A.D. 1800, one hundred and ninety-eight. In time the Society occupied vast areas, especially in China, Indo-China, and Siam. Whether it was more successful than the orders in calling forth vigorous native Christian communities and a native secular clergy is debatable.

Innovations in Roman Catholic missions between A.D. 1500 and A.D. 1800 were not confined to organizations and instruments in Europe. They extended also to methods.

As we have suggested, many of the methods employed by Roman Catholic missions in this period bore a striking similarity to those of earlier centuries. Monarchs made the spread of the faith one of their obligations and they and their subordinates frequently initiated, financed, and supervised missions. Sometimes the motive was as much political as religious. Thus on the frontiers of Spanish America, missions were quite generally employed as a means of extending Spanish rule and of assimilating the Indians to Spanish culture. This, it will be recalled, was very similar to the Saxon policy of Charlemagne and of the programmes of some of the German rulers of the Middle Ages for the Slavs on their borders. Mass conversions were the rule wherever these were possible. In Western and Northern Europe, it will be remembered, whole peoples, led by their princes, had substituted Christianity for paganism as the religion of their community. So in the New World and in parts of India, Ceylon, and the East Indies, peoples abandoned *en masse* their own gods for the God of their white conquerors.

However, in some important respects conditions under which Christianity was propagated between A.D. 1500 and A.D. 1800 differed from those of the preceding thousand years. Other methods were, accordingly, necessary. For instance, in the Americas and the Philippines alien races were kept permanently under the political and ecclesiastical tutelage of whites on a much larger scale than ever before. The closest resemblance in previous centuries was the relation of the Teutonic Knights to their subjects in the lands on the Baltic.

Then, too, alterations in the methods and programme of the Roman Catholic Church in Europe were reproduced or adapted on the expanding frontiers of the faith. Thus the development of catechisms by Roman Catholics in Europe was soon followed by their employment for the instruction of neophytes drawn from paganism.[49]

An extensive literature on problems connected with missions came into existence. The issue of the consistency of the Spanish and Portuguese conquests with Christian ethics; the question of whether force could be employed to effect conversions; the differences of opinion over the propriety of administering the communion to baptized Indians; and controversies over the accommodation of Christian practices and teachings to the ancient cultures of China and India all evoked voluminous writing.[50]

Among the innovations several, of varying importance, call for brief notice. To some of them we will recur more fully in later chapters.

One of these new methods was the specialized preparation of missionaries for their task. We have already noted the Jesuit college established at Coimbra. It became a training school for missionaries to the Indies. From it in the course of two centuries went out sixteen hundred and fifty missionaries.[51] Two colleges were opened in Rome for the preparation of missionaries of two different branches of the Franciscans.[52] In the eighteenth century two colleges for the formation of Franciscan missionaries, one of them with Tibet in view, were opened in Spain.[53] We shall hear of similar colleges or seminaries in the New World. At the very outset of its career, the Propaganda insisted that missionaries study the languages of the peoples among whom they worked. Upon this it continued to insist.[54]

A change in method from the Middle Ages was the almost complete

---

[49] Jann, *Die katholische Missionen in Indien, China und Japan*, p. 193; Berg, *Die katholische Heidenmission als Kulturträger*, Vol. II, p. 30.

[50] Van der Essen in Descamps, *Histoire Générale Comparée des Missions*, p. 309; Schmidlin, *Catholic Mission Theory*, pp. 12-16.

[51] Van der Essen, in Descamps, *op. cit.*, p. 305.

[52] Eduardius Alenconiensis, *Collegii S. Fidelis pro Missionibus Ordinis Fratrum Minorum Capuccinorum*, p. vi; Lemmens, *Geschichte der Franziskanermissionen*, p. 6.

[53] Eduardius Alenconiensis, *op. cit.*, p. viii.

[54] Berg, *op. cit.*, Vol. II, p. 5.

absence, after A.D. 1500, of the use of the Crusading military orders in effecting conquests. These orders had arisen out of the Crusades and had been a favoured method in the struggle of the Cross against the Crescent. The Teutonic Knights and the Knights of the Sword were prominent in the conversion of peoples along the Baltic. In the initial stages of the Portuguese discoveries, in the fifteenth century, the Order of Christ, the successor of the Templars in Portugal, was theoretically prominent, for Prince Henry the Navigator was its grand master. Beyond this, however, the military orders had no prominence in the conquests and missions of the new day. Missions and territorial conquest were often associated, but the function of the missionary and the function of soldier were now separated.

This was related to another alteration in method—the beginning of active opposition of missionaries to the exploitation by Europeans of non-European peoples. In the preceding thousand years, not only was the spread of Christianity sometimes closely intertwined with the conquest of pagan by professedly Christian peoples, but, as well, missionaries seldom protested against the acts of the conquerors. Between A.D. 1500 and A.D. 1800 the expansion of Christianity and the imperialism of Christian powers still went hand in hand. Now, however, the missionary frequently denounced and vigorously sought to counteract the maltreatment of subject peoples.

In part as a phase of the effort of the Roman Catholic Church to achieve the independence of its missions from subordination to the state was the use of vicars apostolic in place of diocesan bishops. Here was an entirely new development. The title of vicar apostolic had been employed centuries before, but not in the sense in which it came to be used in this period. Vicars apostolic were now appointed by the Holy See to lands where a Protestant or a pagan government or the claim to the right of patronage by a Roman Catholic power made the customary hierarchy inadvisable. The vicar apostolic usually was a titular bishop, that is to say, he bore the designation of some extinct see. He exercised most of the usual episcopal powers, but he held these as directly delegated by the Pope and not in his own name. He did not enjoy what in technical language is called the jurisdiction of an "ordinary." Rome exercised its control through the Propaganda.[55]

Relatively new was the deliberate effort of the Propaganda to bring about the creation of a native clergy. In most of Western Europe this had never been a serious problem. Usually within a generation or two the foreign

---

[55] Jann, *op. cit.*, pp. 214, 215; Schmidlin, *Catholic Mission Theory*, pp. 166-170; *Codex Juris Canonici*, Canon 294, Sec. 1. The vicars apostolic possess the same rights as bishops "nisi quid Apostolica Sedes reservaverit."

clergy and hierarchy gave way to one sprung from the soil. Now, however, the foreign clergy tended to perpetuate their control. In the vast Spanish possessions, indeed, if they were Creoles, or colonials by birth, even whites were discriminated against for the higher offices and supervision was kept in the hands of the Spanish-born. In lands where the Spanish or Portuguese crowns exercised the right of patronage, Rome could do little to alter the procedure. However, in regions where the Papacy had direct control, the Propaganda again and again stressed the importance of a native clergy.[56] It welcomed the purpose of the Foreign Missionary Society of Paris to recruit and train an indigenous secular clergy.

For all this effort, however, a native clergy did not develop much if any more rapidly in the lands where the Propaganda's decrees were respected than in those where the Spanish and Portuguese colonial policies prevailed. With the exception of the Uniate bodies, groups from the church of the East which accepted the authority of Rome, and of one or two abortive and brief attempts elsewhere, the European clergy were dominant in the new bodies called into existence by the Roman Catholic missions of this era.

As in the preceding centuries, the lay Roman Catholic Christians of Europe had relatively little direct share in the financial support of missions. In the Spanish and Portuguese possessions some of the funds were contributed directly by the state. Numbers of the missions were partly or entirely self-supporting. The fruits of the labour of the Christians under the direction of the missionaries provided part or all of what was needed. Indeed, missionaries, and especially Jesuit missionaries, were repeatedly accused of engaging in commerce and of being fully as eager to make money as they were to save souls. To be sure, here and there private donors came to the support of missions. Thus the Duchess de Aveiro de Arcos y Maqueda gave liberally to the promotion of Roman Catholic missions in several parts of the world, and was sometimes termed "the mother of missions."[57] The Pious Fund from which much of the support of missions in California was obtained was an endowment accumulated from the gifts of private individuals.[58] Most of these gifts, however, were from a very few wealthy and devout members of the upper classes. We hear of no attempts to obtain contributions

[56] Néez, *Documents sur le Clergé Tonkinois aux XVIIe et XVIIIe Siècles* (Paris, P. Téqui, 1925, pp. ix, 273), p. iv; Huonder, *Der einheimische Klerus in der Heidenländern*, pp. 1, 183, 260, 261.

[57] Rufus Kay Wyllys, *Pioneer Padre, The Life and Times of Eusebio Francisco Kino* (Dallas, The Southwest Press, 1935, pp. xi, 230), p. 19.

[58] Zephyrin Engelhardt, *The Missions and Missionaries of California* (Santa Barbara Mission, Santa Barbara, 2d ed., 2 vols., 1929, 1930), Vol. I, pp. 161-166.

from large numbers of the faithful. For that we must wait until the nineteenth and twentieth centuries. The great masses of Roman Catholic Christians in Europe did not actively concern themselves with the spread of their faith in the lands opened by the discoveries and conquests of the sixteenth, seventeenth, and eighteenth centuries. They left that task to the state, to a few of the clergy, and to orders and congregations whose especial charge it was.

As we have more than once suggested, the nations most active in the propagation of Roman Catholic Christianity in the sixteenth and seventeenth centuries were Spain and Portugal.

The Portuguese sphere was Brazil, the west and east coasts of Africa, the southern and eastern shores of Asia, and the East Indies. Here Portugal rested her claim in part upon discovery and conquest and in part upon Papal bulls. As early as 1418 and 1419 the Pope had encouraged the King of Portugal to conquests in Mauretania, in North-west Africa. In 1455 the Pope granted Portugal extensive rights of conquest in the lands of the Moslems and the pagans. There was a further grant in 1481, and in 1514 a confirmation of earlier privileges. In 1456 the bull of 1455 was made perpetual which gave to the Order of Christ (Portuguese) ecclesiastical jurisdiction over lands taken by Portugal from Capes Lao and Bojador to Guinea and from there to India. In return for Papal support, the King of Portugal was commanded to send and support missionaries and to found and maintain churches, chapels, and monasteries.[59] By the bull *Æquum Reputamus* of 1534, the King of Portugal was bound to provide missionaries and to support them in the Portuguese possessions between the Cape of Good Hope and Japan.[60]

The Spanish sphere of influence was chiefly in the Americas, but also included the Philippines. This, too, rested in part upon Papal bulls. For instance, in 1493 Pope Alexander VI issued several bulls granting Spain exclusive jurisdiction over islands and countries already discovered or to be discovered by Columbus, on condition that the Christian faith be propagated among them.[61]

Spain was much more successful than Portugal in spreading the Christian faith in the allotted territories. The reasons for this are fairly obvious. Spain's colonial territories, while enormous, were not so huge as those to which Portugal aspired. Moreover, they were more compact. Save for the Philippines, practically all of them lay in the New World, and, with the exception

[59] Jann, *Die katholische Missionen in Indien, China, und Japan*, pp. 37-39, 43.
[60] Jann, *op. cit.*, pp. 174-177.
[61] Pastor, *History of the Popes*, Vol. VI, pp. 160-162.

of the West Indies, were continuous. Outside of Mexico and Peru, the subjects of Spain had primitive cultures and, when once conquered, were fairly easy to convert. In Mexico and Peru the populations were so thoroughly subdued that they offered no effective resistance to the nominal acceptance of the religion of their new masters. On the other hand, in Asia Portugal was confronted by ancient and high cultures with well-organized religions. Hinduism, Buddhism, and Islam proved much more doughty adversaries than the crude polytheism and animism which Spanish missionaries faced in the Americas and the Philippines. Moreover, Portugal was a much smaller country than Spain and had a less numerous population. The white Christian element in the Spanish colonies was much larger than that in the Portuguese possessions. Then, too, the union with Spain (1581-1640) worked disadvantageously for the missions of Portugal. In view of all these factors, it is not strange that the achievements of Spain in spreading the faith were much more notable than those of Portugal.

Both Portugal and Spain pushed their missions much less energetically in the latter part of the seventeenth and in the eighteenth century than they had in the sixteenth and in the first half of the seventeenth century. Both powers were declining in vigour and in prominence and the progressive somnolence extended to the propagation of the faith. Neither entirely ceased to maintain missions. Indeed, some of the best remembered of the Spanish achievements were in the eighteenth century. Yet before the eighteenth century the prodigious burst of energy which had carried Spaniards and Portuguese over so much of the earth's surface had largely spent itself.

To a certain extent France came forward to take the place of Spain and Portugal in the spread of the Roman Catholic branch of Christianity. In the seventeenth and eighteenth centuries, France became the most powerful of the states of Continental Europe.[62] She undertook to build a colonial and commercial empire in the West Indies, North America, and India. At the same time, she was the scene of a rising tide of religious life. In the latter part of the seventeenth and in the eighteenth century, therefore, French missionaries were numerous and went to both America and Asia. Yet the French were too engrossed in their European projects to devote more than a small proportion of their energy to exploits across the water. They never quite filled the gap left by the shrinking of Spanish and Portuguese activity.

Italy held the native places of a number of missionaries, but none of the states of Italy had colonial possessions in pagan as distinguished from Moslem

[62] A summary of some of the French missionary activities is in Schwager, *Die katholische Heidenmission der Gegenwart*, pp. 13, 14.

lands. Numbers of Germans became missionaries, and now and again some German prince assisted with financial contributions, but no German state as such had much part in missions.[63]

In general, the eighteenth century was one of decline and stagnation in Roman Catholic missionary activity. To this several factors contributed.[64] The decay of Spain and Portugal brought serious weakness. The Jesuits were swept aside by a rising storm of enmity. In 1759 they were driven out of Portuguese domains. In 1764 the Society was abolished in France and in 1767 those members who remained were expelled. In 1767 the Jesuits were suppressed in the Spanish possessions. In 1773 the Society was dissolved by the Pope. Since the Jesuits had been the most active in missions of all the Roman Catholic orders, their disappearance proved a severe blow. The religious scepticism and indifference which accompanied the Enlightenment undercut much of missionary enthusiasm. On top of all these blows came, in 1789, the French Revolution. This spread through much of Western Europe and was followed immediately by the wars of Napoleon. For more than twenty-five years Europe was the scene of movements which either were opposed to the Roman Catholic Church or dealt cavalierly with it. As a result, Roman Catholic efforts to spread the faith more nearly halted than at any time since the fifteenth century.

The course of the spread of the Protestant forms of Christianity in these centuries, as we have suggested, was almost the exact opposite of that of Roman Catholicism. In the sixteenth century, the heyday of Roman Catholic missionary activity, Protestants made almost no attempt to propagate the faith outside of Europe. In the seventeenth century efforts grew in number and importance. In the eighteenth century, when the Roman Catholic missionary enterprise was slowing down, came a still further increase, and the decade of the seventeen nineties, when Roman Catholic missions seemed almost in their death throes, saw what is often called the beginning of modern Protestant missions and the formation of what later became some of the largest of Protestant missionary societies.

Even in the sixteenth century a few Protestants began to show an interest in propagating their forms of the faith in the lands which were being opened by the geographic discoveries of the age. It is true that in the three centuries between A.D. 1500 and A.D. 1800 Protestants were not nearly so active as were Roman Catholics in transmitting the Christian faith to non-Christian peoples. However, when commerce, conquests, and settlement began to

[63] Schwager, op. cit., p. 14.
[64] See a discussion of these in Schmidlin, Katholische Missionsgeschichte, pp. 358-366.

bring Protestants into intimate relations with non-Christian peoples, from practically the very first here and there were those who were stimulated to use these contacts to give the Christian message to those who had not heard it. Thus in the ill-fated and short-lived attempt (1555-1556) of French Protestants under Nicholas Durand, better known as Villegagnon, to found a colony in Brazil near the present Rio de Janeiro, one of the clergy who accompanied the expedition had intended to endeavour to win some of the natives to the faith, but was discouraged by the savage state and apparent stupidity of those whom he saw.[65] It is significant that this colony, the first effort of Protestants to seek a refuge and establish a settlement in the New World, should be accompanied by the purpose of spreading the faith among non-Christians.

Not far from the same time, Gustavus Vasa, the first Protestant King of Sweden, sent missionaries to the Lapps in the northern portions of his realms, but, since at least some of the Lapps were already nominally Christians, it is a question whether the enterprise was so much for the purpose of extending the geographic boundaries of the Christian faith as for completing the process of drawing whatever of Christianity existed among these peoples into conformity with Protestant ideals.[66]

Dutch commerce and settlements, bringing contacts with non-Christian peoples, as we shall see more at length in several of the succeeding chapters, were accompanied by attempts on the part of Dutch Christians to win these non-Christians to the Protestant form of the faith. Indeed, in 1590, five years before the first Dutch commercial venture set sail for the East Indies, Adrianus Savaria, a Dutch Protestant pastor, came out with the assertion that the command to preach the Christian Gospel to every creature was binding, not merely on the Apostles, but also on the entire Church.[67] In 1618 Justus van Heurn issued in Leyden an appeal for missions to the Indies and in 1622 a missionary seminary was established at Leyden which in the succeeding ten years trained twelve youths who were sent as missionaries to the East.[68]

So, too, in the English colonizing ventures, from the very first, the efforts to win converts from among non-Christian peoples accompanied the attempts to found settlements. In 1587, Hakluyt, an English clergyman who was

[65] Warneck, *Geschichte der protestantischen Missionen*, p. 22; Brown, *History of the Propagation of Christianity among the Heathen since the Reformation*, Vol. I, pp. 1-6; Wiggers, *Geschichte der evangelischen Mission*, Vol. I, p. 22; Lescarbot, *Histoire de la Nouvelle-France*, Book II.
[66] Warneck, *op. cit.*, p. 23; Brown, *op. cit.*, Vol. I, pp. 7-9; Wiggers, *op. cit.*, Vol. I, p. 23.
[67] Warneck, *op. cit.*, pp. 19, 20.
[68] Grössel, *Die Mission und die evangelische Kirche im 17 Jahrhundert*, pp. 21-23; Kalkar, *Geschichte der christlichen Mission unter den Heiden*, Vol. I, pp. 16, 17.

deeply interested in encouraging English voyages and the extension of the British name, in a dedicatory letter to Raleigh of an edition of Peter Martyr Angleri's *De Orbe Novo*, spoke of one object of such adventures as bringing those not knowing God to a reverence for the divine name.[69] In the famous fleeting settlement on Roanoke Island, in Pamlico Sound off the coast of North America, one of its members, Hariot, expounded the contents of the Bible to the Indians, and we hear of them as asking for Christian prayer in time of illness, possibly because they thought that its magic, added to their own, might assist in recovery.[70] The first charter, by James I, for the plantation in Virginia (1606) said that one purpose of the enterprise was the propagation of "the Christian religion to such people as yet live in darkness and miserable ignorance of the true knowledge and worship of God."[71] The second Virginia charter, granted by James I in 1609, declared that "the principal effect which we desire and expect of this action is the conversion and reduction of the people in those parts unto the true worship of God and the Christian religion."[72] Early in the history of Virginia, a project was set afoot for the establishment of a college at Henrico for the education of the children of Indians in the Christian faith. James I issued a letter asking that collections be taken in England for the proposed institution, several hundred pounds were received, and in 1620 George Thorpe was sent out as the college's superintendent.[73]

It was to be expected that in New England, in whose earliest settlements the religious motive was potent, missions to Indians would be especially strong. The first charter of the colony of Massachusetts, granted in 1628, spoke of the royal desire that the settlers by "their good life and orderly conversation" might "win and invite the natives of that country to the knowledge and obedience of the only true God and saviour of mankind and the Christian faith."[74] It is not surprising that the most famous of the early missions by British Protestants, that of John Eliot, should be near Boston. To support the work of John Eliot and to carry on other missions among the Indians of New England, there came into existence what seems to have been the first Protestant missionary society. It was, indeed, without exact counterpart in the earlier spread of Christianity or of any other religion.

[69] *De Orbe Novo Petri Martyris Anglerii Medio Ianensis . . . Labore et Industria Richardi Hakluyti . . . additus est* (Paris, Guillelmum Avvray, 1587, pp. 605).

[70] Anderson, *The History of the Church of England in the Colonies and Foreign Dependencies of the British Empire,* Vol. I, pp. 67-71, 74, 75.

[71] See the text in Lucas, *Charters of the Old English Colonies in America,* p. 2.

[72] See the text in Lucas, *op. cit.,* p. 18.

[73] Anderson, *op. cit.,* Vol. II, pp. 255-258.

[74] See the text in Lucas, *op. cit.,* p. 43.

Through it the Christian impulse was giving birth to a new type of organization. This was "the President and Society for the Propagation of the Gospel in New England." It was incorporated in 1649 by the Long Parliament and the act ordered that a collection be taken through the counties, towns, and parishes of England and Wales for the Society's purposes.[75] Nearly £12,000 was thus received. It was invested and the income was expended for the purposes of the organization. On the Restoration, the charter lapsed, but in 1661 it was renewed by Charles II under the title of the "Company for the Propagation of the Gospel in New England and the Parts adjacent in America" and the celebrated and deeply religious Robert Boyle became its first Governor.[76] It enjoyed a continuing life.

Moreover, Robert Boyle left by bequest a sum for the "propagation of the Christian religion among infidels." For many years the income was remitted to William and Mary College in Virginia for the education of Indian children. After the independence of the Thirteen Colonies, the fund was administered by a new society formed for this purpose, usually known briefly as the "Christian Faith Society," which supported missions of the Church of England in Mauritius and in the British possessions in the West Indies.[77]

To the seventeenth century, too, belongs the inception of missionary effort of the Friends among the Indians. No permanent mission station was established until the last decade of the eighteenth century, but long before then individual Friends, including George Fox himself, had preached to them.[78]

In the seventeenth century, moreover, began that remarkable series of immigrations to the Atlantic seaboard of North America by Protestant groups which eventually led to the emergence of commonwealths of peoples of Western European stock. Many of these settlers were from groups which laboured under disabilities in Europe. Puritans, Independents, Quakers, and Mennonites, they represented earnest and original movements whose members for the sake of conscience and from religious motives could not conform to the official churches of the Old World. In the New World they sought a

[75] Hazard, *Historical Collections*, Vol. I, p. 635; [H. W. Busk], *A Sketch of the Origin and the Recent History of the New England Company by the Senior Member of the Company* (London, Spottiswoode and Co., 1884, pp. 89), pp. 8-10.

[76] Hazard, *op. cit.*, Vol. II, pp. 438, 439; Thomas Birch, *The Life of the Honourable Robert Boyle* (in *The Works of the Honourable Robert Boyle*, London, 1772, Vol. I, pp. vi-ccxviii), pp. lxvi, lxviii; Hole, *Early History of the Church Missionary Society*, pp. xxi, xxii.

[77] Hole, *op. cit.*, pp. xxii, xxiii.

[78] Rayner W. Kelsey, *Friends and the Indians, 1655-1917* (Philadelphia, The Associated Executive Committee of Friends on Indian Affairs, 1917, pp. xi, 291), pp. 19-36.

refuge and opportunity for religious freedom. Here was a form of the expansion of Christianity which differed from the colonies formed by the Roman Catholic powers of the period. To it we must revert in more detail later.

In Germany as well as in England and the Netherlands, the seventeenth century witnessed in Protestantism a rising concern for the propagation of the faith outside of Europe. In the first half of the century several Lutheran writers came forward in advocacy of missions to non-Christians.[79] A small group of young men, apparently law students, from prominent families in Lübeck, became interested in missions. One of them, Peter Heyling, went to Egypt in 1633 and thence to Abyssinia, and after several years died a martyr's death.[80] In the second half of the century, in spite of the wastage wrought in the spiritual and material life of Germany by the recently ended Thirty Years' War, the beginnings of an abounding new life in Protestantism were seen which had as one expression a growing purpose to share the Christian Gospel with non-Christians. Justinianus von Weltz put forward an elaborate suggestion for a society, "the brotherhood of Christ," supported by voluntary gifts, which should further missions among non-Christians. The plan included a *collegium de propaganda fide* for the training of missionaries.[81] At the close of the seventeenth century and early in the eighteenth century the philosopher Leibnitz came out vigorously for missions.[82] The Prussian Society for Philosophical Knowledge, formed in 1700, had as one of its objects the spread of Christianity among non-Christians.[83]

In the seventeenth century the Pietist movement began in Germany, and the fresh impulses for which it was the channel later issued in efforts to carry the Christian faith the world around. Spener, the father of Pietism, expressed his conviction that the spread of the Christian message should not be left to the Roman Catholics.[84]

In the closing years of the seventeenth and in the eighteenth century Pietism gave rise to a large number of missionary enterprises. The scholarly and energetic August Hermann Francke, who succeeded Spener as the outstand-

---

[79] Grössel, *Die Mission und die evangelische Kirche im 17 Jahrhundert*, pp. 13-20; Warneck, *Geschichte der protestantischen Missionen*, pp. 25-29.

[80] Warneck, *op. cit.*, p. 24; Pauli in *Allgemeine Missions-Zeitschrift*, Vol. III (1876), pp. 206-223.

[81] Grössel, *op. cit.*, pp. 33-67; Wolfgang Grössel, *Justinianus von Weltz, der Vorkämpfer der lutherischen Mission* (Leipzig, Akademische Buchhandlung, 1891, pp. 191), *passim*.

[82] Carl Heinrich Christian Plath, *Die Missionsgedanken des Freiherrn von Leibnitz* (Berlin, W. Schultze, 1869, pp. 88).

[83] Plath, *op. cit.*, pp. 47 ff.; Pascoe, *Two Hundred Years of the S. P. G.*, p. 468.

[84] Kalkar, *Geschichte der christlichen Mission unter den Heiden*, Vol. I, p. 16.

ing leader of the movement, gave a great impetus to missions both to Christians and to non-Christians.[85] From Halle, the Pietist university centre, a number of missionaries went. Missions in such opposite climatic and cultural environments as South India and Greenland had their impulse from Pietism. Pietism stressed an inward, transforming religious experience through Christ, and it was this which characterized the Christianity which Pietists propagated.

Most extensive of all the missionary movements in which Pietism was a major factor was that which bears the name Moravian. The Moravians, Brethren, or *Unitas Fratrum*, traced their spiritual descent from Hus and possibly also from Peter Waldo. They had grown greatly in numbers and power in the sixteenth century, but in the seventeenth century had been almost wiped out. Beginning with 1722, a few remnants settled on the estates of Count Zinzendorf in the present Saxony not far from the mountains which there separate Saxony from Bohemia. Here they built a village, Herrnhut, and here they were joined by fragments of other persecuted sects. Nicolaus Ludwig Zinzendorf, their benefactor, was of Pietist parentage and from his youth entered enthusiastically into the Pietist experience. He was educated in part at Halle under strong Pietist influences and early dreamed of an extensive propagation of Christianity among non-Christians. In the settlers at Herrnhut his ardent imagination saw the means for making this vision effective. He became the leader of the group. His conviction proved contagious and persistent. Herrnhut became the centre of a missionary enterprise which extended over much of the world. Zinzendorf's death did not bring the movement to an end. It continued and grew. We are to meet it again and again, particularly before A.D. 1800, but also in later years. Here was a new phenomenon in the expansion of Christianity, an entire community, of families as well as of the unmarried, devoted to the propagation of the faith. In its singleness of aim it resembled some of the monastic orders of earlier centuries, but these were made up of celibates. Here was a fellowship of Christians, of laity and clergy, of men and women, marrying and rearing families, with much of the quietism 'of the monastery and of Pietism but with the spread of the Christian message as a major objective, not of a minority of the membership, but of the group as a whole. Before the end of the eighteenth century the Moravians had begun missions in Russia, in India, in the Nicobar Islands, in Ceylon, among the Indians of the English colonies

---

[85] W. Germann, in *Allgemeine Missions-Zeitschrift*, Vol. XXV (1898), pp. 241-261. For lives of Francke see Gustav Kramer, *August Hermann Francke* (Halle, Verlag der Buchhandlung des Waisenhauses, 1880), and Henry Ernest Guerike, *The Life of Augustus Herman Franke*, translated from the German by S. Jackson (London, R. B. Seeley and W. Burnside, 1837, pp. viii, 296).

in North America, in the Danish and British West Indies, in Surinam, in Central America, on the Gold Coast, in South Africa, among the Lapps, in Greenland, and in Labrador.

The Moravians never sought to bring all other Christians into their Church. After the Pietist pattern, they wished to be a leavening and transforming influence in other communions. As such, they had widespread effect. It was through the Moravians that in 1738 John Wesley entered into the religious experience which proved decisive in bringing Methodism into being. In the Wesleyan revival in England and America and in the growth of world-wide Methodism, the Moravians had their most extensive fruitage.[86]

The closing years of the seventeenth and the opening years of the eighteenth century witnessed the emergence of several Protestant missionary societies. In March, 1699 (1698 by the old style of reckoning) came into existence the Society for Promoting Christian Knowledge. This was formed chiefly by members of the Church of England. The leading figure in its creation was Thomas Bray, Rector of Sheldon and Commissary in Maryland for the Bishop of London. Originally it had as its chief object the strengthening of the Christian faith among the white settlers in the British colonies across the Atlantic, particularly by the distribution of literature and by providing the clergy with libraries. However, it also sought by similar means to raise the level of religious knowledge and living of the masses of nominal Christians in the British Isles and before long it was assisting missions to non-Christians. It had close ties with Pietism. Its inception seems to have been due in part to Pietist influences in England, and it was early hailed by Francke and encouraged somewhat similar movements on the Continent of Europe.[87]

Thomas Bray also had an important share in the founding of the Society

---

[86] On Moravian missions see Karl Müller, *200 Jahre Brüdermission, 1 Band. Das erste Missionsjahrhundert* (Herrnhut, Verlag der Missionsbuchhandlung, 1931, pp. viii, 380); David Cranz, *Alte und neue Brüder-Historie oder kurz gefasste Geschichte der evangelischen Brüder-Unität in den ältern Zeiten und insonderheit in dem gegenwärtigen Jahrhundert* (Burby, Heinrich Detlef Ebers, 1771, pp. 868); J. E. Hutton, *A History of Moravian Missions* (London, Moravian Publication Office, 1923, pp. 550); Otto Uttendörfer and Walther E. Schmidt, *Die Brüder, aus Vergangenheit und Gegenwart der Brüdergemeinde* (Herrnhut, Verein für Brüdergeschichte, 1914, pp. 435).

On Zinzendorf see Hermann Römer, *Nicolaus Ludwig Graf von Zinzendorf* (2d ed., Gnadau, Unitäts-Buchhandlung, 1900, pp. 193); Otto Uttendörfer, *Zinzendorfs Weltbetrachtung. Eine systematische Darstellung der Gedankenwelt des Begründers der Brüdergemeinde* (Berlin, Furche-Verlag G.m.b.H., 1929, pp. 352); Friedrich Adolf Voigt, *Zinzendorfs Sendung, ein Rückblick zur Orientierung über die kirchliche Lage der Gegenwart* (Berlin, Furche-Verlag, 1922, pp. 110).

[87] W. O. B. Allen and Edmund McClure, *Two Hundred Years: The History of the Society for Promoting Christian Knowledge, 1698-1898* (London, Society for Promoting Christian Knowledge, 1898, pp. vi, 551), pp. 1-24, 61-120.

for the Propagation of the Gospel in Foreign Parts, in 1701. This, too, recruited its membership and funds from communicants of the Church of England. It held its initial meeting in Lambeth Palace, the London residence of the Archbishop of Canterbury, and its first president was that dignitary. Its original purpose was the support of clergy in British colonies "for the instruction of the King's loving subjects in the Christian religion" and the winning to the Christian faith of the aborigines and the Negro slaves in these possessions.[88]

In 1709 a society was formed in Scotland for "Propagating Christian Knowledge." It had as its primary object the spiritual welfare of the peoples of the Scotch Highlands but it also subsidized missions to the American Indians.[89]

As the eighteenth century wore on religious awakenings brought new life to British Protestantism, both in the British Isles and in North America. They not only were the beginning of movements which in the nineteenth and twentieth centuries made Protestantism more vigorous and widespread than ever before in its history, but they also eventually made Protestantism more active than any other branch of the Christian movement, even than Roman Catholicism, in the expansion of the faith. Before the middle of the eighteenth century the Wesleys and Whitefield had led in the rise of the Evangelical movement in the British Isles, and the Great Awakening had begun and had commenced to run like wildfire through the Thirteen Colonies. These revivals, like so many others in Christian history, stimulated the expansion of the faith. They brought into a vivid religious experience many of Christian ancestry in the British Isles, and in the English colonies in America helped to plant Christianity firmly among the white stock along the frontier. Out of them also came missions to non-Christians—almost immediately to the American Indians and to Negroes on the English plantations in the New World, and later to other parts of the world.

The intellectual movement, the so-called Enlightenment or *Aufklärung*, which contributed to the decline of Roman Catholic efforts at expansion in the eighteenth century, had repercussions upon Protestantism. The missionary enterprise arising from Pietism was especially affected and slowed down. The war by which the Thirteen Colonies achieved their independence interrupted much of the attempt to win the Indians to the Christian faith. The French Revolution and the wars of Napoleon not only embarrassed Roman Catholic missions

[88] C. F. Pascoe, *Two Hundred Years of the S.P.G. An Historical Account of the Society for the Propagation of the Gospel in Foreign Parts, 1701-1900 (Based on a Digest of the Society's Records)* (London, Published at the Society's Office, 1901, pp. xli, 1429), pp. 3-8; Hole, *Early History of the Church Missionary Society*, pp. xxviii-xxxviii.
[89] Stock, *History of the Church Missionary Society*, Vol. I, p. 27.

but also disturbed those of the Protestants which, like those of the Dutch and the Moravians, drew their support chiefly or entirely from the Continent.

However, the closing years of the eighteenth century witnessed a rapid increase of Protestant missionary activity. The tide of religious life in Great Britain continued to rise. In the last decade of the century, as we are to record more in detail in the next volume, there came into existence the Baptist Missionary Society, the London Missionary Society, the Church Missionary Society, the Glasgow Missionary Society, and the Scottish Missionary Society. These were the pioneers of the remarkable and numerous Protestant missionary societies of the nineteenth and twentieth centuries. The first three have had long and notable careers.

Four general features of this pre-nineteenth century Protestant missionary movement are so striking that they demand especial notice.

The first is one which has already been mentioned. The interest of Protestants in extending their faith to non-Christian peoples increased with each century and did not, like that of the Roman Catholics, have a brilliant rise followed by a discouraging and prolonged decline.

The second has also been recorded. In the Thirteen Colonies of the British there arose in North America through migration a number of churches which were more active in propagating the faith than were any of the Roman Catholic colonial communities, and, indeed, than had been any other Christian communities formed by migration.

From what has already been said, a third feature must be obvious. Protestants were bringing into being new instruments for propagating the Christian faith. The societies which they were forming were without exact precedent in the expansion of Christianity, or, indeed, in the spread of any religious faith. They were organizations, not purely of the clergy, but in which laity and clergy joined. Moreover, several of them did not draw their financial support from the state or from merely a few wealthy donors, as did most of the Roman Catholic missions of the period. They appealed to a large number of donors. In some instances the initial gifts were conserved as an endowment and only the income was expended for the purposes of the society. In others the appeal was continuous. No longer did the expansion of the faith rest upon monastic orders and the state. A widening circle of clergy and laity was enlisted in the active support of missions. Protestantism was without the agencies by which, for a thousand years or more, Christianity had chiefly spread in Europe. It had no monastic orders, and to its missions very few monarchs gave any support. From practically all Protestant rulers the most that could be expected was verbal endorsement. Only here and there was the expansion of the faith used as a political tool. Contemporary Roman Catholicism, it will be recalled, was peculiarly strong in both these traditional aids to its spread. It possessed not only the old, but also new orders which were committed to the missionary obligation. Never had monarchs given quite such persistent and extensive support to the spread of the faith as did those of Spain and some of Portugal. Deprived of these instruments, Protestantism displayed sufficient vitality to develop new ones. The innovations were in part natural outgrowths of its distinctive genius. In accord with the conviction of the priesthood of all Christians, laity shared with clergy in propagating the faith, and the financial burden for the enterprise was assumed by a growing number of the laity and by a non-monastic clergy.

A fourth feature distinctive of the rising Protestant missions was an emphasis upon the conversion of individual non-Christians and a distrust of mass movements of whole communities. As we have repeatedly seen, religions have traditionally been the concern of communities, and have been accepted or abandoned by a community as a whole. It was thus that Christianity had been adopted by the Roman Empire. It was by this process that it had become the faith of Western and Northern Europe. In contrast with this past, most of the forms of Protestantism which gave birth to efforts to propagate Christianity among non-Christians had reacted against much of the superficiality of community Christianity—of state churches—and insisted upon a personal and individual religious experience as the mark of the genuine Christian. This was true of many Puritans, of Quakers, of Congregationalists who were touched by the Great Awakening, of Pietists, of Moravians, of the Wesleys and those moulded by the Evangelical movement, and, indeed, except for a few Anglicans, of practically all Protestants who had much to do with missions. This was in contrast with most of the Roman Catholic missions of the time. Their spectacular successes of this period were by the time-honoured process of the conversion of a tribe or a caste as a whole. The Protestant ideal was historically a development from a community religion and unconsciously presupposed that Christianity was the nominal faith of the group. Could Protestant missions produce the fruits which its supporters expected without the preceding stage of mass conversion? To this question only experience could give the answer.

The length of this introduction has been rather pronounced. It has, however, been necessary. We have had to record the perils which at the close of the fifteenth century seemed about to put an end to the spread of Christianity and to turn expansion into a slow but disastrous retreat. We have had to summarize the movements through which the vitality inherent in Christianity broke out to bring that faith to an unprecedented stage of vigorous life and which were at once the precursors and the channels for the spread of Christianity over a larger area than any religion had previously covered. Christianity, confined by the disasters of the fourteenth and fifteenth centuries chiefly to Europe and threatened even there by the Moslems, and its existence menaced by the emergence of new movements and by internal decay, experienced a series of revivals. In Protestantism the new life expressed itself in a number of new forms, and through the Roman Catholic Reformation it purged the Latin Church of many flagrant ills and brought new orders into being. In Russia the Church displayed increased energy, although not so markedly so as in Western and Southern Europe. Thus reinvigorated, Christianity accompanied the expanding Europe to extensive new frontiers.

It will be recalled that at the outset of the first volume we propounded a number of questions which we said demanded attention. For the period between A.D. 1500 and A.D. 1800 the answers to two of these must now be obvious.

To the inquiry, what was the Christianity which spread, the reply must be, chiefly that of Western Europe and, as a bad second, Greek Orthodoxy in its Russian form. The other types were on the defensive against an aggressive Islam and against a Roman Catholicism which was eager to absorb them. The Christianity of Western Europe had become divided into two main branches, Roman Catholicism and Protestantism. Of these, the former enjoyed the greatest expansion in the three centuries between A.D. 1500 and A.D. 1800. By A.D. 1800, however, while the former was at an ebb, the latter was proving increasingly energetic in spreading the faith.

To the query as to why Christianity spread, the answer must be found partly in the fact that the nominally Christian peoples of Europe were expanding rapidly and partly in the new burst of energy which manifested itself in European Christianity almost simultaneously with this expansion.

Three further generalizations demand mention before we proceed region by region to the account of the process of the spread.

First we must note that in these three centuries much of the expansion of Christianity was by migration. European peoples, whose ancestors had been traditionally Christian, established colonies, some of them of vast extent and destined to attain huge numerical size. The spread of a faith by migration was not new, nor had it been confined to Christianity. However, colonists do not always automatically retain their hereditary faith. Sometimes they surrender it for the religion of the people among whom they settle. We must not regard as a matter of course the extension of Christianity by this means. The processes of its retention and cultivation deserve our notice. We must also record, in their proper place, the effect of Christianity upon these white colonists and the modifying effect of the new environment upon Christianity. Then, too, up to this time no series of migrations by any group of peoples had ever been so extensive and, accordingly, no religion had ever been carried so far and over so wide an area by a *Völkerwanderung*.

In the next place, we must call attention to the growing variety and complexity in our story which the facts make obligatory. Christianity was now carried to more different lands than it or any other one religion had ever before known and became domiciled in a larger variety of cultures and among more different peoples than in any preceding period. We now have to do with the many tribes and cultures of the Americas, with a number of regions of Negro Africa, with practically every portion of Asia, with the East Indies, the Philippines, and with numbers of islands in the Pacific and Indian Oceans. The surviving records of the spread of Christianity also increase in bulk. The materials with which the scholar must deal become discouragingly voluminous, the number of cultures he must know far greater, and the task of summary grows far more difficult. We now must cover most of the globe and narrate events which, because they are relatively recent, are minutely documented and are not readily seen in due perspective.

Last of all we must remark the fact that in these three centuries we have chiefly to do with areas in which Christianity had never before been represented. Between A.D. 1500 and A.D. 1800 Christians still made efforts to spread their faith among the few peoples of Northern Europe who remained pagan, among the Jews, and among the Moslems of South-eastern Europe, the Near East, and Central Asia. Roman Catholics sought to bring into fellowship with their Church the various Christian minorities within Moslem realms. In these areas, however, the numerical successes were comparatively slight. Had the efforts to spread Christianity been confined to the lands to which they had formerly been mainly directed, the story could be quickly told and the outcome of the three hundred years of endeavour would have been a stalemate. The chief expansion of Christianity was now to be in lands where the faith had either never before been introduced or where it had been but scantily represented—the Western Hemisphere, the East Indies, Negro Africa, the Philippines, Japan, China, Tibet, Siberia, Indo-China, Siam, Burma, Ceylon, and India. Of all these lands only India and China had previously known Christian missionary activity, and in these two vast countries the efforts of Western Christianity, while romantic and courageous enough, had been scanty. In the succeeding pages we are compelled to deal for the most part with countries, cultures, and peoples of whom thus far we have said little or nothing. Christianity now for the first time circled the globe.

We must now turn, area by area, to the account of the processes by which Christianity spread. To this we will devote the major part of the volume. Then we must attempt to describe the effect during these centuries of Christianity upon its environment and of the environment upon Christianity.

Chapter II

EUROPE, NORTH AFRICA, AND THE NEAR EAST

FIRST of all in our geographic survey, we must devote a chapter to the areas in which Christianity had heretofore achieved most of its expansion —Europe, North Africa, and the Near East. It is with these that our story has so far chiefly been concerned. Here the majority of Christians had always been found. Here were the strongest churches.

If our history were henceforth to be confined to these regions it would, as we suggested at the close of the last chapter, be much briefer than it will actually prove to be. From A.D. 1500 onward, the geographic gains of Christianity in these portions of the world have been comparatively slight. This is partly because many of the peoples were by this time professedly Christian. It is also because much of the territory had been captured by Islam. From now onward, except in Spain, Islam yielded almost no ground to Christianity, and in Spain by A.D. 1500 the elimination of Islam had been almost completed. Some forms of Christianity made accessions at the expense of other forms. Protestantism arose and tore away large sections of Western Europe from Roman Catholicism. Roman Catholicism regained from Protestantism part of the lost territory. It also attracted numbers from the various Eastern Churches. Fresh conversions to Christianity, however, were chiefly from people previously neither Moslem nor Christian. Of these peoples by A.D. 1500 there were not very many. They were mainly the Jews, still, as throughout Christian history, for the most part stubbornly resistant to this offshoot from the faith of their fathers, and a few pagans in the extreme North and in Russia. This part of our narrative, then, need not long detain us. We will speak first of attempts to win the Jews, then of efforts to gain converts from pagans, next of losses to Islam and of gains from it, and finally of the movements of Christians from one communion to another.

The story of the relations of Jews to Christians and of conversions from Judaism to Christianity is complex and confused. It varies from country to country and from period to period.

In the preceding volume we have seen that near the close of the fifteenth century those Jews who would not accept baptism were expelled from Spain

(1492) and from Portugal (1497). Under pressure, in the attempt to escape exile, in both lands many Jews submitted to the rite. A profession of Christianity made under such circumstances could not fail to be nominal. Many of the converts and their descendants secretly continued some of their old practices. Numbers developed combinations of Jewish and Christian rites and beliefs. Suspicion of the Christianized Jews was rife and often broke out into open enmity. In Spain the Inquisition was indefatigable in hunting down crypto-Jews.[1] In Portugal the Inquisition was not introduced until 1536. In the meantime, the Kings of Portugal had usually taken a mild policy towards the "new" Christians. In several places, however, violence had broken out and numbers of the converts had been killed or brutally handled by the mob. In 1547 and 1579 the Inquisition in Portugal was given increased powers and used them to deal more strictly with those Christians of Jewish descent who clandestinely cherished the faith of their ancestors.[2] For generations a distinction existed in the popular mind between the "new" Christians, descendants of converts, and the "old" Christians, of non-Jewish stock.[3] Moreover, in spite of the vigilance of the Inquisition and the execution through its processes of hundreds of Marranos (secret Jews), many of the "new" Christians cherished half-remembered vestiges of Judaism and in practice their faith was a compound of these and of Christianity. Among the Marranos were even some of the Roman Catholic clergy.[4] Numbers of Marranos, especially of Portugal, sought through migration escape from persecution. Some found homes in North Africa and the Levant, others in Italy, in the Netherlands, in England, and in the Americas, especially in the British Thirteen Colonies. Once away from the Peninsula and the terror of the Inquisition, sooner or later they seem generally to have resumed the open profession of Judaism.[5] Even in the nineteenth and twentieth centuries in both Spain and Portugal numerous nominal Christians of Jewish descent preserved to a greater or less degree some traces of the religion of their forefathers and in Portugal in the twentieth century quite a number once more openly espoused Judaism and organized synagogues.[6]

Jews were numerous in the Papal States and especially in Rome, for the Papacy had often taken a lenient attitude towards them and had sought to

[1] Roth, *A History of the Marranos,* p. 62.

[2] Roth, *op. cit.,* pp. 60-73.

[3] Roth, *op. cit.,* pp. 74, 75.

[4] Roth, *op. cit.,* pp. 146-194; Pastor, *History of the Popes,* Vol. XVII, p. 342; Baron, *A Social and Religious History of the Jews,* Vol. II, pp. 63, 64.

[5] Roth, *op. cit.,* pp. 195-270. On the Netherlands see H. J. Koenen, *Geschiedenis der Joden in Nederland,* pp. 125-171.

[6] Roth, *op. cit.,* pp. 356-376; Baron, *op cit.,* Vol. II, p. 62; George Borrow, *The Bible in Spain* (New York, E. P. Dutton and Co., 1906, pp. xiv, 509), pp. 107-111.

protect them against fanatics and mob violence. Until well along in the six-teenth century the Jews found conditions there more tolerable than anywhere else in Italy.[7] The renewed zeal which arose out of the Catholic Reforma-tion gave birth to efforts to bring the Jews to the Christian faith. Thus Philip Neri, who did so much to revive and deepen religious life in Rome, was earnest in seeking the conversion of the Jews.[8] Loyola and the first Jesuits were active in endeavouring to win the Jews of the Eternal City. They met with some success both among the more prominent and among those of lower social status. It is interesting that the second General of the Society of Jesus, Laynez, was a descendant of Spanish "new" Christians.[9] Out of the activity of the Jesuits arose a centre for the efforts to attract and instruct the Jews in Rome.[10] For a time in 1554 and 1555, the Pope ordered non-Christian Jews to contribute to the support of Jewish missions.[11] A few years later, one of the reforming Popes, Pius V, took measures against the Jews, but also sought to bring them to accept the Christian faith. Perhaps because of his drastic measures, some of the most eminent Jews in Rome became converts. He himself baptized several of them.[12] We hear that in Rome from 1634 to 1790 2,430 Jews were baptized.[13]

In many places in Italy Jews were compelled to attend church on certain occasions and to listen to sermons designed to bring about their conversion. This was true into the eighteenth century.[14] Some of the Jewish children were kidnapped or forcibly taken and baptized.[15] Once baptized, the Church con-sidered them as under its jurisdiction. In a number of Italian cities centres for Jewish catechumens, like that at Rome, were maintained.[16] While a large, perhaps the larger proportion of Jews adhered to their racial faith, many con-verts were made, and of these some rose to high position in the Church.[17]

In the first part of the sixteenth century, Jews were freer from persecution in Poland and Lithuania than in most portions of Western Europe. Their numbers multiplied and they became prosperous.[18] When, in the latter part of

---

[7] Margolis and Marx, *A History of the Jewish People*, p. 504.
[8] Hoffmann, *Ursprung und Anfangstätigkeit des ersten päpstlichen Missionsinstitut*, p. 75.
[9] Hoffmann, *op. cit.*, p. 3.
[10] Hoffmann, *op. cit.*, pp. 2-16.
[11] Hoffmann, *op. cit.*, p. 61.
[12] Pastor, *op. cit.*, Vol. XVII, pp. 334-342.
[13] Cecil Roth, *The Forced Baptisms of 1783 at Rome and the Community of London* (reprint from *The Jewish Quarterly Review*, New Series, Vol. XVI, No. 2, 1925), p. 108, citing Natale, *Il Ghetto di Roma*, p. 245.
[14] Roth, *Venice*, pp. 116, 117.
[15] Roth, *Venice*, p. 117.
[16] Roth, *Venice*, p. 118.
[17] *Ibid.*
[18] Dubnow, *History of the Jews in Russia and Poland*, Vol. I, pp. 66 ff.

the sixteenth and in the seventeenth century, Poland was being rewon to Roman Catholicism and the Jesuits were active, the lot of the non-Christian Jews became harder. The greatest single group of disasters which overtook the Jews in this region arose more from economic and social than from religious factors. In the East a Greek Orthodox Russian peasant population cultivated the estates of Roman Catholic Polish lords. Many of the managers of the estates were Jews. In 1648 the peasants joined with the Cossacks in a revolt against the Polish proprietors. The Jews, as agents of the hated Poles, were massacred in large numbers. Many were forced to accept baptism from the Orthodox. Massacres continued intermittently for about ten years. As soon as they could do so with impunity, a large proportion of the unwilling converts resumed their Jewish faith.[19] In the seventeenth century, too, we hear of riots against Polish Jews led by students in Jesuit schools.[20] As had so frequently been the case in Medieval Europe, the frenzy of the mob was aroused by reports that the Jews had desecrated the host, or that they had been guilty of the ritual murder of a Christian child. Enmity against the Jews was usually as much or more from economic rivalry with Christians and from racial dislike as on religious grounds. On one occasion, the students in a Jesuit school rescued Jews from the fury of the populace.[21]

How many conversions were made of Polish Jews to Roman Catholic Christianity we do not know. We hear of one bizarre episode which brought several hundred into the Church. In the eighteenth century the members of a Jewish sect who had gathered around Jacob Frank and who professed a kind of trinitarian belief were cast out by their orthodox brethren. Thus cut off from Jewry, numbers of the sect, including Frank himself, sought baptism. This was administered, in some instances with marked pomp. Frank fell under suspicion and was imprisoned by the ecclesiastical authorities. After his release he became a Roman Catholic missionary to the Jews in Austria. Suspicion again overtook him, and, fleeing to Germany, he lived as the head of his sect. His followers in Poland remained within the Roman Catholic Church. While for a time cherishing secretly their peculiar beliefs, ultimately they were assimilated to their fellow Roman Catholics.[22]

Obviously a large proportion of the conversions of Jews to Roman Catholic Christianity were brought about by physical force or by social pressure. Some,

[19] Dubnow, *op. cit.*, Vol. I, pp. 139-158.
[20] Dubnow, *op. cit.*, Vol. I, p. 161.
[21] Dubnow, *op. cit.*, Vol. I, p. 166.
[22] Dubnow, *op. cit.*, Vol. I, pp. 216-220; Margolis and Marx, *op. cit.*, p. 584; Hugh J. Schonfield, *The History of Jewish Christianity* (London, Duckworth, 1936, pp. 256), pp. 199-201.

however, were the result of genuine religious conviction. We read of Jews becoming missionaries to their own people. We hear, too, of some who joined religious orders. As a rule those who came over to Christianity in this fashion were isolated individuals. Except under constraint, few if any groups sought baptism collectively.[23]

Efforts were made by Protestants to win the Jews. As in the case of other Protestant missions for non-Christians, these increased with each century.

In the early days of his reforming career, Luther advocated kindness towards the Jews and declared that they could be won through friendship and instruction in the Scriptures. He wished to use the Jews as collaborators in the translation of the Bible. He believed that Jews had been mishandled by the Roman Catholic Church and that a milder, more intelligent policy would be more Christian and more successful. As the years passed and his contacts with members of the race increased, Luther despaired of the Jews ever becoming Christians and grew vigorous in his denunciation of them. He advocated burning their schools and dwellings and compelling their youth to earn their livelihood by manual labour rather than, as he said, by preying on Christians.[24]

Various attitudes towards the Jews were taken by early Protestant leaders. Martin Bucer and some others advised a stern Jewish policy, including the separation of Jews from Christians and the prohibition of any Jew assuming the initiative in debating religious questions with Christians. There was fear lest the latter be shaken in their faith.[25] Some of the early Protestants desired the conversion of the Jews. We read of the compulsory attendance of Jews at Christian preaching and of polemical literature issued to combat Judaism.[26] Beza, the friend and co-worker of Calvin, is said to have prayed daily for the conversion of the race.[27]

In the first few decades of the Protestant movement we hear of a number of converts from Judaism. Some of them attained local prominence as teachers of Hebrew and of the Old Testament. One of the most famous was Tremellius, who, born in Italy, was baptized a Roman Catholic, came under the influence

---

[23] Bernstein, *Some Jewish Witnesses for Christ*, pp. 27-72, gives a number of specific instances of conversions.

[24] De le Roi, *Die evangelische Christenheit und die Juden*, Vol. I, pp. 20-44. This gives pertinent quotations from Luther's writings. For a bibliography of books and articles on Luther's attitude towards the Jews, see Karl Schottenloher, *Bibliographie zur deutschen Geschichte im Zeitalter der Glaubensspaltung 1517-1585* (Leipzig, Karl W. Hiersemann, 3 vols., 1933-1936), Vol. I, pp. 543, 544.

[25] H. Eells, *Bucer's Plan for the Jews*, in *Church History*, Vol. VI, June, 1937, pp. 127-135.

[26] De le Roi, *op. cit.*, Vol. I, p. 44.

[27] De le Roi, *op. cit.*, Vol. I, pp. 51-59.

of a reforming group in his native land, fled to Switzerland in 1542 and there openly joined the new movement. A little later he taught Hebrew at Cambridge and assisted Cranmer in the latter's changes in the Church of England. He was noted as a translator of the Old Testament and a theologian.[28]

In the seventeenth century, especially after the Thirty Years' War, a fairly large literature dealing with Judaism arose in Protestant Germany. Some of it was polemic, some apologetic, and some had an outspoken missionary purpose.[29]

In the same century Protestants in Switzerland developed something of a literature for the Jews. We have seen that many Portuguese and Spanish Jews took refuge in Holland and there cast off the nominal Christianity which had been imposed upon them. Their presence stimulated Protestant efforts to win them. Those who had suffered so severely at the hands of Roman Catholic Christians proved difficult to bring over to the Protestant form of the faith, but a few converts are recorded. With the readmission of the Jews to England by Cromwell came missionary efforts, largely in the form of controversial writings, and a few baptisms followed.[30]

The most famous seventeenth century Protestant missionary to the Jews was Esdras Edzard (1629-1708). He was the son of a Lutheran pastor in Hamburg who is said to have used his contacts with non-Christians in that seaport to win a Turk, a Moor, and several Jews to the Christian faith. After his university education, Esdras Edzard spent most of the rest of his long life in Hamburg. In Hamburg were many Jews, attracted in part by the commerce of the city and in part by the comparative toleration accorded them. Edzard devoted himself to their conversion. He is said to have brought hundreds to baptism, including several men of prominence. His sons continued their father's efforts.[31]

The Pietist awakening in the latter part of the seventeenth and in the eighteenth century and the closely related Moravian movement gave rise to increased efforts by Protestants for the Jews.

The founder of Pietism, Philip Jacob Spener (1635-1705), earnestly desired the conversion of the Jews. He himself knew Hebrew and had studied the Talmud. True to his emphasis upon religious experience and the practice of the Christian virtues rather than upon intellectually correct dogma, he wished to approach the Jews not through polemical or even apologetic writings, as had previously been done by most of such Protestants as paid attention to them,

[28] De le Roi, *op. cit.,* Vol. I, pp. 51-55; Bernstein, *Some Jewish Witnesses for Christ,* p. 505.
[29] De le Roi, *op. cit.,* Vol. I, pp. 72-104.
[30] De le Roi, *op. cit.,* Vol. I, pp. 135-191.
[31] De le Roi, *op. cit.,* Vol. I, pp. 104-114.

but through love and prayer. He would, however, have the civil authorities require the Jews to attend Christian preaching, for otherwise, he held, no correct information concerning the Christian faith would be likely to come to the members of the race.[32]

With its founder so deeply interested, Pietism gave birth to the most active and extensive missions for the Jews which Protestantism had thus far developed. The most notable efforts were connected with the *Institutum Judaicum*. This was established at Halle, the educational centre of Pietism. It was the outgrowth of the work of John Henry Callenberg, who was successively Professor of Philosophy and Professor of Theology at the University of Halle. Callenberg, the son of a farmer, was educated in Pietist circles. He wished to be a missionary to the Moslems and to this end studied Arabic, Persian, and Turkish. He prepared a Christian literature in these tongues and took steps to have it circulated. This interest in Oriental studies led to the foundation of the *Institutum Judaicum*. The Institute was begun in 1728. It had for one of its purposes the preparation, publication, and distribution of Christian literature for the Jews. Indeed, it arose in part out of the effort to print and circulate a book, *Light in the West,* which had been written in the dialect of the German Jews, and which later enjoyed a wide circulation. The Institute was also for the training, direction, and support of missionaries. For missionaries, Christians of non-Jewish stock were preferred. The Institute was deeply concerned for the instruction and care of neophytes and derived part of its income from the gifts of converts. Its missionaries were itinerant and travelled in many lands. Callenberg wished them to go not only to Jews in Europe, but also to Jews outside of Europe. The most famous of them was Stephan Schultz, who, after years spent as a missionary, following Callenberg's death (1760) became Director of the Institute. The most prosperous years of the mission were during the lifetime of Callenberg. Schultz did not have Callenberg's ability as a leader and organizer, conditions were changing, and while the Institute outlasted his time (he died in 1776), its work dwindled. It came to an end in 1792.[33]

By no means all the missionary efforts of Pietists on behalf of the Jews were carried on through Callenberg's Institute. Count Zinzendorf was deeply concerned for them. In his lifetime a number of Jews came over to the Moravians. After his death the Moravians continued missions in their behalf. Indeed, the Moravians were the first Protestant body to make missions to the Jews a part of the programme of the church and not to leave them to the activity of in-

[32] De le Roi, *op. cit.,* Vol. I, pp. 206-215.
[33] De le Roi, *Die evangelische Christenheit und die Juden,* Vol. I, pp. 246-351, Vol. II, pp. 38-46; J. de le Roi, *Stephan Schultz* (Gotha, Friedrich Andreas Perthes, 1871, pp. 279), *passim.*

dividuals. On his return from the West Indies, their first missionary to pagans, Dober, gave himself for work for the Jews. We read of several converts.[34]

Still other enterprises for the conversion of the Jews in Germany were undertaken in the eighteenth century. Thus John Philip Fresenius organized at Darmstadt an institution for the reception of neophytes from Roman Catholicism and Judaism to help them make the transition from the old to the new faith. The undertaking was not long-lived and most of the several hundred who passed through it were former Roman Catholics.[35]

In the first half of the eighteenth century, large numbers of Jews came into the Christian Church. What led the majority of them to make the break we do not know. For many of the more prominent converts, if one may judge from their biographies, the motive was religious conviction. Repeatedly the step was bitterly opposed by their fellow Jews and was taken in the face of persecution.[36]

As the eighteenth century wore on, in Germany the situation was altered. The chief factor in the change was the rationalistic humanism of the Enlightenment. On the one hand this permeated ecclesiastical circles and reduced the zeal of Christians for the conversion of the Jews. The number of active missions and missionaries declined. On the other hand, it penetrated Judaism and led many Jews to drop the customs of their fathers and to adopt the manners of the Christians about them. Jews were encouraged to discard their peculiar dialect in favour of German and to mingle in Christian society. The leading figure in this trend was Moses Mendelssohn. As a result, although Mendelssohn himself remained a Jew, many became Christians. The movement was especially noticeable in Berlin. By the end of the century most of the prominent Jews of Berlin had abandoned their ancestral faith.[37]

While it was in Germany that the most active and numerically the most successful Protestant missions for the Jews were conducted in the eighteenth century, efforts to reach members of the race were made in several other Protestant lands, and conversions occurred. Of the Protestant states outside of Germany, the ones in which Jews were the most numerous were the Netherlands and England. Some were found in Switzerland. Relatively few were in

---

[34] De le Roi, *Die evangelische Christenheit und die Juden*, Vol. I, pp. 359-372.

[35] De le Roi, *op. cit.*, Vol. I, pp. 351-358.

[36] De le Roi, *op. cit.*, Vol. I, pp. 372-407, gives a number of brief biographies of Jewish converts of this period. See also a biography of one convert in Wilhelm Faber, *Herschel-August* (Leipzig, Dörffling & Franke, 2d ed., 1885, pp. 47).

[37] De le Roi, *op. cit.*, Col. II, pp. 18-58; Margolis and Marx, *A History of the Jewish People*, pp. 594-599; Arthur Ruppin, *The Jews in the Modern World* (London, Macmillan and Co., 1934, pp. xxxi, 423; by a Jewish scholar, objective), pp. 274, 328.

Scandinavia and of these the majority seem to have been in Denmark. In all these lands a Christian polemical and apologetic literature appeared for the Jews. In all of them except Sweden, where Jews were not officially admitted until late in the eighteenth century, conversions occurred. Some were from religious conviction and some through marriage with Christians or as part of the process of voluntary assimilation to the life of the country. The disabilities under which Jews laboured must have been a strong inducement to seek escape from them through baptism.[38]

Not all the conversions were in the one direction from Judaism to Christianity. We hear also of conversions of Christians to Judaism.[39] In England an act of Parliament against them was deemed necessary,[40] and the Jews themselves, to allay anti-Jewish feeling, endeavoured to prevent them.[41]

In the Russian realms, some attempts were made at the compulsory conversion of the Jews to the Orthodox form of Christianity. Thus, in 1563, when the Russians occupied the city of Polotzk on the border of Poland, Ivan the Terrible commanded that all the Jews be either baptized or drowned in the Dvina.[42] In 1741 an imperial decree ordered the deportation from the Empire of all Jews who would not submit to baptism. In 1744 a similar ukase was issued commanding that all Jews who were unwilling to be baptized leave Little Russia and Livonia.[43] In Russia, too, the fear that Christians would be converted to Judaism which in the previous volume we have remarked in the fifteenth century reawoke to life periodically in the succeeding centuries. Thus in 1738 a retired captain of the navy was accused of having adopted Judaism, and he and the Jew who had been the means of his conversion were executed and burned.[44]

In general, between A.D. 1500 and A.D. 1800 no such large number of Jews came over to any branch of the Christian faith as had been won by force or persuasion in the Iberian Peninsula before A.D. 1500. In general, too, in Western Europe the use of violence and the imposition by professed Christians of restrictions on Jews decreased as the centuries passed. Not until the nineteenth century did the process of emancipation become very marked, but before A.D. 1800 indications of it had begun to be visible.

---

[38] De le Roi, op. cit., Vol. I, pp. 142-194, 407-432, Vol. II, pp. 58-71; Koenen, Geschiedenis der Joden in Nederland, pp. 268-270; Moses Márgoliouth, The History of the Jews in Great Britain (London, Richard Bentley, 3 vols., 1851), Vol. II, pp. 28, 29, 53-57.

[39] Koenen, op. cit., pp. 270-272; Hyamson, A History of the Jews in England, p. 195.

[40] Hyamson, op. cit., p. 210.

[41] Hyamson, op. cit., pp. 194, 195.

[42] Dubnow, History of the Jews in Russia and Poland, Vol. I, p. 243.

[43] Dubnow, op. cit., Vol. I, pp. 255-259.

[44] Dubnow, op. cit., Vol. I, pp. 251-253.

Before A.D. 1500 open paganism had disappeared from Western and Southern Europe. It survived only in the extreme North and in the East. Roman Catholics were, therefore, not in direct touch with it and after A.D. 1500 had no missions among European pagans.

The Lapps were the only avowedly pagan people in Europe on whom Protestantism bordered. Practically all Protestant missions to European pagans were, accordingly, among them. The Lapps are scattered over the northern portions of the Scandinavian Peninsula and the adjoining mainland. Politically they have been divided between Norway, Sweden, Finland, and Russia. Handicapped by the adverse Arctic climate, they have been backward in culture and subject to exploitation by the more favoured folk on their southern borders.

As we have seen in the preceding volume, long before A.D. 1500 Christianity in its Roman Catholic form was introduced among the Lapps. However, on most of such converts as were made the new faith sat lightly. Pagan beliefs and practices prevailed.

The coming of the Protestant Reformation to Scandinavia did not immediately work much of a change in the Lapps. To be sure, Gustavus Vasa, who both began a new era of Swedish national power and brought about the adoption of Lutheranism, sent itinerant preachers among them and established schools for them. Moreover, in later reigns Swedish pastors were provided. Baptism of children and the Christian celebration of the marriage rite spread. However, few if any of the pastors knew the language of the Lapps and most of the Lapps understood Swedish very little if at all. The majority of the Swedes and Norwegians whom the Lapps knew were derogatory to any comprehension of the Christian faith, for many of these were merchants who debauched them with liquor and robbed them in trade.

As the seventeenth century wore on, conditions began to improve. An occasional earnest missionary appeared who devoted himself through preaching or through a school to making Christianity real. The first mission school was founded in 1632. A prayer book (*Manuale Lapponicum*) appeared in 1648.

In the eighteenth century came a decided rise in missionary activity. The new tides of life associated with Pietism made themselves felt in Scandinavia. This increase in religious interest was particularly marked in Denmark and Norway, then united under Danish monarchs. In the first half of the century missionaries went to India and Greenland. In December, 1714, a royal decree ordered the establishment of a board of missions (*collegium de cursu evangelico promovendo*) in Copenhagen. The following year this was directed to include the Lapps within its purview. Of the missionaries, Fjellstroem was distinguished for literary work among these northern peoples. It was from Norway that the greatest Protestant missionary of the century to the Lapps, Thomas von Westen, carried on his labours. Born in 1682 at Trondhjem, after education elsewhere, he returned as a pastor in that diocese and began preaching a warmer and more vital Christianity than the perfunctory religion which most of the parochial clergy of the time administered. It was natural that he should think of the Lapps, for some of them were in the diocese where he served. With a group of like-minded friends he was chiefly repsonsible for the establishment of a mission to them. He undertook missionary journeys. He recruited and supervised missionaries. He obtained royal support and the assignment for the work of the mission of certain ecclesiastical revenues of the North. Through his zealous and able leadership marked progress was made in the conversion of the Lapps and in the deepening of the faith of those who were already nominally Christian. In the eighteenth century, too, missionaries came from the churches of Sweden and Finland. In 1755 a translation of the New Testament appeared. However, the year 1800 did not see the process of conversion completed. That was still to make progress in the nineteenth century.[45]

It must be pointed out that, so far as the attitude of the governments was concerned, the effort to bring the Lapps into the Christian Church was part of the programme for extending the effective authority of their respective states and to promote the incorporation of the Lapps into the main body of Scandinavian life. The purpose of the Swedish monarchs in furthering this assimilation was to push their territories north to the White Sea to prevent their encirclement by Denmark (which then controlled Norway) and Russia.[46] It seems a fair guess that the Danish monarchs assisted missions in an attempt to counter the Swedish advance. The more earnest and de-

[45] On the mission to the Lapps, see a scholarly account, fairly well documented, in I. Vahl, *Lapperne og den lapske Mission* (Copenhagen, G. E. C. Gads Boghandel, 1866, pp. 174, 189), Part II, *passim*; an older account, employing first-hand sources in Hans Hammond, *Den Nordiske Missions-Historie i Nordlandene, Finmarken og Trundheims Amt til Lappers og Finners Omvendelse, fra første Begyndelse indtil hen udi Aaret 1727 da Lappernes og Finnernes Apostel Hr. Thomas von Westen . . . døde . . .* (Copenhagen, 1787, pp. xxx, 951); and a semi-popular account, based chiefly upon two German publications, in A. Meylan, *Historie de l'Evangélisation des Lapons* (Paris, Société des Écoles du Dimanche, 1863, pp. 115), *passim*. See also K. B. Westman in *The International Review of Missions,* Vol. XXVII, p. 129, and Warneck, *Geschichte der protestantischen Missionen,* p. 23.

[46] Gustav Göthe, *Om Umeå Lappsmarks Svenska Kolonisation från Mitten av 1500—Talet till omkring 1750* (Upsala, Almquist & Wiksells Boktryckeri, 1929, pp. xviii, 484), *passim,* summarized by F. D. Scott, in *American Historical Review,* Vol. XXXVIII (January, 1933), p. 369.

voted members of the missionary body might be entirely innocent of political designs, but the support of the Crown was given from a mixture of motives.

The Moravians, impelled by their daring dream of carrying the Christian Gospel throughout the world, made heroic attempts to conduct missions in the North. In 1735 and 1739 they endeavoured to do something among the Swedish Lapps, but did not persevere. In 1736 they essayed going to Archangel, there to reach the Samoiedes, who dwelt on the Russian shore of the Arctic Ocean. They were, however, detained by the Russian authorities.[47]

The Moravians also envisioned a chain of missions across Asia. As a step towards this end, in 1765, with the consent of the Empress Catharine II, they established a settlement north of the Caspian. There they attempted with some slight success to win converts from among the Kalmyks, a non-Christian Asiatic folk who had migrated to that region.[48]

Some of the Lapps were won to the Russian Orthodox form of Christianity. On the Kola Peninsula, between the White Sea and the Arctic Ocean, were Lapps who were accessible to Russian influence, cultural and political. Here, too, as in the case of the Scandinavian efforts for the same folk, religious zeal joined with political motives.

Even in the fifteenth century a mission to the Lapps had been begun from a monastery on an island in the White Sea.[49]

One of the most distinguished of the missionaries was Tryphon. The son of a priest, he was a simple layman and neither priest nor monk when, in the first half of the sixteenth century, he established himself among the Lapps not far from the North Cape and began seeking to win them to the Christian faith. In the course of time a number of Lapps applied for baptism. Tryphon experienced some difficulty in obtaining a priest to administer the rite. Eventually, however, one came. Tryphon himself became a monk. He obtained a subsidy from Ivan IV, the Terrible, who was seeking to extend the borders of his domains and in the North was encountering Swedish rivalry. He built a church and a monastery. After his death his work was continued by monks from the latter foundation.[50]

Another of the famous Russian missionaries to the Lapps was Theodoret. A contemporary of Tryphon, and a monk, he lived long on the Kola River and near the mouth of that stream erected a church and a monastery in honour of the Trinity. He is said to have baptized as many as two thousand

[47] Müller, *200 Jahre Brüdermission*, Vol. I, pp. 160-162.
[48] Müller, *op. cit.,* Vol. I, pp. 249, 250.
[49] Friedrich Raeder, in *Allgemeine Missionszeitschrift,* Vol. XXXII, p. 356.
[50] Lübeck, *Die Christianisierung Russlands,* pp. 19, 20; Raeder, *in Allgemeine Missionszeitschrift,* Vol. XXXII, p. 357.

Lapps in one day. Driven out of the monastery which he had begun by monks who were rebellious against his strict and strenuous regimen, he retired to Vologda, but, undaunted, twice revisited his mission.[51]

The sixteenth century witnessed an extension of Russian Orthodox Christianity not only among the Lapps, but also among other pagan peoples in Northern and Eastern Europe. Towards the close of the fifteenth century the Russian state which centred around Moscow, the nucleus of the future Russian Empire, threw off the last vestiges of the suzerainty of the "Golden Horde" which since the Mongol irruption in the thirteenth century had controlled much of what is now Russia. The remarkable expansion began through which the Russians pushed their borders westward and southward and particularly eastward until the realm of their rulers attained even grander dimensions than Ivan the Terrible had envisioned when he had himself crowned Tsar—"Caesar"—in alleged succession to the Byzantine and so to the Roman Emperors. The Russian Empire eventually embraced not only Eastern Europe, but also Northern and most of Central Asia.

It was natural that Russian Orthodox Christianity should share in this expansion. Moscow was declared to be the "third Rome," and to have succeeded to the headship of the true Christendom which Rome had abandoned by succumbing to the "heresies" of the Latins and of which Constantinople had been deprived by the Moslem Turkish conquest. In the times of the Mongol rule, as we have seen in an earlier volume, monasteries had multiplied on the northern fringes of Russian settlement and the devotion to the Church, the one institution which then brought the Russians inclusive unity, had increased. Moreover, the autocrats who reigned from Moscow saw in the Church a convenient instrument. By winning to the Russian faith newly subjugated peoples, it could aid in the assimilation of conquered territories and could reinforce the Tsar's rule. Russian missions, therefore, were accorded the support of the state. The Patriarch and the bishops took a large part in the work of conversion. Missions were no longer conducted by single monks on their own initiative, but by entire groups sent by the ecclesiastical authorities. They became better organized and for a time seemed to make more rapid progress than formerly.[52]

Eventually the endorsement by the secular arm entailed for Russian Christianity more embarrassment than assistance. Rulers like Peter the Great brought the Church increasingly under their control and made it a tool for political ends. In the seventeenth century, as we suggested in the previous chapter, the

[51] Lübeck, *op. cit.*, p. 20.
[52] Lübeck, *op. cit.*, pp. 33, 34.

official church was weakened by the secession of the Old Believers—earnest, conservative souls who protested against innovations by the Patriarch Nikon which the latter had wrought in close co-operation with the state. Hampered by state domination, the Church was not flexible enough to contain much of the new life which arose out of fresh religious movements. The latter found expression in dissident sects. The Church ceased to hold the place of leadership in the cultural life of the nation which it had once possessed. No extensive revivals occurred in it comparable to the Catholic Reformation which made over the ancient Church of the West. In the eighteenth century many of the upper classes lost respect for it and, under the secularizing influences from the Enlightenment of Western Europe, preserved only a perfunctory connexion with it. In both the higher and the lower segments of society the official church lost ground.[53] While even some of the worldly rulers of the eighteenth century employed the missions of this state-dominated church as a means to Russification, an ecclesiastical organization which had so little of internal vitality could only rarely be a source of earnest missionaries. The sects were too much subject to persecution to undertake many missions to non-Christians. These are at least some of the reasons why Russian missions, after a promising beginning in the fourteenth, fifteenth, and sixteenth centuries, later displayed a lack of vigour, met with relatively little permanent success among non-Christians, and did not attain the prominence of the Roman Catholic and Protestant efforts to spread the faith.

Here we shall deal only with Russian missions in Europe. Those in Asia and North America are reserved for a later chapter.

In the sixteenth century the Cheremis (also called Tcheremis and Marii) were subdued by the Muscovite state. They were a people speaking a Finnish dialect and in the sixteenth century inhabited a region east of Moscow, on the Volga and Kama rivers, in the neighbourhood of Kazan. They were then pagans, and efforts were soon made to win them to Christianity. An archbishopric was created, with its seat at Kazan. Both the Tsar, Ivan the Terrible, and the head of the Russian Church instructed Gurius, the first Archbishop of Kazan and a man of noble birth, not to use force to bring about the baptism of the Cheremis. In contrast, inducements were offered in the form of presents, of temporary exemption from taxation, and of a promise of freedom for the serfs and those who tilled the soil. Gurius laboured indefatigably for the conversion of his archdiocese. After the death of his successor, German (1567), the mission became less effective. Force was employed to restrain the Cheremis from going over to Islam. Under Peter the Great material advantages continued to be

[53] Vernadsky, *A History of Russia*, p. 115.

offered as inducements to baptism, and we hear of thousands accepting the rite. The tide of conversion reached its height during the reign of Peter the Great's daughter, the Empress Elizabeth (1741-1761). This was because of the advantages which accrued to those who became Christians. Not only were the latter exempted from taxes, but they were also released from forced labour and from military service. Christians accused of crime were to be dealt with leniently. To keep them from contamination from paganism, Christians were to be separated from non-Christians and to be removed to lands at least as good as those they had left. It is said that often after a missionary or a civil official had read in a village the privileges offered to neophytes, practically the entire group asked for baptism, and that under Elizabeth in the district of Kazan alone about one hundred thousand came over to Christianity. Now and then sporadic attempts were made to give some instruction, especially to the children, but these were not pursued. No translation of the Bible into the vernacular was issued and until the nineteenth century not even a vernacular catechism was published. The Christianity of most of the Cheremis remained nominal, at best a mixture of a few Christian conceptions with those inherited from paganism. The old pantheon persisted, perhaps with its members rechristened or its ranks swelled by the addition of some of the Christian saints. Some improvement seems to have come through Russian colonists. These penetrated the lands of the Cheremis, especially after the seventeenth century, and mixed marriages hastened the assimilation. Yet the Christianity of the average Russian peasant had in it much that was akin to paganism, and the faith of the Cheremis was not necessarily purified by the contact.[54]

The Mordvs (also called Mordvinians, Mordva, and Mordvins) spoke a Finno-Ugrian language and inhabited lands on the middle course of the Volga. They, too, were conquered from Moscow. Ivan the Terrible is said to have divided the lands of the Mordvian princes among his *boyars* and to have charged the latter with preparing the Mordvs for baptism. In the sixteenth and seventeenth centuries a number of monasteries laboured for the conversion of the Mordvs. Sometimes the Mordvs offered armed resistance to conversion, possibly because they feared that their lands would be taken from them and given to a monastery. In 1681 an imperial *ukase* ordered exemption of taxation for six years for Mordv neophytes and the confiscation of the goods of those who refused to receive baptism. The exceptional rewards offered by the Empress Elizabeth led here, as among the Cheremis, to wholesale conversions. In 1746 in the eparchy of

[54] Smirnov, *Les Populations Finnoises des Bassins de la Volga et de la Kama*, pp. 1-74, 156; Smirnoff, *A Short Account of the Historical Development and Present Position of Russian Orthodox Missions*, pp. 6-15.

Nijni Novgorod there were reported 50,430 new Christians in one hundred and thirty-two villages. Even when baptized, however, many of the Mordvs are said to have refused to learn Christian prayers and to have treated with contempt the images of the saints. In 1784 the Archbishop of Nijni Novgorod declared that they still observed their old rites. At the beginning of the nineteenth century a pagan reaction occurred, and in the latter part of that century the ancient Mordv religion was still alive, although partly camouflaged under Christian forms.[55]

Slightly north and east of the Cheremis, in the region of the Vyatka River, lived the Votyaks. In the latter part of the sixteenth and in the eighteenth century, several bishops sought their conversion. Here, as among others of the non-Christian peoples, special mundane attractions—gifts, release from taxes, and freedom from military service—played a large part in the reception of baptism. When, in 1746, many of the Votyaks with their horses were called to the colours with the prospect of prolonged service on the borders, in eight months about ten thousand sought exemption through baptism. One priest is said to have administered the rite in nine days to 2,007. Many of the clergy ignored the imperial *ukase* commanding that the neophytes be taught Christian dogmas, prayers, the creed, and the decalogue. It is not surprising that numbers of the Votyaks resented the destruction of the symbols of their old faith, that in 1773-1774 an uprising broke out against the exactions of a mercenary clergy and that twenty priests were killed, and that near the end of the eighteenth century pagan customs revived.[56]

In the seventeenth century some of the Kalmyks, Buddhist by faith, migrated from Asia to the lower reaches of the Volga. In 1771, outraged by attempts to suppress their religion and to convert them to Christianity, several thousand of them decided to return to their old haunts in the Chinese Empire and made the migration through a winter journey rendered tragic by its hardships and enormous loss of life.[57]

In Eastern Europe, then, as late as the second half of the eighteenth century, Russian Orthodox Christianity was being propagated by means of mass conversions induced by the pressure of the state and by this-worldly rewards. Never before had material inducements been so crassly offered on so large a scale to encourage baptism. It is not surprising that in the twentieth century the superficial Christianity so recently acquired and which had had neither time nor opportunity to root itself deeply in the life and affections of the people

[55] Smirnov, *op. cit.*, pp. 280-308.
[56] Lübeck, *Die Christianisierung Russlands*, pp. 55-58.
[57] *Encyclopaedia Britannica*, 14th edition, Vol. XIII, p. 247.

should have shown so little vitality and should have offered such feeble resistance to the anti-Christian propaganda of the Communists.

Between A.D. 1500 and A.D. 1800 the losses of Christianity to Islam were greater than the gains from it. The wave of conquest of the Ottoman Turks did not reach its high watermark until after A.D. 1500. The sixteenth century saw the fall of Belgrade, of Rhodes, and of Cyprus to the Turks. It witnessed the Crescent victorious on the field of battle in Hungary and at the very gates of Vienna. Late in the seventeenth century the Turks again appeared before the walls of Vienna. Turkish fleets ravaged the shores of the Mediterranean as far west as Spain.

Conditions within the Ottoman Empire made for the conversion of Christians to Islam. To be sure, Christianity was tolerated. The wealthy among the Christians were encouraged to settle in the Phanar quarter of Constantinople, and, known as the Phanariots, eventually became powerful in the Turkish state, but they were subject to Moslem rulers. Christians suffered from discriminatory taxes. The Œcumenical Patriarchate, the ranking position in the Greek Church, was under the control of Moslem sovereigns and often was in effect auctioned off to the highest bidder. Other bishops, too, were dominated by the Turks and were taxed heavily. The clergy passed on the burden by heavy exactions from their flocks. Oppressed by a venal hierarchy and belonging to a Church whose corruption had cost it the respect of many of its members, numbers of the Greek Orthodox turned Moslem. Christians were compelled to give up their sons for the Turkish armies, and these lads, reared as Moslems, constituted the powerful and dreaded Janizaries (Yenicheri), more fanatical advocates of Islam than the Turks themselves. In the course of the conquest churches, including the chief cathedral of the Greek Church, St. Sophia, were transformed into mosques. For many years Moslems were zealous in seeking to win Christians to Islam. Then, too, many Christians saw in the military triumph of the Turk convincing evidence that God was on the side of the Prophet and that the Moslems were right in their claim that their faith was superior to Christianity. To the thousands of Christians who were captured and enslaved by the Moslems, this argument must have seemed particularly potent. Moreover, while emancipation did not necessarily follow the acceptance of Islam, many of the Christian slaves deemed it expedient to exchange their faith for that of their masters.[58] Now and then a Moslem ruler attempted to coerce his Christian subjects into the acceptance of Islam. Thus in 1520 one Sultan ordered all churches turned

[58] Fortescue, The Eastern Orthodox Church, pp. 241-244; J. B. Bury in The Cambridge Modern History, Vol. I, pp. 99, 102, 103; Moritz Brosch in op. cit., Vol. III, pp. 128, 129; Arnold, The Preaching of Islam, pp. 145-177; Pastor, History of the Popes, Vol. II. p. 241.

into mosques and all Christians to become Moslems. Only with difficulty did the Patriarch dissuade him from fulfilling his purpose. Later two other Sultans nearly carried out the same plan. In 1670 several thousand Christian children in Crete were taken from their parents, circumcised, and reared as Moslems.[59] In general, however, not much direct constraint was used. Yet, while little force was employed to effect conversions to Islam, other factors worked so powerfully in that direction that it is not surprising to hear of an extensive abandonment of Christianity for Islam.

The full story of the transition from Christianity to Islam of a large proportion of the subjects of the Ottoman Turks will probably never be known. It is clear, however, that the movement was extensive and continued for centuries. In the fifteenth century it had already begun and seems to have reached its height in the seventeenth century. The converts to Islam were drawn from all sections of society. Many from the ruling classes abandoned the Christ for the Prophet. Among them were several members of the imperial family of the Palæologi.[60] Numbers of the clergy, including a Metropolitan of Rhodes and others of high rank, became Moslems.[61] Throngs from the lower and middle classes made the exchange of faith.[62] In Albania the Roman Catholic Church had been strong, and the movement to Islam was late in assuming large proportions. In the seventeenth century, however, it was very marked, and eventually a majority of the population became adherents of the Prophet.[63] Among the Serbs, soon after the Turkish conquest numbers of the nobility went over to Islam but until the seventeenth century the masses continued loyal to the Church. In the course of that century, however, many Christians left the land of their fathers for Hungary, the morale of those who remained declined, an unsympathetic Greek clergy replaced many of the Serbian priests, and numbers appear to have apostatized. In Bosnia a considerable element passed over from the previously popular Bogomilism to the religion of their new masters.[64] However, at least one group, the Laramans, in the mountains between Albania and the later Jugoslavia, while outwardly Moslem, were crypto-Christians, and were secretly ministered to by Christian priests.[65]

It was not only in the Turkish possessions in Europe and in former domains of the Byzantine Empire and of Western Christian powers in the Ægean and in Asia Minor that Christians went over to Islam. The process of the attrition of

---

[59] Fortescue, *op. cit.*, p. 237.
[60] Arnold, *op. cit.*, p. 160; Pastor, *op. cit.*, Vol. II, p. 251.
[61] Arnold, *op. cit.*, p. 165.
[62] *Ibid.*
[63] Arnold, *op. cit.*, pp. 177-192.
[64] Arnold, *op. cit.*, pp. 192-200.
[65] *Fides News Service*, Nov. 26, 1938.

the Eastern Christian Churches by Islam was also marked in other areas. In the seventeenth century the Shahs of Persia subdued the Christian state of Georgia. An heir to the Georgian kingdom, reared in Persia, turned Moslem. In 1634 he came to power and endeavoured to force Islam on the land. When, in 1701, a Christian ascended the throne and attempted to restore Christianity, he was forced out by the fear of Persia and was succeeded by a Moslem. Yet Christianity persisted, perhaps because of Russian assistance.[66] In Abyssinia early in the sixteenth century a Moslem conqueror compelled many of the Christians to apostatize. Several years later, Moslem political rule was overthrown and numbers of the unwilling converts returned to their earlier faith.[67]

In some places where Moslems and Christians lived side by side, each tended to adopt features of the other's religion. Thus in times of an epidemic or of a prolonged drought or of some other natural disaster Christians and Moslems occasionally combined their prayers, at least in one instance in a mosque. Christian shrines of healing were frequented by Moslems. Moslems asked for the body of a Christian saint to carry in procession to stop the cholera.[68] Some Christians felt that if their own saints failed them in time of crisis, the help of Moslem shrines should be invoked.[69] In the sixteenth century several of the Turks had their children secretly baptized, persuaded that the ceremony possessed magic powers for good.[70] In the same century, Turkish mothers believed baptism to be a prophylactic against leprosy, and in the seventeenth century Moslem mothers in Albania had the rite administered as a charm against leprosy, witchcraft, and wolves.[71]

The chief gains of Roman Catholic Christianity against Islam both before and after A.D. 1500 were in the Iberian Peninsula. In the preceding volume we have told most of that story, for the larger part of it falls in the period anterior to the sixteenth century. We have seen that the conquest of Granada in 1492 erased the last of the Moslem kingdoms in the Peninsula and was followed by efforts to win the Moors to the Christian faith. The conciliatory and peaceful methods of the first Archbishop of Granada proved too slow for the zealous, energetic, and powerful Ximenes de Cisneros. Force was applied to hasten

[66] S. C. Malan, *A Short History of the Georgian Church,* translated from the Russian of P. Ioselian, and edited with additional notes (London, Saunders, Otley and Co., 1866, pp. ix, 208), pp. 159-176.

[67] Arnold, *op. cit.,* pp. 114-116; Enno Littmann, in *Deutsche Aksum-Expedition* (Berlin, Georg Reimer, 4 vol., 1913), Vol. I, pp. 58, 59; E. A. W. Budge, *A History of Ethiopia, Nubia, and Abyssinia* (London, Methuen and Co., 2 vols., 1928), Vol. I, p. 155, Vol. II, p. 339.

[68] Hasluck, *Christianity and Islam under the Sultans,* Vol. I, pp. 63-67.

[69] Hasluck, *op. cit.,* Vol. I, pp. 75-82.

[70] Hasluck, *op. cit.,* Vol. I, p. 32.

[71] Hasluck, *op. cit.,* Vol. I, p. 33.

conversion. Many yielded, but others revolted. The rebellion was suppressed (1501) and more conversions ensued.[72] In 1502 Isabella, partly to prevent the contamination of the faith of the converts by their recent fellow Moslems, ordered the expulsion of all Moors from the Kingdoms of Castile and Leon.[73] When, in 1512, Ferdinand conquered Navarre, the Moslems were given the choice of emigration or conversion. Many seem to have gone north of the Pyrenees, to the French portion of Navarre.[74]

In parts of Spain, especially in those under the direct rule of Ferdinand, conversion was slower than in the sections which had been under Isabella. Ferdinand objected to the use of force. The aristocracy found the Moslems valuable, for the latter cultivated the soil and paid large taxes. The transition to Christianity was, therefore, gradual. However, in Valencia in 1520-1522 a revolt, called the *Germanía*, strove to injure the nobles by compelling the Moors who laboured on their estates to accept baptism.[75]

The grandson of Ferdinand and Isabella, Charles V, determined to have religious uniformity in his Spanish domains. With the reluctant consent of Pope Clement VII he put aside his oath of toleration for the Aragonese Moslems, and in 1524 ordered that no Moslem remain in his Spanish realms except as a slave. In spite of rebellions of outraged Moors, thousands were baptized, Korans were burned, and the obdurate were killed or escaped death or baptism by voluntary exile.[76]

Even when formal allegiance to Islam had been extirpated from the Spanish kingdoms by persuasion, assimilation, law, and force, the problem still remained of the converts, the *Moriscos*. Many of these were accused, and probably with reason, of cherishing secretly the religion of their fathers. The transition to Christianity had often been effected by violence, the knowledge of Christianity imparted at the outset was usually superficial in the extreme, and it would have been strange if the resulting religion had not been in practice a combination of the new and the old faith. To bring about full conformity to Christianity the Inquisition was invoked. For decades the Holy Office sought to extirpate Moslem practices.[77] Repeatedly, too, efforts were made to give systematic instruction to the *Moriscos* in the faith which so many had unwillingly adopted *en masse*.[78]

These measures did not fully achieve their objective, and more stringent ones were adopted. Philip II was even more intent upon religious uniformity in his

[72] Lea, *The Moriscos of Spain*, pp. 33-40.
[73] Lea, *op. cit.*, p. 44.
[74] Lea, *op. cit.*, p. 55.
[75] Lea, *op. cit.*, pp. 57-68.
[76] Lea, *op. cit.*, pp. 82-96.
[77] Lea, *op. cit.*, pp. 111-159.
[78] Lea, *op. cit.*, pp. 161-177.

realms than was his father, Charles V, and he was irked by the remnants of Moslem customs. On January 1, 1567, an edict was published in Granada which ordered all the *Moriscos* to learn Castilian, which proscribed the use of Arabic, garments in Moorish style, and various remnants of Moorish customs. In desperation, the unfortunate *Moriscos* rose in a rebellion which for a time assumed alarming proportions. However, the uprising was suppressed with revolting barbarity and the surviving *Moriscos* of Granada were deported to various parts of Spain. Still the *Moriscos* proved annoying to the stricter of the Christians. Finally, in 1609, they were all ordered expelled from Spain. The edict was ruthlessly carried out, and scores of thousands were compelled to leave the realm. While some managed to escape exile, from then onward the *Moriscos* and Moslem customs ceased to be a serious problem for the Inquisition.[79]

It must be added that the religious factor was only one of the causes of the hatred for the *Moriscos*. Added to it were dislike for differences in customs (such as the *Morisco* attitude towards pork and wine), economic rivalry, and the fear that the half-converted Moors might assist the dreaded Turks who were then ravaging the Mediterranean and threatening Christendom.

It was not only in Spain that Moslems were brought over to Christianity. In Italy also conversions were recorded. Here Moslem captives were numerous. Of these a large proportion were baptized. Slaves were encouraged to seek the rite by Papal orders that all baptized bondsmen, at least in Rome, be freed. Apparently in practice this command was a dead letter, for it had to be renewed.[80]

Spanish, Portuguese, and, later, French missionary activity was also extended to North Africa. Here for many years Roman Catholic Europeans had political footholds, chiefly in Tangier and Ceuta, on the African side of the Straits of Gibraltar. In ports of Algiers and Tunis, moreover, were many Christians, some of them merchants and some slaves captured by Moslem corsairs. Clergy were present to care for the Christian residents. Now and again attempts were put forth to win Moslems. Yet seldom if ever were converts made. Politically and religiously the region was overwhelmingly and fanatically Moslem and apostasy from Islam usually would have been followed by death.[81]

As we shall see in a moment, between A.D. 1500 and A.D. 1800 many Roman

[79] Lea, *op. cit.*, pp. 228-270, 292-365.

[80] Hoffman, *Ursprung und Anfangstätigkeit des ersten päpstlichen Missionsinstituts*, pp. 24-26, 30, 38, 90, 91.

[81] Lemmens, *Geschichte der Franziskanermissionen*, pp. 13-18; Schmidlin, *Katholische Missionsgeschichte*, p. 234; Goyau in Descamps, *Histoire Générale Comparée des Missions*, pp. 460-473; *Capucins Missionaires, Missions Françaises*, p. 69.

Catholics went to the Moslem lands of the Near East. Here, however, their efforts were directed chiefly to bringing non-Roman Catholic Christians into communion with Rome. Only infrequently were converts made from Islam. We hear of one of these in 1633, when a chief of the Druses, believing that he owed his recovery from an illness to the prayers of a Roman Catholic missionary, came over to Christianity. His apostasy from Islam created a furor and led to a persecution of Roman Catholics.[82]

Protestants had little direct contact with Moslems in Europe or the Near East. Only in Transylvania and Hungary did they know them intimately, and there merely as suzerains or a menace. In India and the East Indies Protestants were thrown into close proximity with them, as we are to see later, but that was outside the regions dealt with in this chapter. In Europe and the Near East, therefore, Protestants made little effort to win Moslems to the Christian faith. It will be recalled that Callenberg, who from his institute at Halle had been so active in behalf of the Jews, had wished to be a missionary to the Moslems. Although he gave his major attention to the Jews, he did not forget his early dream. He translated portions of the New Testament into Arabic, Turkish, and Persian, and studied Hindustani for the purpose of reaching the Moslems of India. In 1753 he hopefully reported nine converts from Islam, including a Persian prince.[83] The Moravians, who dared to embrace the world in their vision, planned missions in the Near East and included the Turks in their purview. However, before A.D. 1800 most of their efforts in that region were among the Eastern Churches.[84]

The growing domains of the Russian Empire included many Moslems, both in Europe and in Asia. In this chapter we must speak only of Europe. The state-encouraged efforts for the conversion of non-Christians within the Russian realms included not only those missions to the pagans which we have already noticed, but also some for Moslems. As was to be expected, the successes among Moslems were not so striking as were those among pagans. Islam even gained ground, sometimes at the expense of paganism, and sometimes from nominal Christians.[85] Yet conversions were recorded. When, in the sixteenth century, Astrakhan was conquered, one of the Moslem princes with his sons came to Moscow and was baptized there.[86] In 1743, under orders from the Empress Elizabeth, the destruction of mosques was begun, and in nine months in the

[82] Clemente da Terzorio, Le Missioni dei Minori Cappucini, Vol. V, p. 34.

[83] Joh. Heinrich Callenberg, Nachricht von einem Versuch die verlassene Muhammedaner zur heilsamen Erkäntis Christi einzuleiten (Sechstes Stück, Halle, 1753, pp. 92), passim.

[84] Müller, 200 Jahre Brüdermission, pp. 247-252.

[85] Lübeck, Die Christianisierung Russlands, p. 35.

[86] Lübeck, op. cit., p. 30.

district centring in Kazan 418 out of the 536 mosques were destroyed.[87] In 1744-1747, 838 conversions from Islam were reported, and in 1748-1752, 7,535.[88] Under Catherine II (1762-1796) a more liberal policy was adopted. Force was no longer employed and some of the favours previously granted to neophytes were discontinued. The rebuilding of mosques was permitted. After the conquest of the Crimea (1783), Islam, instead of dwindling, spread.[89]

Between A.D. 1500 and A.D. 1800 the expansion of one form of Christianity at the expense of another was very marked in Europe and the Near East. The detailed description of these movements falls outside the purpose of this work. So important was it, however, in determining the religious complexion of Europe and the kind of Christianity which spread outside of Europe, that we must notice it, even though in summary fashion.

The most notable series of losses of one form of Christianity to another during these centuries was accomplished through the secession of the various Protestant groups from the Roman Catholic Church. In the previous chapter we have said concerning this revolutionary development all that we must take the space to record.

The gains of Protestants from other Christians were almost entirely from Roman Catholics. Under the Œcumenical Patriarch Cyril Lucaris (1572-1638) some circles in the Greek Orthodox Church were temporarily affected by Calvinism.[90] Peter Heyling laboured for a time among the Monophysites in Egypt[91] and Abyssinia, and the Moravians made brief contacts with Eastern Christians in Walachia, Persia, Egypt, and Abyssinia.[92]

In the manner in which it recovered from the blows dealt it by Protestantism, experienced a revival, improved its morale, and won back some of the territory which it had lost, Roman Catholic Christianity gave evidence of amazing vitality. Of this counter-advance against Protestantism, no more needs saying than has already been said in the preceding chapter. By the year 1650 these two types of Christianity had reached a kind of stalemate in Europe as against each other. After that date, neither gained much ground from the other.

Roman Catholic missionaries put forth extensive efforts to bring the various Eastern Churches into association with Rome. In no instance were they com-

[87] F. Raeder, in *Allgemeine Missionszeitschrift*, Vol. XXXII (1905), p. 362, giving quotation from Philaret, *Historiya Russkoi Tserkvi*, pp. 392ff.

[88] Lübeck, *op. cit.*, p. 50.

[89] Lübeck, *op. cit.*, pp. 51, 52.

[90] Arnold, *The Preaching of Islam*, pp. 161-165; Richter, *Mission und Evangelisation im Orient*, pp. 55, 56.

[91] Richter, *op. cit.*, pp. 56, 57; *Allgemeine Missionszeitschrift*, Vol. III (1876), pp. 206-223.

[92] Müller, *op. cit.*, pp. 248, 251; Richter, *op. cit.*, pp. 57, 58.

pletely successful. From almost every one, however, they gathered some adherents. Several Uniate Churches were brought into existence. These, while preserving many of their former ecclesiastical customs, were altered sufficiently to come into communion with Rome.

One of the Uniate groups was the Ruthenian. This was made up of former Greek Orthodox, largely of Russian stock, whose ecclesiastical language was Slavonic. Their union with Rome was consummated in 1596 at a congress at Brest. It was the result in part of the control by Poland of a large area inhabited by Russian Orthodox Christians and of dissatisfaction of the Russian bishops with the interference of laymen. Many of these bishops sought relief through submission to Rome. The union was also in part the fruit of the labours of Jesuits.[93]

Not all of the Orthodox of the area entered into the new relationship. However, those in the Ukraine who did not join with Rome, through the long conflict acquired something of the mentality of their opponents. Coming to Moscow in the seventeenth century, they exerted a marked influence upon much of the Russian Church. This made for formal argumentation and theological scholarship.[94]

Rome put forth prolonged efforts to bring the entire Russian Church into union under the Pope. Over much of the period the Jesuits, so aggressive on many another frontier of the Latin communion, were the active agents. Occasionally, as when in the first decade of the seventeenth century a pretender under the name of Dimitri established himself in Moscow with the aid of Roman Catholic Poland and the Jesuits, the outlook seemed favourable.[95] The Jesuits were expelled by Peter the Great, to be succeeded by the Capuchins.[96] Never, however, did the hopes come to full fruition.

In the eighteenth century Roman Catholicism actually lost ground in the Ukraine. Many of the Uniates were compelled by the Russian government to submit to the state church.[97]

South of the Carpathians were large settlements of Little and White Rus-

---

[93] Vernadsky, *A History of Russia*, p. 63; Attwater, *The Catholic Eastern Churches*, pp. 76-80. A full account, by a Jesuit, is in Pierling, *La Russie et la Saint-Siège*, Vol. II, pp. 361 ff.

[94] Vernadsky, *op. cit.*, p. 79.

[95] Pierling, *op. cit.*, *passim*, especially Vol. III; Pastor, *History of the Popes*, Vol. X, p. 366.

[96] Clemente da Terzorio, *Le Missioni dei Minori Cappuccini*, Vol. VII, pp. 156-159, 194, 195.

[97] Stephen Rudnitsky, *Ukraine* (New York, Rand, McNally & Co., 1918, pp. 369; largely Ukrainian anti-Russian propaganda), p. 185.

sians. In 1652 most of these were led into communion with Rome and are known as Podcarpathian Ruthenians.[98]

In 1701 about two hundred thousand Orthodox Rumanians with about fifteen hundred of their priests formally came into communion with Rome. Later a large proportion of these withdrew from the Roman connexion and resumed their Orthodoxy.[99]

In Syria, Palestine, and Egypt, groups of Orthodox of the Byzantine Rite in union with Rome came to be known as Melchites—although that term had also been used to designate the Greek Orthodox in these areas. In Syria and Palestine they were grouped about the Patriarch of Antioch and in Egypt around the Patriarch of Alexandria. From early centuries, in both ecclesiastical successions were occasionally Patriarchs who were in communion with Rome. The final submission to Rome of the Melchite Patriarchs of both centres came in the first half of the eighteenth century. Not all of their flocks followed them, and rival groups, independent of Rome, continued.[100]

No Uniate Church of Greeks was formed. Long before A.D. 1500, communities of Greek Christians had existed in Italy and Sicily, having the Byzantine Rite but in communion with Rome. Most of these were gradually assimilated to the Latin Rite, but in the fifteenth and sixteenth centuries the Byzantine Rite was given a new lease on life by migrations of Albanians in flight from the Turk.[101] Many Greek Christians came over to Roman Catholicism, among them bishops and priests, and in 1576 a college for training priests for Greek-speaking Christians was founded in Rome. However, no distinct organization was created for the Greeks.[102]

From the Copts a few were induced to unite with Rome. Early in the seventeenth century Capuchins established themselves in Cairo. Later in the century Franciscans of the Observance made their way to Upper Egypt. In 1741 a Coptic bishop submitted to Rome and was put in charge of the Roman Catholics of Coptic provenance. Not until the nineteenth century, however, was a Patriarch provided for this group.[103]

In the sixteenth century efforts were put forth to bring the Abyssinian Christians into submission to Rome. The Jesuits were active in the enterprise and had the political support of the Portuguese. For a time the Ethiopians welcomed

[98] Attwater, *op. cit.*, p. 92.
[99] Attwater, *op. cit.*, pp. 101, 102.
[100] Attwater, *op. cit.*, pp. 106 ff.; Fortescue, *The Uniate Eastern Churches*, pp. 195 ff.
[101] Attwater, *op. cit.*, pp. 47-134.
[102] Attwater, *op. cit.*, p. 117.
[103] Attwater, *op. cit.*, pp. 136, 137; Crétineau-Joly, *Histoire de la Compagnie de Jésus*, Vol. I, p. 401.

Portuguese aid against the aggressive Moslem Turks. In 1555 Pope Julius III named a Jesuit as Patriarch of Ethiopia. One head of the Ethiopian state became a Roman Catholic, but because of this defection from the national religion was murdered (1604). His successor, also a convert to Roman Catholicism, had better fortune. For a time he succeeded in inducing the Ethiopian Church to give official acknowledgment to Papal authority and again a Jesuit was appointed Patriarch. The efforts of the Jesuits to erase what they believed to be abuses in the Church led to a violent reaction, persecution ensued, the missionaries were driven out, and not until the nineteenth century could representatives of the Roman Catholic Church once more safely enter the land and live there. However, persistent attempts were made to penetrate the country, especially by the Franciscans. For a time, indeed, in the first decade of the eighteenth century, the Brothers Minor seemed to have established a foothold, only to be driven out a few years later.[104]

Thanks to the Jesuits and the Capuchins, who first came to Syria in the seventeenth century, numbers of the Jacobites became Roman Catholics, and in time had a Patriarch of their own.[105]

Since at least the Middle Ages, the Maronites, living chiefly on the slopes of the Lebanon, have been in communion with Rome. Only in 1516, however, was permanent and uninterrupted contact with the Church of Rome established.[106]

Some of the Armenian Christians were brought by the Crusaders into connexion with Rome, and Roman Catholic missionaries from the West laboured among them. In the eighteenth century the Armenian Roman Catholics were given their own Patriarch.[107]

In the middle of the sixteenth century a disputed succession to the Catholicate of the Nestorians led to a permanent division in the church. One of the aspirants, Sulaka, went to Rome. There he made his submission to the Pope and returned with the coveted title of Patriarch. He became the head of the Chaldean Christians, Uniates from among the Nestorians. In the middle of the seventeenth century the rival Catholicos also submitted to Rome. Both lines, however, later separated from Rome, and in the latter part of the eighteenth century the Pope

---

[104] Charles F. Rey, *The Romance of the Portuguese in Abyssinia* (London, H. F. & G. Witherby, 1929, pp. 319), *passim;* Attwater, *op. cit.,* pp. 150, 151; Adeney, *The Greek and Eastern Churches,* pp. 621-624; Crétineau-Joly, *op. cit.,* Vol. I, pp. 394-396, Vol. II, p. 421; Pastor, *History of the Popes,* Vol. XIII, p. 313; Lemmens, *Geschichte der Franziskanermissionen,* pp. 179-187.

[105] Attwater, *op. cit.,* p. 164.

[106] Attwater, *op. cit.,* p. 182; *The Catholic Encyclopaedia,* Vol. IX, p. 687; Crétineau-Joly, *op. cit.,* Vol. II, p. 418, Vol. V, pp. 8, 9.

[107] Attwater, *op. cit.,* pp. 204, 205; Adeney, *op. cit.,* p. 547.

recognized a metropolitan who applied to him as head of the Uniate Chaldeans.[108]

In the seventeenth century Theatines made their way to Georgia and were received in friendly fashion by the Catholicos—although it is not clear that he ever became a Roman Catholic. Dominicans and Augustinians were also there. Later these were replaced by the Capuchins. We hear of the conversion to Roman Catholicism of two of the heads of the Church and of several princes.[109]

As may be readily gathered, the creation of these groups of Uniates was the result of an extensive and courageous missionary enterprise. In Russia, in many parts of the Turkish Empire, in Persia, and in Ethiopia it was found. In it several orders took part—Jesuits, Franciscans, Capuchins, Dominicans, Theatines, and Discalced Carmelites. Most of these were the product of the Catholic Reformation and were expressions of that abounding new life which carried Roman Catholic Christianity around the globe. Especially prominent were the Jesuits and Capuchins, both distinct expressions of the revival. The missionaries came from various portions of Roman Catholic Europe, but especially, as was to be expected, from Italy, Spain, Portugal, and France. Some of them obtained French protection. As in the Middle Ages, Roman Catholic missions in the Near East were intertwined with the political ambitions and the commercial activities of Western Christendom. Fine heroism and devotion had the incongruous support of princes, diplomats, and merchants who thought of the Christian faith chiefly as a tool for their own selfish ends. Yet but for the zeal of the missionaries, the gains which were registered would not have been possible.[110]

Whether this extensive Roman Catholic effort weakened or strengthened

[108] Aubrey R. Vine, *The Nestorian Churches. A Concise History of Nestorian Christianity in Asia from the Persian Schism to the Modern Assyrians* (London, Independent Press, 1937, p. 227), pp. 170-176; Attwater, *op. cit.*, pp. 228-230; Adeney, *op. cit.*, pp. 497-500.

[109] Michel Tamarati, *L' Église Géorgienne des Origines jusqu'à nos Jours* (Rome, Imprimerie de la Société Typographico-Editrice Romaine, 1910, pp. xv, 710), pp. 401-406, 453-646; Ferro, *Istoria delle Missioni de' Chierici Regolari Teatini*, Vol. I, pp. 14ff, 149, 289-300, 313ff.; *Capucins Missionaires, Missions Françaises*, p. 64; Clemente da Terzorio, *Le Missioni dei Minori Cappuccini*, Vol. VII, pp. 11, 18, 89-113.

[110] A full bibliography of these missions is out of place here. A brief summary, with bibliographical footnotes, is in Schmidlin, *Katholische Missionsgeschichte*, pp. 220-222, 367-372. See also Lemmens, *Geschichte der Franziskanermissionen*, pp. 19-21, 26-28, 41, 49, 60, 67-76, 94; Clemente da Terzorio, *op. cit.*, Vol. II, pp. 33-115, 243 ff., Vol. III, pp. 7-12, Vol. VI, pp. 7-23, 92-111, 159-171; Cesinale, *Storia delle Missioni dei Cappuccini*, Vol. I, pp. 47-73; Pastor, *History of the Popes*, Vol. XX, pp. 483-485; *Capucins Missionaires, Missions Françaises*, pp. 4, 11, 61, 63, 65; Ferro, *op. cit.*, Vol. I, pp. 166-168, 184-197; Crétineau-Joly, *op. cit.*, Vol. III, pp. 219-225, Vol. V, pp. 2, 3, 9-11; *Missionaires Capucins au Levant Syrien Passé et Present* (Beyrouth, Imp. Jeanne d'Arc, 1931, pp. 29); pp. 7-15; Aurelius, *De Kapucijnen en de Missie* (Brasschaat, A. de Bievre, [1927?], pp. 151), pp. 23-41.

Christianity in the Near East is uncertain. On the one hand, it brought division in the Christian forces. In almost every Eastern Church the adherence of part of the group to Rome meant strife with those who remained free from the Roman connexion. On the other hand, Roman Catholic missionaries brought Eastern Christians in touch with the new life which had come with the Catholic Reformation and so added something of vigour. Moreover, the sense of unity with Rome and so with a great body of Christians in the West may have made for added morale.

Between A.D. 1500 and A.D. 1800 Christianity both lost and gained ground in Europe and the Near East. In these areas, the scene of most of its expansion before the year 1500, by the close of the eighteenth century it had about reached the limit of its spread. It had gained a few thousand converts from among the Jews. It had won most of those pagans who had not been reached before A.D. 1500, and by methods reminiscent of the Middle Ages. The last traces of Islam were exterminated from the Iberian Peninsula and in the Russian realms some nominal converts had been made from Islam. Yet Islam had registered notable headway, especially in South-eastern Europe.

The internal religious map of Christendom had been altered, in some regions profoundly. Protestantism had appeared and had torn away from Rome most of North-western Europe. Roman Catholicism, reviving, had recovered some of the ground lost to Protestantism, and had attracted numbers from each of the Eastern Churches.

Christianity had succeeded in perpetuating itself among the descendants of the large majority of the converts of the preceding thousand years. Not only had it held most of its more important territorial gains which were still in its possession at the close of the fifteenth century. It had also come through the crisis of the fifteenth century with increased vigour. While in Roman Catholic, Russian Orthodox, and some Protestant circles the eighteenth century witnessed widespread scepticism and a chilling of enthusiasm, in the eighteenth century Protestantism was showing renewed life.

We must now turn to the more extensive portions of our story of these three centuries, the expansion of Christianity outside the areas which had previously been the scene of most of its triumphs and defeats, to the Americas, Negro Africa, Asia east of Persia, and the East Indies.

Chapter III

SPANISH AMERICA. GENERAL FEATURES OF THE SPANISH
CONQUEST AND OF SPANISH MISSIONS; THE WEST INDIES;
MEXICO; NEW MEXICO AND ARIZONA; TEXAS; CALIFOR-
NIA; FLORIDA AND GEORGIA; CENTRAL AMERICA; VENE-
ZUELA; NEW GRANADA; NEGROES; PERU; CHILE; PARA-
GUAY AND THE ARGENTINE

O F ALL the areas into which Europeans spread between A.D. 1500 and
A.D. 1800, the Americas contained the ones most fully occupied by them.
It was, accordingly, in the Americas that in those same centuries Christianity
made its largest permanent territorial and numerical gains.

Of the various European peoples who settled the Americas, in this particular
period the Spaniards possessed the widest territories and mastered the largest
numbers of the Indians. It was they who conquered the most important centres
of the indigenous civilizations. Before A.D. 1800 their colonies were the greatest
producers of wealth. To the territories held by the Spaniards went the most
missionaries. Here, too, were made the largest numbers of converts from the
native races. To a summary of the spread of the faith in Spanish America,
therefore, we must devote more of our space than to any other geographic
section of our narrative of this period.

The Spanish discoveries and conquests have so often been narrated that only
a brief summary is needed as a background for our story. They began with the
first voyage of Columbus, in 1492. By 1550 in their main outlines they had been
completed. In the intervening years, only a little over half a century, the
achievement of the Spaniards had been amazing. The Atlantic coast line of the
Americas had been explored from Nova Scotia to Cape Horn, and the Pacific
coast line from Oregon to the Straits of Magellan. The globe had been circum-
navigated. In the brief period between 1519 and 1521 a mere handful of men
had conquered the Aztec state in Mexico. Between 1524 and 1535 the realm of
the Incas in Peru had been subdued. Explorers had penetrated into what are
now Arizona, New Mexico, Texas, Louisiana, Alabama, Mississippi, and
Florida. Settlements had been established in the West Indies and Central

America. Hardy adventurers had made their way into the basin of the Orinoco, the valley of the Magdalena, through the passes of the Andes to Quito, up the Paraná and the Paraguay and over the plains and mountains to Peru, across the Andes from the West Coast to the Marañon and thence down the Amazon to the Atlantic, and from Peru into Chile.[1]

By 1574 the Spaniards were said to have in the New World about two hundred cities and towns and a Spanish population of about one hundred and sixty thousand. They were ruling over a tributary Indian population estimated to be more than seven millions. To this were added about forty thousand Negro slaves and many mestizos and mulattoes.[2]

These achievements were by a people who at the same time were waging important and exhausting wars in Europe and who, in the second half of the sixteenth century, were to extend their control across the Pacific and conquer the Philippines. They are evidence of a burst of energy for exploration, conquest, and colonization which until that time had been without equal and which even then was paralleled only by the Portuguese. Adventure was in the air. The incredible appeared possible.

After 1550 the rate of occupation of new territory slowed down. The Spaniards still went on exploring expeditions and reduced new territories to their sway. However, they devoted their energies chiefly to the organization and development of their existing domains. By the close of the seventeenth century decay had progressed far in the mother country. Between 1482 and 1700 the population of Spain is said to have declined from about ten millions to about six millions.[3] Accompanying this decrease was stagnation in economic life and in cultural creativity. Beginning about 1730, in the Spanish American colonies the Creoles, as the American-born whites were called, and the mestizos began to assume a larger place. Restlessness arose against the dominance of the Spanish-born whites. Late in the eighteenth century, taking advantage of the turmoil in Europe, this gave birth to more self-government. Early in the nineteenth century it led to revolts against the rule of Spain and to the independence of all the Spanish possessions in America except Cuba and Porto Rico.[4] For Spanish America, then, as for so much of the Occidental world, the transition from the eighteenth to the nineteenth century was accompanied by marked changes in the political and social structure.

What would be the fate of Christianity in this new world created by the

[1] Bourne, *Spain in America*, pp. 191-193.
[2] Juan Lopez de Velasco, *Geografía y Descripción Universal de las Indias*, edited by Justo Zaragoza (Madrid, Establecimiento Tipográfico de Forlanet, 1894, pp. xiii, 808), p. 2.
[3] Moses, *The Spanish Dependencies in South America*, Vol. I, p. xvi.
[4] Moses, *op. cit.*, Vol. I, p. 4.

Spaniards? Would Christianity display sufficient vitality to accompany the Spaniards on their wanderings and to hold the settlers and their descendants to their hereditary faith? Would it have power to check the brutalities of the conquest and the exploitation of the aborigines, so utterly opposed to its genius? Could it win the Indians and transform them into its likeness? Would it even leave as deep a stamp upon them as it had in earlier periods upon the peoples of the Græco-Roman world and of Northern Europe, where the adoption of the Christian name, although nearly universal and followed by profound changes, had not resulted in anything approaching an approximation to the high standards of Jesus?

As the narrative unfolds, we shall find that Christianity proved singularly potent. As we have seen, the closing years of the fifteenth and much of the sixteenth century witnessed in Spain a burst of new life, not only in discovery and conquest, but also in the Church. From the very beginning a purpose believed to be Christian was prominent in the professed motives of exploration and settlement. Hundreds of missionaries came to the New World and eventually won the large majority of the Indians in the Spanish possessions to an outward acquiescence to the Christian faith. Throughout the colonial period the settlers and their descendants jealously clung to the Christian name. Many of the Negroes, involuntary immigrants from Africa, became Christian. Consciences stirred by Christian precepts placed on the statute books humane legislation in behalf of the Indians and were partially effective in its enforcement. As the wave of secular conquest lost momentum, missionaries, with the support of the state, became the chief agents in extending the Spanish frontiers. Even in the latter half of the eighteenth century, when forces were already at work to disrupt the Spanish regime, missionaries were still extending their borders and multiplying their stations. To be sure, the Christianity so planted did not prove to be so self-propagating as that of Northern and Western Europe. Nor did it succeed in placing the imprint of Jesus so deeply upon the life of the land as had Christianity upon much of Europe. Yet Christianity became an integral part of the life and culture of Spanish America.

The reasons for the lesser influence of Christianity upon Spanish America than upon Europe are to be found partly in the nature of the Spanish colonial regime. From the very outset the Church was kept even more closely under the control of the state than was the Church in the mother country. Moreover, the Church in the colonies, like the rest of the colonial machinery, was under the direction of the home government and of Spanish-born officials. Yet, when the colonies at last broke politically with Spain, their populations displayed much more vigour in forming new governmental than new ecclesiastical patterns. The Church often allied itself with those who opposed the innovations and became a bulwark of the old social, intellectual, and economic order. The creative life displayed in political affairs seems to have been all but absent from the Church. Repression from Spain cannot have been the only cause, or it would have had the same fruits in both realms. To other possible factors we must recur later, in this chapter and in the next volume.

From the very beginning, the spread of Christianity was prominent in the avowed purposes of the Spanish adventure in the Western Hemisphere. In the journal of his first voyage, Columbus declared that the Spanish monarchs sent him "to the countries of India" "to learn their disposition and the proper method of conveying them to our holy faith."[5] The first island which he discovered Columbus named San Salvador in honour of Jesus and the second island Santa Maria de la Concepción in memory of the mother of Jesus.[6] Even on his first voyage Columbus had the conversion of the aborigines on his mind.[7] Of those on the first island which he touched he said in his journal that he "perceived that they could be much more easily converted to our holy faith by gentle means than by force."[8] He also declared that the Indians "have no religion and . . . would readily become Christians, as they have a good understanding."[9] The Indians whom Columbus brought to Spain on his first voyage were instructed in that country and baptized, with the King and Prince Juan as godfathers.[10] On the second voyage of Columbus several of the clergy were included in the company. As might have been expected from their history, Franciscans were among the pioneers.[11]

The control of the Spanish Crown over the propagation of the faith and over the Church in the Spanish dependencies in the New World was absolute. We have seen that in Spain itself the power of the throne over the altar was

[5] Columbus, *Journal of First Voyage to America*, p. 2.

[6] Columbus, *op. cit.*, p. 30.

[7] Differing statements are made about the presence of a priest on this first voyage. Bourne, *op. cit.*, p. 30, declares that no priest went on it. Streit, in *Zeitschrift für Missionswissenschaft*, Vol. IX, p. 133, says that a manuscript exists which gives evidence that Pedro de Arenas went on the voyage and said the first mass in the New World on San Salvador. See Schmidlin-Braun, *Catholic Mission History*, p. 358, p. 17. Engelhardt, *Missions and Missionaries of California*, Vol. I, pp. 719, 720, agrees with Angel Otega, *La Rábida Historia Documenta Critica*, which he cites, that no priest went on the first voyage. He is uncertain as to just when and by whom the first mass on American soil was said, but believes it to have been by some one on the second voyage.

[8] Columbus, *op. cit.*, p. 24.

[9] Columbus, *op. cit.*, p. 36.

[10] Antonio de Herrera, *Historia de las Indias Occidentales* (Madrid, Nicolas Rodriguez Franco, Dec. I-VIII, in 4 vols., 1730), Dec. I, Book II, Chap. 5; Arthur Helps, *The Life of Columbus* (London, Bell and Daldy, 1869, pp. xvi, 262), p. 125.

[11] Villanueva, *Los PP. Franciscanos en las Indias*, p. 7; Helps, *op. cit.*, p. 127.

being rapidly enhanced.[12] In this new area, where no traditional institutions existed from pre-absolutist days to check the Crown, it was to be assumed that the monarch would insist upon domination in ecclesiastical affairs as in other phases of the life of the colonies. To the Crown belonged the selection of all the missionaries. No missionary could go to the New World or, when once there, leave it, without royal permission—usually granted, of course, through the Council of the Indies or one of its associated bureaus. Fines were imposed upon officers of the fleet who carried clerics to Spain from the Indies without a viceregal license. The Pope granted to the Crown all the tithes in the colonies. Partly in return, the state undertook to see that the clergy were maintained. Missionaries were to receive from the Crown their equipment and their stipends. In theory a third of the support came from the royal treasury and the remainder from the landed proprietors, or *encomenderos*, and the Indians. In practice the royal officers frequently declared it impossible to meet their full quota, and the incomes of the clergy were supplemented by legacies and gifts from private individuals. The Pope granted to the Crown the right of appointment to all ecclesiastical benefices in the colonies. In theory Rome reserved the power to confirm the choice, but in fact it often happened that a bishop entered upon the administration of his diocese without awaiting the Papal bulls. All bishops, heads of religious houses, and parish priests were named by the King. The King created new dioceses and determined their boundaries. Sometimes a diocese was created and filled before the Pope was even apprised of its existence. No church, convent, or school could be erected without royal permission. Even the transfer or the dismissal of a sacristan could not be accomplished except with the King's consent. In spite of emphatic protests from Rome, the King would allow no communication to pass from the Holy See to ecclesiastics in the colonies without his *imprimatur*. Nor could a bishop in Spanish America write to Rome without presenting his letter for royal censorship. Actions of ecclesiastical synods in the Americas were all to be submitted to the viceroy or governor. These royal officials had power to overrule them or to send them to the Council of the Indies for such action as that body chose to take. By the end of the reign of Philip II the control of the Church by the King and the royal officials had been thoroughly consolidated. Subsequent events and Papal decrees simply strengthened it.[13]

[12] Pastor, *History of the Popes,* Vol. IV, p. 321, Vol. IX, p. 213, Vol. XVI, pp. 354-362, Vol. XVIII, pp. 1-71.
[13] *Recopilación de Leyes de los Reinos de las Indias,* Book I, Title 6; J. L. Meacham, in Wilgus, *Colonial Hispanic America,* pp. 200-214 and especially the bibliography on pp. 236-239; Ryan, *The Church in the South American Republics,* pp. 19-24; Montalbán, *Das Spanische Patronat und die Eroberung der Philippinen,* pp. 8-26; Mecham, *Church*

This control, it will be seen, was little if any greater than that exerted by the monarchs of Scandinavia in the days when Christianity was winning their realms. However, the ecclesiastical administration of the Spanish Crown was more meticulous than these others and was exerted over much wider areas. Moreover, we must notice that within their domains in the Americas and the Philippines the Spanish monarchs in practice possessed more authority over the Church than did the Portuguese monarchs within their spheres of influence in South America, Africa, and Asia. Portugal was much smaller than Spain and the areas which it endeavoured to control were more scattered, much larger, and more populous than those of Spain. In some of its possessions the Portuguese Crown exercised absolute power over the Church. In others its claims only proved irritating and wrought division in the Christian forces.

The ablest of the Spanish monarchs, particularly Isabella, the Emperor Charles V, and Philip II, took seriously the obligation implied by their control of the Church. They believed it to be their duty to safeguard the Indians from exploitation by the settlers, to prevent them from being enslaved, and to provide them with religious instruction and clerical ministrations. Indeed, the theory under which the monarchs claimed their rights in the Americas implied this obligation. They held not only their ecclesiastical but also their civil powers there by grant of the Pope. The Pope had them to give because, so it was held, as the Vicar of Christ he possessed authority over all men. It was believed to be the duty of the Pope to see that the Christian Gospel was preached to every creature, and no monarch could undertake the task without the express consent of the Pope. When non-Christian peoples were allotted by the Pope to a Christian monarch, the acceptance of the assignment involved the obligation to care for the spiritual and material well-being of the royal wards. So ran the argument.

In practice, the very strongest as well as the weaker monarchs met difficulty in making their will effective. They carried burdens too heavy even for the hardworking Philip II. They had on their shoulders not only the administration of the Indies, but also the rule of Spain and of other portions of Europe, and they were major factors in European politics. Of necessity they delegated many

and State in Latin America, pp. 2, 11-24, 29, 38-44; Lewis Hanke, Pope Paul III and the American Indians, in The Harvard Theological Review, Vol. XXX (April, 1937), pp. 74-81, with an excellent bibliography; A. R. Wright in Wilgus, op. cit., p. 535; Mackay, The Other Spanish Christ, pp. 27, 42, 43, 49-51; Rippy and Nelson, Crusaders in the Jungle, pp. 5, 7, 18, 23; Moses, South America on the Eve of Emancipation, pp. 123-126; Pastor, History of the Popes, Vol. XVI, p. 356; Moses, The Spanish Dependencies in South America, Vol. I, p. xv.

of their duties to subordinates and not all of the latter were competent or zealous.

Moreover, in the New World the royal benevolence encountered many obstacles. The majority of the Spaniards had crossed the Atlantic, not for the purpose of seeking the welfare of the Indians, but to accumulate wealth for themselves. That wealth could be obtained only from mine and field, and to wrest it from the earth much manual labour was required. The Spanish *conquistadores* considered it beneath their dignity to soil their hands with spade, plough, or pick. Eventually Negro slaves were introduced in many regions, but everywhere in the beginning and in most regions later on the only labourers available were Indians. The Indians, then, must be induced to work, by peaceful means if possible, by force if need be. In Mexico and Peru the Indians had been accustomed to toil in the mines and in the fields for their own superiors, and the coming of the Spaniards meant simply, from this standpoint, the exchange of one set of masters for another. In many other areas, however, among them the scene of the first Spanish settlements, the West Indies, the aborigines had not been inured to that kind of discipline. In consequence, the efforts of the Spaniards to obtain labour were accompanied by the greatest cruelty and the grossest barbarities and entailed for the natives untold suffering.

The most flagrant of the abuses seem to have been concentrated in the first years of the settlements. As has so often been the case in the impact of one race upon another, in the first stages the worst passions seemed to be called out in many of the conquerors. At the beginning, a large proportion of the Spaniards came to the New World unmarried or without their wives. Illicit relations with Indian women inevitably followed, with much of violence and lust. Narratives of the time give lurid pictures of rape, of wholesale slaughter, and of great dogs being loosed on the terrified natives.[14] Many of the early slave-traders on the north coast of South America were lawless adventurers over whom the government had no control.[15] Some of the most vivid of the accounts which have reached us may suffer from exaggeration, for they were by men who were seeking to arouse the indignation of the public. When allowance is made for heightened colour, however, they still reveal a picture which is anything but pleasant.

Added to the deliberate cruelties of men were catastrophes which no one

[14] See among others *Colecion de Las Obras del Venerable Obispo de Chiapa, Don Bartolomé de las Casas* (Paris, 2 vols., 1822), especially *Relacion breve de la destruccion de America*, in Vol. I. This is the most famous account and is by an agitator who could not view the situation dispassionately. See also Brion, *Bartholomé de las Casas*, pp. 1-40.

[15] Moses, *The Spanish Dependencies in South America*, Vol. I, p. 57.

planned. Diseases came in with the white man to which, through long contact, he had acquired partial immunity, but which were new in the Americas and so brought appalling mortality to the aborigines.[16]

It took time for the Christian conscience to awaken to the actualities of the situation, to bring effective pressure upon the authorities, and to devise and enforce workable humanitarian legislation.

The problem was complicated by the importation of Negroes. These were brought in as slaves, and for the same reason that the Indians were impressed into service, to supply labour for the mines and estates of the Spaniards. They were particularly numerous where the Indians had died out or were difficult to obtain, notably so in the West Indies, where the Indian population had rapidly declined to the vanishing point, but they were also present in a number of other sections. Their mortality was high, but their numbers were increased by a continuing slave-trade with Africa.[17] Early in the nineteenth century the Negro population of Spanish America was estimated to be seven hundred and seventy-six thousand.[18] On their arrival practically all the Negroes were non-Christians. Their conversion was an added task for the Church, and enactment and enforcement of humane legislation on their behalf constituted another burden for the Christian conscience.

At the outset, some Spaniards believed the Indians not to be really human beings and to be incapable of receiving Christianity.[19] Even a churchman, J. de Quevedo, Bishop of Darien, was found who maintained that the Indians were slaves by nature.[20] However, the Popes and the greater number of Christian scholars emphatically took the opposite position. Thus the most influential Spanish theologian of the first half of the sixteenth century, the Dominican Francisco de Vitoria, asserted that the Indians could be converted, that Christians had the duty to spread the Gospel, and that no one should be forced to accept Christianity.[21] The Pope who spanned the first discoveries, Alexander VI, although notorious for his own unworthy life, declared that the Indians were capable of embracing the Catholic faith.[22] In 1537 Pope Paul III came out with a bull in which he declared in unmistakable terms that the Indians were not brutes, but men who were competent to understand Christianity, and that

---

[16] Bourne, *Spain in America*, p. 212.

[17] Bourne, *op. cit.*, pp. 269-281.

[18] Humboldt, *Travels*, Vol. VI, p. 835.

[19] Berg, *Die katholische Heidenmission als Kulturträger*, Vol. I, pp. 79, 80.

[20] Vanderpol, *La Doctrine Scholastique du Droit de Guerre*, pp. 413-486.

[21] *Ibid.*, containing a summary of Vitoria, *De Indis*. See also Scott, *The Spanish Origin of International Law*, pp. xi, 155.

[22] Lewis Hanke, *Pope Paul III and the American Indians*, in *The Harvard Theological Review*, Vol. XXX, p. 65.

they should not be deprived of their liberty or their property.[23] Some Spaniards, while conceding that Indians should be baptized, held that they were so crude that they were unfit for the heavenly bread of the eucharist and so denied them the privilege of communion, and also would not admit them to confession or administer to them the *viaticum*.[24] However, the weight of official opinion was against these restrictions. In 1658 Pope Alexander VII condemned them.[25] In the latter part of the seventeenth century, the learned Jesuit theologian, José de Acosta, who had spent a number of active years in the Americas, particularly in Peru, who had wide opportunity for observation of Indian Christians, and whose books on the New World were highly esteemed in Europe, was strong in his conviction that Indians should not be deprived of the communion, or confession, or extreme unction.[26] However, he felt the restriction wise which declined to admit Indians and mestizos to the priesthood, for he believed that the high character which should attach to the sacerdotal office might be compromised by the ordination of Indians who had been only recently converted from paganism or of those who, as a rule, were the offspring of irregular unions between white men and Indian women.[27]

Difficult though the task was of protecting the aborigines against the cruelties of the conquest, the excesses of those for whom the transition to America meant freedom from the moral standards of home, and the exploitation of those who were bent on gain, the impulsion of the Christian faith led many to undertake it. Their efforts bore fruit. Humanitarian legislation was placed on the statute books. Indeed, when they dealt with the aborigines, *The Laws of the Indies* were extraordinarily humane and obviously were designed to safeguard the rights of these dusky subjects of the Crown.[28] It was forbidden to reduce the Indians to slavery.[29] The evils against which Christian reformers struggled were never entirely eliminated. The hard facts of human nature and the demands of the ruling white minority for labour were too stubborn ever to be entirely overcome. However, considerable success attended the efforts to curb abuses, and it is significant that the leaders in the long campaign were

---

[23] Hanke, *op. cit.*, pp. 71, 72. See also Pastor, *History of the Popes*, Vol. XII, pp. 518, 519.

[24] Schmidlin, *Catholic Mission Theory*, pp. 452, 454; Huonder, *Der einheimische Klerus in den Heidenländern*, pp. 18-20; Bishop, *The Odyssey of Cabeza de Vaca*, p. 172.

[25] Schmidlin, *op. cit.*, p. 452.

[26] Acosta, *De Promulgatione Evangelii apud Barbaros*, Book VI, Chaps. 1-18.

[27] Acosta, *op. cit.*, Book VI, Chap. 19. The refusal to admit Indians to the priesthood was not confined to Acosta. The first *juntas eclesiasticas* and synods of Mexico and Lima expressly forbade the ordination of Indians.—Schmidlin, *op. cit.*, p. 318.

[28] *Recopilación de Leyes . . . de las Indias*, Book VI.

[29] *Recopilación de Leyes . . . de las Indias*, Book VI, Title 2, Law 1

those who had been profoundly stirred by a Christian conscience and who were sustained by a Christian faith.

Indeed, Christianity was considerably more effective in softening the impact of the Spaniard upon the Indian than it had been in blunting the asperity of the aggression of Teuton on Slav in the centuries before A.D. 1500. The Spanish conquest covered a much larger area and was made over peoples who were much further removed in race and culture from their masters than was the medieval Teutonic imperialism among Slavic and other non-Germanic peoples. Yet the Christian impulse proved more potent in alleviating the one than it had the other. Apparently as the centuries passed it was increasing in strength and in its ability to deal with the mishandling of one race by another.

The story of the efforts on behalf of the Indians, when properly told, is long. Here we cannot even summarize it. We must content ourselves with the barest references to a few of the men and measures that were prominent in it.

In the main, the Crown stood for the protection of the Indians. The devout Queen Isabella, whose endorsement made possible the initial voyage of Columbus, seems to have had sincerely at heart the welfare of her new subjects. In her will she declared that her chief purpose in her enterprise across the ocean was the conversion of the Indians.[30] She charged Bobadilla, who followed Columbus in the governorship of the Indies, to respect the liberty of the Indians.[31] The *encomienda* was early developed. Allotments (*repartimientos*) of Indians were made to grantees (*encomenderos*). In consenting to the system Isabella stipulated that the *encomendero* was to see that his Indians were given Christian instruction, that the Indians were to enter voluntarily into the relationship, were to be treated as free, and were to be paid for their labour, that their wages were to be adequate for the support of themselves and their families, and that the work required was to be non-hazardous and in proportion to the strength of the labourer.[32] *The Laws of the Indies* expressly declared that the motive and origin of the *encomiendas* was the spiritual and temporal welfare of the Indians.[33] These humane stipulations were so frequently ignored that the *encomienda* system became one of the chief targets of the reformers. However, the expressed royal purpose was benevolent. The obligations of the *encomendero* in behalf of his Indians were carefully defined.[34] The enslavement

---

[30] *Recopilación de Leyes.... de las Indias,* Book VI, Title 10, Law 1.

[31] Brion, *Bartholomé de las Casas,* pp. 36-39.

[32] *Ibid.*

[33] *Recopilación de Leyes . . . de las Indias,* Book VI, Title 9, Law 1.

[34] *Recopilación de Leyes . . . de las Indias,* Book VI, Titles 8, 9, 13. See a careful account in Lesley Byrd Simpson, *The Encomienda in New Spain. Forced Native Labor in the Spanish Colonies, 1492-1550* (Berkeley, Calif., University of California Press, 1929, pp. 297), favourable to the Spaniards.

of Indians was expressly forbidden.[35] The Crown, too, appointed officials whose special duty it was to see that the legal rights of the Indians were respected.[36] Although, because of the royal sensitiveness in matters respecting ecclesiastical prerogatives and the unwisdom of antagonizing the powerful monarchs of Spain, the Popes had to tread warily in American issues, more than one of the Pontiffs came out boldly in behalf of the Indians. Thus Pope Paul III took the freedom and the property of the Indians under his protection and made excommunication the penalty for their violation.[37] While, out of regard for the feelings of the Emperor Charles V, he had to revoke the penalties, he did not entirely recede from his position.[38] Pope Pius V again and again called attention to abuses in the West Indies and insisted on better treatment of the aborigines. He insisted, too, that King Philip II see to it that the Indians were provided with Christian preachers and priests and were given instruction in the Christian faith.[39]

Most of the initiative in behalf of the Indians came not from monarchs and Popes, but from private individuals—the larger proportion of them missionaries and other clergy whose calling brought them into close touch with the problems and the sufferings of the aborigines. The Dominicans first arrived in America, in Hispaniola (Haiti), in 1510, less than twenty years after the first voyage of Columbus. Before long they had antagonized the settlers by their outspoken denunciation of the treatment of the Indians.[40] Their Prior, Bernardino de Minaya, repeatedly wrote to Rome, calling attention to the cruelties inflicted on the natives, and eventually went in person to urge the cause of the unfortunates. It was he who was at least partly responsible for the bulls of Pope Paul III on behalf of the Indians.[41]

The most famous Spanish missionary champion of the Indians was Bartolomé de Las Casas.[42] It is significant that his father was one of the company

[35] Recopilación de Leyes . . . de las Indias, Book VI, Title 2.

[36] Recopilación de Leyes . . . de las Indias, Book VI, Title 6; Brion, Bartholomé de las Casas, pp. 110, 111.

[37] Pastor, History of the Popes, Vol. XII, pp. 518, 519.

[38] Hanke, in The Harvard Theological Review, Vol. XXX, pp. 91-93.

[39] Pastor, History of the Popes, Vol. XVIII, pp. 35, 330-332.

[40] Brion, op. cit., pp. 100-106.

[41] Brion, op. cit., pp. 112, 113.

[42] The bibliography on Las Casas is very extensive. A selected one is in Anton Freitag, Historisch-kritische Untersuchung über den Vorkämpfer der indianischen Freiheit Don Fray Bartolomé de Las Casas bis zu seinem Eintritt in den Dominikanermission (Missionsdruckerei in Steyl, 1915, pp. xvi, 106), pp. ix-xiv. A more extensive bibliography, made up of his writings, is scattered through Streit, Bibliotheca Missionum, Vols. I, II. Prominent among his writings are his Historia de Las Indias (Madrid, Miguel Ginesta, 5 vols., 1875, 1876), Coleccion de las Obras (Paris, Rosa, 2 vols., 1822), and, in French translation, his Oeuvres (Paris, Alexis Eymery, 2 vols., 1822). Among the biographical accounts are Marcel Brion, Bartholomé de Las Casas Père des Indiens (Paris, Librairie

on the second voyage of Columbus and that he himself was the first Christian priest ordained in the Americas. Thus did the Christian impulse early make itself felt in rousing the initial representative of the America-ordained clergy to seek indefatigably what he deemed the best interests of the aborigines.

Las Casas was somewhat slow to awake to his mission. A graduate of the famous University of Salamanca, he had received the conventional education of his time. It was natural that in his early manhood he should follow in the family tradition and come to the New World. Here, in the major centre of Spanish settlement of the time, the island of Hispaniola, he lived the life of a well-to-do colonial, probably neither worse nor better than the average, and taking the conventional attitude towards the coercion of the Indians. He shared in the raids against them and had Indians assigned him for his plantation.

In his middle thirties Las Casas sought ordination to the priesthood, and about the same time his conscience was aroused by a Dominican preacher to the enormities of the current treatment of the aborigines.

Las Casas did not immediately sever himself from the system in which he was bound. He took part in the initial expedition for the conquest of Cuba. Although he did what he could to befriend the Indians, baptized their children, and on at least one occasion protested hotly against cruelty to them, he accepted an *encomienda* with a *repartimiento* of aborigines. Before long, however, he became troubled by the system, denounced it in a sermon before the Governor and the settlers, renounced his allotment, and went to Spain to plead the cause of the natives.

In Spain, after long and vexatious delays, he won the favour of the great Cardinal Ximenez. He was appointed Protector-General of the Indians and in 1516 sailed for the New World with a commission of Hieronymite monks to seek the enforcement of the royal laws in behalf of his wards. In the West Indies bitter opposition was encountered, an opposition which was given point by an inopportune Indian rebellion. The Hieronymites were persuaded that Las Casas was a visionary, or worse, and that the Indians could not be handled in the way which he advocated without ruining the colonies. No help was to be had from the local authorities.

Once more Las Casas found himself under the necessity of going to Spain

---

Plon, 1927, pp. 309) (an English translation exists); Freitag, *op. cit.;* Arthur Helps, *The Life of Las Casas, "The Apostle of the Indies"* (London, Bell and Daldy, 1868, pp. xix, 292); and Francis Augustus MacNutt, *Bartholomew de Las Casas, His Life, Apostolate, and Writings* (Cleveland, The Arthur H. Clark Co., 1909, pp. xxxviii, 472). In spite of the volume of material and of original documents, uncertainty exists as to some important phases of the life of Las Casas. We do not know precisely, for instance, the number of trips which he made across the Atlantic.

to plead his cause at court. In Spain he met fresh opposition from those who told the King that without compulsory Indian labour the colonies would be ruined. Las Casas conceived the idea of proving his case by founding a colony in which the Indians would be won by kindly treatment. Again delays followed—due partly to difficulty in obtaining recruits for this benevolent venture.

In 1520 Las Casas sailed for the New World to inaugurate his new enterprise. He had obtained a few white labourers, hoping thus to be freed from the necessity of inducing Indians to do the work of the colony. The place chosen for his experiment was on the northern coast of South America, west of the mouths of the Orinoco. A number of unfortunate incidents combined to make the undertaking a failure before it was fairly launched. Las Casas, temporarily baffled but undefeated, sought refuge with the sympathetic Dominicans in Hispaniola and seems for a time largely to have withdrawn from the world. He there joined the Order of Preachers.

After a number of years, Las Casas was again on his travels. He went to Spain to obtain royal decrees to prevent the then fresh conquest of Peru from being as disastrous for the aborigines as that of the West Indies had been. In 1532 he was back in America, first briefly in Mexico and then for a short visit to Peru to obtain the publication of the King's *cédula* on behalf of the Indians. Thence he went to Nicaragua where, in new missions, he believed that he demonstrated his point that the Indians could be won to the Christian faith through friendship and to assent to Spanish authority without the use of armed force, and that revolts were only due to Spanish cruelty. His work in Central America was cut short by a command to go to Hispaniola to bring to a pacific disposition a native chief who had long brought terror to the colonists. Las Casas induced him to lay down his arms and baptized his followers. Soon he was back on the mainland. For several years he was engaged in the work of a missionary among the Indians of Guatemala. Here again he was challenged to prove a conviction which he had elaborated in a book, that force should not be used against the Indians and that coercion was quite powerless to effect the changes demanded by a true Christian conversion. The doctrine was not new, but he had given it fresh point by its application to conditions in the New World. For a time Las Casas was allowed to continue at the congenial task of experimenting with peaceful measures. However, in the late fifteen thirties he was once more in Spain. Here he continued to plead the cause of the Indians. He sought modifications of the existing laws and probably had large influence upon the provisions of the *Nuevas Leyes* or New Laws which were framed in 1542. Certainly the new legislation was strongly in favour of the Indians and contained much for which Las Casas had pleaded.

Las Casas seemed now to be high in the royal favour. He was offered the see of Cuzco, in some respects the most important in the New World. He declined. Instead he elected to become Bishop of Chiapa, in southern Mexico, and so accepted a diocese which was said to be the poorest in the Americas. He was duly consecrated and at the age of seventy for the last time went to the New World, there to enter upon what he must have known would be one of the most trying tasks of his stormy career.

When he arrived in the Americas, Las Casas found that he was regarded as chiefly responsible for the New Laws. These the settlers were convinced would ruin the colonies. Their enforcement, so they held, would make impossible the Indian labour upon which the prosperity of the Spanish regime depended. In his own diocese, Las Casas met bitter opposition. This was the more violent because he had ordered his clergy to refuse absolution to those Spaniards who continued to treat the Indians under them in ways contrary to the New Laws. Not only did the laymen among the Spaniards of his diocese denounce him, but some even among his clergy also refused obedience. In less than three years after his arrival, he felt it necessary to withdraw. Early in 1547 he was once more on his way to Spain, there to lay before the King his own cause and that of the Indians. In an absolute monarchy such as Spain, repeal of the humane legislation and laxity of enforcement could best be fought by carrying the argument directly to the Throne.

Las Casas was now old and he was never again to see America. Yet his zeal never abated. He entered into a prolonged controversy with Sepúlveda, a distinguished scholar who, contrary to the convictions and practice of Las Casas, argued that the Pope and the Kings of Spain had a right to subdue by war the peoples of the New World. Supported by loyal friends in his Order, he continued to fight infringements on the rights of the Indians. What seems to have been his last treatise was written when he was about ninety. He died in 1566, at the age of ninety-two.

Las Casas had a profound effect upon Spanish policy in the New World. He gave stimulus to much of the humanitarian legislation embodied in *The Laws of the Indies*, which sought to make Spanish rule a blessing and not a curse to the Indian. He did much to shape the ideals, then in process of formation, of the extensive Spanish missions in the Americas. These missions, he held, rather than the exploiting *encomenderos*, should be the vanguard of the Spanish occupation and the tutors of the aborigines. They should be initiated and conducted with either the entire absence or else the very minimum of armed force. He himself travelled widely in the New World in the days when missions were gaining momentum and before mission methods had crystallized. His influence upon them was profound. More than any other one man he embodied the effect of Christianity upon the Spanish conquest.

Yet Las Casas had influence chiefly because Spanish Christianity had produced so many kindred spirits. He was only one of thousands who felt much as he did about the Spanish responsibility in the New World. Indeed, had he never lived, it is probable that this Christian conscience would have made *The Laws of the Indies* substantially what they were and would have created mission methods such as those which were actually put into practice.

As we have suggested, then, Las Casas was only the most famous of many individuals who, from Christian motives, sought to lighten the lot of the aborigines. The names of great numbers of these have perished from memory. Even to cover the work of those whose records have come down to us would prolong this section into a huge tome. For example, Cabeza de Vaca would alone fill a volume.[43] A member of the ill-fated Narváez expedition, as one of the survivors he long wandered among the Indians in Texas and on the northern and western confines of Mexico. At times a captive, he eventually made his way through incredible hardships to men of his own race in Mexico. In the sufferings of these months and through his deliverance—by God, he believed—he formed the purpose of treating the Indians humanely and giving them the Gospel. With this dream he accepted the governorship of the young frontier colony of Paraguay, where unbridled licence marked the treatment of the natives by the settlers. There, in an attempt to give reality to his vision and to restrain the gross cruelties of the Spaniards, he so aroused the anger and resentment of those whom he sought to curb that an insurrection put him in chains and sent him to Spain.

Of another famous enterprise for the welfare of the Indians in the same general region, the Jesuit mission in Paraguay, we are to speak briefly later. We are also to see other frontier missions which sought to make wholesome the initial impact of the white man upon the aborigines.

As time passed, the wave of Spanish secular conquest slowed down. Christian missionaries, usually supported by small companies of soldiers, then became the agents for extending the Spanish frontiers.[44] They attempted, with the minimum of force, to induce the Indians to settle down around the mission, to receive Christian teaching, and to learn the rudiments of European

[43] See a well written account, based upon extensive reading and research, in Morris Bishop, *The Odyssey of Cabeza de Vaca* (New York, The Century Co., 1933, pp. vii, 306).

[44] See a summary description by Herbert E. Bolton, *The Mission as a Frontier Institution in the Spanish-American Colonies,* in *The American Historical Review,* Vol. XXIII, pp. 42-61.

agriculture, industry, and civilization. While frequently they felt themselves compelled to resort to more use of arms than Las Casas would have approved, in general they were in sharp and happy contrast to the earlier *conquistadores*. Christianity was having its effect.

In the treatment of the Negroes, too, Christianity apparently made itself felt. Certainly the laws concerning Negroes were fairly liberal. If a Negro challenged the legality of his enslavement the courts were to hear his cause.[45] If he were cruelly handled he could appeal to the courts and might be declared free.[46] A large proportion of the Negroes were gradually emancipated. Near the close of the eighteenth century, in Porto Rico the free coloured people outnumbered the slaves. In contrast, in the French part of Haiti and in the English Jamaica the proportion of free to enslaved Negroes was then less than one in ten.[47] If one may venture an inference from the motives known to have been back of the legislation on behalf of the Indians, it seems probable that a prominent factor in attempting to ameliorate the lot of the Negroes was Christianity. Certainly it was a member of the Society of Jesus, Alonso de Sandoval, who, writing from America, came out boldly in criticism of the slave-trade.[48] As we shall see a little later, moreover, it was a Jesuit, Pedro Claver, who spent his life in a devoted ministry to the Negroes. In 1789 the King of Spain issued an order to regulate the treatment of Negro slaves in Spanish America. The owner was required to instruct his slaves in the Christian faith and to set aside certain feast days for that purpose in which neither he nor the slaves should work.[49] The masters, too, were commanded to feed and clothe their slaves, to see that the ill were sent to a hospital, to provide for the support of the aged.[50]

One of the outstanding features of the culture which arose out of the Spanish conquests and settlements in the Americas, as we have suggested, was the professedly Christian character of the communities which came into being. This meant that the colonists and their descendants were held to the faith, that many of the imported Negroes and their offspring became Christians, and that the Indians substituted, at least outwardly, the religion of their new masters for their inherited cults.

Much of this result was the outcome of the initiative and active support of the Crown. For instance, in 1526 Charles V expressed the desire that every

[45] *Recopilación de Leyes . . . de las Indias,* Book VII, Title V, Law 8.
[46] Bourne, *Spain in America,* p. 280; Humboldt, *Travels,* Vol. VII, pp. 164-166.
[47] Humboldt, *Travels,* Vol. VI, pp. 820, 824.
[48] Alfonzo de Sandoval, *De Instauranda Æthiopum Salute* (Madrid, 1647), Part I, Book I, Chaps. 23, 27.
[49] *Recopilación de Leyes . . . de las Indias,* Book I, Title I, Law 17.
[50] Moses, *South America on the Eve of Emancipation,* p. 108.

fleet going to the Indies should carry religious charged with preaching the Christian message.[51] *The Laws of the Indies* placed foremost the conversion and spiritual nurture of the Indians, the slaves, the Negroes, and the mulattoes.[52] Again and again, in compliance with the royal purpose, civil officials gave assistance or even took the initiative in propagating the faith.

The Crown was solicitous that no heretical doctrines enter Spanish America. The statutes provided that no one newly converted from Judaism or Islam or his sons should be permitted to go to the colonies without a special royal licence.[53] The Inquisition was introduced. Its jurisdiction was not extended to the Indians, for it was intended to preserve from contamination the faith of the European stock. Within this limitation, however, its officials laboured to keep out Protestantism and all the brood of unorthodox ideas associated with that multiform movement, and to stamp out the tendency to revert to Judaism of those Christians of Hebraic descent who, in spite of the careful safeguards, had found their way to the Americas.[54]

Very early, through royal co-operation and at times through royal initiative, an ecclesiastical structure was created for Spanish America. In 1501, less than ten years after the first voyage of Columbus, an episcopal see was erected in Hispaniola. In 1504 an archiepiscopal see was placed on Hispaniola and under it were two suffragan bishops. By 1530 the American possessions had been divided into seven mission fields, in Hispaniola, Cuba, Mexico, Nicaragua, Honduras, and Venezuela.[55] Before 1548 at least nine sees had been added— two in Mexico, two in Guatemala, three in Peru, one in New Granada, and one for Rio de la Plata. In 1546 archiepiscopal sees had been brought into existence in Mexico and Lima.[56] These many sees were made the centres of missions for the Indians and of clerical ministrations to the Spaniards. Their broad extent, in the West Indies, from Mexico on the north through Central America, into Venezuela, New Granada, and Peru, and to the Rio de la Plata on the eastern slope of South America, is vivid evidence of the vast geographic expansion of the faith which had taken place in the Americas less than two generations after the first discoveries.

The active missionaries were the clergy. On the frontiers of the Church most of the ministry to the *conquistadores* and practically all of the burden of instruct-

---

[51] Van der Essen, in Descamps, *Histoire Générale Comparée des Missions*, p. 329.
[52] *Recopilación de Leyes . . . de las Indias*, Book I, is almost entirely devoted to this topic.
[53] *Recopilación de Leyes . . . de las Indias*, Book IX, Title XXVI, Law 15.
[54] See especially on this Henry Charles Lea, *The Inquisition in the Spanish Dependencies*, Chaps. 6-8. See also Ryan, *The Church in the South American Republics*, pp. 28, 29.
[55] Jann, *Die katholischen Missionen in Indien, China, und Japan*, p. 78.
[56] Pastor, *History of the Popes*, Vol. XII, p. 515.

ing and baptizing the Indians was assumed by the regulars, the members of religious orders. As in the large majority of the missions between A.D. 500 and A.D. 1500 the teaching of the faith and the care of the neophytes had been by monks, so now, it was those who were the outgrowth of the monastic tradition who performed most of the work of conversion. Large numbers of these regulars came to the New World. For example, in 1526, at the command of Charles V, one hundred and twenty Franciscans, seventy Dominicans, and ten Hieronymites were sent out.[57] It was not until a generation after the first voyage of Columbus that the Society of Jesus was founded. Not long after its inception, however, members began arriving in the New World. As we shall see, they instituted some of the most important missions. In 1760, seven years before they were driven out of Spanish territories, 2,171 of them were in the Spanish missions in the Americas and the Philippines.[58] Other orders also came. For instance, the first representatives of the Order of the Hospitallers of St. John of God arrived in the Americas in 1595.[59] Moreover, women joined in the task of missions. Women teachers came from Spain to Mexico to instruct the girls. Before the end of the sixteenth century convents of women were found in several places in the Americas.[60] Here was something relatively new in the spread of Christianity. Not since the early centuries, except in Germany under Boniface, had women been part of the missionary force which pushed forward the geographic frontiers of the faith.

Some trouble was encountered in obtaining enough missionaries.[61] Many, too, when they arrived were dismayed by the difficulties and wished to go on to Japan or China, perhaps in the hope that there the road would be less arduous.[62]

When in a particular district conversion had been completed and the missionary stage was deemed to have passed, the regulars were supposed to give way to the seculars, and the latter took over the care of the parishes. As a matter of fact, in many instances the regulars performed parish duties in the older districts.[63]

The quality of the secular clergy was often poor. Some high posts in the Church were well paid sinecures. Once in one of them, an unworthy prelate was difficult to remove. Then, too, the home government used the colonies as

---

[57] Schlund, *St. Franziskus und sein Orden in der Heidenmission*, p. 32.
[58] Schwager, *Die katholische Heidenmission der Gegenwart*, p. 25.
[59] Lucio Conde, in *Revista de la Exposición Misional Española*, Feb., 1929, pp. 208-211.
[60] Lemmens, *Geschichte der Franziskanermissionen*, p. 344.
[61] Pastor, *op. cit.*, Vol. XIII, p. 290.
[62] Juan Rivero, *Historia de las Misiones de los Llanos de Casanare y los Rios Orinoco y Meta*, p. 350.
[63] Kilgar in *Zeitschrift für Missionswissenschaft*, 1922, pp. 19, 20.

a dumping ground for priests who had given trouble in Spain.[64] The obligation of clerical chastity was chronically ignored.[65] As the colonial period approached its close, the numbers of clergy declined.[66] In the long post-mission decades the quality of the faith which had been transmitted tended to stagnate and even to decline.

Gradually Indians and mestizos were admitted to the ranks of the clergy. As we have seen, men from these two classes were long debarred from holy orders.[67] Indeed, even American-born whites in the ranks of the regular clergy were in the small minority. Rightly or wrongly, it was at first assumed that the Creoles had neither the physical nor the spiritual qualifications for the arduous life of the missionary.[68] In Church as in state, the higher offices were usually filled by natives of Spain, *chapetones* as they were called. By the latter part of the eighteenth century the situation had gradually altered. By the close of the sixteenth century many Creoles had been ordained to the priesthood. Most of these, however, were seculars, and presumably served not as missionaries on the frontiers but in charge of parishes in the regions in which the missionary stage had passed. In 1575 the Archbishop of Mexico reported that of the one hundred and fifty-eight seculars in the archdiocese, seventy-eight were born in America.[69] By the end of the sixteenth century, too, the restriction which kept Indians and mestizos out of the clergy had disappeared.[70] In Mexico exceptions seem to have been made for mestizos before they were made for Indians.[71] The stream of Spanish-born clergy dwindled. The schools long conducted by the clergy in the Americas began to bear fruit in better trained candidates. The concessions which had permitted parishes to be filled by regulars were revoked, and in the long settled portions of the land the proportion of seculars in charge of parishes increased. In their chronic feud with the regulars, the bishops, in order to have enough seculars to fill the parishes, were driven to the ordination of mestizos. In 1768 a royal order commanded that a fourth or a third of those admitted to the seminaries should be Indians or mestizos. In the latter half of the seventeenth century a native of Mexico was

[64] Ryan, *The Church in the South American Republics*, pp. 23, 24; Jorge Juan and Antonio de Ulloa, *Noticias Secretas de America* (London, R. Taylor, Part I, 1826), pp. 489 ff.

[65] Jorge Juan and Antonio de Ulloa, *op. cit.*, pp. 489 ff.

[66] Moses, *South America on the Eve of Emancipation*, p. 139.

[67] Huonder, *Der einheimische Klerus in den Heidenländern*, pp. 20-24; Braden, *Religious Aspects of the Conquest of Mexico*, pp. 269-277.

[68] Lemmens, *Geschichte der Franziskanermissionen*, p. 342.

[69] Braden, *op. cit.*, p. 219, citing Mariano Cuevas, *Documentos Inéditos del Siglo XVI para la Historia de México*, Vol. II, p. 138.

[70] Huonder, *op. cit.*, pp. 24-29.

[71] Braden, *op. cit.*, p. 275.

elevated to the archbishopric of that land.[72] By the end of the eighteenth century a majority of the bishops were natives of America, although most of these were Creoles. In Peru, while in the colonial period all the Archbishops of Lima seem to have been born in Spain, at least fifty-three out of one hundred and eighty bishops were born in America.[73] In the orders the proportion of native-born members increased. In the Mexican Church several important men were of Indian origin.[74] The quality of the faith might leave much to be desired, but the Church was passing under the administration of men sprung from the soil. Christianity had taken root in the New World.

However, opposition to the ordination of Indians remained great and not many were raised to the priesthood. The religious orders were especially reluctant to admit them.[75] To the very end of the colonial period, Christianity continued to be a faith in which those of pure European stock were in control, and those of Indian or mixed blood were passive recipients who were given instruction and the sacraments, and in return bore, through fees and taxation, the chief financial burden of the ecclesiastical structure. Under these circumstances, few of the indigenous races became missionaries. Their faith was not sufficiently compelling to send them out as such. Even had they desired to go, they would have been discouraged from assuming leading rôles in spreading the white man's religion.

The methods employed in propagating Christianity in Spanish America varied from period to period and from region to region. Some of them we are to see as we proceed with our narrative. Several of the main features, however, were found in many widely scattered sections and persisted for centuries.

At the outset, the Americas presented what to the Spaniards was an entirely new set of problems. Heretofore Spaniards had had practically all their close contacts with non-Christians with Jews and Moslems who were approximately on the same level of civilization as themselves. Back of the cultures of Jews, Moors, and Spaniards lay a basis of understanding in the Græco-Roman heritage which was common to all three. Now the Spaniards were brought in touch with peoples of primitive culture or, in Mexico and Peru, of cultures with which they had almost nothing in common. Moreover, never had the Spaniards faced the problem presented by so large a migration of their own people to non-Christian lands. At the beginning of the American experience, then, they were compelled to devise new plans. For a time these were fluid

[72] Bancroft, *History of Mexico,* Vol. III, p. 168.
[73] Means, *The Fall of the Inca Empire,* p. 167.
[74] Huonder, *op. cit.,* pp. 29-37.
[75] Ryan, *The Church in the South American Republics,* pp. 25, 26.

and were modified by methods of trial and error. Only gradually were programmes worked out which remained fairly constant.

In the main, in planting the faith in America the Spanish authorities had
four different groups of problems with which to deal. One was holding to
Christianity and ministering spiritually to the Spanish immigrants and their
descendants, including those in whom the Spanish blood was mixed with that
of the Indians and the Negroes. This was met by sending over clergy from
Spain, by building churches (partly by government funds and compulsory
contributions and partly by private munificence), by creating an ecclesiastical
structure largely modelled on that of Spain, with parishes and episcopal sees,
and by means of schools maintained by the clergy. As we have suggested,
moreover, the Inquisition assisted by stamping out ideas which might contami-
nate the Roman Catholic faith of the whites.

A second type of problems was presented by the civilized peoples. Here were
large societies with towns, cities, highly developed agriculture, and governments controlling moderately large areas. Most of them passed over to Christianity in the sixteenth century. Their conversion was a phase of the Spanish
conquest. It was accomplished fairly easily and promptly. Under orders from
home, the Spanish civil authorities encouraged it, zealous missionaries were its
active agents, and the masses, docile by long tradition to the wishes of their
rulers, acquiesced in it as part of the obedience owed to their new masters.
Some of the Indian youth, trained by the missionaries, became eager assistants
to the foreign clergy. Mass conversions took place on a large scale and, once
the political conquest was accomplished, with very slight use of force.

A third set of problems was presented by the uncivilized tribes. These
peoples varied greatly in types and stages of culture. In the West Indies, as
we have seen, they met a bitter fate. They largely disappeared under the ruthlessness of the first impact of the Spaniards before the Christian conscience
was able to devise safeguards and put them into effect. By the time that the
Spanish occupation had proceeded far on the mainland, however, a body of
legislation was built up and methods evolved which served to give some protection to the Indians and to incorporate large numbers of them into the structure of Spanish colonial life and administration.

In this task of assimilation the missionary played the most important rôle.
In a certain sense the mission became a substitute for the *encomienda* and in
practice had the welfare of the Indian much more at heart than did the latter.
Like the latter, the mission induced the Indians to lead a settled life, to work,
and to accept Christianity. Unlike the latter, however, the main object was
not profit for the whites, but the well-being of the Indians.

In accordance with the principle of the right of patronage exercised by the Crown, new missions were authorized through the royal officials, and in theory and often in practice the expenses were met chiefly from state funds. Equipment was provided partly by the state, and annual stipends, or *sinodos*, were paid by the state to each missionary. The King ordered prelates and religious orders to provide some of the equipment, and in several notable instances funds and endowments were supplied by private lay generosity. As the missions developed, the labour of the Indians was supposed to render them self-supporting. Some missionaries went one by one among the Indians with crucifix and breviary, hoping to persuade them by eloquence to accept baptism. A few of these proved successful. More of them found martyrdom. Usually missionaries went out in bands of two or three, protected by a small guard of soldiers and often accompanied by Christian Indians from older missions. Sometimes a tribe of pagan Indians sent on their own initiative for a *padre*. Efforts were made to induce the Indians to settle down around the mission centre. For this purpose gifts were made and sometimes rations were provided until food could be raised. The number of Indians in a mission varied. In some there were only a few score. In others a thousand or more were to be found. The Indians were taught to raise crops, several of them of plants introduced from Europe. They were also instructed in simple handicrafts.

When fully developed, the mission usually centred about a church built by Indian labour. In front of the church might be a plaza on whose four sides were the arsenal, the house of the missionary, workshops, granaries, storehouses, and the dwellings of the converts. The entire life of the settlement was under the direction of the missionaries and each week-day was an alternation of work, worship, rest, and play. Often each mission had two priests, one charged with the supervision of the spiritual and the other of the temporal affairs of the community. Much attention was paid to the instruction of the children, and repeatedly children were used to convert and instruct their elders. Schools were maintained in which were taught reading, writing, arithmetic, Spanish, music, manual arts, and agriculture. Some of the more adept were trained in painting and sculpture. Usually the missionaries were in complete charge of their wards. Frequently they preferred to have other Spaniards kept at a distance for fear of the contamination of the morals or the exploitation of the Indians. The missions were largely self-contained units.

The missionary attempted to bring his charges to a fairly complete break with their past. Of course this was true in the realm of religion. Old religious beliefs and customs were discouraged. It was also the policy in other phases of native life. So far as possible, the ancient forms of amusement were suppressed and for them were substituted other types of recreation, such as religious processions, Christian fiestas, and dances. New methods of agriculture and industry were introduced and new regulations made to govern the life of the community. The mission itself usually constituted a form of community to which the Indians had been unaccustomed. However, at least one experiment in the conversion of Indians who were permitted to preserve their old tribal life without assembling in a mission ended in disaster.[76]

In many ways the lot of the Indian under the mission regime was far from unpleasant. The religious duties required of the converts were not so exacting as those held up before the Spaniards as ideal. The labour demanded was not excessive. The missionaries carried the responsibility for seeing that their wards were clothed and fed, and that they were protected against hostile Indians and rapacious whites.

The attitudes of the Indians towards the missionary, his message, and his regimen varied. Some Indians, accustomed to the magic of their former faiths, esteemed baptism as having therapeutic value. Some regarded the white man's God as shut up in a house and so as inferior to their own deities, who had the free range of the fields and the forests. Usually they were irked by the discipline of memorizing prayers and the catechism. Many objected to coming to confession. Others annoyed the missionaries by coming too frequently and by professing to have committed sins of which they were quite innocent. Numerous were the uprisings which broke out against the mission and its life. It was to be expected, too, that many, brought by the white man into a life so alien to their traditions, should abandon the mission on the slightest provocation and resume in the wilds their ancestral ways.

These frontier missions were intended by the Spanish authorities to be means of preparing the Indian for incorporation into the normal society of Spanish America. They were, therefore, transitional. After a period of years, sometimes a decade and sometimes longer, when conversion and assimilation were deemed to have proceeded sufficiently, the mission parish was turned over to the secular clergy, and the Indians were fully incorporated into the normal ecclesiastical and civil administration of the older portions of the Spanish possessions.[77]

[76] Engelhardt, *Missions and Missionaries of California,* Vol. II, pp. 371-374.

[77] The summary in these past paragraphs has been gleaned from reading in many books. Excellent accounts are to be found in Rippy and Nelson, *Crusaders of the Jungle, passim,* and especially pp. 50-90, and in H. E. Bolton, *The Mission as a Frontier Institution in the Spanish-American Colonies* (*The American Historical Review,* Vol. XXIII, Oct. 1917, pp. 42-61).

See a summary of mission policy in the first years of the conquest in Anton Freytag, *Spanische Missionspolitik im Entdeckungszeitalter,* in *Zeitschrift für Missionswissenschaft,* Vol. III, pp. 11-28.

This system of missions and these missionary procedures were far from being an unqualified success. The Indians were not taught self-reliance. The programme was paternalistic. When the missionary was withdrawn, the quality of the Indian life usually sagged. In character the seculars seem not to have averaged as high as the regulars whom they displaced. The Christianity of the converts was probably further removed from that of the New Testament than was that of the mother country. In it was much which those accustomed to the Gospels must regard as superstitious and immoral. It was passive and out of it issued few streams of creative life. In extreme instances, as in the famous Jesuit enterprise in Paraguay, even after more than a century of effort, the withdrawal of the missionary was followed by the complete disintegration of the Christian communities.

On the other hand, the missions succeeded in winning the large majority of the Indian population of Spanish America, including thousands from tribes previously uncivilized, to at least the outward acceptance of the Christian faith. They protected millions against the extreme exploitation which had marked the earlier days of the Spanish conquest. They eased the transition to the new regime and were the means of assimilating fairly painlessly the native peoples to Spanish culture and Spanish institutions. As in Northern Europe Christianity had been the vehicle on which had come the culture of the Mediterranean world, so to these native races of Spanish America it was the inspiration and the means of what was meant to be a humane incorporation into the structure of life transmitted from Europe. If in Spanish America the process was not followed by so pulsing a life as it was in Medieval Europe, the cause must probably be sought partly, as we have earlier suggested, in the autocratic paternalism of the Spanish state which did not allow free course to the Christian impulse.

It must be said that, in general, the Spanish missionary effort was more successful among those peoples who had led a settled civilized existence before the coming of the white man than among those which are normally classified as uncivilized. For the former the transition to the Spanish type of civilization did not involve so pronounced a break from their former manner of life as it did for the latter. It was among primitive tribes that missionaries found their task the most difficult. It was among these that lapses of entire groups from Christianity and Spanish culture most frequently followed the withdrawal of the missionary.

The fourth group of problems with which the Spaniards had to deal in transmitting their Christian faith to the Americas was presented by the

Negroes.[78] The Negroes were much less numerous than the descendants of either the Spaniards or the Indians. For them no programme for conversion was instituted which in extent or in the thought devoted to it was at all comparable to that for the Indians. Apparently the missionaries who gave themselves chiefly or entirely to winning the Negroes to Christianity were comparatively few. *The Laws of the Indies* allot far less space to the religious instruction of the Negroes than they do to that of the Indians. Negro slaves were distributed among the plantations of the Spaniards or in other labour groups under white supervision. Free Negroes usually lived in families or in small groups surrounded by Spanish colonial society. Both slaves and freed men tended to pick up more or less imperfectly the language and customs of the dominant groups about them. In general the acceptance of Christianity seems to have taken place in casual fashion as part of the process of assimilation and without much deliberate, organized effort by the ecclesiastical or civil authorities.

From this description of movements and processes which were common to much or all of Spanish America, we now turn to an account region by region of the planting of the Christian faith. Here again we must content ourselves with brief summaries. As with so much else in these volumes, their value must lie not in minute and exhaustive details, but in a comprehensive picture in which the emphasis is on the main outlines.

We begin, as is proper, with the West Indies, for here the first discoveries of Columbus were made and here were the initial Spanish settlements. For a few years, as we have seen, Hispaniola (Haiti) was the chief centre of Spanish power in the New World.

We have also seen that on his second voyage to America, Columbus was accompanied by several priests. One of these, Bernal Boil, is said to have baptized a few natives who accepted the rite under compulsion.[79] Franciscans, Dominicans, and Hieronymites early went to the islands. In a letter of 1500 the Franciscans reported that they had baptized three thousand and that the Indians were eager to receive that sacrament.[80] The Superior of the Dominicans, Pedro de Cordoba, told of preaching, crucifix in hand, through an interpreter, to the Indians.[81] Few of the early missionaries took the pains to learn an

[78] A good treatment of the history of Negroes in Spanish America is Antonio Saco, *Historia de la Esclavitud de la Raza Africano en el Nuevo Mundo y en especial en los Paises Américo-Hispanos* (Barcelona, Jaime Jepús, 1879, pp. 442).

[79] Schmidlin-Braun, *Catholic Mission History*, p. 358.

[80] Schmidlin-Braun, *op. cit.*, p. 359; Streit in *Zeitschrift für Missionswissenschaft*, Vol. XII, p. 173.

[81] Schmidlin-Braun, *op. cit.*, pp. 359, 360.

Indian tongue, and so were badly handicapped in giving instruction.[82] In the course of the years missionaries were sent to Cuba, Porto Rico, Jamaica, Trinidad, and several of the smaller islands.[83]

Much of the conversion must have been very superficial, and the rapid disappearance of the aborigines prevented the emergence of enduring communities of Christian Indians. For many years the clergy were too few adequately to cover the islands. In Jamaica in 1574 the new abbot, the highest ecclesiastical official on the island, reported that confirmation had never been administered. In 1582 another new abbot declared that neither pastor nor prelate had visited Jamaica for eight years, that he could find only one baptismal register, and that even it was in bad condition. However, this particular abbot, Francisco Marques de Villalobos, was in charge of ecclesiastical affairs on the island for about a quarter of a century, and under him the Church made progress.[84]

Presumably the Negro slaves who succeeded the Indians as labourers in the West Indies were slowly assimilated to a more or less nominal acquiescence in the faith of their masters. Now and then we catch glimpses of the process. In 1538 the Emperor Charles V ordered all who owned Negro slaves in the city of San Domingo to send them to church.[85] As late as 1680 a diocesan synod in Cuba took cognizance of the fact that many Negro slaves were not baptized and decreed on pain of fine and excommunication that all who owned such slaves should see that they received the rite within two months and should have them instructed in Christian doctrine, and that those who bought slaves from the importers should have them instructed and baptized within six months after their purchase.[86] From the Cuban action we may gather that the conversion of the Negroes was more slowly accomplished than that of the Indians and was late in coming to completion.

From the West Indies we turn naturally to Mexico.[87] Here, from 1519 to 1521, the Spaniards, led by Hernando Cortés, accomplished their first extensive conquests on the mainland of the Americas—although these were followed almost immediately by others of first-class importance in Peru. Moreover, Mexico constituted the administrative centre and the most populous portion of what its masters denominated New Spain, a viceroyalty which included at one time or another not only the present Mexico, but also most of Central America, the West Indies, Florida, much of the modern Georgia, all the

---

[82] Schmidlin-Braun, *op. cit.*, p. 360.

[83] Schmidlin-Braun, *op. cit.*, pp. 360, 361.

[84] Delany, *A History of the Catholic Church in Jamaica*, pp. 1-25.

[85] Saco, *op. cit.*, p. 175.

[86] Saco, *op. cit.*, p. 286, giving the document.

[87] On the sources and literature for the early missions in Mexico, see a critical essay in Braden, *Religious Aspects of the Conquest of Mexico*, pp. 309 ff.

littoral of the Gulf of Mexico, and vast areas whose northern boundaries were only vaguely defined in the general region of the modern states of Texas, Arizona, New Mexico, and California. It once embraced even Venezuela, and from it the Philippines were governed.

From the beginning, the conquest of Mexico had as one of its purposes the conversion of the inhabitants to the Christian faith. The methods of the conquest were in sharp contradiction to the principles of Jesus, and in their loose relations with the women of the land the *conquistadores* departed widely from the injunctions of the religion which they represented. For all that, the leader, Cortés, was sincere in his piety. He believed that his expedition was a crusade and that God was on his side.[88] Cortés and Martin Luther were contemporaries and a Roman Catholic historian saw in the coincidence a divine providence for winning thousands to the orthodox faith to offset the losses to the Protestant heresy.[89] At the first landing effected, on the island of Cozumel, off the coast of Yucatan, a temple was entered, the images overthrown, an altar set up in their stead, mass celebrated, and the Christian faith preached to the aborigines through an interpreter.[90] The contrast between professed motives and action—although presumably it did not appear to the Spaniards to be such—is seen in some of the earliest baptisms. These were of Indian women who were presented to the Spaniards and who were given the rite and then distributed among the men, including Cortés, as concubines.[91] More than once Cortés might have employed force to effect mass conversions had he not been restrained by Olmedo, a Mercedarian priest, who accompanied him.[92]

After the initial stages of the conquest, more active efforts at conversion were begun. In 1523 a royal letter to Cortés was emphatic that the King's chief interest in New Spain was the conversion of the Indians, forbade the introduction of the *encomienda* and *repartimiento,* declared that the aborigines should be as free as the King's vassals in Castile, and said that they must not be warred against or harmed or deprived of goods without payment, that thus they might be won to the Christian faith.[93] In 1524 Cortés wrote one of his lieutenants commanding that the chiefs be ordered to see that ceremonies in honour of idols cease.[94] In that year, too, Cortés ordered that those who had

---

[88] Francis A. MacNutt, *Letters of Cortés* (New York, G. P. Putnam's Sons. 2 vols., 1908), Vol. I, pp. 206, 207.

[89] Mendieta, *Historia Eclesiástica Indiana*, Book III, Chap. I.

[90] Prescott, *Conquest of Mexico*, Book II, Chap. 4.

[91] Diaz del Castillo, *Historia Verdadera de la Conquista de la Nueva España*, Chap. 72.

[92] Prescott, *op. cit.*, Book II, Chaps. 5, 7.

[93] *Colección de Documentos Inéditos, Relativos al Decubrimiento Conquista y Colonización de los Posesiones Españoles,* Vol. XXIII, pp. 353 ff.

[94] *Colección de Documentos Inéditos* etc., Vol. XXVI, p. 151.

repartimientos of Indians—for the royal prohibition of the system did not prove effective—should ensure that idols be done away with and that provision be made for the instruction of their charges in the Christian faith.[95]

To accomplish the conversion of the Indians, missionaries were sent out. Three Flemish Franciscans early arrived—for Flanders was then under the rule of the Spanish monarchs.[96] The first large group of missionaries was a band of twelve Spanish Franciscans led by the ascetic and devoted Martín de Valencia. They arrived in 1524 and were received by Cortés with great honour.[97] Other Franciscans followed. In 1544, for instance, the King sent to New Spain two hundred and seven members of the order.[98] In 1559 three hundred and eighty Brothers Minor were said to be in eighty different houses in New Spain.[99] Most of the Franciscans were Spaniards, but we hear of a few Portuguese, Italians, and French. Most of them, too, were of the strict branch of the Franciscans known as the Observants.[100] In 1526, very soon after the arrival of the twelve Brothers Minor, came twelve Dominicans, led by Tomás Ortiz.[101] The first Augustinians entered Mexico City in 1533.[102] Reinforcements also reached these orders. By the end of the sixteenth century the Dominicans had from sixty to eighty houses for work among the Indians, and the Augustinians over seventy houses.[103] About 1559 each of these orders had slightly over two hundred members in New Spain.[104] In general the relations between the Franciscans and the Augustinians were friendly, but between Franciscans and Dominicans conflict was not unusual.[105] In 1572 the first of the Society of Jesus came and more soon followed. At the outset the Jesuits gave their attention wholly to Mexico City, chiefly to the Spanish population, and mainly to education, but in 1584 they began to learn the native languages and to labour among the Indians in the cities. Before the close of the century they had commenced missions among at least three different tribes.[106] In 1585

[95] *Colección de Documentos Inéditos* etc., Vol. XXVI, pp. 140-142.

[96] Mendieta, *op. cit.*, Book III, Chap. 4.

[97] Mendieta, *op. cit.*, Book III, Chaps. 8-12; Torquemada, *Monarchia Indiana*, Book XV, Chaps. 5-9; Bancroft, *History of Mexico*, Vol. II, pp. 161-165.

[98] Villanueva, *Los PP. Franciscanos en las Indias*, p. 54.

[99] Streit, *Bibliotheca Missionum*, Vol. II, p. 176, summarizing a *Carta á S. M. el Rey* from Tlaxcala in 1559.

[100] Lemmens, *Geschichte der Franziskanermissionen*, p. 220.

[101] Mendieta, *op. cit.*, Book IV, Chap. 1.

[102] Mendieta, *op. cit.*, Book IV, Chap. 2.

[103] Schmidlin-Braun, *Catholic Mission History*, pp. 421, 442.

[104] Streit, *op. cit.*, Vol. II, p. 176.

[105] Lemmens, *op. cit.*, p. 221.

[106] Jerome V. Jacobson, *Educational Foundations of the Jesuits in Sixteenth-Century New Spain* (Berkeley, University of California Press, 1938, pp. xii, 292), pp. 67 ff.; Schmidlin-Braun, *op. cit.*, p. 422; Crétineau-Joly, *Histoire de la Compagnie de Jésus*, Vol. II, pp. 128, 129; Bancroft, *History of Mexico*, Vol. II, pp. 699-709.

eleven Discalced Carmelites arrived and founded a convent.[107] In 1552 a member of the order of St. John of God reached Mexico.[108] The Benedictines came in 1589.[109] A few seculars also laboured among the Indians,[110] but, as we have said, the great majority of the missionaries were regulars.

A number of factors facilitated the conversion of the Indian population.[111] First of all was the Spanish conquest. The Spaniards were professedly Christian and their new subjects naturally tended to conform to their religion.

This favourable atmosphere was reinforced by the zeal of many of the Spanish civil authorities for the progress of the faith. We have seen that the Spanish monarchs had the propagation of Christianity as one of their most strongly avowed motives for empire. The establishment of the Spanish rule in Mexico coincided with the reigns of two of the most vigorous rulers of Spain, the Emperor Charles V and King Philip II. Monarchs of their force of character and religious purpose could inject something of their will into their subordinates. The purpose of the monarchs was assisted by the active sympathy of the early civil heads of the administration. Of the interest of Cortés we have already spoken. The two viceroys who succeeded him, Mendoza and Velasco, had the spiritual welfare of the Indians at heart.

A third factor was the attitude of the aborigines. For the most part those in the thickly settled portions of the Mexican plateau, in or near the centre of the former Aztec state, proved docile and were amenable to the religious instruction given them. Some were even eager to adopt the faith of their new masters.[112] The submission in which they had been drilled by their former rulers was transferred to their new lords.

A fourth favouring circumstance was the existence of features in the old religion which appeared to the missionaries to have resemblances to Christianity and to predispose the Indians to accept the transition.[113] Under their old cults the Indians seem to have held the cross in reverence, to have practised a form of baptism, to have had a kind of confession, and to have observed a ceremony bearing some resemblance to the Christian communion. They had had a priestly hierarchy, had possessed houses in which young men were trained for the priesthood, had been familiar with the dedication of young women to the

---

[107] Gil González Dávila, *Teatro Eclesiástico de la Primitiva Iglesia de las Indias Occidentales Vidas de svs Arzobispos, Obispos, y Cosas Memorables de svs Sedes* (Madrid, Diego de la Carrera, 2 vols., 1649, 1655), Vol. I, p. 38; Bancroft, *op. cit.*, Vol. II, p. 711.
[108] *Revista de la Exposición Misional Española*, Apr., 1929, pp. 315-320.
[109] Bancroft, *op. cit.*, Vol. II, p. 712.
[110] Schmidlin-Braun, *op. cit.*, p. 424.
[111] See some of these in Braden, *Religious Aspects of the Conquest of Mexico*, pp. 180 ff.
[112] So at least Mendieta believed, *Historia Eclesiástica Indiana*, Book IV, Chap. 21.
[113] See some of these in Braden, *op. cit.*, pp. 61-75; Prescott, *Conquest of Mexico*, Book I, Chap. 3.

service of the gods, and had kept feast days. Myths connected with the god Quetsalcoatl formed a preparation for the acceptance of Christianity. Missionaries from whom our information comes may have misunderstood the native cults and so have exaggerated the likenesses to the Christianity taught by the friars, but that some resemblances existed seems certain.

A fifth and very important assistance in the spread of Christianity was the character of the missionaries themselves. The conquest of Mexico coincided with the rising tide of religious life and zeal in Spain. This new energy and devotion overflowed into New Spain. In the initial stages of the conversion of the Mexicans no figure stands out as prominently as some in other epochs in the expansion of Christianity. There is no one who corresponds to Paul in the first century, to Ulfilas among the Goths, to Patrick in Ireland, to Columba in Scotland, to Boniface in Germany, to Anskar at the beginnings of Scandinavian missions, or to the Francis Xavier who not far from this very time was blazing a trail for the faith in India and the Far East. In place of one dominant leader were a number of men of ability and devotion. To single any of them out from the others for special mention appears almost invidious to their colleagues. Simply as examples may be recorded the names of Martín de Valencia, the leader of the first band of twelve Franciscans and who, although past fifty years of age when he reached Mexico, set for his fellows a high standard of zeal and singleness of purpose; the first Bishop (later Archbishop) of Mexico, Zumárraga; and the gifted Peter of Ghent (Pedro de Gante), a relative of Charles V, a graduate of the University of Louvain, who, while a courtier, had been won to the religious life by two confessors of the Emperor, who did much for the organization of schools[114] and who, declining a bishopric, chose to continue as a lay Franciscan brother. A number of the missionaries seem to have been men of marked ability and the embodiment of the reviving Roman Catholic Christianity of their day.

It may be that a sixth factor entered, a weariness of the Indians with their old religions and a genuine preference for Christianity as a faith. So at least one of the early writers declared.[115]

Obstacles to the spread of the faith were also present.[116] The language barrier was pronounced. Many of the missionaries learned the native tongues, but others never achieved proficiency in them and could give instruction only through interpreters. Not all the Spaniards shared the enthusiasm of the Crown

---

[114] Lemmens, *Geschichte der Franziskanermissionen*, p. 211; Streit, *Bibliotheca Missionum*, Vol. II, pp. 61, 62; Bancroft, *History of Mexico*, Vol. III, pp. 296-300.

[115] José de Acosta, *Historia Natural y Moral de los Indios*, II, 85, cited in Braden, *Religious Aspects of the Conquest of Mexico*, p. 179.

[116] See some of these in Braden, *op. cit.*, pp. 180 ff.

for the conversion of the aborigines. Numbers were lukewarm towards it and by their lives gave to the pagans an unhappy impression of the faith of the conquerors. The cruel treatment of the Indians by many Spaniards could not but create prejudice against the religion of the white man. Then, too, not all of the priests were worthy. Some of them, especially after the pioneer days had passed, appear to have been of inferior quality and belied the morality which the Church officially inculcated. Among the various orders, moreover, jealousy and wrangling were often present and must have hindered the transmission of what is supposed to be the ideal Christian spirit.

The favourable conditions proved stronger than the obstacles, and in spite of the latter Christianity spread among the civilized Indians of Mexico with great rapidity. A mass conversion occurred comparable with the similar movements by which most of the peoples of Europe had first adopted the Christian faith. Zumárraga, writing in 1531, only twelve years after the first landing of Cortés, declared that the Franciscans alone had baptized more than a million persons.[117] In 1536 another missionary estimated the number of baptized at between four and nine millions.[118] Another writer said that the Franciscans and Dominicans had baptized ten and a half millions.[119] In 1541 Bishop Julian Garcés, of Tlaxcala, wrote that each week he baptized at least three hundred, and at the same time confirmed those whom he baptized.[120] This would mean that he alone baptized over fifteen thousand a year. In 1529 Peter of Ghent declared that he and one of his colleagues had often baptized fourteen thousand in one day and that they two had given the rite to more than two hundred thousand.[121] This wholesale baptism was possible partly because the full ritual was followed for only a few out of each group and because for the others merely the baptismal formula was employed. Since this abbreviated method aroused controversy, in 1537 Pope Paul III declared valid what had been done, but ordered that in the future the full ritual should be used.[122] In light of these facts the figures of Zumárraga do not seem excessive and even the extreme total of ten and a half millions appears possible. In the more thickly settled portions of Mexico, following the change of political masters, mass

[117] See Spanish translation of the letter in Mendieta, *Historia Eclesiástica Indiana,* Book V, Chap. 30.

[118] Toribio de Motolinia, *Historia de los Indios de la Nueva España,* Tratado II, Chaps. 2, 3, in Joaquin García Icazbalceta, *Colección de Documentos para la Historia de Mexico,* Vol. I (Mexico, 1858).

[119] Gonzalez Davila, *Teatro Ecles.,* Vol. I, p. 25.

[120] Quoted by Mariano de Cuevas, *Documentos Inéditos de Siglo XVI* (Mexico, 2 vols., 1908), Vol. I, p. 334, cited in Braden, *op. cit.,* p. 224.

[121] Lemmens, *Geschichte der Franziskanermissionen,* p. 203, citing Wadding, an. 1529, Nr. 15.

[122] Lemmens, *op. cit.,* p. 206, citing Wadding, an. 1537, Nr. 6.

conversion on this extensive scale need not surprise us. By the beginning of the seventeenth century the large majority of the population south of the Rio Grande was esteemed nominally Christian.[123]

In this initial generation of missionaries and in the more densely populated sections the methods employed were adapted to mass conversions, but were also designed to bring about a progressive knowledge of the faith so rapidly accepted and to give spiritual nurture to the neophytes and their children. The early missionaries scattered out in small groups over the country.[124] They did not wait to learn the native languages before beginning their instruction. Soon, however, they found it necessary to acquire the tongues of those whom they wished to reach.[125] At the outset the missionaries concentrated upon the children. They gathered them into schools, several hundred of them in an institution, and there instructed them in the rudiments of the faith. At first the creed, the Lord's Prayer, and a few other prayers were taught them, and in Latin. Many of the children learned Spanish. Later, as the missionaries acquired facility in the Indian languages, instruction was given in the vernaculars. The boys who had been in school were encouraged to communicate the Christian message to their elders. The boys, too, were used as interpreters for missionaries who did not feel sufficiently at home in the language.[126] We hear of one prayer book prepared in the native picture-writing.[127] Peter of Ghent noted that in their pagan worship the Indians sang and danced. He therefore composed songs embodying Christian teachings and taught the neophytes to use them.[128] Paintings were employed, again after a native custom, as aids in religious instruction. Adapting a form of organization which they found ready to hand in the villages, the missionaries grouped the neophytes into bands of twenty and one hundred with a captain over each, and it became the duty of the captain to see that his company attended mass and sermons on Sundays and feast days, to ensure that the new-born children were baptized, to induce adults to come to confession at least once a year, to watch against fraud in marriage, and to inform the priest of any drunkenness or sexual irregularity.[129]

Technically little if any force was employed to compel the natives to receive baptism. However, temples and the images of the gods were often destroyed.

[123] Braden, op. cit., p. 3.

[124] Mendieta, op. cit., Book III, Chap. 14.

[125] Mendieta, op. cit., Book III, Chaps. 16, 19.

[126] Mendieta, op. cit., Book III, Chaps. 15, 17, 19.

[127] Keleman, Battlefield of the Gods, p. 137.

[128] Carta de Fr. Pedro de Gante al Rey D. Felipe II in Códice Franciscano, in Joaquin García Icazbalceta, Nueva Colección de Documentos para la Historia de México, Vol. II, p. 224.

[129] Genaro García, Nuevos Documentos o muy Raros para la Historia de México, Vol. II, p. 81, cited in Braden, op. cit., pp. 156, 157.

The boys who had been trained in the Christian schools were encouraged to be active in this systematic elimination of the symbols and shrines of the old cults.[130] In 1531 Zumárraga reported that five hundred temples had been demolished, with more than twenty thousand representations of the gods.[131] Moreover, whipping was employed by missionaries as a form of coercion.[132] The reason offered was that, the Indians being children, they needed the rod for their own good.[133] Presumably it was not used to constrain the Indians to come to the baptismal font.

The content of the instruction given the Indians was set forth in catechisms. One of these, in the native tongue, included the sign of the cross, the Apostles' Creed, the Lord's Prayer, the Ave Maria, the Salve Regina, the fourteen articles of faith, the Ten Commandments, the five commandments of the Church (to hear mass on Sundays and feast days, to make confession during Lent, to take communion at Easter, to fast, and to pay tithes and first-fruits), the seven sacraments, the venial and mortal sins, the seven virtues, the commended works of mercy (such as feeding the hungry, giving drink to the thirsty, clothing the naked, visiting the sick, redeeming captives, showing hospitality to travellers, and burying the dead), the spiritual works (such as comforting the sad and forgiving injuries), the gifts of the Holy Spirit, the eight beatitudes, a list of strong points and the enemies of the soul, the gifts of the glorified body, the obligations of god-parents, and a general confession. This particular catechism ended with a blessing for use at the table and a formula of thanks for the close of the meal. While this was a standard body of teaching for neophytes, not all of it was required of the old.[134]

The question of marriage gave the missionaries much concern. Apparently the arrival of the Spaniards, with customs different from those to which the Indians had been accustomed, had encouraged chaos. Many of the Indians repudiated their former marital ties without adopting the Christian *mores*.[135] The friars required monogamy. A Papal ruling confirmed their insistence and said that in case a pagan had more than one wife, before baptism he must put away all but one, keeping her to whom he had been first married, or, in case he could not recall which had been first, her whom he preferred. Marriages dating from pre-Christian times, if legal according to native custom, were held valid—

---

[130] Mendieta, *op. cit.*, Book III, Chap. 21.

[131] Spanish translation of Zumárraga's letter given in Mendieta, *op. cit.*, Book V, Chap. 30.

[132] Mendieta, *op. cit.*, Book III, Chap. 51.

[133] *Ibid.*

[134] See the document in *Códice Franciscano* in García Icazbalceta, *Nueva Colección de Documentos para la Historia de México*, Vol. II, pp. 30-61.

[135] Mendieta, *op. cit.*, Book III, Chap. 48.

apparently an attempt to check the licence which had entered with the shift from one culture to another.[136]

Earnest efforts were made by at least some of the missionaries to improve the physical lot of the natives. Some frowned upon the use of wines and liquors.[137] Several of the Jesuits and the friars laboured to familiarize the Indians with European medicine and surgery.[138] Zumárraga is said to have fostered the cultivation of silk, linen, and cotton, to have imported agricultural implements from Spain, to have called in artisans for the instruction of the Indians in handicrafts, and to have founded a large hospital in Mexico City.[139] Zumárraga, too, was the officially appointed Protector of the Indians.[140] He contributed to the life of the entire community, white as well as Indian, by laying the foundations of the University of Mexico, an institution which originally professed for its chief purpose the preparation of candidates for the priesthood.[141] He had a large share in instituting the first printing press in Mexico. The precise date of the beginning of the enterprise is somewhat in doubt, but it seems to have been about the year 1535. A leading objective was the issuance of literature to facilitate the religious instruction of the Indians.[142]

The authorities were careful to see that the Indians were not given sufficiently advanced education to bring them out of the state of tutelage. If they did much independent thinking, they might depart from the teachings of the Church. A higher school for the Indians, the Colegio de Santa Cruz en Tlatelulco, was opened in 1536, and for a time appeared to be performing a most acceptable function in training Indian teachers. However, some of its products fell under suspicion for heresy. Indeed, in spite of the general rule that the Indians were not subject to the Inquisition, one of the college's former pupils was the first to be burned in Mexico through condemnation of the Holy Office.[143] It is not strange, therefore, that the institution languished.

The first generation of missionaries witnessed among these civilized peoples of Mexico a remarkable religious revolution. After the mass movement was once well under way, the new faith was received with great enthusiasm. The Indians displayed unusual zeal in coming to confession, so much so that at times the friars found themselves embarrassed by the throngs who pressed

---

[136] Mendieta, *op. cit.,* Book III, Chaps. 47, 48.

[137] Mendieta, *op. cit.,* Book III, Chap. 31.

[138] Berg, *Die katholische Heidenmission als Kulturträger,* Vol. III, pp. 15-17.

[139] Lemmens, *Geschichte der Franziskanermissionen,* p. 209.

[140] Lemmens, *op. cit.,* p. 208.

[141] Mariano Cuevas, *Historia del la Iglesia en Mexico* (Vol. I, Tlalpam, D. F., Mexico, 1921), p. 244.

[142] Streit, *Bibliotheca Missionum,* Vol. II, pp. 86, 87.

[143] Mendieta, *Historia Eclesiástica Indiana,* Book IV, Chap. 15; Braden, *op. cit.,* pp. 149, 150; Lea, *The Inquisition in the Spanish Dependencies,* p. 196.

them to obtain this clerical ministration.[144] Before the end of the sixteenth century, and, indeed, earlier, in the more thickly settled portions of the land the ancient cults had disappeared, or at least had retired from public view.

However, this period of enthusiasm was followed by one of problems and discouragement, and, in places, of moral and spiritual retrogression. The second half of the sixteenth century was marked by despondency. The clergy were too few to give adequate care to the huge parishes and the great throngs of half-instructed converts which were assigned them. Dioceses were too large to be thoroughly covered by their bishops.[145] Many priests and bishops did not know the language of their charges and had to use interpreters in whom they could place little confidence.[146] Numbers of friars were discontented, made no effort to learn the vernaculars, and wished to return to Spain. The high enthusiasm of the first generation had waned.[147] Even in the first half of the century Zumárraga said that many of the clergy who came to America did not know their offices, and he lamented their ignorance, corruption, and immorality.[148] Complaints were made of the heavy pecuniary exactions of the clergy and in at least one instance of the unnecessary burden placed on the Indians by the erection of an excessively sumptuous church.[149] Seculars were accused of simony. Some bishops were said to be too autocratic. Conflict divided the clergy into jealous and warring camps. Chapters were at outs with their bishops, between bishops and regulars friction existed, and ill will and suspicion were chronic between regulars and seculars.[150] We hear of one case in which a Dominican was tried on the accusation that he had used the confessional to attempt to seduce women penitents.[151] Whether true or false, the charge detracted from esteem for the clergy.

How far, moreover, the ancient beliefs and practices had been eradicated is in doubt. Some declare that the old gods persisted in Christian guise and under Christian names and that the old attitudes and even some of the ancient customs lived on.[152] Many of the early converts were said to place the images of the gods behind the crosses which they venerated or to offer worship to

---

[144] Mendieta, *op. cit.,* Book III, Chaps. 41-44; Braden, *op. cit.,* pp. 233-237.

[145] *Relacion del Arzobispo al Consejo Real,* in *Colección de Documentos Inéditos, Relativos al Decubrimiento Conquista y Colonización de las Posesiones Españolas,* Vol. IV, pp. 492 ff.

[146] Letter of Juan de San Román in 1571, in García Icazbalceta, *Nueva Colección de Documentos,* Vol. I, p. 105.

[147] Mendieta, writing in 1562, in García Icazbalceta, *op. cit.,* Vol. I, pp. 3, 4.

[148] J. L. Mecham in Wilgus, *Colonial Hispanic America,* p. 229.

[149] Genaro García, *Documentos Inéditos ó muy Raros para la História de México,* Vol. XV, pp. 83, 132, 133.

[150] Van der Essen in Descamps, *Histoire Générale Comparée des Missions,* p. 340.

[151] Lea, *History of Sacerdotal Celibacy,* Vol. II, p. 289.

[152] As in J. L. Mecham in Wilgus, *Colonial Hispanic America,* p. 224.

them in secret localities.[153] In parish after parish the priest came infrequently, preached in a language which the natives did not understand, and so conveyed to his hearers little of what was in his mind. Even in the twentieth century pre-Christian dances were said to persist and with some modifications to be performed in the churches.[154] More than once it has been noted that the Christian shrine which of all those in Mexico has most captured the imagination and affection of the Indians, that of the Virgin of Guadelupe, is on the spot on which, in 1531, when Christianity was first winning its way in Mexico, the vision is said to have appeared to a humble Indian which gave rise to her cult, and that this site is not far from that of the chief temple of an aboriginal goddess of fertility.[155] In 1930 a traveller found in a mountain village in Oaxaca offerings, including the fresh blood of a turkey, in front of a sculptured monolith.[156] In the twentieth century, on the border between Mexico and Guatemala, a church has been noted which was in charge of a group of twenty men who were said to be in fact priests of an old Maya cult.[157] In another place images of the Virgin and of Christ were venerated through a priestess in a manner reminiscent of pagan days.[158] Such instances might be multiplied indefinitely.

On the other hand, in some regions the old gods are said to have disappeared. Thus among the Zapotec Indians the ancient deities are declared to survive only in folk tales and then under disguised names, and in Mitla their rituals are reported to be barely remembered.[159]

Apparently, as might have been expected, on the main plateau and near the large cities where the Spaniards were strongest, the elimination of the old was fairly thoroughly accomplished. For instance, a careful study of the village of Tepoztlán, in the state of Morelos, one of the densely settled portions of the plateau not from from Mexico City, shows most of the Aztec marriage customs to have been displaced by those of the Church and the chief festivals to be those of the ecclesiastical calendar.[160] It is in the mountains and more remote regions that something of the ancient cults remains.[161]

---

[153] Bancroft, *History of Mexico*, Vol. II, p. 179.

[154] Starr, *In Indian Mexico*, p. 395; Auguste Genin, *Notes on the Dances, Music, and Songs of the Ancient and Modern Mexicans*, in *Annual Report of the Smithsonian Institute*, 1920, pp. 669-677.

[155] Braden, *Religious Aspects of the Conquest of Mexico*, pp. 47, 297-306; Camargo and Grubb, *Religion in the Republic of Mexico*, pp. 5, 6.

[156] Chase, *Mexico*, p. 86.

[157] Chase, *op. cit.*, p. 99.

[158] Starr, *op. cit.*, pp. 252-255.

[159] Parsons, *Mitla*, pp. 210-214.

[160] Redfield, *Tepoztlán, A Mexican Village*, pp. 90-93, 140.

[161] Parsons, *op. cit.*, pp. 210-214.

From what we have seen in the earlier volumes of the survival of pre-Christian customs, beliefs, and even deities into areas and centuries which accepted Christianity, and from what we know of the persistence of earlier religious practices and convictions among peoples who have adopted Islam, Buddhism, or Hinduism, we would be amazed if something of the old had not carried over into a Mexico which professed to be Christian.

In general, the persistence of the indigenous religion was displayed in four ways. (1) Some of the old dances, although usually in modified form, were used in connexion with Christian festivals. (2) Here and there some of the pagan feasts were conserved, but under a Christian guise. (3) Offerings familiar in pagan days, of copal, flowers, and animals, were made before images bearing Christian names. (4) Occasionally sacred sites persisted and functions attributed to pagan deities were transferred to the Virgin or to one or more of the saints.[162] However, this, as we have said, is not peculiar to Mexico, but has been found in many religions in other lands and climes. Some of it was the result of conscious adaptation by the early clergy. Some of it arose without deliberate planning.

In Mexico, as in other countries, the adoption of Christianity as the community faith worked real changes. Not only were Christian objects of worship and Christian rites substituted for those of paganism. Alterations were also wrought in morals and customs. Human sacrifices, so wholesale under the old cult, disappeared. Monogamous marriage, solemnized by Christian rites, took the place of polygamy and sanctions of pagan origin. To be sure, the laxity in sexual matters so common in Spain was reproduced in the New World, but, whatever the departures from it, the official teachings of the Church enjoined chastity. Then, too, what the Christian esteemed as virtues were held up for honour and what the Church denounced as sins were censured. Practice and precept might be poles apart, but precept could not be utterly without effect. Popular religious hymns and even many of the religious dances were inspired by the Christian faith and were woven around themes of Christian origin.[163] It was a Spanish Christianity which was propagated and in the main it was reproduced with remarkable fidelity.

Thus far we have confined our account of the spread of Christianity in New Spain to the conversion of the densely populated, civilized regions of the Mexican plateau. However, the movement towards the faith of the Spanish conquerors was not confined to that region.

[162] Braden, *op. cit.,* pp. 280 ff., gives many instances. See also Anita Brenner, *Idols Behind Altars* (New York, Payson and Clarke, 1929, pp. 359; semi-popular), *passim.*
[163] Redfield, *op. cit.,* pp. 175-178.

Missionaries, especially Franciscans, early extended their efforts to Yucatan. In spite of the opposition of the Spanish military forces in the peninsula, about 1534 the Brothers Minor established themselves there.[164] Luis de Villalpando prepared a grammar and dictionary of the native language.[165] Lorenzo de Bienvenida founded a number of monasteries and mission stations and wrote the first description given by a European of the remarkable archæological remains of the region. Later he became a pioneer in Costa Rica and, going to Spain for reinforcements, returned to Costa Rica with thirty new recruits.[166] The second Bishop in Yucatan, Diego de Landa, was interested in the native lore and in one of his works professed to give something of the hieroglyphic writing of the Mayas.[167] He also stood up stoutly for the rights of his Indian charges against the tyranny of exploiting Spaniards.[168] By the close of the sixteenth century the Franciscans had established thirty-four mission stations in the peninsula,[169] and in the last quarter of the century these had so far accomplished the task of conversion that in some sections the pioneer stage was deemed complete and the parishes were transferred to the secular clergy.[170]

From the Mexican plateau as a base, Christianity spread northward over a wide area and continued to do so until, early in the nineteenth century, political upheavals in Mexico brought in a new era. As we have earlier suggested, missions and missionaries constituted the first wave of the advancing Spanish frontier. To recount even the main features of the history of all the missions of this vast area and this long stretch of time would prolong this chapter into a volume. Here we must confine ourselves to the main outlines of the movement, to some specific examples, and to a few outstanding individuals. Large as was the territory covered and numerous though the missionaries were, we must remember that the story embraces only one phase of a Spanish missionary activity which extended over Central America and over much of South America and which overflowed from Mexico to the Philippines.

The principal agents in the propagation of Christianity north of the Mexican plateau were the Dominicans, the Jesuits, and the Franciscans. Of these the latter two were the more widely spread. As time passed, the Franciscan enter-

[164] Mendieta, *Historia Eclesiástica Indiana*, Book IV, Chap. 6. Here Mendieta gives the date as 1534. In Book V, Chap. 42, he gives it as 1531. 1534 is the preferred year. Lemmens, *Geschichte der Franziskanermissionen*, p. 223; Pastor, *History of the Popes*, Vol. XIII, p. 303.

[165] Mendieta, *op. cit.*, Book IV, Chap. 6.

[166] Mendieta, *op. cit.*, Book IV, Chap. 6; Streit, *Bibliotheca Missionum*, Vol. II, pp. 142, 143.

[167] Streit, *op. cit.*, Vol. II, pp. 192, 193.

[168] Mendieta, *op. cit.*, Book IV, Chap. 6.

[169] Pastor, *op. cit.*, Vol. XIII, p. 303.

[170] *Ibid.*

prises tended to be placed under the auspices of three seminaries for the training of missionaries—one in Querétaro, founded in 1684, one in Zacatecas, founded in 1704, and the College of San Fernando in Mexico City, officially recognized by the Viceroy in 1731.[171] Theoretically the missions were supported financially by the state. In practice the chronically over-strained treasury found the task difficult. For the Californian missions the public subsidies were supplemented and largely made needless by the Pious Fund, created by private benefactions.[172]

Very early, in 1525, following the submission of the leading chief or "king" of Michoacán, west of Mexico City, Franciscans entered the region and met with substantial success.[173] In 1546 friars went to wild tribes in the northern part of what became later the state of Zacatecas and there gathered converts from tribes which had previously been hostile.[174] Between 1550 and 1590 the Franciscans extended their efforts north and west of Zacatecas, into Durango, Sinaloa, and Chihuahua. A number of mission stations were founded, but in places no permanent work could be undertaken and several of the missionaries won the coveted martyr's crown.[175]

In 1590 the Jesuits, some of whom had previously made tentative journeys into the region, entered seriously upon enterprises in the area. In the next few years they founded a number of missions.[176] By the close of the century, Jesuits had established missions with substantial churches along the Rivers Sinaloa and Mocorito, near the lower end of the Gulf of California, and had visited tribes still farther north.[177] In the first decade of the seventeenth century the Spanish advance had penetrated to regions along the east side of the Gulf of California. Several of the tribes were defeated in war, and on more than one occasion the Indians were persuaded by their reverses to ask for missionaries. Before the first half of the seventeenth century was ended, converts had been made in the valley of the Sonora.[178] Northward, along both the west and the east slopes of the Sierra Madre, the Jesuits made their way. Now and again a missionary was killed, but his colleagues, undaunted, continued to push the frontier northward and into the sierras on the east. Eventually the Jesuits occupied what are now

[171] Lemmens, *op. cit.*, p. 228. Engelhardt, *The Missions and Missionaries of California,* Vol. I, p. 729, gives 1682 as the date of the founding of the Querétaro College, and says that the College of San Fernando was established by authority of the Pope and King Ferdinand VI in 1734.

[172] Engelhardt, *op. cit.*, Vol. I, p. 497.

[173] Mendieta, *op. cit.*, Book IV, Chap. 5.

[174] Bancroft, *North Mexican States,* Vol. I, p. 99.

[175] Bancroft, *op. cit.*, Vol. I, pp. 100-119.

[176] Bancroft, *op. cit.*, Vol. I, pp. 119-127.

[177] Bancroft, *op. cit.*, Vol. I, p. 150.

[178] Bancroft, *op. cit.*, Vol. I, pp. 212 ff.

Lower California, the states of Durango, Chihuahua, Sinoloa, Sonora, and part of Arizona.[179]

The most famous Jesuit missionary in Northern Mexico was Eusebio Francisco Kino.[180] Kino was born in the Tyrolese Alps, north-west of Trent, at a date not certainly determined. He was baptized August 10, 1645, which was very possibly the day of his birth. His family was known by the name of Chino rather than Kino, and was of Italian blood and tongue. He studied in the Jesuit College in Trent. Here he must have heard much of the world-wide enterprises of the Society, because the members were already scattered over much of the Americas, here and there along the coast of Africa, in Southern Asia, and in the Far East. A serious illness sealed his purpose and he registered a vow to his patron saint, the great Jesuit missionary, Francis Xavier, that if he recovered he would seek admission to the Society and himself endeavour to become a missionary. Kino, his illness gone, apparently never wavered from his purpose. In honour of Xavier he added the name Francisco to his own. He went through his novitiate, received a thorough education, and for a time taught. In due course he received his desire and was appointed a missionary. He had wished to go to Asia, but, by the casting of lots, he was assigned to America. He reached Mexico in 1681. There he was appointed to a new Jesuit venture, a mission to Lower California. Late in 1685 a royal order commanded the suspension of the effort to conquer California and Kino transferred his energies to Pimería Alta, a region which included what is now the southern portion of Arizona and the northern section of Sonora. Here he began what proved to be his major achievements.

In 1687, although he was in his early forties and past the energy of his youth, Kino pushed out beyond the then frontier of the settled Jesuit establishments and in a fertile mountain valley laid the foundations of a new mission, Nuestra

---

[179] Bolton, *Rim of Christendom*, p. 6.

[180] The literature on Kino is extensive. The standard modern biography, very well done by a competent scholar, is Herbert Eugene Bolton, *Rim of Christendom. A Biography of Eusebio Francisco Kino, Pacific Coast Pioneer* (New York, The Macmillan Co., 1936, pp. xiv, 644). For a bibliography see pp. 597-627 of Bolton's biography. An account, largely autobiographical, is Herbert Eugene Bolton, *Kino's Historical Memoir of Pimería Alta. A Contemporary Account of the Beginnings of California, Sonora, and Arizona, by Father Eusebio Francisco Kino, S.J., Pioneer Missionary Explorer, Cartographer and Ranchman, 1683-1711* (Cleveland, The Arthur H. Clark Co., 2 vols., 1919). A brief account of the manuscript of which this latter work is a translation is by Herbert E. Bolton, *Father Kino's Lost History, Its Discovery and Its Value*, in *Papers of the Biographical Society of America*, Vol. VI, 1911, pp. 9-34. See also Rufus Kay Wyllys, *Pioneer Padre. The Life and Times of Eusebio Francisco Kino* (Dallas, The Southwest Press, 1935, pp. xi, 230), based upon manuscript and printed sources and pertinent secondary works. See a good brief summary in Lockwood, *Story of the Spanish Missions of the Middle Southwest*, pp. iii-vi.

Señora de los Dolores. Here for nearly twenty-five years he made his head-quarters. From Dolores he pushed on north and west. He founded a chain of stations along the Altar and Magdalena rivers and another in a north-easterly direction. He established missions within what are now the confines of the state of Arizona. To induce them to ask for missionaries and to settle down around the missions he sent presents to distant tribes. He went on many an exploring expedition, teaching and baptizing as he journeyed. Again and again he reached the Gila River. He voyaged down the Colorado and finally reached the mouth of that stream. He proved that Lower California was a peninsula, not an island as had been currently believed, and that it could therefore be reached by land. Much of his incessant travel was for the purpose of supervising his missions, for he was always and primarily the missionary.

To provide an economic basis for the missions and to supply their populations with food, Kino developed ranching and stock-farming. This he did almost entirely with Indians whom he and his colleagues had trained. He saw that vineyards and orchards were begun. He introduced European trees and plants.

Kino was courageous. His exploring expeditions required daring of no usual order. On the one hand he had to deal with the complaints of Spanish settlers who accused him of depriving them of Indian labour. On the other hand he met disgruntled Indians who believed that he and his colleagues were working them too hard. He is known to have faced an Indian uprising alone. To his adoring companions he appeared modest, gentle, humble, a man of prayer, sparing of sleep and food, ascetic in drink and clothing, devoted first of all to the spiritual welfare of the Indians to whom he had come to bring the Christian message. He dreamed of converting the truculent Apaches and of establishing communication with his fellow Jesuits in French America. He died in 1711, as he probably had wished, at work and on one of his tours.

In the early part of the eighteenth century the Jesuit enterprise in northern Mexico suffered from a shortage of men. However, about the middle of the century reinforcements came and the borders were pushed beyond those which Kino had occupied.[181] For instance, in the seventeen twenties the Nayarit Indians, on the west coast, who had long resisted Spanish authority and had declined to receive missionaries, were conquered. Jesuits followed the troops and laboured faithfully and with success.[182]

Before Kino's death, moreover, Jesuit missions had been resumed in the scene of Kino's first endeavour, Lower California.

[181] Bolton, *The Rim of Christendom*, pp. 594, 595.
[182] Bancroft, *History of Mexico*, Vol. III, pp. 316-330.

The transient venture in Lower California in which Kino had engaged in his first years in America had not been the first in that inhospitable peninsula. In the initial generation of the conquest of Mexico, no less a person than Hernando Cortés brought about the Spanish discovery of California. With him as chaplains were Franciscans who were also intended to be missionaries to the Indians. From 1535 to the abandonment of the settlement in 1537 the friars were in the peninsula.[183] In the next few years Mendoza, the Viceroy in New Spain, sent several expeditions towards the North-west Coast, but after his transfer to Peru (1551) these were discontinued. For about fifty years not much thought was devoted to California.[184] The occupation of the Philippines in the latter part of the sixteenth century gave rise to a new interest in the West Coast, for the islands were reached by way of Mexico.[185] In 1602-1603 an expedition under Vizcaino explored the California littoral. With it were Discalced Carmelites, but no permanent establishments were made.[186] We have seen the brief and unsuccessful attempts at settlement with which the Jesuits were associated in the sixteen eighties. Kino and Juan Maria Salvatierra put forth persistent efforts to obtain permission from the Spanish secular and ecclesiastical authorities for the renewal of the mission. Royal consent was obtained in 1697, and, losing no time, in that very same year Salvatierra began a settlement at Loreto, in the peninsula.[187]

The enterprise in Lower California thus renewed by the Jesuits was pursued with diligence and persistence. The field was unpromising. The physical surroundings and the climate were adverse. The Indians, affected by prolonged residence in the adverse environment, were distressingly low in the scale of civilization, were semi-nomadic, and were quite without experience in the settled, agricultural existence which the missionaries sought to induce them to adopt.[188] The missionaries found difficulty in obtaining the promised royal subventions. Friction with the civil authorities and the white settlers, unfortunately chronic through much of Spanish America, proved annoying.[189] While, in time, the missions of the North prospered, epidemics in 1742, 1744, and 1748 carried off about five-sixths of the natives in the South.[190] Yet the Jesuits kept

[183] Engelhardt, *The Missions and Missionaries of California*, Vol. I, pp. 17-23, citing the various sources.

[184] In 1606 Vizcaino was commanded by the King to find a suitable stopping place in California for ships from the Philippine Islands.—Clavigero, *The History of [Lower] California*, Lake and Gray translation, p. 133.

[185] Bolton, *Spanish Exploration in the Southwest, 1542-1706*, p. 43.

[186] Bolton, *op cit.*, pp. 52-54, 85, 104-134.

[187] Clavigero, *op. cit.*, p. 148; Engelhardt, *op. cit.*, Vol. I, pp. 98-106.

[188] Engelhardt, *op. cit.*, Vol. I, pp. 181-186.

[189] Engelhardt, *op. cit.*, Vol. I, pp. 106-113, 115-128, 136-144.

[190] Engelhardt, *op. cit.*, Vol. I, pp. 226-271.

at their task. By rations of grain they persuaded Indians to come for catechetical instruction, they trained the children, and eventually they built up a settled mission life.[191] Private beneficence in the form of the Pious Fund came to their assistance. By about 1700 approximately six hundred Indians were under instruction and not far from two hundred children had been baptized. In 1745 the peninsula was served by thirty-seven mission stations and sixteen settled missions under resident missionaries.[192]

In 1767 came an event which brought drastic changes in many different parts of the Spanish colonial empire. The Jesuits had fallen into bad odour with the Crown and were ordered driven out of all the Spanish dominions. In that very year the execution of the order was begun in the New World. At the time of their expulsion the Jesuits are said to have had in Mexico one hundred and three missions and one hundred and four priests.[193] In Northern Mexico and California most of the Jesuit missions were transferred to the Franciscans, although some went to the Dominicans.

The Franciscans had already extended their outposts on the northerly frontiers of New Spain. At various times in the course of the sixteenth century several Franciscans penetrated into New Mexico.[194] However, no permanent Spanish occupation was effected or missions established in the region until the close of the century. In 1598 and 1599 Juan de Oñate took possession of the region of El Paso and journeyed beyond that area. He was accompanied by Franciscans who inaugurated various missions.[195] Then a slight recession ensued, followed in the early part of the seventeenth century by the founding of Santa Fé, which, like so many others of the Spanish settlements, bore in its very name evidence of the professed faith of the conquerors. Various missions were developed, and in 1630 it was reported that about fifty missionaries were shepherding over sixty thousand converts in ninety pueblos.[196] Even before the coming of the Spaniards a large number of Indians were living a settled agri-

[191] Engelhardt, *op. cit.*, Vol. I, pp. 106-113.

[192] Engelhardt, *op. cit.*, Vol. I, pp. 266-271. On the Jesuit missions in Lower California see also Bancroft, *North Mexican States*, Vol. I, pp. 407-476, and Clavigero, *op. cit.*, *passim*, which carries the story down to the expulsion of the Jesuits.

[193] Bancroft, *History of Mexico*, Vol. III, p. 431.

[194] Bancroft, *History of Arizona and New Mexico*, pp. 27 ff.; Bolton, *Spanish Exploration of the Southwest, 1542-1706*, pp. 3-5, 151, 158; Schmidlin-Braun, *Catholic Mission History*, p. 429; Bancroft, *North Mexican States*, Vol. I, pp. 127-129; Maas, *Misiones de Nuevo Méjico*, p. v.

[195] Bancroft, *History of Arizona and New Mexico*, pp. 110 ff., Bancroft, *North Mexican States*, Vol. I, p. 129; Bolton, *op. cit.*, pp. 199-206.

[196] Bancroft, *History of Arizona and New Mexico*, pp. 146 ff.; Bancroft, *North Mexican States*, Vol. I, pp. 373, 374; Maas, *op. cit.*, p. vi, says that in 1630 the native population was c. 500,000, and that the number of baptized was 86,000 and the number of Franciscans more than one hundred.

cultural existence and thus were somewhat more readily and quickly reached by the missionary and adjusted to Spanish life than were the semi-nomadic tribes. In 1680 a major revolt drove the Spaniards out of New Mexico and cost the lives of twenty-one Franciscans. After 1690 Spanish rule was re-established, missionaries re-entered, and new missions were founded.[197] In the eighteenth century, in New Mexico, the missionary staff varied in size from twenty-five to forty, and the Indian Christians from ten to fifteen thousand. In the latter third of the century several of the missions nearest the Spanish settlements were considered to have progressed sufficiently in the process of assimilation to be transferred from the regular to the secular clergy.[198] By a combination of civil authority, armed force, the immigration of Spaniards, and the labours of missionaries, large portions of New Mexico were being transformed into a settled, nominally Christian community with a tincture of Spanish culture.

The Franciscans also pressed on into Texas. In the sixteenth century various expeditions of Spaniards, including the famous and ill-starred one led by Hernando de Soto in 1539-1542, covered much of the territory bordering on the Gulf of Mexico from Florida to the Rio Grande.[199] In the sixteenth century and the first three-quarters of the seventeenth century, a number of Franciscans penetrated at various times into regions which might be termed Texan, but no permanent settlements or missions were brought into existence.[200] It was the danger of French penetration which stirred the Spaniards to more determined action. In 1682 La Salle descended the Mississippi River to its mouth and in the next five years attempted to found a colony in Louisiana. The Spaniards, alarmed, exerted themselves to extend their effective occupation beyond the Rio Grande.[201] To fulfil this purpose, the mission, as the characteristic Spanish frontier instrument of this period, was invoked. In 1689 and 1690 Franciscans founded two missions near the Neches River in East Texas, the first Spanish settlement in the area called Texas.[202]

The Texan Indians were divided into a number of groups of varying grades of culture, ranging from some in Eastern Texas with a settled agricultural

---

[197] Bancroft, *History of Arizona and New Mexico*, pp. 174 ff.; Bancroft, *North Mexican States*, Vol. I, pp. 374, 375; Schmidlin-Braun, *op. cit.*, p. 517.

[198] Bancroft, *History of Arizona and New Mexico*, pp. 197 ff.; Bancroft, *North Mexican States*, Vol. I, pp. 603, 604. Maas, *Las Órdenes Religiosas de España y la Colonización de América*, Vol. II, p. 25, says the number of Franciscans in c. 1779 was thirty-four priests and two or three lay brothers.

[199] Heusinger, *Early Explorations and Mission Establishments in Texas*, pp. 1-13.

[200] Bolton, *op. cit.*, pp. 284-343; Heusinger, *op. cit.*, pp. 15-20; O'Rourke, *The Franciscan Missions in Texas (1690-1793)*, pp. 5-15. On what were included under the name Texas, see Bolton, *Texas in the Middle Eighteenth Century*, p. 1.

[201] O'Rourke, *op. cit.*, pp. 5, 6.

[202] Bolton, *Spanish Exploration of the Southwest, 1542-1706*, pp. 348-423.

existence to some between the Rio Grande and the San Antonio who were weak, poverty-stricken, and semi-nomadic hunters and fishers.[203] The missions were under the direction of the Franciscan missionary seminaries, or colleges, which we have already noted, of Querétaro, Zacatecas, and San Fernando in Mexico City, principally the first two.[204] After the expulsion of the Jesuits from New Spain, the Querétaro fathers assumed so much of the work of the Society that they felt constrained to turn over to the seminary of Zacatecas all of their missions in Texas.[205]

As usual with these frontier missions, the state was deeply interested. The Viceroy exercised his authority in determining whether a new mission should be planned, a small guard of soldiers was often provided, and, except for the gift of one private individual, Don Pedro de Terreros in 1757 for work among the Apaches, stipends were paid by the government.[206]

In the course of the years, about twenty-five missions were founded in Texas, the first being in 1689 and the last in 1793.[207] The years 1745 to 1762, or down to the transfer of Louisiana to Spain by France, saw a fairly extensive development. Obviously one of the causes was the fear of the French, an incentive which disappeared after 1762.[208] In these years, too, efforts were made to reduce the warlike Apaches to a settled, peaceful existence. This meant continued attacks by the enemies of the Apaches and several of the missions were destroyed or came to naught.[209] Yet the older missions among other tribes flourished, and by 1762 in the four missions of the Querétaro College alone forty-four hundred Indians had been baptized.[210]

The missions varied in their gains. For instance, in contrast with the numbers mentioned in the last sentence, in one mission for the difficult coast tribes between 1754 and 1758 only twenty-one had been baptized, and these in *articulo mortis*.[211] In 1754 in four Zacatecan missions in East Texas, in more than thirty years merely a few children and an occasional adult on his death bed had been baptized.[212]

[203] Bolton, *Texas in the Middle Eighteenth Century*, pp. 2-4.
[204] Bolton, *Texas in the Middle Eighteenth Century*, pp. 10-13.
[205] O'Rourke, *op. cit.*, pp. 22-40.
[206] Bolton, *op. cit.*, pp. 10-13.
[207] O'Rourke, *op. cit.*, pp. 22-40.
[208] Bolton, *op. cit.*, pp. 42, 43; Bolton, *The Founding of the Missions on the San Gabriel River, 1745-1749* (*The Southwestern Historical Quarterly*, April 1914, Vol. XVII, No. 4, pp. 323-378).
[209] Bolton, *Texas in the Middle Eighteenth Century*, pp. 78-94.
[210] Bolton, *Texas in the Middle Eighteenth Century*, pp. 95-101.
[211] Bolton, *The Founding of Mission Rosario; a Chapter in the History of the Gulf Coast* (*Texas Historical Association Quarterly*, Vol. X, Oct. 1906, pp. 113-139), *passim*.
[212] Bolton, *The Founding of Mission Rosario*, p. 129.

In 1751 the Querétaro College, confronted with more tasks than could be compassed with its limited resources, turned over to the seculars two of its stations on the Rio Grande.[213] From 1762 until 1788 the Spanish government in this area was either preparing for or actually engaged in war with England, and as part of the programme North-eastern Texas was to be given back to the Indians.[214] The process of retrenchment had begun.

In California the latter part of the eighteenth century was marked by a rapid expansion. Here again the inciting motives were mixed. Politically the Spanish fear of Russian encroachments from the North-west led to efforts by the state to extend the Spanish occupation northward, and religiously the zeal of the friars provided personnel for punctuating the frontier with missions. In 1768, for instance, a royal order commanded the occupation of the ports of Monterey and San Diego to save them from the Russians. Franciscans were sent to establish missions at the two centres and at a point midway between them.[215] At approximately the same time, the Franciscan College of San Fernando in Mexico City was placed in charge of the missions in Lower California from which the Jesuits had just been expelled. Although the College felt its resources stretched to the breaking point by the assignment, it accepted it.[216]

In 1770 reinforcements came from Spain in the form of forty-four new friars. Although the older Franciscan missions in the Sierra Gorda were in desperate need of strengthening, thirty of the new men were sent to California and the pressure in the Sierra Gorda was relieved by transferring some of the missions there to seculars.[217] In the newly chosen Superior of the California mission, Junípero Serra, the expanding enterprise was given an able leader. Born on the Island of Majorca in 1713, of humble parents, after a brilliant career as a scholar, at his own request Serra was appointed, in 1749, to the post of missionary.[218] He and his pupil and biographer, Palóu, came together, were assigned to the missions of the College of San Fernando, served for nine years in the difficult Sierra Gorda, and then for seven years in Texas. Serra was therefore already in his early fifties and seasoned by missionary experience when he was placed in this new and responsible post.

[213] Bolton, *Texas in the Middle Eighteenth Century*, p. 239.
[214] Bolton, *Texas in the Middle Eighteenth Century*, pp. 102 ff., 377-379.
[215] Engelhardt, *Missions and Missionaries of California*, Vol. I, pp. 373-382.
[216] Engelhardt, *op. cit.*, Vol. I, pp. 325, 326; Palóu, *Historical Memoirs of New California* (Bolton's translation), Vol. I, pp. 3 ff.
[217] Engelhardt, *op. cit.*, Vol. I, p. 434.
[218] Engelhardt, *op. cit.*, Vol. I, p. 326; Bancroft, *California Pastoral, 1768-1848*, pp. 169-172; Palóu, *op. cit.*, Vol. I, pp. xxiii ff. The standard life of Serra is by his friend and companion, Francisco Palóu, *Relación Histórica de la Vida y Apostolicos Tareas del Venerable Padre Fray Junípero Serra y las Misiones que fundó en la California Septentrional* (Mexico, Imprenta de Don Felipe de Zúñiga y Ontiveros, 1787, pp. 344).

In 1772 the Dominicans, at their earnest request, were given the missions in Lower California which had been developed by the Jesuits and which, after the expulsion of the latter, had been transferred to the Franciscans. The Franciscans were thus able to concentrate more of their energies upon the new frontier in what is now the State of California.[219]

Under the Dominicans the missions in Lower California, difficult at best, deteriorated. To be sure, the Dominicans used much the same methods as those of their predecessors, the Jesuits and the Franciscans. However, funds at the disposal of the missions declined, missionaries changed frequently, and there was a resulting lack of a continuing, experienced personnel. The main causes of the decline seem to have been a poor water supply and the entrance of epidemics which decimated the scanty Indian population.[220] As we shall see in the next volume, disastrous blows were dealt these missions, as to so many others, by the changes of government in Mexico in the early part of the nineteenth century.

The Franciscans, released from the burden of Lower California and encouraged by civil rulers who feared the Russian menace, rapidly expanded their missions in Upper California. In the last decades of the Spanish colonial regime and on the eve of the eclipse of the spread of Spanish Christianity, on this section of the frontier missions had a remarkable growth. The native stocks among whom the missions were established were said to be of poorer quality and on a lower scale of culture than were even those of the peninsula. They were reputed not to have been cultivators of the soil, but to have lived on wild seeds, fruits, and game. From the standpoint of those who sought to reduce them to the orderly life of the mission, so different from their former customs, they seemed filthy, lazy, stupid, and improvident.[221] At its height in the missionary period the total population has been estimated as between seventy-five thousand and a hundred and fifty thousand.[222] Great diversity in tongues enhanced the difficulties presented to the missionaries, for the languages were many and often were reciprocally unintelligible.[223] However, the weaknesses also had their advantages. Groups of Indians so divided and on such a low scale of culture could offer no effective armed resistance to the small armed forces which the Spaniards sent in. Junípero Serra died in 1784, and under his able and energetic leadership and with the aid of the state, by the time of his

[219] Meigs, *The Dominican Mission Frontier of Lower California,* pp. 2, 3; Engelhardt, *op. cit.,* Vol. I, pp. 503-511.

[220] Engelhardt, *op. cit.,* Vol. I, pp. 569-572; Meigs, *op. cit.,* p. 155.

[221] Palóu, *Historical Memoirs of New California* (Bolton's translation), Vol. III, p. 226; Engelhardt, *op. cit.,* Vol. II, p. 245.

[222] Engelhardt, *op. cit.,* Vol. II, p. 246.

[223] *Ibid.*

passing a string of missions had been established from San Diego in the south to San Francisco in the north.[224] In 1781 Upper California had eight missions and seventeen friars.[225] In 1789, five years after Serra's death, the Franciscan enterprise in California numbered eleven missions, twenty-three missionaries, and seventy-three hundred and five neophytes.[226] In 1791 two new missions were founded,[227] and in 1797-1798 five more were added.[228]

The funds for the missions came largely from the Pious Fund, an endowment, as we have seen, of private origin. [229] At the request of Serra, the state granted to the missionaries exclusive control over the baptized Indians, including all rights of punishment and discipline except the death penalty.[230] This, however, was not exceptional. In one form or another control of the missionaries over their converts was usual.

The regulations governing the missions and the methods employed were largely those which had been tested by the Franciscans elsewhere in New Spain, particularly in Texas and by the College of San Fernando in the Sierra Gorda.[231] A site marked by good soil and water, a convenient supply of timber, and a numerous Indian population was chosen. As in other missions, the Indians were encouraged to live an orderly, settled existence, and were trained in agriculture and handicrafts. The religious instruction given consisted in attendance at public worship, including daily morning and evening prayers, the sign of the cross, the Lord's Prayer, the Hail Mary, the Creed, the Confiteor, the act of contrition, the acts of faith, hope and charity, the Ten Commandments, the precepts of the Church, the seven sacraments, the six necessary points of faith, and the four last things. While some of the missionaries learned the native tongues, others used interpreters and by royal command the teaching of Spanish to the Indians was obligatory.[232] At one time a royal decree made illegal the use of the vernaculars. This, however, proved impossible of enforcement.[233]

What were the results of the missions in Upper California? The answer to that question would carry us beyond this volume, for the story was not com-

[224] Bancroft, op. cit., pp. 169-172; Engelhardt, op. cit., Vol. II, pp. 44-49. A plan of 1781 called for eleven missions along the coast from San Diego to San Francisco, and a similar line of missions inland.—Engelhardt, op. cit., Vol. II, pp. 105-109, 350-354.

[225] Engelhardt, op. cit., Vol. II, p. 404.

[226] Engelhardt, op cit., Vol. II, pp. 464, 465.

[227] Engelhardt, op. cit., Vol. II, p. 471.

[228] Engelhardt, op. cit., Vol. II, pp. 512-515.

[229] Engelhardt, op cit., Vol. II, pp. 29-32, 147.

[230] Engelhardt, op. cit., Vol. II, pp. 135-140.

[231] Engelhardt, op. cit., Vol. II, p. 267.

[232] Engelhardt, op. cit., Vol. II, pp. 267-278; Bancroft, California Pastoral, 1768-1848, Vol. II. pp. 220-247.

[233] Engelhardt, op. cit., Vol. II, p. 490.

pleted until the nineteenth century. The period of greatest prosperity seems to have been in the first decade of that century.[234] Here we may be permitted to say that at the dawn of the nineteenth century about fifty thousand Indians are reported to have been connected with the missions. In the first half of that century, however, epidemics of measles and smallpox wrought havoc and the Indians deteriorated in numbers and morale.[235]

How much permanent transformation did the Christianity taught by the missionaries effect in the lives of the less civilized peoples in Northern Mexico and the neighbouring frontier lands? Undoubtedly this varied with the tribe. Even among many of the remote peoples the results were often marked. In the twentieth century, for instance, we have a study of the Tarahumara, said to be the largest tribe of Indians north of Mexico City who have maintained an aboriginal American culture little modified by contacts with the Europeans.[236] In the second quarter of the seventeenth century, the Jesuits founded missions among them. As a consequence of the work then begun, the majority of the Tarahumara have become nominal Christians, although some have persisted in their paganism. The church building, where one exists, forms the centre of the community. The knowledge of Christian doctrine is very meagre. Two leading divinities are recognized, God ("that God our father") and the Virgin Mary ("that God our mother"). The rosary and crucifix are in use, and the manner of making the sign of the cross is transmitted. A few names of saints, Spanish names, the custom of god-parents, a few church ceremonies, and Sunday services in abbreviated forms conducted by a lay *maestro* in the absence of the priest (who often makes only one visit a year to the church), with the use of Spanish prayers which probably even the leader seldom understands, and the mixture of Christian ideas in the *fiestas*, are said to be the chief observable effects.[237] If in such a remote tribe even these influences are found, presumably the impress of Christianity has been more marked upon others more closely in contact with European culture and accorded more careful clerical ministrations.

In the south-eastern portion of North America, Florida and the adjoining areas, notably Georgia, missionaries penetrated. However, no such lasting

[234] Engelhardt, *op. cit.*, Vol. II, p. 619.

[235] Bancroft, *op. cit.*, pp. 220-247. For a popular account of the missions and their history and of the remains as they were in the early part of the twentieth century, see Charles Francis Saunders and J. Smeaton Chase, *The California Padres and Their Missions* (Boston, Houghton Mifflin Company, 1915, pp. xi, 418). For another popular account which gives the history of the individual missions with their legends and romances, see Mrs. Fremont Oliver, *California Missions and Their Romances* (New York, Coward-McCann, 1938, pp. xxiv, 314).

[236] Bennett and Zingg, *The Tarahumara*, p. vii.

[237] Bennett and Zingg, *op. cit.*, pp. 296, 319, 320.

effects followed in the life of the Indians as in Mexico and parts of the South-west. The English menace proved disconcerting and eventually disastrous. The Indians were not at a stage of civilization readily to adjust themselves to European culture, no strong adjacent centre of Spanish rule existed such as was provided by the Mexican plateau, and none of the missions was as per-sistent and continuous as were the more prominent of those in the West. Many of the efforts were brilliant and heroic, but they did not issue in enduring results.

Only the briefest possible summary can be given of the attempts to spread Christianity in the South-east. Here, as in Texas and California, the missions had a political as well as a religious purpose. They were intended to help stem the advance of the English and the French. Various sporadic and relatively unsuccessful expeditions and efforts to found missions were made in the six-teenth century before 1565. Notable among these was one by a group of Dominicans led by Luis Cancer de Barbastro, who in 1549 endeavoured to put into practice the principles of which their order, and particularly Las Casas, made so much, and to approach the Indians without the use of force. Cancer had had extensive experience as a missionary, notably in Guatemala, where as a companion of Las Casas he had met with success with this kind of method. However, the experiment in Florida was terminated by the early martyrdom of Cancer, on a spot usually conjectured to have been near Tampa Bay.[238]

In 1565 a continuing Spanish occupation was begun under Pedro Menendez de Avila, and St. Augustine was founded. In 1566 some Jesuits came out to co-operate with the enterprise and penetrated as far north as Chesapeake Bay. Their venture, however, proved disastrous. A number of misfortunes cul-minated in the massacre of some of the missionaries, including their leader, Segura, in 1571.[239] The Jesuit effort thereupon came to an end.

The Franciscans soon arrived to take up the task thus sadly interrupted. In spite of various vicissitudes, they extended their lines, founded several mis-sions of the general type with which we have already become familiar on the Spanish American frontier, and in 1634, at the zenith of their prosperity, were said to have had in what are now Florida and Georgia thirty-five missionaries,

---

[238] V. F. O'Daniel, *Dominicans in Early Florida* (New York, The United States Cath-olic Historical Society, 1930, pp. xii, 230; sympathetic, based on extensive research), pp. 30-69; Shea, *History of the Catholic Missions among the Indian Tribes of the United States, 1529-1854*, pp. 46-49.

[239] Priestley, *Tristán de Luna*, pp. 52, 53; Pastor, *History of the Popes*, Vol. XVIII, p. 345; Walsh, *American Jesuits*, p. 18; Shea, *op. cit.*, pp. 55 ff.; Lanning, *The Spanish Missions of Georgia*, pp. 33 ff.

forty-four centres, and about thirty thousand Indian Christians.[240] Indian wars punctuated the history of the Spanish regime and disturbed the missions. To these were added attacks by the English. In the first half of the eighteenth century the Florida and Georgia missions virtually came to an end.[241] From 1763 to 1783 Florida was in the hands of the English, and conditions did not favour Roman Catholic missionary activity.

It was not only to the north of Mexico that missionaries helped to enlarge the Spanish frontiers. Extensive enterprises were also carried on to the south, in Central America. These were begun early and were pursued throughout the colonial period, although latterly with diminished energy. In general they met with success and brought about at least the nominal allegiance to Christianity of the vast majority of the Indians of the region.

In Central America dwelt a great variety of tribes speaking numerous different languages. The mountains broke the country into many valleys and plateaus. In places, notably in Guatemala, the Indians had developed fairly high cultures, some of them akin to those of Yucatan and Mexico. In these civilized portions were settled agricultural populations. Columbus himself explored the eastern coastline of Central America and planted the first settlement of Europeans. About the time of the conquest of Mexico, Guatemala was subdued by the Spaniards. Eventually all of Central America except Panama was organized administratively into a captaincy-general. Where the Indian populations had been leading an organized agricultural life, the Spanish occupation at the outset meant for the masses chiefly a change of masters. As in Mexico, Christianity was adopted at the behest or under the encouragement of the new lords. However, a large proportion of the population was in uncivilized tribes whose conversion to Christianity and assimilation to Spanish culture was a slower and more difficult process.

It was in 1510, at a town founded in that year by Balboa on the Isthmus of Panama, that what was said to be the first church building on the American Continent was erected. In 1513 this church was made a cathedral. The first bishop was a Franciscan, Juan de Quevedo, who arrived in 1514.[242]

The oldest extensive Central American missions among the Indians were not in Panama, but in Guatemala and Nicaragua. The first missionaries seem to have visited Guatemala in 1526.[243] In 1530 Francisco Marroquin arrived and began the study of the language. In 1533 he was made the first bishop of

[240] Lanning, *op. cit.*, pp. 59 ff.; Schmidlin-Braun, *Catholic Mission History*, pp. 436, 437; Maynard Geiger in Wilgus, *Colonial Hispanic America*, pp. 538-550.
[241] Lanning, *op. cit.*, pp. 59 ff.
[242] Rojas y Arrieta, *History of the Bishops of Panama*, pp. 1-6.
[243] Lemmens, *Geschichte der Franziskanermissionen*, p. 224.

Guatemala. He encountered difficulty in trying to induce the *conquistadores* to attend church,[244] but he succeeded in attracting clergy to his assistance. In 1533 some Mercedarians came.[245] Dominicans arrived early.[246] Las Casas had been dared by the heads of the Spanish colony to demonstrate that his programme of approach to the Indians without the use of force was feasible. He accepted the challenge and chose as the field for demonstration an area in the north of Guatemala called the Terra de Guerra which the Spaniards had so far been unable to conquer. He and his colleagues composed couplets in the native tongue telling something of the story of man's creation, fall, and redemption. These they taught Christian Indian merchants who penetrated the mountains, sang them, aroused the curiosity of the Indians to hear more, and so procured an invitation for the friars. The latter went and made converts.[247] Franciscans arrived in 1539.[248] Before the end of the sixteenth century Guatemala contained twenty-two houses of Franciscans and fourteen of Dominicans. The Mercedarians had six districts, and the seculars twenty-two.[249] The Jesuits, too, had established a college in Guatemala.[250]

In Nicaragua the first bishop, Diego Alvarez Osorio, was appointed in 1531, two years earlier than the first bishop of Guatemala.[251] Las Casas had helped to introduce the Dominicans to that diocese a few years before his mission in Guatemala.[252] Franciscans also came.[253] In 1616 the Jesuits arrived.[254] We hear of the baptism of thousands, at so rapid a rate that much preliminary instruction was impossible. Thus between September, 1538, and March 5, 1539, 52,558 are said to have received the rite.[255]

In Costa Rica, too, the sixteenth century witnessed missionary activity by the Franciscans. One of the missionaries is said to have used twelve Indian dialects.[256]

The missionary frontier in Central America continued to be advanced throughout the seventeenth and eighteenth centuries. Only a few of the many examples can be given. In 1600 in Panama Dominicans, Franciscans, Augustin-

---

[244] Bancroft, *History of Central America*, Vol. II, pp. 133-140.
[245] Pedro N. Pérez, *Apostolado de los Mercedarios entre los Indios de América*, in *Revista de la Exposición Misional Española*, No. 2, Nov. 1928, pp. 50-54.
[246] Pastor, *History of the Popes*, Vol. XIII, p. 304.
[247] MacNutt, *Las Casas*, pp. 190 ff.
[248] Mendieta, *Historia Eclesiástica Indiana*, Book IV, Chap. 7.
[249] *Ibid.*
[250] Pérez, *La Compañiá de Jesus en Colombia y Centro-América*, Part I, p. xiv.
[251] Bancroft, *op. cit.*, Vol. II, pp. 168-171.
[252] MacNutt, *op. cit.*, p. 185.
[253] Mendieta, *op. cit.*, Book IV, Chap. 9.
[254] Pérez, *op. cit.*, Part I, p. xiv.
[255] Bancroft, *op. cit.*, Vol. II, p. 184.
[256] Bancroft, *op. cit.*, Vol. II, pp. 431, 432.

ians, and Mercedarians, reinforced by the zeal of the Bishop, were labouring for the conversion of the Indians.[257] In the second quarter of the seventeenth century the Indians of Darien, who had only recently massacred a number of Spaniards, seemed to accept missionaries, but a little later they again rose in revolt.[258] In 1646 the Capuchins began a mission in Darien which persisted until 1689.[259] In the seventeenth and eighteenth centuries the frequent raids of the buccaneers retarded the progress of missions on the Isthmus,[260] but efforts at conversion were renewed again and again, and in the latter part of the eighteenth century seemed to be meeting with success.[261] In the seventeenth century a number of attempts were made to subdue to the faith the Indians in the difficult regions between Yucatan and Guatemala, but with only slight results. We hear of one tribe which accepted Christianity, but who renounced it when they found by sad experience that the Spaniards would not protect them against the attacks of pagan neighbours.[262] In 1712 and 1713 an Indian cult arose in Chiapas, on the western edge of Guatemala, which was a medley of Indian and Christian ideas. A prophetess led in a revolt against the Spaniards. She was supported by an Indian who declared that St. Peter had appointed him his vicar on earth with power to ordain priests. A bishop was consecrated and mass celebrated. However, the Spaniards quickly suppressed the revolt.[263] Down into 1783 we hear of attempts, most of them futile, to convert the Indians in the mountains of Tilaran.[264] In the latter part of the seventeenth century the Franciscan efforts between Honduras and Nicaragua prospered.[265] For a time, too, in the sixteen eighties, the Brothers Minor made spectacular gains among the Indians of Talamanca, in an area where a few years before a governor of Costa Rica had seemed to meet with similar success. In five years two Franciscans, without the protection of troops, are said to have baptized forty thousand Indians and to have established fourteen villages. Yet the results were transient.[266] In the eighteenth century the Franciscans had the mission college of Nueva Guatemala de la Asuncion, with missions in Panama, Talamanca (Costa Rica), and Honduras.[267] It was only slowly, and with many

[257] Rojas y Arrieta, *History of the Bishops of Panama*, pp. 29-35.

[258] Rojas y Arrieta, *op. cit.*, pp. 37-44.

[259] Terzorio, *Manuale Historicum Missionum Ordinis Minorum Capuccinirum*, pp. 357-359.

[260] Rojas y Arrieta, *op. cit.*, pp. 63-67, 93-95.

[261] Rojas y Arrieta, *op. cit.*, pp. 147-149.

[262] Bancroft, *History of Central America*, Vol. II, pp. 672-679.

[263] Bancroft, *op. cit.*, Vol. II, pp. 696-705.

[264] Bancroft, *op. cit.*, Vol. II, pp. 613-616.

[265] Bancroft, *op. cit.*, Vol. II, pp. 643, 644.

[266] Bancroft, *op. cit.*, Vol. II, p. 446.

[267] Maas, *Las Órdenes Religiosas de España y la Colonización de America*, Vol. II, pp. 77 ff.

reverses, that Christianity made its way through the jungles and mountain fastnesses of Central America. Even nominal conversion was not universal when the political upheavals of the first part of the nineteenth century brought the colonial era to an end.

In the Spanish portions of South America the progress of Christianity was fully as chequered as in Central and North America. Between the two regions marked likenesses existed in the spread of the faith. In both at the coming of the Spaniard there were populous centres of civilization on high mountain plateaux—north of the Isthmus in Guatemala and Mexico, and south of it in Peru. Among the civilized peoples of both Mexico and Peru formal conversion followed quickly the political conquest and for much the same reasons. Each became the headquarters of political and ecclesiastical administration over a vast area. In both continents were many wild tribes who proved less amenable to the *conquistadores* and the missionaries. In South America conditions were, if anything, more difficult, for here many of the mountains were more forbidding and some of the jungles along the great rivers and their tributaries more formidable than anything known on the northern continent. Probably in South America more tribes remained untouched by Christianity or more fiercely and successfully resistant to Spanish control and to Spanish culture, including Spanish missions. In North, Central, and South America, however, in their main outlines the methods used by missionaries bore a common family likeness and the larger proportion of the Indians were more or less affected by Christianity. As in the other sections of the story, we must proceed geographically.

We go first to what is now called Venezuela, for not only does that region lie on the northern shore of South America, but also in it Spanish exploration and occupation began early, and administratively it was long included in what was called the Kingdom of New Spain, which embraced the Spanish possessions in the Caribbean and in Central and North America.[268]

Slave hunters, fishers for pearls, and merchants early visited the northern shores of South America, and most of them thought of the Indians only as a possible means of gain. Two Dominicans, Pedro de Cordova and Juan Garcés, built what was said to have been the first monastery in South America, and in 1513 celebrated what is reported to have been the first mass. However, they met martyrdom at the hands of Indians who, enraged by the treachery of some pearl-fishers, took indiscriminate vengeance on white men.[269] A few

---

[268] Bourne, *Spain in America*, p. 229.

[269] Humbert, *Les Origines Vénézuéliennes*, pp. 206 ff.; Moses, *The Spanish Dependencies in South America*, Vol. I, p. 32; Rippy and Nelson, *Crusaders of the Jungle*, pp. 105-108.

years later, Franciscans and Dominicans attempted to renew the mission, but in 1520 a massacre again wiped out the Dominican enterprise.[270] We have already noted the unsuccessful effort of Las Casas at colonization. After his departure the Franciscans were also erased.[271] With the famous and futile attempt of the Welsers in the first half of the sixteenth century to develop Venezuela twenty Dominicans were associated, but in general the Welser rule meant suffering for the natives.[272] Sixteenth century efforts on the Island of Trinidad[273] and by the Brothers Minor on the Orinoco[274] also failed. In 1531 a bishopric was established at Coro.[275]

In spite of these heroic ventures, continuous and successful missions were not established in Venezuela until the middle of the seventeenth century. The man from whom stemmed the first missions which enjoyed a continuing existence was a friar whose original name was Tiburcio de Redin, but who is better known by the designation which was his after he abandoned the world for the religious life, Francisco de Pamplona. He was born in 1597, of aristocratic lineage, and for many years was a soldier and a sailor. Ardent, quick-tempered, courageous, he lived a life of action and adventure, part of it in the New World, until, as a result of a profound religious change, in his fortieth year he joined the Capuchins. In 1650, when he had reached his early fifties, he led some of his fellow Capuchins to undertake a mission in Cumaná, in Northern Venezuela, near the mouths of the Orinoco. Although he died the following year, in 1651, and for a time the enterprise which he had initiated was interrupted, before 1660 two missions had arisen, one of the Capuchins in the region of Cumaná, and the other of the Observant Franciscans, just to the west of the Capuchins.[276] The first contingent of the Observants arrived in 1656, led by Juan de Mendoza, who had been head of the province of his order in Florida, and so was experienced in missions to the Indians. A second contingent came in 1660 and others followed.[277]

The tasks which confronted these missions were most baffling. Few of the Indians were settled in villages. Some were cannibals.[278] Much difficulty was

[270] Humbert, op. cit., pp. 210, 211; Moses, op. cit., Vol. I, p. 33.

[271] Schmidlin-Braun, Catholic Mission History, p. 368.

[272] Ibid.

[273] Moses, op. cit., Vol. I, p. 37.

[274] Schmidlin-Braun, op. cit., p. 369.

[275] Lemmens, Geschichte der Franziskanermissionen, p. 276.

[276] Rippy and Nelson, Crusaders of the Jungle, pp. 108-110; Froylán de Rionegro, Relaciones de las Misiones de los PP. Capuchinos en las Antiguas Provincias Españolos hoy República de Venezuela, 1650-1817, Vol. I, p. 83; Terzorio, Manuale Historicum Missionum Ordinis Minorum Capuccinorum, pp. 359-361.

[277] Blanco, Conversion en Piritu, pp. 76, 77, 134-139, 144, 145.

[278] Froylán de Rionegro, op. cit., Vol. I, pp. 55 ff.

encountered in learning the native idioms, in giving instruction in them, and in finding words which would convey the meaning of Christian concepts.[279] Yet progress was made. Such statistics as we have must be in part conjectural. Still, they may help to indicate what was accomplished. About 1678, or when the missions had been under way for about twenty-five years, the number of Indians baptized by the Capuchins and the Observants was put at about forty-five hundred.[280] In 1779 a summary by a missionary said that since the beginning of the mission one hundred and thirty-eight Observants had come to the field (but of these twenty-eight had died early or had returned to Spain ill or discouraged), that they had baptized fifty-eight thousand, and that about twelve thousand converts were then living.[281] In 1780, the prefect of the Capuchin missions reported that nearly fifty-three thousand had been baptized since the inception of missions of his order in that region, and that slightly over twelve thousand were then living under the tutelage of the Capuchins.[282] Both Capuchins and Observants did much to promote agriculture and stock-raising. Great herds of horses, mules, and cattle came into existence. Sugar, bananas, maize, cassava, rice, and beans were extensively cultivated.[283] Cacao and coffee plantations were developed, with irrigation works.[284]

As in other parts of Latin America, the civil authorities regarded the mission stage as temporary. By the end of the seventeenth century they were attempting to extend their control over the Indians who were under the friars. The missionaries succeeded in obtaining from Spain a postponement of the step, pleading that the time was not ripe and that, if the Indians were compelled to pay tribute, what had been accomplished at the cost of so much labour would be ruined.[285] However, before the end of the eighteenth century fully half of the missions had been transferred to the secular clergy and the civil officials.[286] At the same time the birth rate seems to have been falling,[287] but whether this was because of the passing of the missions or because of the altered conditions of life brought by the missions is uncertain.

Farther west, in the plains south of the coast mountains which lay back of Carácas, the Capuchins also had establishments. The field was adverse. In the

[279] Froylán de Rionegro, op. cit., Vol. I, p. 114; Blanco, op. cit., pp. 176 ff.
[280] Froylán de Rionegro, op. cit., Vol. I, p. 115.
[281] Caulin, Historia Coro-graphica, p. 376.
[282] Rippy and Nelson, op. cit., p. 114, citing Simón Torrelosnegros in Relacion Históricas de las Misiones de Padres Capuchinos de Venezuela, in Colección de Libros Raros ó Curiosos que Tratan de América, Vol. XXII.
[283] Caulin, op. cit., p. 8.
[284] Rippy and Nelson, op. cit., p. 115.
[285] Caulin, op. cit.. pp. 300, 301, 421, 422.
[286] Rippy and Nelson, op. cit., p. 116.
[287] Ibid.

rainy season the lowlands were flooded. During the dry season much of the land was parched. The Indians were semi-nomadic and usually were scattered into families rather than tribes. They were, accordingly, peculiarly difficult to bring into a settled, agricultural existence such as was entailed in the life of a mission.[288] Yet in the century between 1658 and 1758 the Capuchins founded about a hundred different stations. Many of these were short-lived, some became the nuclei of Spanish towns, but in perhaps fifteen or thirty at a time the typical routine of a mission went on. Missions in this region continued until the decline brought by the wars of independence.[289]

The Capuchins also, as we have said, had centres in Darien.[290] In 1678 a group of the same order went to the Island of Trinidad to found a mission.[291] The Capuchins were also in North-west Venezuela, in the regions of Maracaibo.[292]

South of the Capuchins in Venezuela, along the course of tributaries of the Orinoco which rose in mountain glades of the Andes, chiefly the Casanare and Meta Rivers, the Jesuits long had missions. Politically they were in New Granada and they looked to Bogotá as a centre, but they lay east of the mountain passes. The first of the Jesuits reached the plains of the Casanare early in the seventeenth century.[293] Between 1629 and 1660 the Jesuits paid little attention to the area. About 1659 or 1661 they began again more vigorously, but were hampered by the ill will aroused by Spanish slave-hunters. Shortly before 1767, the year in which it was driven from the Spanish possessions, the Society had on the Casanare six missions with a population of about twenty-two hundred. After the expulsion the Society's farms were sold for a song, the churches were despoiled, and many of the Indians resumed the wild life.[294]

Subsequent to the enforced departure of the Jesuits, Franciscans, Dominicans, and Augustinians entered and attempted to build on the ruined foundations. In 1793 the Dominicans on the Casanare were reported to have about as many Indians under their care as the Jesuits had had in that region a quarter of a century before, and in 1794 the Augustinians were said to have on the Meta about forty-three hundred in charge. In that same year the Brothers Minor,

[288] Froylán de Rionegro, op. cit., Vol. II, pp. 249 ff.; Rippy and Nelson, op. cit., pp. 118-120.
[289] See a description of the state of these missions, dated 1745, in Froylán de Rionegro, op. cit., Vol. II, pp. 249 ff.; Rippy and Nelson, op. cit., pp. 121-125.
[290] Froylán de Rionegro, op. cit., Vol. II, pp. 80 ff.
[291] Froylán de Rionegro, op. cit., Vol. II, pp. 158, 159.
[292] Terzorio, Manuale Historicum Missionum Ordinis Minorum Capuccinorum, p. 363.
[293] Rivero, Historia de las Misiones de los Llanos de Casanare y los Rios Orinoco y Meta, pp. 49 ff.; Rippy and Nelson, Crusaders of the Jungle, pp. 126-128.
[294] Rivero, op. cit., passim; Rippy and Nelson, op. cit., pp. 129-141.

who were on the Guaviare a little farther south, were reported to have gathered between twelve hundred and seventeen hundred Indians.[295] South and east of the Orinoco lay what was known as Spanish Guiana. Much of it was debatable land. English and Dutch traders and corsairs and fierce Caribs disputed with the Spaniards for its possession. Missions in it were late in beginning. In 1595 a Franciscan "convent" was established on the lower Orinoco.[296] For several years subsequent to 1664 the Jesuits attempted to establish missions in Guiana, but, after serious loss of life, found it necessary to retire to the plains of the Casanare.[297] In 1681, for at least a time the Society formally left the region to the Capuchins of Catalonia. These, as we have seen, had recently opened a mission on Trinidad, then under the same governor as Guiana. As early as 1680, indeed, the Capuchins had sent some of their order to begin operations.[298] Between 1687 and 1728 forty-six Capuchins served in Trinidad and Guiana. Of these twenty-three had died, but the order was said to have succeeded in founding twelve missions and baptizing more than eight thousand Indians.[299] However, until about 1724 most of the strength of the mission was in Trinidad. Only after this year were the friars able to begin numerous establishments in Guiana. In 1755 the Capuchins were reported as having eleven missions with 2,901 Indians, and as having founded seven others which had meanwhile been discontinued.[300] In the second half of the eighteenth century the Observant Franciscans also founded a number of missions on the south side of the Orinoco.[301] In 1761 an official report showed that in the region the Capuchins had sixteen missions, the Jesuits four, and the Observant Franciscans three. The Capuchin missions were said to have a population of 4,406, but epidemics of smallpox and measles and attacks by Caribs and the English had cost the lives of many Indians; eight missions which had once existed had been destroyed, and nearly seventeen hundred Indians had returned to the forest.[302] Conflicting contemporary reports were given at various times in the latter half of the eighteenth century, but on the whole the missions seem to have continued to grow.[303] Between 1797 and

---

[295] Rippy and Nelson, op. cit., pp. 142, 143.

[296] Rippy and Nelson, op. cit., p. 145; Lemmens, Geschichte der Franziskanermissionen, p. 278.

[297] Rivero, op. cit., pp. 171 ff.; Rippy and Nelson, op. cit., pp. 146, 147. Some Jesuits seem to have been in the region as early as 1652, although the real origin of their missions was in 1664.—Humbert, Les Origines Vénézuéliennes, p. 296.

[298] Humbert, op. cit., pp. 297, 298; Froylán de Rionegro, op. cit., Vol. II, p. 215.

[299] Froylán de Rionegro, op. cit., Vol. II, p. 231.

[300] Humbert, op. cit., pp. 304, 305.

[301] Rippy and Nelson, op. cit., p. 149.

[302] Rippy and Nelson, op. cit., p. 153.

[303] Rippy and Nelson, op. cit., pp. 160-165.

1813 the Capuchins were said to have thirty missions in the region and to have baptized 34,667. The population of the missions is reported as having increased from 16,139 in 1797 to 21,246 in 1813.[304] Like so many others in Spanish America, the missions were disrupted by the disturbances which ushered in political independence.[305]

In one other region in what can be called Venezuela, missions were established. About 1670 Jesuits began to push their way towards the upper reaches of the Orinoco, largely on the eastern side. For the next twenty-five years heroic attempts were made to found permanent enterprises in the area. Each, however, ended in failure—except that several of the missionaries obtained the coveted martyr's crown.[306] At various times in the eighteenth century, Jesuits, Capuchins, Observant Franciscans, and Dominicans were on the upper Orinoco and founded missions which persisted for considerable periods. At one time in the second half of the century, in an effort to occupy territory which was disputed with Portugal, the Spanish civil authorities encouraged the Capuchins to push their activities southward. While for a time dissension over the transfer of the missions to the secular clergy led to the withdrawal of the Capuchins from the upper Orinoco, at the end of the century the friars were again at work and had well established centres.[307]

In the introduction of Christianity to Venezuela, the Franciscans, Capuchins and Observants played, as we have seen, the major role. However, the Jesuits had also been prominent. Lesser shares of the burden were assumed by Dominicans, Augustinians, Mercedarians, and Candelarians.[308]

In general, the subjugation of Venezuela to Spanish rule and the conversion of the aboriginal population to Christianity were much more delayed than in some other portions of Spanish America. The physical and climatic obstacles were great. The ferocity of the Caribs, the wandering and disorganized nature of most of the Indian groups, and raids by Dutch and English added to the difficulties. Apparently, too, the region was less well supplied with missionaries than were some other sections. Here, too, as elsewhere, the secular clergy proved of poorer quality and less efficient than the regulars in the care of the Indians. In the latter part of the eighteenth century, moreover, the Church seemed to be losing its hold on the white population and on sections which had been longer under Spanish rule. Only among the missions on the frontiers

[304] Humbert, op. cit., pp. 320, 321.
[305] Rippy and Nelson, op. cit., pp. 165-167.
[306] Rivero, Historia de las Misiones de los Llanos de Casanare y los Rios Orinoco y Meta, pp. 252-285, 296 ff.
[307] Rippy and Nelson, op. cit., pp. 171-177.
[308] Watters, A History of the Church in Venezuela, 1810-1930, p. 8.

was it still gaining ground. Yet, while the imprint of Christianity and of Spanish culture was stamped less deeply upon Venezuela than upon some other sections of Spanish America, the Church had been responsible for most of whatever formal education was available for whites and mestizos. Christian missionaries had laid the foundations of many Spanish towns, they had induced thousands of Indians to begin a settled existence, they had helped in the introduction of certain types of agriculture and of stock-farming, and they had led tens of thousands of Indians to at least the outward acceptance of the Christian name and faith.[309]

In New Granada, in the area which is now embraced in the republic of Colombia, Christianity early made its way and obtained a firm foothold. It seems, indeed, to have been much stronger than in Venezuela. The high plateaux, particularly in the neighbourhood of Bogotá, favoured a denser and more settled Indian population which more readily adapted itself to Spanish ways and to Christianity than did the scattered, primitive folk of Venezuela, and also made possible a larger Spanish population. In the lowlands, Negroes eventually constituted an important element. Yet, while the successes were greater than in Venezuela, they were not so marked as in Mexico and Peru, for the scale of the indigenous culture was lower than in these two lands and the numbers of civilized Indians much smaller. Here, as elsewhere, wild tribes offered a formidable problem.

The Spanish conquest of what came to be known as New Granada was begun in the first half of the sixteenth century. In its initial stages it was characterized by marked cruelty to the aborigines.[310] In 1525 a Spanish settlement had been formed at Santa Marta, near the mouth of the Magdalena River. From this as a base, in 1536-1538 Jimenez de Quesada, with a small force of armed men, penetrated with great hardship up the valley of the Magdalena to the tableland of Bogotá and Tunja and there made himself and his fellows masters of the Chibchas, the civilized folk who dominated that area.[311]

With Quesada were Dominicans and a secular priest. As was to be expected, conversions began almost at once. Presumably the Indians deemed it best, as in Mexico and Peru, to acquiesce in the faith of their new masters. More Dominicans and seculars followed. A temple at Bogotá was transformed into a church and within two years the entire population had become professedly Christian.[312] The Franciscans came,[313] and in 1585 their Provincial estimated

[309] Watters, op. cit., pp. 3-52.
[310] Las Casas, Brevissima Relacion, translated in MacNutt. Las Casas, pp. 401-411.
[311] Moses, The Spanish Dependencies in South America, Vol. I, pp. 121 ff.
[312] Schmidlin-Braun, Catholic Mission History, pp. 371, 372.
[313] Civezza, Storia delle Missioni Francescane, Vol. VII, Pt. 2, pp. 20, 22.

the number baptized by them as more than two hundred thousand.[314] About the middle of the sixteenth century Augustinians arrived.[315] Between 1562 and 1569 the Dominican, Luis Beltrán (Louis Bertrand), later canonized and declared the patron saint of New Granada, is said to have gone about preaching, barefooted, armed only with Bible and breviary, often without guides, and to have brought to the Christian faith more than twenty-five thousand Indians.[316] He came from a successful career as a popular preacher in Spain and had only seven years in the New World. He had great respect for Las Casas and was prominent as a champion of the Indians against exploiting Spaniards.[317] In 1553 the see of Santa Marta was removed to Bogotá and raised to an archbishopric.[318] In 1598 the initial contingent of Jesuits reached Bogotá. At first they addressed themselves to the Spanish population but before long they were at work among the Indians.[319]

It is not surprising that at the outset a large proportion of the conversions were superficial. In 1550 an ecclesiastic lamented the fact that many of the Indians who had received baptism, on returning to their villages, reverted to the old gods.[320]

Only slowly, moreover, was the faith carried to the less civilized Indians in mountain fastnesses and in the lowlying valleys. We have seen how the Jesuits, from Bogotá as a base, penetrated to the Indians on the Casanare and other tributaries of the Orinoco. From a college established in 1756 at Cali, south and west of Bogotá, Franciscans spread to several fields, including, after 1780, a mission in the western part of Colombia.[321]

In New Granada, as elsewhere, efforts were made by some of the missionaries to learn the native tongues. We hear, for instance, of a Dominican who was a teacher of the Indian languages in a Dominican monastery and prepared a catechism for use in the missions.[322] Here, too, the use of force to induce Indians to receive Christian instruction was prohibited by the ecclesiastical authorities, although presumably not with entire success, and efforts were

---

[314] Lemmens, *Geschichte der Franziskanermissionen*, p. 280, citing Lopez in *Arch. Ib.-Am.*, Vol. XV, p. 135.

[315] Schmidlin-Braun, *op. cit.*, p. 373.

[316] Pastor, *History of the Popes*, Vol. XVIII, pp. 345, 346.

[317] Moses, *op. cit.*, Vol. I, pp. 290, 291; José Espina, in *Revista de la Exposición Misional Española*, June, 1929, pp. 418-422. Espina puts the number baptized by Beltrán at fifteen thousand.

[318] Rojos y Arrieta, *History of the Bishops of Panama*, pp. 12, 13.

[319] Perez, *La Compañía de Jesus en Colombia y Centro-América despues de su Restáuración*, Part I, p. xi; Crétineau-July, *Histoire de la Compagnie de Jésus*, Vol. III, pp. 203-205.

[320] Lemmens, *op. cit.*, p. 280, citing *Arch. Ib-Am.*, Vol. XX, p. 151.

[321] Lemmens, *op. cit.*, p. 283, citing Compte, *Varones*, Vol. II, p. 104.

[322] Moses, *The Spanish Dependencies in South America*, Vol. II, p. 84.

made by the Church to induce the *encomenderos* to provide priests and chapels for their Indian wards.[323]

In the latter half of the sixteenth century, in some sections a decline of population occurred, but this seems to have been in spite of rather than to have arisen from the work of the missionaries, and to have been attributable to smallpox, to work in the mines, and to discouragement brought on by the disappearance of the old order.[324]

We must not pass from New Granada without making mention, even though briefly, of two remarkable missionaries to the Negroes. Both had as the centre of their labours the city of Cartagena, long the chief port of entry for the slave-ships from Africa. Here Alfonso de Sandoval, a Jesuit from a wealthy family, gave himself devotedly to the Negroes and died in their service. More famous was his successor, Pedro Claver. Pedro Claver was born in Catalonia in 1581, of a noble family, and, like so many other of the high-born youths of the day, was early caught up in the Jesuit movement. He arrived in Cartagena in 1615 and was profoundly influenced by Sandoval, under whose tutelage he served his apprenticeship in the work for the Negroes. Until his death, nearly forty years later, in 1654, he spent himself on the poor wretches whom the greed of men had torn from their homes in Africa. On their arrival he visited the slave-ships, foul with the stench of crowded and ill-tended humanity, and carried food, fruit, wine, and tobacco to their black cargoes. He ministered to the ill, baptized the infants, gave religious instruction, and attempted to inculcate Christian ideals of morality, including especially chastity. He met the multiplicity of languages of his charges by training catechists who had some of the many tongues. Naturally shy, he could be bold as a lion in behalf of the oppressed and proved an able organizer. He insisted upon receiving the Negroes into the Jesuit church on the basis of equality with the whites, although in doing so he aroused intense opposition on the part of some of the latter. He made long journeys to visit the blacks in the mines and on the plantations. He braved the enmity of slave-dealers and slave-owners. He is said to have baptized more than three hundred thousand, and while one distrusts estimates in round numbers it is clear that his ministry reached thousands. It was eminently fitting that eventually the Church should honour his memory with canonization and make him the patron saint of missions to Negroes.[325]

[323] José Manuel Groot, *Historia Eclesiastica y Civil de Nueva Granada* (Bogotá, 3 vols., 1869, 1870), Vol. I, Appendices 2, 3.

[324] Moses, *The Spanish Dependencies in South America*, Vol. I, p. 279.

[325] See a brief biography by Pierre Suau with a bibliography, in *The Catholic Encyclopedia*, Vol. XI, p. 763. See brief notices in Crétineau-Joly, *Histoire de la Compagnie de*

The main centre of Spanish colonial power in South America was Peru. What Mexico was in North America, that Peru, as we have suggested, was in the southern continent. In each the basis was the same. In Peru as in Mexico a fairly high civilization had existed before the coming of the white man. In both countries a numerous Indian population was living an ordered life founded upon settled agriculture. In both, the Spanish conquest was accomplished within a generation after the first arrival of Columbus in America, and by a handful of men. In each a ruling Spanish minority displaced the former native rulers. In both regions, too, the outward acceptance of Christianity took place rapidly. The masses acquiesced in it as the will of their new masters. On the fringes of both lands, moreover, uncivilized or semi-civilized peoples existed among whom Spanish civilization and the Christian faith made progress much more slowly and only through the continued efforts of generations of missionaries supported by the Spanish colonial regime.

The conversion of the Indians was, as in so much of the Spanish activity in the Americas, one of the avowed purposes of the conquest of Peru. This is not the place for the story of that conquest. It has often been told.[326] After preliminary voyages which gave some knowledge of the west coast, the expedition which brought about the actual beginning of the conquest set out from Panama in January, 1531. It was led by Francisco Pizarro, a hardy adventurer. With it were several priests, notably the Dominican, Vicente de Valverde.[327] Indeed, the royal capitulation of 1529 under which the conquest was inaugurated required that priests be taken along to effect the conversion of the natives.[328] Here, as about a decade before in Mexico, a little band of Europeans with ruthlessness and courage made themselves masters of an empire. Their lust for gold and power was combined in at least some of them with activity in supplanting the native cults with their faith. Thus in the initial stages of the conquest an image in one of the more prominent of the Indian shrines was destroyed and a cross set up in its place,[329] and the Inca, Atahuallpa, was prevailed upon to accept baptism before his execution.[330] When the Inca capital,

---

Jésus, Vol. III, pp. 187-192, and Rojas y Arrieta, *History of the Bishops of Panama*, pp. 56-58. See a longer biography by a fellow Jesuit, Bertrand-Gabriel Fleuriau, *La Vie du Vénérable Père Pierre Claver*, (Revised edition, Clermont-Ferrand, 2 vols., 1834-1835).

[326] The classic account in English has long been William H. Prescott, *History of the Conquest of Peru* (Preface, Boston, 1847). A more recent account is Philip Ainsworth Means, *Fall of the Inca Empire and the Spanish Rule in Peru: 1530-1780* (New York, Charles Scribner's Sons, 1932, pp. xii, 351).

[327] Means, *op. cit.*, p. 27.

[328] Prescott, *op. cit.*, Book III, Chap 1.

[329] Prescott, *op. cit.*, Book III, Chap. 6.

[330] Pedro Sancho, *An Account of the Conquest of Peru* (translated by P. A. Means, New York, The Cortes Society, 1917, pp. 203), pp. 17, 18.

Cuzco, was taken, Valverde became its bishop. Before long a Dominican monastery was erected on the site of the House of the Sun.[331] Yet Pizarro had no such zeal for the propagation of Christianity as had Cortés, the conqueror of Mexico,[332] and Valverde seems not to have sought to put forth a restraining hand for mercy towards the Indians as did Olmedo, the leading priest who accompanied Cortés.[333]

Las Casas is said to have visited Spain in 1530, although the accuracy of the report is questioned, in an attempt to prevent a repetition of the cruelties towards the natives of Peru which had characterized the reduction of Mexico.[334] In 1532, when the conquest of Peru was only well begun, Las Casas reached the country carrying a royal *cédula* which prohibited the enslavement of the aborigines. The commanders of the *conquistadores* solemnly assured him that they would give it obedience. This having been accomplished, and the land being still too much upset for the foundation of monasteries, Las Casas and his party believed their mission to be ended and left the country.[335] A later attempt of Las Casas to revisit the land to ensure the observance of the royal order was frustrated.[336] In 1564, at the age of ninety, Las Casas was still solicitous for the Peruvians and wrote a treatise on their behalf.[337]

In the generation following the conquest, numbers of missionaries arrived to assist in the conversion of the multitudes thus made accessible. The Dominicans who accompanied the first expedition were reinforced by others of their order.[338] Franciscans arrived early and soon extended their activities throughout large portions of the former Inca realms. They were active in the modern Ecuador, into which the Inca empire extended, and in Peru. We hear of a lay brother, Mateo de Xumilla, who practised extreme austerities, who held a skull in one hand as he preached to the Indians, and who taught children rhymed summaries of Christian doctrine and had them repeat these in villages to which he went.[339] In the neighbourhood of Quito a number of Franciscans from Flanders laboured and employed some of the same methods which their brethren in Mexico were using.[340] Mercedarians and Augustinians also came

---

[331] *Oeuvres de Don Barthélemi de las Casas,* edited by J.-A. Llorente, Vol. II, p. 183.

[332] Prescott. *op. cit.,* Book IV, Chap. 1.

[333] Prescott, *op. cit.,* Book IV, Chap. 6.

[334] MacNutt, *Bartholomew de Las Casas,* p. 181.

[335] MacNutt, *op. cit.,* pp. 183-185.

[336] MacNutt, *op. cit.,* pp. 187, 188.

[337] *Oeuvres de Don Barthélemi de las Casas,* edited by J.-A. Llorente, Vol. II, pp. 181 ff.

[338] Schmidlin-Braun, *Catholic Mission History,* p. 376.

[339] Henrion, *Histoire Générale des Missions Catholiques,* Vol. I, p. 421.

[340] Lemmens, *Geschichte der Franziskanermissionen,* p. 284. The standard account of Franciscan missions in Peru is Bernardino Izaguirre, *Historia de las Misiones Franciscanas y Narracion de los Progresos de la Geografía en el Oriente del Peru* (Lima, 12 vols., 1922-1926).

early.[341] The first Jesuits arrived in 1568.[342] In 1613 there were three hundred and sixty-five of them in Peru.[343]

By the end of the sixteenth century most of the civilized population of Ecuador was professedly Christian.[344] By that time, too, the majority of the former subjects of the Incas elsewhere had been baptized. The conversion, as we have said, was rapid. The population lived in fairly dense communities, it was easy of access from the coast, it was accustomed to subservience to its rulers and to priests and so acquiesced readily to the wish of its new masters, and the climate of the coast and the plateaux was congenial to Europeans.[345] By about A.D. 1600 the missionary period among the civilized Indians was deemed to have ended and the parishes were transferred to the seculars.[346]

It seems almost unjust to the unnamed to choose for special mention a few among the many missionaries who had a share in the conversion of Peru and the adjacent lands. Yet two have been selected by the Roman Catholic Church for canonization and both seem to have been worthy.

One was the second Archbishop of Lima, Toribio Alfonso de Mogrovejo y Robles. Born in 1534 of a noble family, highly educated, before his appointment to the See of Lima, Toribio had taught at the University of Salamanca and had been connected with the Inquisition in Spain. He was then still a layman, but was duly given clerical orders before his departure for the New World (1581). In Peru he lived an austere life and travelled extensively over his vast archdiocese, generally on foot and often alone and without military escort. Although well along in middle life when he reached America, he went to the trouble of learning the Quechua tongue the better to serve his flock. He himself baptized and preached, and he is said to have administered confirmation to about eight hundred thousand. He built roads, schools, chapels, and hospitals. In the thirteen diocesan and three provincial synods which he assembled, he introduced the reforming decrees of the Council of Trent and had measures taken in defence of the Indians and of the religious rights of the Negro slaves. He died as he had lived, in harness.[347]

The other missionary in the Peruvian area whom we must note was Francis

---

[341] Schmidlin-Braun, *op. cit.*, pp. 377, 378; Pedro N. Pérez in *Revista de la Exposición Misional Española*, April, 1929, pp. 289-294.

[342] Crétineau-Joly, *Histoire de la Compagnie de Jésus*, Vol. II, pp. 125-128.

[343] Van der Essen in Descamps, *Histoire Générale Comparée des Missions*, p. 345.

[344] Lemmens, *op. cit.*, p. 286.

[345] Rippy and Nelson, *Crusaders of the Jungle*, pp. 190, 191.

[346] Lemmens. *op. cit.*, p. 290.

[347] Carlos Garcia Irigoyen, *Santo Toribio. Obra Escrita con Motivo del Tercer Centenario de la Muerte del Santo Arzobispo de Limo* (Lima, Libraria de San Pedro, 4 vols., 1906); Pastor, *History of the Popes*, Vol. XX, p. 502; Means, *Fall of the Inca Empire*, p. 175.

Solanus, a Franciscan. Born in 1549 in Andalusia, he attended a Jesuit school, but joined the Brothers Minor at the age of twenty, choosing the strict branch of the Observants. He had wished to go to Africa as a missionary, but instead, when he was forty, was appointed to South America. He was sent to a difficult frontier, across the Andes, to the region of Tucumán, on the edge of the Gran Chaco. There he laboured indefatigably for twelve years for Spaniards and Indians, acquiring a remarkable command of several of the Indian tongues. He journeyed widely, barefoot, crucifix in hand, preaching. He accompanied with his violin the chanting of the psalms. His hearers would join with him in the singing, at times dancing. His body proved unequal to the burdens which he placed upon it, and in 1602 ill health compelled him to accept a less arduous life. He went to Lima, and there enforced in his monastery the exacting discipline of the Recollects, prepared younger missionaries, preached, and visited the prisoners and the sick. Death came in 1610.[348]

Attention must also be called to Francisco de Toledo, who arrived in Peru in 1569 and who as Viceroy sought the welfare of his dusky charges. In Cuzco and Lima he founded colleges for the sons of prominent Indians. He wished to place Indians on the council of each colony and so to give them a voice in determining their own affairs. He found that many of the Indians, so recently baptized, tended to fall back secretly into their former cults. He did much to increase the provision for the religious instruction of the Indians, seeking to have one priest for each four or five hundred of the natives, and at the same time he strove to limit the exactions made by the ecclesiastics from their flocks. He urged that no priest be placed in charge of a parish unless he knew the local vernacular. To assist in making this ideal feasible, he set up a special department in the young University of Lima for the study of the native tongues and sought to require candidates for Indian parishes to pass an examination before this faculty.[349]

In Peru, as in other parts of Spanish America, the Church introduced and conducted whatever formal education was given, not only for Indians, but also for Spaniards and mestizos. The schools ranged from those of elementary grade up through the universities.[350]

In Peru, too, missionaries introduced new cultivated plants from Europe.

[348] *Acta Sanctorum,* July, Vol. V, pp. 847-910; Schlund, *St. Franziskus und sein Orden in der Heidenmission,* pp. 44-53; Civezza, *Storia delle Missioni Francescane,* Vol. VII, Pt. 2, pp. 94-117; G. Goyau in Descamps, *Histoire Générale Comparé des Missions,* pp. 400, 401.

[349] Pastor, *op. cit.,* Vol. XVIII, pp. 339, 340; Moses, *The Spanish Dependencies in South America,* Vol. I, pp. 318-320.

[350] Ryan, *The Church in the South American Republics,* p. 36; Moses, *op. cit.,* Vol. I, p. 328.

Thus, about 1560, Donna di Retezi, one of the first of the nunnery of St. Clare in Cuzco, brought the cultivation of flax to that region.[351]

The conversion of the uncivilized tribes proved a much more prolonged and difficult task than did that of the civilized peoples. The latter required less than two generations and was substantially completed by A.D. 1600. The former was still unfinished when the upheavals of the wars of independence brought to an end the colonial era and interrupted the progress of the faith. The difficulties were partly physical and partly cultural. Most of the wild tribes lived to the east of the main plateaux, in the valleys which led down from the great mountains which flanked the coast to the Amazon and Paraná. Numbers of these valleys were difficult to reach and the lower courses of many were miasmic and clogged with tropical jungles. Some areas were semi-arid. Few of the tribes were large or lived a settled, agricultural existence. They did not readily conform to the alien, ordered regimen of the missions.

Limitations of space forbid even a summary account of all of the missions among the wild tribes. Only a few can so much as be mentioned. These, however, can be assumed to be fairly typical.

In the seventeenth century the Franciscans pushed their frontiers along the ridges between the Huallaga and Ucayali rivers, both of them tributaries of the upper reaches of the Marañon which in turn is a branch of the Amazon.[352] In 1650 we hear of one tribe said to have been about twenty thousand strong whose members were declared to be competing for baptism.[353] Of another tribe, the Panatahuas, we read that more than seventy thousand are reported to have been baptized.[354] Early in the eighteenth century misfortunes overtook some of these missions. An irruption of pagan Indians destroyed a number of the Christian communities.[355] In the course of the years, several of the missionaries suffered martyrdom.[356] In parts of the same region Jesuits also laboured, and a division of territory had to be arranged between them and the Brothers Minor.[357]

The Franciscan missions were given a fresh impetus by the founding of the mission college of Santa Rosa de Ocapa. The creator of this college bore as his religious name the designation of Francisco de San Jose, but before he had

---

[351] Civezza, *op. cit.,* Vol. VI, p. 719.

[352] Izaguirre, *Historia de las Misiones Franciscanas y Narracion de los Progresos de la Geografia en el Oriente del Peru,* Vol. I, *passim;* Villanueva, *Los Franciscanos en las Indias,* pp. 42, 43.

[353] Izaguirre, *op. cit.,* Vol. I, p. 133.

[354] Izaguirre, *op. cit.,* Vol. I, p. 138.

[355] Izaguirre, *op. cit.,* Vol. I, pp. 137, 138.

[356] Izaguirre, *op. cit.,* Vol. I, pp. 226 ff., 290 ff.

[357] Izaguirre, *op. cit.,* Vol. pp. 285-290.

entered the Order he had been known as Francisco Jiménez. Born in Guadalajara in 1654, he had served as a soldier in Flanders, had then joined the Brothers Minor, and had gone to America as a missionary. There he served for two years in Mexico in connexion with the college at Querétaro. For several years he shared in missions in Central America. Thence, in 1708, he came to Peru. The remainder of his life, about twenty-eight years (he died in 1736) he spent in Peru. In the course of time he built up an enterprise along the Ucayali and on the Pampas del Sacramento, to the west of the Ucayali. As a centre for his missions, on the models with which he had become familiar in Mexico and Central America, he developed a college. This had first been located on the coast south of Lima, at Pisco, but was soon moved to a point nearer the missions, to Ocapa, in the valley of the Jauja, east of Lima.[358] In the year of his death, the field supervised by the college had fifty-eight stations and 8,519 Christians.[359]

In 1742 a revolt began which was headed by Juan Santos, who professed to be a descendant of the Inca, Atahuallpa. In the course of the uprising the Ocapa missions were largely destroyed.[360] However, the members of the Ocapa college were given other fields—to the north in the Western Andes in Cajamarquilla, to the south in Bolivia in the Province of Charcas where a centre was chosen at Tarija, and in Chile, where a college was erected at Chillán.[361]

Northward, in the departments of Huánuco and Cajamarquilla, the latter near the northern edge of what is now Peru, and along the valley of the Huallaga, one of the tributaries of the Marañon, the second half of the eighteenth century witnessed a number of Brothers from Ocapa.[362] In that period, too, missionaries from that same centre made their way along the valley of the Apurimac, one of the branches of the Ucayali, and established reductions, or settlements, of Indians in the mountains which bordered it.[363] In the mountains on the frontiers of Tarma, not far from Ocapa, in the last quarter of the eighteenth century some of the Indians were won.[364]

In the second half of the eighteenth century, from Tarija, the Franciscans founded missions over a wide range of territory in what are now Bolivia, the northern part of Argentina, and the southern part of Peru, in the modern provinces of Tucumán, Salta, Santa Cruz de la Sierra, La Paz, and Arequipo. In Bolivia in 1775 the abandoned Jesuit college of Moquegua was given to

---

[358] Izaguirre, op. cit., Vol. II, pp. 1-103.
[359] Lemmens, Geschichte der Franziskanermissionen, p. 295.
[360] Izaguirre, op. cit., Vol. II, pp. 107-185; Villanueva, op. cit., p. 43.
[361] Izaguirre, op. cit., Vol. II, pp. 189 ff.
[362] Izaguirre, op. cit., Vol. VI, pp. 19-274; Villanueva, op. cit., pp. 46, 47.
[363] Izaguirre, op. cit., Vol. VI, pp. 275 ff.
[364] Izaguirre, op. cit., Vol. VII, passim.

Tarija. In 1796 the missionary college of Tarata arose from Tarija.[365] New missions were begun right up to the close of the eighteenth century and into the first decade of the nineteenth century. Beginning with 1799 uprisings wrought damage to some of the missions.[366] However, the destroyed stations were restored. In 1810 a report declared that among the Chiriguanos, on the north-western edge of the Gran Chaco, the Franciscans had, in fifty-five years, founded twenty-two missions and had made 16,425 converts.[367]

The Maynas, as an irregular and none too closely defined territory in the upper part of the Amazon Valley was called, was entered from the Spanish settlements on the west coast. In it were many tribes. Most of the missionaries in the area were drawn from the Jesuits and the Franciscans. In 1599 Rafael Ferrer, a Jesuit, penetrated the borders, with no other white man, carrying only his Bible, his breviary, and a crucifix. He is said to have induced a number of Indians to begin a settled village life. Before his martyrdom, in 1611, he had led two others of his Society to share his labours.[368] In 1633 some Franciscans entered the region.[369] A little later in that same decade, Brothers Minor made their way from Quito to the Marañon and thence down the Amazon to the Portuguese post at Pará, at the mouth of the mighty river and back to Quito.[370] In 1637 the Jesuits began an extended mission in the Maynas. By 1661 they were said to have baptized 6,880, of whom about three thousand were under six years of age, but in 1660 an epidemic reduced the population.[371] Most of the Jesuits were from the seminary of San Luis in Quito, founded by their Society in 1594. As in many other missions in the Americas, gifts were used to attract the Indians.[372] The Indians of the Maynas were much less tractable than those of the famous Jesuit reductions in Paraguay,[373] and the diversity of languages and the opposition of the Portuguese (who laid claim to part of the country) prevented the missions from enjoying a rapid growth.[374] Still, it is said that before the expulsion of the Society from the Spanish domains (1767) one hundred and fifty-seven Jesuits had served in the Maynas and had carried the Christian message to half a million Indians.[375] A little

---

[365] Lemmens, *Geschichte der Franziskanermissionen*, p. 321.
[366] Izaguirre, *op. cit.*, Vol. III, pp. 191-295.
[367] Rippy and Nelson, *Crusaders of the Jungle*, p. 230.
[368] Rippy and Nelson, *op. cit.*, pp. 199, 200.
[369] Figueróa, *Relación de las Misiones de la Compañia de Jesus en el Pais de los Maynas*, p. vii.
[370] Rippy and Nelson, *op. cit.*, pp. 201, 202.
[371] Figueróa, *op. cit.*, pp. 6, 16-18, 161.
[372] Rippy and Nelson, *op. cit.*, p. 194.
[373] Moses, *The Spanish Dependencies in South America*. Vol. II, pp. 178, 179.
[374] Figueróa, *op. cit.*, pp. 293-339.
[375] Rippy and Nelson, *op. cit.*, pp. 203-215.

earlier, in 1745, the Jesuit missions of the Maynas and Quixos were said to have 12,853 in their charge, of whom 9,858 were baptized.[376] This latter figure may be excessive, for at no time do the Jesuits seem to have had much more than ten thousand aborigines living under their supervision.[377]

After the expulsion of the Jesuits, for a time seculars were placed in charge of the Maynas missions. However, they proved unsatisfactory and Franciscans were soon substituted. Some of these were from the College of Santa Rosa at Ocapa.[378] Others, on the Caquetá and Putumayo, northern tributaries of the Amazon, were from the College of Popoyan in New Granada.[379] By A.D. 1800 the Maynas missions were said to be in a sad state of decline. The population is declared to have decreased by fifty per cent, not enough priests were available to care for the reductions which remained, and some of the few who were there were said to be too ignorant to say mass and not interested in their work.[380]

The conquest of Chile by the Spaniards was begun soon after that of Peru. The expedition which is looked back upon as having begun effective Spanish domination was led by Valdivia and reached the present Santiago. No great civilized Indian populations existed in Chile. Throughout the colonial period, a fierce people, the Araucanians, proudly maintained their independence and from time to time wasted the Spanish settlements. Some others of the aborigines submitted, and here, as elsewhere in the Spanish possessions, efforts were made by many who had had their consciences quickened by Christianity to lighten the lot of the conquered.[381]

Christian missionaries early entered Chile—at first Mercedarians, Franciscans, and a secular.[382] Later came Jesuits.[383] In much of the country, wars with the Araucanians long made missions difficult and dangerous. In 1641 a treaty brought a formal peace by conceding to the Araucanians the territory from the Bio-Bio, at Concepción, southwards. Missions were eventually conducted even south of this line. For a time in the eighteenth century the Franciscans left the Araucanians to the Jesuits.[384] In 1756, however, Franciscans from the missionary College of Ocapa founded a daughter institution at Chillán, not far

[376] Jorge Juan and Antonio de Ulloa, *Noticias Secretas de America*, p. 364.
[377] Rippy and Nelson, *op. cit.*, pp. 216, 217.
[378] Izaguirre, *op. cit.*, Vol. VIII, *passim*.
[379] Rippy and Nelson, *op. cit.*, pp. 217, 218.
[380] Rippy and Nelson, *op. cit.*, p. 218, citing José Pardo y Barreda, *Arbitraje de Límites entre el Perú y el Ecuador* (Madrid, 2 vols., 1905), Vol. I, pp. 182, 183.
[381] Moses, *The Spanish Dependencies in South America*, Vol. I, pp. 169-184, Vol. II, pp. 49-57, 111-120.
[382] Civezza, *Storia delle Missioni Francescane*, Vol. VII, Part 2, p. 162; Lemmens, *Geschichte der Franziskanermissionen*, p. 307.
[383] Crétineau-Joly, *Histoire de la Compagnie de Jésus*, Vol. II, p. 422.
[384] Lemmens, *op. cit.*, p. 310.

from Concepción and the Araucanian territory. Missions were carried south-ward to the island of Chiloé and to other islands on the south coast. After the expulsion of the Jesuits the former missions of the Society were placed (1771) directly under the College of Ocapa, and by the end of the eighteenth century most of the population of Chiloé and the adjacent archipelago was said to be nominally Christian,[385] On the mainland the missions were under the College of Chillán.[386]

In connexion with Francis Solanus and the College of Ocapa we have al-ready mentioned the missions which were conducted to the east of the Andes in what are now Bolivia, Northern Argentina, and Paraguay. Here, in what is now Bolivia, in the seventeenth and eighteenth centuries the Jesuits had successful missions among the Mojos. These Indians seemed responsive to the missionaries. In 1705 thirty Jesuits were reported to have among them fifteen or sixteen towns and between twenty-five and thirty thousand Indians under their tutelage.[387] When in 1767 the Jesuits were expelled, they were said to have fifteen towns with a population of about thirty thousand. They were re-placed by Franciscans, but the missions did not fully recover from the blow given by the transfer.[388]

The Jesuits also had missions among the Chiquitos, a group of tribes on what are now the borders between Bolivia and Brazil. In 1732 the Jesuits were said to have among them seven towns with about forty-two hundred families. In 1766, on the eve of the end of the Jesuit regime, the missions were ten in number and possessed a population of 5,173 families consisting of 23,788 persons.[389]

As we have seen in several of the last paragraphs, Spanish missions were widely extended in the broad territories east of the Andes in the modern Bolivia, Argentine, and Paraguay. The Spanish penetration of that region began early. The Rio de la Plata was entered in 1516. Buenos Aires was founded in 1535. Asunción in Paraguay was established three years later.[390] It was in this latter frontier settlement that Cabeza de Vaca, of whom we have already spoken, met tragic failure in an attempt to enforce humane treatment of the Indians. To these lands Franciscans penetrated at the time of the earliest settlements.[391]

Tucumán had some famous bishops. In 1595 there came to the see Fernando

[385] Izaguirre, op. cit., Vol. IV, pp. 11 ff., Vol. V, pp. 157 ff.
[386] Lemmens, op. cit., pp. 312, 313.
[387] Rippy and Nelson, op. cit., p. 224.
[388] Rippy and Nelson, op. cit., p. 225.
[389] Rippy and Nelson, Crusaders of the Jungle, p. 227.
[390] Moses, The Spanish Dependencies in South America, Vol. I, pp. 188-199.
[391] Civezza, Storia delle Missioni Francescane, Vol. VI, p. 726.

de Trejo i Sanabria, a Franciscan, an American-born white. In the nineteen years of his episcopate he was a stout defender of Indians and Negroes. He was also a promoter of education and founded (1613) a university at Cordova.[392] Tomas de Torres, a Dominican, Bishop of Asunción in 1620 and of Tucumán in 1626, zealously set about a reform of the morals of the Spaniards as, supposedly, an essential preliminary to successful missions among the Indians.[393]

The most famous of the missions, in this area, and, indeed, one of the most prominent anywhere in this entire period were those developed by the Jesuits in Paraguay.[394] Various tentative beginnings were made in the sixteenth century. Not until the first decade of the seventeenth century was the system really instituted. The plan adopted was not novel. Foreshadowings of it had long been seen in both Spanish and Portuguese America and in the missions of other orders as well as of the Society of Jesus. In most of its main outlines, it was the programme followed by missions of several orders in many parts of the Spanish possessions. The purpose was the conversion of the Indians and their protection against the vices and exploitation of the colonies. The essence of the system was the collection of the Indians into villages under the supervision of the missionaries. Here the aborigines were afforded protection, were given Christian instruction, were taught to work, and were organized into a closely regulated communal life. Each village had a church, and on this building and its elaborate services the Jesuits, in characteristic fashion, lavished

---

[392] Moses, *South America on the Eve of Emancipation*, pp. 143 ff.

[393] Goyau in Descamps, *Histoire Générale Comparée des Missions*, p. 401.

[394] On the Jesuit missions in Paraguay a large literature exists. An old standard account, by a Jesuit, is Pierre François Xavier de Charlevoix, *Histoire du Paraguay* (Paris, Desaint, 6 vols., 1757). A collection of pertinent documents, with extensive notes, also by a Jesuit, is Pablo Pastells, *Historia de la Compañia de Jesús en la Provencia del Paraguay* (Madrid, Librería General de Victoriano Suárez, 5 vols., 1912-1933). One extensive study from a Protestant, anti-Roman Catholic viewpoint is J. Pfotenhauer, *Die Missionen der Jesuiten in Paraguay* (Gütersloh, C. Bertelsmann, 3 vols., 1891-1893). A more scholarly study is Maria Fassbinder, *Der "Jesuitstaat" in Paraguay* (Halle, Max Niemeyer, 1926, pp. ix, 161). Another, not so carefully documented, is E. Gothein, *Der christlich-sociale Staat der Jesuiten in Paraguay* (Leipzig, Duncker und Humblot, 1883, pp. viii, 68). A monograph which is not so much a history as a study of the economic organization and ethics of the missions is Johann Sebastian Geer, *Der Jesuitstaat in Paraguay* (Nürnberg, Krische und Co., 1928, pp. 112). A popular account is W. H. Koebel, *In Jesuit Land. The Jesuit Missions of Paraguay* (London, Stanley Paul & Co., no date, pp. 381). An older account is Muratori, *Relation des Missions du Paraguai* (translated from the Italian, Paris, Veuve Bordelet, 1757, pp. xxiv, 402). An excellent brief account is Bertrand, *Les Missions ou Reductions des Jesuites au Paraguay*, in *Revue d'Histoire des Missions* (Dec., 1928), Vol. V, pp. 555-571. Some material exists in *Lettres Edifiantes et Curieuses* (Paris, 4 vols., Mairet et Fournier, 1838-1843), Vol. II. Scholarly summaries, with excellent bibliographies, from the Roman Catholic viewpoint, are A. Huonder in *Catholic Encyclopedia*, Vol. XII, pp. 688-700, and Schmidlin-Braun, *Catholic Mission History*, pp. 388 ff.

wealth and devotion. The music and the choirs of these churches were widely celebrated. Cattle-raising and agriculture were carefully nurtured and supervised, and the Indians were taught various handicrafts. The missions obtained their financial support through the sale of their products. They entered extensively into commerce. The missionaries had civil as well as religious and economic supervision. With the consent of the Spanish King they organized armed forces of Indians to protect the reductions against raids of slave-traders. The reductions constituted a kind of state within a state. They were, too, a method of guarding the frontier against foreign—in this case Portuguese— aggression. They were used by the state, as were the California, Texas, and Florida missions, as a method of extending and securing Spanish rule on the borders.

The missions were scattered over a wide territory and embraced a number of tribes. They extended over portions of what are now Bolivia, the Argentine as far as Northern Patagonia, Paraguay, Uruguay, and the Brazilian states of Paraná and Rio Grande do Sul. The largest single tribal group was the Guaranis.

Statistics are somewhat uncertain, but the total number of Indians in the missions probably never much exceeded 150,000 at any one time. At the expulsion of the Jesuits, about 106,000 Indians were said to be living in thirty-eight villages and under eighty-three missionaries. Epidemics took serious toll. More than once, especially in the earlier part of the period, slave-raiders from the Brazilian frontier wrought havoc. Yet for a century and a half the missions went on, and for the majority of their inhabitants afforded a regulated, peaceful life, with religious instruction and nurture, and a mild but firm supervision of morals and social life.

The expulsion of the Jesuits in 1767 brought disaster. The Society had always had enemies among the colonists who looked with covetous eyes upon the fancied riches of the missions and resented the stout refusal of the fathers to allow their wards to be enslaved or recruited for the plantations or mines of the whites. Critics, too, were fond of saying that the Jesuits were shrewd business men who were competitors with lay folk in trade and were as much interested in making money as they were in saving souls. About 1750, indeed, serious disturbances began Moreover, friction between the Jesuits and secular and episcopal authorities was chronic. After 1767 attempts were made to replace the Jesuits with other orders, notably the Franciscans. The Franciscans valiantly strove to keep the transition from being disastrous. In 1786 they founded the mission college of San Carlos at San Lorenzo on the Paraná, the better to provide personnel and supervision for the former Jesuit field. However, most of the missions rapidly declined. Slave-raiders worked their will on the now almost defenceless villages, and the Indians were killed, carried off, or scattered. If in no other section of Spanish America had a group of missions among uncivilized tribes arisen to such prominence, in no other was the eventual ruin so sadly spectacular.

No other of the European powers of the sixteenth, seventeenth, and eighteenth centuries so systematically and effectively propagated the Christian faith over so wide a range of territory as did Spain. To the vast areas in the New World covered by Spanish missions must be added the Philippines, to which we are to come in a later chapter. The Portuguese attempted to cover a larger proportion of the surface of the globe, but their missions were neither so comprehensive nor so effective. In diversity of peoples and lands approached, the Protestant Moravians surpassed the Roman Catholic Spaniards, but in the total number of converts they were far behind them. The Russians, too, claimed vast regions, but their missions were far less numerous. Indeed, up to this time no other government had so nearly succeeded in winning the acceptance of its official faith by the majority of the inhabitants of so many square miles of land.

We can best summarize the Spanish religious achievement in the Americas by seeking to give, in brief compass, answers to the major questions which we raised at the outset of this work.

First, what was it that spread? It was Spanish Roman Catholic Christianity. It was, of course, Christianity, and was in the stream of the impulse given by Jesus. It was Roman Catholic, for the Spaniards were proud of the name Catholic, their rulers were stern against all departures from Catholic orthodoxy, and their Catholicism was of the kind which centred at Rome. The Christianity was Spanish. It was a lineal descendant of the faith which had been planted in the Iberian Peninsula in the early Christian centuries, it had developed a crusading form in the long struggle with the Moslem, and in the later years of its political triumph over Islam it had become intolerant and at times fanatical. It was a Christianity which was more and more controlled by the Crown and which became, therefore, in part, an adjunct of the state. This Spanish Roman Catholic Christianity had, too, felt profoundly the new religious life of the sixteenth century which led to reforms in the old Church. Many of the missionaries were the product of this reformation. Yet much of Spanish Christianity was but little touched by the revival, was formal, and tolerated many priests who found the clerical status a convenient source of livelihood and power and in practice were often ignorant and departed widely from the ethical standards of the New Testament.

Why did this Christianity spread? It was partly because the Spaniards automatically remained professing Christians. It was even more because the state supported it and used it as an instrument for the assimilation of the aborigines to Spanish culture and for the extension of the frontiers of the Spanish occupation. Christianity spread, too, among the masses of civilized Indians because it was the faith of the *conquistadores* and because it was easier than not to acquiesce in the religion of the new masters. Still more important than state initiative and support was the zeal of missionaries. Hundreds of men actuated in part and some of them primarily by a devotion to the Christian faith as they understood it, endured physical hardship and separation from all but a few others of their race, acquired alien tongues, and persevered in the long, slow, difficult task of inducing Indians to settle down around a mission and of inculcating a religious faith, methods of agriculture and industry, and manners and customs which were quite different from those with which these children of nature had been familiar.

By what processes did Christianity spread? Little compulsion was used. Force might be invoked to induce the Indian to submit to the Spaniard, but seldom were the aborigines confronted with the hard alternative of the sword or baptism. Among the civilized peoples, clergy quickly persuaded the submissive thousands to accept baptism, destroyed the images of the old cults, demolished or transformed into Christian shrines the native fanes, and imparted a minimum of instruction in Christian dogmas and practices. Lay masters of the natives were required to see that their wards were given spiritual care. As for the uncivilized tribes, they were persuaded to gather into communities about a church where they were organized into villages, were inducted into an ordered economic and social life, and, as an essential part of that life, were taught the main tenets of Spanish Roman Catholic Christianity and were given regularly the spiritual ministrations of the Church.

What effect did this Spanish Roman Catholic Christianity have upon its environment? First of all, for the large majority of the Indians in the Spanish colonial domains, this Christianity displaced the cults which it found in possession. Here and there these cults secretly persisted or elements from them were carried over into the succeeding Christianity, but for the most part they disappeared. What survived was attitudes which they had bred: their former adherents expected of Christianity what had been demanded of the old religions. In the next place, Christianity served to soften the harshness of the Spanish domination. The Spaniards felt that they must have cheap labour and they continued to be the dominant race. However, stirred by the Christian impulse, many Spaniards, from monarchs, governors, and the higher clergy down to humble members of religious orders, sought to make of the Spanish rule a blessing and not a curse. On page after page, *The Laws of the Indies* and the records of the Spanish administration bear witness to the power of Christianity to mitigate the evils of the conquest and rule of one race by another. Thanks to the official exponent of Christianity, the Church, Spanish America was provided with a system of schools from primary grades through the university. That educational system might leave much to be desired, but it was all that the colonies could boast. Moved by their Christian purpose, missionaries became intrepid explorers and pioneers of Spanish rule. They reduced Indian tongues to writing, prepared grammars and dictionaries, and wrote the beginnings of a vernacular literature. They introduced grains, fruits, and new types of domestic animals. They taught new methods of agriculture and fresh handicrafts. They brought thousands of Indians to a settled existence. They were the chief recorders of the pre-Spanish cultures. They were pioneers of Spanish culture and the Spanish language. They abolished polygamy (although in practice sex standards were often not improved and in some instances may have deteriorated). They helped to eliminate inter-tribal warfare, head-hunting, and the use of torture. They fought slavery and the slave traffic. It is clear that in many phases of its life, Spanish colonial America was profoundly affected by Christianity.

Yet it must be noted that in many respects the life of the Church in Spanish America fell very far short of the New Testament ideal. A large proportion of the clergy, and especially of the seculars, to whom the parishes in the regions which had longest been Christian were entrusted, were notorious for their evil living. The situation seems to have become worse as the centuries wore on.[395] It is cold comfort to say that conditions were as bad among many of the clergy of Europe in the Middle Ages. In Spanish America there were never the pulsing movements for reform welling up from below which in Medieval Europe were evidence that the Christian message had ploughed deeply into the popular mind and conscience and was giving rise to fresh efforts to make it effective. Few if any new monastic movements arose and only a few sects. Spanish American Christianity was passively content to reproduce what had been transmitted from Europe. It must be noted, moreover, that when the missionaries were withdrawn, as happened occasionally in the colonial period and more

---

[395] As in Juan and Ulloa, *Noticias Secretas de America*, pp. 489 ff.; Ryan, *The Church in the South American Republics*, pp. 6-8; Schmidlin-Braun, *Catholic Mission History*, pp. 502-505.

markedly after political independence, numbers of the Christian Indians apostatized. Christianity had not taken sufficiently deep root to go on without the continued injection of life from the Church in Europe. By A.D. 1800 Christianity had been present in Spanish America about as long as it had in the Roman Empire before Constantine. Yet in the former it had not begun to stir the human spirit to anything like the creativity in thought and organization that it had in the latter.

Much of the passivity and lack of new life in Spanish American Christianity must be ascribed to environment. It was partly the effect of Spain upon the Christianity which was transmitted to the New World, and partly the effect of racial, political, and social conditions in the Americas. By A.D. 1800 Christianity in Spain had ceased to send out many new shoots or to produce great saints. In this it shared in the general stagnation of the nation—a stagnation which was no less marked because its causes are debatable and obscure. The land from which missionaries came was in a decay which contrasted lamentably with the abounding vitality of the fifteenth and sixteenth centuries. In the Americas the entire colonial system was one of regimentation and repression. In Church, state, and society the whites dominated the Indians, Negroes, and mixed stocks. In Church and state, too, the Spanish-born whites rather than the Creoles were in power. The Inquisition was at hand to stamp out every suspicion of variation from Roman Catholic doctrine. The Church was under the close control of the Crown. It had life, but no independent life. It is not strange that under these circumstances Spanish American Christianity was stereotyped and displayed little originality.

Yet it must also be said that if the processes by which Christianity was introduced and perpetuated in Spanish America were accountable for the weaknesses of the resulting religious life, they had at least had marked successes. Because of them the large majority of the population of the Spanish colonial possessions were professedly Christian and Spanish American culture bore marked evidence of the impress of Christianity. Moreover, decadent and stagnant though much of Spain had become, right down to the revolutions brought by political independence, and in spite of the serious dislocations wrought by the expulsion of the Jesuits, on several frontiers missions were extending their borders. The day of the pioneering by secular *conquistadores* had passed. It was missionaries, acting under the propulsive power of Christianity, who were continuing to enlarge the Spanish domains. It was only Christianity which was able to galvanize the somnolent Spanish soul into effective, expansive action.

Chapter IV

PORTUGUESE AMERICA

IN ITS general outlines, the spread of Christianity in Portuguese America resembled that in Spanish America. In both areas a Roman Catholic power was in possession. In both the Crown obtained from the Pope a grant of patronage which entailed practically absolute control over the Church and over the direction of missions. In both regions Christianity was confronted with the triple challenge of retaining its hold upon the white settlers, traditionally of that faith but many of them prone to let it sit lightly upon them in the new environment, of winning the Indians, and of bringing within its fold the Negroes who were imported from Africa to provide labour for the white colonists. In both zealous regulars conducted missions among non-Christians. In both a type of mission was conducted in which the Indian was induced to lead a settled life under the tutelage and protection of the missionary. In Brazil the missions were called *aldeas* or *doutrinas*, but the essential principles were the same. In both Spanish and Portuguese America Christian missionaries fought the exploitation of the aborigines by the whites, stirred the Crown into enacting protective measures for the Indians, and thereby won the enmity of a large proportion of the lay community. In both a nominal Christianity eventually prevailed.

Yet marked differences existed between Spanish and Portuguese America in the expansion of Christianity. In Portuguese America no great bodies of Indians with an indigenous civilization existed, such as the Spaniards had found in Mexico and Peru, who quickly followed political submission with religious acquiescence. Portuguese missions were, therefore, among uncivilized tribes who, as in Spanish America, constituted a more perplexing problem. Vast areas of Brazil were, too, for reasons of climate and geography, difficult of access, more so than any similarly extensive regions in the Spanish possessions. Moreover, Portugal was a smaller country than Spain, and yet its colonial ambitions led it to attempt to control a much larger proportion of the earth's surface. It had footholds in Africa, India, Ceylon, the East Indies, the Malay Peninsula, and China. Even had race and geography not been so adverse, it could not, therefore, have occupied Brazil as effectively as the Spaniards did their sections of the Americas. Then, too, Portuguese rule in Brazil was more disturbed by incursions of other European powers than was that of Spain in most of its American possessions. For a few years after 1555 the French occupied the harbour of Rio de Janeiro. From 1580 until 1640 Portugal was united with Spain under the Spanish Crown. From 1630 to 1661 the Dutch had control of territory around Pernambuco. All of these factors combined to make the spread of Christianity in Brazil more nearly incomplete than in Spanish America. A larger percentage of country remained comparatively untouched, and the effect of Christianity in much of the area covered was more superficial than in some sections of Spanish America.

Christian missionaries shared in the very first contact of the Portuguese with Brazil. On the voyage in which he discovered Brazil, in 1500, Cabral was accompanied by Franciscans. It was the leader of these Brothers Minor who celebrated the first mass on the shores of Brazil. Indians are said to have observed the ceremony with reverence. To the land thus revealed the name of Santa Cruz was piously given.[1] However, no permanent settlement was made nor were missions begun at this time.

Gradually the Portuguese commenced occupying the shores of the vast land thus disclosed to them. At various times in the first half of the sixteenth century and for periods of shorter or longer duration, spiritual sons of Francis of Assisi laboured among the Indians of the region and made converts.[2]

A new and more vigorous period of Portuguese government and missions opened in 1549. In this year King John III united the administration of his Brazilian possessions under a Governor-general and appointed to that post Thomé de Sousa, a man of energy and ability who had already acquired colonial experience in Africa and India. The capital was established at Bahia, in a city named significantly São Salvador.[3] In 1551 Pope Julius III granted to the kings of Portugal a right of patronage in Brazil which put the monarchs in control of the ecclesiastical affairs of the colony.[4]

The youthful Society of Jesus was a rising power in Portugal. Following a request of John III, Francis Xavier had already sailed to the East and was in the full tide of his brilliant career. It is not surprising, therefore, that with

---

[1] Maghalhães, *The Histories of Brazil,* translated by Stetson, Vol. II, pp. 20-22; Southey, *History of Brazil,* Vol. I, pp. 9 ff.; Lemmens, *Geschichte der Franziskanermissionen,* p. 270; Villanueva, *Los Franciscanos en las Indias,* p. 10.

[2] Civezza, *Storia delle Missioni Francescane,* Vol. VI, pp. 768-775; Lemmens, *op. cit.,* p. 270; Elsner, *Die deutschen Franziskaner in Brazilien,* pp. 14-19; Jaboatam, *Nova Orbe Serafico Braisilico,* Vol. II, pp. 11 ff.

[3] Vasconcellos, *Chronica da Companhia de Jesu do Estado do Brasil,* Book I, Chap. 25; Southey, *op. cit.,* Vol. I, pp. 221, 222.

[4] Rippy and Nelson, *Crusaders of the Jungle,* pp. 233-237.

Thomé de Sousa a contingent of Jesuits should sail for Brazil. The leader was Manoel de Nobrega, a Portuguese of noble family.[5] The establishment at São Salvador (Bahia) of a bishopric, the first in Portuguese America, soon followed.[6] The continued and growing influence of the Society at the Portuguese court ensured the prominence of the Jesuits in the religious life of Brazil. Other orders followed, the Carmelites in 1580 or 1581, the Benedictines in 1581,[7] and the Capuchins in 1642.[8] The Capuchins were first from Brittany and later from Italy.[9] The Observant Franciscans continued. However, it was the Jesuits who long held the most prominent place in the missions of the land. Before the close of 1555, the members of the Society were at four centres and a province of the Society had been created for Brazil with Nobrega as its head.[10] The Jesuits attempted to inculcate a higher standard of morals among the colonists.[11] In 1550 they introduced Portuguese orphans from Lisbon who they hoped would learn the native tongues and help instruct the Indians. Some of these later entered the Society.[12] Schools were organized in which native children were taught.[13]

The labours thus begun so energetically by the Jesuits did not save the progress of Christianity in Brazil from serious problems. The first Bishop of São Salvador was zealous but sometimes far from wise. The seculars whom he brought with him were from the dregs of the priesthood and by their lives and their indiscriminate administration of the sacraments undid much of what the Jesuits had attempted to accomplish with the white population. In 1556 the Bishop himself was captured by cannibal Indians and eaten.[14] Many of the Portuguese, too, were criminals who had been transported to the colony and who gave the missionaries much trouble. They mistreated Indian women, encouraged intertribal wars, and are even said to have participated in cannibalism.[15]

---

[5] Vasconcellos, *op. cit.*, Book I, Chaps. 8 ff.; Southey, *op. cit.*, Vol. I, pp. 222-224; Nobrega, *Carta I* (from Bahia, 1549) in Vasconcellos, *op. cit.*, Vol. II, appendix, pp. 289-292.

[6] Jann, *Die katholischen Missionen in Indien, China, und Japan,* p. 296.

[7] Lemmens, *op. cit.*, p. 271; Marie, *Histoire des Instituts Religieux et Missionaires,* p. 34.

[8] *Capucins Missionaires. Missions Françaises,* pp. 72, 73; Terzorio, *Manuale Historicum Missionum Ordinis Minorum Capuccinorum,* p. 313.

[9] Terzorio, *op. cit.*, pp. 313-318.

[10] Robert Ricard, *Les Jésuites au Brésil Pendant la Seconde Moitié du XVIe Siècle (1549-1597),* in *Revue d'Histoires des Missions* (Vol. XIV, pp. 321-366, 435-470), p. 328.

[11] Pastor, *History of the Popes,* Vol. XIII, p. 292.

[12] Ricard, *op. cit.*, p. 333.

[13] Ricard, *op. cit.*, p. 334.

[14] Pastor, *op. cit.*, Vol. XIII, p. 292: Ryan, *The Church in the South American Republics,* p. 82.

[15] Ryan, *op. cit.*, pp. 83, 84.

In spite of obstacles, the Jesuits expanded their efforts and their enterprises prospered. Between 1549 and 1583 or 1584 they are said to have made about one hundred thousand converts in Brazil.[16] They developed villages of Christian Indians—a device which we have often seen in Spanish America and which we are to find Christian missionaries using in one form or another among primitive folk in many lands. Not all of the Christian villages had a resident missionary, but each had a church and many also had a school.[17] In 1559, or ten years after the first contingent, more than forty Jesuits were at work.[18] Five years later, in 1564, the number had increased to fifty-two.[19]

In 1553 there arrived in Brazil one of the most notable of the Jesuit missionaries to that land, Joseph de Anchieta.[20] Born in the Canaries in 1533 or 1534, Anchieta had studied at the University of Coimbra. Once in Brazil, he displayed an unusual capacity for learning the native tongues. Most of his earlier labours were in the South, in São Paulo and on the adjacent coast. Eventually he became Provincial of his Society, and in connexion with his duties travelled extensively through the land. He died June 9, 1597, and, fittingly, in an Indian village.

Another famous Jesuit of the sixteenth century was Ignacio de Azevedo. He was from one of the most distinguished families of Portugal and was a brother of a Viceroy of the Indies. In 1565 he was named as Visitor General of his Society in Brazil. After a prolonged tour of inspection in Brazil, he returned to Europe, partly for the purpose of obtaining recruits for the mission. In 1570 he was on his way back with large reinforcements, when he and his company were captured at sea by French Huguenots and were killed.[21]

This disaster checked for a time but did not permanently stop the growth of the Jesuit force. In 1584 the Society had a staff of a hundred and forty-two, of whom sixty-six were priests.[22]

During the sixteenth century the missionary efforts of the Jesuits were furthered by a succession of civil Governors who were favourable to them. Some of these took positive measures to protect the villages which were under the Society, and particularly to keep out those who wished to raid them to obtain slaves.[23] One of the most deeply religious of the Governors, Mem de Sá,

[16] Ricard, op. cit., p. 337.
[17] Ricard, op. cit., pp. 359 ff.
[18] Vasconcellos, op. cit., Book II, Chap. 65.
[19] Vasconcellos, op. cit., Book III, Chap. 35.
[20] Vasconcellos, op. cit., Book I, Chap. 136; Ricard op. cit., pp. 445 ff.
[21] Vasconcellos, op. cit., Book IV; Pastor, op. cit., Vol. XVIII, pp. 326-330; Crétineau-Joly, Histoire de la Compagnie de Jésus, Vol. II, pp. 109-118.
[22] Ricard, op. cit., p. 453.
[23] Ricard, op. cit., pp. 460-463.

came out in 1558.[24] He wished to hasten the conversion of the aborigines. He also forbade any Indian from one of the Christian communities being sold as a slave and even prohibited, except on authorization from himself, the restoration to their masters of runaway slaves who had taken refuge with the missionaries.[25]

The Jesuits addressed themselves not only to the Indians who had not been brought into captivity by the white man, but also to the slaves, both Indians and Negroes. We hear of the baptism of slaves, of opportunities given them for the confessional, of sermons preached to them, and of the sacraments of baptism and the communion administered to them.[26]

As in so many other regions in the Americas, the missionaries engaged in a prolonged and at times discouraging struggle to protect the Indian from those who would enslave him. Not always were the Governors' orders for the security of the Christian settlements respected.[27] The battle had again and again to be renewed, for, as in the Spanish colonies, the white settlers were in need of labour if they were to make their holdings profitable, and sought it by reducing the Indians to servitude.

In the seventeenth century a staunch advocate of the Indians was the Jesuit, Antonio Vieira. In his youth he served five years among the Indians and Negroes of Brazil. He then returned to Portugal and became one of the most distinguished preachers of his day. Against the initial opposition of the King, who did not wish to lose him, he insisted upon going back to Brazil (1652). Once in that country, he was appalled by the spiritual and moral condition of the colonists. He found that many of the Portuguese settlers did not go to mass throughout the year, that few observed the holy days, that churches and priests were entirely too few, that such priests as there were had been banished from Portugal for misconduct or had come because they had been unable to win a living elsewhere, and that episcopal supervision was entirely inadequate. He discovered that the laws allowed the enslavement of Indians taken in just wars, that under this guise wars were frequent and the Indians were being exterminated, and that those Indians who were called free were even more exploited by the Portuguese than were the slaves. Vieira wrote the King what he found. He also preached to the settlers, denouncing their treatment of the Negroes and the Indians. Finding that protests in Brazil were ineffective, he returned to Portugal to lay the situation in person before

[24] Vasconcellos, op. cit., Book II, Chaps. 47, 48.
[25] Ricard, op. cit., p. 465.
[26] Ricard, op. cit., pp. 467, 468. On a general summary of the early work of the Jesuits, see Maghalhães, The Histories of Brazil, Stetson's translation, Vol. II, Chap. 13.
[27] Ricard, op. cit., p. 465.

the King. He obtained a decree (1655) which was designed to cure the worst abuses and which placed the Indian settlements under the Jesuits. Thereupon he returned to Brazil, partly to see that the law was enforced and partly to continue his mission to the Indians. The edict aroused resentment against the Jesuits, and a popular tumult deported a number of the Society, including Vieira. However, eventually the law wrought improvement in the lot of the Indians. Vieira made his way back to Brazil and died there (1697) at an extreme old age. Not only was he one of the great preachers of his day, who commanded a rapt hearing equally in Rome, Lisbon, the cities of Brazil, and among the aborigines. He was also a master of prose style, an unwearied champion of the Indians and the poor, and an indefatigable missionary. He is said to have baptized tens of thousands and to have organized scores of Indian towns north of the Amazon.[28]

Vieira's long life of efforts on behalf of the Indians did not end the struggle. Again and again the Jesuits came forward in defence of the aborigines. Repeatedly they incurred the enmity of planters and slave-traders, and accusations against them were made to the King. Various measures were taken to protect the Indians, until, in 1755, the enslavement of Indians was definitely forbidden.[29]

The lack of episcopal supervision which Vieira lamented was only slowly remedied. São Salvador (Bahia) remained the sole see until 1676 and 1677, when it was raised to metropolitan rank and suffragan dioceses were created for Pernambuco, Maranhão, and Rio de Janeiro.[30] Throughout the colonial period the provision for the religious care of the white and mixed population and of the Christian Indians outside the missions of the regulars remained inadequate. Intellectually Brazil was distinctly behind Spanish America. The stipends for the seculars were niggardly and few men of the better classes took up the calling. Settlements on the coast and in the interior were scattered, and except for the larger cities usually were forced to be content with the services of itinerant priests. In the cities conditions were better, for here the religious orders had houses, and here not only was religious care given, but also various institutions were founded under ecclesiastical auspices for orphans, the sick, the poor, and travellers.[31]

The progress of the Christian faith in Brazil was dealt a serious blow by

[28] Southey, op. cit., Vol. II, pp. 456-548, Vol. III, pp. 33, 34; J. C. Reville in Catholic Encyclopedia, Vol. XV, pp. 415, 416; Ryan, op. cit., pp. 85, 86.

[29] Ryan, op. cit., p. 85; Crétineau-Joly, Histoire de la Compagnie de Jesus, Vol. V, pp. 89-98.

[30] Jann, op. cit., pp. 211, 212, 296.

[31] Ryan, op. cit., pp. 86, 87.

the suppression of the Jesuits in the Portuguese possessions (1759). This act was in consequence of a rising tide of criticism against the Society in various parts of Europe, but in the Portuguese domains was hastened by an Indian revolt which broke out over the attempt of the civil authorities to remove from one place to another some of the Paraguay missions of the Jesuits. Over four hundred members of the Society were transported to Lisbon. Since the Jesuits were the leading order in the missions of Brazil, and since their colleges had a dominant place in what little education the region possessed, the reverse to the Christian forces was serious.[32] Moreover, because of the restrictive policy of the state towards regulars in general in the latter part of the eighteenth century, it was impossible for other orders to step in, as they did in Spanish America, and make good the loss.

Although the Jesuits were the most prominent of the religious orders in Brazil, they were not the only regulars. We have seen that Franciscans had preceded them, and that Capuchins, Benedictines, and Carmelites were present. In 1724 the Capuchins were said to have nine residences among the Indians with a total population of about 280.[33] Mercedarians and the Oratorians of Olinda were also at work.[34]

The Franciscans were especially strong. Soon after the union with Spain, Philip II, ever zealous for his faith, encouraged the sending out of Brothers Minor. In 1585 a contingent arrived in Pernambuco. Before the end of the century missions for the Indians had been begun not only around Pernambuco but also in the regions of Pará and Maranhão. The Dutch occupation in the middle of the seventeenth century brought difficulties but after the restoration of Portuguese rule further progress was registered. Shortly after the middle of the seventeenth century what had been known as a custody was erected into a province of the order, and before the end of the century a second province was carved out in the South from the first. In 1680 the northern province had thirteen monasteries with two hundred and thirty members, and the southern province ten houses and one hundred and seventy members. In 1724 the state forbade the foundation of new houses, and in the middle of the eighteenth century hostility on the part of the civil authorities led to decline. However, partial compensation was found in the North, among the Indian tribes of the Amazon. Here in 1740 forty mission stations were counted.[35]

[32] Schmidlin-Braun, *Catholic Mission History*, p. 504.
[33] Terzorio, *op. cit.*, p. 320.
[34] Schmidlin-Braun, *op. cit.*, p. 505.
[35] Lemmens, *op. cit.*, pp. 271-274; Elsner, *op. cit.*, pp. 20-49; Cletus Espey, *Festschrift zum Silberjubiläum der Wiedererrichtung der Provinz von der unbefleckten Empfängnis*

In general, as we have indicated, Christianity made less impression upon Brazil than it did upon Spanish America. A smaller proportion of its population adopted the Christian name, much of such Christianity as existed was even more superficial, education was more backward, measures in behalf of the aborigines were more tardily enacted and enforced, and the second half of the eighteenth century witnessed a much more serious decline in the activity of the orders. Whereas in Spanish America, to the very end of the colonial period, in many places the frontier of Christianity was pushed forward, in Portuguese America it had begun to contract.

Yet Christianity had not been without marked effects in Brazil. Most of the Portuguese had been held to an outward profession of the Christian name, tens of thousands of Indians and Negroes had been brought within the fold of the Church, and, thanks chiefly to missionaries and the Christian conscience, more and more stringent measures had been taken to protect the Indians against ruthless exploitation.

in Süden Braziliens, 1901-1926 (Werl i. Westf., Franziskus-Druckerei, 1929, pp. 175); Antonio de Santa Maria Jaboatam, Novo Orbe Serafico Brasilico ou Chronica dos Frades Menores da Provincia do Brasil, passim.

Chapter V

FRENCH AMERICA, ACADIA; CANADA; THE MISSISSIPPI VALLEY; THE WEST INDIES; GUIANA

THE part of the French in planting Christianity in the New World was picturesque, the narrative is marked by much of heroism and devotion, and the territories embraced were extensive. Measured in continuing Christian Indian communities, the results, while important, were not so impressive as those which followed the Spanish endeavour. This, however, was chiefly because of the sparseness and primitive character of the Indian population. In a continuing white community intensely loyal to Roman Catholicism the French enterprise was more successful than was that of the Spaniards and Portuguese.

Effective French efforts towards establishing permanent footholds in the Western Hemisphere were late in beginning. Sporadic enterprises commenced early in the sixteenth century, but not until the seventeenth century were significant permanent settlements made.

Then, for more than a century, a great French empire seemed in process of building. In vast areas in North America, in Canada and the Mississippi Valley, New France was coming into being. The future seemed to lie, not with British, but with French culture. Had it endured, New France would in the nineteenth and twentieth centuries have been one of the most powerful states on the globe, comprising what later became the Dominion of Canada and some of the wealthiest and most populous portions of the United States. Islands in the West Indies were acquired. A section of Guiana, on the northern shore of South America, was roughly staked out.

To this fair prospect the second half of the eighteenth century brought disaster. French political dominion on the mainland of North America was obliterated. Only small islands off the coast of Newfoundland, a few fragments in the West Indies, and the inhospitable Guiana were left to French rule.

The causes of this tardy beginning, this meteoric burst of empire, and this ruinous collapse must be sought in the history of Europe and especially of France. Civil dissension in France itself, brought partly by the conflict between Roman Catholics and Protestants, was chiefly responsible for the initial delay. A divided nation had little surplus energy for overseas adventures. At the close of the sixteenth century the accession to the throne and the conversion to Roman Catholicism of Henry IV brought domestic peace. In the seventeenth century Richelieu, Mazarin, and Louis XIV made France the dominant power in Western Europe, and imperial enterprises were begun abroad with vigour and promise. Then, in the eighteenth century, European wars in which she became embroiled, and particularly the Seven Years' War (1756-1763), left France still powerful, but stripped of most of her American possessions. Acadia was conquered by the English in 1690 and restored to France in 1697. In 1713 France ceded to England Hudson Bay, Newfoundland, and Nova Scotia, and in 1763 Canada was finally surrendered to England, with Cape Breton and all French lands east of the Mississippi except the lowest reaches of that river and New Orleans. A few weeks before, in 1762, France had ceded to Spain this latter area and her territory west of the Mississippi. France also surrendered to England title to the West Indian islands of Tobaga, Dominica, Grenada, and St. Vincent, although these latter did not then come permanently into British hands.

During the century and a half of French prominence in the Americas, French missions were extensive. They were not Protestant. As an outcome of the domestic strife, Protestantism in France became confined to minority enclaves, on the defensive and eventually restricted by severe persecution. The sixteenth century Huguenot efforts to plant the Reformed faith in the New World proved abortive. Only through scattered exiles in the English colonies and through the influence of the great Calvin on Dutch, English, Scots, and Germans did the Protestantism of France contribute to the building of Protestantism in the Americas. The characteristic French missions were Roman Catholic. As we have seen in an earlier chapter, in France the seventeenth century was a time of abounding life, not only in the consolidation of the monarchy and the achievement of a leading place among the European powers, but also in the Roman Catholic Church. As so frequently has happened, religious revival and national vigour went hand in hand.

The American missions of this awakened French Roman Catholicism were under severe handicaps. Not only was the time available for their expansion under French political rule in most areas relatively brief, but they also suffered from the character of the non-Christian peoples whom they sought to win. None of these tribes were in settled, civilized communities. Most of them were in a hunting, semi-agricultural stage of culture and found it difficult to adjust themselves to the white man's rule. The aboriginal population of most of New France was sparse. It was fluctuating and some of it was inclined to a frequent change of habitat.[1] Inter-tribal wars decimated it and destroyed some of the most promising missions. In the West Indies the majority of the Indians who survived until the French occupation were intractable Caribs whom the white man killed off but could not subjugate. The Negroes who were imported to the West Indies were somewhat more assimilable, but under slavery could not have a vigorous Christian life of their own.

In spite of obstacles, the French achievement in the propagation of Christianity was noteworthy. Missionaries traversed vast distances and by patient labour succeeded in making numbers of converts. Sometimes they were the pioneers of French influence. Often they went hand in hand with lay explorers and with fur-traders, for the chief wealth of colonial New France was in furs and the main economic incentive to westward expansion was their acquisition. Since furs were relatively scarce in Eastern Canada, the urge was westward to richer supplies. Then, too, many of the early explorers were driven by a desire to see new regions and to build a vast empire. The frontier moved westward by progressive stages—first islands off the east coast used for fishing centres, then the Lower St. Lawrence and the eastern maritime districts, then what is now Ontario and New York State, and eventually the region of the upper Great Lakes and the Mississippi Valley. It was on this rapidly moving frontier that missionaries were found—although they also remained in the older districts to care for such Indians as persisted in the rear. Yet along this frontier the French occupation, in contrast with that of the English Thirteen Colonies, was not consolidated. Only a few scattered forts, wandering fur-traders, and an occasional small white village represented the French power.

The expansion of New France differed markedly from the course in Spanish America. In the latter, after the initial burst of conquest, missionaries constituted the chief agents for extending the frontier. In New France the French secular urge of exploration and conquest had not spent itself when the British curbed it, and the search for furs sent the trader ever onward. Missionaries were not the only and frequently not the chief representatives of an expanding Europe.

Then, too, in Canada, through immigration and a high birth rate, a French population came into existence. Until the end of the French occupation it remained small, for the main interest of the colony, as we have said, was the fur-trade. Usually agriculture was ancillary, and the quest for pelts meant a widely scattered but scanty white population. The French Canadians proved to be loyally Roman Catholic. To be sure, after the end of French rule their fidelity to that branch of the faith was in part the result of an effort to preserve their

[1] Parkman, *The Jesuits in North America*, p. 3.

cultural integrity against the politically dominant British. Yet in the nineteenth and twentieth centuries they were more aggressive and had a greater share in the spread of Christianity beyond their eighteenth century borders than did the Roman Catholics of either Spanish or Portuguese America.

The contrast with the course of Christianity in British America was also marked. In Canada the chief interest of the French, in the fur trade, was in sharp contradistinction from that of the adjacent British Colonies, where the white settlers came primarily to build homes. In the Thirteen Colonies of the English, therefore, the transplanting of Christianity by immigration was foremost, and missions to Indians were incidental. In French North America Indian missions held the centre of the stage. Moreover, in the Thirteen Colonies the desire for religious freedom was prominent as a cause of white settlement and the type of Christianity propagated was primarily Protestant, and of the kinds which were persecuted in Europe. In French America the longing for religious liberty was not a factor in inducing immigration and the Christianity was entirely Roman Catholic. The religious picture, therefore, differed widely between the British and the French possessions.

Early in the sixteenth century French fishermen began frequenting the shores of Newfoundland.[2] Apparently the first attempts by the French to spread their faith among the Indians were in 1534-1536 in connexion with the earlier expeditions of Jacques Cartier, the first seaman seriously to undertake the exploration of the region of the St. Lawrence on behalf of France. Cartier is said to have made the sign of the cross over some sick Indians and to have told them of the passion of Christ.[3] Three of those whom Cartier brought with him to France were baptized.[4]

The civil wars in France prevented an early successful continuation of these promising beginnings. When the domestic conflicts were once over, efforts were resumed. In the first ten years of the seventeenth century, a settlement was effected at Port Royal, near the present Annapolis in Nova Scotia. Here, in that decade, a number of Indians were baptized by a secular priest,[5] but their conversion was superficial, and within a few years they were said to have forgotten even the Christian names which had been given them.[6] In 1611 two Jesuits, Biard and Masse, came to Port Royal and earnestly began efforts to win the Indians. They set about learning the language. Reinforcements arrived. A new

[2] Thwaites, *France in America*, p. 5.
[3] Lescarbot, *Histoire de la Nouvelle-France*, Book III, Chap. 17.
[4] N. E. Dionne, *La Nouvelle-France de Cartier à Champlain, 1540-1603* (Quebec, C. Darveau, 1891, pp. 395), p. 103.
[5] See accounts in several contemporary documents in Thwaites, *Jesuit Relations*, Vol. I, pp. 74 ff., 108-113, 120-123, 160, 161.
[6] Letter of Biard in Thwaites, *Jesuit Relations*, Vol. I, pp. 162, 163, Vol. III, pp. 3 ff.

settlement was formed on Mt. Desert Island, in the present Maine. Scarcely had this been done, however, when English from Virginia appeared (1613), killed two of the Jesuits, and carried the other two away captive.[7]

In the meanwhile what proved to be a more fortunate step was taken. In 1608 a settlement was formed by Champlain at what came to be known as Quebec. Quebec was farther removed from English attacks than Acadia and commanded access to a vast interior.[8] Soon a small colony arose, recruited from mechanics and farmers from France.[9] The spiritual oversight of the French immigrants was entrusted to the Recollects, that sixteenth century offshoot of the Franciscans which was one of the expressions of the rising tide of French religious life. The first of the Recollects arrived in 1615.[10] From the very outset steps were taken to bring the Christian message to the Indians. The vernaculars were studied, and in the course of the next few years in several places missions were begun and a number of neophytes were baptized. Through great hardships, Joseph le Caron made an approach to the Hurons. Reinforcements came and a novitiate was begun.[11] However, in 1624 Le Caron reported that few real conversions had been effected among the Indians.[12]

Beginning in 1619 Recollects of the province of Aquitaine undertook the religious oversight of Acadia[13] and continued in it for several years.[14]

In 1625, at the initiative of the Recollects, a contingent of Jesuits arrived in Quebec, thus beginning a long and noteworthy enterprise of that Society in the vast region tributary to the St. Lawrence.[15] The Jesuits established themselves near the Recollects and began the study of the vernacular. However, in 1629 Quebec fell into the hands of the English and the Jesuits were deported to England and thence permitted to return to France.[16]

In 1632 Canada was restored to France, and a new distribution of territory among the religious orders followed. The Recollects were not returned to the

[7] Letters of Biard in Thwaites, *Jesuit Relations*, Vol. II, pp. 4 ff.; *Relatio Rerum Gestarum in Novo-Francica Missione Annis 1513 & 1614*, in Thwaites, *Jesuit Relations*, Vol. II, pp. 194 ff.; Jouvency, *Canadicae Missionis Relatio*, in Thwaites, *Jesuit Relations*, Vol. I, pp. 226 ff.; Leger, *The Catholic Indian Missions in Maine, 1611-1820*, pp. 20, 21.

[8] Le Clerq, *First Establishment of the Faith in New France*, translated by J. G. Shea, Vol. I, p. 65.

[9] Le Clerq, *op. cit.*, Vol. I, pp. 62, 69.

[10] Le Clerq, *op. cit.*, Vol. I, pp. 70-85.

[11] Le Clerq, *op. cit.*, Vol. I, pp. 86-137, 175-198.

[12] Le Clerq, *op. cit.*, Vol. I, p. 214.

[13] Le Clerq, *op. cit.*, Vol. I, pp. 199, 200.

[14] See a discussion of the dates, which are somewhat uncertain, in Leger, *The Catholic Indian Missions in Maine, 1611-1820*, pp. 29, 30.

[15] Le Clerq, *op. cit.*, Vol. I, pp. 229 ff.

[16] Letters of Lalemant, one of the Jesuits, in Thwaites, *Jesuit Relations*, Vol. IV, pp. 190 ff.; Thwaites, *France in America*, p. 22.

St. Lawrence Valley. Quebec and the area tributary to it were assigned to the Jesuits.[17] Although they made repeated efforts to obtain permission, not until 1670 were the Recollects allowed to resume operations.[18]

However, some years before 1670 the spiritual sons of St. Francis, in the persons not of the Recollects, but of the Capuchins, had undertaken (1632) the care of the maritime regions included in the vaguely defined term of Acadia. In a number of places in what later became Nova Scotia and New Brunswick they established missions. This effort was, however, brought to an end by the English occupation of the region in 1654, an occupation which lasted until 1667.[19]

In the meantime another religious force entered New France and founded an idealistic settlement at Montreal. This enterprise is connected with the names of Jerome de Royer de la Dauversière, a receiver of taxes in France, and Jean Jacques Olier (1608-1657). Olier was a priest, and was at once a product and one of the chief leaders in the religious revival in France associated with such spirits as Francis de Sales and Vincent de Paul. He it was who took over in Paris the parish of St. Sulpice, said to have been the most difficult and degraded in the French capital, transformed it, and founded there a seminary for the training of priests which became the centre of the Society of St. Sulpice. The Montreal enterprise was one of his earlier ventures. The two men organized the Society of Notre-Dame de Montreal. The purpose was to found at Montreal a Christian centre of secular priests who would carry on missions for the Indians and have spiritual oversight of the colonists. The plan also included a community of nuns who would nurse the sick and teach the children, both white and red. A fund was raised in France, largely through the contributions of devout women, and the island of Montreal was purchased. In 1640 the initial contingent sailed and the settlement which they founded was christened Villemarie de Montreal and was dedicated to the Holy Family.[20]

After a time the enterprise seemed to languish. In 1657 the group in Montreal had declined to five or six persons. The remnant, quite naturally, turned to another creation of Olier, the Seminary of St. Sulpice, and asked it to come to the rescue. This it did. Priests from the Seminary reached Montreal, and eventually the island was transferred to that more sturdy child of Olier's zeal.[21] At the same time, in 1657, a contingent of hospital sisters of Anjou came out,

[17] Le Clerq, op. cit., Vol. I, pp. 310 ff.; Thwaites, France in America, p. 22.

[18] Le Clerq, op. cit., Vol. II, p. 72.

[19] Leger, op. cit., pp. 34-36; Terzorio, Manuale Historicum Missionum Ordinis Minorum Capuccinorum, p. 419.

[20] Parkman, The Jesuits in North America, pp. 281-303; Fenlon in Catholic Encyclopedia, Vol. XI, pp. 240-242; Le Clerq, op. cit., Vol. II, pp. 39 ff.

[21] Parkman, The Old Régime in Canada, p. 84.

backed by an endowment from a generous benefactor. In 1659 an initial group of three women arrived to found a school for girls.[22]

In the ecclesiastical leadership of Canada it was the Jesuits and not the spiritual sons of Olier who had the determining voice. For years the Archbishop of Rouen had considered Canada to be under his jurisdiction. This, however, was unsatisfactory, for a resident bishop was essential if the Church were really to take permanent root. Through the influence of the Jesuits the post was given to François Xavier de Laval-Montmorency. Laval, to give him the name by which he is best known, was of distinguished lineage and a man of marked force of character. Although not a member of the Society, he had been reared under strong Jesuit influence. Deeply religious, he was one of the little group whose missionary vision led to the formation of the Société des Missions Étrangères of Paris. His initial appointment was as vicar apostolic, the device employed to give episcopal powers to those friends of his who at about the same time were being dispatched to the Far East. While Laval's designation was made with the consent of France, as vicar apostolic he was more directly under Rome than if he had been Bishop of Canada.[23] He sailed for Canada in 1659. In 1674, at the urgent request of Laval and the Pope, the King allowed him to become Bishop of Quebec, the first to hold the title.[24]

As Laval gave thought to providing a clergy for his vast diocese, it was to be expected that he would seek to accomplish his purpose through a seminary akin to that which formed the basis of the Société des Missions Étrangères. Indeed, the Quebec seminary was placed under that of Paris.[25] Laval opened the seminary in 1668 and later transferred to it grants of land which had been given him in New France.[26] A tie between the Quebec institution and the Paris society was maintained until the conquest of Quebec by the English (1759).[27] The plan of the Quebec seminary contemplated the creation of a secular clergy for the new land, but knit into a closer fellowship and into more of a mobile missionary force than would have been possible under the type of diocesan organization which prevailed in France itself.

The chief missions of the Quebec seminary were in Acadia, in the present New Brunswick and Nova Scotia. Here they ministered both to Indians and to

[22] Le Clerq, op. cit., Vol. II, pp. 45-48.
[23] Parkman, The Old Régime in Canada, pp. 87 ff.; Launay, Histoire Générale de Société des Missions Étrangères, Vol. I, pp. 38 ff.; Mulvey, French Catholic Missionaries in the Present United States (1604-1719), pp. 8, 9; Brasseur de Bourbourg, Histoire du Canada de son Église et de ses Missions, Vol. I, Chap. 5.
[24] Parkman, The Old Régime in Canada, p. 160.
[25] Launay, op. cit., Vol. I, pp. 156 ff., 258-261.
[26] Parkman, The Old Régime in Canada, pp. 160 ff.
[27] Launay, op. cit., Vol. II, pp. 24-27.

French colonists, but the expulsion of the Acadians from Nova Scotia by the British dealt them a fatal blow.[28] The seminary also extended its activities to the Mississippi Valley—the Illinois region and the Arkansas.[29]

Still another body entered Canada to share in giving the Christian message to that land. A wealthy widow of noble family, Madame de la Peltrie, fired by the reports of the labours of the Jesuits in New France, determined to devote herself and her fortune to the native women. She turned for help to the Ursulines, who had been begun in the previous century for the express purpose of teaching girls. The initial contingent, led by Marie de l'Incarnation and with Madame de la Peltrie as a member, came out in 1659 and was established at Quebec. There they opened a school for Indian girls. Marie de l'Incarnation developed an unusual capacity both for leadership and for the mastery of the Indian tongues.[30]

On the ship with the first group of Ursulines came, through the initiative of a niece of the great Richelieu, the Duchess d'Aiguillon, nuns whose purpose it was to found a hospital at Quebec.[31]

For years the most prominent of the missionaries in New France were the Jesuits. Le Jeune, who headed the mission at Quebec which had been restored in 1632, set about the acquisition of one of the Indian vernaculars and in the autumn and winter of 1633-1634 spent several months with a company of Indians, sharing the discomforts of their wandering life.[32]

Not far from Quebec a settlement of Algonquin converts was formed. It was given the name of Sillery, in honour of a benefactor who had contributed a fund to make the effort possible.[33]

During the middle decades of the seventeenth century, the outstanding French missions were those of the Jesuits among the Hurons. Along the lower courses of the St. Lawrence River the Indians seem to have been comparatively few. In the second quarter of the century the Hurons were the chief accessible group. They were a semi-agricultural people, belonging to the widely flung Iroquoian family, but held in bitter and chronic enmity by the Iroquois proper. At the time of which we speak, they were a fairly compact group, living in towns, some of which were fortified, mostly between Lake Simcoe and

---

[28] Launay, *op. cit.*, Vol. II, pp. 5-20.

[29] Launay, *op. cit.*, Vol. I, pp. 441-450; Thwaites, *Jesuit Relations*, Vol. LXV, p. 61, Vol. LXVI, pp. 260, 261, Vol. LXVII, p. 248.

[30] Parkman, *The Jesuits in North America*, pp. 260 ff.; Le Clerq, *op. cit.*, Vol. II, pp. 26 ff.

[31] Le Clerq, *op. cit.*, Vol. II, pp. 26, 27, 32, 36.

[32] Parkman, *op. cit.*, pp. 101-128.

[33] Parkman, *op. cit.*, p. 275.

Georgian Bay in the modern Ontario. In 1639 they were said to number about twenty thousand.[34]

Jesuit contacts with the Hurons had begun before the three year (1629-1632) occupation of Canada by the English. From 1626 to 1629 Jean de Brébeuf, of a noble family of Normandy, had lived in the Huron country.[35] In 1634 Champlain, that seasoned explorer and civil governor, now near the end of his life, induced Hurons who were on a trading visit at Quebec to take back some Jesuits to reside among them. His chief motive seems to have been the extension of French influence. At the head of the band was Brébeuf. Supporting the group were four French soldiers with arquebuses.[36] The expedition bore a marked resemblance to those which at that time were extending the Spanish frontiers. At the outset the Jesuits planned to establish a residence in each of the chief towns, but in 1639 they decided instead to form one main station, partly for protection and partly as a centre to which to bring neophytes and so remove them from the contaminations of paganism.[37] Again the resemblance to the Spanish and Portuguese missions was striking. With the Jesuits were *donnés*, laymen who from religious devotion had attached themselves to the missions and served without pay.[38]

Progress was fairly rapid. During the initial years baptisms were, perforce, limited to children and the dying. Not until 1637 was the first able-bodied adult baptized.[39] Not unnaturally, the Hurons, looking to their own background for a parallel, regarded the Jesuits as professionals in magic, held them responsible for crop failures and epidemics, and praised them when crops were abundant.[40] Before long, however, a number of converts were gathered. In 1640 a beginning was made at Quebec of a college and seminary for Huron children.[41]

However, before the Huron mission could be more than well begun, the disasters of war brought it to an early and tragic end. The Iroquois obtained firearms from Dutch traders in New York. Strengthened by this superior equipment, they fell upon the Hurons.

The incursions continued for a number of years. For instance, in 1642 a party of Iroquois attacked a band of Hurons with whom were three missionaries. Some were killed outright and others taken into a captivity marked by cruel torture. Among the victims was Isaac Jogues, a Jesuit. In spite of his sufferings,

[34] Parkman, *op. cit.*, p. 10.
[35] Parkman, *op. cit.*, pp. 92, 144.
[36] Parkman, *op. cit.*, pp. 129-154.
[37] Parkman, *op. cit.*, p. 230.
[38] Parkman, *op. cit.*, p. 309.
[39] Parkman, *op. cit.*, p. 202.
[40] Parkman, *op. cit.*, pp. 204-214.
[41] Parkman, *op. cit.*, p. 246.

he baptized children as he had opportunity and sought to win to his faith his adult captors. Through the aid of the Dutch, he eventually escaped and reached France. Yet the pull of his calling would not let him rest content and he returned to Canada. He longed, too, to go as a missionary to the Iroquois. He welcomed, then, an appointment as an envoy of the French to the Mohawks, one of the Iroquois confederacy. His errand completed and peace seemingly assured, he reported to the French authorities and made his way back to the Mohawks, as he had wished, as a missionary. However, the temper of the Indians changed. Disease had attacked their persons and a blight was destroying their corn. Jogues was held accountable and was killed (1646).[42] His death and the consequent failure of efforts for peace may have contributed to a renewal of the war on the Hurons.[43]

As, from 1645 to 1648, the attacks of the Iroquois increased, many of the Hurons became more responsive to the missionaries. Some, to be sure, laid at the door of the Jesuits the disasters which had overtaken them: had not the misfortunes multiplied with the increase of the Black Robes? A large proportion, however, in their desolation and despair came to the missionaries for succour, and in some towns Christians increased to a majority.[44] It was noted, too, that Christians rarely participated in the time-honoured custom of burning enemy prisoners and sometimes even opposed it.[45] From the side of the Hurons, the effect of the Christian message was to lessen the horrors of war.

In 1649 came the end. The Iroquois delivered an overwhelming blow. The Jesuits remained by the Hurons and strove to nerve them to resistance. Several priests perished. Brébeuf himself was tortured and killed. The surviving Hurons fled. The foe, relentless, followed. A few Hurons were led by the Jesuits to Quebec and near there effected a permanent settlement. Some were taken captive and constituted Christian nuclei among the Iroquois. Others scattered in various directions, some making their way to what later became the United States. However, the distinctive Huron mission was terminated.[46]

The missions of the Jesuits were not confined to the Hurons. We have noted the group of Algonquins at Sillery, near Quebec. The Jesuits also penetrated to the Kennebec, in the present Maine. The Abenaki, an Algonquin people,

[42] Francis Talbot, *Saint Among Savages. The Life of Isaac Jogues* (New York, Harper & Brothers, 1935, pp. ix, 466), *passim;* Parkman, *op. cit.,* pp. 305-334, 396-403.
[43] Mulvey, *French Catholic Missionaries in the Present United States (1604-1791),* pp. 21-23.
[44] Parkman, *op. cit.,* pp. 449-452.
[45] Parkman, *op. cit.,* p. 450.
[46] Parkman, *op. cit.,* pp. 480-537. Also on the Huron mission see original documents in Thwaites, *Jesuit Relations,* Vols. VII, VIII, X, XI, XIII-XXX, XXXII-XXXIV, XXXVII-XL, LX, and in Auguste Carayon, *Première Mission des Jésuites au Canada Lettres et Documents Inédits* (Paris, L'Écureux, 1864), pp. 165 ff.

had for some time been frequenting Sillery, and it was natural that they should be followed to their homes. In 1646 and again in 1650, Druillette visited them, the latter time on his way to New England in a futile attempt to negotiate an alliance with the English colonists against the Iroquois.[47] When drink, disease, and war had reduced to a feeble remnant the Indian community at Sillery, Abenaki, in flight from the English and the Iroquois, for a time swelled the numbers.[48] Later settlements of Christian Indians were made a little farther up the St. Lawrence and south of Quebec.[49] Jesuits were also on the St. John River, in the present New Brunswick, and in the present Maine on the Saco, the Kennebec, and the Penobscot.[50] The missions among the Abenaki persisted well into the eighteenth century.[51] In some of these areas the Jesuits shared the field with priests from that Quebec seminary in whose founding Laval had had a part.[52]

The Jesuits also had missions among the five tribes or "nations" who made up the Iroquois confederacy, the Mohawks, Oneidas, Onondagas, Cayugas, and Senecas. These resided in what are now the central and western parts of the State of New York—beginning with the Mohawks in the east and ending with the Senecas in the west. The story is complicated by many factors, among them the shifting relations between the various tribes and the French and particularly the recurrent wars between the French and the English. The Iroquois were on the border between the French and the English possessions and, naturally, were courted by both sides. In effect, although not necessarily always in deliberate purpose, the Jesuits were often the main vanguard of the French. In a number of places captive Christian Hurons, dispersed among the Iroquois, constituted a nucleus for the activity of the missionaries. However, the Jesuits never acquired really strong footholds among the Iroquois. Their greatest successes in winning converts were among tribes which, from the military standpoint, were relatively weak. From the most vigorous tribes of Canada and the West they gathered comparatively few.

[47] Thwaites, *Jesuit Relations*, Vol. XXXVI, pp. 82 ff. Also on the Huron mission see the semi-popular account, John J. Wynne, *The Jesuit Martyrs of North America* (New York, The Universal Knowledge Foundation, pp. xi, 246), *passim*; P. F. J. Bressani, *Relation Abrégée Quelques Missions des Pères de la Compie de Jesus dans la Nouvelle France* (Macérata, 1653, pp. 336), *passim*; Brasseur de Bourbourg, *Histoire du Canada de son Église et de ses Missions*, Vol. I, Chaps. 3, 4; Parkman, *op. cit.*, pp. 419-430; Leger, *The Catholic Indian Missions in Maine (1611-1820)*, pp. 40 ff.

[48] Leger, *op. cit.*, p. 55.

[49] Leger, *op. cit.*, pp. 57-64.

[50] Leger, *op. cit.*, pp. 90 ff.

[51] Thwaites, *Jesuit Relations*, Vol. LXV. pp. 86 ff., Vol. LXVI, pp. 174 ff., Vol. XLVII, pp. 84 ff.

[52] Leger, *op. cit.*, p. 91.

The missions to the Five Nations began soon after the ruin of the Hurons and when Iroquois attacks on the sparse white settlements on the St. Lawrence had brought French power in that region to a low ebb. In 1653 came an Onondaga offer of peace.[53] This was followed, in 1656, by the establishment, at the request of the same Indians, of a French settlement with a Jesuit mission on Lake Onondaga, not far from the present Syracuse, New York.[54] One of the motives of the Onondagas may have been a desire for immediate access to the European goods of which their neighbours, the Mohawks, had a more direct source of supply through the Dutch. The mission had a chequered history.

Missions were also begun among the Mohawks, the Oneidas, the Cayugas, and the Senecas. Converts were made, among them some of the chiefs. Drunkenness was one of the chief evils which the missionaries were forced to combat. They attempted to prohibit the sale of brandy to the Indians, but in vain.

Christians from several tribes were collected in a settlement not unlike the reductions of the Jesuits in Portuguese and Spanish America. At first it was opposite Montreal, but a little later it was moved slightly above Montreal, to Caughnawaga, near the rapids of the St. Lawrence.

During the various wars between the French and the English, in the latter part of the seventeenth and in the eighteenth century, the missions among the Iroquois, being in debatable land, naturally suffered. When, in 1713, by the Treaty of Utrecht, the French recognized the suzerainty of the British over the Iroquois, Jesuit missions among the tribes in their native haunts came to an end. However, the Christian settlements continued.[55]

No one of the Iroquois tribes became professedly Christian. In 1693 the Superior of the Jesuits in New France reported that in the past three years in all the Canadian missions over two thousand had been baptized.[56] However, by no means all of these were among the Iroquois. Between 1668 and

[53] Parkman, *The Old Régime in Canada*, pp. 3 ff.; Shea, *History of the Catholic Missions among the Indian Tribes of the United States, 1529-1854*, pp. 205 ff.

[54] Thwaites, *Jesuit Relations*, Vol. XL, pp. 219, 220, Vol. XLII, pp. 48 ff., Vol. XLIII, pp. 156 ff.; Parkman, *The Old Régime in Canada*, pp. 16 ff.; Shea, *op. cit.*, pp. 228 ff.

[55] Thwaites, *Jesuit Relations*, Vol. XLIV, pp. 20 ff., Vol. XLVII, pp. 67 ff., Vol. LI, pp. 166 ff., Vol. LII, pp. 116 ff., Vol. LIII, pp. 52 ff., Vol. LIV, *passim*, Vol. LV, pp. 55 ff., Vol. LVI, pp. 18 ff., Vol. LVII, pp. 21 ff., Vol. LVIII, pp. 170 ff., Vol. LXI, pp. 18 ff., 159 ff., Vol. LXII, pp. 54 ff.; Mulvey, *op. cit.*, pp. 23-35; Parkman, *op. cit.*, pp. 316 ff. Also on the Iroquois missions see Charlevoix, *Histoire et Description Générale de la Nouvelle France* (Paris, Ganeau, 3 vols., 1744); Brasseur de Bourbourg, *op. cit.*, Vol. I, Chaps. 4, 7; Alexander M. Stewart, *A Guide to the Map of the Seneca Villages and Jesuit and French Contacts* (Published by the Author, Rochester, N. Y., 2d ed., 1931, pp. 12); *passim*.

[56] Thwaites, *Jesuit Relations*, Vol. LXII, pp. 190, 191.

1678 only about 2,220 of the Iroquois are said to have been baptized.[57] The majority remained pagan.

The Jesuits expanded their activities north and west of the Great Lakes. By 1674 they had missions among the Ottawas, at Sault Ste. Marie (between Lakes Huron and Superior), at Green Bay (in the present Wisconsin), at Chequamegon (on the south-west shore of Lake Superior), and at St. Ignace (on the Strait of Mackinac, between Lakes Michigan and Huron).[58] Jesuits went as far north as Hudson Bay and recorded baptisms in that region.[59] Efforts were put forth to win the tribes in the central part of Wisconsin. Thus we hear of Allouez, who spoke five different languages of that territory, and of a group of young warriors who, inspired by the story of Constantine, believed that they had been victorious because of their use of the sign of the cross.[60] Allouez had been appointed by Laval as Vicar General and Superior of the Western missions. He attracted some able men to his assistance and came to be known as "the Apostle to the North-west."[61]

Before the close of the seventeenth century the wide-ranging, dauntless Black Robes had traversed much of the valley of the Mississippi. There they made contacts with several tribes and ministered to the scattered French settlements which followed in their wake. In 1673 Marquette, a Jesuit, was with the party which pioneered in the exploration of the Mississippi, and died in 1675 while engaged in an attempt to establish a mission among the Illinois.[62] Missions were soon begun in Illinois,[63] and in 1750 the largest of these had a population of over six hundred, of whom the major part had been baptized. Yet here, as in so many other centres, the brandy sold by French traders proved demoralizing, and at least one missionary believed that his chief accomplishment was the baptism of dying infants.[64] A futile attempt was made to found a mission among the Sioux.[65] Some missionaries pushed even farther westward, to the Lake of the Woods.[66] Something was done

[57] Mulvey, French Catholic Missionaries in the Present United States (1604-1791), pp. 35, 36.

[58] Thwaites, Jesuit Relations, Vol. LVI, pp. 91 ff., Vol. LIX, pp. 169 ff.

[59] Thwaites, Jesuit Relations, Vol. LVI, pp. 148 ff.

[60] Thwaites, Jesuit Relations, Vol. LVI, pp. 139 ff.

[61] Mulvey, op. cit., pp. 37-51.

[62] Thwaites, Jesuit Relations, Vol. LIX, pp. 86 ff.; Parkman, La Salle and the Discovery of the Great West, pp. 48 ff.

[63] Thwaites, Jesuit Relations, Vol. LX, pp. 148 ff., Vol. LXIV, pp. 158 ff.

[64] Thwaites, Jesuit Relations, Vol. LXIX, pp. 200 ff.

[65] Parkman, A Half-Century of Conflict, Vol. II, pp. 26, 27.

[66] A. G. Morice, History of the Catholic Church in Western Canada (Toronto, The Musson Book Co., 2 vols., 1910), Vol. I, Chaps. 2-4.

for the Choctaws.[67] At New Orleans was a Jesuit centre.[68] There were mission posts among the Arkansas, the Yazoos, and the Alibamons.[69]

At no one time does the number of Jesuits in New France seem to have been very large for so vast an area. Thus in 1748 the total, including lay brothers, was only fifty-one, and of these twenty-one were in the college at Quebec.[70]

The end of the French Jesuit missions was almost coterminous with French rule in North America. In 1762-1763 the Society was suppressed in France, and in 1763 a decree was issued expelling the Black Robes from Louisiana.[71] In 1762, however, New Orleans and French claims west of the Mississippi had been transferred to Spain, and in 1763 Canada and the French claims east of the Mississippi were formally ceded to Great Britain. In the territory transferred to Great Britain a few Jesuits continued, although, of course, reinforcements could not be had from France. As late as 1789 four former members of the Society were still in Canada.[72]

As we have suggested, the Jesuits, while long the most prominent, were by no means the only French Roman Catholic missionaries in New France. The Sulpicians extended their activities outside Montreal. In 1667 they took over from the Jesuits the care of an Iroquois settlement at Quinte Bay, north of Lake Ontario.[73] They had a mission on the Lake of Two Mountains, not far from Montreal.[74] In 1748 Piquet, a Sulpician, founded a settlement of Iroquois, mostly from the Onondagas and Cayugas, on the St. Lawrence, on the site of the present Ogdensburg, New York. Since missions among the Iroquois within the British sphere were impossible, the hope was that here, too, near the British border, a centre could be established. For a time it prospered, but suffered in the war which brought French rule to its final end.[75] Sulpicians started with La Salle in 1669 on the latter's famous journey of discovery in the Mississippi Valley, but parted company with him and made their way along Lake Erie and Lake Huron and eventually back to Montreal.[76]

Priests of the Foreign Missions from the seminary in Quebec had a part in the introduction of Christianity to the Mississippi Valley. In 1698 three

[67] Thwaites, *Jesuit Relations*, Vol. LXIX, pp. 74-77.
[68] *Ibid.*
[69] Delanglez, *The French Jesuits in Lower Louisiana (1700-1703)*, pp. 430 ff.
[70] Thwaites, *Jesuit Relations*, Vol. LXIX, pp. 74-77.
[71] Thwaites, *Jesuit Relations*, Vol. LXX, pp. 211 ff.
[72] Thwaites, *Jesuit Relations*, Vol. LXXI, pp. 100 ff.
[73] Shea, *History of the Catholic Missions among the Indian Tribes of the United States,* p. 254.
[74] Shea, *op. cit.,* p. 335.
[75] Shea, *op. cit.,* pp. 336, 337.
[76] Parkman, *La Salle and the Discovery of the Great West*, pp. 10-21.

of them left Quebec with that destination in mind and began missions there.[77] Some friction with the Jesuits arose, in part because of the conflict between the Society of Jesus and the members of the Paris Seminary over the Chinese rites—a story to which we are to come in a later chapter.[78] Early in the eighteenth century priests arrived in Louisiana directly from the Paris Seminary.[79] They were inclined to confine their activities to the settlers at Mobile, although some effort was put forth for the Indians.[80]

To the Mississippi Valley also came Capuchins, the initial contingent arriving in 1722.[81] A few Carmelites were likewise found in the broad region known as Louisiana.[82] To New Orleans came Ursulines, directly from France, in 1727, to care for the sick and to teach.[83]

The Recollects were very widely scattered. We have seen how they early made their way to Canada and then, after an interruption, returned in 1670. As was to be expected, the initial contingent of the renewed mission built a church at the capital of New France, Quebec.[84] They were at Fort Frontenac, near the lower end of Lake Ontario,[85] and at Montreal.[86] Recollects accompanied La Salle on the western expedition which began in 1678.[87] For a time Recollects were in Illinois.[88] They were brought by Cadillac to provide chaplains for Detroit.[89] We hear of them in New Orleans and in other parts of Louisiana.[90] In the eighteenth century they were active in several parts of what are now the Maritime Provinces.[91]

For the care of the white population, in addition to the regulars, a secular clergy gradually arose. Between 1700 and 1714 fifteen seculars are said to have arrived from France, and in that same period eighteen were ordained in Canada. From 1714 to 1719, six are said to have come from France and four to have been ordained at Quebec.[92]

[77] Delanglez, *The French Jesuits in Lower Louisiana (1700-1763)*, pp. 21-23.
[78] Delanglez, *op. cit.*, pp. 32 ff.
[79] Delanglez, *op. cit.*, pp. 52, 55.
[80] Delanglez, *op. cit.*, pp. 72, 73.
[81] Delanglez, *op. cit.*, p. 96; Mulvey, *French Catholic Missionaries in the Present United States (1604-1791)*, pp. 89-94.
[82] Delanglez, *op. cit.*, pp. 94 ff; Mulvey, *op. cit.*, pp. 89-94.
[83] Delanglez, *op. cit.*, pp. 134-136.
[84] Le Clercq, *First Establishment of the Faith in New France*, translated by Shea, Vol. II, pp. 73 ff.
[85] Le Clercq, *op. cit.*, Vol. II, p. 86.
[86] Le Clercq, *op. cit.*, Vol. II, p. 99.
[87] Le Clercq, *op. cit.*, Vol. II, pp. 108 ff.
[88] Mulvey, *op. cit.*, pp. 58-76.
[89] Mulvey, *op. cit.*, pp. 52-57.
[90] Delanglez, *op. cit.*, pp. 94, 318, 429.
[91] Rochemonteix, *Les Jésuites de la Nouvelle-France au XVIIIe Siècle*, Vol. I, pp. iii ff.
[92] Rochemonteix, *op. cit.*, Vol. I, p. 97.

The substitution of British for French rule inevitably brought marked religious changes. Since Great Britain was a Protestant power, an influx of Protestants followed, in part from the British Isles and in part from the Thirteen Colonies, soon to become the United States. Of this Protestant development we are to speak in the next volume, for it leads so continuously into the nineteenth century that the real dividing line is not 1800 but 1763 and the American Revolution, and it can best be treated with the later period.

For the Roman Catholic Church the transition was momentous. The free exercise of the Roman Catholic faith was guaranteed by the capitulation of Quebec in 1759, by that of Montreal in 1760, and by the Treaty of Paris (1763). There were then said to be about seventy thousand Roman Catholics in Canada, most of them French.[93] The Treaty of Paris, however, restricted this freedom by the clause, "so far as the laws of Great Britain permit," and the instruction to the first British Governor was "not to admit any ecclesiastical jurisdiction of the See of Rome."[94] At the outset the Bishop of Quebec was forbidden to carry on any correspondence with Rome. Only gradually did the Bishops win concessions.[95] However, to ensure the loyalty of the Canadians in the American Revolution the British Governor proved conciliatory.[96] The Quebec Act of 1774 and the Constitutional Act of 1791 reaffirmed religious toleration.[97] The penal laws against the Roman Catholics existing in England at the time were not extended to Canada.[98] The privilege of jury service was accorded to Canadian Roman Catholics in 1764, twenty-seven years before it was granted in England.[99]

Under the French régime, Gallicanism had been strong in the Canadian Church, as it was in France, and Rome had but little more control than it did in the Spanish possessions. The effect of British rule was to drive the Canadian Catholics closer to Rome. For years the British struggled against this tendency and efforts were made to claim for the King of England the rights over the Church which had been exercised by the King of France. In time, however, the restraints were withdrawn, and eventually the authority of Rome became greater than it had ever been in the days of French rule.[100] The French Canadians were strengthened in their allegiance to their ancestral faith, for the Roman Catholic Church in Canada was the one

[93] E. H. Oliver, *The Winning of the Frontier*, p. 79.
[94] Lindsey, *Rome in Canada*, p. 127; Oliver, *op. cit.*, pp. 82-84.
[95] Oliver, *op. cit.*, p. 104.
[96] Oliver, *op. cit.*, pp. 84-88.
[97] Oliver, *op. cit.*, p. 92.
[98] Lindsey, *op. cit.*, p. 120.
[99] Oliver, *op. cit.*, p. 81.
[100] Lindsey, *op. cit.*, pp. 5. 122-124.

great institution which was solely theirs and it was identified with their French heritage.

For the Indian missions the coming of British rule was a serious blow. The supply of fresh recruits from France was cut off. The suppression of the Jesuits in France, practically contemporary with the transfer to Britain, added to the seriousness of the situation. In the great sections ceded to Spain, some Spanish clergy entered, but probably not enough to make up the losses.[101] The Indians were disintegrating from contact with the white man's diseases and strong liquors. This, and the lack of clergy, proved benumbing to the weak and incipient Indian Christian communities.

In such of the West Indies as belonged to France, some efforts were made to give spiritual oversight to the colonists and to win the Negroes and Indians. When, in the first half of the seventeenth century, French rule was established in several of the islands, seculars first came out. Almost immediately, however, the French authorities called in regulars. Capuchins were on St. Christopher, Gaudeloupe, and Martinique. Dominicans were on the latter two islands and Haiti. Jesuits also arrived and in 1682 are said to have had four houses for Negroes on Martinique, one in Guadeloupe, and two on St. Christopher.[102] In the difficult French Guiana, where French efforts at development and colonization long encountered indifferent success and even failure, Capuchins for a time laboured and then, for a much longer period, Jesuits.[103]

As we have said at the outset, French rule on the North American Continent was much more brief than that of Spain or England. The Indian population was scanty, not easily reduced to an ordered life, and dwindled through war, disease, and alcohol. Missions among the Indians, although their annals are marked by heroism and martyrdoms, had sparse results in the form of continuing Christian communities. However, the French settlers remained true to their faith and by the English conquest were led to adhere to it the more tenaciously as the symbol and guarantee of their French heritage. While, at the time of the British annexation, they numbered only a few thousand,

[101] Mulvey, *op. cit.*, pp. 105-109.

[102] Joseph Rennard, *Les Caraïbes la Guadeloupe 1635-1656 Histoire des vingt premières années de la Colonisation de la Guadeloupe d'après la Relations du R. P. Breton* (Paris, G. Ficker, 1929, pp. 182), *passim;* Aurelius, *De Capucijnen en de Missie,* p. 40; Crétineau-Joly, *Histoire de la Compagnie de Jésus,* Vol. III, pp. 224-226, Vol. V, pp. 103-105; Schmidlin-Braun, *Catholic Mission History,* pp. 363, 513, 514; J. Rennard, *Les Mission Catholiques aux Antilles,* in *Revue d'Histoire des Missions,* Vol. XII, pp. 241-249, 407-426, Vol. XIII, pp. 68-77.

[103] Schmidlin-Braun, *op. cit.,* pp. 369, 512.

thanks to a high birth rate they multiplied rapidly and in the course of the nineteenth century constituted a large and influential Roman Catholic enclave, one of the strongest Roman Catholic groups in the Americas. In the French West Indies Roman Catholicism became the nominal faith and gained a foothold in French Guiana.

May we summarize the effect of the French Christianity upon the environment? On the North American continent, Christianity did not, as in Spanish and Portuguese America, have to contend with the slave trade, for—except in the Lower Mississippi Valley and then chiefly after the French period—the type of agriculture developed did not require the plantation or cheap, servile labour, and mining did not exist. Rather Christianity was forced to face intertribal wars, accentuated by the use of the white man's fire-arms, and the demoralization of the Indians by the white man's diseases and liquor—to which the red man was unusually susceptible. Christianity, through the missionaries, helped to mitigate the asperities of war by inducing Christian Indians to forego some of the torture applied traditionally to captive foes. It also fought the use of liquor and the sale of liquor by white traders. That some remnants of Indians survived the impact of the European and persisted, often fairly happily, in the new society, was due in no small degree to the missionary and so to Christianity. As for the white population, the Church succeeded in retaining the allegiance of the settlers. For this population, too, the Christian impulse provided some schools and some hospital care. In higher education French America was behind Spanish and British America. In this respect Christianity did not prove so effective as in these other two colonial empires.

As to the effect of the environment on Christianity. The scattered and semi-nomadic nature of the aboriginal population at the advent of the white man worked against the emergence of any such large or continuing Christian communities as were to be found in Spanish America. The early incidence of British rule accentuated the loyalty of the French for the Roman Catholic form of the faith and so tended to make French Canadian Roman Catholicism unusually conservative in the effort to preserve the French heritage free from contamination by British Protestant culture. Yet, perhaps because it was on the defensive, no such exuberant new movements arose from it as came from the Protestant groups which constituted so important an element in the British Thirteen Colonies.

Chapter VI

PROTESTANTISM IN THE AMERICAS. THE THIRTEEN BRIT-
ISH COLONIES; THE WEST INDIES; SURINAM; GREENLAND;
LABRADOR

BEFORE A.D. 1800 several of the forms of Christianity usually grouped
under the name of Protestantism had acquired footholds in the New
World. They did not cover so large an area as did Roman Catholicism.
They did not institute as many missions for Indians and Negroes, nor did
they win nearly so many of these to the Christian faith. They did not play
so outstanding a rôle in protecting non-European peoples from exploitation
by Europeans. Before A.D. 1800 the settlements effected by Protestants were
not so extensive in square miles as those founded by Roman Catholics. Yet,
from the standpoint of the future of Christianity, the spread of Protestantism
to the Americas before A.D. 1800 was even more significant than the spread
of Roman Catholicism. Protestantism became the major factor in determining
the religious complexion of the United States, the most powerful of the American
nations of the nineteenth and twentieth centuries. Even before A.D. 1800 it
exhibited more inherent vigor in the New World than did Roman Catholicism.
It required less continuous injection of new blood from Europe than did the
latter. It was at least as influential as Roman Catholicism in shaping the
religious life of nineteenth and twentieth century Canada. In the United
States and Canada, and especially in the United States, out of this transplanted Protestantism arose what was in many ways a new type of Christianity. In the twentieth century from these two nations came the majority of
the personnel and more than half the funds which made possible the remarkable expansion of the Protestant forms of Christianity in that period. In
contrast, in the nineteenth and twentieth centuries, Roman Catholicism in
the Americas, while displaying a rapid extension in the United States and
Canada, proportionately had only a minor, even though a growing part in
the propagation of the Roman Catholic form of Christianity in other portions
of the world. For these reasons we must devote a slightly larger chapter
to the pre-nineteenth century spread of Protestantism in the New World than
the actual situation in this period would seem to warrant.

First we must speak of the transfer of Christianity through the migration of Europeans to those thirteen English colonies which later became the United States. Then we must recount the attempts to win to the Christian faith the Indians and Negroes of the Thirteen Colonies. After that we must go on to the British West Indies, and from there to areas not under British control—the Danish West Indies, Surinam, Greenland, and Labrador.

Chronologically we will not always bring the narrative down plump to A.D. 1800. For the Thirteen Colonies, the achievement of independence from Great Britain rather than events in A.D. 1800 constituted the decisive transition. For the territories to the north of the United States which remained under the British flag, the important years were those which in the various provinces marked the permanent establishment of British rule. For some of the other regions, other dates towards the close of the eighteenth century seem natural divisions between one period and the next.

We turn first of all to the spread of Christianity in the Thirteen Colonies by the migration of European peoples.

At the outset it is important to note the kind of Christianity which was brought across the Atlantic to what later became the United States.

It was, as we have said, predominantly Protestant. Some Roman Catholics there were, but, so far as they were Christian, the pre-Revolutionary immigrants were overwhelmingly Protestant by tradition. Sentiment against Roman Catholicism was strong. In this the Colonies reflected the attitude which prevailed in the Great Britain of that day and in the sections of the European Continent from which the settlers came. The feeling was strengthened by the political threat from the Roman Catholic French possessions on the north.[1]

This Protestantism was varied. Almost all the chief European strains were represented—Anglicanism, Congregationalism, Lutheranism in several of its forms, Reformed or Calvinism of more than one national type, Anabaptists, Quakers, and Pietists.

No one type was in the ascendant. Several churches were represented which in their respective countries on the other side of the Atlantic enjoyed the exclusive support of the state. The Church of England, the Church of Scotland, the Reformed Church of the Netherlands, and the Church of Sweden were among them. Yet no one of them prevailed. In some of the colonies the Church of England was accorded by law and custom a preferred position, yet in no colony was it relatively as powerful as in the mother country. In

---

[1] Mary Augustina Ray, *American Opinion of Roman Catholicism in the Eighteenth Century* (New York, Columbia University Press, 1936, pp. 456), *passim*.

1700 its strength was chiefly in Virginia and Maryland. Under Dutch rule for a time the Reformed Church of the Netherlands had a legal monopoly of religion in what later became New York.[2] In most of New England (Massachusetts, Connecticut, and New Hampshire) what came to be known as Congregationalism, an outgrowth of the blending of Independents and Puritans, was supreme. Yet even in Massachusetts and Connecticut, while as the "Standing Order" it was closely allied to the state, Congregationalism was not established in the sense in which that word was used in the mother country to describe the relation between government and church. In Rhode Island the principle of toleration, adopted from the beginning, put the various Christian groups on an equal footing. In Maryland for a time partial religious freedom existed.[3] Pennsylvania (which long included Delaware) was designed by its great creator, William Penn, to have religious freedom as one of its basic principles, and in the number of Christian groups became a coat of many colours. In at least the larger proportion of the colonies the particular church which enjoyed the favour of the state did not, as in the Old World, have the allegiance of the majority. As a minority church it was constrained to enter upon active efforts to increase its numbers.[4]

In the Thirteen Colonies, moreover, the radical tendencies of Protestantism were more strongly represented than in Great Britain or on the Continent of Europe.[5] Some of the largest and strongest of the Thirteen were begun as havens in which to escape persecution and to worship and to live as radical minorities believed their Christian faith called them to do. Many of these minorities had endeavoured to go back to the New Testament for their model and counted as corruptions of the primitive and valid Christian message all accretions since New Testament times. They dreamed, too, of establishing societies in which the Christian purpose would be fully lived out. In this respect they resembled many of the reform movements in monasticism, except that they did not believe in the traditional monastic vows of poverty, celibacy, and obedience. They gave a bent to the Christianity of the Thirteen Colonies and so to the succeeding United States which has never been effaced.

---

[2] The Church of England was established by law in the five southern colonies, Virginia, Maryland, North Carolina, South Carolina, and Georgia. Manross, *A History of the American Episcopal Church*, pp. 40-43. See also McConnell, *History of the American Episcopal Church*, p. 87. In New York and New Jersey the royal governors attempted to make it the established church, but did not succeed. Weigle, *American Idealism*, p. 67. On the Dutch Reformed Church in New York, see Corwin, *A Manual of the Reformed Church in America*, p. 23.

[3] Andrews, *The Colonial Period of American History*, Vol. I, p. 427; Weigle, *op. cit.*, p. 34.

[4] Douglas, *Church Unity Movements in the United States*, p. 26.

[5] Sweet, *The Story of Religions in America*, pp. 2, 3.

Moreover, even some groups which in the Old World were the majority churches, in the New World were largely dominated by those who took Christianity seriously. Thus those stemming from Pietism had the leading place in moulding Lutheranism, and Presbyterianism owned much of its spread and its strength to men controlled by the spirit of the Great Awakening.

As in the expansion of Roman Catholicism it was the regulars, those who took their faith more seriously than the majority, who were the active agents, so in the Thirteen Colonies it was generally those who in Protestantism most nearly corresponded to them, earnest and enthusiastic Congregationalists, Baptists, Quakers, Pietists, and products of revivals, who took the lead in propagating Christianity, both among those of European stock and among Indians and Negroes.

It is also important to note the means by which Christianity spread. In contrast with Spanish America, the Crown accorded very little assistance. Most of such help as it gave was by way of formal decrees and not in the substantial form of money. Although in England the monarch was in theory in fuller control of the Church than was the King in the Spanish realms, in practice the latter gave much more active support to the propagation of Christianity. Some aid came through societies in the Old World. The chief of these we have already mentioned—the Company for the Propagation of the Gospel in New England and the Parts Adjacent in America, the Society for Promoting Christian Knowledge, and the Society for the Propagation of the Gospel in Foreign Parts.[6] Bray, to whom the inception of the last two societies owes more than to any other one man, had visited Maryland as the Commissary of the Bishop of London[7] and so was peculiarly interested in the American colonies. In New Netherland the Dutch West India Company was supposed to provide preachers, schoolmasters, and "comforters of the sick," but in general the Dutch churches were under the oversight of the Classis of Amsterdam and remained so even after the colony had passed under English rule.[8] The Reformed churches in Holland contributed clergy

---

[6] Up to the close of the American Revolution the Society for the Propagation of the Gospel in Foreign Parts had maintained about three hundred missionaries and had expended £ 227,454; Alfred W. Newcombe, *The Appointment and Instruction of S. P. G. Missionaries,* in *Church History,* Dec., 1936, Vol. V, 340-358; Pascoe, *Two Hundred Years of the S. P. G.,* pp. 86, 87. At least seventy-nine of the three hundred were American-born, Newcombe, *op. cit.*

[7] Allen and McClure, *Two Hundred Years: The History of the S. P. C. K., 1698-1898,* pp. 13 ff.

[8] *Ecclesiastical Records, State of New York,* Vol. III, pp. 2088-2091; Corwin, *op. cit.,* p. 21. In the earlier days of the colony several of the synods in Holland shared in the supervision of New Netherland; *Ecclesiastical Records, State of New York,* Vol. I, *passim,* and especially p. 138.

and money to the German Reformed churches in Pennsylvania.[9] From time to time sums were raised by private subscription in Great Britain and Ireland for special projects in the colonies, as, for instance, the College of New Jersey, Rhode Island College, Wheelock's Indian Charity School, and King's College.[10] Money was given in Germany to aid the German churches in Pennsylvania.[11] As churches came into existence in the colonies they themselves began to help establish congregations in the newer settlements. At their own initiative and frequently at their own expense pastors preached in places which they could easily reach from their own charges. When individual congregations commenced to associate in organized ecclesiastical bodies, often they began together missionary effort for unchurched communities. Later, in the eighteenth century, religious movements swept the colonies, notably what was known as the Great Awakening,[12] and through them and men touched by them the spread of Christianity was accelerated. Under the direction of ministers colleges were early formed, chiefly for the training of a native American clergy. Here, as in Latin America, ecclesiastical leaders, in endeavouring to prepare clergy, were giving the best education that the colonies knew. In other words, Christianity spread not through state aid, but chiefly through private efforts of ecclesiastical bodies in the Old World, and by the spontaneous endeavour of Christian colonials.

Yet Christianity did not expand unopposed or easily. The majority of the immigrants came to the Thirteen Colonies not from religious but from economic motives. They wished to better their lot financially and, many of them, socially. In the mother countries they had had a formal connexion with the Church as a matter of law or of community custom. In the New World that nominal Christianity tended to drop away and the majority lost all ties with the Church. At the time that the Thirteen Colonies achieved their political independence, and in spite of the efforts of the churches for more than a century and of some marked religious awakenings, only a minority of the population had membership in any religious body. The proportion of those possessing a church connexion varied from colony to colony. Presumably it was larger in New England, where the religious motive had been strong in the original settlements, and was smaller in colonies like Virginia where religion had not been prominent as a cause of immigration. In Vir-

---

[9] *Minutes and Letters of the Coetus of the German Reformed Congregations in Pennsylvania 1747-1792*, pp. iii-v.

[10] Richardson, *An Indian Preacher in England*, pp. 14, 15; Sweet, *op. cit.*, pp. 245, 246.

[11] Dubbs, *History of the Reformed Church, German*, p. 285.

[12] See Joseph Tracy, *The Great Awakening* (Boston, Tappan and Dennet, 1842, pp. xviii, 433), *passim*; Gewehr, *The Great Awakening in Virginia*, *passim*.

ginia at the end of the seventeenth century, the lower classes were practically untouched by the Church.[13] However, even in settlements where the founders had been impelled by a Christian impulse, the second and third generations were marked by a decline in zeal and for a time the original urge seemed waning.

Of the repeatedly told story of the introduction of Christianity to the Thirteen Colonies only the barest summary is needed. We will first approach it by geographic sections and then by the more prominent religious groups.

In New England the chief initial settlements were made by those in whom the religious motive was either prominent or dominant. The famous colony of the Pilgrims at Plymouth, in 1620, was founded by Independents or Separatists, who believed that a true church is a body of Christians under the guidance of pastors elected by "the Lord's godly and free people," who had broken with the established Church of England, had suffered persecution, had sought refuge in Holland, and then, after several years, had decided to go to America. Their purpose in making the momentous change was declared by one of their leaders to be partly economic (an easier living than was theirs as an alien minority in a Dutch city), partly the desire to keep their children loyal to Christian truth as they saw it and removed from the contaminations which surrounded them in the Netherlands, and partly "a great hope . . . of laying some good foundation . . . for the propagating and advancing of the gospel of the kingdom of Christ" in America.[14] It was also later declared that they were moved by a desire not to lose their interest in the English nation, but to extend the King's dominions.[15] This company, while small, because of the halo given it by later generations had an influence upon the ideals of New England and of the United States out of all proportion to its size.

More numerous were the groups who settled around Massachusetts Bay. At the outset their avowed purpose was to "raise a bulwark against the kingdom of anti-Christ which the Jesuits labour to rear up in all parts of the world" and to escape from the corruptions which afflicted the inhabitants of the Old World.[16] They were Puritans who sought to remain within the Church of England, but who wished to eliminate from it what they deemed "corruptions and disorders." For a time some clung to the Book of Common Prayer and even those who did not do so are said to have disclaimed any intention of separating from the Church of England. Yet while they were not

[13] Gewehr, *The Great Awakening in Virginia*, pp. 33 ff.
[14] Bradford, *History of Plymouth Plantation*, Chap. 2.
[15] Mather, *Magnalia Christi Americana*, Book I, Chap. 2, §2.
[16] Mather, *op. cit.*, Book I, Chap. 4, §5.

willingly Separatists, a large proportion of the early clergy seem from the outset to have preferred for the Church a Congregational polity,[17] and those who clung to the Book of Common Prayer were sent back to England.

The four oldest communities out of which arose Rhode Island—at Providence (1636) founded by Roger Williams, at Portsmouth (1639) and Newport (1639) begun by William Coddington, and at Warwick by Samuel Gorton—were established by religious radicals who had proved obnoxious to the authorities on Massachusetts Bay.[18]

In the oldest English colonies in Connecticut, the religious motive was not important if, indeed, it was present. The dominant impulse was the desire for better economic opportunity. Yet those who effected the settlements were Puritans, mostly from Massachusetts, and carried that type of Christianity with them.[19] Thomas Hooker, who as a minister came to have a prominent place in the new colony, encouraged more participation by freemen in the control of state and Church than did John Cotton, who was the outstanding ecclesiastical figure in the older settlements around Boston.[20]

In contrast with these Connecticut settlements, that of New Haven (1638) was founded by a company of strict Puritans who had left the mother country primarily from religious conviction.[21]

While the leading motive in most of the earliest migrations which laid the foundations of New England was religious, and while many who subsequently joined these colonies came from the same purpose,[22] before many years other factors became prominent. The pioneers had been controlled by religious ideals, but many who came later were attracted by the economic advantages in the new land which the others had opened.[23] The fathers did not always succeed in transmitting to their children and grandchildren their own experiences and convictions. Church membership had been conditioned upon the relation of a personal transformation by what was believed to be the grace of God. The children of such members were baptized, but often, because of the lack of such an experience, could not become full members of a church. Eventually their children, in turn, were also baptized, although on the propriety of administering them the rite sharp controversies arose. Unless they could present evidence of "regeneration" such persons were not admitted to full membership or to the communion. Since for admission to this partial

---

[17] Mather, *op. cit.*, Book I, Chap. 4, §8; Miller, *Orthodoxy in Massachusetts*, pp. 119 ff.

[18] Andrews, *The Colonial Period of American History*, Vol. II, pp. 3 ff.

[19] Andrews, *op. cit.*, Vol. II, p. 82.

[20] Andrews, *op. cit.*, Vol. II, pp. 84 ff.

[21] Calder, *The New Haven Colony*, pp. 83, 260-263.

[22] John Higginson in introduction to Mather, *op. cit.*, Vol. I, p. 7.

[23] Miller, *Orthodoxy in Massachusetts, 1630-1650*, pp. xi, xii.

membership, or "half-way covenant," as it was nicknamed by its critics, acquaintance with the chief Christian teachings and a promise to walk in the fellowship and under the moral discipline of the church were required, the compromise was, in effect, a device for transmitting something of Christianity from one generation to another.[24] However, it was not long before the fires of religious devotion were burning much lower than in the first days of high sacrifice.

While union was early achieved between the Independents and the Puritans and what was termed Congregationalism became the prevailing form of Christianity in New England, in spite of initial resentment and even persecution other forms of Christianity either arose by separation from the Standing Order or were introduced from the outside. They flourished especially in Rhode Island, where from the outset much of religious toleration existed. Such diverse groups as the Church of England,[25] Quakers,[26] and Baptists were present. Missionaries of the Society for the Propagation of the Gospel in Foreign Parts were active in seeking to win adherents to the Church of England. Sprinklings of Huguenots came, although they were soon assimilated and did not form permanent ecclesiastical bodies of their own.[27]

Through New England, Christianity exerted a greater influence upon the Thirteen Colonies and the subsequent United States than through any other section of the country. New England was a major although by no means the only source of that Great Awakening which brought to all the colonies the greatest religious revival that they had known. Out of New England parentage came the two greatest leaders of nineteenth century nation-wide revivals, Charles G. Finney and Dwight L. Moody. In New England arose early American efforts to carry Protestant Christianity to non-Christian lands. It was in New England that the Student Volunteer Movement for Foreign Missions began and from it spread throughout the Protestant world. It was in New England that, also in the nineteenth century, the Young People's Society of Christian Endeavour came into being, an organization which soon had branches in many lands. From New England stock were sprung the founders of two somewhat eccentric outgrowths of the Christian impulse, the Church of the Latter-day Saints of Jesus Christ (the Mormons) and Christian

[24] Walker, *A History of the Congregational Churches in the United States*, pp. 170-180.
[25] On the Church of England, see Perry, *The History of the American Episcopal Church*, Vol. I, Chaps. 6, 10, 12, 14, 15; McConnell, *History of the American Episcopal Church*, pp. 93, 94, 127-146, 190 ff.
[26] On the Quakers in New England, see Jones, *The Quakers in the American Colonies*, pp. 3 ff.
[27] Fosdick, *The French Blood in America*, pp. 125 ff.; Chinard, *Les Réfugiés Huguenots en Amerique*, pp. 23 ff.

Science. The firebrand of the Abolition movement, William Lloyd Garrison, was born and reared in New England. From a New England family were two of the most prominent of the Christian philanthropists of the first half of the nineteenth century, Arthur and Benjamin Tappan. From New England Christianity came most of the founders of the earliest American peace movements. It was out of a New England parsonage that there arose one of the greatest expounders of American idealism, Ralph Waldo Emerson. A New England clergyman, in the days of his theological course, was the author of the popular hymn, *America*, which more than any other song has been used to voice and to shape the American dream. From New England colleges, founded through the influence of Christianity, long came the preponderant currents in American higher education. In these and scores of other ways the Christianity of New England moulded the entire United States and had repercussions which were felt the world around.

In New Netherland, later the Colony of New York, much religious diversity existed. Here the major motive in effecting the original settlement was not, as in New England, religious. Nor was the quest of refuge from religious persecution usually an important cause of immigration. To be sure, the Dutch regime was fairly tolerant religiously, and numbers found there a refuge from persecution.[28] Only for a brief time under the vigorous Governor Peter Stuyvesant, himself an active churchman, do the Dutch seem to have engaged in serious efforts to restrain dissent—against Quakers, Baptists, and Lutherans.[29] At the outset the English rule was lenient to the variant forms of Christianity[30] and some who were persecuted elsewhere sought its protection. However, from the beginning, New Amsterdam, later New York City, was a commercial centre. Its inhabitants were drawn from quite a variety of sources and in the majority of instances from economic motives.

In New York under Dutch rule the Reformed Church and under English rule the Church of England enjoyed a preferred position. The Dutch Reformed Church continued strong after the cession of the colony to England.[31] In 1701 no congregation of the Church of England existed in the province outside of New York City. Early in its existence the Society for the Propagation of the Gospel in Foreign Parts appointed missionaries to remedy the situation and a number of accessions were won from other denominations, including,

[28] Jones, *op. cit.*, p. 215.

[29] Sweet, *The Story of Religions in America*, p. 129; Mode, *Source Book of American Church History*, p. 132; *Ecclesiastical Records, State of New York*, Vol. I, p. 361.

[30] Mode, *op. cit.*, p. 133.

[31] Quirinus Breen, *Domine Everhardus Bogardus*, in *Church History*, Vol. II, pp. 78-90.

in Albany, several of the Dutch.[32] Members of that far-flung dispersion, the Huguenots, who contributed to Protestantism in so many lands, were in the company which first settled on Manhattan Island. Others followed. Many came to New York. In its very name New Rochelle bears evidence of its Huguenot origin. Staten Island especially became a Huguenot centre. When, in 1685, the Edict of Nantes which had assured them religious toleration in France was revoked, the exodus of Protestants from France swelled to a flood. Being Calvinist in theology and polity, like the Dutch, the Huguenots easily fused with the Dutch Reformed. Assimilation to still other Protestant groups was also rapid. Some separate Huguenot congregations were formed, but, where these survived, they became incorporated into other denominations.[33] A few Waldensians came, and a church was early built for them on Staten Island.[34] Some of radical religious views, among them those with Anabaptist tendencies and who for that reason were made uncomfortable in New England, moved to Long Island.[35] Quakerism, the most prominent of the English radical religious movements of the second half of the seventeenth century, was early introduced. The first Friends who are known to have reached New Amsterdam arrived in 1657. Later they increased in numbers, in part by additions from those in the colony who were dissatisfied with existing churches.[36] Some English Separatists arrived by way of Holland.[37] A few Congregational churches came into being on Long Island.[38] In 1760, in the early flush of its enthusiastic career, Methodism reached New York City and Methodist meetings began.[39] Baptists were in the colony, for a few years after 1714 a Baptist church existed in New York City, and there were those of that persuasion on Long Island.[40] Presbyterians and Lutherans were also there.[41] German Lutherans, Calvinists, and Roman Catholics came from the Palatinate.[42] For a brief period, 1683-1688, under the favouring rule of James II, Jesuits were in New York City and conducted a school. Although, in 1688, when James II was driven from England

[32] Pascoe, *Two Hundred Years of the S. P. G.*, pp. 57-78.

[33] Fosdick, *op. cit.*, pp. 212 ff.; Chinard, *op. cit.*, pp. 36 ff.; Pannier and Mondain, *L'Expansion Française Outre-Mer et les Protestants Français*, pp. 29-31.

[34] Goodman, *Glimpses of the Story of the Waldensians*, p. 16.

[35] Jones, *op. cit.*, p. 216.

[36] Jones, *op. cit.*, pp. 219 ff.

[37] Jones, *op. cit.*, p. 224.

[38] Walker, *A History of the Congregational Churches in the United States*, p. 310.

[39] Luccock and Hutchinson, *The Story of Methodism*, p. 145.

[40] Vedder, *A Short History of the Baptists*, pp. 303, 304.

[41] Mode, *op. cit.*, pp. 131, 145; *Ecclesiastical Records, State of New York*, Vol. I, pp. 360, 396.

[42] Knittle, *The Early Eighteenth Century Palatine Emigration*, p. 35.

they had to flee, for thirty years or so they carried on their labours sur-reptitiously.[43]

However, the prevailing atmosphere of the colony was commercial and secular. The Dutch were a little tardy in developing church life, and probably for the majority of the population, religion, when it received attention at all, was given a minor place.

New Jersey was later than New York in acquiring many Europeans. A few Dutch came. French Huguenots settled there.[44] To it removed some who found New England too restricted religiously. Thus a protesting minority mi-grated from New Haven to Northern New Jersey.[45] The influence of New England Puritanism became strong in Eastern New Jersey. After the territory embraced in New Jersey passed into the hands of the English, leading Quakers acquired proprietary interests in the region. The vicissitudes of their title need not detain us. Naturally, however, settlements of Quakers followed. Indeed, Quakers had begun to move there before these rights had been acquired. George Fox had found meetings in New Jersey in 1672. By the close of the seventeenth century Quakers were very numerous in both divisions of the province, East and West Jersey. They were particularly prominent and influential in East Jersey, where the Quaker proprietorship had begun earlier.[46] It was in New Jersey that the well-known and greatly loved Quaker, John Woolman, was born (1720). Yet in 1701 a report that the youth in East New Jersey were "very debauched and very ignorant and the Sabbath Day there seems to be set apart for rioting and drunkenness" helped to decide the Society for the Propaga-tion of the Gospel in Foreign Parts to send missionaries to the province.[47]

Opposite Southern New Jersey, on the other side of the Delaware River, near the present Wilmington, in 1638 a Swedish commercial company bought land from the Indians and founded Fort Christina. The project had been de-vised under Gustavus Adolphus, and part of the purpose of that energetic monarch was the conversion of the Indians, that Protestantism might become dominant in the New World. A clergyman came with the second contingent, in 1639.[48] Other Swedish settlements followed and the number of clergy in-creased. When, in 1655, the Dutch eliminated Swedish rule, two of three resi-dent Swedish clergymen were expelled, and the Dutch declared that the one

[43] Walsh, *American Jesuits*, pp. 42-50.
[44] Pannier and Mondain, *op. cit.*, pp. 29-31.
[45] Sweet, *The Story of Religions in America*, p. 87.
[46] Jones, *The Quakers in the American Colonies*, pp. 357-390.
[47] Pascoe, *Two Hundred Years of the S. P. G.*, pp. 52-56.
[48] Maurer, *Early Lutheran Education in Pennsylvania*, pp. 22-24; Sweet, *op. cit.*, p. 130; Wentz, *The Lutheran Church in American History*, p. 41; Jacobs, *A History of the Evangelical Lutheran Church in the United States*, p. 81.

who was permitted to stay was given to drunkenness and brawling.[49] Yet numbers of the Swedes remained, not only in Delaware, but also in Pennsylvania and Southern New Jersey, and their congregations continued. When difficulty was experienced in obtaining clergy, in 1697, at the direction of King Charles XI, three ministers arrived from Sweden. Until the end of the colonial period Lutheran ministers continued to come from Sweden. The Church of Sweden maintained close relationships with the American congregations and the latter flourished. About 1760 the communicants numbered not far from three thousand. The cost to Sweden was between $100,000 and $200,000. Gradually, however, Swedish gave place to English in the services. In 1791 the connexion with Sweden ended.[50] Some of the Swedish clergy had received assistance from the (English) Society for the Propagation of the Gospel in Foreign Parts and at least one served congregations of the Church of England as well as those of Swedish Lutherans. The Society also supported British missionaries who helped build up the Church of England in the colony.[51] Eventually most of the Swedish congregations became affiliated with the Church of England or its successor, the Episcopal Church. The transition was not difficult, for the Church of England and the Church of Sweden had close similarities. Both, for instance, were episcopally governed.

Pennsylvania was at the outset a "holy experiment." Like the earliest settlements in New England, it owed its inception primarily to the Christian impulse. The region on the Delaware passed from the Dutch to the English. The Quakers had long been dreaming of a refuge in the New World, and one of their great early converts, the wealthy and powerful William Penn, made this aspiration a reality by acquiring, in 1681, a charter which gave him what was called, in honour of his father, Pennsylvania. In this grant was included not only the present state of that name, but also what later became the state of Delaware. William Penn had been educated in an Anglican school in which Puritan influence was strong. While not yet in his teens he had a profound religious experience. At Oxford as a student he belonged to a group of earnest men who met for prayer and exhortation. Later he aligned himself fully with

---

[49] *Ecclesiastical Records, State of New York,* Vol. I, p. 395.

[50] C. J. I. Bergendoff, *The Swedish Church on the Delaware,* in *Church History,* Vol. VII, pp. 215-230; Wentz, *op. cit.,* pp. 43-45; Jacobs, *op. cit.,* pp. 87-109. See a list of the ministers sent from Sweden to America in Carolus David Arfwedson, *A Brief History of the Colony of New Sweden,* pp. 40-44, in *The Pennsylvania German Society Proceedings,* Vol. XVIII.

[51] Jacobs, *op. cit.,* pp. 94, 147; Edgar Legare Pennington, *The Reverend George Ross, S. P. G. Missionary at New Castle, Delaware (Proceedings of the American Antiquarian Society,* Oct., 1936), *passim.*

the Quakers and in time became the leader of the Dissenters.[52] It was not strange that Penn, coming from this background, should plan in his vast new domains a community in which Christian principles as he understood them should be the basis of society. He made religious toleration part of the cornerstone of the colony. He gave to his capital the name of Philadelphia, "the City of Brotherly Love." Instead of seizing the lands of the aborigines by force, he entered into a treaty of amity with the Indians.[53] Here in Pennsylvania was a deliberate and conscientious attempt to put Christianity into practice on a large scale and to build a society governed by the Christian ideal. It reminds one of the dream of some of the Spanish princes, of numbers of Portuguese and Spanish ecclesiastics and laymen, and of early Independents and Puritans in New England—that in the New World, from the very beginning, free from the evil traditions of the Old World, a society should be built on Christian foundations.

In attracting settlers, however, Penn appealed not only to the religious motive, but also to what he deemed a legitimate desire for a larger economic opportunity than Europe and England afforded. In this, too, he must have believed that he was acting as a Christian. He told of the excellent land, the sweeping forests, the possibilities of the fur trade, and the social and political liberty of the colony.[54] Those who responded were impelled by a variety of desires. Many sought both freedom from religious, social, and political oppression, and a greater store of this world's goods. In some, especially in later years when the colony had become prosperous, the religious incentive was slight or entirely missing.

Several different religious groups came. Active efforts to recruit settlers were made not only in the British Isles, but also on the Continent of Europe.

Of course Quakers were numerous. In the second half of the seventeenth century they were multiplying in England. They were then what Independents and Puritans had been a generation or two earlier, the most prominent and aggressive of the groups who declined to conform to the Church of England. Persecution and enthusiasm combined with the generous opportunity afforded by their powerful fellow-believer to send them out to Pennsylvania. From nearly all parts of the British Isles they came. In the first year two thousand are said to have arrived. At the outset they provided the overwhelming majority of the immigrants.[55]

Before long, Dutch and Germans began to filter in. Penn made three journeys

[52] William Hull, *William Penn, A Topical Biography* (Oxford University Press, 1937, pp. xvi, 362), *passim*.
[53] Jones, *op. cit.*, pp. 417 ff.
[54] Jones, *op. cit.*, p. 420.
[55] Jones, *op. cit.*, pp. 421, 422, 459.

to the Continent of Europe, seeking out kindred spirits and groups and attempting to win them to fellowship with the Quakers.[56] Out of these arose the beginnings of emigration to his colony. In 1682 an organization was formed at Frankfurt to promote the movement to Pennsylvania. It bought several thousands of acres in Penn's domains.[57] The first shipload of Germans arrived in 1683.[58] Germantown, near Philadelphia, was founded in 1683, chiefly by Dutch.[59] As the years passed the tide of German immigration swelled. Most of it came from the Rhine Valley, South Germany, and Switzerland. A very large part of it was from the Palatinate, where wastage by successive wars and, later, persecution by Roman Catholic rulers, made conditions intolerable for many, particularly (although not exclusively) Protestants.[60] The tyrannous exactions of German princes added to the unrest, and ship-owners and shipping companies spread broadcast enticing pictures of the American paradise.[61] Between 1727 and 1775 nearly sixty-nine thousand Germans are said to have landed at Philadelphia, and by the latter date Germans are said to have comprised about one-third of the population of Pennsylvania.[62]

Several Christian bodies were represented among these Germans. Some were Quakers when they arrived. Of these a number had first been Mennonites and had become Quakers through missionaries of the latter group who had visited them in Germany.[63] Many were Mennonites when they reached Pennsylvania. Some of these traced their religious descent through Swiss Brethren and some through Dutch Anabaptists.[64] Numbers of the Mennonites were assisted by Quakers to cross the ocean.[65] Some of the settlers were Dunkers or Tunkers, or, as they preferred to be known, Brethren, or the Church of the Brethren. The initial group arrived in 1719 and first made their home at Germantown. Others followed. Eventually the members were scattered in various parts of the colony and in New Jersey and Maryland. Active efforts were made by the Germantown congregation to nourish the faith of those dispersed elsewhere, and in 1742 an Annual Meeting was begun which was designed to bring all

[56] Hull, *William Penn and the Dutch Quaker Migration to Pennsylvania*, p. 58.
[57] Hull, *op. cit.*, pp. 180-183.
[58] Faust, *The German Element in the United States*, Vol. I, pp. 34, 35.
[59] Hull, *op. cit.*, pp. 178-180.
[60] Faust, *op. cit.*, Vol. I, pp. 52 ff.; Maurer, *Early Lutheran Education in Pennsylvania*, p. 9; Bittinger, *The Germans in Colonial Times*, pp. 11 ff.; Knittle, *The Early Eighteenth Century Palatine Emigration*, pp. 1 ff.; Strassburger and Hinke, *Pennsylvania German Pioneers*, Vol. I, pp. xiii-xv.
[61] Faust, *op. cit.*, Vol. I, pp. 60 ff.
[62] Faust, *op. cit.*, Vol. I, p. 128; Maurer, *op. cit.*, p. 9; Strassburger and Hinke, *op. cit.*, Vol. I, p. xxxi.
[63] Wenger, *History of the Mennonites of the Franconia Conference*, pp. 7-11.
[64] Wenger, *op. cit.*, pp. 4-6.
[65] Wenger, *op. cit.*, p. 14.

the congregations into fellowship and to confirm them in the tenets of the Brethren.[66] From 1731 to 1737 came the Schwenkfelders, a small group who traced their origin to a contemporary of Luther.[67]

Naturally the largest German groups were those which were in the majority in the regions from which the immigrants came, the Lutherans and the Reformed. In 1759 the Lutherans were said to number about thirty-five thousand and the German Reformed thirty thousand, or together about a fourth of the population of Pennsylvania.[68] At the outset much co-operation existed between Lutherans and Reformed. Often the two worshipped in the same buildings and were served by the same pastors.[69]

The first Lutherans did not bring teachers and pastors with them. In the early days ecclesiastical tramps of dubious character took advantage of their desire for religious services to prey on them. Soon, however, preachers of a different stripe arrived. Some of them showed great devotion in travelling among the settlers, holding services, baptizing children, and encouraging the erection of church buildings.[70]

The great early leader of the Lutherans in America, the one who did more than any other of the colonial period to multiply their congregations, to organize them, and to mould their temper, was Henry Melchior Muhlenberg. Muhlenberg was born in 1711 in Hanover. As a young man he was brought under the influence of Pietism. After his graduation at Göttingen he taught in the Orphan House and the charitable institutions connected with it in the great Pietist centre, Halle. For a time he expected to go to India to the missions maintained there by the Pietists. The door to that enterprise seemed closed to him, and he fulfilled his missionary purpose by accepting a call to America. This had come through Ziegenhagen, Lutheran preacher at the German Court Chapel maintained in London in connexion with the ruling house—which hailed from Hanover. German congregations in London had naturally developed a lively interest in the Germans in the American colonies. Muhlenberg was the choice of G. A. Francke, the son and successor of A. H. Francke as the director of the Pietist institutions at Halle. The appointment was hastened by the desire to counteract the activities of Zinzendorf, who was in Pennsyl-

[66] Otho Winger, *History and Doctrines of the Church of the Brethren* (Elgin, Ill., Brethren Publishing House, 2d ed., 1920, pp. 320), pp. 23-58; Martin Grove Brumbaugh, *A History of the German Baptist Brethren in Europe and America* (Mount Morris, Pa., Brethren Publishing House, 1899, pp. xxii, 559), *passim*.

[67] Wenger, *op. cit.*, pp. 82, 83.

[68] Klett, *Presbyterians in Colonial Pennsylvania*, p. 35.

[69] Faust, *op. cit.*, Vol. I, p. 116; Maurer, *Early Lutheran Education in Pennsylvania*, pp. 50, 51, 65.

[70] Wentz, *The Lutheran Church in American History*, pp. 57-60.

vania seeking to bring about a kind of union of some of the Protestant groups which seemed dangerous to the Halle leaders.

Additional personnel and money came from Halle, and voluminous reports were sent back by the Pennsylvania missionaries. Although some non-Halle ministers came from Germany, it was Halle Pietism which was most active in moulding the Lutheranism of Pennsylvania, and the impress of that Pietism was much stronger upon colonial Lutheranism than it was upon the Lutheranism of Germany as a whole.

Muhlenberg reached Pennsylvania in 1742. He adopted as his motto *Ecclesia Plantanda*, and most ably lived up to his slogan. He founded many congregations, brought order and life into others, organized a synod (1748), helped in the adoption of a uniform liturgy, and dreamed of a native ministry. Before his death (1787) the Colonies had achieved their independence, the Lutheran Church was thriving, and sons of the soil had begun to pour into the ministry. Lutheranism had become an integral part of American life.[71]

The Reformed, like the Lutherans, were late in developing an organization and a body of clergy. Pioneers in a given locality usually set apart a farm for the support of a clergyman and of a school. The schoolmasters were expected to teach the children the catechism, and on occasion they officiated at funerals. Several of the teachers had been unable to obtain employment in Europe because of their unworthy character, but others seem to have laboured well in laying the foundations of church as well as school.[72] Laymen of deep religious conviction did much to nourish congregations. One of these, John Philip Boehm, served several congregations and eventually was ordained.[73] The *Oberconsistorium* of the Palatinate, with headquarters at Heidelberg, paid the travelling expenses to America of young ministers or *candidati*.[74] However, the ecclesiastical authorities in the Palatinate found themselves too impoverished to give the help that was needed and commended the German Reformed churches to the Synods to Holland (1728). These latter acted through the

---

[71] William J. Mann, *Life and Times of Henry Melchior Muhlenberg* (Philadelphia, General Council Publication Board, 1911, pp. xvi, 547), *passim*; Wentz, *op. cit.*, pp. 65-77; Jacobs, *A History of the Evangelical Lutheran Church in the United States*, pp. 209-306. Many of the pertinent contemporary documents, including some of the papers of Muhlenberg, are in *Nachrichten von den Vereinigten Deutschen Evangelisch-Lutherischen Gemeinen in Nord-America absonderlich in Pensylvanien mit einer Vorrede von D. Johann Ludewig Schulze . . . Halle . . . 1787* (new edition, 2 vols. Vol. I, Allentown, Pa., Brobst, Diehl and Co., 1886, Vol. 2, Philadelphia, P. G. C. Eisenhardt, 1895).

[72] Dubbs, *History of the Reformed Church, German*, pp. 240-242.

[73] *Minutes and Letters of the Coetus of the German Reformed Congregations in Pennsylvania, 1747-1792*, pp. 1-31; Dubbs, *op. cit.*, pp. 247 ff.

[74] Dubbs, *op. cit.*, p. 255.

Classis of Amsterdam, which, as we have seen, had oversight of the Dutch Reformed churches in New York.[75]

As a representative of the Dutch Synods there arrived, in 1746, Michael Schlatter, who performed for the Reformed churches a mission somewhat similar to that which Muhlenberg, who had come four years before, accomplished for the Lutherans. Schlatter was born July 14, 1716, in St. Gall, Switzerland. He was well educated, was ordained, and had been in Holland. It was not strange that the Dutch Synods called him to the American mission. He was responsible for gathering ministers and elders into a *Coetus*, or Synod, which proved an enduring organization. He helped to bring order into congregations and to induce them to contribute to the support of a ministry. In 1751-1752 he was in Europe and there raised about £12,000 as an endowment for the American churches and pastors—although as a condition of this aid the *Coetus* was required to be subordinate to the Classis of Amsterdam. He brought back with him six young ministers. In England, as an outgrowth of Schlatter's work, there was organized a Society for the Promotion of the Knowledge of God among the Germans, and the money collected was devoted to the establishment of charity schools for Germans of all denominations in Pennsylvania. The charity school was a type of education which had wide vogue in the British Isles in the eighteenth century and was for the purpose of giving education and religious instruction to the poor. In Pennsylvania Schlatter became the superintendent of the movement. However, a fierce resentment against the charity schools developed among the Germans on the ground that they sought to deprive the German children of their native tongue and to make them servants of the English proprietors—and it must be acknowledged that the schools were in part designed to assimilate the Germans to their English colonial environment, on the theory that in the long struggle with the French the large foreign element was dangerous. Under the wave of criticism, Schlatter, discouraged, resigned. Although he continued to live in America and did not die until 1790, he ceased to be a leader in the Reformed churches.[76]

The Moravians were active in Pennsylvania. Apparently the first to reach the colony, and, indeed, any of the Thirteen Colonies, came in 1734 with the Schwenkfelders with the expectation that he would become an itinerant missionary among the religiously destitute German settlers.[77] In 1735 a group of

---

[75] Dubbs, *op. cit.*, pp. 278, 279.

[76] Dubbs, *op. cit.*, pp. 279-289; A. G. Weng in *Church History*, Vol. V, p. 361. A mine of information about the Reformed churches is in *Minutes and Letters of the Coetus of the German Reformed Congregations in Pennsylvania, 1747-1792*, which were sent as reports to Holland.

[77] Hamilton, *A History of the Unitas Fratrum, or Moravian Church, in the United States of America*, p. 439.

Moravians, led by Augustus Gottlieb Spangenberg, reached Georgia, but by the end of 1740 the survivors had moved to Pennsylvania. Beginnings of settlements were made at Nazareth and Bethlehem.[78] Late in 1741 the great patron of the Moravians, Zinzendorf himself, arrived in Philadelphia, and was in America until early in 1743. His months in America were shortly before the period when leadership from Europe effected adequate ecclesiastical organization for the Lutherans and Reformed. He was deeply impressed by the religious destitution of many of the settlers and the divisions among the Christian bodies who were serving the Germans. He wished to bring together in co-operation the several groups and to unite them to serve the colonies and to reach the Indians. His visit led to an extensive missionary activity among the colonists, to systematic work for the Indians, and to some new Moravian congregations.[79] Spangenberg, a man of marked energy and intellectual gifts, became the great leader of the American Moravians in their formative period. With the development of denominational organizations by other groups, the dream of inclusive union faded, but congregations of Moravians arose in a number of places and a fellowship was formed to tie them together.[80]

Centring in Philadelphia there came into existence a Baptist Association which was stronger and more uniform than any other developed by that group in colonial times. The first Baptist church in Pennsylvania seems to have been organized in 1684 by an Irishman.[81] The religious liberty in Pennsylvania and New Jersey favoured a rapid growth of Baptist churches. Some arose from immigration, and some as the result of the preaching of earnest missionaries. Many Baptists came from Wales. Others were English and Irish. Some were from New England. In the first decade of the eighteenth century what came to be known as the Philadelphia Association was formed. This helped to give cohesion and strength to a movement which by its very nature tended to lack centralization.[82] In 1762 the Association included twenty-nine churches with a membership of 1,318 in Pennsylvania, New Jersey, New England, New York, Virginia, and Maryland. In 1776 forty-two churches were reported with a membership of 3,013.[83] The Association assisted destitute congregations and sent out missionaries to the colonists.[84] Eventually it adopted a confession of faith which was Calvinistic in theology and in so doing helped to give a

[78] Hamilton, *op. cit.*, pp. 440-442; Bechler, *August Gottlieb Spangenberg und die Mission,* pp. 18 ff.

[79] Hamilton, *op. cit.*, pp. 446-451.

[80] Hamilton, *op. cit.*, pp. 452-473. On Spangenberg see Bechler, *op. cit., passim.*

[81] Newman, *A History of the Baptist Churches in the United States,* p. 201.

[82] Newman, *op. cit.*, pp. 202-215.

[83] Newman, *op. cit.*, p. 273.

[84] White, *A Century of Faith,* p. 27.

prevailingly Calvinistic tinge to the Baptists of America. Arminian influence had been strong among Baptists in other sections.[85] Numbers of Baptist churches existed which did not affiliate themselves with the Association.

A strong Presbyterian element arose in Pennsylvania through the Scotch-Irish. Under James I large numbers of Presbyterian Scotch had moved to Ulster. Under Charles II and James II they were persecuted by the Anglicans and developed a strong consciousness of religious and racial unity as against the Irish Roman Catholics on the one hand and the Anglicans on the other. Most of them belonged to the middle and lower classes. As time passed they were harassed by mounting rentals and tithes and by limitations on their industry and trade. In the seventeenth century a few of these Scotch-Irish began to find their way to America. Beginning with the close of the second decade of the eighteenth century the trickle became a flood. In 1728 and 1729 about two thousand left Dublin for Pennsylvania, and in the seventeen seventies before the outbreak of the War of Independence about one hundred and fifty thousand embarked for America. While they scattered widely through the Colonies, a large proportion of them settled in Pennsylvania, for they were attracted by the religious toleration in the colony and by the reputed wealth of the natural resources.[86] In most of the Colonies they tended to go to the unoccupied lands on the frontiers. A few were Roman Catholics, but the great majority were Presbyterians by tradition. Indeed, because of the persecution which they had suffered in Ireland, they tended to be tenacious of their Presbyterianism. At the outset they were desperately poor, clergy were few, and some of such clergy as came were of poor quality. One of the early ministers, Francis Makemie, however, travelled up and down as a missionary, ranging from South Carolina to New York. It was he who became the leader in organizing the first Presbytery in the Colonies, formed in Philadelphia.[87] Before many years the rapid growth of congregations and clergy brought about the enlargement of this organization to a synod with four subordinate presbyteries.[88]

Religious toleration made possible resident Roman Catholic priests in Pennsylvania for the settlers of that church.[89]

---

[85] Coe Hayne, *Trends in Theological Thought among Early Baptists in the United States* (Ms. used with the author's permission).

[86] Klett, *Presbyterians in Colonial Pennsylvania*, pp. 1-24.

[87] Thompson, *A History of the Presbyterian Churches in the United States*, pp. 18, 19. For a biography of Makemie, see I. Marshall Page, *The Life Story of Rev. Francis Makemie* (Grand Rapids, Mich., Wm. B. Eerdman Publishing Co., 1938). The exact date of the organization is uncertain. It appears to have been in 1705 or 1706, although some kind of informal council seems to have been held in 1701.

[88] Thompson, *op. cit.*, p. 25.

[89] O'Gorman, *A History of the Roman Catholic Church in the United States*, pp. 238-245; Sister Mary Augustina Ray, *American Opinion of Roman Catholicism in the*

The Church of England had to work against the overwhelming strength of other groups and enjoyed no especially preferred position. Yet churches were built in Philadelphia and clergy came from England, some of them sent by the Society for the Propagation of the Gospel in Foreign Parts.[90]

The Christianity of Pennsylvania, then, had a leading role in the Thirteen Colonies and so of the later United States. Its effect upon the total life of the subsequent nation was not as great as was that of New England. The Quakers lost control in the colony much earlier than did the Puritans in New England. Yet because of the size and fertility of the province and the purpose and programme of Penn (inspired by the latter's Christian faith) the influence of the Christianity of Pennsylvania was second only to that of New England —and may have been greater than that of any one New England colony. Because of the toleration adopted from the inception of the "holy experiment," more different denominations were present than in any other colony and more groups there first achieved a denominational organization. In this variety and this denominational organization Pennsylvania was more typical of the coming United States than any other colony or section.

The founders of Maryland, the Calverts, were Roman Catholics. With the first party of settlers, in 1634, came Jesuits, and seculars followed.[91] As the only one of the Thirteen Colonies in which Roman Catholics enjoyed this favoured position, it is not strange that Maryland was the centre of Roman Catholicism in colonial days, and that after the War of Independence Baltimore became the see of the first Roman Catholic bishop in the United States. From Maryland Jesuit missionaries penetrated into Delaware, New Jersey, and Pennsylvania, to care for the Roman Catholics.[92]

Yet Maryland was not primarily Roman Catholic. Out of expediency or of necessity the founders granted religious toleration, and so far as its population had church affiliations the colony became overwhelmingly Protestant. The Church of England was slow in developing. In 1676 only three of its clergy were said to be in Maryland.[93] In 1689-1690 a local revolution led to the overthrow of the Roman Catholic political control and in 1692 the Church of Eng-

Eighteenth Century (New York, Columbia University Press, 1936, pp. 456), p. 70; Griffin, The Contribution of Belgium to the Catholic Church in America (1523-1857), pp. 53 ff.
[90] Pascoe, Two Hundred Years of the S. P. G., pp. 33-40; Manross, A History of the American Episcopal Church, pp. 124-132.
[91] O'Gorman, A History of the Roman Catholic Church in the United States, pp. 220-223; Walsh, American Jesuits, pp. 37, 38; Griffin, The Contribution of Belgium to the Catholic Church in America (1523-1857), pp. 24 ff., 55 ff.
[92] O'Gorman, op. cit., p. 245.
[93] Perry, The History of the American Episcopal Church, Vol. I, p. 134, giving a letter of John Yeo, from Maryland, of that year.

land was given by law a privileged position. Francis Nicholson, who became governor shortly thereafter, actively encouraged the building of residences and the setting aside of glebes for the clergy of the Church of England. The Calverts became members of the Established Church. Before many years the strength and life of that Church became not unlike that in the neighbouring Virginia, except that the average parish was smaller.[94] In 1696 Thomas Bray, who later had a prominent part in organizing missionary societies in England, was appointed Commissary, or agent, of the Bishop of London, for Maryland. Through him the legal position of the Church of England was strengthened.[95] In 1701 the colony had a population of about twenty-five thousand, and possessed thirty parishes, of which about half had clergy. So much better were conditions than in some of the other colonies that the Society for the Propagation of the Gospel in Foreign Parts gave only occasional help.[96]

Various other Protestant groups were represented in Maryland. Puritans were early there. They had first settled in Virginia, had obtained clergy from Boston, were persecuted by the Virginia authorities, and removed to Maryland.[97] By 1661 the Quakers had a number of regular meetings, and that in spite of opposition.[98] Quaker missionaries arrived, among them the founder, George Fox. In 1672 the Baltimore Yearly Meeting, the second oldest in America, came into being.[99] Itinerant ministers visited isolated Quaker families, held meetings, and effected conversions.[100] Many Lutherans were there, and before the War of Independence a Synod had been constituted in Maryland.[101] Maryland vied with New York as the earliest centre of American Methodism. To Maryland came, in the seventeen sixties, Robert Strawbridge, a Methodist local preacher, from Ulster. He made his home there and became an independent itinerant preacher in Eastern Maryland, Delaware, and Pennsylvania.[102]

Virginia, although the oldest and most populous of the Thirteen, did not occupy nearly so prominent a place in the religious life of the Colonies as did some others. In contrast with the earliest settlements in New England, and with Pennsylvania and part of New Jersey, religious motives were either absent or played a subordinate role in its founding and in most of its immigra-

[94] Manross, op. cit., p. 74; Perry, op. cit., Vol. I, pp. 136, 137; Allen and McClure, Two Hundred Years: The Story of the S. P. C. K., 1698-1898, pp. 224, 225; McConnell, History of the American Episcopal Church, pp. 105 ff.
[95] Perry, op. cit., Vol. I, pp. 138-143.
[96] Pascoe, op. cit., p. 31.
[97] Goodwin, The Colonial Church in Virginia, p. 97.
[98] Jones, The Quakers in the American Colonies, p. 279.
[99] Jones, op. cit., pp. 280-283.
[100] Jones, op. cit., pp. 291-294.
[101] Jacobs, A History of the Evangelical Lutheran Church in the United States, p. 263.
[102] Sweet, Methodism in American History, pp. 50-53.

tion. To be sure, as we have seen, one of the purposes avowed in the first charters was the conversion of the Indians to Christianity, but among the initial settlers the desire for monetary gain seems to have been uppermost.

Yet from the beginning Christianity had a place in the life of the colony. Provision was made for services according to the Church of England. Alexander Whitaker, first minister of Henrico Parish, the second to be organized in Virginia, was a man of means who is said to have come to the dangers and discomforts of the crude, new world from purely religious motives.[103] "Dale's Laws," enacted 1611 for the government of the colony, were Draconian in their attempt to enforce on all settlers daily attendance at Morning and Evening Prayer and in their penalties for blasphemy.[104] They were never really carried out, but their milder successors gave the Church of England a privileged place. The law required conformity to the Church of England in public services.[105] As in England, the land was divided into parishes. In 1680 these were said to number forty-eight and to be served by thirty-five ministers. In 1784, when the church was disestablished, ninety-five organized parishes and a dozen or more nominal parishes existed.[106]

However, neither an episcopate nor a full set of church courts was provided, and in colonial days the church was never a fully grown organism in the sense in which it existed in England.[107] In the seventeenth century difficulty was experienced in obtaining enough clergymen.[108] The General Assembly once offered a bonus of £25 to any one bringing to the colony a clergyman in priest's orders.[109] In 1680 the complaint was made that parishes were too large and were permitted by the planters to lie vacant to save expense, that laymen were commissioned to preach and enjoyed the income of four or five parishes, and that clergy still only in deacon's orders administered the sacraments and held more than one parish.[110] Even in the eighteenth century the new settlements on the western frontier were sadly neglected.[111] Some of the clergy, too, were said to be of poor quality. Yet the average of the clergy, morally and education-

[103] Francis L. Hawks, *A Narrative of Events Connected With the Rise and Progress of the Protestant Episcopal Church in Virginia*, pp. 29 ff.; Manross, *History of the American Episcopal Church*, p. 9; McConnell, *History of the American Episcopal Church*, pp. 19; Weigle, *American Idealism*, p. 71.

[104] Manross, *op. cit.*, p. 8; Andrews, *The Colonial Period of American History*, Vol. I, pp. 114-116; Weigle, *op. cit.*, p. 68.

[105] Manross, *op. cit.*, pp. 10 ff.

[106] Goodwin, *The Colonial Church in Virginia*, p. 74.

[107] Manross, *op. cit.*, pp. 10 ff.; McConnell, *History of the American Episcopal Church*, pp. 173 ff.

[108] Manross, *op. cit.*, p. 17; McConnell, *op. cit.*, p. 195; Hawks, *op. cit.*, p. 35.

[109] Goodwin, *op. cit.*, p. 80.

[110] Godwyn, *The Negro's and Indian's Advocate*, pp. 171, 172.

[111] Manross, *op. cit.*, p. 72.

ally, is declared to have been good. A large proportion were graduates of Oxford or Cambridge and were of excellent social background.[112] The Society for the Propagation of the Gospel in Foreign Parts regarded Virginia as so much less needy than some of the other colonies that it confined its assistance to contributions of religious books and to gratuities to two clergymen.[113] Moreover, James Blair, who came to the colony in 1685 as a missionary and in 1689 was appointed Commissary of the Bishop of London and held that office for forty-four years, gave the church pugnacious but upright and vigorous leadership.[114]

In spite of the favoured position accorded the Church of England, dissenting groups appeared in Virginia. Most of these were not of spontaneous origin, but arose from immigration and the efforts of missionaries from outside the colony. In the first half of the seventeenth century Puritans settled in Norfolk County and obtained ministers from Boston, but were persecuted by the civil authorities.[115] Huguenots and Waldensians came at intervals, and the former had at least one congregation of their own.[116] As early as 1657 Quakers appeared, and in 1660 and 1662 laws were enacted against them.[117] Quaker preachers persisted in coming, among them George Fox himself, and the number of adherents rose.[118] Beginning about 1725, moreover, and continuing until the War of Independence, large numbers of Quakers moved in from the northern colonies, chiefly from the desire to better their economic status.[119] For instance, in 1754 a meeting was organized at Lynchburg.[120] By the early years of the eighteenth century, a few scattered Baptists existed. Some of these wrote to fellow Baptists in London for ministers, and in response two were sent in 1714. In 1737 two other ministers came. Partly through the assistance of these missionaries, a few churches were organized.[121] In the second half of the eighteenth century, the Baptists grew apace. This was largely because of religious revivals arising out of the Great Awakening and through the preaching of evangelists from other colonies.[122] By the outbreak of the War of Independence, Baptists were said to number ten thousand. They were drawn largely from the frontier and the lower classes, areas and groups not effectively

[112] Goodwin, *op. cit.*, pp. xix, 80, 92.
[113] Pascoe, *Two Hundred Years of the S. P. G.*, p. 30.
[114] Goodwin, *op. cit.*, p. 82; Weigle, *op. cit.*, p. 73.
[115] Goodwin, *op. cit.*, p. 97.
[116] Fosdick, *The French Blood in America*, pp. 345 ff.; Hawks, *op. cit.*, pp. 78, 79.
[117] Jones, *The Quakers in the American Colonies*, pp. 268-272; Hawks, *op. cit.*, p. 71.
[118] Jones, *op. cit.*, pp. 282-292, 306, 307.
[119] Jones, *op. cit.*, pp. 295-297.
[120] Douglas Summers Brown, *A History of Lynchburg's Pioneer Quakers and Their Meeting House, 1754-1936* (Lynchburg, J. P. Bell Co., 1936, pp. viii, 180), p. 35.
[121] Newman, *A History of the Baptist Churches in the United States*, p. 230.
[122] Newman, *op. cit.*, pp. 284 ff.

touched by the Church of England.[123] In the second half of the eighteenth century German Lutherans from Pennsylvania pressed southward into the Shenandoah to occupy the virgin lands of that fertile valley and immigrants also came directly from Germany. Peter Muhlenberg, the distinguished son of the great organizer of colonial Lutheranism, moved to Virginia to help supply as pastor the spiritual needs of these pioneers.[124] Before the middle of the eighteenth century, itinerant Moravian missionaries were visiting settlements in Virginia.[125] The flood of Scotch-Irish immigration also reached Virginia and helped to give Presbyterians a strong foothold. In 1738 the Synod of Philadelphia began extending its care to the Presbyterians on either side of the Blue Ridge.[126] Beginning about 1736 itinerant missionaries commenced regular visits to Presbyterians on this frontier.[127] Beginning in 1683 Francis Makemie did much to help Presbyterianism in Southern Maryland and in the adjoining part of Virginia, east of Chesapeake Bay. Samuel Davies organized Presbyterianism in the eastern counties.[128] From 1755 onward, the New York Synod sent missionaries to Virginia.[129] As may be surmised from these dates, Presbyterianism in Virginia owed much of its growth to the Great Awakening. Until the seventeen seventies it was the most powerful of the dissenting denominations.[130] Before the outbreak of the War of Independence, Methodism had been introduced. In 1773 one hundred members were reported, and the numbers grew rapidly.[131] By the time that Virginia ceased to be a colony and became one of the new United States, Christianity, represented by these groups outside the Church of England, was beginning to take deeper hold upon the non-aristocratic masses of the Old Dominion.

North Carolina was backward. In spite of the fact that ephemeral English settlements were made there as early as the sixteenth century, it was not until the second half of the seventeenth century that important permanent colonization was effected. Natural obstacles—the lack of good harbours, rocks, shoals, and falls in the rivers—worked to the disadvantage of the region.[132] In 1729 the white population probably did not exceed thirty thousand, and

[123] Gewehr, The Great Awakening in Virginia, pp. 19-39, 106.
[124] Jacobs, A History of the Evangelical Lutheran Church in the United States, p. 295.
[125] Gewehr, op. cit., p. 35.
[126] Gewehr, op. cit., p. 40.
[127] Gewehr, op. cit., pp. 43, 44.
[128] William Henry Foote, Sketches of Virginia (Philadelphia, William S. Martin, 1850, pp. v, 568), pp. 40 ff., 119-146, 157 ff.; Gewehr, op. cit., pp. 68 ff.; Hawks, op. cit., pp. 106 ff.
[129] Gewehr, op. cit., p. 90.
[130] Gewehr, op. cit., pp. 34, 35.
[131] Gewehr, op. cit., p. 145.
[132] Johnson, Ante-Bellum North Carolina, pp. 3-5.

most of this was confined to the coastal plain. By 1760 the settlements extended to the Blue Ridge. In 1790 the white population was only 289,181, of whom 83 per cent were of English, 11.2 per cent were of Scotch, 2.8 per cent of German, 2.3 per cent of Irish, .3 per cent of French, and .2 per cent of Dutch stock. The Scotch were both from the Highlands and from the North of Ireland. The latter had come in, like most of the Scotch-Irish, by way of Philadelphia.[133]

Under these circumstances, North Carolina was slow in developing religiously and owed its Christianity largely to continued activity of missionaries from Europe and the northern colonies.[134] The Quakers were the first religious body to obtain a foothold and until the close of the seventeenth century were the most prominent denomination. The Quaker, William Edmundson, is said to have preached the first sermon in the province (1671). George Fox was there in 1672.[135] A chain of meetings was established along the coast.[136] Most of the gentry on the coastal plain, like those of tidewater Virginia, belonged to the Church of England.[137] In 1715 the colonial Assembly divided the province into nine parishes and fixed the salaries of the ministers. However, such Church of England clergy as came were largely missionaries of the Society for the Propagation of the Gospel in Foreign Parts. One arrived in 1703. Two more were sent in 1707. In 1717 the Governor reported that he could find only one clergyman of the Church of England, and that he was a missionary of the Society. In 1732 the Society declared that not one clergyman was in the province and so appointed an itinerant. In 1752 a missionary of the Society wrote that in seven or eight years he had travelled fourteen thousand miles and had baptized a little over six thousand children.[138] At least three types of Baptists were found in the colony. Missionaries were sent by the Philadelphia Association. Others came from New England. They were zealous in spreading their faith and the numbers of adherents grew.[139] Presbyterian ministers were active as missionaries, and Lutherans and Moravians were represented.[140] The Society for the Promotion of Christian Knowledge aided in supplying the Lutherans

---

[133] Johnson, *op. cit.,* pp. 8-11.

[134] Johnson, *op. cit.,* p. 410.

[135] Johnson, *op. cit.,* p. 353; Jones, *The Quakers in the American Colonies,* pp. 283-286.

[136] Jones, *op. cit.,* p. 299.

[137] Johnson, *op. cit.,* p. 18.

[138] Humphreys, *Historical Account of the Incorporated Society for the Propagation of the Gospel in Foreign Parts,* pp. 129-143; Pascoe, *Two Hundred Years of the S. P. G.,* pp. 20-25.

[139] George Washington Paschal, *History of Wake Forest College* (Wake Forest College, Vol. I, 1935, pp. viii, 681), Vol. I, pp. 16-18.

[140] Johnson, *op. cit.,* pp. 18, 411; William Henry Foote, *Sketches of North Carolina* (New York, Robert Carter, 1846, pp. 557), pp. 77-83, 158-182, 231 ff.

with pastors.[141] In 1753 a Moravian settlement was made by a group from Bethlehem, Pennsylvania, and this was swelled by immigrants from Europe. Salem became a Moravian centre from which missionaries were sent as far south as Georgia.[142]

In South Carolina the first permanent settlements were slightly later than those in North Carolina. However, partly because of the excellent port at Charleston, the smaller of the Carolinas forged ahead of its northern sister. Along the coastal plain a wealthy planter aristocracy arose, and Charleston became an important city, a centre of wealth and culture.

In the second half of the sixteenth century transient attempts at settlement by French Huguenots for a brief period brought Protestantism to South Carolina. After the English began what proved to be permanent colonization, French Huguenots came in several contingents and constituted an important element, religiously as well as racially. They organized congregations and built churches, but for the most part these were assimilated to the Church of England.[143] As in the other southern colonies, the Church of England was given by a law a privileged position. Yet many of the white population showed little regard for religion. Only slowly did intermittent Commissaries of the Bishop of London, missionaries of the Society for the Propagation of the Gospel in Foreign Parts, and free lance clergy (some of them of questionable character), build up the church.[144] German Palatinates received, at their own invitation, a minister from the Society.[145] Baptists early arrived and throve. In 1751 the Charleston Association of Baptist Churches was formed.

As in Virginia and North Carolina, the back country of South Carolina was settled by a variety of racial and religious groups. After the Great Awakening particularly, itinerant preachers did much to create Baptist nuclei in this part of the colony.[146] In the first quarter of the eighteenth century a Presbytery was formed, largely of Scots.[147] Not many years before the War of Independence, extensive German contingents arrived. Congregations, most of them Lutheran, but at least one of them Reformed, were organized.[148]

---

[141] Jacobs, *A History of the Evangelical Church in the United States*, p. 296.

[142] Hamilton, *A History of the Unitas Fratrum, or Moravian Church, in the United States of America*, pp. 460, 468.

[143] Arthur Henry Hirsch, *The Huguenots of Colonial South Carolina* (Durham, Duke University Press, 1928, pp. xv, 338), pp. 5-16, 47-90.

[144] Humphreys, *op. cit.*, pp. 81-127; Pascoe, *op. cit.*, pp. 12 ff.; Perry, *A History of the American Episcopal Church*, Vol. I, pp. 372 ff.

[145] Pascoe, *op. cit.*, p. 19.

[146] Leah Townsend, *South Carolina Baptists, 1670-1805* (Florence, S. C., The Florence Printing Co., 1935, pp. 391), pp. 3, 5, 7, 9, 61, 111, 122-125.

[147] Thompson, *A History of the Presbyterian Church in the United States*, p. 47.

[148] Faust, *The German Element in the United States*, Vol. I, pp. 226, 227.

Georgia, the last of the Thirteen Colonies to be settled, owed its inception to the double motive of constructing a bulwark against Spanish Florida and French Louisiana and of providing a refuge for underprivileged from Britain and for persecuted Protestant groups from the Continent of Europe. The founder, James Edward Oglethorpe, gave little vocal expression to his religious faith and seemed to the zealous Wesley to be lax in his church attendance, but he was a friend of Bray, who had so much to do with the founding of the Society for Promoting Christian Knowledge and the Society for the Propagation of the Gospel in Foreign Parts, and, as a trustee of Bray's estate and in accordance with Bray's known interest, used some of Bray's property to aid in the settlement of poor families in Georgia.[149] The charter, granted in 1732, guaranteed liberty of conscience. The first settlers, accompanied by Oglethorpe, arrived early in 1733. With them was a clergyman of the Church of England.[150] From late in 1735 until late in 1737 John Wesley was in Georgia, ministering to the settlers with a strictness which brought about his retirement from the colony.[151] In 1758 the Assembly of the colony ordered the creation of eight parishes and made provision for the building of churches and the support of the clergy, but as late as 1769 only two churches of the establishment existed. The progress of the Church of England was slow and the numerous dissenters objected to some of its privileges.[152] The great evangelist, George Whitefield, came to Georgia in 1738, and while the inward compulsion to itinerant preaching never allowed him to remain long in the colony, he raised large sums for an orphanage there, on his repeated trips to America revisited Georgia again and again, and towards the end of his life (he died in 1770) was planning to transform the orphanage into an academy.[153] To Georgia came fragments of the Salzburgers, persecuted German Protestants who were being exiled for their faith and whom philanthropic Englishmen were helping to find new homes. The first of the Salzburgers arrived in Georgia in 1734, accompanied by two ministers from the Pietist circles of Halle. More Salzburgers came, and Moravians were in an early contingent.[154] It was through contacts with the Moravians in Georgia that John Wesley entered upon the path which shortly was to lead him to the profound religious experience from which can be traced the world-wide

[149] Ettinger, *James Edward Oglethorpe*, pp. 111-137, 158.

[150] Pascoe, *op. cit.*, p. 26.

[151] *The Journal of the Rev. John Wesley*, Oct. 14, 1735-Feb. 1, 1737/8.

[152] Marjorie Daniel, *Anglicans and Dissenters in Georgia, 1758-1777*, in *Church History*, Vol. VII, pp. 247-262; Pascoe, *op. cit.*, p. 28.

[153] Gledstone, *The Life and Travels of George Whitefield, passim;* Perry, *op. cit.*, Vol. I, pp. 346-359.

[154] Faust, *op. cit.*, Vol. I, pp. 226, 227; Allen and McClure, *Two Hundred Years: The History of the S. P. C. K.*, pp. 388-395.

Methodist movement. To Georgia also came Scotch Highlanders, Presbyterians.[155] Before the War of Independence Georgia had three or four Baptist churches.[156] The Quakers obtained only a slight hold[157]: by the middle of the eighteenth century the wave of Quaker expansion was subsiding. Large numbers of settlers entered from the other English colonies. Most of these were attracted by the economic opportunities and had at best only a secondary interest in Christianity.

On the eve of the War of Independence, English settlement had begun to flow across the mountains into Kentucky. So far as is known, the earliest religious service in Kentucky was by a clergyman of the Church of England, in 1775, at the opening of the first legislative assembly.[158] At least two Baptist ministers arrived in 1776, but no Baptist church was organized until 1781.[159] The story of this westward migration and of the ensuing remarkable expansion of Christianity falls in a later period and is therefore reserved for the next volume.

From the preceding pages it must be clear that as the eighteenth century wore on the tide of religious life was rising. Some of the initial settlements had had a pronounced religious purpose, but even in New England and Pennsylvania these had been followed by a flood of immigrants for the majority of whom Christianity was at best only a nominal profession. Uprooted from their accustomed life in the Old World, they tended to drop the religious practices which had been part of the traditional social pattern that they had left behind them, and many of their children grew up without instruction in the Christian faith. However, by the middle of the eighteenth century the situation was beginning to be distinctly altered. Thanks to missionaries and financial assistance from Europe and the British Isles and to the initiative of some of the colonists, churches and ministers were multiplying and comprehensive religious organizations were coming into existence. More and more of the population were being reached.

To be sure, no denomination had as yet an organization embracing all the Colonies. Of them all, the Church of England was the most widely represented. In several of the Colonies it enjoyed a privileged legal position. Yet, taken together, the Presbyterian and Congregational churches were spread as generally through the Colonies and were numerically much stronger. The Church of England had no resident bishop and was still ecclesiastically dependent upon the Bishop of London. Lutherans, Presbyterians, Baptists, and Quakers

[155] Ettinger, op. cit., pp. 168-180.
[156] Newman, A History of the Baptist Churches in the United States, p. 318.
[157] Jones, The Quakers in the American Colonies, p. 300, n. 3.
[158] Arnold, A History of Methodism in Kentucky, Vol. I, pp. 1-3.
[159] Arnold, op. cit., Vol. I, pp. 4-12.

were beginning to construct organizations which embraced more than one colony. Francis Asbury, to whom more than to any other one man was due the later comprehensive structure of Methodism, had landed, but by the outbreak of the Revolutionary War he had barely begun his gargantuan labours. The Roman Catholic Church was represented by only a feeble minority and as yet had no bishop. The Christianity of what was soon to become the United States, like the new nation as a whole, was in its infancy and was still in large part a conscious apanage of Europe.

In the eighteenth century came a religious movement which to a large extent was American in its immediate origin, which assumed forms peculiar to the new country, and which brought into a vital allegiance to Christianity thousands whose connexion with that faith had been nominal, extremely tenuous, or non-existent. It was a kind of mass movement, akin to those by which so many thousands in other lands had been brought to accept Christianity. Only in the Thirteen Colonies it did not substitute Christianity for another religion, but led to an active adherence to the faith of those whose ancestry was Christian. It went by the name of the Great Awakening. In part it was the product of the contemporary movement across the Atlantic through which the Protestantism of Europe was experiencing a growing vigour—Pietism, the Moravians, and the Evangelical revival led by the Wesleys and Whitefield. In part it sprang spontaneously out of the religious life of the Colonies. In some of its phases it was explosive and gave rise to bitter controversies. Through it, however, Christianity enjoyed phenomenal expansion, chiefly among those of European stock, but, to a less extent, among the Indians and Negroes.

The earliest series of revivals which blended into the Great Awakening arose out of the labours of Theodorus Jacobus Frelinghuysen in New Jersey. Frelinghuysen was of German birth but of Dutch training. In 1720, in response to a request of the Dutch Reformed, he came as pastor to the Raritan Valley. He preached with great force the necessity of a thoroughgoing conversion. Under him revivals soon began in the Raritan Valley and spread to other places.[160] Contagion from Frelinghuysen helped to set on fire young Gilbert Tennent, of Irish birth, who in 1726 had become pastor of a Presbyterian church in New Brunswick, where was one of Frelinghuysen's congregations. He developed into a leading preacher of the revival.[161] William Tennent, Junior, a brother, was also prominent,[162] and William Tennent, Senior, later began, for the train-

---

[160] Maxson, *The Great Awakening in the Middle Colonies*, pp. 11 ff.; *Dictionary of American Biography*, Vol. VII, pp. 17, 18.

[161] Maxson, *op. cit.*, pp. 26 ff.; *Dictionary of American Biography*, Vol. XVIII, pp. 366-368.

[162] *Dictionary of American Biography*, Vol. XVIII, pp. 370, 371.

ing of ministers, what was known derisively as the Log College, the fore-runner of the College of New Jersey and of Princeton University. In it a number of the young clergy caught the new spirit.[163] The religious experience and enthusiasm of the Tennents, while encouraged by Frelinghuysen, was independent of him and went back to Irish and Calvinist sources.

Quite independently, in 1734 a revival broke out at Northampton, Massachusetts, through the preaching of one of the ablest minds of the century, Jonathan Edwards. Revivals had been known at Windsor, Connecticut, under the preaching of the father of Edwards, and at Northampton, under the ministry of Stoddard, the maternal grandfather and predecessor of Edwards. However, the movement which began under Edwards was of unusual power and had repercussions on both sides of the Atlantic.[164]

The Great Awakening was augmented throughout the Colonies by the preaching of George Whitefield. He first visited America in 1740 and came on additional visits in 1744, 1754, 1764, and 1770. His fervid oratory and burning conviction had striking and widespread results.[165] Many preachers of lesser distinction carried the message of the Awakening to the towns, cities, and rural districts of all the Colonies.

The Great Awakening was not confined to any one branch of the Church or to any single age group. Its leading spirits were from the New England Congregationalists, the Dutch Reformed, and the Presbyterians. Whitefield, who reinforced it, was a clergyman of the Church of England. It greatly stimulated the spread of the Baptists, for the insistence of the revival upon a conscious and transforming experience as a prerequisite to church membership was akin to what Baptists had historically advocated. Yet it also led to the growth of other denominations. At its outset it was led by youth, for at its inception all of its outstanding exponents were in their twenties or thirties. Yet in time it touched all ages.

[163] Maxson, *op. cit.*, pp. 25, 26; *Dictionary of American Biography*, Vol. XVIII, pp. 369, 370.

[164] See an account by Edwards in *The Works of President Edwards*, Vol. III (New York, Robert Carter and Co., 1864), pp. 231-428. Excellent biographies are Arthur Cushman McGiffert, *Jonathan Edwards* (New York, Harper & Brothers, 1932, pp. 225), and Alexander V. G. Allen, *Jonathan Edwards* (Boston, Houghton Mifflin Co., 1889, pp. xi, 401).

[165] See a popular, but thoughtful account, in Frank Grenville Beardsley, *A History of American Revivals* (New York, American Tract Society, 1904, pp. 352), pp. 31 ff. An old standard account is Joseph Tracy, *The Great Awakening* (Boston, Tappan and Dennet, 1842, pp. xviii, 433), pp. 35 ff. See also George Leon Walker, *Some Aspects of the Religious Life of New England* (Boston, Silver, Burdett and Co., 1897, pp. 208), pp. 83-125. On Whitefield see L. Tyerman, *The Life of the Rev. George Whitefield* (New York, Anson D. F. Randolph and Co., 2 vols., 1877), *passim;* Gledstone, *The Life and Travels of George Whitefield, passim;* and John Gillies, *Memoirs of Rev. George Whitefield* (New Haven, Whitmore & Buckingham and H. Mansfield, 1834, pp. 648), *passim.*

The Great Awakening helped to give the Christianity of the later United States one of its most characteristic features, revivals, waves of religious fervour through which thousands were led to an active profession of the Christian faith. It was largely—although by no means entirely—by revivals that Christianity spread in the latter part of the colonial period and through the nineteenth century. Revivals were akin to the mass movements by which so much of the spread of Christianity had taken place in other lands. The Great Awakening, too, brought marked moral changes. It denounced most of the gamut of practices which to the Christian are sins and led many to abandon them. Out of it came an impulse for more schools. It was one of the forces making for democracy.[166] As we shall see in a moment, it spread to the Indians and the Negroes. Nothing quite like it occurred in Spanish, Portuguese, or French America. It was a Protestant movement through which Christianity became a more active force in the Thirteen English Colonies.

Enterprises to win the Indians of the Thirteen Colonies to the Christian faith were numerous and were carried on by members of several Protestant groups. Like the French missions, they faced the obstacles of a sparse and semi-wandering Indian population which subsisted chiefly by hunting and fishing.[167] As in the case of the Spanish and Portuguese missions, those attempts at conversion which met with anything more than transient success were accompanied by efforts to induce the Indians to live in settled, agricultural communities. Moreover, as was usual in the impact of the whites on the red man, the missionaries had to contend with fellow-countrymen who wished to exploit him.[168] Then, too, the Indian tended to die off through the white man's diseases and the white man's rum. If extensive Indian Christian communities did not arise out of the endeavours of the Protestants, the failure must be ascribed more to the nature of the Indian population and the difficulty of helping it make its adjustment to the very different culture introduced by the Europeans than to lack of wisdom or of zeal on the part of the missionaries.

It must also be noted that increasingly the initiative and the personnel in Indian missions were from American-born whites. At the outset, of course, the missionaries were natives of the British Isles and of the Continent of Europe. To the end of the colonial period, financial assistance continued to come from the European side of the Atlantic. Yet, to a much larger extent than in Spanish, Portuguese, and French America, by the middle of the eighteenth century the active leadership had been largely assumed by those of American birth. In the

[166] Gewehr, *The Great Awakening in Virginia*, pp. 187 ff., 219-250.
[167] Wheelock, *A Plain and Faithful Narrative of the Original Design . . . and Present State of the Indian Charity School at Lebanon, Conn.*, p. 15.
[168] *Ibid.*

religious as in the political realm, the Thirteen Colonies were more nearly independent of the mother country than were their Spanish, Portuguese, and French colonial contemporaries.

Even to mention all the individual missions to the Indians within the borders of the Thirteen Colonies would unduly prolong these pages. We can take space only for some of the more prominent. The arrangement will be by sections or colonies.

We have seen that the first charter of Massachusetts expressly declared that the chief object of the colony was the conversion of the Indians. Not many colonists took this statement with sufficient seriousness to attempt to carry it into effect. About two decades elapsed after the initial settlements before active efforts were made to win the Indians to the Christian faith. To be sure, it is said that before his death one of the Indians who had most loyally befriended the original group at Plymouth asked the white men to pray for him that he might go to their God in Heaven.[169] Roger Williams laboured assiduously to prevent wars between Indian tribes and between Indians and whites.[170] He preached to the Narragansetts. Yet he despaired of any conversions being made.[171] In November, 1644, the General Court of Massachusetts interested itself in the religious instruction of the Indians and in 1646 it directed that the ministers appoint two of their number each year to undertake missions among the aborigines.[172]

The earliest extensive mission to the Indians of New England was on the island of Martha's Vineyard and on the smaller Nantucket and the Elizabeth Islands, south of Cape Cod. In 1641 Thomas Mayhew and his son, also named Thomas, purchased these islands.[173] The Indian population was then not very large. One estimate places that on Martha's Vineyard in 1642 at three thousand.[174] Another says that in 1694 the population of Nantucket was about five hundred adults,[175] a total of possibly less than a thousand individuals. The first settlement by the Mayhews was effected about 1642.[176] The younger Thomas Mayhew began a mission to the Indians and unstintedly devoted himself to it. Converts soon began to be won. The growth of the faith was accelerated by an epidemic in 1645 in which the Christians suffered less than the non-Christians[177]

---

[169] Mather, *Magnalia Christi Americana*, Book I, Chap. 3.
[170] Andrews, *The Colonial Period of American History*, Vol. II, pp. 21, 22.
[171] *Dictionary of American Biography*, Vol. XX, p. 287.
[172] Byington, *The Puritan as a Colonist and a Reformer*, p. 208.
[173] Banks, *History of Martha's Vineyard*, Vol. I, pp. 81-83.
[174] Banks, *op. cit.*, Vol. I, p. 57.
[175] Mather, *op. cit.*, Book VI, Chap. 6, §2.
[176] Banks, *op. cit.*, Vol. I, p. 87.
[177] Banks, *op. cit.*, Vol. I, p. 214.

and by which evidence seemed to be given that Christianity was the superior religion. In 1651 Mayhew reported that one hundred and ninety-nine professed to be Christians.[178] Financial support came from England, at first from private persons and soon from the Society for the Propagation of the Gospel in New England.[179] In 1657 the younger Thomas while on his way to England was lost at sea.[180] The elder Thomas then took up the burden, and in spite of his duties as governor of the island carried it until his death, in 1682.[181] The mission was extended to Nantucket, and in 1682 that island had two churches with over forty members.[182] On the death of Thomas, Senior, John, the youngest son of Thomas, Junior, assumed the task. John, in turn, was succeeded, on his death, by his eldest son, Experience. Experience had an unusual mastery of the Indian vernacular and prepared something of a literature in it.[183] Experience died in 1758, and his son, Zachariah, took over the family mission and maintained it until his own death, in 1806. In his day the Indian population had dwindled until only about three hundred were left.[184] In the course of the years a number of Indians had been trained to assist in the mission. Some had been ordained. A few had gone as missionaries from Martha's Vineyard to Nantucket and the mainland.[185] One had even graduated from Harvard.[186] For over a century and a half scions of the Mayhews had laboured, a persistent family missionary effort which for length has few if any equals in the history of the spread of Christianity. Not even the line of Gregory the Illuminator in Armenia was so prolonged in its leadership.

Not long after the younger Thomas Mayhew had commenced on Martha's Vineyard, a numerically larger mission was begun by John Eliot near Boston. John Eliot (born in 1604) was a native of England, graduated from Cambridge, and while in England had been under the influence of the Puritan, Thomas Hooker. He arrived in America in 1631 and the following year became pastor of the church in Roxbury, on the outskirts of Boston. Along with a number of other Puritan clergymen, he set about acquiring a knowledge of the Indian

[178] Banks, *op. cit.,* Vol. I, p. 223.

[179] Banks, *op. cit.,* Vol. I, pp. 219, 225.

[180] Banks, *op. cit.,* Vol. I, p. 230.

[181] On Thomas, Senior, see Lloyd C. M. Hare, *Thomas Mayhew, Patriarch to the Indians (1593-1682)* (New York, D. Appleton and Co., 1932, pp. xii, 231), *passim.*

[182] Banks, *op. cit.,* Vol. I, p. 245.

[183] Banks, *op. cit.,* Vol. I, pp. 246, 252.

[184] Banks, *op. cit.,* Vol. I, pp. 254-256.

[185] Experience Mayhew, *Indian Converts* (London, 1727, pp. xxiv, 310), *passim;* Mather, *op. cit.,* Book VI, Chap. 6, §2; *Some Correspondence between the Governors and Treasurers of the New England Company in London and the Commissioners of the United Colonies in America* (London, Spottiswoode & Son, 1896, pp. xxxii, 127), pp. 97 ff.

[186] Hare, *op. cit.,* p. 136. A building was erected in connexion with Harvard for the education of Indians. *Some Correspondence . . . of the New England Company, etc.,* p. xx.

tongue. Proving unusually proficient in the language, he commenced the translation of prayers and of parts of the Bible. In 1646, with others, he began to preach to the Indians. The Indians were greatly impressed, and soon converts were made. Within less than a year Eliot had gathered the Christians into a separate village, at Nonantum, thus, probably quite unconsciously, using a method akin to that employed by Roman Catholic missionaries in Spanish and Portuguese America. Some financial assistance was given by the General Court. In 1649, as we have seen, there was organized in England to support his work and other missions like it the President and Society for the Propagation of the Gospel in New England. A larger settlement was begun (1651) for the "praying Indians" at Natick, eighteen miles south-west of Boston, houses were built in semi-European style, and a government was set up modelled in part on the eighteenth chapter of Exodus. In the course of the following decades other villages of Christians were founded on the pattern of Natick, and in 1674 these were said to number fourteen with a Christian population of eleven hundred. Not until 1660 was the first church organized, for Eliot did not believe it wise to admit the converts to full communion until after a period of testing. A few other churches were formed and a native ministry trained. Eliot, too, prepared a translation of the entire Bible, the New Testament being printed in 1661 and the Old Testament in 1663. A revised edition appeared later.[187]

Simultaneously with the labours of Eliot, others of the clergy were active as missionaries in other parts of Massachusetts, and in Rhode Island and Connecticut. By 1675 the Old Colony in Eastern Massachusetts and the islands were said to contain twenty-five hundred Christian Indians. About 1700, approximately thirty Indian congregations existed in Southern Massachusetts, although the Indian population had declined in the past half century. We hear, too, of ministers in New London and Norwich, Connecticut, preaching to the Indians. One of these pastors gave the Indians some of his own land and taught them to cultivate it.[188]

In 1675 and 1676 a general Indian outbreak against the whites, known as King Philip's War, wrought devastation among the Christian settlements. The converts were distrusted by both pagan Indians and whites; by the former because they had adopted the white man's religion and supposedly were allied with him, and by the latter because they were Indians. Yet during the war

---

[187] Byington, op. cit., pp. 209-258; Mather, op. cit., Book III, Part III; Pascoe, Two Hundred Years of the S. P. G., Vol. I, pp. 2, 3; Hazard, Historical Collections, Vol. I, p. 635, Vol. II, pp. 438, 439; Some Correspondence . . . of the New England Company, etc., passim.

[188] Byington, op. cit., p. 259; Harold Clayton Bradshaw, The Indians of Connecticut (1935, no place of publication given, pp. 64), pp. 30 ff.; Some Correspondence . . . of the New England Company, etc., pp. ix, xviii, 83.

Eliot did what he could to give relief and after the war sought to gather together the survivors and restore their morale. He lived on until 1690, to the ripe age of eighty-five.[189] The Great Awakening led to a heightened missionary activity in New England for the Indians. Samson Occom, an Indian born near New London, Connecticut, was touched by one of the itinerant preachers of that movement and became a missionary to the Montauks on the eastern tip of Long Island. Later, endorsed by Whitefield, he went on a successful mission to England to raise funds for Indian missions, and eventually he led in moving some of the New England Indians to lands in New York.[190] Eleazer Wheelock, a clergyman who was active in the Great Awakening, undertook the instruction of Samson Occom, and from that was led to organize a school in Lebanon, Connecticut, where he was pastor, for the education of Indian youth as missionaries to their own people. To him came pupils from the Delawares of New Jersey and the Iroquois of New York, and some of them went back as teachers. In 1770 Wheelock removed his residence to Hanover, New Hampshire, where he laid the foundations of Dartmouth College.[191] John Sergeant (1710-1749) became a missionary to the Indians at Stockbridge, in Western Massachusetts.[192] Here, too, for a time Jonathan Edwards himself was a pastor. David Brainerd (1718-1747), a Connecticut youth, was touched by the Great Awakening and, supported by the Scotch Society for Propagating Christian Knowledge, became a missionary first between Stockbridge and Albany, and later in New Jersey. Extraordinarily sensitive, a mystic, deeply devoted, although he died young he exercised a profound influence. His diary was widely read and helped to inspire many to become missionaries, not only in America, but also in other parts of the world.[193] In his efforts for the Indians of New Jersey he was succeeded by his brother John.[194]

[189] Byington, *op. cit.*, pp. 258-270.

[190] *Dictionary of American Biography*, Vol. XIII, pp. 614, 615; Leon Burr Richardson, editor, *An Indian Preacher in England, Being Letters and Diaries Relating to the Mission of the Reverend Samson Occom and the Reverend Nathaniel Whitaker in England*, etc. (Dartmouth College, 1933, pp. 376), *passim.*

[191] *Memoirs of the Rev. Eleazer Wheelock* (Newburyport, Edward Little & Co., 1811, pp. 336), *passim; Dictionary of American Biography*, Vol. XX, p. 58; Eleazer Wheelock, *A Plain and Faithful Narrative of the Original Design, Rise, Progress, and Present State of the Indian Charity-School at Lebanon, Connecticut* (Boston, 1763, pp. 55), *passim;* Eleazer Wheelock, *A Continuation of the Narrative of the State . . . of the Indian Charity-School at Lebanon* (Boston, 1765, pp. 25), *passim.*

[192] *Dictionary of American Biography*, Vol. XVI, pp. 587, 588.

[193] *Memoirs of Rev. David Brainerd. . . . Based on the Life of Brainerd Prepared by Jonathan Edwards, D.D., and afterwards Revised and Enlarged by Sereno E. Dwight, D.D., edited by J. M. Sherwood* (New York, Funk and Wagnalls Co., 1884, pp. lxxx, 354), *passim.* On the Scottish society see Mackichan, *The Missionary Ideal in the Scottish Churches*, pp. 69-72.

[194] *Dictionary of American Biography*, Vol. II, p. 593.

Much of this missionary activity was subsidized by what was variously known as the Society for the Propagation of the Gospel in New England, the Company for the Propagation of the Gospel in New England and Parts Adjacent in America, and the New England Company. The funds were held in England, but were administered through commissioners in America.[195]

In New York missions were carried on among the Iroquois. This was partly for the purpose of offsetting French influence. These missions were particularly active and successful among the Mohawks. Late in the seventeenth and early in the eighteenth century Bernardus Freeman or Freerman, a Dutch Reformed minister at Schenectady, became proficient in the Mohawk tongue and translated into it prayers and parts of the Old and New Testaments.[196] At the instance of the Earl of Bellomont, Governor of New York, who urged it as a matter of state policy, the newly organized Society for the Propagation of the Gospel in Foreign Parts undertook missions among the Iroquois. Early efforts proved fruitless. However, missionaries continued to be sent and eventually with better results. One of the most successful of the missionaries was Henry Barclay, a native of Albany, New York, and later rector of Trinity Church, New York City. By the middle of the century, quite a large number of Mohawks had been baptized. The mission was continued up to the Revolutionary War.[197] One of the converts was the famous Mohawk chief, Joseph Brant, who, after the Revolutionary War, led his people into the British possessions and helped establish "the Old Mohawk Church."[198] Under the impulse of the Great Awakening a Connecticut youth, Samuel Kirkland, who prepared for college in Wheelock's school at Lebanon, went to the Oneidas, won their confidence, established a church among them, induced them to prohibit the sale of liquor in their territory, and in later years began an institution for the joint education of whites and Indians which eventually became Hamilton College.[199]

In New Jersey and Pennsylvania the Quakers had extensive relations with the Indians. George Fox, himself, on his trip to America, in 1672, addressed the Indians in Delaware and North Carolina and found them, so he records,

[195] [H. W. Busk] *A Sketch of the Origin and the Recent History of the New England Company* (London, Spottiswoode & Co., 1884, pp. 89). Hazard, *Historical Collections*, contains many pertinent documents.

[196] *Dictionary of American Biography*, Vol. VII, pp. 8, 9.

[197] Perry, *The History of the American Episcopal Church*, Vol. I, pp. 322-334; Humphreys, *Historical Account of the Incorporated Society for the Propagation of the Gospel in Foreign Parts*, pp. 276-311; Pascoe, *Classified Digest of the Records of the Society for the Propagation of the Gospel in Foreign Parts*, pp. 66-71, 86, 136, 137; Weigle, *American Idealism*, p. 78.

[198] *Dictionary of American Biography*, Vol. II, p. 604.

[199] *Dictionary of American Biography*, Vol. X, pp. 432-444.

"very loving."[200] Even before Fox's visit, Quakers had preached to them.[201] At different times in the latter half of the seventeenth and in the eighteenth century a number of Quakers went among the Indians on brief missions.[202] Not until after the independence of the Colonies, however, and so in a division of our story which belongs in the next volume, did any of the Quakers begin a continuing mission among them.[203] However, the Quakers were notable for their efforts to put into practice in their dealings with Indians Christian principles as they understood them. Particularly in Pennsylvania, but also in other colonies where they had influence—in New Jersey, Rhode Island, and the Carolinas— the Quakers sought to win the Indians to the Christian faith by showing by their lives what the faith would do for conduct. Thus again and again Quakers were scrupulous in seeing that lands occupied by them were sold to them, and willingly, by the Indians.[204] The Quaker conscience increasingly became uneasy over the enslavement of Indians.[205] For nearly two generations, or from 1683 to 1755, the Quaker policy preserved peace with the Indians in Pennsylvania. In 1755 war broke out, and in 1756 Quakers permanently lost control of the government of the colony. However, while some Quakers supported the war as defensive, others sought another way and attempted to mitigate the horrors of the conflict.[206]

Along the lower reaches of the Delaware River some of the early Swedish settlers endeavoured to win the Indians to the Christian faith. In 1643 John Campanius, a clergyman, came. He was primarily a pastor to the whites, but he studied the Indian tongue, prepared Christian literature in it, and, with his son, used it in an effort to convert the Indians.[207] In the first quarter of the eighteenth century Andrew Hesselius, pastor of the Swedish Lutheran Church at Wilmington, laboured for the Indians.[208]

It was to be expected that the Moravians, so active in attempts to win non-Christians in various parts of the earth, would seek from their settlements in the Colonies to carry the Christian message to the Indians. In 1740 Henry Rauch began a mission among the aborigines, in what is now Dutchess County,

[200] *Journal of George Fox* (Everyman's Library edition), pp. 295, 300.
[201] Kelsey, *Friends and the Indians*, pp. 23, 24.
[202] Kelsey, *op. cit.*, pp. 24-37.
[203] Kelsey, *op. cit.*, pp. 89 ff.
[204] Kelsey, *op. cit.*, pp. 38-55.
[205] Kelsey, *op. cit.*, pp. 55-58.
[206] Kelsey, *op. cit.*, pp. 60 ff.; Brookes, *Friend Anthony Benezet*, pp. 110-118.
[207] Maurer, *Early Lutheran Education in Pennsylvania*, pp. 23, 24; C. J. I. Bergendoff in *Church History*, Vol. VII, pp. 220, 221.
[208] Jacobs, *A History of the Evangelical Lutheran Church in the United States*, p. 99.

New York, and the first baptisms followed in 1742.[209] In 1742 Zinzendorf himself visited the Iroquois.[210] From the labours of Rauch and those who followed him, a number of converts were gathered in Dutchess County, and in the adjoining Litchfield County, in Connecticut. In 1744, through fear that the Germans and their converts would support the enemy in the chronic wars with the French, the colonial authorities closed the mission.[211] Soon a mission station was begun by the founding of Gnadenhütten on the Mahony in the later Carbon County, Pennsylvania.[212] At the Moravian centre at Bethlehem Spangenberg instituted the preparation of candidates for missions to the Indians.[213] One of the students was David Zeisberger. Zeisberger was the most famous of the eighteenth century Moravian missionaries to the Indians. He became an adept at the Mohawk language. He gained the confidence of the Iroquois and was initiated into some of their tribes. However, he and the other Moravians eventually concentrated upon the Delawares, first in the Wyoming Valley, in Pennsylvania, and then, as colonial policies pushed the Delawares westward, he and his colleagues followed them into Ohio and there helped them form settlements in the Tuscarawas Valley.[214] To narrate the tragic fate of these settlements would carry us into a later period. Prominent, too, among the Moravian missionaries was Christian Frederick Post, a restless, erratic wanderer, who laboured among the Indians of Pennsylvania and the West, in Labrador and in Central America, and eventually was disowned by the Unitas Fratrum.[215]

In the early days of the Maryland settlement, Jesuits were successful in seeking the conversion of the Indians.[216]

We have seen that in Virginia, as in New England, one of the purposes of the first settlements, as avowed in the charters, was the conversion of the Indians,[217] and that very early money was raised for the College of Henrico for the induction of Indian youth into the Christian faith.[218] Whitaker, the first minister of Henrico Parish, was also a missionary to the Indians. A famous

---

[209] Loskiel, *Geschichte der Mission der evangelischen Brüder unter den Indianern in Nordamerika*, pp. 217 ff.; De Schweinitz, *The Life and Times of David Zeisberger*, pp. 97, 106.

[210] Loskiel, *op. cit.*, pp. 237 ff.; De Schweinitz, *op. cit.*, pp. 107 ff.

[211] De Schweinitz, *op. cit.*, pp. 116, 117.

[212] De Schweinitz, *op. cit.*, p. 141.

[213] De Schweinitz, *op. cit.*, p. 120.

[214] De Schweinitz, *op. cit., passim;* Loskiel, *op. cit.*, pp. 353 ff.

[215] *Dictionary of American Biography*, Vol. XV, p. 113.

[216] O'Gorman, *A History of the Roman Catholic Church in the United States*, p. 222.

[217] Lucas, *Charters of the Old English Colonies in America*, pp. 2, 18.

[218] Anderson, *The History of the Church of England in the Colonies and Foreign Dependencies of the British Empire*, Vol. I, pp. 255-258.

early convert was the Indian princess, Pocahontas, who was instructed in the faith by Whitaker.[219] After her untimely death in England, James I, at the request of the Virginia Company, sent out a letter through the Archbishops of the Church of England, urging popular contributions for missions to the Indians.[220] One of the six professorships of the College of William and Mary was designated for teaching the Indians—although after the Revolution it was diverted to the modern languages.[221]

We have seen that the first missionary activity of the English in the Thirteen Colonies was through the fleeting settlement on Roanoke Island in the later North Carolina.

In North Carolina, too, the Moravians, from the beginning of their settlement, included missions to the Indians in their plan.[222] Here, moreover, the missionaries of the Society for the Propagation of the Gospel in Foreign Parts baptized a few Indians.[223]

In South Carolina the first missionary of the Society for the Propagation of the Gospel in Foreign Parts, S. Thomas, laboured among the Indians.[224]

Early in the history of Georgia contributions were made by various benevolently disposed persons for the conversion of the Indians in that colony.[225]

From north to south, then, by various Christian bodies and over the entire range of the colonial period, efforts were made to convert the Indians. A large part of the financial support and the personnel came from the other side of the Atlantic, but increasingly the initiative was from American-born whites. In many instances the missions succeeded, and Christian communities arose. Disease decimated the communities of Christians, as of non-Christians, and pressure from the land-hungry whites led to the removal of some of them to the West. Others persisted, and while obscured by the overwhelming white population, some even continued into the twentieth century.

Before the Thirteen Colonies tore themselves away from the mother country, the Negro had begun to form an element in their population. As in Spanish and Portuguese America, he was brought in as a slave. He was present in the large majority of the Colonies, but naturally was more prominent in those

---

[219] Perry, *The History of the American Episcopal Church*, Vol. I, p. 61; McConnell, *History of the American Episcopal Church*, p. 19.

[220] Goodwin, *The Colonial Church in Virginia*, pp. 52-62.

[221] Anderson, *op. cit.*, Vol. III, pp. 108-109.

[222] Hamilton, *A History of the Unitas Fratrum . . . in the United States of America*, p. 460.

[223] Pascoe, *Two Hundred Years of the S. P. G.*, p. 222.

[224] Pascoe, *op. cit.*, pp. 12-19.

[225] Perry, *op. cit.*, Vol. I, p. 361.

from Maryland southward, for there the plantation system created a demand for his labour.

Here was an additional problem for Christianity in the Colonies. Not only was this Christianity confronted with the necessity of holding the allegiance of the thousands of white immigrants who had been removed from the conventional ecclesiastical associations of the Old World and with the challenge of winning the red man and helping to save him from the destruction threatened by contact with the white man's culture. It had also to determine its attitude towards Negro slavery and to seek to bring the Negroes into its fold. By 1776 only a beginning had been made.

At the outset, efforts to instruct the Negroes in Christianity met the conviction, inherited from the Middle Ages, that a Christian could not be held as a slave, and, therefore, that if the Negro were baptized he would by that act be emancipated and lost to his master.[226] In at least some of the Colonies, legislation was enacted which explicitly declared that baptism did not have this effect.[227] The way was thereby opened for missionary activity among the Negroes. Some of the agents of the Society for the Propagation of the Gospel in Foreign Parts gave much attention to them. We hear of a school for them in South Carolina and of baptisms in North Carolina, Georgia, Pennsylvania, and New Jersey.[228] In 1724 a Church of England clergyman wrote the Bishop of London that in Maryland a large proportion of the American-born Negroes had been instructed and baptized. In 1727 the Bishop of London wrote a general letter to masters and mistresses urging them to baptize their slaves and sent another letter to Anglican missionaries encouraging them to zeal in this labour.[229] Moravians planned efforts for Negroes,[230] but did not accomplish nearly so much as they did in the West Indies. The Great Awakening spread to the Negroes. In their revivals, Presbyterians, Baptists, and Methodists made a marked appeal to the blacks.[231] However, by the time the Colonies achieved their independence, the Methodist and Baptist successes among the Negroes, later so notable, had only barely begun.

So, too, at the outbreak of the Revolutionary War the protest of the Christian

[226] Sweet, *The Story of Religions in America*, p. 135.

[227] Anderson, *The History of the Church of England in the Colonies and the Foreign Dependencies of the British Empire*, Vol. II, p. 344, Vol. III, p. 130; Townsend, *South Carolina Baptists*, p. 255; Godwyn, *The Negro's and Indian's Advocate*, p. 140.

[228] Pascoe, *op. cit.*, pp. 22, 28, 38, 54; Anderson, *op. cit.*, Vol. III, p. 321; Mode, *Source Book of American Church History*, p. 552.

[229] Humphreys, *Historical Account of the Incorporated Society for the Propagation of the Gospel in Foreign Parts*, pp. 257-275; Manross, *A History of the American Episcopal Church*, p. 77.

[230] Hamilton, *op. cit.*, p. 440.

[231] Gewehr, *The Great Awakening in Virginia*, pp. 235-250.

conscience against Negro slavery was only in its beginnings in the Colonies. The Quakers led the way. In 1688 Germantown Mennonites sent to the Quarterly and Yearly Meetings of Friends a petition against Negro slavery.[232] At Newport, Rhode Island, the most important centre of the slave trade in the Colonies, in 1717 the Yearly Meeting of the Quakers expressed doubts about the propriety of importing and keeping slaves, and in 1727 censured the traffic.[233] In 1773 the Yearly Meeting which was the highest legislative body of New England Quakers came out explicitly for the emancipation of all slaves held by Friends.[234] By the middle of the seventeen sixties the New York Quakers were against the slave trade.[235] About the same time, Quakers living in the Southern Colonies became increasingly uneasy about slavery.[236] In 1758 the influential Philadelphia Yearly Meeting began action against the institution.[237] The outstanding early leader in stirring the Quakers to action was John Woolman, whose *Journal* is among the classics of religious literature.[238]

While most pronounced among Quakers, the anti-slavery movement was not confined to them. Samuel Hopkins, a product of the Great Awakening and one of the formative figures in what came to be known as New England Theology, when a pastor at Newport denounced slavery (although many in his congregation profited by the slave trade and fiercely resented his strictures), sought to raise money to free the slaves, and joined with a fellow clergyman, Ezra Stiles, in an appeal for funds to train Negro missionaries for Africa.[239] The Great Awakening, too, was accompanied by exhortations to masters to be kind to their slaves.[240]

The tide of conviction was beginning to rise and in the next century was to sweep Negro slavery away. Both in Great Britain and in the United States the anti-slavery movement was chiefly Christian in origin and a large proportion of its leaders were the product of the religious awakenings of the eighteenth and the first part of the nineteenth century.

The beginning of the anti-slavery movement is a convenient transition to the

[232] Mode, *Source Book of American Church History*, pp. 552, 553.

[233] Jones, *The Quakers in the American Colonies*, p. 157.

[234] Jones, *op. cit.*, p. 164.

[235] Jones, *op. cit.*, p. 256.

[236] Jones, *op. cit.*, pp. 321 ff.

[237] Jones, *op. cit.*, p. 397; Mode, *op. cit.*, pp. 555, 556.

[238] John Woolman, *Some Considerations on the Keeping of Negroes Recommended to the Professors of Christianity of Every Denomination, first printed in the Year 1754.*— In his *Works*, Philadelphia, fourth edition, 1806, pp. 233 ff. John Woolman was reinforced in his anti-slavery stand by Anthony Benezet, a Quaker of Huguenot origin.—Brookes, *Friend Anthony Benezet*, pp. 76-109.

[239] *Dictionary of American Biography*, Vol. IX, p. 217.

[240] Gewehr, *op. cit.*, pp. 235-250.

next general heading of our story, the effect of Christianity upon the Thirteen Colonies.

Some of these effects are clear. The preceding pages have made it obvious that from the outset Christianity had been one of the causes of the migrations which gave rise to the Thirteen Colonies. It was by no means the only one. In some of the Colonies it was almost negligible in bringing about the settlements. Even in New England, Pennsylvania, Maryland, and Georgia, where it was prominent at the beginning, for probably a majority of the later immigrants it was at best only a minor factor in inducing the change of habitat to the New World. Yet the fact that for some Christianity was the primary impulse which led them to cross the ocean was significant. Through them the Christian faith had an important part in shaping the ideals and the life of the nascent nation.

It is also clear that Christianity was increasingly successful in retaining or in winning the allegiance of the population of the Thirteen Colonies. The large majority of the settlers had come, not from religious motives, but to better their social and economic status. They tended to leave behind the nominal church connexion which had been theirs in the Old World, and their children often grew up without religious instruction. The degree to which Christianity retained its hold varied from colony to colony and even in different parts of the same colony. In Virginia, for instance, on the eve of the Great Awakening, the masses were practically untouched by the Church.[241] In the eighteenth century, however, Christianity made decided headway. Particularly through the Great Awakening it won thousands who had previously been indifferent. More and more it reached out to the Indians and to the Negroes.

As in Spanish America, Christianity gave rise to most of such institutions of learning, and particularly of higher learning, as came into existence.[242] Practically all of the colleges were founded by members of churches, with a Christian purpose as avowedly primary. Some of them were explicitly for the training of the clergy. It is significant, as indicative of the effect of Christianity, that the Great Awakening gave an impetus to education.[243]

Obviously Christianity tended to bring the ethical standards and practices of the Colonies into accord with its own. In this it was by no means wholly successful. Never, from that standpoint, has any community ever been entirely

---

[241] Gewehr, *op. cit.*, pp. 33 ff.

[242] Most of this is too well known to require supporting footnotes. It is significant that the first effective efforts to educate the Lutherans of Pennsylvania were made by Pietists, and that the English charity schools, mentioned above, supplemented them.—Maurer, *Early Lutheran Education in Pennsylvania*, pp. 167, 184.

[243] Gewehr, *op. cit.*, pp. 219-239.

Christian. However, again and again we hear of the Christian impulse resisting sexual irregularities, profanity, faithlessness to promises, drunkenness, quarreling, and gambling.[244]

As in Spanish and Portuguese America, Christianity tended to ameliorate the lot of the non-white peoples and to resist the ruthless exploitation of Indians and Negroes. No Las Casas arose, and no benevolent *Laws of the Indies* were enacted. This was because the Indian population was much more sparse than in the Spanish domains and the initial cruelties much less marked. However, the Christian conscience impelled some to obtain lands by purchase from the Indians rather than to seize them by force. Often, too, we find whites moved by a Christian impulse labouring for peace between their fellow-countrymen and Indians.[245] Scores of missionaries by Christian teaching and secular education strove to help the Indian to take his place wholesomely in the white society which was submerging him. Moreover, by the end of the colonial period from the Christian conscience movements to abolish Negro slavery and the slave trade were beginning to emerge.

Less obvious but no less important was the contribution of Christianity to the development of democratic ideals and institutions. In part these went back to Anglo-Saxon roots. In part, too, they were favoured by conditions on the frontier. Before ascribing them exclusively to the frontier, however, it is well to remember that on some other frontiers they did not develop. They were notably absent in Spanish and Portuguese America, and in French Canada they did not have a spontaneous growth. In large part they are attributable to the fact that radical groups of the Protestant movement had so large a place in the settlement of the colonies. These groups tended to emphasize the direct access of every Christian to God and the priesthood of all believers. In their forms of church government the democratic element was strong. In some of them, such as the Quakers, the Congregationalists, the Presbyterians, and the Baptists, every member had a voice. It is not surprising that in Virginia the Great Awakening gave rise to churches which, by their polity, accustomed their members to democratic self-government.[246] Nor is it strange that in New England, the stronghold of Congregationalism, the clergy preached most of the doctrines which later led to the American Revolution—the inalienability of rights which came from nature and nature's God, the theory that all men are born free, the duty

---

[244] Gewehr, *op. cit.*, pp. 260-262; *Minutes and Letters of the Coetus of the German Reformed Congregations in Pennsylvania, 1747-1792*, pp. 264-266; Klett, *Presbyterians in Colonial Pennsylvania*, p. 116. See, too, sermons of the preachers of the Great Awakening, including Jonathan Edwards.

[245] As in Brookes, *Friend Anthony Benezet*, pp. 110-137.

[246] Gewehr, *op. cit.*, pp. 187 ff.

of resistance to encroachments on these rights, and the popular element in government.[247] To be sure, the New England clergy preached the sanctity of property and a large proportion of them looked askance at pure democracy. Then, too, many of their ideas were in part derived from the reading of contemporary English thinkers. However, the strain of English tradition from which they drew inspiration may well have gone back to a pre-Reformation English dissent[248] and some of the political theorists who provided them with arguments were indebted ultimately in large part to the Christian impulse. It must also be added that the motive which led them to make use of this intellectual ammunition sprang from their religious background. Indubitably, the political and especially the growing democratic ideals of the Thirteen Colonies had some of their main roots in Christianity. The "American dream" of equality of opportunity for all is in part derived from the Christian impulse.

Did time permit, it would be interesting to seek to trace the extent to which the variations of culture appearing in the different Colonies had their sources in the different religious traditions of the groups which settled them. New England, with its form of government, its educational tradition, and its mid-nineteenth century flowering of literature, bore the imprint of its predominant form of Christianity. Pennsylvania, with its many denominations and its diversified cultural traditions, was in part the product of the numerous national and religious strains which were attracted through Penn's Quaker policy of toleration. All this, however, we must dismiss with only a passing hint.

By the time of the outbreak of the Revolutionary War the effect of the environment upon the Christianity of the Thirteen Colonies was already beginning to be apparent.

One pronounced consequence was variety. The religious toleration practised in some of the Colonies, the differing national origins (Swedish in Delaware, Dutch in New York, English and German in Pennsylvania, French in sprinklings of Huguenots, and English elsewhere) with the transplanting of more than one national church, and the failure of the Church of England fully to occupy the field even in the Colonies in which it was established by law, contributed to give a variety to the Christianity of the land which was unequalled in contemporary Europe.

A second outstanding effect of the environment was the growth of religious toleration. With two of the Thirteen Colonies, Pennsylvania and Rhode Island,

---

[247] Alice M. Baldwin, *The New England Clergy and the American Revolution* (Durham, N. C., Duke University Press, 1928, pp. xiii, 222), pp. 3-5, 36, 82; Weigle, *American Idealism*, pp. 45, 58.

[248] Thomas Cuming Hall, *The Religious Background of American Culture* (Boston, Little, Brown and Co., 1930, pp. xiv, 347), *passim.*

consistently espousing it from the beginning, and with the many kinds of Christianity represented and the impossibility of any one form gaining exclusive control, the movement towards toleration was irresistible. Toleration was hastened by the Great Awakening, for by that movement non-conforming groups were greatly strengthened. Not until after independence did full toleration prevail in all the Colonies, but the tide had begun to flow in that direction.

Closely connected with toleration was the separation of Church from state. In the majority of the Colonies this had not been completed before the achievement of political independence. Yet the movement towards toleration made impossible the support of any one branch of the Church by the state and rendered difficult the subsidy by the state of all the varieties of Christianity represented. To be sure, the severance of Church and state never became complete, even in the United States of the nineteenth and twentieth centuries. The armed forces and some of the legislative bodies had chaplains, "in God we trust" was stamped on the coins, and official Thanksgiving days and even fast days existed. Yet not since Constantine had so little connexion between Church and state existed in any land where Christianity was the prevailing form of religion.

The separation of Church and state meant the principle of voluntaryism. Churches tended to be maintained, not by public taxation, but by the gifts of the members and the well disposed. To be sure, in most of the Colonies some support of one form of Christianity from public funds continued down to the Revolution and even beyond—of Congregationalism in much of New England and of the Church of England in several others. However, increasingly bodies arose which enjoyed no subsidy through the state, and the principle of public taxation for the Church was clearly doomed.

We must remind ourselves again, moreover, that, because so many of them sought haven in the Colonies, the radical forms of Protestantism were proportionately much more strongly represented than in the Old World and tended to give their complexion to the Christianity of the nascent nation. Quakers, Congregationalists, Baptists, Moravians, and Anabaptists of many stripes were more prominent than in Europe.

This made for the separation of the Protestantism of the Colonies from the stream of European religious tradition. The radical groups wished to go back to the New Testament for their model and regarded the intervening developments in Christianity as corrupt accretions. In the Thirteen Colonies, then, Christianity seemed to be making a new beginning, and, accordingly, to display marked peculiarities.

Revivalism became a feature of this novel Christianity. The Great Awakening gave a decided impulse to this form of the spread of Christianity, an impulse which was strengthened in the nineteenth century.

In part as an outgrowth of revivalism was what came to be known as the New England Theology. Calvinistic in its roots, it had its rise in Jonathan Edwards and was further developed by Joseph Bellamy and Samuel Hopkins. By the end of the eighteenth century its main outlines had appeared. It was at once a product of revivals and helped to stimulate them. Strict Calvinism with its doctrine of predestination made difficult or impossible the preaching of revivals with the appeal to the individual to exert his will and repent. Here was a modification of Calvinism which still clung to election, the divine decrees, and the majesty of God, but which in effect gave somewhat more freedom to the will and emphasized the mercy and love of God.[249] New England Theology became influential not only in New England but also in other parts of the country.

Partly as a fruit of revivalism, and partly as a result of the urge which drove each of the groups to seek recruits in a new land in which the majority had no church connexion, there arose a tradition of aggressive missionary effort, the endeavour to bring all the population to a Christian experience and into fellowship with the Church. In the Old World, with its state churches and its tradition that all, by reason of their birth in a country, were baptized into the Church, this did not seem so essential. In the Thirteen Colonies, with the absence or weakness of a state church and the tendency of nominal Christians to lapse, active missions became necessary if Christianity were to go on.

Sects tended to multiply. Because of the movement towards toleration and the separation of Church and state, and because of revivalism, divisions increased. This was not so apparent in colonial times. Then few new sects came into existence.[250] Yet the Great Awakening brought disruption to some local congregations and led to a growth of New Lights and Baptists. After political independence was achieved and the country became less colonially minded, the emergence of new bodies rapidly increased. It must be remembered, moreover, that New England Congregationalism, while having its roots in the Old World, was an American development.

Activism, long present in Western Christianity, was accentuated. The Christians of the Thirteen Colonies were inclined to expect the Kingdom of God

---

[249] Frank Hugh Foster, *A Genetic History of the New England Theology* (The University of Chicago Press, 1907), *passim.*

[250] Minor sects appeared, such as the celibate Ephrata Society, an offshoot of the Brethren (Brumbaugh, *A History of the German Baptist Brethren in Europe and America*, pp. 438-470), and The Contented of the God-loving Soul, from the Quakers (Hull, *William Penn and the Dutch Quaker Migration to Pennsylvania*, p. 187).

to appear in the New World. This tendency was accentuated by the Great Awakening, with its transformation of individual and community life.[251] From this expectation of something to be brought in by the act of God the step was fairly easily taken towards man's assistance in the coming of the Kingdom of God. It was not strange that movements to mitigate the lot of the Indian and the Negro and to abolish Negro slavery came out of the Great Awakening.

Here, then, as a joint product of environment and of what had been inherited from Europe, was beginning a new type of Christianity. Most of its essential features had appeared in colonial days. In the succeeding United States it was to experience a striking growth.

The English possessions in the New World were not confined to the Thirteen Colonies, to Newfoundland, and to the vast areas which in the nineteenth century coalesced into the Dominion of Canada. They also included Bermuda, several islands in the West Indies, and footholds in Honduras and on the Mosquito Coast in Central America. Because of their importance as producers of tropical products, and particularly of sugar, the British colonies in the West Indies, when compared with those on the mainland of North America, seemed relatively more important in the seventeenth and eighteenth centuries than they did later. They had white settlers, chiefly artisans and planters, and a few remnants of Indians, but their population was made up largely of Negro slaves. From the standpoint of the expansion of Christianity, the problem was partly the preservation and deepening of the nominal faith of the white colonists, partly the winning of the Negroes, and partly the protection of the Negroes against heartless exploitation. Before the end of the eighteenth century, progress had been made towards the solution of the first two phases of the problem. Agitation had been begun towards the solution of the third, but the main part of that story, including the abolition of Negro slavery, belongs to the nineteenth century.

For decades almost the only active propagation of Christianity in the British West Indies was by the Anglican communion. Thus it was reported that in the first quarter of the eighteenth century the Bermudas contained nine churches and one clergyman.[252] It was in Bermuda that Bishop Berkeley planned to establish an ideal community which should be a new centre of civilization. He wished to found a college in which clergy could be trained for the churches, not

---

[251] H. Richard Niebuhr, *The Kingdom of God in America* (Chicago, Willett, Clark and Co., 1937, pp. xvii, 215), pp. 141-148.
[252] Pascoe, *Two Hundred Years of the S. P. G.*, pp. 102, 103.

only of Bermuda, but also of the colonies on the mainland. He was disappointed in obtaining funds and did not reach Bermuda, but he was in Rhode Island for a time. His effort resulted in some money for the Georgia project.[253] As early as 1680 Barbados had eleven churches, about half of which had ministers.[254] However, the planters objected to the baptism of their Negroes, arguing that Christian instruction would make the slaves less governable, would interfere with Sunday labour, and might lead to insurrection.[255] In 1712, under the will of Christopher Codrington, formerly Captain General and Commander-in-Chief of the Leeward Islands, two plantations on the island of Barbados, with their slaves, passed into the possession of the Society for the Propagation of the Gospel in Foreign Parts. The expressed purpose of the bequest was the establishment of a school for instruction and practice in medicine, surgery, and theology. The ownership of the plantations with their slaves brought serious problems, but the Society maintained a succession of missionaries for the Negroes and hundreds were reported to have become Christians.[256] Beginning with 1731, missionaries of the Society served the white population of the Bahamas. In some of the islands they found that the colonists were almost illiterate religiously and that the Negroes were quite without instruction in the Christian faith. Jamaica, the largest and most prominent of the British-owned possessions in the West Indies, was seized by the English in 1655. Within a decade the island was divided into parishes, but the number of clergy seems long to have been insufficient.[257] In 1738 a school was opened in the Bahamas for Negroes.[258] Grenada was permanently transferred from France to Great Britain by the treaty of 1783. The following year the colonial assembly made provision for stipends for five clergymen of the Church of England. The glebe lands which under the French regime belonged to Roman Catholic priests became the property of the Crown and were granted to the Assembly for the support of the clergy, both Roman Catholic and of the Church of England.[259]

The Church of England was by no means the only form of Christianity represented in the British West Indies. In the latter part of the seventeenth century two-thirds of the white population of the Bermudas were said to be Presby-

[253] John Wild, *George Berkeley* (Harvard University Press, 1936, pp. ix, 552, thoroughly documented), pp. 287-330.

[254] Godwyn, *The Negro's and Indian's Advocate*, p. 137.

[255] Godwyn, *op. cit.*, pp. 107-150.

[256] Pascoe, *op. cit.*, pp. 196-206; F. J. Klingberg, *British Humanitarianism at Codrington*, in *The Journal of Negro History*, Vol. XXIII, pp. 451 ff.

[257] Pascoe, *op. cit.*, p. 228; J. B. Ellis, *The Diocese of Jamaica* (London, Society for Promoting Christian Knowledge, 1913, pp. 237), pp. 24-60.

[258] K. S. Malden, *Broken Bonds. The S. P. G. and the West Indian Slaves* (Westminster, The Society for the Propagation of the Gospel in Foreign Parts, 1933, pp. 101), p. 33.

[259] Coke, *A History of the West Indies*, Vol. II, p. 58.

terians, and among the remaining one-third were Independents, Anabaptists, and Quakers. In Jamaica, as was natural from the fact that the island came into English hands during the Commonwealth period, non-conformists were numerous in the early years after the Stuart restoration.[260] In 1671 George Fox, on a visit to Barbados, urged the Quakers there to train their Negro slaves in the Christian faith.[261] However, of the groups of Christians outside the Church of England, until after A.D. 1800 only three, the Moravians, the Methodists, and the Baptists, were particularly aggressive in propagating their faith, and these were not present until the latter half of the eighteenth century. Of these three, moreover, the Methodists were only partly outside the Church of England. Moravian, Methodist, and Baptist missionaries were evidence of that rising tide of life in Protestant Christianity whose effects we have already seen in the Thirteen Colonies and which was to come to flood in the nineteenth century.

Before A.D. 1800 Moravian missionaries were at work in several of the British West Indies—Jamaica, Antigua, Barbados, St. Kitts, and Tobago. They directed their efforts primarily towards the conversion of the Negro slaves. In each of these islands they received assistance from white residents, and in three of them they entered through the invitation of planters. In Jamaica the first of the Moravians arrived in 1754. For their support they were given a plantation by the friendly planters through whose initiative they had come and were encouraged to approach the slaves on several other estates. Only slowly, however, were converts gathered. During the eighteenth century the Jamaica mission did not flourish. Antigua was entered in 1756. For the first fourteen years only slight progress was registered. However, under the leadership of Peter Braun, who was on the island from 1769 to 1791, phenomenal gains were made, and the number of neophytes rose to over seven thousand. On Barbados various untoward circumstances prevented much growth. On St. Kitts, in the twenty-three years between the inception of the mission, in 1777, and 1800, about two thousand converts were gathered. On Tobago only beginnings were made before 1800.[262] Moravian missions continued after 1800.

Methodism seems to have first reached the West Indies in 1760. While in England, Nathaniel Gilbert, a planter and lawyer of Antigua and at one time Speaker of the Assembly of the island, heard John Wesley and through him came into a contagious religious experience. Two of his Negroes were baptized

---

[260] Anderson, *The History of the Church of England in the Colonies and Foreign Dependencies of the British Empire,* Vol. II, pp. 286, 333, 334.

[261] *Journal of George Fox* (Everyman's Library edition), p. 277.

[262] Hutton, *A History of the Moravian Missions,* pp. 50-56; Müller, *200 Jahre Brüdermission,* pp. 60-85; J. H. Buchner, *The Moravians in Jamaica: History of the Mission of the United Brethren's Church to the Negroes in the Island of Jamaica, from the Year 1754 to 1854* (London, Longman, Brown & Co., 1854, pp. 175), pp. 24-45.

by Wesley. In 1760 he returned to Antigua. There, in spite of the opposition of the island aristocracy, he preached, especially to the slaves, and before his death (1774) he had gathered a Methodist Society of about two hundred. Methodists and Moravians worked together and made of Antigua the strongest early centre of Protestantism among the Negroes of the West Indies.[263] In 1778 Gilbert's work was resumed by John Baxter, a shipwright who accepted an opportunity on Antigua to practise his trade that he might use his spare time to preach. By the close of 1786, thanks chiefly to Baxter's faithful labour, nearly two thousand Methodists, the overwhelming majority of them Negroes, were found on the island.[264] Late in 1786 Thomas Coke visited Antigua. Of a well-to-do family, a graduate of Oxford, and a clergyman of the Church of England, as a young man Coke whole-heartedly cast in his lot with John Wesley. He became the outstanding early Methodist leader in carrying Christianity to non-Christians outside the British Isles. The visit of 1786 kindled the enthusiastic imagination of Coke. He went to several of the islands. He even touched at the Dutch St. Eustatius, where a Negro slave who had been converted through the Methodists in North America was preaching. Again and again he revisited the West Indies. In 1788, 1790, 1792, and 1793, he came, bringing new missionaries, initiating fresh enterprises, preaching, and building up the Methodist societies. In his last visit ten circuits were mapped out for the islands. For these twelve missionaries were available. Methodism had become the church of the blacks. It then numbered 6,570. Only a few score whites and possibly slightly more of mixed blood were found in it. A brief and unsuccessful attempt had been made to win the Carib Indians on St. Vincent. The vast majority of the members were full-blooded Negroes. In spite of the gaps in the thin ranks brought by climate and disease, recruits from Great Britain replenished the missionary forces. Methodism continued to flourish. In the more than twenty years which intervened between the last visit and the death (1814) of Coke the Methodist membership increased to seventeen thousand.[265]

In 1783 there came to Jamaica from the United States a freed Negro, George Liele, a Baptist. He began preaching, finding his physical support in the work of his hands. In spite of persecution, out of his labours arose a congregation at

[263] Findlay and Holdsworth, *The History of the Wesleyan Methodist Missionary Society,* Vol. II, pp. 29-31; Coke, *A History of the West Indies,* Vol. II, pp. 427, 428; Walker, *The Call of the West Indies,* pp. 28-32.

[264] Findlay and Holdsworth, *op. cit.,* Vol. II, pp. 32-37; Coke, *op. cit.,* Vol. II, pp. 428-437; Walker, *op. cit.,* pp. 34-36.

[265] Findlay and Holdsworth, *op. cit.,* Vol. II, pp. 36-62; Coke, *op. cit.,* Vol. I, pp. 411 ff., Vol. II, pp. 65 ff., 131 ff., 251 ff., 350 ff., 436 ff.; Walker, *op. cit.,* pp. 38-48; Peter Duncan, *A Narrative of the Wesleyan Mission to Jamaica* (London, Partridge and Oakey, 1849, pp. xii, 396), pp. 1-66.

Kingston. Before the end of the century, from his associates and converts other groups of Baptists arose.[266]

Protestantism in the New World was by no means completely confined to the British colonies. For a few years just after the middle of the sixteenth century a fleeting Huguenot settlement under the leadership of Villegagnon was made in Brazil, on the bay of Rio de Janeiro.[267] In the first half of the seventeenth century the Dutch seized Bahia and held it for a brief time. For a quarter of a century they had possession of Pernambuco. During the Dutch regime several clergymen came, an ecclesiastical organization in the form of a classis was set up, and at least two of the clergy laboured for the Indians and had converts among them.[268] In the sixteen sixties one of the earliest of the German Protestants to advocate missions to non-Christians, Justinianus von Weltz, was consistent in carrying out the purpose to which he called others and sailed for Surinam, Dutch territory on the northern shore of South America. Here he died.[269]

The first foreign mission of the Moravians was to the Negro slaves of the Danish West Indies. In 1730, while in Copenhagen for the coronation of his friend, Christian VI of Denmark, Zinzendorf came in contact with a Negro from the Danish West Indies who declared that missionaries would be welcome. Zinzendorf was deeply stirred and on his return to Herrnhut reported what he had heard. Some of the Moravians felt called to go. In 1732 two of them arrived on the island of St. Thomas. Gradually reinforcements came, others of the Danish islands were entered, and new stations were opened. The missionaries were self-supporting. Tropical diseases made heavy inroads on the staff, but others came to fill the places of those who fell. Like the Wesleyans in the British West Indies a generation later, the Moravians gave themselves to the Negro slaves. Converts were won, and "native helpers" were trained.[270]

[266] John Clark, W. Dendy, and J. M. Phillippo, *The Voice of Jubilee: A Narrative of the Baptist Mission, Jamaica, from Its Commencement* (London, John Snow, 1865, pp. xx, 359), pp. 30-36.

[267] Jacques Pannier and Gustave Mondain, *L'Expansion Française Outre-Mer et Les Protestants Française* (Paris, Société des Missions Evangeliques, 1931, pp. 179), pp. 10-23; Braga and Grubb, *The Republic of Brazil*, pp. 18, 47.

[268] *Archief voor de Geschiedenis der Oude Hollandsche Zending*, Vol. II (Utrecht, C. Van Bentum, 1885), pp. 215 ff.; Braga and Grubb, *op. cit.*, p. 47; Warneck, *Geschichte der protestantischen Missionen*, pp. 41-47; *Ecclesiastical Records, State of New York*, Vol. I, pp. 111, 122.

[269] Wolfgang Grössel, *Justinianus von Weltz* (Leipzig, Akademische Buchhandlung, 1891, pp. 191), pp. 151, 152.

[270] Hutton, *op. cit.*, pp. 14-49; Müller, *op. cit.*, pp. 17-59; C. G. M. Oldendorps *Geschichte der Mission der evangelischen Brüder auf den caraibischen Inseln S. Thomas,*

Again through the vision and initiative of Zinzendorf, in 1735 a band of Moravian missionaries went to the Dutch possessions on the northern coast of South America. By the missions thus inaugurated, persistent attempts were made to win the Arawak Indians, the Negro slaves on the plantations, and the "bush Negroes." The bush Negroes were those who had escaped from the plantations, had set up independent groups beyond the control of the whites, and were often a terror to the planters. Converts were made among the Negroes, but here, too, disease worked havoc in the missionary staff, and for a time after 1813 effort for the bush Negroes ceased.[271] Support for the mission came largely through the profits of a business house which was established in 1765 at the chief port, Paramaribo.[272]

Climatically almost at the other extreme from the West Indies and Surinam were Greenland and Labrador. Here, too, were Protestant missions. The ones in Greenland and Labrador were established first. As we have seen in the previous volume, Christianity existed in Greenland from a time not far from the year 1000 into the fifteenth century. Its stronghold had been on the west coast, and it had disappeared when the descendants of the Scandinavian settlers died out. Contacts between Greenland and Scandinavia seem to have ceased in the fifteenth century. In the seventeenth century they were intermittently renewed. The first enduring settlement in the new day was effected in 1721 by a Norwegian Lutheran pastor, Hans Egede. For years Egede had dreamed of beginning a mission on that desolate island. Eventually he obtained the support of the King of Denmark, for Norway was then joined to Denmark, and under royal auspices took his family to Greenland. In order to reach Greenland, he associated himself with a commercial enterprise. This for him, however, was only a means to his end. He was deeply interested in the fate of the former Scandinavian population, and when he did not discover survivors on the west coast he hoped that they might be found on the less accessible east coast. None were there, however, and, perforce, he confined his efforts to the Eskimos and on the west side of the island. He learned the Eskimo language, but for years he seemed unable to make any impression religiously, for his faith, as he described it, appeared to his hearers not to offer anything which they desired. Some of his fellow settlers had been recruited from Danish jails

S. Croix und S. Jan, herausgegeben durch Johann Jakob Bossart (Barby, Christian Friedrich Laux, 2 parts, 1777), passim; A. v. Dewitz, In Dänisch-Westindien. Hundert und fünfzig Jahre der Brüdermission in St. Thomas, St. Croix und St. Jan, Teil I, Die erste Streitezeit in des Grafen von Zinzendorf Tagen von 1732 bis 1760 (Niesky, Missions-Institut, 1882, pp. 373), passim.

[271] Hutton, op. cit., pp. 117-125; Müller, op. cit., pp. 17-59.
[272] Hutton, op. cit., pp. 250, 251.

and were an obstacle rather than a help. For fifteen years he persevered in the face of difficulties and discouragements. Then when, in 1736, he returned to Denmark, he headed a seminary for the training of missionaries for Greenland and continued his literary labours. In Greenland he was succeeded by his son Paul. Other helpers also came. In 1741 the enterprise had four missionaries and two catechists. Converts were few, and in the twenty years between 1721 and 1741 only twenty or thirty aged persons and about a hundred younger ones had been baptized.[273]

To Greenland, attracted by the news of Egede's enterprise, came Moravian missionaries. The first arrived in 1733. They, too, had a discouraging period without converts. Eventually, when success began to be theirs, they gathered their converts into a settlement at New Herrnhut in which they could control the entire life of the community. Before a half century after their initial landing, the single settlement had increased to three. Thus a method was worked out not unlike the Spanish Roman Catholic missions among the Indians.[274]

The Moravians also went to the Labrador. In 1752 they sent an emissary to spy out the land. He was killed by the Eskimos, but his death inspired a Danish Moravian, Jens Haven, to take up his fallen mantle. Haven made his way to Greenland, learned the Eskimo tongue, and in 1764 went to the Labrador in the dual capacity of an agent of the British Government (for the region had passed to Great Britain through the Peace of Paris in 1763), and of a missionary. Reinforcements arrived, and the mission became the especial charge of a Society for the Furtherance of the Gospel which had been organized in London in 1741. The Society was given a large grant of land, and thus could control the contacts with other Europeans and guard the Eskimos from ruthless whites. As in Greenland, the Eskimos were encouraged to congregate in settlements under the supervision of the missionaries. The mission obtained its support, much as did the Jesuit missions in Paraguay, by selling in Europe the products of the natives. Christianity gradually spread, and in 1804 a marked religious

---

[273] Hans Egede, *Ausführliche und wahrhafte Nachricht vom Anfange und Fortgange der gronländischen Mission* (Hamburg, Christian Wilhelm Brandt, 1740, pp. 288), *passim*; Hans Egede, *A Description of Greenland* (London, T. and J. Allman, 2d ed., 1818, pp. cxviii, 225), *passim*; H. M. Fenger, *Bidrag til Hans Egde og den grønlandske Missions Historie 1721-1760* (Kjøbenhavn, 1879, pp. xv, 345), *passim*; David Crantz, *The History of Greenland* (London, J. Dodsley, 2 vols., 1767), Book IV, Chap. 2.

[274] Fenger, *op. cit., passim;* Crantz, *op. cit.,* Books V-X; [F. L. Kölbing], *Die Missionen der evangelischen Brüder in Grönland und Labrador* (Gnadau, Hans Franz Burkhard, 1831, pp. viii, 254, 180), pp. 1-254.

movement along the coast brought a moral revolution with a widespread adoption of Christian ethical standards.[275]

In the West Indies the Church of England succeeded in holding most of the white population to at least a nominal adherence to Christianity and, at times, to more. In the eighteenth century the rising tide of Protestant vigour began, through Methodists, Moravians, and Baptists, to bring the Negro slaves to the Christian faith and to prepare the way for the emancipation which came in the nineteenth century.

In Greenland and Labrador Protestant missionaries led the way in effecting permanent settlements of Europeans, protected the Eskimos from much of the selfish exploitation which would otherwise have been their lot, led many of them to the Christian faith, and began the process of helping them to construct a community life in accordance with Christian principles.

In the New World before A.D. 1800 Protestant forms of Christianity, while not as extensively spread as Roman Catholic Christianity, had obtained footholds along most of the Atlantic coast of North America, had been firmly established in the West Indies and Guiana, and had been introduced to Greenland. In these regions Protestant Christianity was growing in power among peoples of European descent, had won many of the Indians, and was beginning to attract the Negroes and the Eskimos. It was helping to offset the exploitation of non-European by European peoples and was becoming an integral and growing factor in the new nation which was emerging from the Thirteen Colonies. In this new nation, moreover, Christianity was beginning to develop novel characteristics. A new type of Christianity was emerging which was even now proving unusually potent. In the nineteenth century it was to increase in vitality and to play an important rôle in world-wide Christianity.

[275] F. L. Kölbing, *op. cit.*, Part II; Hutton, *op. cit.*, pp. 131-145; Müller, *op. cit.*, pp. 145 ff.

Chapter VII

WEST, SOUTH, AND EAST AFRICA, AND THE NEIGHBOURING ISLANDS

BETWEEN A.D. 1500 and A.D. 1800 only the fringes of Africa were touched by Christianity, and they but slightly. Politically practically all of the shore of North Africa was in the hands of Moslems. Two or three ports on the African side of the Straits of Gibraltar were held by the professedly Christian powers of Europe. In some of the other ports were Christian captives and merchants. In Egypt the Copts constituted a substantial Christian minority, and in the mountains of Abyssinia an ancient church held out against the encircling Islam. Because of the Moslem control, however, conversions from the predominant Islam were all but impossible. South of the Sahara and the Nile Valley, Africa was overwhelmingly pagan. That paganism was of a primitive kind which presumably would succumb before an energetic approach by a more highly organized religion, whether it were Christianity or Islam. Before A.D. 1800 that type of approach was not made. Here and there Moslems touched the east coast, but gained no extensive populations. Portuguese, English, Dutch, and French skirted the coast on the way to India and the Far East. To them, however, Africa was chiefly an obstacle which stood in the way between them and the rich commerce of Southern and Eastern Asia. Here and there trading posts were established. Before A.D. 1800 the chief contact of Negro Africa with European peoples was through the traffic in slaves for the white man's economic enterprises in the New World. As such the record is one of heartless cruelty and untold suffering. The internal wars and raids in Africa by which one black tribe seized victims from another for the European traders, the horrors of the trans-Atlantic passage and the servitude in the New World are among the darkest pages of man's inhumanity to man. The Christian conscience was slow in awaking to this palpable contradiction of Christian ideals. Not until the latter part of the eighteenth century did it bestir itself to bring the evil to an end and not until the nineteenth century did it succeed in reducing it to a minimum. Here and there before A.D. 1800 Christian missionaries laboured for longer or shorter periods at various places in neighbouring islands and on the mainland. Only a few enduring communities were gathered. Most of the missions were

Roman Catholic. In the eighteenth century a few were by Protestants. On the southern tip of Africa colonization by Protestants was begun which in the nineteenth and twentieth centuries was to expand into a new nation and an active centre of the Christian faith. By A.D. 1800, however, this had barely commenced. The story of Christianity in this portion of the world between A.D. 1500 and A.D. 1800 can, accordingly, be summarized in a very few pages. Yet it must be noted that, while making but a small impression on Negro Africa in these centuries, Christianity was being planted. No other one faith had ever before been brought to so much of the periphery of the continent. Christianity was thus being carried to the edges of vast regions which it had never previously touched.

For the most part, Roman Catholic missions to Negro Africa in this period were under Portuguese auspices. The early explorers who opened the route around Africa to the Indies were Portuguese and those under Portuguese direction. The Portuguese padroado held for the west and east coasts, and Roman Catholic missions there were, accordingly, under the control of the Crown.[1] The fact that the shores of Africa were no better covered by Roman Catholic missions must be ascribed in part to the vast amount of territory over which Portugal sought a political, economic, and ecclesiastical monopoly. Portugal was a smaller country than Spain, yet it endeavoured to occupy a much larger proportion of the earth's surface than did the latter. Brazil, Africa, Southern Asia, the East Indies, and the Far East with their huge populations were included in the area which it had staked out as its own. It could not possibly cover them effectively. However, even after its brief commercial supremacy had been shattered and its political control had dwindled to a few footholds, it struggled to maintain its direction of ecclesiastical affairs in all these regions. While it by no means entirely succeeded in the attempt it often embarrassed Roman Catholic missions.

The original Portuguese advance along the west coast of Africa in the fifteenth century had in part what professed to be a Christian motive. Henry the Navigator was the master spirit behind it. One of his purposes, or at least so a Papal bull declared, was to unite with the Christians of India against the Moslems and pagans of that land and to spread the Christian faith.[2] Henry became the Grand Master of the Order of Christ, a military monastic body which in Portugal had succeeded to the property of the Templars, and it was under the auspices of this organization, in something of the guise of a Crusade, that much of the early exploration was accomplished.[3]

[1] Jann, *Die katholischen Missionen in Indien, China, und Japan*, pp. 67-70.
[2] Jann, *op. cit.*, p. 32.
[3] Jann, *op. cit.*, pp. 29-39.

In the fifteenth century a beginning was made in the colonization of the Azores, the Madeiras, and the Cape Verde Islands. Before their discovery by Europeans the first two groups and probably the third were without inhabitants. On all three the Franciscans were active very early.[4] In the fifteenth century, too, missions began on the west coast of Africa. In 1489 a chief of Senegambia and a number of his notable men were baptized at Lisbon, but on his return home he expelled the Dominicans who attempted to work through him for the conversion of his people. Before the end of the century a chief of Benin was also baptized.[5]

At longer or shorter intervals through the sixteenth, seventeenth, and eighteenth centuries various orders conducted missions at several points along the Guinea Coast. In the seventeenth and eighteenth centuries Portuguese Franciscans, with their base on the Cape Verde Islands, had missions at various centres, including Sierra Leone.[6] At the beginning of the seventeenth century the Jesuits came, and we hear of chiefs becoming Christian, including one of Sierra Leone.[7] In the seventeenth century both French and Spanish Capuchins laboured at different times and places on the west coast.[8] We read of Dominicans and Augustinians.[9] In the eighteenth century a French secular had marked but brief success.[10] No permanent Christian communities seem to have arisen.

The most spectacular of the Roman Catholic missions in Africa in this period were in what was called the Kingdom of Congo. In the lower part of the Congo Valley, with its capital south of the river and a few score miles from the mouth, was a native state by that name. The Congo River was discovered by the Portuguese in 1482 or 1483.[11] Towards the close of that decade some of the Negroes from that region were brought to Portugal and baptized.[12] In 1491 the first missionaries reached the Congo, probably secular Canons of St. John the Evangelist from Lisbon, although that is in dispute.[13] Before long the paramount chief, the "King of Congo," accepted baptism, possibly in the hope of obtaining aid in a war. He soon went back to his old religion, but his son, known to the Portuguese as Alfonso, who succeeded him, had been opposed

[4] Lemmens, *Geschichte der Franziskanermissionen*, pp. 189-194.

[5] Schmidlin-Braun, *Catholic Mission History*, p. 242.

[6] Civezza, *Storia Universelle delle Missioni Francescane*, Vol. VII, Part 3, pp. 306-353.

[7] Crétineau-Joly, *Histoire de la Compagnie de Jésus*, Vol. II, p. 420.

[8] Henri Labouret and Paul Rivet, *Le Royaume d'Arda et son Évangelisation au XVIIe Siècle* (Paris, 1929), *passim*; Schmidlin-Braun, *op. cit.*, pp. 281-283, 469, 470.

[9] Schmidlin-Braun, *op. cit.*, p. 470.

[10] *Ibid.*

[11] Eugen Weber, *Die portugiesische Reichsmission im Königreich Congo. Von ihren Anfängen 1491 bis zum Eintritt der Jesuiten in die Kongomission in 1548*, p. 6.

[12] Weber, *op. cit.*, p. 17.

[13] Weber, *op. cit.*, pp. 119-125; Civezza *op. cit.*, Vol. VI, pp. 180, 181.

by the pagan elements, apparently owed his post to Portuguese aid, and was a zealous Christian. He was active in preaching his faith, more missionaries arrived, and a large proportion of his subjects, following his example, were baptized. Alfonso supplied the Portuguese with hundreds of slaves for export, but this did not prevent the growth of the Church. Schools were established by the missionaries, and in 1513 Alfonso sent an embassy to the Pope. In 1518 a son of Alfonso, Henry, was consecrated bishop, so far as we know the first Negro to be elevated to that dignity, and had his see at the capital, Baji, or San Salvador. Some others of the Negroes were ordained to the priesthood. Here was an experiment in creating an indigenous clergy which was in sharp contrast with the contemporary policy in the Americas. Apparently it proved unsuccessful. The Christianity of the populace was superficial, and when, in 1534, a bishopric was created with its seat on the island of São Thomé, the clergy of the Congo, who were made subject to it, proved insubordinate.[14] Jesuits arrived about 1548 from Coimbra and were in the Congo at intervals during much of the remainder of the sixteenth century.[15] A large proportion of the nominal Christianity seems to have died out from lack of clerical care. Towards the end of the sixteenth century Franciscans reappeared.[16] As late as 1777 we hear of a company of Portuguese Brothers Minor going to the Congo.[17] In the latter part of the sixteenth century we read of the arrival of Discalced Carmelites.[18] In the seventeenth and eighteenth centuries several hundred Capuchins came to the Congo and to Angola. They were of more than one nationality, but the majority were Italians. While they had the support of the Propaganda, they also obtained Portuguese permits and a large proportion of them sailed from Lisbon.[19] In time Christianity died out, but in the latter half of the nineteenth century traces of it were still found at San Salvador—such as crucifixes and images of the saints which were kept as fetishes in the compound of the chief and were occasionally brought out in parade in an effort to dispel a drought.[20]

[14] Weber, op. cit., passim; Schmidlin-Braun, op. cit., pp. 276-279; G. Goyau, Les Débuts de l'Apostolat au Congo et dans Angola (1482-1590), in Revue d'Histoire des Missions, Vol. VII, pp. 481-514.

[15] Huonder, Der hl. Ignatius von Loyola und der Missionsberuf der Gesellschaft Jesu, p. 26; Goyau, op. cit.; Schmidlin-Braun, op. cit., p. 279; Crétineau-Joly, op. cit., Vol. I, pp. 397, 398.

[16] Civezza, op. cit., Vol. VII, Part 3, p. 356.

[17] Civezza, op. cit., Vol. VII, Part 3, p. 369.

[18] Pastor, History of the Popes, Vol. XX, p. 482; Florencio del Barcelona Niño Jesús, in Revista de la Exposición Misional Española, Oct., 1928, pp. 39-42.

[19] Quelque Notes sur les Anciennes Missions des Capuchins au Congo et dans l'Angola, in Revue d'Histoire des Missions, Vol. XI, pp. 329-345, Vol. XIII, pp. 53-67; Schmidlin-Braun, op. cit., pp. 279, 280, 471.

[20] H. L. Hemmens, George Grenfell, Pioneer in Congo (London, Student Christian Movement, 1927, pp. 248), pp. 68, 69.

Just south of the Congo lay Angola, with its centre at Loanda. Here Portuguese influence was especially strong. Both commerce and missions began later than in the Congo, but by the end of the sixteenth century several chiefs and thousands of their followers had been baptized and some districts, notably Loanda, were said to be completely Christian.[21] In the seventeenth and eighteenth centuries, the Capuchins were there as well as in the Congo.[22] We hear, too, of the arrival in the eighteenth century of members of several other orders, including other branches of the Franciscans.[23] Christianity seems to have persisted better in Angola than in the Congo.

In the latter half of the eighteenth century some French clergy made an attempt to found a mission in Loango, just north of the Congo, in an area which had been neglected by the Portuguese.[24]

In the first decade of the sixteenth century, Portugal acquired footholds on the east coast of Africa at Mombasa and Mozambique.[25] In 1560, Jesuits, attracted by the report that a chief of Imhambane was favourable to Christianity, went to East Africa, but after initial successes met Moslem opposition and for a time retired.[26] In the first half of the seventeenth century, however, the Jesuits had several stations on the Zambesi, the Dominicans had established centres, and the Augustinians were at Mombasa and Malindi.[27] In 1612, the better to supply the east coast with episcopal ministrations, Mozambique, which had previously been under the Archbishopric of Goa, was made a vicariate apostolic.[28] It is charged that towards the middle of the eighteenth century both Dominicans and Jesuits were chiefly engaged in commerce in slaves and in firearms and gunpowder.[29] However, in the twentieth century what may have been traces of the Christianity of the earlier centuries were found among the Negroes of the Zambesi in ceremonies which suggested baptism and the eucharist, and in the words and music of songs.[30]

In the sixteenth and seventeenth centuries at various times efforts were made

---

[21] Van der Essen in Descamps, *Histoire Comparée des Missions*, pp. 314, 315; Schmidlin-Braun, *op. cit.*, pp. 280, 281.

[22] *Quelque notes, etc.*, in *Revue d'Histoire des Missions*, Vol. XI, pp. 329-345, Vol. XIII, pp. 53-67.

[23] Civezza, *op. cit.*, Vol. VII, Part 4, p. 314.

[24] G. Goyau in Descamps, *op. cit.*, pp. 481-483.

[25] Jann, *op. cit.*, p. 61.

[26] Crétineau-Joly, *op. cit.*, Vol. I, pp. 398-400; Van der Essen in Descamps, *op. cit.*, p. 315.

[27] G. Goyau in Descamps, *op. cit.*, pp. 484-486; Schmidlin-Braun, *op. cit.*, p. 285.

[28] Jann, *op. cit.*, p. 117.

[29] Eduardo Moreira, *Portuguese East Africa* (London, World Dominion Press, 1936, pp. 104), p. 18.

[30] Clemen, *Der Einfluss des Christentums auf andere Religionen*, p. 17; Basil Mathews, *Consider Africa* (New York, Friendship Press, 1936, pp. vi, 181), p. 25.

by the Portuguese to plant Christianity in Madagascar. In the seventeenth century the French, particularly through the then youthful (Lazarist) Congregation of the Mission, also made heroic attempts. None, however, led to permanent Christian communities.[31]

The islands of Réunion (Bourbon) and Mauritius (Île de France), occupied by the French in the seventeenth and eighteenth centuries, had white settlers and Negro slaves. The Lazarists were active in winning the slaves to the Christian faith and in serving the European population.[32] In the second half of the eighteenth century the Sisters of Saint Paul of Chartres went to both islands to care for the sick and to open schools.[33]

The strongest Protestant foothold in Africa before A.D. 1800 was on the extreme southern tip of the continent. Here, as an important point on the route to the Indies, the Dutch built up a community. The first settlement was formed in 1652,[34] and in 1795, when the English seized the colony, the population numbered twenty-one thousand whites, more than twenty-five thousand slaves, and fourteen thousand Hottentots.[35] For several years the colony had no resident minister, but sermons were preached and the sacraments administered by clergy passing to and from the East Indies.[36] In 1665 the first resident clergyman arrived. He began the custom of baptizing some of the children of slaves. Between 1665 and 1731 the records show the baptism of 1,121 slave children and forty-six adults. A church was built for them in Capetown and in 1683 a regulation declared that baptism made the slave free.[37] Beginning with 1685, Huguenots, members of the widespread dispersion brought by the persecution in France, came to South Africa, but they never numbered more than an eighth of the white population and religiously were so akin to the Dutch that their assimilation presented no serious problem, especially since at an early date the East India Company forbade the ministers to preach in French.[38] The churches, like those of the Dutch Reformed in North America, were under the Classis of Amsterdam, and an attempt of the local ministers to

---

[31] Coste, *The Life and Works of St. Vincent de Paul*, Vol. II, pp. 51-117; *Revue d'Histoire des Missions*, Vol. IV, pp. 217 ff., Vol. V, pp. 407 ff., Vol. XIII, pp. 82 ff.; *Zeitschrift für Missionswissenschaft*, Vol. XII, pp. 194 ff.; Léon Derville, *Madagascar-Betsiléo* (Paris, Dillen et Cie, 1930, pp. 126), p. 33; Coste, *La Congrégation de la Mission*, pp. 193-195.

[32] Schmidlin-Braun, *op. cit.*, p. 473.

[33] Jean Vaudon, *Histoire Générale de la Communauté des Filles de Saint-Paul de Chartres . . . 1694 à 1800* (Paris, Pierre Téqui, 1922, pp. vii, 524), pp. 323-364.

[34] John McCarter, *The Dutch Reformed Church in South Africa*, pp. 2-7.

[35] McCarter, *op. cit.*, p. 13.

[36] J. Du Plessis, *The Life of Andrew Murray of South Africa*, p. 78.

[37] McCarter, *op. cit.*, p. 14.

[38] Colin Graham Botha, *The French Refugees at the Cape* (Cape Town, Cape Times, 2d ed., 1921, pp. 171), *passim*; McCarter, *op. cit.*, pp. 7, 8.

form a classis of their own was quashed by the government.[39] The salaries of the ministers were paid by the East India Company.[40] In 1795 the colony had seven Dutch Reformed congregations and ten ministers.[41] As time passed, the zeal for the conversion of the slaves cooled,[42] but the white population remained professedly Christian.

To South Africa came a Moravian, George Schmidt. From 1737 to 1743 he was there and made a few converts among the Hottentots. However, opposition developed from the Dutch clergy, chiefly over his baptizing those whom he had won, and he withdrew.[43] Not until the last decade of the eighteenth century, through movements which are to be described in a subsequent volume, were efforts for the non-Christian tribes renewed.

The latter half of the eighteenth century witnessed the beginning of British missions in Africa. In 1752 an Anglican clergyman, Thomas Thompson, an appointee of the Society for the Propagation of the Gospel in Foreign Parts, arrived at Cape Coast Castle, on the Guinea Coast, and began an effort to reach the Negroes. After four years he returned to England, broken in health. However, he sent three Negro boys to England to be educated, and the one of these who arrived was in time ordained, returned to Africa (1766) as a missionary of the Society, and continued as such, although with few tangible results, until his death, in 1816.[44] In the last decade of the century the rising tide of humanitarianism and missionary interest in Great Britain brought the beginnings of missions on the west coast and gave rise to a settlement of freed Negroes in Sierra Leone,[45] but that development belongs to a later period.

In A.D. 1800 Negro Africa, so far as Christianity was concerned, was the Dark Continent. In none other of the five continents was Christianity so sparsely represented. However, it was present, and at a number of points on the periphery. From some of these footholds it was to have a rapid expansion in the nineteenth and twentieth centuries.

[39] McCarter, *op. cit.*, pp. 20, 21.
[40] Du Plessis, *op. cit.*, p. 78.
[41] McCarter, *op. cit.*, p. 13.
[42] J. Du Plessis, *A History of Christian Missions in South Africa*, pp. 36 ff.
[43] Du Plessis, *A History of Christian Missions in South Africa*, pp. 50 ff.
[44] Pascoe, *Two Hundred Years of the S. P. G.*, pp. 254-259.
[45] J. Du Plessis, *The Evangelisation of Pagan Africa* (Cape Town, J. C. Juta and Co., 1930, pp. xii, 408), pp. 61 ff.

Chapter VIII

INDIA. THE RISE AND GROWTH OF ROMAN CATHOLIC
MISSIONS; THE RETARDMENT OF ROMAN CATHOLIC
MISSIONS; THE BEGINNINGS OF PROTESTANT
MISSIONS; THE EFFECT OF CHRISTIANITY;
THE EFFECT ON CHRISTIANITY

WHEN the Portuguese carried the Cross around the southern tip of
Africa and disclosed a new route from Western Christendom to
Southern and Eastern Asia they opened a new chapter in the expansion of
Christianity. No longer did Western Christians confront an impenetrable barrier of Moslems when they faced the East. They had turned the flank of
Islam. To be sure, Islam was also spreading eastward and long continued to
make greater numerical gains there than did Christianity. However, in many
areas it was only getting under way and was still a minority faith. Christianity
had a chance, and a good one, of forestalling it.

In Southern and Eastern Asia both Christianity and Islam faced high cultures
closely integrated with ancient religions. Until these cultures should weaken,
neither could hope to become the majority faith. Before A.D. 1800 these cultures
remained substantially intact. In the major lands, India, China, and Japan,
and in most of the minor lands, Christianity won only inconsiderable minorities.
Before A.D. 1800 in no great country did Christians constitute more than a
small fraction of one per cent of the population. In a few islands the Christian minority was substantial. In only one group, the Philippines, was Christianity accepted by the majority. In Southern and Eastern Asia Christianity
had to wait until the nineteenth and twentieth centuries to see the disintegration of the chief opposing cultures usher in its great day of opportunity.

The first land in Southern and Eastern Asia touched by Western Europeans
was India. Here were established what by A.D. 1800 became their major territorial possessions in the East. Here was much of their most active missionary
endeavour.

In India Christianity and Christian missionaries met a situation which differed markedly from any which had confronted them in the New World or
in Africa. In the first place, in India, in contrast with the Americas, the

Christian Europeans did not establish extensive settlements. Theirs were primarily merchant communities which always remained a small minority. No large populations of European descent came into existence. The Christian Church had the problem of holding these traders to their hereditary faith and, what was even more difficult, had the task of making their hereditary faith something more than nominal. Even though the Europeans retained the Christian name, at the best they were small ruling enclaves amid an overwhelming non-European population. There was no possibility of bringing into existence new Christian nations of European stock. In the second place, until almost the close of the eighteenth century, Europeans exercised political control over only a small proportion of the territory of India. Indeed, in the sixteenth century, not long after the first of the Europeans to arrive, the Portuguese, had begun to gain footholds on the coast of India, Moslem invaders from the North founded an empire, known by the name of Mogul, which brought a large part of the peninsula under its sway. In only small sections, therefore, could political pressure be applied to induce non-Christians to accept Christian instruction and baptism, and with only relatively minor groups would political, economic, or social expediency come to the assistance of missionaries in bringing about conversion. During most of the period the political advantage in India lay chiefly not with Christianity, but with its doughty hereditary rival, Islam. When it was carried around the Cape of Good Hope the Cross had not completely outflanked the Crescent. In the three centuries between A.D. 1500 and A.D. 1800 the Prophet gained many more followers in India than did the Christ. In the third place, in India the non-European cultures proved more resistant to European penetration than in the Americas. They did not collapse as did those of Mexico and Peru. They remained intact. They were more highly developed than were those of the Americas and Negro Africa. The religions associated with these cultures proved very resistant. Here were religious systems, notably Hinduism and Islam, which always have offered stubborn opposition to other faiths and which have been accustomed themselves to absorb or conquer other religions rather than to be displaced. They yielded much less readily to Christianity than did the animism or the somewhat crude polytheism of the American Indians and the African Negroes. In the fourth place, in India Christian communities existed which long antedated the European discoveries and invasions of the sixteenth, seventeenth, and eighteenth centuries. Here were the so-called Syrian Christians whose origins are lost, but whose history goes back unquestionably many generations before the advent of the Portuguese, the Dutch, the English, and the French. In India Western

Europeans were not, as in the Americas and Negro Africa, the first to introduce Christianity.

Between A.D. 1500 and A.D. 1800 Christianity was propagated in India by more than one people and by both Roman Catholics and Protestants. The Portuguese were first. Then came the French, the Dutch, and the English. The most widely spread and numerically successful missions were those of the Roman Catholics. Protestants were late in beginning and were more restricted geographically. We will, therefore, first recount the story of Roman Catholic missions and next tell of the Protestant efforts.

In the preceding volume we have seen that Roman Catholic Christianity was represented in India in the thirteenth and fourteenth centuries.[1] However, its converts then seem to have been few and no continuing bodies of adherents came into existence.

The reintroduction of Roman Catholicism into India was associated with the Portuguese. The primary purpose of the Portuguese in India was economic. They wished to capture the rich overseas trade and to divert it from the Arabs and from the Italian cities to Lisbon. To this end they sought to sweep the Arabs off the Indian Ocean and to establish themselves at strategic centres along the trade routes. In 1498 they reached India. Within sixteen years they had taken Ormuz and Malacca, which commanded respectively the entrance to the Persian Gulf and the best approach to the Far East, and had acquired footholds in India. Cochin became their first headquarters, but in 1530 Goa was made permanently the chief seat of Portuguese rule. By the middle of the sixteenth century, the Portuguese empire in the East had reached its apex. Portuguese commerce extended from Japan, China, and the East Indies to India, the Persian Gulf, and around Africa to Europe. However, the Portuguese contented themselves with the mastery of the high seas and the possession of a few strategic ports. Never did they attempt extensive territorial conquests in India.

The Portuguese regime both aided and embarrassed Roman Catholic missions. It aided them by conquering footholds from which they could operate and by giving active support to the work of conversion. Within Portuguese territories the state frequently enforced upon non-Christians instruction in Christianity and in other ways furthered the formal acceptance of Christianity. In some instances the hope of Portuguese protection encouraged the request for baptism. On the other hand, the lives of many of the Portuguese could not but bring disgrace upon the Christian name. The Portuguese were guilty of unspeakable acts of cruelty and barbarism. Large numbers of them were

[1] *The Thousand Years of Uncertainty*, pp. 333, 334.

rapacious. Many gave bridle to their lusts. If the atrocities were not so great as those perpetrated by the Spaniards in the New World, it was because the Portuguese met with more resistance and did not conquer so much territory. To Indians, with their tradition of caste, to become Christian seemed tantamount to becoming a Portuguese, and those who scorned the Portuguese connexion were disinclined to take that step. Then, too, the Portuguese claimed the right to control all Roman Catholic missions in India, and prolonged friction ensued with Rome and with non-Portuguese missions which weakened the Church and persisted into the twentieth century. Papal decrees gave to the King of Portugal extensive powers over ecclesiastical affairs in India and South-eastern Asia. As Grandmaster of the Order of Christ, as Christian conqueror, and as the possessor of the right of patronage to bishoprics of the area, the King had been granted large authority over the Church and its agents. The dispute largely centred about the interpretation of these bulls. The Portuguese Crown and Portuguese officials averred that the royal control extended outside Portuguese territories and that, since the Archbishop of Goa was the primate of Southern Asia and the Far East and since he was under the control of the King of Portugal, the ecclesiastical authority of the Throne should also run current over all that vast area. On the other hand, Rome claimed that except by specific Papal grants Portuguese rights over the Church did not extend outside Portuguese territories.[2] The Portuguese government was charged by Rome to provide missionaries and clergy for its territories between the Cape of Good Hope and Japan and to support them. For a time the Crown fulfilled this obligation. However, before the end of the sixteenth century, especially after the union of the Spanish and Portuguese Crowns, complaints became frequent that churches were without clergy and that many of such clergy as were present were unworthy.[3] Jealousy between the two nations prevented much assistance from the Spanish Church, for Spanish clergy were not supposed to be permitted in Portuguese territories.[4] While within Portuguese possessions the support of the state had its advantages in obtaining outward adherence to the Church, even here it had its limitations. Outside Portuguese territories the padroado was again and again a handicap. In the sixteenth and seventeenth centuries these difficulties multiplied and were among the causes of the retarded growth of Roman Catholicism in India and the Far East in these decades.

From the very beginning of Portuguese activities in India, Roman Catholic missionaries were at work. Two Trinitarians sailed from Lisbon with Vasco

[2] Jann, Die katholischen Missionen in Indien, China und Japan, pp. 43, 177-182.
[3] Jann, op. cit., pp. 174-177.
[4] Jann, op. cit., p. 183.

da Gama in 1497 on the famous voyage which first brought the Portuguese to India. One of these died on the way out, but the other landed at Calicut in 1498. He began preaching and in that very year won the martyr's crown, but we do not know that he made any converts.[5] On the second Portuguese voyage to India, in 1500, under Cabral, went several seculars and Franciscans. The latter did some preaching in and near Cochin.[6] In Calicut they made converts, including several Hindus of prominence, but were driven out when Moslems alarmed the ruler by telling him that the missionaries were forerunners of a Portuguese army of conquest.[7] During the first quarter of the sixteenth century Dominicans reached India.[8] However, in the first years of the enterprise the Brothers Minor predominated.[9] Not until 1548 did the Dominicans establish houses of their order in India.[10] Before the middle of the sixteenth century Franciscans had laboured at a number of places on the coast, including Goa and the islands of Salsette and Bassein. Temples had been destroyed and churches erected. We hear of the conversion of about twelve thousand Moplas in or near Quilon, of a church in the suburbs of Madras, and of other centres of missionary effort on both the east and the west coast.[11] Seminaries, notably at Goa, had been begun for the preparation of a native clergy.[12] In the fifteen thirties Goa was made a bishopric[13] and in the late fifteen fifties it was elevated to an archbishopric.[14] Yet early efforts of Portuguese officials to win Hindus to baptism by gifts of money and the unions of Portuguese with women of lower castes tended to bring Christianity into disrepute among the more prominent. To the controlling classes of Hindus this Roman Catholicism of the Portuguese seemed to be a mercenary religion and only for the common folk.[15]

Marked impetus was given to the spread of Christianity in India and the rest of South-eastern and Eastern Asia by the coming of the Jesuits. The first of the Society to arrive was one of the most famous missionaries in the entire history of the Church, Francis Xavier.[16]

[5] Müllbauer, *Geschichte der katholischen Missionen in Ostindien*, pp. 42-44.
[6] *Ibid.*; Lemmens, *Geschichte der Franziskanermissionen*, p. 95.
[7] Lemmens, *op. cit.*, p. 95.
[8] Van der Essen in Descamps, *Histoire Générale Comparée des Missions*, p. 317; Müllbauer, *op. cit.*, p. 57.
[9] Van der Essen in Descamps, *op. cit.*, p. 57; Jann, *op. cit.*, pp. 79-89.
[10] Müllbauer, *op. cit.*, pp. 44-47; D'Sa, *The History of the Diocese of Damaun*, p. 30.
[11] D'Sa, *History of the Catholic Church in India*, Vol. I, pp. 37-43.
[12] Müllbauer, *op. cit.*, pp. 54, 56.
[13] Jann, *op. cit.*, pp. 79-89.
[14] Müllbauer, *op. cit.*, p. 83; Jann, *op. cit.*, pp. 118-120. Cochin and Malacca were its first suffragan sees.
[15] Lemmens, *op. cit.*, p. 98.
[16] The Literature on Xavier is extensive. See some of it listed in Streit, *Bibliotheca Missionum*, Vol. IV, pp. 123-135, 142, 143, 146, 150-153, 156, 158-165. A brief, popular

Francis Xavier was born in 1506 on the Spanish side of Navarre, not far from the Pyrenees. He was of Basque stock and of noble blood. The youngest son in his family, he spent his boyhood in the family castle. He was reared devoutly. Although lithe and athletic, he was fond of books and had no desire to follow the soldier's calling. In 1525, when not yet twenty, he went to the most famous of the universities of the day, that of Paris, with the purpose of preparing himself for an ecclesiastical career. He was there eleven years. While in Paris he was for a time attracted by a group with Protestant tendencies. However, he also came in contact with Ignatius Loyola. Loyola was older by about fifteen years and had already gone through the religious transformation which made him the greatest single force in the Catholic Reformation. In time he made a profound impression upon his young, brilliant, charming fellow-countryman and won him from his Protestant leanings and the lure of a lucrative and easy career in the Church to a complete dedication of his life. Xavier became one of the little, devoted, enthusiastic band which first constituted the Society of Jesus. With the group he went to Italy and was in Rome when informal Papal approval was given to the constitution of the Society.

While in Rome, Loyola received a request of King John III of Portugal, through the Portuguese Ambassador, for missionaries for the Indies. The request was for four. Loyola felt that his small company could not spare that number. He was, however, prepared to respond with two. One of the two chosen fell ill. The day before the Ambassador was to return to Lisbon, Loyola asked Xavier to fill the vacant place. Xavier had already dreamed of India, possibly because the head of his college in Paris had been interested in propagating Christianity through the Portuguese enterprise in the East. He promptly and gladly agreed to go and with less than twenty-four hours' notice left for Portugal, on the first stage of what was to be the great work of his life. He was delayed for a time in Lisbon and employed the interval to preach and to seek to win to a more earnest Christian life those whom he touched in that port. Rodriguez, who was originally assigned to go with him, was retained in Portugal for religious work. Xavier sailed in 1541, with the endorsement of the King and with a Papal commission as Apostolic Nuncio. With him were two companions. On a voyage which was filled with unusual hardships, even for those days of overcrowded ships, slow passage, and poor food, he gave him-

biography is Edith Anne Robertson, *Francis Xavier* (London, Student Christian Movement Press, 1930, pp. 207). Fairly good is Henry James Coleridge, *The Life and Letters of St. Francis Xavier* (London, Burns and Oates, 2 vols., 1872), by a Jesuit. A standard life, in whose footnotes are references to the pertinent sources and literature, and also sympathetic, is A. Brou, *Saint François Xavier 1506-1548* (Paris, Gabriel Beauchesne & Cie, 2 vols., 1912).

self unstintedly to the physical and spiritual welfare of his fellow travellers. His two colleagues remained at Mozambique to care for the sick who were left there, so that Xavier was the first of his Society to reach India. Between Mozambique and India, his ship touched at Socotra. There Xavier found Christians, presumably Nestorians, and Moslems. The Christians, he discovered, did not have baptism. Xavier baptized a number of children and wished to remain on the island, but the Portuguese Governor, with whom he was, would not allow it. Later he saw to it that missionaries went to the island.

Once in the Indies, Xavier did not confine himself to any one spot. He believed his mission to be to the entire area, incredibly vast and populous, touched by the Portuguese enterprise in the East. His was the vision and the task of the explorer and the pioneer, to blaze new trails, to open doors, and to lay foundations. He had only slightly more than ten years in the East, but in that brief span of time he ranged over parts of India and Ceylon, to Malacca, and to the East Indies; he began Roman Catholic missions in Japan, and he died, towards the close of the year 1552, off the coast of China while endeavouring to gain entrance to that vast empire. A devoted friend, intensely interested in individuals, seeking by love, gayety, and a timely word to lead men into the Christian faith or into a deeper Christian life, Xavier also had an imagination which covered vast areas and peoples. He endeavoured to raise the level of Christian living of the Portuguese adventurers and of their nominally Christian mixed-blooded offspring. He strove, through his Society, to bring the Christian Gospel to the many lands and peoples opened to the West by Portuguese discoveries and commerce. He recruited members for the Society, sought new missionaries from Europe, and made provision for the training of natives of the East for the service of the Church.

In Goa Xavier cared for the sick and the prisoners, heard confessions, preached, and taught children their prayers, the Creed, and the Commandments. His example of teaching the children was followed by the Bishop, who ordered the custom adopted by other priests. With the cordial approval of the Governor, a college was established at Goa for training in the Christian religion youths of various nations in the hope that they would eventually become missionaries to their fellow-countrymen. The Governor desired that Jesuits be sent to take charge of the institution.

From Goa after a few months Xavier went to the Paravas, a pearl-fishing, low-caste group north and east of Cape Comorin. About 1534 these had become nominally Christian. They had sought the protection of the Portuguese against the Moslems, and in return for it had accepted baptism. About twenty thousand are said to have received the rite. However, they were left without religious instruction, and about the only evidence of their change of faith was the Portuguese baptismal names which they had received.[17] They had joined the "Portuguese caste," but beyond that their Christian faith meant little. They were without the sacraments, without priests, and without instruction, except such little as could be given them on infrequent visits by the Franciscans of Cochin.[18] To these Xavier went. He devoted a large part of two years to teaching them, administering the sacraments, and eradicating pagan customs. He learned something of the vernacular, and had translations prepared in it of a catechism, the Apostles' Creed, the Ten Commandments, and some prayers, including the Lord's Prayer. He taught these, with explanations, to the Christians. He concentrated his attention on the children, for they, he felt, being still impressionable, had a better chance of becoming good Christians than did their elders. He encouraged the children to teach what they had learned to the older members of the community. The children, too, proved zealous in destroying idols and other symbols of the old cults. In each of the thirty Christian villages he appointed catechists, salaried by the Portuguese Governor, to preside over meetings on feast days at which he suggested that the Christians assemble and sing together what they had learned. He also baptized many. He spoke of often in a single day baptizing whole villages and of scarcely being able to use his hands because of the fatigue from that labour and of losing his voice from repeating the formulæ in which he instructed the neophytes. He longed, too, for reinforcements from the universities of Europe, especially his own *alma mater*.[19] It is interesting to record that the descendants of the Paravas on whom he expended so much devotion continued to be Christians, that many of them rose to wealth and eminence, and that in the twentieth century they constituted a stronghold of Roman Catholicism.[20]

Xavier could not be confined to the Paravas. He journeyed into other regions in South India, among them especially Travancore, and into Ceylon. In Travancore the prince, presumably from a desire for the friendship of the powerful Portuguese, showed Xavier favour and allowed liberty of preaching and of conversion. Assisted by some priests of Indian birth, Xavier made several thousand converts. Most of these seem to have been from a fisher caste, akin to the Paravas, but more degraded than these latter. Almost no accessions could be obtained from the upper classes.

---

[17] Brou, *op. cit.*, Vol. I, pp. 138, 139; Müllbauer, *Geschichte der katholischen Missionen in Ostindien*, pp. 58, 59.

[18] Brou, *op. cit.*, Vol. I, p. 179.

[19] See especially the letter of Xavier of December 31, 1543, translated in Coleridge, *op. cit.*, Vol. I, pp. 151-163.

[20] *Fides News Service*, March 9, 1935.

From India, in 1545, Xavier went to Malacca, and then to the Moluccas, where the Portuguese had established trading posts. In 1548 he was once more in India. He revisited the Christian communities in the South, giving directions to the missionaries there. Cochin and Ceylon saw him. In Goa he directed much attention to the college. On another trip to the Fisher Coast he found the Parava mission better manned and better disciplined than any other in India. In Cochin he founded a college. In 1549 Xavier was off again, this time to inaugurate a mission in Japan. Early in 1552 he was once more in India for a brief sojourn, and then he embarked for the China adventure in which, towards the end of the year, his life came to its close.

Before his death, only a decade after his arrival in India, Xavier had seen the Society of Jesus, in whose inauguration he had shared, strongly reinforced in the East. Some of the accessions were from among the Portuguese already in the Indies. Some were by fresh recruits from Europe.[21] In 1542, the very year of Xavier's arrival in India, a Jesuit college had been founded in Portugal at the famous university centre at Coimbra, as a *seminarium missionis Indicæ*. In 1546 it had an enrolment of eighty and in the following year of one hundred and fifteen, some of them from the best families of the kingdom.[22] In 1546 ten Jesuits sailed for India.[23] To be sure, discouragements met the young mission. In the fifteen forties and fifties so few pagans in India had accepted baptism that some Jesuits felt that so unfruitful a field should be abandoned. However, the General of the Society, far from being disheartened, ordered it continued.[24] In 1557 Philip Neri, from whom arose the Oratorians, was so thrilled by Jesuit reports that only the advice of their confessor deterred him and a score of his followers from starting for India.[25]

A few notes, somewhat at random, will serve to indicate the progress made by the Jesuits. In Goa the process of conversion continued, assisted by the state. Even during the lifetime of Xavier, a royal decree forbade the practice of Hinduism in the Portuguese domains and commanded the destruction of idols.[26] Brahmins, the leaders of the pagan cults, were required to attend the Sunday disputations of the missionaries.[27] Baptisms of pagans were celebrated with great public festivals. Each year thousands were administered the rite.

[21] As in Coleridge, *op. cit.*, Vol. II, pp. 389-395.
[22] Huonder, *Der hl. Ignatius von Loyola und der Missionsberuf der Gesellschaft Jesu*, pp. 23, 24.
[23] Huonder, *op. cit.*, p. 26.
[24] Müllbauer, *Geschichte der katholischen Missionen in Ostindien*, pp. 77-79.
[25] Hoffmann, *Ursprung und Anfangstätigkeit des ersten päpstlichen Missionsinstituts*, p. 75.
[26] Müllbauer, *op. cit.*, pp. 77-79.
[27] Müllbauer, *op. cit.*, pp. 79-81.

In 1560 the Jesuits are said to have baptized nearly thirteen thousand in the vicinity of Goa. While the number receiving baptism diminished, in the fifteen eighties it was still between fifteen hundred and two thousand a year.[28] In the Bombay region temples were pulled down and the materials used to build churches. Mosque revenues were diverted to churches.[29] By the close of the sixteenth century practically all in the vicinity of Goa were professing Christians.[30] Paganism proved stubborn on the island of Salsette, about three miles from Goa. Riots broke out against the Jesuits. In 1567, the Viceroy commanded the destruction of mosques and temples and the baptism of orphans under fourteen years of age.[31] By the end of the seventeenth century most of the island of Salsette, near Bombay, belonged to the Jesuits. Here, however, the majority of the converts were from the poorer classes.[32] In 1601 the Jesuits had seven residences on the Fisher Coast, where Xavier had laboured, and at Tuticorin, their stronghold, they had schools, including a seminary with about thirty students.[33] At the beginning of the seventeenth century they founded a mission for a robber tribe and won converts.[34] For a time the ruler of Travancore withdrew from the Portuguese alliance and persecuted Christians, but the Portuguese sent a fleet against him and compelled him to renew the association and to give the Jesuits permission to preach. As a result, several hundred converts were made each year.[35] In 1595 the Jesuits established a mission for the Christian Paravas at Madura, but no conversions followed as yet among the non-Christians there.[36]

One of the most interesting of the Jesuit missions was at the court of the Great Mogul.[37] As we have seen, the sixteenth century witnessed the establishment of

---

[28] Müllbauer, op. cit., pp. 81-83.

[29] Hull, *Bombay Mission History*, Vol. I, pp. 12, 13.

[30] Müllbauer, op. cit., pp. 81-83.

[31] Müllbauer, op. cit., pp. 96-103.

[32] Fernandes, *Bandra, Its Religious and Secular History*, pp. 11, 15.

[33] Müllbauer, op. cit., p. 123.

[34] *Ibid.*

[35] Müllbauer, op. cit., pp. 114-119.

[36] Müllbauer, op. cit., p. 125.

[37] On this mission to the Mogul Court, see Edward Maclagan, *The Jesuits and the Great Mogul* (London, Burns Oates and Washbourne, 1932, pp. xxxi, 434); *Akbar and the Jesuits. An Account of the Jesuit Missions to the Court of Akbar by Father Pierce du Jarric, S.J., Translated with Introduction and Notes by C. H. Payne* (London, George Routledge and Sons, 1926, pp. xlviii, 288); *Jehangir and the Jesuits with an Account of the Travels of Benedict Goes and the Mission to Pegu From the Relations of Father Fernão Guerreiro, S.J., Translated by C. H. Payne* (London, George Routledge and Sons, 1930, pp. xxix, 287); and Filippi, *An Account of Tibet. The Travels of Ippolito Desideri of Pistoia, S.J., 1712-1727*, pp. 68-71. The succeeding paragraphs are based upon these accounts.

two vigorous foreign conquerors in India, the Roman Catholic Portuguese on parts of the seaboard and the Moslem Moguls over much of the interior.

Shortly after the middle of the century there came to the Mogul throne a most remarkable ruler, Akbar. Very able, he increased the domains of the Mogul Empire. For a generation he was the most prominent figure in India. Akbar seems first to have had his attention attracted to Christianity in 1576 when two Jesuits in Bengal evoked his admiration by declining to give absolution to some Christian merchants who had defrauded the Mogul government of taxes. Akbar was deeply interested in religion. This was partly from a personal concern which dated from his boyhood and partly from policy of state. The religious differences in his realms, particularly between Moslems and Hindus, constituted then, as now, a serious obstacle to political unity. Akbar searched for solutions of the problem. He broke with orthodox Islam, instituted conferences between the representatives of the various religions, and ultimately worked out a new religion, a type of monotheism, which he endeavoured to substitute for the others. In the course of his search he induced a Christian priest, Julian Pereira, to come to his court. Through Pereira he learned of the Jesuits in the College of St. Paul, in Goa. He sent, accordingly, an embassy to Goa (1579) asking for priests and books. The authorities in Goa were a little fearful that the missionaries would be treated as hostages, for they were well aware that Akbar looked upon the Portuguese as intruding rivals. However, three Jesuits were sent, Aquaviva (the son of an Italian duke and nephew of the Aquaviva who later became the General of the Jesuits), Monserrate (a Spaniard), and Henriquez (a Persian convert from Islam). Aquaviva especially seems to have impressed Akbar by the sincerity and austerity of his life. The Jesuits aspired to the conversion of Akbar and through him of the inhabitants of the Mogul Empire. They were living in the days when a handful of Spaniards or Portuguese might hope to overthrow a vast kingdom, and to them the dream of winning India to the Cross did not appear fantastic. Akbar subsidized the Jesuits, outwardly took tolerantly their strictures on his polygamy, and listened to their disputations with the Moslem scholars. He was still sufficiently a Moslem to find difficulty with the Christian doctrines of the Incarnation and the Trinity. Presumably there was never any likelihood of his conversion, but at one time his supposed leaning towards Christianity was a contributory factor to revolts against him. Akbar's friendliness cooled, Aquaviva returned to Goa in 1583, and from then until 1590 we hear nothing of the interest of the Mogul Emperor in Christianity. At Akbar's request a second mission came from Goa in 1590, but, discouraged, soon left. In 1594, again at the instance of Akbar, a third mission was appointed, this time headed by Jerome Xavier, a nephew of Francis Xavier.

This third mission had a much longer life. A church was built at Lahore, reinforcements came, and about 1601 Akbar gave an order allowing his subjects to accept the Christian faith. Akbar's successor, Jehangir, before his accession had been very friendly to the Jesuits. With one short exception he remained so. The missionaries were daily at his audiences, he employed some Christian symbolism in his palaces, and he allowed three of his nephews to be instructed and publicly baptized. A few converts were made from Moslems and Hindus. At one time or another the Jesuit mission had missionaries or adherents at Agra, Lahore, Delhi, Kabul, Peshawar, Srinagar, and Garhwal. Yet the number of baptisms was never large, the three nephews of Jehangir apostatized, and the mission dwindled.

The death of Jehangir (1627) brought an orthodox Moslem, Shah Jehan, to the throne. Difficulties with the Portuguese led to restrictions on the Jesuits, and while these were eventually relaxed, the mission was obviously waning.

Aurangzeb, who succeeded Shah Jehan in 1658, was fanatically Moslem. For a time he continued subsidies to the Jesuit mission, but restrictions increased. For instance, statues of Christ, of the Virgin, of the Apostles, and of various saints and angels had to be taken down and hidden. Yet adherents of the Jesuit mission were found at Agra, Lahore, and Delhi.

Thanks partly to the influence of Donna Juliana Diaz da Costa, a Christian who was high in favour at court and who had charge of the education of several of the princes, the four succeeding monarchs were more friendly.

Gradually, however, the mission waned, subventions from the princes ceased, the college at Agra lost its endowments, and in the second half of the eighteenth century the expulsion of the Jesuits by the Portuguese and then the dissolution of the Society by the Pope brought Jesuit efforts to an end.

Although the Jesuits had prepared Christian literature, had won friends by their knowledge of painting and their scholarship, and had maintained their religious services with pomp, those who sought their ministrations were principally foreign Christians—merchants, artisans, and soldiers—and converts were scarce and chiefly from low-caste servants in the households of non-Indian Christians.

A few efforts were made to establish missions in the Mogul realms outside the chief cities. For a time in the latter part of the seventeenth century a landowner in Bengal was a zealous convert and under his influence several thousands were baptized. Augustinians and Jesuits ministered to them. However, the landowner deteriorated through debt and drink and the Christian communities disintegrated.[38] In the first half of the eighteenth century a Rajput chief of Jaipur through his concern for astronomy became interested in the Jesuits, for these put him in touch with European findings in the subject. He supported Jesuits at his court, but after his death attention to astronomy and Christianity dwindled.[39] Christian communities in the Mogul's domains were at best few and small.

A Jesuit mission which, like that at the court of the Great Mogul, was for the purpose of reaching the higher classes in the hope that, in the fashion of the missions of Medieval Europe, they would lead the masses into the faith, centred at Madura. Its founder was one of the ablest and most original of the missionaries of these centuries, Robert de Nobili.[40] Nobili was born in 1577 of a distinguished Italian family. He was a nephew of Bellarmine, Jesuit, theologian, and Cardinal, and was related to Pope Julius III. In 1597 he joined the Jesuits and in due course at his own request was sent as a missionary. He reached India in 1605. After a brief period on the Fisher Coast he was assigned to Madura where, as we have seen, were some of the Parava Christians. He found that here, as practically everywhere in India outside the Portuguese possessions and spheres of influence, few converts were being made. Christians were regarded by their neighbours as Portuguese and were despised. To accept baptism was to break with one's own caste and to join that of the Christians. Since most of the native Roman Catholic Christians were from the lowest social groups, they were looked down upon by their neighbours. Obviously under such circumstances the hope of the conversion of all India was vain. Some way must be found of ending the identification of Christians with Portuguese.

In Madura Nobili lived apart from his Portuguese colleague (although he kept in contact with him), built a hut in the Brahmin quarter, repudiated the

[38] Maclagan, *The Jesuits and the Great Mogul*, pp. 121-133.
[39] Maclagan, *op. cit.*, pp. 133-135; Josson, *La Mission du Bengale Occidental*, Vol. I, p. 131.
[40] On Nobili, see Peter Dahmen, *Robert de Nobili, S.J. Ein Beitrag zur Geschichte der Missionsmethode und der Indologie* (Münster i.W., 1924, pp. xii, 82); Pierre Dahmen, *Un Jésuite Brahme. Robert de Nobili, S.I., 1577-1656, Missionaire au Maduré* (Bruges, Charles Beyaert, 1925, pp. x, 103); *Robert de Nobili l'Apôtre des Brahmes Première Apologie, 1610. Texte inédit latin traduit et annoté par le P. Pierre Dahmen, S.J., de la Mission du Maduré* (Paris, Éditions Spes, 1931, pp. 205); J. Bertrand, *La Mission du Maduré d'après des Documents Inédits* (Paris, Librairie de Poussielgue-Rusand, 4 vols., 1847-1854. Largely made up of documents).
A brief account by a Protestant is Richter, *Indische Missionsgeschichte*, pp. 64-77. A somewhat longer account, also still brief and by a Protestant, is J. S. Chandler, *History of the Jesuit Mission in Madura South India in the Seventeenth and Eighteenth Centuries* (Madras, M. E. Publishing House, 1909, pp. vii, 72), based chiefly upon the published letters of members of the mission.

name *prangui* by which Portuguese and Christians were indiscriminately denominated, and proclaimed himself an ascetic and a Roman rajah. In this he
was both astute and honest, for he was Italian, not a Portuguese, and he lived
the ascetic life. He devoted himself to mastering the language and within six
months could preach in Tamil. He studied Sanskrit and the sacred books in
that language. He also acquired Telugu. So far as he could do so without what
he believed to be compromise of essential Christian principles and practices,
he adopted Indian methods and customs and accommodated himself to Indian
prejudices. He lived like an Indian holy man, or *sannyasi*, and, later, more like
an Indian *guru*, or teacher. He adopted the vegetarian diet deemed by the
Hindus consistent with the religious profession and employed a Brahmin cook.
In conformity with the custom of the Indians, he admitted only Brahmins to
his meals, although he would eat with other missionaries. For a time he wore
a cord, somewhat in the fashion of the upper castes, but with a cross appended.
He wore a sandalwood paste, also in resemblance to an Indian custom, and
went through ceremonial ablutions before saying mass. For Christian concepts
he adopted Tamil terms which differed from some of those previously employed
by missionaries. He prepared an extensive literature in Indian tongues. He
seriously considered the use of Sanskrit as the liturgical language for the Church
in India. He wished to found a college for the training of a native clergy in
which the instruction would be given in Sanskrit instead of Latin, but was
prevented by lack of funds. From the church which he built he excluded the
Parava Christians, fearing that otherwise the higher castes would not come.
In defence he pled the refusal of the St. Thomas Christians to admit low-caste
people to their churches and the fact that a separate church had be erected
for members of a fisher group with whom the Christian Paravas declined to
associate. For his Brahmin converts, he substituted a cord which he himself
had blessed and which had a cross hung from it. He permitted them to retain
the tuft of hair which was one of their caste privileges. He also had them wear
sandalwood paste as a caste mark. Here was an ingenious attempt to acclimatize
Christianity in India, and to win the upper classes and through them the entire
country.[41] Nobili did not neglect the lower classes, for he interested himself in
the Pariahs, but he sought to reach India through what appeared to him to be
the natural leaders.

His methods brought down on Nobili a storm of criticism, partly from non-
Christians, but chiefly from his fellow missionaries.[42] The colleague who had

[41] In general these methods are summarized from Nobili's own description of them,
chiefly in his apology of 1610 as contained in Dahmen, *Robert de Nobili . . . Première
Apologie.*
[42] Much of the documentary material on this controversy is in Bertrand, *op. cit.*, Vol. II.

preceded him in Madura and who had ministered to the Parava Christians led in the attack. Nobili was accused of compromising with paganism. The General of the Jesuits and his own uncle, Bellarmine, were scandalized. However, Nobili defended himself ably, his archbishop supported him, and in the bull *Romanæ sedis antistes* (Jan. 31, 1623) Rome pronounced in his favour, albeit guardedly. Nobili laboured on until, in 1643, the increasing infirmities of age compelled his retirement. He died in 1656.

At Nobili's initiative and in general pursuing his methods, other Jesuits joined the Madura mission and expanded into other parts of South India.[43] At the instance of Nobili, two kinds of missionaries were developed, one of the *sannyasi* type for the higher castes, and another which served as well members of the lower social groups. Several very able men joined the mission. Joseph-Constant Beschi, an Italian, who reached Madura about 1710, acquired a knowledge of Tamil which won him great respect. He composed poems in Tamil and a number of other works, including grammars and dictionaries. Accorded high honours by the ruler of Tanjore, so far did he go in holding to the upper castes that he became almost inaccessible and appeared in public only in state. Yet he gave himself unstintedly to his mission and ended his days among the Paravas on the Fisher Coast.[44] Giovanni Éttore de Britto was the son of a viceroy to Brazil and was reared in the Portuguese court. He joined the Jesuits, in 1673 went to India, and in India lived as a *sannyasi*. He served in Mysore, Tanjore, and in other places in South India. He is said to have baptized many thousands. He came to a martyr's end, in 1693, at the command of the Prince of Marawa.[45] To Italian and Portuguese Jesuits were added, in 1695, French members of the Society.[46] They extended their labours into the Telugu country.[47] They composed in Telugu poems on sacred subjects, narratives of Biblical history, and translations of prayers.[48] One of the French Jesuits, La Fontaine, who adopted the method of life of a *sannyasi*, gained the goodwill of a rajah and numbered several Brahmins among his converts.[49]

The mission which had Nobili as its greatest missionary met with considerable success. By the death of Nobili the annual number of baptisms among adults

[43] For part of the succeeding history of the mission, especially the pertinent letters from missionaries, see Bertrand, *op. cit.*, Vols. III, IV.

[44] Bertrand, *op. cit.*, Vol. IV, pp. 342 ff.; Jenks, *Six Great Missionaries of the Sixteenth and Seventeenth Centuries*, p. 137; Schwager, *Die katholische Heidenmissionen der Gegenwart*, p. 334.

[45] Jenks, *op. cit.*, p. 136; Schwager, *op. cit.*, p. 334; [Zaleski], *Les Martyrs de l'Inde*, pp. 148-172.

[46] Müllbauer, *Geschichte der katholischen Missionen in Ostindien*, pp. 237-239.

[47] Paul, *History of the Telugu Christians*, p. 15.

[48] Paul, *op. cit.*, pp. 36, 37.

[49] Paul, *op. cit.*, p. 4.

was said to have been more than a thousand. Then years later the Madura mission is reported to have had forty thousand Christians. By 1688 the total is declared to have risen to seventy-five thousand and at the beginning of the eighteenth century to ninety thousand.[50] Other estimates place the number of Christians in 1699 at one hundred and fifty thousand and in 1703 at two hundred thousand.[51]

However, while a few of these Christians were Brahmins, the overwhelming majority were Sudras and Pariahs.[52] The number of missionaries was never large. It was usually only eight or ten, and at most twelve or fifteen. Moreover, two of these were generally in one place, one to minister to the higher and one to the lower castes.[53] Nobili's enterprise, then, while proving that converts in fairly large numbers could be made outside areas touched by Portuguese political and commercial power, was far from effecting the conversion of India or of even one of the states of India. Nor did it bring into the Christian faith any appreciable proportion of the higher castes. In spite of efforts designed to go as far towards allaying prejudice as was consistent with the most liberal interpretation of the Roman Catholic faith and practice, very few of the socially prominent were won. Then, as later, the large majority of Christians were drawn from the lower social strata. Even more than in the contemporary China, where at about the same time Jesuits were endeavouring by similar methods to win the dominant elements of society, the higher classes either ignored Christianity or persecuted it. Only an occasional individual of rank was converted. Nor was the main structure of Indian life and thought appreciably modified.

It must not be thought that the Jesuits were the only Roman Catholic missionaries in India. Prominent though the Society of Jesus was, other orders had a share in attempting to win the land. As we have seen, Franciscans were in India before the Jesuits. They continued to be active. One Brother Minor destroyed about two hundred pagan shrines on the island of Salsette and in their place built eleven churches.[54] It must be noted, incidentally, that in conformity with Roman Catholic principles, the first provincial council of Goa, held in 1567, forbade any one to be constrained to be a Christian by force or intimidation. It forbade Christians to compel Hindus to eat with them and so to break caste. Nor could children be baptized without the consent of their parents or

---

[50] Dahmen, *Robert de Nobili . . . Première Apologie*, p. 18.
[51] Schwager, *op. cit.*, pp. 333, 334.
[52] Müllbauer, *op. cit.*, pp. 260, 261.
[53] Schwager, *op. cit.*, pp. 333, 334; Müllbauer, *op. cit.*, p. 236.
[54] Lemmens, *Geschichte der Franziskanermissionen*, p. 99.

slaves without the permission of their masters.[55] We have little news of the Franciscan missions in India in the seventeenth and eighteenth centuries, but it is said that in 1587 members of the order were ministering to forty thousand Christians.[56] As we have seen, Dominicans were also early in India. However, they were not firmly established until 1548, when, at the command of King John III, the head of the Portuguese Province sent out a contingent which founded a house at Goa. Dominicans were present in a number of places— among them Bassein, Damaun, Diu, Cochin, and Bengal.[57] The Order of St. John of God, which developed in the sixteenth century chiefly for the care of the sick, spread to India. The mother house in the East was at Goa and other houses were established at several Portuguese centres.[58] The Theatines, one of the early fruits of the Catholic Reformation among the aristocracy, came to India. Peter Avitabile, one of the order who had been a missionary in Georgia in the Caucasus, was responsible for the initiation of their effort. In 1639, with the support of the Pope and of the general chapter of the order, he and two others went to India. For a time they were in Bijapur. They opened a mission in Golconda. In spite of the fact that, because they were under the Propaganda and supposedly inimical to the Portuguese padroado, they were banned by royal decree from all Portuguese possessions, they managed to maintain a house at Goa.[59] The Augustinians came and founded houses in several Portuguese centres. At Goa they had a school for the sons of Brahmins. Their chief field was in Bengal.[60] In the second quarter of the seventeenth century the Oratorians were represented by a flourishing community of Indian priests who were living according to the rule of Philip Neri.[61] The Carmelites had houses.[62] In the second half of the seventeenth century the French began establishing themselves on the south-east coast. French Capuchins early settled at Pondicherry.[63] Yet, in spite of the labours of these other orders, the Jesuits had the most prominent missions in India.

One phase of Roman Catholic activity which can only briefly be touched upon is the story of the relations with the so-called Syrian or St. Thomas Christians. As we have seen, when the Portuguese inaugurated continuing Roman Catholic missions in India, fairly large Christian communities were already in existence.

[55] D'Sa, *History of the Catholic Church in India*, Vol. I, pp. 114-122.
[56] Lemmens, *op. cit.*, p. 99.
[57] Müllbauer, *op. cit.*, pp. 331-338.
[58] D'Sa, *History of the Diocese of Damaun*, pp. 54, 55.
[59] Müllbauer, *op. cit.*, pp. 350-358.
[60] Müllbauer, *op. cit.*, pp. 339-344; D'Sa, *op. cit.*, p. 51.
[61] Müllbauer, *op. cit.*, pp. 349, 350.
[62] Schmidlin-Braun, *Catholic Mission History*, p. 305.
[63] Müllbauer, *op. cit.*, p. 262.

On the Malabar Coast dwelt several thousand of these Christians. They were Nestorians in doctrine and historically were affiliated with the Nestorians of Mesopotamia. They had, in effect, become a caste, proud of their standing but not reaching out to make fresh converts. Quite naturally the Roman Catholic missionaries strove to bring them into fellowship with Rome. Since we are not, in our story of the expansion of Christianity, primarily concerned with the efforts of one group of Christians to win over adherents of other groups of Christians, we must not go extensively into the account of what was attempted or of the outcome. We must, however, briefly summarize developments, for they are essential to an understanding of the later complexion of Christianity in India.[64]

The initial relations between the Portuguese and these Malabar Christians were friendly. Each welcomed the other's help against non-Christians, especially Moslems. Soon Roman Catholic clergy made efforts to bring conformity with Rome. A Dominican persuaded a congregation in his charge at Quilon to allow the celebration of mass in Latin. Franciscans brought several thousand into union with Rome. A Franciscan established a seminary to train candidates for the Syrian priesthood in the Roman spirit, but the effort failed because of the lack of a knowledge of the Syriac language. The situation became complicated by a number of factors. In the second half of the sixteenth century came the Jesuits. They established a seminary which proved more successful than the other and prepared a literature. For a time they enjoyed a monopoly of Roman Catholic missions among great sections of the Syrian Christians. In the second half of the sixteenth century the struggle over the succession to the Patriarchate of the Nestorians had repercussions on the Malabar Coast, for each wing of the Mesopotamian Church attempted to gain control over the co-religionists in India. The leadership of each wing made its submission to Rome. The Portuguese authorities claimed the right of ecclesiastical control over the Malabar Christians and resented what they deemed infringements on their prerogatives, either by the representatives of uniate Patriarchs in Mesopotamia or by agents of the Propaganda. Rome took a direct hand, often to the irritation of the Portuguese.

For a time it seemed that the Malabar Christians had entered safely into the Roman Catholic communion. In 1599 the Synod of Diamper, attended by over eight hundred of the laity and clergy, adopted decrees bringing the Malabar

---

[64] Accounts from which the following summary is made are Richter, *Indische Missionsgeschichte*, pp. 82-99; Jann, *Die katholischen Missionen in Indien, China, und Japan*, pp. 145-173, 361-379; *History Album of St. Joseph's Apostolic Central Seminary, Verapoly-Puthenpally-Alwaye, South India*, pp. 7-12; Lemmens, *Geschichte der Franziskanermissionen*, p. 96; and Civezza, *Storia delle Missioni Francescane*, Vol. VI, pp. 281, 282.

Church largely into conformity with the Roman pattern and within a few years a Jesuit was made the head official of the Church with the title first of Bishop and then of Archbishop.

However, resentment soon arose against this Jesuit Archbishop of Cranganore, his autocratic ways, and the efforts which he and his fellow Jesuits made to root out what they considered to be abuses and to enforce Roman Catholic practices, including clerical celibacy. The native clergy, headed by one of their number, Archdeacon George, headed a revolt which withdrew the large majority of the Malabar Christians from the Roman fellowship.

Slowly Roman Catholicism won back part of the lost ground. This was done largely by Carmelite missionaries, though for a time Jesuit influence was strong and an Indian Theatine of Brahmin stock, Thomas de Castro, had ecclesiastical jurisdiction over some of the Syrian Christians who adhered to Rome. In the seventeenth century the Dutch supplanted the Portuguese on the Malabar Coast and placed obstacles in the way of Roman Catholic missions. However, under certain restrictions, they allowed the presence of Carmelites from nations which had no commercial or political ambitions in India.

To obtain consecration for their bishops, since this could be had through Jacobite prelates from the Near East, the Syrian Christians who remained aloof from Rome abandoned their Nestorianism for Monophysitism.

At the close of the eighteenth century, the Syrian Christians were divided into three main groups—those who had submitted to Rome and had Latin as their ecclesiastical language, those who adhered to Rome but preserved many of their old customs and had Syriac for their ecclesiastical language, and those who were Jacobites.

In the seventeenth and eighteenth centuries a number of untoward circumstances militated against Roman Catholic missions in India.

First was the decay of the Portuguese power. The Portuguese proved unable to extend their control over all the vast area in Asia on whose borders they had staked out claims. Indeed, they lost many of the strongholds and most of the commerce which had once been theirs. A declining power, they were no longer able to give the energetic support to missions which they had formerly provided, either in personnel or in financial and political undergirding. It is significant that the large majority of the church buildings in the Bombay region were erected between 1534 and 1600, that few were built between 1600 and 1650, still fewer between 1650 and 1700, and at most one after 1700.[65] Then, too, the quality of the Portuguese clergy shared in the general sag of Portuguese morale. Rome charged the Goanese clergy with refusing com-

[65] Hull, *Bombay Mission History*, Vol. I, p. 11.

munion to the poor, even on their death bed, with allowing pagans to sacrifice in Christian churches, and with forcing the poor to give their labour gratuitously in building churches.[66] Lamentable and noteworthy was the decline of the Franciscans, accentuated by decay of missionary zeal in the monasteries, by dissensions between the home authorities and the Indian branches of the Order, by friction between the branches of the Order in India, and by objections of full-blooded Portuguese in the Order to granting full equality to their brethren who had Indian blood in their veins.[67]

In the second place, the Portuguese were being largely displaced by Protestant powers, notably the Dutch and the English. Both the Dutch and the English were inclined, because of their long struggle against Roman Catholic Spain, to be suspicious of Roman Catholic missionaries. Certainly the latter could expect no favours from them and at times encountered opposition. For instance, when in 1633 the Dutch took Cochin they ordered all Roman Catholic missionaries to leave. In 1671 Matthew of St. Joseph, a Discalced Carmelite and a distinguished botanist and physician, arrived. By his learning he gained the respect of the Dutch governor and gradually other Carmelites were allowed to enter.[68] In Bombay friction between the English and Portuguese arose, for the latter objected to the transfer of the port to the former. In the first quarter of the eighteenth century the Portuguese clergy were expelled on the charge that they were implicated in an anti-English plot. Italian Carmelites were put in their stead and in 1800 the Roman Catholics on the island were said to number ten thousand. From 1748 to 1775 the English expelled the vicars apostolic from Bombay.[69]

In the third place, a conflict arose between the Portuguese authorities, both lay and clerical, and Rome. Rome was eager to strengthen its missions in India and saw clearly that if this were to be done it could not be through the waning Portuguese power. Missionaries must come directly from other nations and an ecclesiastical structure must be developed which was not tied to a decaying colonial and commercial regime which was fast losing whatever prestige it had once enjoyed. Not all missionaries to the East, for example, were content to go out by way of Lisbon as the Portuguese insisted.[70] Early in the

[66] De Bussierre, *Histoire du Schisme Portugais dans les Indes,* pp. 41 ff.

[67] Jahn, *Die katholischen Missionen in Indien, China, und Japan,* pp. 267-306, 340-346; Goyau in Descamps, *Histoire Générale Comparée des Missions,* p. 447; Lemmens, *Geschichte der Franziskanermissionen,* p. 102.

[68] *History Album of St. Joseph's Apostolic Central Seminary Verapoly-Puthenpally-Alwaye, South India,* pp. 13-28.

[69] Hull, *op. cit.,* Vol. I, pp. 22-33, 211; D'Sa, *The History of the Diocese of Damaun,* pp. 96-106.

[70] Jann. *op. cit.,* pp. 267-306.

seventeenth century Rome removed this restriction.[71] On the other hand, the Portuguese stubbornly contended for the right of patronage which they had long claimed and in support of which they could adduce Papal grants and long practice. Non-Portuguese missionaries who came to Goa were often hampered by the Inquisition on the ground that they did not have royal permission.[72] The situation differed from that in the Spanish possessions. In these latter the political control of the Spanish Crown was practically co-extensive with its ecclesiastical claims. The Papacy, accordingly, did not seriously dispute the claims of the Kings of Spain to exercise the patronage which Rome had so incontestably granted them. Nor did Rome challenge the claims of the Kings of Portugal to the padroado in areas obviously under the civil authority of these monarchs. The contention arose over areas in which the Portuguese political regime was either non-existent or merely nominal. The difficulty was that Portugal attempted to dominate the Church throughout much of India and the Far East, whereas her political rule was confined to a few footholds which more and more declined in commercial significance. Moreover, Portugal was much less able or inclined to provide funds and men for the missions in the vast territories to which she extended her insistence upon ecclesiastical control than was Spain for the Americas and the Philippines. Often sees claimed by Portugal were allowed to go unfilled. Thus after 1652 even the important Archbishopric of Goa was vacant for nearly twenty-three years. Some Portuguese appointed to Indian sees were reluctant to take up their residence in the East. The quality of the Portuguese clergy often left much to be desired. Some declined to use the native tongues. Some exacted burial fees which the poor could not afford. Some engaged in commerce. Rome felt constrained to step in.[73] The result was prolonged controversy which embarrassed the spread of Roman Catholic Christianity, although in decreasing measure, down into the twentieth century. Indeed, it is not certain that the conflict has even yet been finally resolved.

Much of the friction centred about the vicars apostolic. Vicars apostolic were a device employed by Rome to provide episcopal jurisdiction in the lands of Southern and Eastern Asia, in part to solve the problem presented by the Portuguese padroado. In 1657 or 1658 while in Rome Matthæus de Castro was consecrated bishop and appointed Vicar Apostolic in the native state of Bijapur, inland from Goa. Matthæus de Castro was of the Brahmin stock of Goa, had been won by the Theatines, had received his theological education in the College of the Propaganda at Rome, and while in Rome had joined the Oratory of

[71] Jann, *op. cit.,* pp. 189-191.
[72] *Ibid.*
[73] Jann, *op. cit.,* pp. 267-306.

Philip Neri. In Bijapur were Italian Carmelites who had there found a field when, because they were not Portuguese, they had been expelled from Goa. Eventually Matthæus de Castro established his headquarters at Bicholim, just outside the borders of Goa. The Portuguese authorities gave him much trouble and the Archbishop of Goa declined to recognize him. Although bound by oath to the Pope as well as to the King, in times of conflict between the Curia and the Crown the Archbishop of Goa invariably sided with the latter.[74] To defend himself Matthæus de Castro had to journey to Rome, and near the end of his life he went permanently to Rome and there died, in 1668 or 1669.[75] He was succeeded by another Indian, also of Brahmin blood, an Oratorian who had been educated at Rome. This successor, however, managed to remain on friendly terms with the Portuguese.[76] Usually, the Indo-Portuguese clergy sided with the padroado against the vicars apostolic.[77] In 1633 Rome had threatened with excommunication all who hindered missionaries from going to India and China. In 1674 this ban was extended to those who placed obstacles in the way of the vicars apostolic.[78] Insistent though Rome was on the rights of the latter, it also confirmed the Portuguese padroado. When the union of the crowns of Spain and Portugal was ended, and in 1640 the House of Braganza came to the Portuguese throne, some fear was felt that Rome might refuse the padroado to the new royal line. In 1670, however, the Pope formally conferred the coveted right on the Braganza monarchs.[79] The vicariate apostolic which had been established for Bijapur became in time what was known as the Vicariate Apostolic of the Great Mogul, and embraced a large area. It was entrusted to the Italian Carmelites. To these non-Portuguese prelates the Portuguese strongly objected, and chronic disputes arose over the efforts of the Portuguese to extend their ecclesiastical control to vicars apostolic and to the territories and clergy under these Papal appointees.[80] When, in 1671, Rome appointed Thomas de Castro, a relative of Matthæus de Castro, Vicar Apostolic of Canara, the Archbishop of Goa considered the act an infringement on his rights.[81] In the first quarter of the eighteenth century the English recognized the Carmelite Vicar Apostolic as having jurisdiction over the Roman Catholics in Bombay and expelled the Goanese Franciscans, but the local congregations

[74] Jann, *op. cit.*, pp. 94-96, 112.
[75] Jann, *op. cit.*, pp. 306 ff.; Hull, *op. cit.*, Vol. I, p. 53.
[76] Jann, *op. cit.*, pp. 306 ff.; Hull, *op. cit.*, Vol. I, p. 54.
[77] De Bussierre, *op. cit.*, pp. 43-49.
[78] Jann, *op. cit.*, pp. 306 ff.
[79] Jann, *op. cit.*, pp. 231 ff.
[80] Jann, *op. cit.*, pp. 306 ff.
[81] Do Rego, *L'Apostolo di Ceylan, P. Guiseppe Vaz*, p. vi.

sympathized with Goa and embarrassed the Vicar Apostolic.[82] In 1789 the Bombay Government, acting under instructions from the Directors of the East India Company, turned over the Carmelite churches to a representative of the Archbishop of Goa. However, in 1791 the Directors, under the impression that the Roman Catholics of Bombay were opposed to this action, ordered that jurisdiction be restored to the Carmelites.[83]

Friction, too, arose over the insistence of Portugal that all missionaries to the East go out via Lisbon. Although, as we have seen, in the first half of the seventeenth century Rome removed this restriction, some missionaries found it difficult to make their way to India by another route, and if they did succeed in doing so, in India the Portuguese authorities embarrassed them and even, through the Inquisition, imprisoned them.[84] In practice the Inquisition had as its chief object in India the enforcement of the padroado.[85] When non-Portuguese clergy did go out to assist the bishops who were subject to Goa, they were required to take an oath of fealty to the Portuguese King, to assume Portuguese names, and to remain long enough in Lisbon and Goa to acquire the Portuguese language and customs.[86]

These three factors were enough in themselves to slow down the progress of Christianity in India. To them, in the early part of the eighteenth century, was added a fourth, disheartening dissension over the methods which the Jesuits had employed to allay Indian prejudices and to acclimatize Christianity in India. For more than fifty years, since shortly before the middle of the seventeenth century, in China a controversy had been raging over a similar issue. The Jesuits had many enemies, and some of their bitterest critics were in rival orders.[87]

In India the dispute which had arisen in the first half of the seventeenth century over the methods of Robert de Nobili had died down, quieted by the Papal decision of 1623. In South India the Jesuits had continued to apply the general principle adopted by Nobili of conforming so far as possible to Indian customs. In doing so they had developed methods some of which went beyond those of Nobili. In the second half of the sixteenth century the French Capuchins lodged complaints at Rome against what they alleged to be Jesuit procedure. The Capuchins are said to have been angered by what they deemed the in-

[82] Jann, op. cit., pp. 324-361.

[83] D'Sa, The History of the Diocese of Damaun, p. 111; De Bussierre, op. cit., pp. 59, 60, 257.

[84] Jann, op. cit., pp. 191-205.

[85] Jann, op. cit., pp. 189-191.

[86] Jann, op. cit., p. 186.

[87] For a summary of the dispute see Müllbauer, Geschichte der katholischen Missionen in Ostindien, pp. 262-276; Jann, op. cit., pp. 394-422, 473-485, 500-512.

trusion of the Jesuits into a field which the former had held at Pondicherry among the Tamils. In March, 1703, a Capuchin presented to the Propaganda his criticisms of the Jesuits.

A few weeks before there had sailed from Europe Charles Maillard de Tournon, titular Patriarch of Antioch and *Legatus a latere* to the Indies and China, commissioned with the publication of a Papal decree against some of the Jesuit practices in China and charged with reporting to the Holy See on conditions in the East. He went out on a French ship and without the approval of Portugal, and so constituted a direct affront to the ecclesiastical claims of the latter country. He was of noble stock, but was young, infirm in health and temper, and proved an unfortunate choice. In the dispute between the Jesuits and the Capuchins over Pondicherry, Tournon decided in favour of the Jesuits. However, the Capuchins laid before Tournon their charges against the Jesuits on what came to be known as the Malabar rites—the Jesuit accommodations to Indian customs. Here Tournon came out with a decree (June 23, 1704) against the Jesuits. He forbade omitting any features of the Roman Catholic baptismal ceremony, such as spittle and salt. He declared that the baptized must take the names of saints from the Roman martyrology and not pagan names or the names of idols. Since parents often put off the baptism of their children, he commanded that missionaries set a time within which a child must be brought to baptism. He proscribed child marriages and ordered that marriage be only by Christian forms. He prohibited to Christian women the wearing of the sign of a non-Christian God and ordained instead the sign of the cross. He forbade the use of the cord which designated the upper castes. The practice of purification of women after menstruation by pagan rites was to be given up and a girl's first menstruation was not to be celebrated by a feast. Pariahs were not to be forbidden the sacrament when ill and missionaries must themselves bring it to the house—a blow to the separation of castes. Christians were not to be musicians in pagan temples. Baths of purification were allowed, but they were not to be according to pagan ritual. The use of the ashes of cow dung to mark the body was condemned. The reading of pagan books was forbidden to Christians. These were not necessarily an accurate portrayal of what the Jesuits had permitted. Indeed, some of them the Jesuits denied having allowed. They were, rather, what their critics accused the Jesuits of condoning. Some of them, however, the Jesuits tolerated and defended.

The decree met violent opposition in India. As was to be expected, the Jesuits and the Portuguese bishops had no use for it. The French *conseil supérieur* of Pondicherry came out against it. On the other hand, Rome supported its legate. A Jesuit went to Rome to present the case of the Society. A subsequent Papal

legate, Mezzabarba, who before going to the East had submitted to the Portuguese claims and obtained Portuguese recognition, in 1720 set aside Tournon's
decree. However, in 1727 Rome, after prolonged consideration, reaffirmed the
decisions of Tournon. At the request of some of the Jesuits, Rome again went
into the issues and in 1733 and 1734 made a few concessions. Yet, when the
Jesuits submitted further requests, a Papal brief of 1739 refused them and decreed that each missionary in South India must take an oath to abide by the
decision of 1734. Again the Jesuits asked Rome to reconsider. Rome proved
adamant and in 1744 finally ended the controversy by a bull which confirmed
earlier decrees and briefs on the Malabar rites and forbade further dispensa-
tions. However, not all for which the Jesuits had stood was disallowed. For
instance, separate missionaries were allowed for the Pariahs, and thus caste was
recognized not as a religious institution which the Church must condemn, but
as a civil institution which the Church could tolerate.

To the factors which led in the sixteenth and seventeenth centuries to troubled
days for Roman Catholic missions was added another, political disturbances in
India. In the latter part of the sixteenth and in the first half of the eighteenth
century the wars waged by the Marathas brought distress to several of the
Christian communities. Between 1737 and 1740 the loss was especially severe.
The Marathas then captured several of the Portuguese centres, among them
Bassein and Bandra. The Marathas were aggressively Hindu. While they
promised to Christians liberty of worship, they razed churches and chapels,
Christians were carried into captivity, some migrated to areas where they
would be safe, and some went over to Hinduism.[88] In the South, in the second
half of the eighteenth century, Hyder Ali of Mysore, and especially his son,
Tipu Sultan, who was an ardent Moslem, wrought destruction. The damage to
the Christian cause was the greater from the fact that some of the strongholds of
Christianity were in the very regions overrun by Tipu. Tipu was particularly
enraged because of the help which Christians gave to his enemy, the English.
Many Christians were killed or died of starvation, thousands were enslaved,
thousands adopted Islam, and other thousands moved to territories which were
outside Tipu's domains.[89]

In addition, in the second half of the eighteenth century, the expulsion of the
Jesuits from the Portuguese and the French possessions and the eventual dis-

[88] D'Sa, The History of the Diocese of Damaun, pp. 60-62, 86 ff.; Fernandes, Bandra.
Its Religious and Secular History, pp. 23, 40-57; Müllbauer, Geschichte der katholischen
Missionen in Ostindien, pp. 239, 240; Hull, Bombay Mission History, Vol. I, pp. 11, 74-79.
[89] Mascarenhas, A Brief History of the Catholic Community of Mangalore, passim;
Schwager, Die katholische Heidenmission der Gegenwart, pp. 327, 343, 344, 394, 395;
Launay, Histoire des Missions de l'Inde, Vol. I, pp. 134 ff.

solution of the Society here, as in many other parts of the world, brought embarrassment to Roman Catholic missions. The Madura mission, for instance, suffered severely. It had depended very little on Portuguese financial assistance and had not been seriously affected by the stagnation which overtook Portuguese missions. The expulsion of the Jesuits from Portuguese possessions in 1759 dealt the mission a serious blow and the suppression of the Society by Rome in 1773 was even more of a disaster. A small remnant of ex-Jesuits remained and the Missions Étrangères of Paris sent in a few men, but the loss was not fully made good.[90] So, too, in the Carnatic the Missions Étrangères attempted to fill the gap left by the Jesuits. They had only fairly begun work, however, when the French Revolution disrupted their support from home. In some places the number of Christians declined.[91]

If Roman Catholic Christianity made less headway in India than in Spanish and Portuguese America, the reasons are not far to seek. Here were much more resistant religions, Hinduism and Islam. Portugal and France, the Roman Catholic commercial and political powers, never conquered more than coastal footholds: by far the major part of the land remained under non-Christian rulers or, towards the close of the eighteenth century, began to pass into the hands of the Protestant British. The chief Roman Catholic power, Portugal, lost in vigour and possessions. Controversies, such as the church in Latin America never knew, distracted the attention of missionaries. Wars by aggressive non-Christians made inroads into the Christian ranks.

In spite of all these handicaps, Roman Catholic Christianity continued and even in the eighteenth century here and there registered gains. In Goa the Portuguese Lazarists tried to make good the losses sustained by the expulsion of the Jesuits.[92] In Goa, too, after the departure of the Jesuits, two diocesan seminaries were established for the education of Indian priests.[93] In the latter part of the seventeenth century the coming of the French brought a reinforcement and extension to Roman Catholic missions which persisted through most of the eighteenth century. The French attempted to establish themselves as a political and commercial power, and in connexion with them came missionaries. French Capuchins and Jesuits arrived.[94] Ursulines were added,[95] an interesting instance, of which there were very few in this period, of women having

[90] Hull, *Bombay Mission History*, Vol. I, pp. 279, 280.
[91] Paul, *History of the Telugu Christians*, pp. 41-50.
[92] Coste, *La Congregation de la Mission*, p. 209.
[93] D'Sa, *The History of the Diocese of Damaun*, pp. 230-232.
[94] Clemente da Terzorio, *Le Missioni dei Minori Cappucini*, Vol. VIII, pp. 20-22; Josson, *La Mission du Bengale Occidental*, Vol. I, pp. 134 ff.; Launay, *op. cit.*, Vol. I, pp. xxx, xxxi.
[95] Launay, *op. cit.*, Vol. I, p. xxxvii.

an active share in the personnel of missions in the South and East of Asia. How-ever, the French were too engrossed in Europe ever to make India a major in-terest, and their activities there, whether commercial or religious, were never as extensive as were those of Portugal in her prime. In Bengal missions were found in the seventeenth and eighteenth centuries. In 1576 Jesuits came from Goa.[96] Augustinians first arrived at the very close of the sixteenth century. To these were added, in the opening years of the following century, Dominicans.[97] Augustinians penetrated as far as Assam.[98] One estimate declares that in 1666 there were thirty-three thousand Christians in Bengal.[99] Naturally these cen-tred about the Portuguese trading establishments. In 1620 it is said that Hugli contained fourteen thousand Christians.[100] In the early part of the eighteenth century the bishop found that a large proportion of the Christians were Portu-guese speaking. He discovered, too, a number of "hidden Christians," Moslems who had been privately baptized but had made no public profession of their faith.[101] About 1775 the number of Christians in Calcutta was estimated as being between twenty and twenty-five thousand.[102] By the end of the eighteenth century, however, the morale of the Bengal Christians was low. Most of the foreign priests had died and the clergy were predominantly Goanese, pro-fessedly of Brahmin ancestry, who were arrogant, quarrelsome, and ignorant of the vernacular.[103]

Accurate statistics of the strength of the Roman Catholic communities in India in this period are not obtainable. One estimate says that in 1700 the num-ber of Roman Catholics in India was about one million, of whom about half a million were in the Portuguese possessions on the West Coast, and about four hundred and fifty thousand on the Fisher Coast and in Madura and the asso-ciated missions.[104] Other estimates put the total as high as two and a half mil-lions.[105] By 1800 the number seems to have declined. Estimates vary from 475,000 to 1,200,000.[106] The morale, too, appears to have deteriorated.

Yet the Indian Roman Catholic community possessed enough vitality to pro-duce martyrs and missionaries. For instance, Nilakandam-Pullay, a convert of the Malabar Coast, baptized in 1744, in the century of decadence, was earnest

[96] Josson, op. cit., Vol. I, pp. 48-58.
[97] Josson, op. cit., Vol. I, pp. 59-60.
[98] Josson, op. cit., Vol. I, pp. 85-87.
[99] Ibid.
[100] Josson, op. cit., Vol. I, p. 79.
[101] Josson, op. cit., Vol. I, pp. 109-124.
[102] Josson, op. cit., Vol. I, p. 153.
[103] Josson, op. cit., Vol. I, pp. 151, 152, 155.
[104] Schwager, Die katholische Heidenmission der Gegenwart, pp. 343, 344.
[105] Ibid.
[106] Ibid.; Richter, Indische Missionsgeschichte, pp. 99-103.

in propagating his new faith and in 1752 was put to death for it.[107] In the following chapter we shall see that Joseph Vaz (1651-1711), of old Indian Christian stock, with fellow Goanese priests revived the Roman Catholic communities in Ceylon which had been threatened by the Dutch occupation.

Throughout much of this period efforts were made to bring into existence an indigenous clergy. As early as 1542 the Seminary of Santa Fé was begun in Goa by two seculars for the purpose of training for the priesthood youths of all nations. By 1560 the seminary was preparing sufficient men to enable the Archbishop to appoint seculars to a number of churches which had previously been filled by regulars.[108] From this seminary came the two Parava deacons who accompanied Xavier to the Fisher Coast. Xavier, it will be recalled, took over the seminary and transformed it into a Jesuit college.[109] Theatines and Carmelites worked for a native clergy.[110] The attempt was made to exclude members of lower castes from the priesthood. In 1592 the provincial council of Goa decreed that ordination should be limited to those of Brahmin or other high-caste blood.[111] In the course of the years the native clergy seem to have become almost too numerous in Goa, for in 1705 the Viceroy reported that twenty-five hundred native seculars were there.[112] We hear, too, of other seminaries than the one in Goa—of schools for the training of a clergy for the Syrian Christians, and of one opened by the Jesuits in Pondicherry.[113] With a few rare and notable exceptions these native priests evinced little interest in spreading the faith. In the seventeenth century an occasional native priest was raised to the episcopate.[114] However, the appointments were followed by so much friction that Rome, discouraged, did not repeat the experiment until the nineteenth century.[115] Clergy of European birth, moreover, were inclined to look with distrust or disdain upon those of Indian blood.[116] To be sure, Indians of higher caste were admitted to the ranks of the Franciscans, the Dominicans, and the Augustinians, and a native congregation of Oratorians arose at Goa. However, prolonged bitter controversies arose over the status of those of Indian blood, especially among the Franciscans.[117] Not until the twentieth century did the movement for a native

[107] Zaleski, The Martyrs of India, pp. 231-255.
[108] D'Sa, The History of the Diocese of Damaun, p. 56.
[109] Huonder, Der einheimische Klerus in den Heidenländern, pp. 57-60.
[110] Huonder, op. cit., pp. 66, 67.
[111] Huonder, op. cit., p. 69.
[112] D'Sa, op. cit., p. 59.
[113] Huonder, op. cit., pp. 62-65.
[114] Maclagan, The Jesuits and the Great Mogul, pp. 111-113; Müllbauer, Geschichte der katholischen Missionen in Ostindien, pp. 349, 350.
[115] Huonder, op. cit., pp. 261, 262; Schmidlin, Catholic Mission Theory, p. 330.
[116] Lemmens, Geschichte der Franziskanermissionem, p. 102.
[117] Huonder, op. cit., pp. 66, 67.

clergy and episcopate come fully into its own. Yet not only was Roman Catholic Christianity stronger numerically in India than in any other land in Asia before A.D. 1800; here also, with the possible exception of the Philippines, it made greater progress towards creating a native clergy and episcopate than in any other land in Southern and Eastern Asia.

Some advance was registered towards providing tools for the study by missionaries of Indian tongues and towards the creation of a Christian literature in the languages of India. In the opening years of the Portuguese adventure in India, missionaries acquired little or no knowledge of the local speech and depended upon interpreters. As early as 1575, however, the Jesuits determined upon the founding of language schools in which missionaries might learn the various vernaculars.[118] In the seventeenth century Roman Catholic literature was prepared in at least seven of the languages of India.[119] The achievements in Tamil of the Italian Jesuit Beschi have been regarded by native scholars as literary accomplishments of the first rank. Beschi is especially famous for a poem in higher Tamil in honour of St. Joseph.[120] The English Jesuit, Thomas Stephens, who reached India in 1579 and spent most of a long life among the Roman Catholic Brahmins of Salsette, prepared a Christian *purana* which contained a summary of Old Testament history and of the life of Christ and which was held in great esteem by Christians of the middle and lower classes. It was widely used in churches and families to instruct and nourish in the Christian faith.[121] Somewhat later, a metrical account of the birth, passion, death, resurrection, and ascension of Christ, the coming of the Holy Spirit, the Virgin Mary, the sacraments, and the Trinity was published in Marathi.[122] In Sanskrit, in the style of the Vedas, was composed a summary of Christian teaching.[123]

Tieffentaller, a German Jesuit missionary of the eighteenth century, wrote an important geographical work on India, based upon his own observations.[124] Another Jesuit, Fenicio, wrote an account of Hindu mythology from which the European scholars of the seventeenth and eighteenth centuries derived much of their impressions of Hinduism.[125] Missionaries were not only conveying Christianity to India. They were also interpreting India to the Occident.

Whether, outside Christian circles, Roman Catholicism had much influence on the culture of India is doubtful. It is asserted and as positively denied that

[118] Dahmen, *Robert de Nobili*, pp. 12, 13.
[119] Berg, *Die katholische Heidenmission als Kulturträger*, Vol. II, pp. 78, 79.
[120] *Ibid.*
[121] Saldanha, *The Christian Purana of Father Stephens of the Society of Jesus, passim.*
[122] Saldanha, *op. cit.*, p. xli.
[123] Berg, *op. cit.*, Vol. II, p. 81.
[124] Berg, *op. cit.*, Vol. II, p. 293.
[125] *Fides News Service*, July 14, 1934.

Tulsi Das (Tulasi Dasa), the great poet of Northern India, was dependent on Christianity.[126] It is declared that in the Bhaktamala of Nabhadas, of about 1600, Christian influences are apparent,[127] and that the poems of Tukaram show infiltrations from the Gospels.[128] However, much of this is at least debatable. Much clearer is the effect of the Indian environment upon Roman Catholic Christianity. As we have repeatedly seen, caste continued in Christian circles, although not so prominently as outside them. The tendency was, moreover, to make of the Roman Catholic community a separate caste. We have also seen that many of the Jesuits, with Nobili as the path-breaker, sought consciously, so far as they could so so without denaturing Christianity, to bring Hindu customs into the Christian community. The accusations against the Jesuits laid at the door of the Society practices which went even farther on the road of accommodation to Hinduism. Outside Jesuit circles, as we have said, the ecclesiastical authorities found it necessary from time to time to take action against the use of pagan customs by Christians. We also hear of what may well be a contribution of popular paganism, that in time of drought, in case processions and prayers for rain were unavailing, statues of the Virgin and the saints were chained and immersed in water long enough to ensure rain and were then restored to their niches.[129] Much of the conversion had been so superficial and Hinduism is so powerful an absorbent of other faiths that it is not surprising that popular Roman Catholic Christianity in India bore marks of contact with the dominant religion.

Roman Catholicism was not the only type of Christianity represented in India between A.D. 1500 and A.D. 1800. We have noted the antecedent presence of Nestorian Christianity and the interesting fact that those Nestorians who did not unite with Rome became Jacobites. Armenian Christians were also present. They were immigrants and under the Moguls formed communities in Delhi, Lahore, and Agra. In Agra they had a bishop and clergy.[130] Apparently, however, they made little or no attempt to win converts.

Protestant Christianity also came to India. Especially in South India active and persistent efforts were made by Protestants to spread their faith, which laid

[126] Clemen, *Der Einfluss des Christentums auf andere Religionen*. Advocating the influence is Richard Garbe, *Indien und das Christentum* (Tübingen, J. C. B. Mohr, 1914, pp. viii, 301), pp. 280 ff., and against it is Charles Eliot, *Hinduism and Buddhism* (London, Edward Arnold & Co., 3 vols., 1921), Vol. II, p. 247.
[127] Clemen, *op. cit.*, p. 94; Garbe, *op. cit.*, pp. 280 ff.
[128] Clemen, *op. cit.*, p. 94.
[129] Jann, *Die katholische Missionen in Indien, China, und Japan*, p. 198.
[130] Jann, *op. cit.*, p. 282.

the foundations for some of the strongest Christian communities of the nineteenth and twentieth centuries.

Protestant forms of Christianity were first brought to India in the seventeenth century in the persons of Dutch, British, and Danish traders. Each of these groups, Protestant by profession, had chaplains or preachers who ministered primarily to the Europeans, their families, and their servants. The Dutch *predickant* Abraham Rogerius, who was at Pulicat, not far from Madras, from 1631 to 1641, wrote *Gentilismus Reseratus,* an extensive account of the Hinduism of South India.[131] In the very early days of the English East India Company some of the London merchants who joined in it were eager for the conversion of the peoples of India. In 1614 the Company resolved to educate an Indian youth who had been brought to England that "he might upon occasion be sent unto his country where God may be so pleased to make him an instrument in converting some of his nation."[132] In 1657 the East India Company "having resolved to endeavour the advance and spreading of the Gospel in India" sought from Oxford and Cambridge a minister for that purpose, but without success.[133] Long before that time chaplains had been sent out to the Company's factories in India.[134] Moreover, although the Company tolerated Roman Catholicism and non-Christian religions in its territories, it wished the children of Englishmen to be reared as Protestant Christians.[135] Robert Boyle, who had been interested in spreading the Christian faith in the New World, as a director of the East India Company promoted the use of the English contacts with India as a door for the propagation of Christianity in the East, and by the end of 1682 a fund had been raised for that purpose.[136] The charter of 1698 of the English East India Company made provision for a Christian minister in each garrison and superior factory of the Company and ordered that all such ministers should learn Portuguese (the *lingua franca* of these posts) the better to instruct the servants and slaves of the Company and its agents in the Protestant religion.[137] The hostility to missions which characterized the policy of the Company in the latter part of the eighteenth century was a late development.

In spite of these earlier efforts, Protestant missions in India are generally counted as beginning in 1706, with the inception of an enterprise in which, in the course of the next few decades, Danes, Germans, and English joined. Since 1620 the Danes had had their chief trading post in India at Tranquebar. At the

[131] *The Cambridge History of India,* Vol. V, p. 53.
[132] Penny, *The Church in Madras,* pp. 14-16.
[133] Penny, *op. cit.,* pp. 35, 36.
[134] Penny, *op. cit.,* pp. 1 ff.
[135] Penny, *op. cit.,* pp. 71-73.
[136] Penny, *op. cit.,* pp. 95-98.
[137] Penny, *op. cit.,* pp. 122-124.

Danish fort were Lutheran chaplains, but they seem to have done nothing to spread the Christian faith outside the Danes and Germans who were found at the factory and in the immediate vicinity.[138]

The originator of a more active mission was King Frederick IV of Denmark who, although of irregular marital habits, had for some reason come to feel an obligation to see that missionaries were sent to the non-Christians touched by Danish colonies and trade. He found encouragement and able assistance in his court preacher, a German, Franz Julius Lütkens. Men fitted and willing to undertake the projected mission were not to be had in Denmark. Through Lütkens they were discovered in Germany. The two pioneers, Bartholomäus Ziegenbalg and Heinrich Plütschau, were both from the circles of the then youthful Pietism and both had been students at the Pietist centre, Halle.[139] Of the two, Ziegenbalg, although seldom really well, had the greater initiative and he is thought of as the real founder of the mission. The two arrived at Tranquebar on July 9th, 1706. They were not welcome. The Danish chaplains already on the ground regarded them as intruders and the Pietist convictions of the missionaries increased the friction. The Danish Commandant alternately persecuted and favoured them. For a time in 1708 and 1709 the Commandant had Ziegenbalg imprisoned. Yet the missionaries persevered. They ministered to the Germans. They learned Portuguese and won to Lutheranism some of the nominal Roman Catholics of mixed Portuguese and Indian blood who were numerous in Tranquebar as in other ports where Europeans had commerce. They studied Tamil. Ziegenbalg especially acquired facility with that language. They translated into Portuguese and Tamil Luther's catechism and Lutheran prayers and hymns. Ziegenbalg compiled a Tamil grammar and wrote books in that language. Converts were gathered from Hinduism, although some of them were attracted by the hope of employment and financial support which the missionaries felt it necessary to give to those who, because of their Christian faith, had been cut off from their previous occupations and social connexions. Communication with Europe was slow and irregular. Reinforcements, when they came, made for dissension. One shipment of money was lost through carelessness when it was being landed at Tranquebar. In 1711 Plütschau returned

---

[138] One of these chaplains, Jacob Worm, on his epitaph (he died Dec. 17, 1691) is called "the Danish Apostle of India," but doubt exists as to the nature and success of his efforts.— Fenger, *History of the Tranquebar Mission*, pp. 11-13.

[139] The standard account of Ziegenbalg and Plütschau is W. Germann, *Ziegenbalg und Plütschau, Die Gründungsjahre der Trankebarschen Mission. Ein Beitrag zur Geschichte des Pietismus nach handschriftlichen Quellen und ältesten Drucken* (Erlangen, Andreas Deichert, 2 Parts, 1868). The second part is made up of letters and other sources. A brief popular account in English is H. M. Zorn, *Bartholomaeus Ziegenbalg* (St. Louis, Concordia Publishing House, 1933, pp. 150).

to Europe, permanently. Ziegenbalg made one trip to Europe, in the interests of the mission, but resumed his work in India.

Help came from a variety of sources. Some members of the Danish royal family were interested. In Pietist circles in Germany active sympathy existed. In England the Danish consort of Queen Anne had a German Lutheran chaplain, Anton Wilhelm Böhme, who was deeply committed to the Tranquebar project. Böhme urged the recently founded Society for the Propagation of the Gospel in Foreign Parts to aid the mission. When it decided that by its charter it was limited to British plantations and colonies, the sister Anglican organization, the Society for Promoting Christian Knowledge, which was not so restricted, came forward with substantial assistance.[140]

Ziegenbalg's last months were saddened by differences between himself and the head of the organization in Copenhagen which supported him. The latter felt that the missionaries should remain unmarried, that they should move about from place to place proclaiming the Gospel, not giving financial subsidies to converts, schools, or churches, but insisting that the Christian communities provide for themselves what was needed in material equipment. Only thus, he believed, could Christianity gain a permanent vital foothold in Asia and cease to be an unhealthy parasite on the Christianity of the West. Ziegenbalg was married and his methods involved prolonged residence in one spot and a fairly heavy investment of European funds. The criticisms from Europe aggravated the decline in his health. He died February 23, 1719, at the early age of thirty-five. Similar criticism helped to bring to a premature grave Ziegenbalg's leading colleague, Gründler.

The deaths of Ziegenbalg and Gründler by no means ended the mission.[141] Converts had been gathered, churches built, and in Denmark, Germany, England, and even in New England the enterprise had friends. Reinforcements arrived. The personnel was still Lutheran, predominantly German, and chiefly Pietist, most of it selected by Francke of Halle (only a very few were from the mission college in Copenhagen), but financial support came also from Den-

[140] Allen and McClure, *Two Hundred Years: The History of the S. P. C. K. 1698-1898*, pp. 260 ff.

[141] On the further history of this mission, see especially J. Ferd. Fenger, *Den Trankebarske Missions Historie* (Copenhagen, C. A. Reitzel, 1843, pp. 371) (there is an English translation of a German translation, *History of the Tranquebar Mission*. Tranquebar, Evangelical Lutheran Mission Press, 1863, pp. 324); Johann Lucas Neikamp, *Kurtzgefasste Missions-Geschichte oder historischer Auszug der Evangelischen Missions-Berichte aus Ost-Indien* (1705-1767. Halle, 2 vols., Waisenhaus, 1740, 1772) (there is a Latin translation and extension of the first volume published at Halle at the Orphanage in 1747); Georg Christian Knapp, editor, *Neuere Geschichte der evangelischen Missions-Anstalten zu Bekehrung der Heiden in Ostindien* (Halle, Waisenhaus-Buchhandlung, 6 vols.); Chatterton, *A History of the Church of England in India*, Chap. VI; Richter, *Indische Missionsgeschichte*, pp. 104-137.

mark and Great Britain. Before the death of Ziegenbalg the mission had begun to expand its activities beyond the constricted limits of Danish Tranquebar. It continued to do so. Schultze, who, after Gründler's death, was the next outstanding figure in the mission, aided by the Society for Promoting Christian Knowledge, translated the Bible into Telugu and translated the New Testament and part of the Old Testament into Hindustani. He put in part of his life in Madras, an English centre.[142] At Madras he was succeeded by Philip Fabricius. Fabricius became an accomplished Tamil scholar and his translations of the Bible and Christian hymns into that tongue were notable achievements. Although the wars of the eighteenth century brought interruptions, outstations were opened from Madras, and a mission was formed at another centre of English trade, Cuddalore. One of the Cuddalore staff, Kiernander, later moved to Calcutta and there laboured for many years.

Most notable of all the German missionaries of the second half of the eighteenth century was Christian Friedrich Schwartz.[143] Born in 1726, he was educated in Halle, landed in India in 1750, and died there in 1798. He remained unmarried and gave himself with singleness of heart to the work of the mission. Of marked purity of mind and motive, transparently unselfish, he won the confidence of high and low, of Indians and English. The first part of his life in India was spent at Tranquebar. Later he transferred the centre of his life in India to the adjoining state of Tanjore. Here English influence was very strong and Schwartz was on friendly terms with the English officials. He also had the confidence of the local rajah. He came to be powerful in the administration of Tanjore. Yet he was always primarily the missionary. If converts were attracted because of his political connexions, he sought to give sound instruction in the Christian faith. In the wars which plagued South India in the second half of the eighteenth century, he and another of the missionaries, Gericke, sometimes acted as mediators and helped to allay the suffering.

Before the end of Schwartz's life the fires of missionary enthusiasm in Halle were burning low and recruits were slow in coming. At the close of the eighteenth century, however, the Christians attached to the German-Danish-English mission are estimated to have numbered between eighteen and twenty thousand, chiefly in Tranquebar, Tanjore, Trichinopoly, Madras, Cuddalore, and Tinnevelly.[144] They were mainly from the Sudras, the Pariahs, and the mixed stock

[142] Allen and McClure, op. cit., pp. 260 ff.

[143] On Schwartz, see Hugh Pearson, *Memoirs of the Life and Correspondence of the Reverend Christian Frederick Swartz* (New York, D. Appleton and Co., 1835, pp. xiv, 414) ; W. Germann, *Missionar Christian Friedrich Schwartz. Sein Leben und Wirken aus Briefen des Halleschen Missionsarchives* (Erlangen, Andreas Deichert, 1870, pp. 408).

[144] Richter, *Indische Missionsgeschichte*, p. 137. Estimates vary as to the total number of baptized since the mission's inception. Richter, *op. cit.*, p. 137, relying on Hough,

which went by the name of Portuguese. As in Roman Catholic circles, some concessions to caste differences had been made. The descendants of these converts, especially those of Sudra ancestry, constituted the most stable elements in the Lutheran communities in South India in the nineteenth and twentieth centuries.

To the Lutheran missionaries were added Moravians.[145] The first of these arrived in Tranquebar in 1760. They were regarded by the Lutherans with suspicion and as interlopers. An attempt, costly in life, was made to plant a mission on the Nicobar Islands, to which the Danes were then endeavouring to extend their power. Ephemeral footholds were won in connexion with Danish factories at Patna and Serampore, and, apart from the Danes, in Calcutta. The obstacles proved so great that the posts were one by one given up and in 1803 the last of the Moravians left the soil of India. The little company of the Unitas Fratrum, which so gallantly sought to carry the Christian Gospel throughout the world and which had pioneered in so many difficult fields, had here met defeat.

Before the end of the eighteenth century the rising tide of religious life in England had ceased to be content with fulfilling its sense of duty towards the millions revealed by the rapidly growing British possessions in India through financial support of the Danish-German mission. A series of chaplains with strong Evangelical convictions went out under the English East India Company. One of the earliest of these, David Brown, laboured in Calcutta from 1787 to 1812. He did not confine his efforts to the European population, but opened a boarding school for Hindus. His correspondence with England was one of the sources out of which arose the Church Missionary Society, the creation of the Anglican Evangelicals. Another, Claudius Buchanan, who arrived in 1797, had a part, through one of his printed sermons, in stimulating the formation of the American Board of Commissioners for Foreign Missions. Still another, Henry Martyn, whose brilliant but brief career in India fell entirely in the nineteenth century, we must reserve for a later volume.[146] In 1793, five years before the death of Schwartz, there landed in Calcutta William Carey, who was to begin a new era in Protestant missions, not only in India, but also in the entire world. The waning of the Danish-Halle-English mission was to be many times compensated by the new stream from Great Britain, America, and the Continent of Europe which in its inception

---

History of Christianity in India, Vol. III, places it at about forty thousand. Sherring, *The History of Protestant Missions in India* (New edition by F. Storrow, London, The Religious Tract Society, 1884, pp. xv, 463), p. 49, puts it at "not less than fifty thousand."

[145] Fenger, *Den Trankebarske Missions Historie,* pp. 277 ff.; Müller, *200 Jahre Brüdermission,* Vol. I, pp. 252 ff.

[146] Chatterton, *A History of the Church of England in India,* pp. 108 ff.

owed so much to the Moravians and so to the Pietism out of which had come most of the personnel of the older enterprise.

As we bring to a close this brief account of the spread of Christianity in India between A.D. 1500 and A.D. 1800, it may assist our perspective to give a summary of what has been narrated according to the now familiar categories of this work.

The Christianity which was propagated in India in these centuries was not of one kind but of several. In addition to the older Nestorian communities which became divided between the Roman Catholics and the Jacobites, there were Roman Catholic, Armenian, and at least four forms of Protestant Christianity. Of these Roman Catholicism was the most active.

The reasons for the spread were at least two, the commercial and political activities of the Europeans and the new religious life which arose within the Christianity of Western Europe beginning with the sixteenth century. In the territories controlled by them Europeans enjoyed a prestige which predisposed many in favour of their faith. In the case of the Paravas conversion was due at the outset to the hope of Portuguese aid against Moslem oppressors. In Portuguese domains special inducements were sometimes offered by the civil authorities to multiply baptisms, and force was occasionally employed to suppress non-Christian worship and non-Christian shrines. Compulsion was rare in the propagation of Protestant Christianity, but we hear of the forcible baptism by Danes of some whom they sold as slaves.[147] As throughout so much of the course of the spread of Christianity, prestige and the efforts of civil authorities were supplemented by the labours of professional missionaries, some of them men of great devotion and beauty of character who embodied the spirit of Jesus. From a Francis Xavier or a Christian Friedrich Schwartz something of Jesus and the New Testament must have proved contagious.

The processes of the spread of Christianity reflected the reasons for the spread. Support came from the state to Roman Catholicism chiefly from the Crown of Portugal, and to a less extent to Protestantism from the Danish Crown. Through their chaplains the commercial companies of the Dutch, the Danes, and the English gave assistance. Much of the financial undergirding, particularly of Protestant missions, was supplied by private individuals in Europe. Conversion, especially to Roman Catholicism, was often by groups and with little or no initial instruction. A large proportion of the Protestant and many of the Roman Catholic converts came one by one and were baptized only after fairly extensive preliminary training. The majority of the conversions were in the territories, limited in area, under the control or the influence of European powers.

[147] Fenger, *op. cit.*, p. 13.

The effect of Christianity was seen chiefly in the substitution of Christian for non-Christian religious beliefs and customs in the Christian communities. So far as our evidence goes, the erasure of the old by the new was fairly thorough. The Christianity of the majority of those who bore the name may have been nominal, but at least it involved outward adherence to the Christian cultus. The inner transformation of life and the appearance of what Paul called the fruits of the Spirit—love, joy, peace, longsuffering, kindness, goodness, meekness, self-control—are more tardy of growth and more difficult to ascertain. Indian Christianity was still predominantly foreign in leadership and depended largely upon contact with Europe for such vigour as it displayed. However, an indigenous clergy was appearing. It was found chiefly among the oldest groups, the Syrian Christians, but it was also developing among the Roman Catholic and the Protestant communities. The Goanese Roman Catholicism had sufficient vitality to impel missionaries to go to Ceylon to seek to resurrect there that form of the faith which had been submerged by the Dutch. Upon the morals of the majority of the Europeans the inherited Christianity had but little effect. Of all nationalities it was true, as it was to be in the nineteenth century, that east of Suez the Ten Commandments did not hold. Avarice, lust, and cruelty had free course. No movement to curb the exploitation of the dark races by the Westerner came out of the Christian impulse comparable to that of which Las Casas was the outstanding exponent in the New World. Yet upon many individuals Christianity exerted a restraining influence. Xavier laboured mightily to improve the morals of the Portuguese, and not without success. Other less famous men did likewise. Not until the nineteenth century did Christian rulers attempt on a large scale to apply Christian principles to their rule in India and to regard their empire as a trust held in behalf of the Indians. Still, it must be said that Christianity had prompted many, both Roman Catholic and Protestant, even of those whose lives did not comply with their convictions, to regard their contacts with India as carrying with them an obligation to work for the betterment of the Indians—although that betterment might be interpreted as bringing "salvation" through rather mechanical means. The Christian impulse was already beginning to serve as a corrective to heartless conquest and conscienceless profit-making.

Upon Christianity, the major effect of the Indian environment seems to have been to impregnate the Christian communities with something of the caste tradition. The Christian groups themselves became a kind of caste, inclined to identify themselves with the Europeans, holding to their faith as an hereditary possession. Within the Christian groups, too, the pre-Christian caste divisions often persisted. However, there were not wanting protests against caste as un-

Christian, and the caste cleavages were not so marked as in non-Christian circles.

In spite of its weaknesses, Indian Christianity had been greatly augmented in these centuries after A.D. 1500—in numbers, variety, and morale. The foundations had been laid for the larger growth of the succeeding nineteenth and twentieth centuries.

Chapter IX

CEYLON

IN CEYLON, between A.D. 1500 and A.D. 1800, Christianity made proportionately greater gains than in India. At the dawn of the period no Christians seem to have been found on the island. At the end of the period a larger percentage of the population were professing Christians than in India.

This was to be expected. In these three centuries European peoples established their political control over a much larger proportion of Ceylon than of India. Indeed, although it was not until the latter half of the eighteenth century that Europeans became formidable territorially in India, as early as the sixteenth century they effected the conquest of considerable sections of the coast of Ceylon and throughout all but the earliest decades of the three centuries were a major factor in the life of most of the island. Ceylon, so prominent on the route from India to the East Indies, could not but be important to those who sought to control the sea-borne commerce of Southern and Eastern Asia. It was not so large, moreover, but that the littoral could be mastered by the European armed forces of the day. The Portuguese were the first of the European rulers. Their occupation began in the initial quarter of the sixteenth century with the erection of a fort at Colombo. Intermittent and frequent wars with the native states followed, and by the close of the century, although some native rulers still held out, Philip II, then master of Portugal as well as of Spain, was formally recognized as King of Ceylon. In the middle decades of the seventeenth century, the Dutch ejected the Portuguese and became masters of almost all of the coast. The Dutch ruled until the closing decade of the eighteenth century, when they were supplanted by the British. Under the ægis of the Portuguese Roman Catholic missionaries made thousands of converts. The Dutch introduced Protestantism and attempted to induce their Roman Catholic subjects to accept it. To a brief elaboration of this story we now turn.

In 1505 the Portuguese seem to have made their earliest landing in Ceylon. They established a factory at Colombo. There the first mass was said by Vicente, a Franciscan.[1] For nearly a generation the Portuguese foothold was tenuous

---

[1] Queyroz, *The Temporal and Spiritual Conquest of Ceylon*, pp. 176 ff.; Prakasar, *A History of the Catholic Church in Ceylon. I. Period of Beginnings, 1505-1602*, pp. 17-21.

and little effort was put forth to win converts. Chaplains sent to care for the Portuguese made some attempts to reach the natives. The first priest regularly stationed at Colombo (1518) is said to have had a number of converts in the adjacent villages and to have erected some chapels.[2] In the fifteen thirties the Portuguese gave assistance to one of the native rulers, in Jaffna, in the North, in a civil war. Thanks to Portuguese aid, the ruler was successful. He sent to Lisbon an effigy of his grandson, the heir to his throne, to be crowned. As a result of this dependence on the Portuguese, missionaries were asked for. In response to the request, Franciscans were sent and arrived in 1543. While the King declined to receive baptism, he gave the Brothers Minor a friendly welcome and two of his sons were later taken to India and baptized.[3]

Not far from this time, Francis Xavier extended his activities to Ceylon. On the island of Manar, or Manaar, near the west coast, were those who heard of the labours of Francis Xavier among the Paravas on the Fisher Coast in the adjacent India. They sent to Xavier, asking that he come and baptize them. Their motives we can only conjecture. Perhaps, like the Paravas, they hoped for Portuguese protection against their oppressors. Xavier himself could not go, but sent in his stead another priest. The latter baptized a large number, and the King of Jaffna, whose subjects they were, presumably fearing that by becoming Christians they would remove themselves from his jurisdiction and place themselves under the Portuguese (a not unwarranted apprehension as the event proved), had a number of them put to death.[4] Xavier himself paid a flying visit to Ceylon.[5]

Into all the many details of the spread of Christianity in Ceylon we must not take the time to go. The progress of the faith was associated with the extension of Portuguese rule. To be sure, many of the Portuguese contradicted by their lives the religion which they professed. We hear of earnest attempts of a Jesuit and the Franciscans to win them to higher standards of Christian living, and of a temporary improvement.[6] Yet in general, conversions were wrought not by laymen but by professional missionaries. For a time the Kings of Portugal granted the Brothers Minor a monopoly of the missions in Ceylon,[7] but we

[2] Kuruppu, *The Catholic Church in Ceylon*, pp. 3-9.

[3] Pieris and Fitzler, *Ceylon and Portugal*, Part I, pp. 1-36, Prakasar, *op. cit.*, pp. 31-38.

[4] Letter of Xavier, Jan. 27, 1545, in Coleridge, *Life and Letters of St. Francis Xavier*, Vol. I, pp. 281-283; *Catholic Negombo*, p. 7.

[5] Letter of Xavier, Jan. 27, 1545, in Coleridge, *op. cit.*, Vol. I, pp. 281-283. See also Schurhammer and Voretzsch, *Ceylon zur Zeit des Königs Bhuvaneka Bāhu und Franz Xavers, 1539-1552*, p. 4.

[6] Prakasar, *op. cit.*, pp. 94-98.

[7] Queyroz, *The Temporal and Spiritual Conquest of Ceylon*, p. 257.

read of a Dominican and an Augustinian as being early in the island.[8] Jesuits were active (although the Franciscans objected to what they regarded as an intrusion on their preserves)[9] and eventually sections of the island were apportioned to these three orders—as well as to the Brothers Minor.[10]

Before the close of the sixteenth century thousands of converts had been made. A King of Kotte, in the region of Colombo, had been baptized, with many of his nobles, and this, not unnaturally, was followed by the baptism of thousands of his subjects.[11] A King of Kandy, the leading state in the island, was baptized, apparently in the hope of Portuguese political support, but later, fearing that these allies might become his masters, proved antagonistic to the missionaries.[12] About 1551 a King of Trincomalee, on the east coast, was baptized in the expectation of thus obtaining Portuguese assistance against his rivals.[13] Many of the conversions seem to have been by social groups. In 1556 seventy thousand Careas (also known as Karaiyar, Karawa, and Karawola), a fisher caste on the coast between Colombo and Negombo, were received into the Church.[14] About 1560 Manar came into the possession of the Portuguese and by 1583 the island is said to have had forty-three thousand Christians. On it the Paravas, who were pearl fishers, and the Careas, embraced the faith *en masse*.[15] Conversions also were made on the adjacent coast of Ceylon.[16] In 1590 Portuguese overlordship in Jaffna was re-established by force of arms, and in consequence entire villages were converted and churches multiplied.[17] In one case a friar, to acquire possession of a site which he wished for a church, had fire set secretly to a mosque which occupied it and then obtained it from the King.[18] Towards the close of the century, one of the native rulers of the island transferred to the Franciscans all of the temples of his realm, with their endowments and revenues. However, the King of Portugal, acting on the advice of the Bishop of Cochin (who had ecclesiastical jurisdiction on the island), allowed the friars to have only such portions of the income as were adjudged necessary to support their work.[19]

[8] Queyroz, *op. cit.*, pp. 176 ff.; Prakasar, *op. cit.*, pp. 81-88.
[9] Prakasar, *op. cit.*, p. 261.
[10] Pieris, *Ceylon. The Portuguese Era*, Vol. II, p. 39.
[11] Lemmens, *Geschichte der Franziskanermissionem*, p. 105.
[12] Schurhammer and Voretzsch, *op. cit.*, pp. 6-8; Prakasar, *op. cit.*, pp. 70-80; Lemmens, *op. cit.*, pp. 105, 106.
[13] Prakasar, *op. cit.*, pp. 89, 90.
[14] Prakasar, *op. cit.*, pp. 114-124.
[15] Prakasar, *op. cit.*, pp. 140-167.
[16] Robert Streit, *Maddu, Die Geschichte eines Heiligtums in den Urwäldern von Ceylon* (Fulda, 3d ed., 1913, pp. 62), pp. 11, 12.
[17] Prakasar, *op. cit.*, pp. 208-222; Queyroz, *op. cit.*, pp. 661-685.
[18] Queyroz, *op. cit.*, pp. 661-685.
[19] Pieris, *op. cit.*, Vol. II, pp. 39-41.

Obviously much of this Christianity was superficial. When Portuguese suffered reverses on the field of battle, the Christian ranks shrank.[20] One of the native rulers complained that Christians were unwilling to pay taxes due him, and that some of his subjects became Christians in the hope of obtaining freedom from laws governing inheritances and land tenure and of escaping punishment for murder and robbery.[21] We hear, too, that after their conversion many of the pearl fishers tried to abandon their hereditary occupation and sought exemption from the dues which they had been accustomed to pay. Later the Portuguese Viceroy agreed to be content with an annual contribution just sufficient to cover the cost of the armed vessels which the government gave the fishers as a protection.[22] We also are informed that many in Ceylon crowded to the baptismal font because they feared that if they did not become converts their lands would be taken from them and given to Christians.[23] In general the tendency of converts was said to be to adopt Portuguese manners along with their Portuguese Christian names.[24] Presumably many of the thousands who sought baptism hoped that by becoming Christians they would acquire the privileges of their Portuguese masters and be freed from some of the galling social, legal, and financial restrictions and obligations that had been theirs under the old order.

In the first decades of the seventeenth century, before the Dutch conquest, the numbers of Christians probably continued to increase. Between 1600 and 1636 the Franciscans are reported to have baptized fifty-two thousand. In 1644 the Jesuits are declared to have had twelve residences with more than thirty-two thousand Christians in their charge, in addition to over five thousand Christians on the island of Manar.[25] We read that in 1623 the baptism of a prince, together with his mother and sisters, was made the occasion of public ceremony, with a procession, dances and plays, and was graced by the presence of Portuguese officials and soldiers.[26] It is reported that the following year a hundred and fifty persons of consequence were baptized with much pomp and circumstance.[27] By 1628 the Franciscans were said to have baptized more than seventy-one thousand in the Kingdom of Kotte.[28] By the time that the Dutch supplanted the

---

[20] Queyroz, *op. cit.*, p. 257.

[21] Pieris and Fitzler, *Ceylon and Portugal*, Part I, pp. 1-36, 87.

[22] Pieris, *Ceylon. The Portuguese Era*, Vol. II, pp. 69-71.

[23] Pieris and Fitzler, *op. cit.*, pp. 1-36.

[24] *Ibid.*

[25] Joh. Rommerskirchen, *Die Oblatenmissionen auf der Insel Ceylon im 19 Jahrhundert 1847-1893* (Hünfeld, Verlag der Oblaten, 1931, pp. xi, 247), pp. 8, 9.

[26] Queyroz, *The Temporal and Spiritual Conquest of Ceylon*, pp. 685-696; Pieris, *Ceylon. The Portuguese Era*, Vol. II, p. 154.

[27] Queyroz, *op. cit.*, pp. 652-659.

[28] Queyroz, *op. cit.*, pp. 710-718.

Portuguese, the population in some portions of Ceylon was declared to be predominantly Christian, notably in Galle, Negombo, and Jaffna.[29]

In common with much of the popular belief of the time, some of the Portuguese saw the miraculous in their successes. Thus in 1611 a vision of the Virgin Mary was said to have nerved a Portuguese army on to victory.[30] On another occasion an image of the Virgin was alleged to have given oral assurance to two friars of victory in battle on the morrow.[31] At still another time a Christian who swore to a lie on an image of the Virgin died within a few hours, to the great awe of both Christians and non-Christians.[32]

The Portuguese were intolerant of the Moslems, for the latter were regarded with dislike as rivals in commerce and with abhorrence because of their faith. In 1626 the adherents of Islam were expelled from the portions of the island under Portuguese control.[33]

In the seventeenth century the Portuguese star was waning in the East. The Dutch star was coming into the ascendant. In Ceylon the Portuguese had alienated many of the population by taxation and oppression.[34] The King of Kandy was not averse to playing off one group of Europeans against another and sought the help of the Dutch against their rivals. The Portuguese were not quickly eliminated. The Dutch began to attack early in the seventeenth century, but not until 1658 did they finally triumph and expel the Portuguese from their last strongholds on the island.

The Dutch sought to erase Roman Catholicism from Ceylon. This was to be expected. The Portuguese were defeated rivals, but still rivals, and in Ceylon Roman Catholicism was associated with them. At the time of the Dutch conquest, the Roman Catholic clergy actively asserted themselves on behalf of the Portuguese,[35] and this must have heightened Dutch enmity against them. Moreover, in Dutch minds the memory of the struggle for the independence of the Netherlands and of the sufferings at the hands of a Roman Catholic power was still vivid. The Dutch looked upon Roman Catholicism with abhorrence.

The Dutch policy towards Roman Catholicism was to seek to eliminate it and to substitute for it their own form of Protestantism, the Reformed faith. The first Protestant clergyman arrived in 1642, before the completion of the conquest.[36] The images in Roman Catholic churches were defaced, Roman

[29] Pieris, *op. cit.*, Vol. II, pp. 358, 359.
[30] Queyroz, *op. cit.*, pp. 612-614.
[31] Queyroz, *op. cit.*, p. 451.
[32] Queyroz, *op. cit.*, p. 492.
[33] Queyroz, *op. cit.*, p. 727.
[34] Pieris, *op. cit.*, Vol. II, pp. 232-263.
[35] Pieris, *op. cit.*, Vol. II, p. 358.
[36] Tennent, *Christianity in Ceylon*, p. 39.

Catholic clergy were expelled, and in the year of the Dutch triumph (1658) a proclamation decreed the death penalty for harbouring a Roman Catholic priest.[37] This seems to have been disobeyed, for it was repeated in 1733 and in 1745.[38] Many Roman Catholic churches were converted to Protestant uses. Public and private meetings of Roman Catholics were forbidden.[39]

The Dutch also attempted to win non-Christians to the Christian faith. Political disabilities were placed upon non-Christians as well as upon Roman Catholics: both were declared ineligible for office.[40] At least some non-Christian ceremonies were prohibited and Buddhist worship was suppressed in a temple a few miles from Colombo.[41] Fines are said to have been imposed for non-attendance at church and forfeiture of a third of one's property is reported to have been the penalty for refusing to accept baptism.[42]

To effect the spread of the Reformed faith the Dutch developed an ecclesiastical structure. Clergy were sent out from Holland. Schools were supposed to be erected in every village. Attendance at these was compulsory. Through them baptism was administered and marriages performed.[43] Consistories were organized. Vigorous efforts were made to prevent Christians from marrying non-Christians.[44] Later help came from the Protestant missions in the adjacent South India. Both in the South India and the North Ceylon missions Tamil was the language employed. From the South India mission came type, printers, trained men, and occasionally missionaries.[45]

The Dutch efforts, although covering approximately the same period of time as the Portuguese, were not attended by as substantial lasting results as were the latter. To be sure, in the northern kingdom of Jaffnapatam by 1663 there were said to be sixty-five thousand converts.[46] One estimate puts the number of Protestant Christians on Ceylon in 1722 at 424,392, of whom 189,388 were Tamils in Jaffna, 55,159 were in the Galle district, and the remainder were Singhalese in other places.[47] Another account declares the number of Protestants in 1801 to have been 342,000.[48] Yet the clergy were too few and most of them too unacquainted with the vernacular to give adequate

---

[37] Tennent, op. cit., pp. 40, 41.
[38] Tennent, op. cit., p. 41.
[39] Ibid.
[40] Tennent, op. cit., p. 53.
[41] Tennent, op. cit., p. 54; P. E. Pieris, Ceylon and the Hollanders, 1658-1796, p. 37.
[42] Tennent, op. cit., p. 56.
[43] Tennent, op. cit., pp. 40-48.
[44] Pieris, op. cit., pp. 6, 88.
[45] Tennent, op. cit., pp. 61, 62.
[46] Tennent, op. cit., p. 44.
[47] Tennent, op. cit., p. 63. (See also pp. 73, 74.)
[48] Ibid.

supervision. Between 1642 and 1725 the number of clergy who served was said to have been ninety-seven, and of these we are told that only eight could preach in the vernacular. In 1747 it is reported that all Ceylon had only five ministers and that of these only one understood the local tongue.[49] More than once the ecclesiastical authorities bewailed the superficiality of most of the nominal Christianity of the converts.[50] Yet earnest attempts were made to provide a clergy acquainted with the country. In Jaffna and in Colombo were seminaries, both opened in the year 1690. In practice they were chiefly for the training of teachers and catechists, but a few ministers seem to have come from them. Most of their students were of mixed European and native blood.[51] Moreover, translations were published of the New Testament into Tamil, and of at least part of the New Testament into Singhalese.[52]

In spite of Dutch efforts to eliminate it, Roman Catholicism persisted, and in 1801 was said to have more adherents than Protestantism.[53] Some of the Roman Catholics fled to the domains of the King of Kandy, outside the area of direct Dutch control.[54] Others, while perforce submitting their children to Protestant baptism and instruction, also gave them Roman Catholic baptism and teaching.[55] Famous for maintaining the morale of Roman Catholic Christians was Joseph Vaz.[56] Vaz was an Indian, born in 1651, near Bombay, of Brahmin stock that had long been Christian. He was educated at Goa, was ordained priest, and early achieved fame as an ascetic, a preacher, and a confessor. Later he became head of a community of native priests at Goa which lived according to the rules of the Oratory of Philip Neri. After service in the mission at Canara, he went to Malabar to learn Tamil, as a tongue which would give him access to a large part of the population of Ceylon. Through Ceylon he travelled, sometimes disguised as a slave, sometimes as a beggar. For two years he was imprisoned by the King of Kandy as a possible Portuguese spy and employed his leisure to study Singhalese and to prepare a dictionary in it. He ministered to Roman Catholics, won back apostates, and brought non-Christians into the faith. Other Goanese clergy joined him. Before

---

[49] Tennent, *op. cit.*, pp. 62, 68.
[50] Tennent, *op. cit.*, pp. 64, 65; Pieris, *op. cit.*, p. 133.
[51] A. Schreiber, in *Allgemeine Missionszeitschrift*, Vol. XII, p. 472.
[52] I have seen editions of these, the one in Tamil published in Colombo in 1759, and the one in Singhalese published in Colombo in 1776.
[53] Tennent, *op. cit.*, p. 64.
[54] Kuruppu, *The Catholic Church in Ceylon*, p. 15.
[55] *Catholic Negombo*, pp. 29, 30.
[56] On Joseph Vaz, see D. R. Luis, *Life of the Venerable Father Joseph Vaz* (Mangalore, J. M. Saures Codialbail Press, 1916, pp. 154); Sebastião do Rego, *L'Apostolo di Ceylon P. Guiseppe Vaz della Congregazione dell' Oratorio di S. Filippo Neri* (after the edition of 1753, Mangalore, 1897).

his death (1711) he and his colleagues had brought about a revival of Roman Catholicism. Successors maintained the work which he had begun. Occasionally persecutions broke out, led by Buddhists. In 1746, as a result of one of these, many Christians lapsed into Buddhism.[57] In the latter part of the eighteenth century, in Dutch territory the restrictions on Roman Catholicism were relaxed.[58]

The Roman Catholics of the period formed the basis of a large and continuing body of Christians which in the nineteenth and twentieth centuries were to become even more numerous. The reason for their greater strength as compared with Protestantism is probably not to be found in the policies of the Portuguese and Dutch civil administrations. If anything, the latter appear to have given Protestantism more aggressive and systematic support than the former had accorded to Roman Catholicism. At least one cause for the more secure foothold of Roman Catholicism was the larger number of missionaries from outside Ceylon who propagated and nourished it. The Protestant missionary forces were much smaller and the resulting Protestant Christianity was, accordingly, more nominal and had less of the inward vitality which is transmitted through devoted personalities.

In the eighteenth century Buddhism also seems to have enjoyed a revival. The Dutch were less energetic than formerly in seeking to curb it and a great leader injected new life into it.[59]

By the close of the eighteenth century, then, Christianity was firmly planted in Ceylon, but was paralleled by a vigorous Buddhism. Protestantism, always without much inward vitality in the island, was waning, but Roman Catholicism had survived the testing of Dutch rule and was strong. The growth of Christianity was due in part to the long political control by professedly Christian governments, but the missionary had had an indispensable share in the outcome.

[57] Rommerskirchen, *Die Oblatenmissionen auf der Insel Ceylon*, pp. 11, 12.
[58] Tennent, *op. cit.*, p. 62.
[59] Pieris, *Ceylon and the Hollanders*, pp. 64, 65.

Chapter X

BURMA, THE MALAY PENINSULA, SIAM, AND INDO-CHINA

THE European expansion of the sixteenth, seventeenth, and eighteenth centuries carried Christianity into the various states and regions of South-eastern Asia—Burma, the Malay Peninsula, Siam, and parts of what are known collectively as Indo-China. In all this area, until late in the eighteenth century, the only important territorial foothold acquired by Europeans before 1800 was Malacca. Except here, and in Cambodia, Cochin China, and Annam (where at times native rulers leaned heavily on European support), Christianity, without the advantage of political backing, gained very few adherents. Such Christianity as entered was almost entirely Roman Catholic. Before 1800, except in Malacca, Protestant Christianity won no followers. Yet in a number of centres commercial contacts were established and gave opportunity for missions. Beginnings were made, notably in Indo-China, for what in the nineteenth and twentieth centuries became large Christian communities.

In Burma the first Roman Catholic missionaries seem to have been two Franciscans who reached Pegu in the fifteen-fifties and laboured, fruitlessly, for three years.[1] In that same decade, too, Jesuits were making a few converts at Bassein.[2] By the end of the sixteenth century a number of churches had been built, by Jesuits, Dominicans, and Franciscans, who came with European, most of them Portuguese, mercenaries in the service of native princes. Early in the seventeenth century, however, war brought these efforts to an end.[3] Yet it was near the beginning of the seventeenth century that Franciscans succeeded in establishing themselves at Syriam, where the Portuguese were engaged in commerce.[4] Not far from the same time Jesuits were also in Syriam, and Dominicans were in Pegu.[5] In Syriam a Portuguese adventurer, Philip de Britto, had a stronghold. Between 1613 and 1616, however, the King of Ava conquered Syriam and led into captivity the Portuguese there, including two Jesuits.[6] In 1617 the King of Arakan wrote to Hugli, asking

[1] Lemmens, *Geschichte der Franziskanermissionen*, p. 108.
[2] Pastor, *History of the Popes*, Vol. XIII, p. 307.
[3] Schmidlin-Braun, *Catholic Mission History*, p. 3.
[4] Lemmens, *op. cit.*, p. 108.
[5] Schmidlin-Braun, *op. cit.*, p. 309.
[6] Müllbauer, *Geschichte der katholischen Missionen in Ostindien*, p. 131.

for a missionary, and declaring that in his realm were twenty-three hundred Christians. A priest was sent and received an ovation.[7] About 1680 a Theatine arrived in Arakan, but apparently remained only a short time. In the first quarter of the eighteenth century, a Portuguese priest was found at Syriam and another at Ava.[8] These little glimpses indicate the presence of Christian communities, probably weak, in more than one of the ports of Burma.

In 1722 Mezzabarba, a Papal legate, on a special mission to the Far East, appointed Calchi, one of the Congregation of Clerks Regular of St. Paul, better known as Barnabites, as Vicar Apostolic of Pegu, Ava, and Martaban, to found a mission. In Ava he won toleration from the King, and an Armenian merchant provided him with a church.[9] This was the beginning of a mission of the Barnabites which continued through most of the eighteenth century. Burmese dictionaries and catechisms were composed, and translations were made of several books of the Bible. Towards the end of the period, however, the Barnabite mission came to an end. It had been troubled by the wars which wracked Burma, and its course was not prosperous.[10] Between 1559 and 1800, thirty-eight missionaries, most of them Barnabites, had laboured in the Burmese mission.[11] Presumably they had never been able to reach outside of the Buddhist Burmese, from whom later missionaries were to win comparatively few, into those animistic peoples of the hills among whom the phenomenal gains of the nineteenth and twentieth centuries were chiefly to be effected.

On the Malay Peninsula and its fringing islands Christianity made but slight progress. Moslem traders had preceded those of the Christian faith. Through them Islam had obtained a firm foothold and, as usual, offered stubborn resistance to the spread of Christianity. Until almost the close of the eighteenth century, the only continuing settlement of Europeans was at Malacca. This was the chief mart of the Straits of Malacca and as such commanded that route to the coveted Spice Islands of the East Indies, the goal of the European commercial enterprise in the East in the sixteenth and much of the seventeenth century. Malacca, then, became practically the only Christian centre in the Malay Peninsula until the closing decades of the

---

[7] Josson, *La mission du Bengale Occidental . . . Province Belge de la Compagnie de Jésus*, Vol. I, p. 68.

[8] Ferro, *Istoria delle Missioni de' Chierici Regolari Teatini*, Vol. II, pp. 448 ff.

[9] Luigi Gallo, *Storia del Christianesimo nell' Impero Barmano Preceduta dalle Notizie del Paese*, Vol. I, pp. 92-161; Michelangelo Griffini, *Della Vita di Monsignor Gio Maria Percoto della Congregazione di S. Paolo Missionario ne' Regni di Ava e di Pegu' Vicario Apostolico e Vescovo Massulense*, pp. 84-122.

[10] Gallo, *op. cit.*, Vol. III, pp. 170-172; Griffini, *op. cit.*, *passim*.

[11] Gallo, *op. cit.*, Vol. III, pp. 159-164.

eighteenth century. In 1511 the Portuguese took it. They kept it until 1641. The Dutch then dispossessed them and held it for a century and a half. In 1795 the British captured it, but did not obtain permanent possession until 1824. During the Portuguese period churches were built. With the coming of the Dutch, the Roman Catholic clergy fled and the churches were either transformed into Protestant houses of worship or were diverted to secular purposes.[12]

In Siam Roman Catholicism was the only form of Christianity which attempted missions before the nineteenth century. Its course was chequered. At times it knew persecution. At other times the state was friendly. For some years Portuguese mercenaries were employed by the monarch. In the latter part of the seventeenth century amicable relations were established with France. Under both circumstances the way became open for missionaries. Yet no marked numerical successes followed. The land was predominantly Buddhist, a factor which militated against conversions. Foreign wars and internal political vicissitudes also created unfavorable conditions. In the sixteenth century, Portuguese Dominicans and Franciscans penetrated the country. Some of them made converts, but some paid for their temerity with their lives.[13] At the capital, Ayuthia, priests served the Portuguese mercenaries and their native wives. For a time in the first half of the seventeenth century at the invitation of a monarch who was attempting to develop the commerce of Bangkok, missionaries of several orders arrived and were well received.[14] Jesuits came from the Philippines.[15] Siam became a centre of the Société des Missions Étrangères, which was formed in the second half of the seventeenth century, in part for the training of an indigenous clergy in the neighbouring Cochin China and Tongking. To Siam came, in 1662, La Motte Lambert, one of the pioneers of the Paris fellowship. Here, too, in 1664, arrived Pallu, the outstanding early leader of the Society.[16] Siam seemed a more secure place for the founding of a school in which to give training to candidates for an indigenous priesthood than were the adjacent states of Indo-China. Accordingly, in 1664, on the outskirts of Ayuthia, a beginning was made of what became the Society's *collège général* in the Far East, its central institution for the fulfilment of this purpose. The school remained here until, in 1769, an invasion from Burma made advis-

[12] Jann, *Die katholischen Missionen in Indien, China und Japan*, pp. 210, 211.
[13] Schmidlin-Braun, *op. cit.*, p. 310; Lemmens, *op. cit.*, p. 109.
[14] Jann, *op. cit.*, pp. 200, 207, Schmidlin-Braun, *op. cit.*, p. 310.
[15] *Relation of 1626*. Translation in Blair and Robertson. *The Philippine Islands*, Vol. XXII, pp. 138 ff.
[16] Launay, *Histoire Generaie de la Société des Missions-Étrangères*, Vol. I, pp. 17, 60, 75.

able its removal to French territory, at Virampatnam, near Pondicherry, in India.[17]

East of Siam were the regions which in the nineteenth century were brought under European rule as French Indo-China. Cambodia, Cochin China, Annam, Laos, and Tongking were the chief territorial divisions. In the sixteenth century Portuguese by way of Malacca and Spaniards from the Philippines established contacts at various points along the coast and missions followed. In the course of that century Portuguese and Spanish Dominicans and Franciscans spent longer or shorter times in Cambodia and Cochin China. A few converts were made and we hear of persecution and martyrdom.[18] In 1595 the ruler of Cambodia asked for Spanish help against Siam and, probably for that reason, was friendly to missionaries and the converts.[19] An expedition sent from Manila in 1596 in response to this request was shipwrecked and the survivors returned, crestfallen, to Manila.[20] In 1603 another similar invitation from a Cambodian ruler reached Manila. A few soldiers were sent with some Dominicans, but the initial successes which were obtained proved fleeting.[21] Another Dominican attempt in Cambodia in about 1628 proved a failure.[22]

In 1615 Jesuits, driven from Japan by severe persecutions, established a mission in Cochin China which met with considerable success and which led to important and lasting developments. Early in their mission the Jesuits were accused by popular opinion of responsibility for a drought which afflicted the land and were expelled. They found a foothold in a Japanese settlement, the King recalled them, abundant rains followed, and the attitude of the populace changed.[23] Within the next few years several thousand converts were made. In Tongking, too, the first half of the seventeenth

[17] Néez, Documents sur le Clergé Tonkinois aux XVIIe et XVIIIe Siècles, pp. vi, vii.

[18] Schmidlin-Braun, op. cit., pp. 310, 311; Lemmens, op. cit., p. 110; Blair and Robertson, The Philippine Islands, Vol. IX, pp. 161 ff.; Louvet, La Cochinchine Religieuse, Vol. I, pp. 223 ff.

[19] Blair and Robertson, op. cit., Vol. IX, pp. 161 ff.

[20] Aduarte, Historia de la Provincia del Santo Rosario de Filippinas, etc., translation in Blair and Robertson, op. cit., Vol. XXXI, pp. 76 ff.

[21] Aduarte, op. cit., translated in Blair and Robertson, op. cit., Vol. XXXI, pp. 175 ff. See also Antonio de Morga, Sucesos de Islas Filipinas, translated in Blair and Robertson, op. cit., Vol. XV, p. 279, and Bartolome Leonardo de Argensola, Conquista de las Islas Molucas, translated in Blair and Robertson, op. cit., Vol. XVI, pp. 254 ff.; Louvet, op. cit., Vol. I, pp. 231 ff.

[22] Aduarte, op. cit., translated in Blair and Robertson, op. cit., Vol. XXXII, pp. 168 ff.

[23] Schmidlin-Braun, op. cit., p. 311; unsigned letter from a Jesuit in Manila, July 12, 1619, translated in Blair and Robertson, op. cit., Vol. XVIII, p. 213; Louvet, op. cit., Vol. I, pp. 233 ff.

century saw several Jesuits at work, and in 1639 the Christians were said to number eighty-two thousand.[24]

In Cochin China a Jesuit, Alexander of Rhodes, laboured, and with much success. He became convinced that if Christianity were to be adequately planted and have an enduring life through a continuing church, native clergy were essential. When, not far from the middle of the century, persecution drove him out of the country, he went to Rome and submitted his suggestions to the authorities there. He found receptive ears, for the recently organized Congregation for the Propagation of the Faith had already recommended the establishment of a hierarchy for Japan, China, Tongking, and Siam.[25] Encouraged, he sought recruits to implement his vision. In Paris he came in contact with a deeply religious group of young men who were under the spiritual direction of a Jesuit. Two of these, François Pallu and La Motte Lambert, were appointed as Vicars Apostolic (the new device for missionary administration developed by Rome in that century) over Tongking and Cochin China. Both of them reached their fields.[26] Out of this movement arose the Société des Missions Étrangères of Paris.

To both the Portuguese and the Spaniards, the activities of these Vicars Apostolic seemed an infringement of the right of patronage which had been granted them by Rome. The Portuguese and Spaniards were the more hostile because they feared, and not without ground, that Pallu and his colleagues would prove an opening wedge for French imperialism. A bitter controversy developed and only with difficulty did Rome succeed in making a place for these French ecclesiastics.[27]

In the course of the years the Société des Missions Étrangères was more and more active in Indo-China. Gradually it became more prominent than the Jesuits.[28] Catechists were trained, and some of them were raised to the priesthood. Among the latter were those too advanced in years to be given a prolonged education, but at least they knew enough Latin to say mass. They were seldom ordained before the age of forty. In general these native

[24] Schmidlin-Braun, *op. cit.*, pp. 311, 312; Goyau in Descamps, *Histoire Générale Comparée des Missions*, pp. 452-454.

[25] Launay, *op. cit.*, Vol. I, p. 9.

[26] Jann, *op. cit.*, pp. 218-229, 245, 246; François Pallu, *Relation Abregé des Missions et des Voyages des Evesques François Envoyez aux Royaumes de la Chine, Cochinchine, Tonquin, et Siam* (Paris, Denys Bechet, 1668, pp. 148), pp. 9-18, 25-60.

[27] Jann, *op. cit.*, pp. 231-245.

[28] Jann, *op. cit.*, p. 229; Virgile Pinot, *La Chine et la Formation de l'Esprit Philosophique en France (1640-1740)* (Paris, Paul Geuthner, 1932, pp. 480), p. 17. Friction developed between the Jesuits and the Paris Society.—Pinot, *op. cit.*, pp. 68, 69.

priests seem to have been faithful and earnest in their ministry, and the records show them reaching out among non-Christians and making converts.[29] In 1771, moreover, one of the catechists became a pioneer in Laos.[30] In 1780 the Paris society was in charge of Cochin China, Cambodia, Siam, and the western part of Tongking. In 1755 Cambodia and Cochin China were said to have 22,370 Christians, and in 1786 Tongking was said to hold 130,000.[31] Occasionally persecution ,broke out, churches were burned, missionaries were imprisoned, and Christians were killed.[32] In spite of reverses, however, Christianity continued to attract adherents. A body of Christian literature, too, began to be developed in the vernacular.[33]

Other groups of European priests shared with the fathers of the Paris society in the propagation of the faith in Indo-China. Spanish Dominicans came, an extension of the province of that order which had headquarters in Manila. In 1676 they began a mission in Tongking. In 1761 they were given exclusive charge of the eastern of the two vicariates into which Tongking had been divided in 1678.[34] Towards the close of the seventeenth century Franciscans arrived and were especially active in Cochin China.[35] Some of them were from Bavaria and Italy. One report declares that in 1750 they had in Cochin China and Cambodia forty-four churches and thirty thousand Christians.[36] Augustinians were also present.[37] It was not until the second half of the eighteenth century that the Jesuits ceased to help. They had followed the plan which they had pursued so successfully in China in winning a hearing for the faith and had become court mathematicians in Cochin China.[38]

The question of the attitude towards local religious customs which so vexed Roman Catholic missions in China and India in the seventeenth and eighteenth centuries had repercussions in Indo-China. The clergy were required to conform to the bull *ex quo singulari* which in 1745 brought the

---

[29] Néez, *op. cit.*, pp. 11-68, 85-109, 271.

[30] Launay, *op. cit.*, Vol. II, p. 71.

[31] Launay, *op. cit.*, Vol. II, p. 147.

[32] Schmidlin-Braun, *op. cit.*, p. 490; Goyau in Descamps, *op. cit.*, p. 457; Néez, *op. cit.*, pp. 131, 138; Lemmens, *op. cit.*, pp. 112-117.

[33] Francis Trochu, *Théophane Vénard* (Lyons, Librairie Catholique Emmanuel Vitte, 1929, pp. xvi, 537), p. 360.

[34] *Los Dominicos en Extreme Oriente*, pp. 123, 124; Jann, *op. cit.*, p. 251.

[35] Lemmens, *op. cit.*, pp. 111-117; Civezza, *Storia Universelle delle Missioni Francescane*, Vol. VII, Part 3, pp. 104-106.

[36] Lemmens, *op. cit.*, pp. 112-117.

[37] Néez, *op. cit.*, pp. 2-10.

[38] Néez, *op. cit.*, pp. 2-10; Schmidlin-Braun, *op. cit.*, p. 490; Louvet, *op. cit.*, Vol. I, pp. 374 ff.

long controversy to an end. However, the conflict was not so severe as in China.[39]

Roman Catholic missions became a means for extending European political control over Indo-China. In 1778 the Spanish government expressed to Rome a desire to bring part of the region under its ecclesiastical patronage. Had Rome approved this might have led to political jurisdiction. However, the Propaganda declined to give its consent.[40] In the latter part of the eighteenth century Pigneau de Behaine, of the Paris society and Vicar Apostolic in Cochin China, was obliged by a successful rebel power to leave his territory. While an exile, he met a monarch of Cochin China who had been ousted from the throne by this same rebellion. Pigneau de Behaine offered the dispossessed king to procure for him French aid to replace him on his throne. He went to Paris to consummate the transaction and there obtained a promise of French naval and military assistance. In return France was to receive the island of Pulo Condor, off the mouths of the Mekong, and the port of Tourane on the Annam coast. The expedition was successful, the friendly monarch was restored to his throne and founded a dynasty in Annam which survives to this day, and Christianity, having proved thus politically useful, was favoured.[41] In the course of the nineteenth century this French beginning expanded into a colonial empire, and, under French ægis, Roman Catholic missions flourished and made hundreds of thousands of converts.[42]

The chief cause of the fairly large size of the Christian communities which ushered in the nineteenth century was not the political support of European governments, for until the closing decades of the eighteenth century that had been slight, but the continuing presence and zeal of missionaries and the absence of well organized religions which could offer effective resistance to the coming of a new faith. Buddhism, Confucianism, and the other pre-Christian cults were not nearly so strong as the Buddhism of Siam and Burma. Christianity found its path less obstructed than in any other part of South-eastern Asia.

[39] Néez, op. cit., p. 5.
[40] J. Beckmann in Zeitschrift für Missionswissenschaft, Vol. XXVII, pp. 164-172.
[41] Launay, op. cit., Vol. II, pp. 229 ff.
[42] Also on this area see Adrien Launay, Histoire de la Mission de Cochinchine 1658-1823. Documents Historiques (Paris, P. Tequi, 3 vols., 1923-1925), and Adrien Launay, Histoire de la Mission du Tonkin. Documents Historiques (Paris, Librairie Orientale et Americaine Maisonneuve Frères, Vol. I, 1658-1717, 1927).

Chapter XI

THE EAST INDIES (THE MALAY ARCHIPELAGO)

SOUTH and east of Indo-China and the Malay Peninsula stretches a vast congeries of islands known to Europeans as the East Indies or the Malay Archipelago. It extends east and west over a distance broader than the North American Continent. To it through the centuries successive waves of immigration have come, each leaving its deposit of peoples. Several cultures are present, from the most primitive to the most advanced. Ruins overgrown by jungle testify to half-forgotten, populous, and civilized realms of the past. Religion, like culture, is in several layers. Animism and forms of polytheism are there. By the sea have come some of the great systems of Asia. Hinduism, Buddhism, Islam, and Christianity have all been present. Islam and Christianity were the last to arrive. Of these two, Islam was first and pre-empted the ground in many of the islands, notably in the most populous, Java. Yet Christian missionaries did not despair of the race because they entered it late. In some islands they were able to gain a foothold before Islam. Moreover, in recent centuries they have made headway against even Islam, so easygoing has the latter been in a languorous climate.

To the European explorers and merchants of the sixteenth, seventeenth, and eighteenth centuries, the East Indies proved a strong attraction. Here were the chief sources of some of the spices which had lured them eastward. Spurred by desire for gain and by age-long religious hatred for the Moslem, these adventurers of the West sought to oust the Arabs who had preceded them and to make themselves masters of the coveted springs of wealth. Portuguese, Spaniards, Dutch, and English strove for the prize. The Portuguese and the Spaniards were first. The Portuguese arrived in the second decade of the sixteenth century. They established numerous forts and factories, notably in Amboina, Ternate, the Banda Islands, Celebes, and Halmahera. Their greatest administrator was the historian, Antonio Galvão, governor from 1536 to 1540. The Spaniards were only shortly behind the Portuguese. They mastered the Philippines more completely than ever the Portuguese did the islands farther south. So important was their accomplishment that it must be reserved for a separate chapter. In the sixteenth century the Dutch and the English began to invade what the Portuguese and Spaniards regarded as their preserves. Except in the Philippines, for the most part the Dutch prevailed. In the second half of the sixteenth century the Portuguese power waned. The English were not so successful as the Dutch. Through their East India Company, incorporated in the opening years of the seventeenth century, the Dutch made themselves dominant commercially. They placed their headquarters at Batavia and controlled islands and bits of territory at various places in the archipelago. It was not, however, until the nineteenth and twentieth centuries that the great expansion of their political empire in the islands was accomplished.

The commercial and political history was paralleled by the religious history. At the advent of the Portuguese and Spaniards, Islam, the faith of the Arab traders, was already making rapid progress. The Portuguese and Spaniards brought Roman Catholicism. The Dutch introduced and propagated their form of Calvinistic Protestantism. To a brief summary of the progress of Christianity we must now address ourselves, first Roman Catholicism and then Protestantism. Together these missions, and especially those of the Protestants, laid the foundations for what in the twentieth century became some of the numerically strongest Christian groups in the Far East. Indeed, in the twentieth century, the Protestant communities in the Dutch East Indies were larger than the total of those in any other of the lands of the Far East, including Japan and China.

Roman Catholicism entered the East Indies chiefly from two directions —from the west by way of Malacca through the Portuguese, and from the north by way of the Philippines through the Spaniards. We here have room merely for a few fragmentary notes which give only glimpses of the Roman Catholic activity and achievements. The first missionaries seem to have been Franciscans who in the fifteen twenties arrived in the Moluccas under Portuguese auspices.[1] Before the middle of the century we hear of a Portuguese merchant, Antonio de Payva, who is said to have won two chiefs at Supa, in Macassar, on the west coast of Celebes,[2] and of a secular priest from Malacca.[3] The Jesuit pioneer in the east of Asia, the indefatigable Francis Xavier, with the energy, the vision, and the daring that made him the great Christian pioneer of India and the Far East, reached Amboina early in 1546. He found that seven villages on the island were already Chris-

[1] B. J. J. Visser, *Onder Portugeesch-Spaansche Vlag. De Katholieke Missie van Indonesië 1511-1605*, pp. 6 ff.

[2] Visser, *op. cit.*, pp. 26 ff.

[3] Schmidlin-Braun, *Catholic Mission History*, p. 313.

tian. He went on to Ternate and was there for several months.[4] Following him more Jesuits came to the East Indies, among other places to Celebes, Ternate, and Amboina. In Amboina about fifty served before the time when, in the opening years of the seventeenth century, the advancing power of the Dutch made it impossible for more of them to labour there.[5] On Celebes we read of a Jesuit who baptized a chief with several hundred of his followers.[6] In 1569 the Jesuits were said to have in the Moluccas eighty thousand Christians in their charge.[7] In the sixteenth century Dominicans had marked success on Solor, Timor, and Flores.[8] On Ternate, Franciscans, seconded by Portuguese laymen, were early active in propagating their faith. When, in the latter part of the century, the Dutch drove out the Portuguese, some of the Christians are said to have remained faithful.[9] In 1606 the Spaniards took the island and Augustinians, Dominicans, Jesuits, and Franciscans followed. To the Brothers Minor was given the chief Moslem mosque.[10] In 1670 a prince of Siau, an island north of Celebes, came to Manila and asked for priests to teach his people. Some Jesuits responded and before they were driven out by the Dutch advance made a number of converts.[11] To Borneo in 1656 went Jesuits from the Philippines.[12] To Borneo, too, came representatives of the aristocratic Theatines. Antonio Ventimiglia, of Palermo, although he had only a few years on the island (from 1688 to 1692 or 1693) before his untimely death brought his mission to an end, was termed the Apostle of Borneo, and in 1692 he was appointed the first incumbent of the vicariate apostolic which Rome created for Borneo and entrusted to his order.[13] However, both Portuguese and Spanish authority in the East Indies was waning, and before the end of the seventeenth century the Roman Catholic communities were dwindling.[14] Wars and the

[4] Visser, *op. cit.*, pp. 44 ff.; Crétineau-Joly, *Histoire de la Compagnie de Jésus,* Vol. II, pp. 129-131.

[5] C. Wessels, *De Geschiedenis der R. K. Missie in Amboina vanaf haar Stichting door den H. Franciscus Xaverius tot haar Vernietiging door de O. I. Compagnie 1546-1605* (Nijmegen, N-V. Dekker & Van de Vegt en J. W. Van Leeuwen, 1926, pp. xxviii, 204), *passim.*

[6] Crétineau-Joly, *op. cit.,* Vol. I, p. 387.

[7] Schmidlin-Braun, *op. cit.,* p. 315.

[8] *Ibid.*

[9] Schmidlin-Braun, *op. cit.,* pp. 314, 315.

[10] Lemmens, *Geschichte der Franziskanermissionen,* pp. 118-121.

[11] Casimiro Diaz, *Conquistas,* translation in Blair and Robertson, *The Philippine Islands,* Vol. XLII, pp. 121 ff.

[12] Colin, *Labor Evangelica,* translation in Blair and Robertson, *op. cit.,* Vol. XXVIII, p. 98.

[13] Ferro, *Istoria delle Mis oni de' Chierici Regolari Teatini,* Vol. II, pp. 466-617; Jann, *Die katholischen Missionen in Indien, China und Japan,* p. 252.

[14] Colin, *op. cit.,* translation in Blair and Robertson, *op. cit.,* Vol. XXVIII, pp. 99-102.

absence of spiritual guides brought death or coldness of faith. Islam and Christianity often competed for the same community and in some instances Islam was successful.[15] The rise of the Dutch power brought with it Protestantism. In 1598 what were called "sick visitors" or "comforters of the sick," were sent out on Dutch ships.[16] This seems to have been due largely to the initiative of the Classis of the chief Dutch port, Amsterdam.[17] The East India Company regarded the promotion of Christianity as one of its functions and assigned clergy to care for the Europeans and to win the natives to the faith. The Church became a branch of the Company's activities and the governors dealt with it and its ministers fairly autocratically.[18] The local civil colonial authorities seem to have been in fuller control of the Church than were those in Portuguese and Spanish colonies. Conversion to Christianity, too, was regarded by the natives as a kind of naturalization, entitling the baptized to some of the privileges of the Dutch rulers.[19] Just as in Ceylon and much of India the adoption of Roman Catholic Christianity appeared to the convert and to his non-Christian neighbours to be tantamount to becoming a Portuguese, so in the seventeenth and eighteenth centuries in the East Indies the acceptance of Protestant Christianity seemed to many to be assimilation to the Dutch.

Although in the Indies the government was in control of the Church, in Holland the Church took an independent interest in missions. No missionary society was formed, but several of the *classes* concerned themselves with the Indies.[20] In the Indies, the civil officials determined which territories should have missionaries, the languages which should be used in religious services, where schools should be opened and what salaries should be paid, and assigned the personnel to their posts. However, the Church in Holland examined those who were sent and carried on correspondence with them after they reached the East.[21] Several of the *classes* appointed *deputati ad res Indicas*, and in time the suggestion was made that a *coetus correspondentium* for joint communication with the Indies be formed.[22] For several years in the sixteen twenties and thirties, a seminary was maintained at Leiden,

[15] T. W. Arnold, *The Preaching of Islam* (New York, 1913), pp. 388-392.
[16] Rauws *et alii*, *The Netherlands Indies*, p. 33.
[17] Van Boetzelaer van Dubbeldam, *De Gereformeerde Kerken in Nederland en de Zending in Oost-Indië*, pp. 20-29.
[18] Vandenbosch, *The Dutch East Indies*, p. 227.
[19] Vandenbosch, *op. cit.*, p. 196.
[20] Van Boetzelaer van Dubbeldam, *op. cit.*, pp. 20-29, 50-58.
[21] Van Boetzelaer van Dubbeldam, *op. cit.*, pp. 120-125.
[22] Van Boetzelaer van Dubbeldam, *op. cit.*, pp. 72-110.

under the leadership of Walæus and at the expense of the East India Company, for the training of men for religious service in the Indies. However, this was discontinued, at least partly because of the expense.[23] The Church in Holland appears to have made no effort to raise funds by private subscription either for the training or the support of missionaries. Yet an active missionary interest existed. The work which Hugo Grotius wrote in support of Dutch missions, *De Veritate Religionis Christianæ*, was translated into Malay.[24] The earnest Justus Heurnius wrote *De legatione evangelica ad Indos capessenda admonitio* (1618).[25]

The Dutch East India Company, although, like its English contemporary, a commercial organization which gauged its success by its profits, did not, as did the latter at times, oppose the preaching of Christianity to non-Christians, but encouraged it. To be sure, it subordinated the propagation of Christianity to its financial and political interests. In its tolerance for Islam for political reasons occasionally it became almost intolerant of Christian missions. For instance, in spite of a storm of protest in Holland, it observed a treaty into which it had entered with the Sultan of Ternate not to allow a change of religion.[26] Yet that Christianity was propagated at all was due largely to the support given by the Company.

One of the main obstacles to the spread of Christianity in the East Indies was, as we have suggested, the presence of Islam. The Crescent had antedated the Cross in the islands and eventually won the majority of the population. It was chiefly in regions where it had not penetrated, particularly among those of animistic cults, that Christianity made the greatest progress.

Another hindrance was language. The East Indies had many vernaculars. Malay formed a kind of *lingua franca*, but to a large proportion of the population it was unintelligible. Portuguese was understood by numbers of those who had had contact with Europeans. Some of the Dutch clergy learned Malay. Several laboured on translations of the Bible into that tongue. The question arose as to whether the translations should be into high or low Malay, that of the educated, or that of the masses, and whether they should be printed in Latin or in Arabic characters. In 1734 the entire Bible appeared in Malay in the Latin alphabet, and in 1759 in Arabic letters.[27] The New Testament in Malay formed the main textbook in the schools.[28]

---

[23] Van Boetzelaer van Dubbeldam, *op. cit.*, pp. 72-92, 166-174; Warneck, *Abriss einer Geschichte der protestantischen Missionen*, p. 44.
[24] Warneck, *op. cit.*, p. 24.
[25] Warneck, *op. cit.*, p. 43.
[26] Rauws, *op. cit.*, p. 34; Warneck, *op. cit.*, p. 71.
[27] Van Boetzelaer van Dubbeldam, *op. cit.*, pp. 144-157.
[28] Rauws, *op. cit.*, p. 35.

In 1682 a translation of the New Testament into Portuguese prepared by a former Roman Catholic priest was ready, and in 1745 a Portuguese translation of the Old Testament was published in Batavia.[29]

A problem which caused much discussion, both in the Indies and in Holland, had to do with the sacraments. Particularly acute was the debate over the admission of the nominal converts to the Lord's Supper. Thousands of these had been baptized, but many of them knew little of the Christian faith. Should they be allowed to come to the Lord's Table? The controversy began in the seventeenth century and was particularly acute in the eighteenth century.[30]

It is beyond question that much of the Christianity of the East Indies was superficial. It is said that in Amboina the chiefs were commanded by the civil officials to have a number ready for baptism every time a clergyman appeared, and that the latter was paid a specified sum for each person baptized.[31] It is not surprising that Amboina is reported to have contained forty thousand Christians at the end of the seventeenth century.[32] The number of clergy, too, was insufficient for the vast area. In 1660 the complaint was made that there were only twenty-one ministers in the Indies when formerly there had been twenty-eight.[33] In 1730 the number is said to have been thirty-four and in 1776 twenty-two, of whom only five could preach in any other language than Dutch.[34] However, clergy were not the only agents of the Church. Moreover, at least some of the clergy were men of zeal and imagination. Famous was Justus Heurnius, the son of a professor at the University of Leiden. He went to the Indies in 1624 and became a preacher of the large Dutch congregation in Batavia. He was not content to remain there, but went on to Amboina and to other centres to labour among the nominal Christians. He attempted to acquire one of the vernaculars in addition to Malay. However, in 1638 ill health compelled his return to Holland.[35]

Since the Church was dependent upon the East India Company for support, the vigour and numbers of its leadership paralleled in part the strength of the Company. While the Company was not abolished until 1798, by the end of the seventeenth century its trade had begun to decline.[36]

[29] Van Boetzelaer van Dubbeldam, *op. cit.*, pp. 144-157.
[30] Van Boetzelaer van Dubbeldam, *op. cit.*, pp. 184-237.
[31] Warneck, *op. cit.*, p. 45.
[32] Warneck, *op. cit.*, p. 46.
[33] Van Boetzelaer van Dubbeldam, *op. cit.*, p. 110.
[34] Rauws, *op. cit.*, p. 37.
[35] Julius Richter, *Die evangelische Mission in Niederländisch-Indien*, p. 12.
[36] Clive Day, *The Policy and Administration of the Dutch in Java* (New York, The Macmillan Co., 1904, pp. xxi, 434), p. 75.

It is not surprising that when the Company was finally brought to its end only seven clergymen remained.[37]

We must not here attempt to give island by island the history or even the numerical strength of the Church. We hear of large numbers of Christians in Amboina, in Ceram, to the north of Amboina, in the Banda islands, in Timor, in the far north of the archipelago, in Talaur and the Sangi Islands (where in 1700 the Christian community was estimated at twenty-six thousand), and in the island of Roti, south of Timor, where in 1760 the Christians were said to number nearly six thousand. Batavia, as the capital, had several churches. In 1721 it is reported to have had eleven clergymen, five for Dutch congregations, three for Malay, and three for Portuguese.[38] In Batavia much of the work of the Church was among slaves.

How many Christians the East Indies contained at the close of the eighteenth century we do not know. The number is estimated at between sixty-five thousand and two hundred thousand.[39]

Superficial though much of the Christianity of these thousands was, here in A.D. 1800 were the largest groups of Protestant Christians east of India and Ceylon and some of the largest bodies of Christians of any kind in the Far East. Here, too, was a substantial nucleus in preparation for the large expansion in the Dutch East Indies in the nineteenth and twentieth centuries. The state church which had been founded and nourished by the clergy sent out under the East India Company was one of the most prominent features of the Christianity of the archipelago of a later day.

[37] Rauws, *op. cit.*, p. 37.

[38] Rauws, *op. cit.*, pp. 34-37. See also *Archief voor de Geschiednis der Oude Hollandsche Zending*, Vols. V and VI, *De Molukken* (Utrecht, C. Van Bentum, 1890, 1891), *passim;* J. Mooij, *Geschiedenis der Protestantsche Kerk in Nederlandsch-Indië*, Vol. I, 1602-1636 (Landsdrukkerij-Wettevreden, 1923, pp. viii, 494), *passim;* and H. Dijkstra. *Het Evangelie in Onze Oost. De Protestantsche Zending in het tegenwoordige Nederlandsch Indië van de Eerste Vestiging tot op Onzen Tijd.* Part I (Leiden, E. Donner, 1900, pp. 217), *passim.*

[39] Richter, *op. cit.*, p. 12.

Chapter XII

THE PHILIPPINE ISLANDS

THE one land in the general region of the South and South-east of Asia and the adjoining islands where the majority of the inhabitants became professedly Christian between A.D. 1500 and A.D. 1800 was the Philippine Islands. Indeed, the Philippine Islands are still the largest area in this part of the globe in which the faith of the majority is or ever has been Christianity.

This exceptional circumstance must be ascribed to at least two factors. One was the character of the population when the Europeans first arrived. The Filipinos were then in a fairly primitive state of culture with forms of religion of the type which readily give place to "higher" faiths. Of the great religious systems of the mainland of Asia only Islam had made much impression, and it had only begun to gain a foothold. Significantly, where it had become firmly established Christianity was never to make much headway. Presumably, if, as in Java, the majority had been previously impregnated with Buddhism, Hinduism, or Islam, Christianity would have made but a slight impression. In the Philippines the Crescent antedated the Cross. Before the coming of the Spaniards, Moslem merchants from Borneo were coming and teaching their faith.[1] Had Islam been given a century or two more of leeway it is conceivable that the islands would have become predominantly Moslem rather than predominantly Christian. The Spanish missionaries were just in time. It is, of course, well known that in the South there were and are many Moslems. Moreover, in 1573, a few years after the beginning of the Spanish conquest, it was reported that some of the natives of the great northern island, Luzon, especially on the coast, were Moslems.[2] In the South the further spread of Islam was partly countered by the Governor's order to a chief on Mindanao that no more preachers of Islam be admitted, that the houses where Islam was proclaimed be destroyed, and

---

[1] Antonio de Morga, *Sucesos de Islas Filipinas* in Blair and Robertson, *The Philippine Islands*, Vol. XVI, pp. 134, 135.

[2] Guido de Lavezaris from Manila, June 29, 1573, translation in Blair and Robertson, *op. cit.*, Vol. III, pp. 179-188.

that Christian teaching be allowed.[3] In the North Christianity was in time to prevent Islam from obtaining a secure foothold.

The other factor making for the adoption of Christianity was the nature of the contacts with the Occident. The dominant power was Spain. Spain was much larger and more powerful than either Portugal or the Netherlands, which until the eighteenth century were the most aggressive of the European nations in the South and East of Asia. In contrast with the others, moreover, the Philippines were almost her only possession in this part of the world. She was not there attempting to cover so much ground as did the others and could more nearly concentrate her energies upon it than could they in any one of their territories. Then, too, the missionary had relatively a much larger part in the Philippines than in any of the other European posts in the South and South-east of Asia. Elsewhere the primary purpose of the Westerner was commerce, and the extension of the Christian faith was secondary. In the Philippines commerce was less prominent than missions and political conquest was ancillary to the labours of the heralds of the Cross. To be sure, the civil and the ecclesiastical groups of Spanish officials were often at variance and commerce existed, but all contacts with Spain had to be by way of Mexico, and freight to Spain had to cross the Pacific, be carried over Mexico, and then be shipped across the Caribbean and the Atlantic. Even had Spain desired it, commerce with the Philippines and the Far East would, under this handicap, have proved extremely difficult. Philip II, in whose reign the effective occupation of the islands was begun and for whom the islands were named, was a religious zealot, and it is not strange than an enterprise set in motion under his supervision should have the spread of the Christian faith as its major objective. The Philippines, as the Spanish outpost in the Far East, although having some commerce, were chiefly a base for Christian missions, in which missionaries won the larger part of the population, and from which missionaries went to the East Indies, Indo-China, China, Formosa, and Japan. Indeed, at the outset, the Philippines were esteemed primarily as a strategic centre for Spanish political and religious conquest in the Far East.[4]

Magellan, sailing under instructions from the Emperor Charles V to discover the lands which belonged to the latter as King of Spain under the Papal demarcation of the globe between himself and the Kings of Portugal, was the first to lead a group of Europeans to the Philippines (1521) and lost

---

[3] Letter of Governor Francisco de Sande, May 23, 1578, translation in Blair and Robertson, *op. cit.*, Vol. IV, pp. 174 ff.

[4] Montalbán, *Das spanische Patronat und die Eroberung der Philippinen,* pp. 7, 93.

his life there at the hands of natives. Although the formal extension in 1529 to the antipodes of the demarcation line placed the Philippines in the Portuguese half of the earth, the Spaniards set about the occupation of the islands. After an unsuccessful expedition under Villalobos sent in 1542, in the third quarter of the sixteenth century the beginnings of the real conquest of the islands were made under the direction of Legaspi.[5]

The occupation of the Philippines was an extension of the Spanish conquests in the New World. Legaspi's expedition was in ships built in America and was under the direction of men who had had experience there. The phenomenal burst of energy which had carried the Spaniards across the Atlantic and over so much of the Western Hemisphere also sent them across the Pacific and made them the masters of a larger area in Asia than was under any Western European power before the eighteenth century. Never had a similarly large group of peoples been won to any religion whose centre of propagation was so remote as was Spain from the Philippines. The conversion of the Philippines was a most remarkable achievement and was due to the zest for conquest and the zeal for souls.

Although efforts had been made by Magellan and under Villalobos for the conversion of the Filipinos, the permanent planting of Christianity, like the political conquest, began under Legaspi. The official instructions to Legaspi directed that all in the expedition should acquit themselves like Christians, honour the name of the Lord and his Mother, accord good treatment to the natives, and not engage in the slave trade. Private soldiers were not even to cross the field of a native without the latter's consent.[6] With Legaspi went five Augustinians, of whom three remained in the islands. Until 1570 the missionaries fixed their attention chiefly on China and little was done for the conversion of the Filipinos, but very shortly the Philippines were given more care, reinforcements came, and a number of stations were established.[7]

To the Augustinians were added in the course of time representatives of other orders. In 1577 a contingent of Franciscans arrived. The province that was constituted was given the name of Gregory, from Pope Gregory the Great who had had so much to do with the spread of the faith nearly a thousand

[5] E. G. Bourne, *Discovery, Conquest, and Early History of the Philippine Islands,* in Blair and Robertson, *op. cit.,* Vol. I, pp. 27 ff.; Blair and Robertson, *op. cit.,* Vol. II, pp. 11-13.

[6] Montalbán, *op. cit.,* pp. 61, 62. Magellan promised a native chief a suit of armour if he would be baptized. This chief, his wife, and his leading men accepted the rite. Magellan instructed them to destroy their idols and to set up a cross in their place and to adore it daily with clasped hands.—Antonio Pigafetta, *Primo Viaggio intorno al Mondo* (Ms. 1525), translation in Blair and Robertson, *op. cit.,* Vol. XXXIII, pp. 142-159.

[7] Montalbán, *op. cit.,* pp. 103-108.

years before. This Franciscan enterprise was the outgrowth of an effort to found a mission in the Solomon Islands, a group which had been disclosed to European eyes by an expedition from Peru in the preceding decade. By order of the King the Brothers Minor who had been recruited for the Solomon Islands were diverted to the Philippines, although only part of those enlisted actually arrived.[8] The Dominicans entered in company with the first bishop of the islands. In 1578 a Papal bull ordered the erection of the diocese and cathedral church of Manila.[9] To the new see was appinted Domingo de Salazar, a Dominican who had come to Spain from Mexico to plead at court against the wrongs committed against the Indians.[10] A little later, apparently originally at the instance of some of the order in Mexico, the Dominican Province of the Holy Rosary was created with the Philippines as its centre.[11] Salazar reached the Philippines in 1581. With him also came Jesuits.[12] Some time later Augustinian Recollects arrived.[13] The royal permission for the establishment of the order was obtained in 1604.[14] In 1617 royal approval was given for the transfer to the Philippines of the hospital order of St. John of God,[15] but the first evidence of the presence of this group seems to be from 1641.[16] Some seculars also came.[17] The main burden of the conversion of the islands was borne by the Augustinians, the Franciscans, the Dominicans, the Jesuits, and the Augustinian Recollects. Within about a generation of the beginning of the conquest under Legaspi all five of these were represented.

To prevent overlapping, duplication of effort, and friction, in 1594 a royal command directed that no two orders labour in any one province.[18]

As in Spanish America, provision was made by the Crown for the financial undergirding of missions. Thus in 1579 the King directed that the expenses

[8] Montalbán, *op. cit.,* pp. 103-108; Raucaz, *In the Savage South Solomons,* pp. 12-28.
[9] Bull of Gregory XIII, Feb. 6, 1578, translation in Blair and Robertson, *op. cit.,* Vol. IV, pp. 119 ff.
[10] Montalbán, *op. cit.,* pp. 103-108; Pastor, *History of the Popes,* Vol. XX, p. 479.
[11] Papal decrees of Sep. 15 and Oct. 20, 1582, translation in Blair and Robertson, *op. cit.,* Vol. V, p. 199. See also *Los Dominicos en el Extremo Oriente,* pp. 41-49; Galarreta, *Vida del Martir Ilmo Fr. Jerónimo Hermosilla* (Barcelona, Tip. Ariza, 1906, pp. 336), p. 16.
[12] Blair and Robertson, *op. cit.,* Vol. V, p. 9, Vol. XII, p. 193.
[13] Antonio de Morga, *Sucesos de la Islas Filipinas,* translation in Blair and Robertson, *op. cit.,* Vol. XVI, pp. 150 ff.
[14] Blair and Robertson, *op. cit.,* Vol. XIII, p. 247.
[15] Juan Francisco de S. Antonio, *Chronicas,* translation in Blair and Robertson, *op. cit.,* Vol. XXVIII, p. 143.
[16] Juan J. Delgado, *Historia General,* translation in Blair and Robertson, *op. cit.,* Vol. XXVIII, p. 176.
[17] Montalbán, *op. cit.,* pp. 103-108; Antonio de Morga, *op. cit.,* translation in Blair and Robertson, *op. cit.,* Vol. XVI, pp. 150 ff.
[18] *Recopilación de Leyes de las Indias,* Book I, Title 14, translation in Blair and Robertson, *op. cit.,* Vol. XXXIII, pp. 67 ff.

ɔf the newly founded bishopric for the Philippines, as previously for the Augustinians and Franciscans, be at royal charge and that where *encomiendas* existed, monasteries be built at the expense of *encomenderos* by native labour.[19] A little later we hear of tithes collected from the Indians and of a royal order that *encomenderos* pay for the religious instruction of natives.[20] Apparently the royal command was not always obeyed, for we read that the support earlier ordered for the Augustinians had been accorded with some irregularity.[21] At times the royal grants proved insufficient.[22]

Further provision for the episcopal supervision of the Philippines was early made. In 1591, at the request of Bishop Salazar, Manila, the seat of the Bishop, was erected into an archdiocese with three suffragan bishops.[23]

Before the close of the sixteenth century more than four hundred and fifty regulars had embarked for the islands. While some of these died on the long and arduous journey, and while others were detained in Mexico on the way out,[24] a very considerable number reached their designated field.

However, in the early years especially, much difficulty was experienced in holding missionaries in the Philippines and there was a chronic shortage of priests. To many the lure of the Continent of Asia, particularly of China, proved irresistible. In 1582 the Governor advised the King that missionaries be sent directly from Spain to the Philippines and not be permitted to remain any length of time in Mexico, for the prosperity of the latter land and the progress of the faith there were so great that those friars who had been in that country became discouraged by the poverty and pioneer conditions in the Philippines and wished either to return to New Spain or to go elsewhere.[25] In the face of the express command that no missionary leave the Philippines for the Continent without official permission, several succeeded in doing so.[26]

In spite of the shortage of missionaries, the conquest and conversion of the Philippines went on apace. The land was divided politically and could offer little effective resistance. No highly organized cultural structure stood in the

---

[19] Translation of royal order of May 13, 1579, in Blair and Robertson, *op. cit.,* Vol. IV, pp. 141-143.

[20] Translation of royal order of Aug. 9, 1589, in Blair and Robertson, *op. cit.,* Vol. VII, pp. 141 ff.

[21] Translation of royal order of Apr. 24, 1584, in Blair and Robertson, *op. cit.,* Vol. VI, p. 45.

[22] Diego Aduarte to the King, 1606, translation in Blair and Robertson, *op. cit.,* Vol. XIV, pp. 90 ff.

[23] Chirino, *Relación de las Islas Filipinas,* translation in Blair and Robertson, *op. cit.,* Vol. XII, p. 204.

[24] Montalbán, *op. cit.,* pp. 103-108.

[25] Letter of Governor Peñalosa to the King, June 16, 1582, translation in Blair and Robertson, *op. cit.,* Vol. V, pp. 23 ff.

[26] Blair and Robertson, *op. cit.,* Vol. IV, p. 308.

way. Tact, the show of arms, and the efforts of the missionaries, with very small contingents of troops and very slight bloodshed, brought about, in an amazingly brief period, the political and religious submission of the non-Moslem peoples of the lowlands.[27] By the time the first Franciscans arrived, the Augustinians are reported to have baptized more than one hundred thousand.[28] By 1586, or only about a quarter of a century after the coming of Legaspi and the first Augustinians, the total number baptized by all the orders is declared to have been more than four hundred thousand.[29] Though one instinctively distrusts these large round numbers and in 1586-1588 Bishop Salazar reported that the total of pacified (and supposedly) Christian Filipinos was considerably less, or 146,700,[30] even this latter figure is very considerable. In 1610 the ninety-one Jesuits in the islands are said to have baptized 2,383 adults in one year.[31] About 1612 statistics gathered at royal command show that the four major orders, the Augustinians, the Franciscans, the Dominicans, and the Jesuits, had 461 members in 143 establishments and in the island of Luzon ministered to 322,400 souls.[32] In 1621-1622 the Archbishop of Manila reported that in all the Philippines the total of those under religious instruction (apparently not counting children) by the regulars and seculars was not far from half a million.[33] A little over a century later, in 1735, a table shows 837,182 in the islands served by the regulars and the seculars.[34] In 1750 the number of those over seven years of age under the spiritual care of regulars and seculars was reported to be 904,116, or, if children under seven be included, over a million. These were said to live in 569 different villages.[35]

As among the uncivilized Indians of Latin America, the missionaries in the Philippines sought to induce the natives to gather into settlements in which supervision would be easier than in scattered households over the countryside.[36] Often, however, the Filipinos offered obstacles to this procedure, preferring their hereditary method of living.[37]

[27] Bourne, in Blair and Robertson, *op. cit.*, Vol. I, p. 38.

[28] Mendoza, *Historia del Gran Reyno de China,* translation in Blair and Robertson, *op. cit.*, Vol. VI, p. 126.

[29] Mendoza, *op. cit.*, in Blair and Robertson, *op. cit.*, Vol. VI, p. 148.

[30] Blair and Robertson, *op. cit.*, Vol. VII, pp. 29 ff.

[31] *Annuae Litterae Societatis Iesu 1610,* translation in Blair and Robertson, *op. cit.*, Vol. XVII, pp. 53, 54.

[32] Blair and Robertson, *op. cit.*, Vol. XVII, pp. 189 ff.

[33] Serrano to the King, translation in Blair and Robertson, *op. cit.*, Vol. XX, pp. 226 ff.

[34] Juan Francisco de S. Antonio, *Chronicas,* translation in Blair and Robertson, *op. cit.*, Vol. XXVIII, p. 160.

[35] Juan J. Delgado, *Historia General,* translation in Blair and Robertson, *op. cit.*, Vol. XXVIII, p. 178.

[36] Chirino, *Relacion de las Islas Filipinas,* translation in Blair and Robertson, *op. cit.*, Vol. XIII, p. 91; Domingo Perez in Blair and Robertson, *op. cit.*, Vol. XLVII, pp. 289 ff.

[37] Serrano to the King, translation in Blair and Robertson, *op. cit.*, Vol. XX, pp. 226 ff.; Keesing, *Taming Philippine Headhunters,* p. 63.

In teaching the Filipinos, it became necessary for the missionaries to learn the native languages. Indeed, royal commands ordered that no missionary should go among the natives without a knowledge of the vernacular.[38] The tongues were fairly numerous, but since several of them were interrelated, the acquisition of one was of assistance in becoming familiar with some of the others.[39] We hear of one of the early Jesuits who within six months had gained sufficient knowledge of the language of his district to preach in it.[40]

Efforts were not confined to the Filipinos, but were extended to the Chinese and the Japanese who were resident in the islands. The former outnumbered the latter.[41] The Chinese apparently offered no very great opposition to outward conformity to the faith of the masters of the islands, and some of the priests learned their language the better to minister to them.[42] The Spaniards, always relatively few in numbers, from time to time feared that the Chinese would displace them, and repeatedly the apprehension broke out in massacres in which the Chinese suffered most cruelly. Some converts were won from among the Japanese, and at a time when Christianity was making progress in Japan itself.[43]

The process of conversion, while becoming more sluggish after the initial impulse of the conquest, continued throughout the seventeenth and eighteenth centuries, and, indeed, into the nineteenth century. To be sure, the expulsion of the Jesuits from the Spanish domains in 1768-1769[44] brought some inconvenience, but the Society was never so prominent in the Philippines as in some other areas of the globe and its absence did not prove a major inconvenience. More potent in slowing down the advance were two other factors. First was the fact that the initial conquests and conversions had been, as was natural, in the more accessible valleys, plains, and ports, and that later extension of the boundaries of Christianity and Spanish rule was chiefly in difficult mountain terrain among less docile tribes. Second was the growing lethargy and exhaustion in Spain which were reflected in the wide-flung Spanish colonial empire. Yet in spite of handicaps, fresh conversions were still made. Thus in 1671 entrance was effected among Filipinos in Mindanao who until that time had been

[38] Blair and Robertson, op. cit., Vol. XX, p. 249.

[39] Chirino, op. cit., translation in Blair and Robertson, op. cit., Vol. XII, p. 235.

[40] Letter of Dasmariñas to Philip II, Dec. 6, 1595, translation in Blair and Robertson, op. cit., Vol. IX, pp. 193, 194.

[41] Antonio de Morga, Sucesos de las Islas Filipinas, translation in Blair and Robertson, op. cit., Vol. XVI, p. 198.

[42] Chirino, op. cit., translation in Blair and Robertson, op. cit., Vol. XII, pp. 216 ff., Vol. XIII, p. 39 ff.; Santiago de Vera to Philip II, June 13, 1589, translation in Blair and Robertson, op. cit., Vol. VII, p. 91; an account by an anonymous author, Manila, Apr. 20, 1572, translation in Blair and Robertson, op. cit., Vol. III, pp. 141 ff.

[43] Antonio de Morga, op. cit., translation in Blair and Robertson, op. cit., Vol. XVI, p. 198.

[44] Blair and Robertson, op. cit., Vol. L, p. 269.

pagan and independent of Spain.[45] In 1739 thirty-nine missionaries in twenty-one centres were engaged in working for the pagans who dwelt in the mountains.[46] In 1739 Dominicans, at the cost of the lives of four of their number, penetrated into an area in Central Luzon. They found it advisable to exercise care in admitting applicants to baptism, for many sought the rite to escape creditors or tyrannical lords, but in six years they had erected seven churches and baptized 970.[47] After several unsuccessful attempts, in 1783 the Dominicans began a permanent mission on the Bátan Islands, to the north of Luzon.[48]

The Spanish extended their missions beyond the Philippines. We have seen them in Siam, in Indo-China, and in the adjoining East Indies. In the succeeding two chapters we are to find them in Japan and China. In the second half of the seventeenth century a successful mission was begun by Jesuits on the Ladrones or Mariana and the Caroline Islands.[49] In 1772 and 1774 Franciscans from the college at Ocapa in Peru took part in expeditions to Tahiti.[50]

This phenomenal advance of Christianity was not made without loss of life and reverses. In the seventeenth century we hear of revolts and of the killing of missionaries.[51] In some instances the uprisings were against the oppression of the Spaniards, but even more they were led by chiefs who wished to restore the old order with its non-Christian cults.[52] In 1662, moreover, the Spaniards decided to abandon their forts in Mindanao and the Sulu Archipelago. This led to the temporary disappearance of Spanish rule in that region and to the apostasy of most of such Moslems as had become Christian.[53]

It was not only opposition from the Filipinos which embarrassed the spread of Christianity in the Philippines. Friction within the Church and between civil and ecclesiastical authorities also proved a weakness. In spite of the principle adopted by the state that except in the cities no two orders should work in the same area, disputes sometimes arose over the possession of a particular

[45] Pedro de San Francisco de Assis, *Recollect Missions in the Philippines,* translation in Blair and Robertson, *op. cit.,* Vol. XLI, p. 137.

[46] Fernando Valdés Tamón, Manila, 1739, translation in Blair and Robertson, *op. cit.,* Vol. XLVII, p. 143.

[47] Bernando Ustáriz, O.P., in pamphlet published at Manila in 1745, translation in Blair and Robertson, *op. cit.,* Vol. XLVIII, pp. 123 ff.

[48] *Los Dominicos en el Extremo Oriente,* pp. 102, 103.

[49] Crétineau-Joly, *Histoire de la Compagnie de Jésus,* Vol. V, pp. 20-22; Schmidlin-Braun, *Catholic Mission History,* pp. 499, 500. Bolton, *Kino's Historical Memoir of Primería Alta,* Vol. I, p. 34, says that of the Jesuits who sailed from Genoa with Kino in 1681, four went to the Marianas and that three of these suffered martyrdom.

[50] Izaquirre, *Historia de las Misiones Franciscanas . . . en el Oriente del Peru,* Vol. III, p. 15.

[51] Luis de Jesús, *Historia de los Religiosos Descalzos de San Augustin,* translation in Blair and Robertson, *The Philippine Islands,* Vol. XXXV, pp. 65 ff.

[52] Blair and Robertson, *op. cit.,* Vol. XXXVIII, pp. 87 ff.

[53] Blair and Robertson, *op. cit.,* Vol. XLI, pp. 277 ff.

territory.[54] In theory, as in Spanish America, the task of the regulars was to be temporary. The friars were to be the missionaries, and when the conversion of a district was completed, secular priests were to take over the parishes. In practice, the regulars were very reluctant to submit to the transfer. They remained much more prominent in the Church than in Spanish America. Conflicts arose over the tenacity of their hold. The regulars objected, too, to another phase of the transition from the mission stage to the ordinary life of the Church, episcopal supervision and visitation. As early as 1621 an Archbishop of Manila was saying that friars should leave the settled parishes and go to the missions and that there were sufficient seculars to care for all the parishes which the regulars might surrender.[55] In 1636 one of the bishops complained to the King that the friars declined to let him make an episcopal visitation and recommended that they be replaced by seculars.[56] In 1638 a royal order stated that many of the graduates of the local colleges were unemployed and directed that all benefices which had been taken in the past twenty years by the regulars be restored to the seculars.[57] In 1666 a friar set forth reasons why seculars should not be substituted for regulars and why the latter should not be under episcopal supervision.[58] As late as 1767, when a new Archbishop of Manila attempted episcopal visitation, of the regulars only the Dominicans submitted. The Archbishop appointed seculars to vacant curacies, and since the number of available Spaniards was small, he made up the deficiency by ordaining Filipinos. This led to resentment among the regulars and their adherents, particularly since the critics could argue that the Filipino seculars were lacking in both morals and education.[59] In 1753, the civil authorities, to bring an end to the friction over episcopal visitation, had ordered that all parishes be handed over to seculars. This caused trouble. In 1774 and again in 1776 and 1778 the Crown commanded that a body of Filipino seculars be formed so that parishes could be transferred to them.[60] In spite of efforts to unseat them, the regulars remained powerful and in the provinces were usually practically absolute, with little regard either for bishops or for the civil authorities.[61] The islands were kept predominantly

[54] Concepción, *Historia de Philipinas,* translation in Blair and Robertson, *op. cit.,* Vol. XLI, pp. 231 ff., Vol. XLVI, pp. 56 ff.

[55] Blair and Roberston, *op. cit.,* Vol. XX, pp. 76 ff.

[56] Blair and Robertson, *op. cit.,* Vol. XXV, p. 301.

[57] Blair and Robertson, *op. cit.,* Vol. XXIX, pp. 106, 107.

[58] Blair and Robertson, *op. cit.,* Vol. XXXVI, pp. 264 ff.

[59] Montero y Vidal, *Historia de Filipinas,* translation in Blair and Robertson, *op. cit.,* Vol. L, pp. 29 ff.

[60] Sinibaldo de Mas, *Informe sobre el Estado de las Islas Filipinos en 1842,* translation in Blair and Robertson, *op. cit.,* Vol. XXVIII, pp. 226 ff.

[61] Le Gentil, *Voyages dans les Mers de l'Inde* (Paris, 1781), translation in Blair and Robertson, *op. cit.,* Vol. XXVIII, p. 218.

in the mission stage. Such native seculars as existed were not the controlling force in the Church. Many of the regulars bore an excellent name as to character, but others were charged with neglecting their duty to the Filipinos and with being avaricious, tyrannical, and meddlesome.[62] Then, too, civil and ecclesiastical authorities were frequently at loggerheads.[63] For instance, we hear the complaint that the civil officials permitted bishoprics to remain vacant, and that episcopal incomes were small, were collected at the will of the governors, and were grudgingly doled out by them to the incumbents of the sees.[64] It was in spite of a great deal of dissension within the dominant Spanish minority that Christianity made gains and became firmly established among the Filipinos.

The effect of Christianity upon the Philippine Islands was very marked. First of all was the erasure of pre-Christian cults and the substitution of Spanish Roman Catholic Christianity. To be sure, pre-Christian beliefs yielded but slowly and for a long time much of the Christianity was superficial. In the very early days of the Spanish occupation in one district baptism was forcibly administered with no instruction beyond the giving of Christian names. Under the circumstances the Filipinos objected, perhaps thinking the rite a curse, and washed off the holy oils.[65] The Filipinos were very slow at first to come to confession.[66] In the second quarter of the seventeenth century a friar, arguing the necessity of giving to the missionaries the authority to punish the natives, declared that the latter detested the Church and loved their pagan beliefs and customs.[67] As late as the eighteenth century an Augustinian complained that the Christian Filipinos were still paying reverence to the manes of their ancestors and to other spirits and declared their beliefs to be a compound of paganism and Christianity.[68] Also in the eighteenth century a Dominican told of a tribe among whom his colleagues had been labouring for seventy years where the missionary could visit each settlement only once or twice a year to

[62] Blair and Robertson, *op. cit.*, Vol. X, pp. 53 ff., Vol. XII, pp. 98 ff.

[63] Blair and Robertson, *op. cit.*, Vol. XXXIX, is largely given to the records of such disputes.

[64] Pedro Diaz del Cosio, Procurator-General in Madrid of the Dominicans, to the Crown, Aug., 1674, translation in Blair and Robertson, *op. cit.*, Vol. XXXVIII, pp. 72-75.

[65] Aduarte, *Historia de la Provincia del Santo Rosario . . . en Philippinas* (Manila, 1640), translation in Blair and Robertson, *op. cit.*, Vol. XXX, p. 163.

[66] Aduarte, *Historia de la Provincia del Santo Rosario de Filipinas* (1693), translation in Blair and Robertson, *op. cit.*, Vol. XXXI, p. 27.

[67] Juan de Medina, *Historia de la Orden de S. Augustin de Estas Islas Filipinas* (written 1630), translation in Blair and Robertson, *op. cit.*, Vol. XXIII, p. 269.

[68] Tomás Ortiz, *Práctica del Ministereo*, translation in Blair and Robertson, *op. cit.*, Vol. XLIII, pp. 103 ff.

give instruction and of whom most of the baptized remained really pagan.[69] This need not surprise us. In the course of our narrative we have again and again witnessed similar phenomena, particularly in areas where entire groups as groups accepted the faith. Nor need we be astonished to learn that some of the features of Spanish Roman Catholicism which seem to many a superstitious excrescence on Christianity appeared in the Philippines. Thus a cross with relics was raised in a field as a protection against a pest of locusts.[70] An image of the infant Jesus, perhaps left by Magellan, had been sacrificed to by the pagan Filipinos. Later the clergy found it, gave it high honour, and many miracles, especially on behalf of women in child-birth, were said to have been wrought through it.[71] In Manila the Jesuits introduced a "procession of blood" in which during Lent the faithful indulged in gory self-flagellation.[72] A priesthood trained in the Spanish tradition quite naturally permitted or encouraged such practices. The fact remains that whatever may have been its features, due to the labours of Spanish missionaries supported by the Spanish civil authorities, long before A.D. 1800 Christianity became the dominant faith in the Philippine Islands. Only in the mountains did overt paganism survive and only in the South did substantial Moslem communities hold out against the Cross.

A second effect of Christianity in the Philippines was akin to what we have found in the Americas—the mitigation of the harshness of conquest and the endeavour to make the coming of the Occidental a blessing to the Filipinos and not a curse. In the Philippines the task of those who sought to protect the native peoples against heartless exploitation was not so difficult as in many sections of Latin America. White colonists demanding native labour for mines and plantations were much less prominent than in Spanish or Portuguese America. The advocates of the Filipinos, therefore, had a much less rocky path than did a Las Casas. To be sure, force was employed in the conquest of the Philippines, and to its use at least some of the missionaries gave not only consent but active endorsement.[73] From practically the very beginning of the conquest, however, clergy, moved by what they believed to be a Christian motive, came forward in behalf of the Filipinos. In 1573 we hear that Diego de Herrara, an Augustinian, had gone to Spain to lodge complaints against the extortions of soldiers from the Filipinos.[74] In 1574 Martin de Rada, the leader

[69] Vincente de Salazar, *Historia de el Santissimo Rosario* (Manila, 1742), translation in Blair and Robertson, *op. cit.,* Vol. XLIII, pp. 40 ff.

[70] Chirino, *Relacion de las Islas Filipinas,* translation in Blair and Robertson, *op. cit.,* Vol. XIII, p. 36.

[71] Chirino, *op. cit.,* translation in Blair and Robertson, *op. cit.,* Vol. XII, p. 180.

[72] Chirino, *op. cit.,* translation in Blair and Robertson, *op. cit.,* Vol. XIII, p. 45.

[73] Blair and Robertson, *op. cit.,* Vol. VIII, p. 199.

[74] Blair and Robertson, *op. cit.,* Vol. III, p. 209.

of the Augustinians in the islands, declared that he and his colleagues regarded the conquest as unjust, denounced acts of oppression, and declared that the tribute exacted was three times what it should be.[75] The first Bishop and Archbishop of Manila, Domingo de Salazar, was notable as a champion of the Filipinos. For nearly a generation he had been a missionary in Mexico and there had been known as an advocate of the Indians against white oppression.[76] In 1573 the King had forbidden the enslavement of the Filipinos and had ordered slaves freed.[77] No sooner had Salazar landed in the islands than he called a council of the leading men in the various orders to support him in the publication of the royal ban on slavery.[78] From the Philippines, as soon as he had had time to become acquainted with conditions, he wrote to the King insisting that missionaries should go about their work without the support of a military escort and imploring redress for the Filipinos for the wrongs suffered at the hands of Spanish officials.[79] The royal decree ordered the establishment of an *audiencia* in Manila as a superior court and assigned to the new body among other duties the task of seeing that the Filipinos were well treated and that crimes against them were punished.[80] In 1591 Pope Gregory XIV ordered that all Filipino slaves be emancipated and that restitution be made for losses caused to the Filipinos in the conquest of the islands.[81] In 1620 a Franciscan memorialized the King, telling of acts of cruelty suffered by the Filipinos and asking that the forced service and tribute exacted of the latter for shipbuilding and public works be abolished.[82]

Missionaries strove to improve the morals of their Filipino charges. They fought drunkenness.[83] They sought, not without success, to curb usury.[84] They introduced the Christian family and raised the status of women.[85]

Missionaries did much for the improvement of agriculture. They instructed the Filipinos in irrigation and in methods of tillage and brought in cattle and plows.[86] They introduced better rice culture, brought in cacao and Indian corn

[75] Blair and Robertson, *op. cit.,* Vol. III, pp. 253 ff.
[76] Aduarte, *Historia de la Provincia del Santo Rosario de Filipinas,* translation in Blair and Robertson, *op. cit.,* Vol. XXXI, pp. 39 ff.
[77] Montalbán, *Das Spanische Patronat und die Eroberung der Philippinen,* pp. 75-82.
[78] Blair and Robertson, *op. cit.,* Vol. XXXIV, pp. 325-331.
[79] Blair and Robertson, *op. cit.,* Vol. V, pp. 9, 188 ff., 210 ff.
[80] Blair and Robertson, *op. cit.,* Vol. V, pp. 274 ff.
[81] Blair and Robertson, *op. cit.,* Vol. VIII, pp. 70 ff.
[82] Blair and Robertson, *op. cit.,* Vol. XIX, pp. 71 ff.
[83] Chirino, *op. cit.,* translation in Blair and Robertson, *op. cit.,* Vol. XIII, pp. 37 ff.
[84] Chirino, *op. cit.,* translation in Blair and Robertson, *op. cit.,* Vol. XIII, pp. 56 ff.
[85] Bourne, in Blair and Robertson, *op. cit.,* Vol. I, p. 85.
[86] Antonio Mozo, *Noticia Histórica Natural* (Madrid, 1763), translation in Blair and Robertson, *op. cit.,* Vol. XLVIII, pp. 59 ff.

from America, and developed the growth of indigo, coffee, and sugar cane.[87]

The clergy cultivated the love of music and introduced new songs. Thus some of the earliest Dominicans, noticing that the Filipinos were fond of singing, composed for them, in their own tongue and in their own style of music, songs on Christian themes and taught these to them.[88]

To the Christian impulse was due the founding of hospitals and provision for the organized care of the unfortunate. We hear of endowments for hospitals maintained by the religious orders and of a brotherhood of Santa Misericordia.[89]

The Philippines owed to the Church and so to Christianity most of such literature and formal education as was theirs. The missionaries early began preparing religious pamphlets and books in the vernaculars and introduced printing presses for their dissemination.[90] Schools were founded and conducted. In some of these Spanish was taught,[91] although familiarity with that language did not become widespread. The schools were the work of the clergy, usually of the orders. Thus the Jesuits inaugurated a number of secondary schools.[92] The first university in the islands, that of San Ignacio, was developed by them.[93] The Dominicans had charge of the University of Santo Tomás, initiated through the bequest of an Archbishop of Manila who was a member of that order.[94] Between 1645 and 1735 that university enrolled 12,265 students in philosophy and 2,050 in theology.[95] The Dominicans also had schools for orphans and for girls.[96] Literacy was probably as widely spread as in the rural districts of Europe of the day.[97]

Missionaries, too, prepared an extensive literature on the islands-chronicles, and on geography, geology, ethnology, languages, plants, and animals.[98]

As in Spanish America, the policy both of state and of Church was paternalistic. The Filipinos were kept under the control of Europeans and strict

[87] Bourne, in Blair and Robertson, *op. cit.*, Vol. I, p. 42.

[88] Aduarte, *op. cit.*, in Blair and Robertson, *op. cit.*, Vol. XXXII, pp. 51 ff.

[89] Juan Baptista de Uriarte, *Manifiesta y Resumen Historico de la Fundación de la Venerable Hermandad de la Santa Misericordia* (Manila, 1728), translation in Blair and Robertson, *op. cit.*, Vol. XLVII, pp. 23 ff.

[90] Berg, *Die katholische Heidenmission als Kulturträger*, Vol. II, p. 76; *Los Dominicos en el Extremo Oriente*, p. 282; Alzona, *A History of Education in the Philippines*, pp. 32-40.

[91] Alzona, *op. cit.*, pp. 18-22.

[92] Alzona, *op. cit.*, pp. 24-28.

[93] Alzona, *op. cit.*, pp. 28-31.

[94] *Los Dominicos en el Extremo Oriente*, pp. 56-66; Blair and Robertson, *op. cit.*, Vol. XVII, pp. 155 ff., Vol. XXXVII, p. 11.

[95] *Los Dominicos en el Extremo Oriente*, p. 272.

[96] *Los Dominicos en el Extremo Oriente*, pp. 77-103.

[97] Bourne, in Blair and Robertson, *op. cit.*, Vol. I, p. 80.

[98] Berg, *op. cit.*, Vol. II, p. 303.

supervision was exercised from Spain. Civilization remained relatively static and learning and thought were stagnant. Objections were raised by some of the missionaries on the ground of the inherent weaknesses of the race to raising the Filipinos to the priesthood[99]—an instance of the sense of benevolent superiority which Europeans continued to cherish towards non-Europeans down into the twentieth century. However, a Filipino clergy was gradually developed,[100] and while as a rule these priests were kept subordinate to the Spaniards, by A.D. 1800 mestizos and even full-blooded Filipinos had been elevated to the episcopate.[101]

The Philippines were probably happier than were any other of the European possessions in Asia before the nineteenth century.[102] Probably, too, the Filipinos were more care-free than were any others of the peoples of the Far East between A.D. 1600 and A.D. 1800. The rank and file of the Filipinos seem to have fared as well as did the peasantry of the period in most countries in Western Europe. Under the Spanish regime the population increased substantially—in itself an evidence of security and prosperity.[103]

To this relative well-being several factors contributed. The close restriction of foreign commerce by the Spanish mercantile system kept the islands comparatively isolated. Spain bore the burden of defence and so forestalled the fear of foreign aggression. The government, while paternalistic and often corrupt, was usually mild.

Yet much of the relatively fortunate lot of the Filipinos must be ascribed to the Christian impulse which worked against oppression by the whites and which sent forth the missionaries who raised the level of civilization and were the chief agents of the benevolent Spanish rule. If, as seems to have been the case, the Filipinos were happier under Spanish rule than were the rank and file of the Indians in the Americas, it was because the missionary and the Christian purpose were more prominent.

Whether the benevolent paternalism which characterized the policy of both state and Church was ultimately good for the Filipinos the centuries before A.D. 1800 did not tell. It was to be left to events of the twentieth century to supply data for an answer to this question.

The Christianity which became the prevailing faith of the islands displayed, as we have suggested, the effects of its environment. It gave evidence of the

---

[99] Gaspar de San Agustin, writing in 1720, translation in Blair and Robertson, *op. cit.,* Vol. XL, pp. 273 ff.

[100] Alzona, *op. cit.,* pp. 146-152; Huonder, *Der einheimische Klerus in den Heidenländern,* pp. 47, 48.

[101] Huonder, *op. cit.,* pp. 264-266.

[102] Bourne, in Blair and Robertson, *op. cit.,* Vol. I, pp. 70-76.

[103] Bourne, in Blair and Robertson, *op. cit.,* Vol. I, p. 86.

Spanish vehicle by which it had arrived. In it the pre-Christian beliefs and customs were slow to die. Occasionally a Filipino attempted to effect a deliberate combination of the ancestral faith with the imported religion. Thus in the seventeenth century a Filipino announced that the spirits of the first ancestors of his nation in the islands had commissioned him. He called himself the Eternal Father, named one of his associates the Son, dubbed another the Holy Ghost, and denominated a woman the Virgin Mary. He appointed apostles, popes, and bishops. The cult gave rise to an insurrection which the Spaniards found it necessary to suppress.[104] Moreover, the Christianity of the Filipinos was passive. So far as the faith spread from the Philippines to other parts of the Far East and even in the islands themselves, it was carried chiefly by Spanish priests and not by the Filipinos. Yet the Christianity of the Philippines was in the historic stream which arose in Galilee and Judea. It wrought marked changes in the islands and had sufficient vitality to survive and to retain the allegiance of the large majority of the population.

[104] Diaz, *Conquistas,* translation in Blair and Robertson, *op. cit.,* Vol. XXXVIII, pp. 217 ff.

Chapter XIII

JAPAN

IF CHRISTIANITY was more successful in the Philippine Islands in winning the formal allegiance of the population than in any other land of the Far East, in Japan during these centuries its course was more meteoric and more marked by the blood of martyrs than in any other region in Southern or Eastern Asia.

The clue to the situation is to be found largely in conditions in Japan. In the sixteenth century, at the very time when Portuguese commerce was first reaching the Far East and when Christian missionaries, coming in their train, were first knocking at the doors of the Land of the Rising Sun, several factors were preparing the Japanese to be singularly receptive to Christianity. The Ashikaga shogunate was drawing to its close, and in the debility which marked its concluding years the central administration was less able, even if it had been so inclined, to keep out foreign ideas than it had long been. In the turbulence and civil wars of the times, old patterns of life were being weakened and were, accordingly, less resistant to innovations than for many years previously. Japanese were venturing overseas as never before and the land was more susceptible to fresh impressions than it had been for centuries. To many, Buddhism, which had been the dominant religion, was proving unsatisfactory, and the way was open for the entrance of a new faith.[1] From the fifteen sixties until his death, in 1582, the leading political and military figure was Oda Nobunaga. Nobunaga had bitter enemies in the warrior Buddhist monks who had been prominent in the state. He fought against them and subdued them. He was inclined to welcome as possible counterweights to the Buddhist priests the Christian missionaries who were arriving, and his defeat of the Buddhists weakened the latter in their resistance to Christianity. Moreover, the *daimyo*, or feudal lords, in Kyushu, the island where were the chief marts of the Portuguese trade, were eager for the leading share in the lucrative foreign commerce. They were, accordingly, inclined to favour the missionaries in the hope of attracting the merchants who outwardly paid reverence to these representatives of the Church. The peculiarly auspicious conditions in Japan

---

[1] Anesaki, *A Concordance to the History of Kirishitan Missions*, pp. 1, 2.

coincided with the flood tide of Portuguese and Spanish colonizing, commercial, and missionary activity. Then it must be remembered that the Japanese had for centuries been learning from the Chinese. Most of their civilization was an adaptation and outgrowth of what they had received from China. Having been accustomed to tuition from one alien nation, it is not strange that they should be willing to listen to what others had to teach. The result of this combination of factors was a phenomenal growth of Christianity in the second half of the sixteenth century.

However, because of other conditions, partly outside and partly inside Japan, almost inevitably this rapid spread of Christianity was followed by a spectacular decline. In nearly every land into which it expanded between A.D. 1500 and A.D. 1800, Christianity was closely associated with political conquests by European powers. The Japanese became aware of this fact. Then, as now, they were highly patriotic and proud of their independence and military prowess. They fiercely resented any activity which might be an opening wedge for aggression from without. Moreover, Christianity made for internal dissension and weakness. The missionaries were intolerant of Buddhism. When attempts were put forth to restrict them or to keep them out of the country they defied the laws of the land. In this they were abetted by their Japanese adherents. To obtain security, they threw their weight with a particular leader or party. The main effort of the outstanding political figures of the time was the unification of Japan. Nobunaga had favoured the missionaries because he had believed that they would help him in this task. His successors, Toyotomi Hideyoshi and Tokugawa Iyeyasu, in time felt Christianity to be a threat to this, their cherished objective, and took steps against it. The heirs of Iyeyasu, bent upon completing the consolidation of the rule of their family, the Tokugawa, adopted even more vigorous anti-Christian measures. As a consequence, in a series of bloody persecutions, Christianity was all but stamped out.

It was apparently in 1542 (the date is somewhat uncertain) that the Portuguese first landed in Japan.[2] Less than a decade later, in 1549, active Christian missionary effort was begun there. Fittingly, the leader of the initial band of missionaries was the pioneer Jesuit in the Far East, Francis Xavier. While in Malacca, on the way back from the Moluccas, Xavier heard of Japan. At Malacca, too, he found a Japanese, Yajiro or Anjiro,[3] who in Japan had sought refuge on a Portuguese ship to escape punishment for murder. From the Portuguese Yajiro had learned of Christianity and of Xavier. Eventually he was sent

[2] See a long discussion of the first Portuguese landing in Haas, *Geschichte des Christentums in Japan*, Vol. I, pp. 20 ff.
[3] On the name, see Haas, *op. cit.*, Vol. I, p. 57, who conjectures the Japanese form to have been Hachiro. See also Brou, *Saint François Xavier*, Vol. I, p. 429.

to the College of St. Paul at Goa, and then was baptized. Two other Japanese were also baptized, Yajiro's servant and another who had been sent by Xavier to Goa. Xavier, with the imagination which ranged far and was quick to seize strategic opportunities, saw in the opening Portuguese commerce with Japan and in Yajiro a challenge to introduce Christianity into virgin territory. The Portuguese ships would provide the transportation and Yajiro would be at once interpreter and guide. After a visit of several months to India, Xavier set out for Japan. He was accompanied by the three Japanese and by three fellow Jesuits. The first landing was effected at Kagoshima, the home of Yajiro. The local *daimyo* received the group in friendly fashion. The first converts were from among the family of Yajiro and others followed. Xavier pressed on to the capital of the country, Kyoto, but did not have a long stay there. At Yamaguchi, where a less hurried halt was made, a number of converts were won. Xavier went on to Bungo, a daimyate on the east coast of Kyushu. Here the *daimyo*, Otomo Yoshishige, was very cordial, possibly because he hoped thus to encourage the profitable Portuguese trade. From Bungo Xavier left for Malacca and India (November 20, 1551). He had accomplished his purpose. He had planted Christianity in Japan and had left behind him colleagues to carry on what he had begun.[4]

For nearly a generation after Xavier, Christianity in Japan enjoyed marked prosperity and rapid growth. As we have suggested, Japanese culture was at its lowest ebb. Many were led by a genuine religious hunger to accept this newly arrived faith. They were distressed by the morals of many of the Buddhist monks, by the divisions between the various schools of Buddhism, and in contrast with the vague idealism of the dominant Buddhist school, Zen, were eager for convincing and tangible evidences of salvation and were impressed by the note of authority in Christianity.[5] Naturally, the earliest strongholds of Christianity were in the South. The first main centres were in the cities of Yamaguchi and Hirado and in the daimyate of Bungo.[6] From about 1560, the faith began to make important gains in the central provinces, especially in Miyako (Kyoto).[7] There several of the higher classes were converted, including members of the Takayama family. One of these, Justus Takayama Ukon, became a striking example of a combination of a Japanese warrior and an ardent Roman Catholic. When Nobunaga in 1568 entered Kyoto, he showed marked favour to Chris-

---

[4] On Xavier in Japan, see Brou, *op. cit.*, Vol. II, pp. 88-240; Haas, *op. cit.*, Vol. I, pp. 67-236.

[5] Anesaki, *History of Japanese Religion*, p. 242; Anesaki, in *Harvard Journal of Asiatic Studies*, Vol. I, pp. 13-27.

[6] Cary, *A History of Christianity in Japan*, Vol. I, pp. 52 ff.

[7] Haas, *op. cit.*, Vol. II, pp. 113 ff.

tians and the Church (and that in spite of the fact that the Emperor, at the instance of Buddhist monks of the Tendai School, had proscribed Christianity).[8] The strongest centre of Christianity became Nagasaki and its environs. The *daimyo* of Omura, Omura Sumitada, who had been baptized in 1562 or 1563, a few years later entrusted this port to the Jesuits. Nagasaki grew rapidly in importance as an *entrepôt* for foreign trade and here, although the civil administration was not long allowed to remain in their hands, the Jesuits had their headquarters.[9] Sumitada may originally have been moved primarily by a desire to attract Portuguese commerce, but he seems to have become enthusiastically zealous for his new faith and to have persevered in it to his death.[10] Christianity also found prosperous entrance into the Goto Islands, off the west coast of Kyushu, and into Arima, not far from Nagasaki.[11] The *Daimyo* of Satsuma, for a time after his first experience with the missionaries less friendly to the new faith, fearing the loss of the lucrative foreign trade to rivals more cordial to Christianity, wrote to the Portuguese Viceroy of the Indies, assuring him of a welcome to missionaries.[12] About 1571 one of the missionaries estimated the number of Christians in Japan as thirty thousand.[13] By the time of the death of the friendly Nobunaga, in 1582, churches were said to number about two hundred and converts about 150,000. This latter is estimated to have been about one per cent of the population of Japan, or a larger proportion than Christians form at the present time.[14] In 1582 Christian *daimyo* sent an embassy to the Pope. It was away several years and was received in Europe with great acclaim.[15]

The number of missionaries who achieved this remarkable spread of Christianity was not large. In 1563 they did not exceed nine.[16] In 1582 the priests were variously said to total twenty-two or twenty-eight, with twenty-five other foreigners in the missionary body.[17] Steps had been taken to raise up a Japanese clergy. In 1580 in two places were the beginnings of seminaries, with pupils

---

[8] Anesaki, *History of Japanese Religion*, pp. 243, 244; Haas, *op. cit.*, Vol. II, pp. 176 ff.; G. B. Sansom, *Japan. A Short Cultural History* (New York, D. Appleton-Century Co., 1936, pp. xvi, 537), p. 409.

[9] Paske-Smith, *Western Barbarians in Japan and Formosa in Tokugawa Days*, p. 285; Steichen, *The Christian Daimyos*, pp. 18-20.

[10] Haas, *op. cit.*, Vol. II, pp. 233-236.

[11] Haas, *op. cit.*, Vol. II, pp. 246 ff.

[12] Haas, *op. cit.*, Vol. II, pp. 194 ff.

[13] Pastor, *History of the Popes*, Vol. XX, p. 449.

[14] Anesaki, *History of Japanese Religion*, p. 243; Delplace, *Le Catholicisme au Japon*, Vol. I, p. 209.

[15] Steichen, *op. cit.*, pp. 112 ff.

[16] Haas, *op. cit.*, Vol. II, p. 274.

[17] Delplace, *op. cit.*, Vol. I, pp. 198, 209.

largely from the upper classes.[18] However, these had not yet yielded substantial results, and in 1582 only twenty-one Japanese brothers, catechists, and novices were included on the Church's staff.[19]

The rise of Hideyoshi to power in place of the dead Nobunaga did not at first bring any reverse to the fortunes of Christianity. Hideyoshi seemed to be friendly. In 1583 the commander of his fleet became a Christian. Another convert was the personal physician of Hideyoshi. Other Christians held high office and some of the Christian *daimyo* were shown marked favour.[20]

Eventually, however, the transition to Hideyoshi brought a change of atmosphere and official attitude which worked adversely for Christianity. Hideyoshi gave the country political unity and a strong rule. With unity and internal peace after the long and disheartening civil disorder came a new current of confidence and a revival of national pride. The native Shinto became stronger and in Hideyoshi found an object of hero-worship. Zen monasteries became centres of an awakened zeal for learning. This national revival and this quickening in the non-Christian faiths were both directed in part against the foreign religion.[21] Hideyoshi became hostile, just why is not clear, but possibly out of caprice and a desire for an apotheosis which the missionaries could not grant.[22] It may be, too, that he wished to have no one in the realm whom he could not control.[23] In 1587 Hideyoshi came out with an edict against Christianity. It declared that Japan was the land of the gods and so could not tolerate a religion which denounced its national deities as false. Missionaries were ordered to leave the country within twenty days and the Portuguese merchants were forbidden to bring more.[24]

In spite of the hostility of Hideyoshi and the rising tide of nationalist feeling against the foreign faith, Christianity continued to grow. Persecution was not new. While adverse action by the central authority was a novelty, locally violent opposition had been encountered again and again. For the time Hideyoshi was not disposed to follow up his edict with vigorous measures. Missionaries were given six months in which to leave the country and even at the expiration of that time the majority remained on, although in hiding, presumably with his knowledge.[25] A nephew of Hideyoshi's wife became a Christian.[26] In one of

[18] Delplace, *op. cit.*, Vol. I, pp. 194, 195; Alfors Kleiser, in *Monumenta Nipponica*, Vol. I, No. 1, p. 72.

[19] Delplace, *op. cit.*, Vol. I, p. 198.

[20] Cary, *A History of Christianity in Japan*, Vol. I, pp. 98-100.

[21] Anesaki, in *Journal of Asiatic Studies*, Vol. I, pp. 13-27.

[22] *Ibid.*

[23] Cary, *op. cit.*, Vol. I, pp. 103-105.

[24] Anesaki in *Transactions of the Royal Asiatic Society of Japan*, 2d Series, Vol. VII, pp. 1-15. See translation of the edict in Cary, *op. cit.*, Vol. I, p. 106.

[25] Cary, *op. cit.*, Vol. I, pp. 106-118.

[26] Cary, *op. cit.*, Vol. I, p. 107.

the two chief divisions of the Japanese armies which Hideyoshi sent to conquer Korea the commanding officer and many of the soldiers were Christians. In this division new converts were won by a missionary and his Japanese assistant.[27] The *Daimyo* of Arima ordered the populace of three cities which had recently come into his possession to become Christian and two thousand are said to have complied.[28] For years Japan had theoretically been in the see of Macao, but the bishop of that diocese had never visited the country. In 1588 a bishopric for Japan was created and placed under the Portuguese padroado.[29] The initial appointee died on the voyage out and it was not until 1596 that a bishop actually reached the country. He was received by the Christians openly and with great pomp.[30]

Although in 1585 Rome had specifically reserved Japan to the Jesuits and had forbidden members of any other order to perform any ecclesiastical function there without express permission from the Pope, both Dominicans and Franciscans succeeded in effecting an entrance. Spanish friars, who regarded the recently occupied Philippines as a vantage point for the missionary occupation of the Far East, were thrilled by the news of Jesuit successes in Japan and longed to share in the harvest of souls. In 1592 a Dominican arrived on a Spanish diplomatic errand and ten years later an active Dominican mission was established in the South.[31] Even before 1592, in 1584, a Franciscan had reached Japan from Macao.[32] In 1593 a group of Franciscans left the Philippines for Japan. They pled exemption from the Papal monopoly granted the Jesuits on the ground that they were coming as diplomatic representatives and that a later Papal brief had annulled, so far as the Brothers Minor were concerned, the earlier restriction in favour of the Jesuits.[33] They began active mission work in Kyoto. At first Hideyoshi appeared well disposed towards them. One of the Franciscans, indeed, reported to the Pope that Hideyoshi had given them permission to dwell anywhere in Japan, to preach, and publicly to say mass. Franciscan centres were opened at Nagasaki and Osaka. The Jesuits were annoyed by what they deemed an intrusion on their preserves. The friction was intensified by the fact that the Jesuits came out under Portuguese auspices and the Brothers Minor were mostly Spaniards. The Franciscans, too, employed methods which to the Jesuits, experienced in Japan, seemed unwise. It is not surprising that the

[27] Cary, *op. cit.*, Vol. I, p. 115.
[28] Cary, *op. cit.*, Vol. I, p. 108.
[29] Jann, *Die katholischen Missionen in Indien, China, und Japan*, pp. 125-129.
[30] Cary, *op. cit.*, Vol. I, p. 122.
[31] *Los Dominicos en el Extremo Oriente*, p. 164; Henri Bernard, in *Monumenta Nipponica*, Vol. I, No. 1, pp. 122 ff.
[32] Lemmens, *Geschichte des Franziskanermissionen*, pp. 155-173.
[33] *Ibid;* Bernard, in *Monumenta Nipponica*, Vol. I, No. 1, pp. 122 ff.

Bishop, a Portuguese Jesuit, attempted to induce them to leave the country and forbade the faithful to hear mass or preaching by the obnoxious poachers.[34] Late in 1596 Hideyoshi followed up his anti-Christian decree, now nearly a decade old, with active persecution. The cause of this sudden accession of activity is partly conjectural. Some were inclined to find it in the indiscreet public activity of the Franciscans.[35] Enemies of the Society of Jesus represented it to the Pope as fear of the excessive power of the Jesuits.[36] The more usual explanation is that when a Spanish galleon on its way from Mexico to Manila was forced by a storm onto the shores of Japan and the local *daimyo* declared that by the law of the land the cargo was confiscated, the pilot, in a vain effort to intimidate the Japanese, pointed out on a map the vast domains of the King of Spain and declared that in effecting conquests he first sent missionaries who, by weaning away the inhabitants from their old religious allegiance, prepared the way for annexation.[37] Whether this incredibly tactless remark was made in the bald form in which it has come down to us we do not know. Even if it were uttered in somewhat more guarded language, it might well have been a sufficient irritant to inflame the temper of the autocratic and belligerent Hideyoshi. Being himself engaged in a foreign expedition aimed at the conquest of China, he was in no mood to tolerate even a fancied insult to the dignity and integrity of Japan. It is said, too, that the refusal of the Philippines to acknowledge him as suzerain had aroused Hideyoshi to wrath. Soon twenty-six Christians, Spanish Franciscans and Japanese, among the latter some attached to the Society of Jesus, were arrested, taken to Nagasaki, and executed by crucifixion. *Daimyo* were forbidden to become Christians, and missionaries were ordered assembled at Nagasaki preparatory to deportation. Most of the missionaries succeeded in remaining in the country, but several scores of churches were destroyed and in some places Japanese Christians were persecuted.[38] Fortunately for the Christians, Hideyoshi died in September, 1598, and in the transition to a new regime the persecution lagged.[39]

For a time after the death of Hideyoshi persecution was relaxed and Christianity flourished as it had at no previous time. Hideyoshi had attempted to transmit his authority to his son, Hideyori, who was a mere lad when his father died. In fact, however, power rapidly passed into the hands of Iyeyasu. Iyeyasu

---

[34] Lemmens, *op. cit.*, pp. 155-173.

[35] *Ibid.*

[36] Charlevoix, *Histoire du Christianisme au Japon*, Vol. II, p. 25.

[37] Charlevoix, *op. cit.*, Vol. II, pp. 19 ff.; Delplace, *Le Catholicisme au Japon*, Vol. II, pp. 29 ff.

[38] Cary, *A History of Christianity in Japan*, Vol. I, pp. 125-131; Charlevoix, *op. cit.*, pp. 41 ff.; Delplace, *op. cit.*, Vol. II, pp. 31 ff.

[39] Cary, *op. cit.*, Vol. I, p. 131.

succeeded where Nobunaga and Hideyoshi had failed and placed his family, the Tokugawa, so firmly in control of the country that, seated in the shogunate, the office which in theory derived its position from the fountain of authority, the sacrosanct Emperor, but by which the land was actually ruled, it governed Japan until 1867.

Iyeyasu at first favoured foreign trade and Christianity[40] and in the opening years of the seventeenth century Christianity reached its zenith in Japan. In 1600 there were said to be one hundred and nine Jesuits in the country, of whom fourteen had arrived that year. The Jesuits are reported to have rebuilt fifty churches and to have baptized fifty thousand in the year.[41] In 1603 the Bishop wrote that in less than two years they had baptized seventy thousand.[42] In 1606 and 1607 the annual letters of the Jesuits reported the baptism of fifteen thousand adults. The population of Nagasaki was said to be predominantly Christian. It contained churches not only of the Jesuits but also of the Augustinians, the Franciscans, and the Dominicans.[43] The position of these orders had received Papal sanction when in 1600 Clement VIII opened Japan, China, and the islands of the Far East to members of the mendicant orders on the condition that the passage out be by way of Portugal and Goa.[44] In 1608 this latter restriction was removed, and missionaries were permitted to go by any route.[45] However, it must be noted that rivalries between the orders continued, and that the division extended to the Japanese Christians.[46] Most of the non-Jesuit missionaries came by way of the Philippines. From time to time Iyeyasu showed favour to the missionaries. He gave them financial assistance.[47] He received the Bishop with marked honour.[48] Churches were built in his capital, Yedo, the later Tokyo.[49] He was inclined to allow the various *daimyo* to deal with the Christians in their own domains as they liked.[50] Some *daimyo* were very friendly. Even in the north of Japan, in Sendai, Christianity was gaining a footing. Through an enterprising Franciscan, Sotelo, and the *Daimyo* of Sendai, efforts were made to open direct trade with Mexico and an embassy was sent to Mexico and Europe several of whose members were baptized.[51]

[40] Cary, *op. cit.*, Vol. I, pp. 135, 136.
[41] Pagés, *Histoire de la Religion Chrétienne au Japon depuis 1598 jusqu'a 1651*, Vol. I, p. 16.
[42] Translation in Pagés, *op. cit.*, Vol. II, p. 43.
[43] Delplace, *op. cit.*, Vol. II, p. 64.
[44] Text in Pagés, *op. cit.*, Vol. II, pp. 3-7.
[45] Text in Pagés, *op. cit.*, Vol. II, pp. 82-85.
[46] Cary, *op. cit.*, Vol. I, p. 146.
[47] Cary, *op. cit.*, Vol. I, p. 150.
[48] Cary, *op. cit.*, Vol. I, p. 155.
[49] Cary, *op. cit.*, Vol. I, pp. 136, 145.
[50] Cary, *op. cit.*, Vol. I, p. 161.
[51] Cary, *op. cit.*, Vol. I, pp. 167 ff.; Civezza, *Storia delle Missioni Francescane*, Vol. VII, Part 2, appendix.

How many Christians Japan contained at the maximum strength of the Church there we do not know. The Bishop placed those in 1603 actually ministered to by missionaries at two hundred thousand.[52] He said that in 1600, before certain civil wars, it had been about three hundred thousand.[53] Another estimate says that in 1605 the total was seven hundred and fifty thousand.[54] Amid such variations it is difficult to arrive at even approximate accuracy.

To reinforce the Church a fairly elaborate structure of schools was developed. As a substitute for the education provided by Buddhist temples or to give education where none existed, elementary schools were conducted. Higher schools were provided to train catechists and interpreters. There were normal schools for teachers and seminaries for the preparation of a secular clergy.[55] In Manila a seminary was founded to train Japanese for holy orders.[56]

Western medicine was introduced.[57] A Christian literature in Japanese was prepared.[58]

Financial support came from a variety of sources—partly from the Portuguese and Spanish governments, partly from grants by the Pope, partly from private gifts by Europeans, merchants and others, and partly from the Japanese themselves.[59]

This prosperity of the Church always rested, so far as Japan was concerned, upon shaky foundations. The anti-Christian edicts of Hideyoshi seem not to have been repealed.[60] Here and there *daimyo* instituted persecutions within their possessions.[61]

In 1612 began persecutions engineered by the Tokugawa themselves which eventually expelled the missionaries, closed the country to all trade with Roman Catholic lands, enforced a strict censorship of the importation of Chinese books by which translations of Christian works in Chinese might enter the country, instituted and continued the death penalty for all who held to their Christian faith, with tests to ensure that none should become Christians, placarded the land with anti-Christian edict-boards, and drove Christianity underground. In no other country in these centuries were such thoroughgoing and persistent efforts made to stamp out the Christian faith.

The reasons for Iyeyasu's change of policy were several. Only gradually

[52] Translation in Pagés, *op. cit.*, Vol. II, p. 51.
[53] Translation in Pagés, *op. cit.*, Vol. II, p. 50.
[54] Pagés, *op. cit.*, Vol. I, p. 10.
[55] Schilling, *Das Schulwesen der Jesuiten in Japan (1551-1614)*, pp. 4, 29-39.
[56] Blair and Robertson, *The Philippine Islands*, Vol. XXI, pp. 84 ff.
[57] Schilling, *op. cit.*, pp. 40-68.
[58] Schmidlin-Braun, *Catholic Mission History*, p. 345.
[59] Schilling, *op. cit.*, pp. 13-28.
[60] Cary, *A History of Christianity in Japan*, Vol. I, pp. 149, 155.
[61] Cary, *op. cit.*, Vol. I, pp. 143 ff., 150 ff.

did he become inexorable, and his successors in the shogunate were progressively more severely anti-Christian. Iyeyasu resented, as a possible threat to Japanese sovereignty, the fact that Spaniards made soundings along the coast of Japan. The sharp practices of two outstanding Christians won his dislike.[62] He was alarmed by the unwillingness of Christians to give up their faith at the command of their feudal superiors and by the veneration which Christians showed for their fellows who, as a punishment for their obstinacy in refusing to obey the law and apostatize, had suffered martyrdom.[63] Will Adams, an Englishman and a Protestant, who had found favour with Iyeyasu, reflected the attitude of many of the English of the time and had little good to say of the Spanish and Portuguese "Papists."[64] Some Christians had been prominent in uprisings against Iyeyasu and some, too, had backed Hideyori in his resistance to the Tokugawa.[65] Iyeyasu had grown to manhood in a period of internal anarchy and rebellion and had as his chief object the unity of the land under the sway of his family. Christianity probably seemed to him abhorrent chiefly because it appeared to him to threaten that order which had been won with such difficulty. It was conceivable that the missionaries and the Japanese Christians might back an opponent of Iyeyasu and be a determining factor in the substitution of some other family for the Tokugawa in the seat of the shogun. It is significant that in the decree which Iyeyasu issued against Christianity in 1614 he declared that Christians "have come to Japan . . . longing to disseminate an evil law, to overthrow right doctrine, so that they may change the government of the country and obtain possession of the land. This is the germ of great disaster and must be crushed."[66]

The same political motive animated the successors of Iyeyasu. They felt themselves driven to more and more severe measures by the contumacy of missionaries and Japanese Christians. In direct violation of the laws missionaries either attempted to remain in Japan or persisted in striving to obtain entrance. While many Christians apostatized at the behest of their rulers, hundreds went to their death rather than deny their faith. To the alarmed Tokugawa shoguns here seemed to be a major threat to the integrity of the land. First Iyeyasu's immediate successor, Hidetada, and then the succeeding shogun, Iyemitsu, adopted stern measures. Iyemitsu, who, to complete the extirpation of Christianity, eventually all but closed the doors of Japan against European trade, was conceited, sensitive, and temperamental, and was irritated beyond endurance

---

[62] Cary, *op. cit.*, Vol. I, p. 164.
[63] Cary, *op. cit.*, Vol. I, pp. 174, 175.
[64] Cary, *op. cit.*, Vol. I, p. 142.
[65] Cary, *op. cit.*, Vol. I. pp. 137, 138, 185.
[66] See translation in *Transactions of the Asiatic Society of Japan*, Vol. VI, pp. 46 ff.

by the persistence of Christians, by this time mostly common folk and *ronin* (warriors who had renounced their allegiance to their lawful lords), in holding to their faith against his clearly expressed will.[67]

Here is neither space or need for going into the tragic story of the long persecution.[68] Room exists for only the briefest summary. Iyeyasu commanded the *daimyo* to send all the missionaries to Nagasaki for deportation, to destroy all churches, and to compel Christians to give up their religion. Every one in the Empire was required to have a certificate of membership in some form of Buddhism through adherence to a Buddhist temple. Following the decree of 1614 some missionaries were deported, but several remained on in hiding and others returned disguised as merchants, slaves, and sailors. New missionaries seeking to enter Japan from the Philippines went clothed as merchants and several days before they sailed would go about Manila in that garb so that the Japanese there might come to think of them as engaged in commerce.[69] Many Japanese Christians were exiled to the Philippines or sought refuge in Indo-China. Under Hidetada several missionaries were executed, and numbers of Japanese Christians were put to death. Many Christians obeyed their government and renounced their faith. This was to be expected. Presumably numbers had become Christians under the encouragement or from the example of their feudal superiors. When the latter changed their religious allegiance many of the former again were willing to follow them. However, enough remained firm to drive the rulers to more severe measures. Some of the executions were by beheading. Others were by crucifixion. Large numbers were burned, some by slow fires. Many were put to a peculiarly harrowing torture by suspension head downwards and bound in such fashion as to intensify an agony which might last for several days before death came to the relief of the sufferer. Only infrequently did a missionary under pressure renounce his faith. A Jesuit, Ferreira, apostatized, became an active assistant in the persecution, and was the author of a large part of a work written in refutation of Christianity. He, however, was the rare exception. In 1637 and 1638 several thousand Christians rose in what has been known as the Shimabara Rebellion. This was in part against the persecution and in part against the exorbitant taxation of the rulers of Arima,

[67] Anesaki in *Harvard Journal of Asiatic Studies*, Vol. I, pp. 13-27.

[68] See accounts of the persecution in Cary, *op. cit.*, Vol. I, pp. 175 ff.; Delplace, *Le Catholicisme au Japon*, Vol. II, pp. 125 ff.; Pagés, *La Religion Chrétienne au Japon*, Vol. I, pp. 251 ff.; Charlevoix, *Histoire du Christianisme au Japon*, Vol. II, pp. 152 ff.; Steichen, *The Christian Daimyos*, pp. 273 ff.; Profillet, *Le Martyrologe de l'Église du Japon 1549-1649* (Paris, Tequi, 3 vols., 1895-1897); Anesaki, *A Concordance to the History of Christian Missions*, pp. 28 ff., giving a list of those who suffered for their faith; Anesaki, in *Transactions of the Royal Asiatic Society of Japan*, 2d Series, Vol. VII, pp. 1-15.

[69] Blair and Robertson, *The Philippine Islands*, Vol. XX, p. 88.

which had long been a Christian centre. The insurgents finally took refuge in a deserted castle and there defied the authorities. They were reduced only after several weeks and by overwhelming force. Practically all the defenders were slain.

The Shimabara Rebellion was followed by still more drastic anti-Christian measures. It had sent a shiver of fear throughout ruling Japan. Here, so it was believed, was proof conclusive that Christianity meant disunion and anarchy. The persistence, too, of missionaries in coming to the country in various disguises aroused distrust of all Spanish and Portuguese commerce. Foreign trade, once so eagerly desired, was now envisioned as a threat to the integrity and independence of the Empire. Special officers existed for the detection of Christians. The shogun himself personally attended the examinations of many of the accused. Those suspected of the faith were required to trample upon a cross or a representation of Christ. As late as the last half of the eighteenth century, all the inhabitants of Nagasaki, once a strong Christian centre and still the port for such European trade as was allowed, were required annually to tread on such an image. Even before the Shimabara Rebellion, Japanese ships and Japanese subjects had been forbidden to go to other lands, Japanese returning to their native land had been ordered killed, and commercial intercourse with the Philippines had been prohibited as a source of infection. Now, in 1639, notice was served that if any Portuguese ship reached the country it would be destroyed and those it carried put to death. An attempt of the Portuguese in 1640 to reopen trade led to the burning of the ship and the execution of the envoys and a number of their companions. Of the Europeans, only the Dutch, who had displayed no inclination to propagate Christianity in the land, were permitted to continue their commerce, and they were strictly regulated and confined to one port, Nagasaki. Whenever a Dutch ship arrived all objects on it connected with the Christian faith were either concealed or else were put in a chest and placed in charge of a Japanese. Since Christian books entered in the Chinese language, which was familiar to educated Japanese, and by Chinese ships, a list of forbidden Chinese titles was published and restrictions were placed on Chinese trade.[70]

In spite of the severity of these measures, Christian missionaries persevered in efforts to reach Japan. Thus in 1642, after the Shimabara Rebellion, a party of Jesuits from Macao entered the country, were imprisoned, tortured, and

---

[70] Paske-Smith, *Western Barbarians in Japan and Formosa in Tokugawa Days*, p. 123; Shio Sakanishi in *Journal of the American Oriental Society*, Vol. LVII, pp. 290-303; M. Anesaki, *Prosecution of Kirishitans After the Shimabara Insurrection*, in *Monumenta Nipponica*, Vol. I, No. 2, pp. 1-8.

killed.[71] Early in the eighteenth century, an Italian priest, Sidotti, fired from youth by stories of the persecuted Church in Japan, made his way to the Philippines, there studied Japanese from shipwrecked sailors of that tongue, succeeded in effecting an entry into the Empire, was imprisoned, and before his death won to his faith two of those who served him.[72]

Moreover, Christianity persisted. In the hills of Kyushu and on the Goto Islands survivors of the persecutions secretly handed down their beliefs to their children. Baptism was administered. The Ten Commandments, some Christian doctrines, and several Christian prayers were transmitted. Shortly after the middle of the nineteenth century, missionaries, now once more in the country, were thrilled by the disclosure of these communities who had kept the faith.[73] By other Japanese, objects of Christian worship were passed on as talismans from father to son with little or no knowledge of their original significance.[74]

In spite of its sanguinary course and its seeming extirpation, between A.D. 1500 and A.D. 1800 Christianity had a marked effect on Japan. It had won many thousand adherents and had given rise to communities some of which succeeded in surviving, albeit against the strictest prohibitions rigidly enforced and for about two centuries without contact with Christians of other lands. It was in the effort to exclude Christianity that the Tokugawa all but hermetically sealed the country against foreign commerce and inaugurated the policy of isolation which was to last for over two hundred years. Since, in the measures adopted against the hated faith, all families were required to show some formal Buddhist connexion, Buddhism was strengthened as the established religion.[75] It is also conjectured that Christian influence was strongly felt by some of the non-Christian religions and philosophies. Toju Nakae, the founder of the Oyomei school of Confucianism which perpetuated in Japan the teaching of the Chinese philosopher Wang Yang-ming and which had wide currency among the educated, is said to have declared his belief in the fatherhood of one infinite and absolute God and to have owed this to contact with a Christian.[76] It is also suggested that the Shinto revival of the eighteenth century which was one of the contributory forces to the eventual overthrow of the shogunate and to the restoration of the Emperor may have been indebted to Roman Catholicism and to some ideas of Christian provenance which filtered in by way of the Dutch.[77]

[71] Cary, A History of Christianity in Japan, Vol. I, pp. 233-235.
[72] Cary, op. cit., Vol. I, pp. 237-240.
[73] Cary, op. cit., Vol. I, pp. 282 ff.
[74] One such example is given in Fides News Service, Aug. 31, 1935.
[75] Anesaki, History of Japanese Religion, p. 260.
[76] Kagawa, Christ and Japan, p. 98.
[77] Kagawa, op. cit., p. 76.

The sacrifices of missionaries and martyrs were not without lasting effects. Christianity had helped to make Japan a different country. Although some of the major results were the exact opposite of those desired by the missionaries and contradicted the spirit of Christianity, they were no less potent in shaping the future of the nation. Here as elsewhere Christianity created a tension. In Japan the forces which fought against Christianity appeared to triumph, but in their victory they paid tribute to the power of their rival by adopting extreme measures and by striking modifications in their own structure.

How far did the Japanese environment mould the imported Christianity? Somewhat, and that in spite of the inherited Roman Catholic form through which it had been transmitted. We hear of a dance performed in connexion with a feast of the most holy sacrament.[78] The cherishing by converts of peculiarities of particular religious orders through which they had received the faith may reflect the feudal and clan loyalties which have been so marked a feature of Japan. In the years of obscurity and of separation from Christians of other lands, the hidden Christian communities developed idiosyncrasies which many were unwilling to surrender when, in the nineteenth century, Roman Catholic missionaries, re-entering, sought to bring them into fellowship and conformity. Yet, persecuted, this Japanese Christianity, although having sufficient vitality to perpetuate itself, was too harassed to give birth to vigorous new movements or markedly distinct schools and sects. In the main, so far as it was able, it was loyal to what had been transmitted from the missionaries and the early converts.

[78] Blair and Robertson, *The Philippine Islands,* Vol. XII, p. 200.

Chapter XIV

THE CHINESE EMPIRE. FORMOSA, TIBET, AND KOREA

FROM the standpoint of the numbers of individuals involved, the Chinese Empire presented to Christianity the chief challenge of the three centuries between A.D. 1500 and A.D. 1800. About the middle of the period China fell under the domination of the Manchus. Under the two greatest of the Manchu Emperors, K'ang Hsi and Ch'ien Lung, the combined length of whose reigns covered nearly four-fifths of the second half of the period, A.D. 1650 to A.D. 1800, the Chinese Empire reached the greatest territorial extent and the largest population in its long history. In area it came to embrace China Proper, Manchuria, Mongolia, Chinese Turkestan (Sinkiang or the New Dominion), and Tibet, and a more or less shadowy suzerainty was acknowledged by Nepal, Burma, Annam, and Korea. In square miles covered, the Chinese Empire ranked with those of Spain and Russia as the most extensive of the day. Through the order maintained by the early Manchu Emperors, the inhabitants of China Proper increased until by the close of the eighteenth century they were not far from four hundred millions. China was thus the most populous realm of the era. Indeed, in A.D. 1800 the Manchus reigned over more people than were to be found in all Europe and America, and the Chinese were probably almost twice as numerous as the total of those who professed the Christian name throughout the world.

Chinese culture opposed a solid and forbidding front to the entrance of Christianity. Its political structure was based upon one of the leading non-Christian systems, Confucianism. The land was ruled through those who had been trained in an intellectual discipline dominated by Confucianism. Socially and in the realm of thought these Confucian *literati* were even more in control than they were in the state. Family life was built upon Confucian precepts. Industry and trade were dominated by guilds each of which had a patron non-Christian god. Religiously the land was pre-empted by faiths that combined popular appeal with philosophies which were the product of profound and mature reflection—Confucianism, Buddhism, and Taoism. Islam was represented by a strong minority. To gain much of a foothold, Christianity would either need to wait until some other force had weakened the structure of

Chinese life or would have the difficult task of adjusting itself to Chinese civilization. It could scarcely do the latter without compromises which would be a surrender of most of its own essential features and for the former it had to wait until the closing years of the nineteenth and the opening years of the twentieth century.

Moreover, in effecting an entrance into China, Christianity enjoyed less support from the commerce and the political imperialism of the Occident than in any other major land at whose doors it knocked during these centuries. The Chinese government and the vast majority of the Chinese people had no desire for trade with Europe. During much of the period, maritime commerce with the West was confined to one port, Canton, and direct overland trade with Europe was only with the Russians and was a mere trickle. The territorial holdings of Europeans were restricted to Macao, a small peninsula on an island not far from Canton. The Chinese deemed their culture superior to all others, economically the Chinese Empire was almost completely self-contained, and the Manchu rulers of the seventeenth and eighteenth centuries were powerful enough to repel any foreign invasion.

It must be said, however, that this *piedàterre* at Macao, although slight, proved significant. Macao became a port of entry for many missionaries. Under Portuguese control, it gave to Portugal a prominent part in Roman Catholic missions in China and, unfortunately, also made for dissension between those missionaries who came through Lisbon and those who did not.

Christianity faced the discouraging fact that twice in the preceding thousand years it had acquired a foothold in China only to disappear completely without leaving any clearly demonstrable lasting impression. From the seventh into the eighth or ninth century, and again from the thirteenth into the fourteenth or the fifteenth century, it had had adherents in the Middle Kingdom. Some of these had been active missionaries. Yet nothing but a few written records and physical remains and debatable influences on other religions survived to testify to the former presence of the faith.

In the face of this huge population, this solid opposition, this paucity of adventitious aids, and this discouraging history, could Christianity hope now to win for itself a permanent place in China and to transform the life of the land?

One of the most signal achievements in the history of any religion is that in spite of these handicaps and conveyed by a mere handful of missionaries, Christianity won a body of adherents who, although widely scattered and numerically not large in any one place, totalled in A.D. 1800 not far from two hundred thousand and formed nuclei from which in the nineteenth and twentieth centuries, under more favourable circumstances, Roman Catholicism expanded to impressive dimensions.

Fittingly, the reintroduction of Christianity was begun by Francis Xavier. Xavier had touched at Canton on his way to Japan.[1] In Japan he met Chinese and formed a high opinion of them. From Portuguese merchants, too, he learned of the populousness and high culture of the land. He determined to go there and hoped that the way might be opened not only for Jesuits but also for members of other orders. He believed that if the Chinese accepted Christianity, the Japanese would give up the faiths which the Chinese had taught them.[2] So Xavier, with his kindling imagination and his faith, dreamed of the time when through the labours of his Society the Chinese would be Christians and the Japanese would follow them into the Church.[3] For his undertaking he made careful preparation. Thanks to the use of Chinese characters by the Japanese, he had had written in the former a book setting forth the main Christian doctrines.[4] He went to India and there elaborated a design for an embassy to the Emperor of China by which he hoped to set free Portuguese held in captivity, to negotiate an alliance between the Portuguese and China, and to begin the Christian mission. He asked the King of Portugal for missionaries for China.[5] At Malacca, however, Xavier met firm opposition from the Portuguese Commandant, Alvaro de Ataide, and the project of the embassy was, perforce, abandoned. Yet Xavier himself was allowed to go on to China. There he joined the Portuguese merchants at the island of Shang Ch'uan, off the south coast not far from the estuary of the West River and Canton, where the Portuguese had made their temporary headquarters after they had been excluded from the large ports. From Shang Ch'uan Xavier tried in vain to obtain passage to the mainland. He fell ill, and on the island, towards the end of 1552, he died, his dream seemingly a pitiful failure.[6] The greatest of the missionary pioneers in the South and East of Asia in these centuries perished, baffled, before the closed doors of the greatest empire which he had faced.

Even had Xavier not given his life for the opening of China, efforts of Roman

---

[1] Letter of Xavier, Nov. 5, 1549, translated in Coleridge, *The Life and Letters of St. Francis Xavier*, Vol. II, p. 232.

[2] Letter of Xavier, Jan. 29, 1552, translated in Coleridge, *op. cit.*, Vol. II, pp. 347, 348.

[3] Xavier to Loyola, Jan. 29, 1552, translated in Coleridge, *op. cit.*, Vol. II, pp. 373, 374.

[4] Xavier to Loyola, Jan. 29, 1552, translated in Coleridge, *op. cit.*, Vol. II, p. 374.

[5] Xavier to the King of Portugal, Apr. 10, 1552, translated in Coleridge, *op. cit.*, Vol. II, pp. 497, 498.

[6] Brou, *Saint François Xavier*, Vol. II, pp. 319 ff.; Coleridge, *op. cit.*, Vol. II, pp. 510 ff. See also Joseph de la Servière, *Saint François-Xavier et la Chine* in *The New China Review*, Vol. II, pp. 197-206. On the exact day of Xavier's death (probably the night of Dec. 2 and 3), see Servière, in *op. cit.*, Vol. II, p. 201, n. 3. See also Bernard, *Aux Portes de la Chine*, p. 50.

Catholic missionaries to penetrate the country could not long have been delayed. Within less than two decades from the death of the great Apostle to the Indies Macao had been permanently occupied by the Portuguese, and the Philippines, with Manila as the capital, by the Spaniards. Such was the missionary urge from the Portugal and Spain of the time that with such bases from which to operate, emissaries of Roman Catholic Christianity were certain soon to be knocking at the doors of the Middle Kingdom. Long before the close of the sixteenth century repeated efforts had been made to win an entrance to China, by way both of Macao and of the Philippines. In these, Jesuits, Augustinians, Franciscans, and Dominicans were engaged.[7] No one order had a monopoly on pioneering enthusiasm and heroism. In 1576, moreover, Macao became the centre of an episcopal see and the King of Portugal agreed to make financial provision for the bishop and the cathedral staff.[8]

It was, however, fitting that when at last Roman Catholic Christianity succeeded in gaining something more than an ephemeral footing in China, the outstanding agents should be members of Xavier's society. It was Allessandro Valignani, Visitor of the Jesuits in the Indies, a man of energy, breadth of vision, imagination, and gifts of leadership, who was immediately responsible. At times the obstacles seemed to him all but insuperable, and it is recorded of him that, looking towards China from the Jesuit College in Macao, he once cried "with a loud voice and the most intimate affection of his heart, speaking to China, 'Oh, Rock, Rock, when wilt thou open, Rock?'"[9] Valignani had sent to China Michael Ruggerius, or Roger, an Italian Jesuit, and arranged to have him begin the study of the language.[10] Within a few years Ruggerius was reinforced by Matteo (Matthew) Ricci. Ricci became the chief pioneer of his Society in China. It was he who was the most prominent leader in devising and first putting into practice methods which gained for Christianity much of such standing as it held in China before 1800. It was he, too, who adopted attitudes towards Chinese culture that later aroused the protracted and bitter controversy in Roman Catholic circles which was one of the causes of the retardation in the growth of Christianity in China in the eighteenth century.

Ricci was, strangely enough, born only a few months before the death of Xavier. He was a native of Macerata and in his youth was a student of law in

---

[7] A number of these attempts are enumerated, with citations to the appropriate authorities, in Latourette, *A History of Christian Missions in China*, pp. 88-90. See also Montalbán, *Das Spanische Patronat und die Eroberung der Philippinen*, pp. 100-102; Bernard, *op. cit.*, pp. 53-136.

[8] Jann, *Die katholischen Missionen in Indien, China und Japan*, pp. 123, 124.

[9] Semedo, *The History of the Great and Renowned Monarchy of China*, pp. 170-172.

[10] See letters of Ruggerius in Tacchi Venturi, *Opere Storiche del P. Matteo Ricci*, Vol. II, pp. 396-413; Bernard, *op. cit.*, pp. 139 ff.

Rome. There, like so many other of the able Roman Catholic young men of his day, he was caught up in the enthusiasm of the rapidly growing Society of Jesus. He had instruction in mathematics, cosmology, and astronomy. He studied with Christopher Clavius, a Jesuit distinguished for his attainments in mathematics and for his part in reforming the calendar under Pope Gregory XIII. This training was to be of marked advantage to him in China. His novitiate was passed under the direction of Valignani, and it may have been the influence of his master which drew him to the Far East. In 1577, at his own request, he was sent to the Indies. After a few years in Goa, in 1582, at the behest of Valignani, he went to Macao and began his China career.[11]

Ruggerius and Ricci saw that if they were to win toleration for Christianity they must first gain the respect and friendship of the ruling classes. This had repeatedly been the policy of missionaries, both Christian and Buddhist, in preceding centuries, and it was one which the Jesuits followed in many other parts of the world. Presumably as a step in this direction, in 1583 Ruggerius and Ricci established their residence at Chaoch'ing, a city not far from Canton, and at that time the capital of the province of Kwangtung. There they obtained access to officials and scholars. Ricci's training in mathematics proved an open sesame, and clocks, as more ingenious timekeepers than the Chinese had known, proved attractive. Ricci, too, prepared a map of the world which opened to the astonished eyes of the *literati* Europe and the Americas. Indeed, it was through their scientific knowledge and mechanical skill, especially in the realm of mathematics, the making of maps, and the regulation of the calendar, that the Jesuits were henceforth to acquire and to hold most of that respect which assured to them and to missionaries of other orders whatever opportunity was theirs to propagate the faith in the Middle Kingdom. The European geographic discoveries of the age and the advances in the calendar associated with the name of Pope Gregory XIII, an older contemporary of Ricci, were to bear unexpected fruit in pushing ajar the door for the entrance of Christianity into China.[12]

Ricci soon became the head of the mission, for in 1588 Ruggerius left, permanently as it proved, for Europe, on what turned out to be a futile attempt to induce some European monarch to send an embassy to China to obtain formal toleration for the faith.[13] In the absence of such an embassy, Ricci and his colleagues were forced to depend upon their skill in making friends with influen-

[11] Brucker in *The Catholic Encyclopedia*, Vol. XIII, pp. 34 ff.; *Lettres Édifiantes*, Vol. III, p. 2.

[12] Tacchi Venturi, *op. cit.*, Vol. I, pp. 141, 142. On the map of the world see Augustin Bernard, *La Mappemonde Ricci du Musée Historique de Pékin* (Peking, Imprimerie de la "Politique de Pekin," 1928, pp. 13).

[13] Brucker, in *The Catholic Encyclopedia*, Vol. XIII, p. 36.

tial scholars and officials to win official acquiescence in the preaching of their faith. Ricci made himself familiar with the Chinese classical books on which the *literati* looked with reverence and composed treatises in Chinese, both on European science and on the Christian faith.[14] He adopted Chinese garb, first that of Buddhist monks, and then, when he found that these were not highly esteemed, that of the Confucian scholar, the most respected of the social classes in China.[15] To make a point of connexion between the Christian message and the venerated Chinese past, he employed as names for God terms which were found in the ancient classics of the land, *Shang Ti* and *T'ien*. He came to feel that the ceremonies in honour of the ancestors and of Confucius which constituted so integral a part of the family life and of the routine of the scholars and officials did not possess a religious significance in a sense which would make participation in them compromising for Christians. He therefore permitted his converts to continue in them. Thus he rendered it possible for one reared in the Confucian tradition to become a Christian without being disloyal to two institutions esteemed by the Chinese as basic. Ricci was, in other words, endeavouring to meet the solid opposition offered by the structure of Chinese life by maintaining that Christianity was not antagonistic either to the family or the state, and that it was congenial to much in the Classics. Ricci wished, too, to adapt for Christian uses the pagoda, prominent in the Chinese landscape, and to have the form of Christian worship as nearly Chinese as possible.[16]

In his methods Ricci met with amazing success, rather more, indeed, than did his younger contemporary, Nobili, who adopted somewhat similar attitudes in India. For longer or shorter intervals he lived at Ch'aochou, an important city near the coast north of Canton, in Nanch'ang, the capital of the province of Kiangsi, and in Nanking, formerly the capital of the then reigning dynasty, the Ming. He saw that if he were fully to realize his purpose he must establish a mission in the actual capital of the Empire, Peking, and there, at the centre of authority, lay siege to the imperial court. Here, too, after one discouragingly brief sojourn, he succeeded. In 1601 he reached Peking and was allowed to remain. Thus was begun a mission which was to endure, with various vicissitudes, until the dissolution of his Society, and which was then to be transferred to another missionary body. Before his death, in 1610, Ricci had seen the conversion of a number of important scholars and officials and of an imperial prince. Of these the most distinguished in Christian circles was Hsü Kuang-ch'i, or

---

[14] See an account of some of Ricci's works in Alexander Wylie, *Notes on Chinese Literature* (Shanghai, American Presbyterian Mission Press, New edition, 1902, pp. xxxix, 307), pp. 109, 110, 172, 174.

[15] Semedo, *op. cit.*, p. 175.

[16] Berg, *Die katholische Heidenmission als Kulturträger*, Vol. II, p. 125.

Paul Hsü. Fittingly, the present chief headquarters of Jesuit missions in China are in the home village of Hsü's family, Zikawei, on the outskirts of Shanghai, and on ground donated by Paul Hsü.[17]

So well had Ricci laid its foundations that his death did not check the mission which he had established. Indeed, in 1611, only the year after his passing, an imperial decree placed the Jesuits in charge of a correction of the Chinese calendar.[18] Support for the mission came from Europe. Additional recruits arrived. Of these one of the most famous was Johann Adam Schall von Bell.[19] Born in 1592, a scion of an aristocratic family which had close connexions with Cologne and which had given a number of its offspring to religious orders, he was educated in Rome and there entered the Society of Jesus. At his own initiative he was sent to China and in 1619 arrived at Macao. In 1623 he came to Peking and there won prestige among the officials by the accuracy of his prediction of an eclipse of the moon. After a period in Hsianfu he again took up his residence in Peking and became the leading figure in the mission. Financial assistance also came. Thus in 1616 the Duke of Bavaria promised an annual subvention which was paid fairly regularly for at least a century.[20]

In 1616 and 1622 persecutions for a time threatened the existence of the nascent Christian communities. The enemies of the missionaries charged the latter with introducing a seditious movement which was plotting with foreigners in Macao to overthrow the dynasty. The missionaries were forced to leave Peking and some were transported to Macao. However, the scholars whose friendship the Jesuits had won proved towers of strength in the hour of need, the edict against the missionaries was not uniformly enforced, and in 1629 members of the Society were again placed in control of the calendar.[21]

About the middle of the seventeenth century occurred a change of dynasty. In 1644 the Manchus occupied Peking and drove the native rulers, the Ming, southward, until, in 1662, Kuei Wang, the last of that line to claim the throne, perished near the southern frontier. Much of the land was thrown into confu-

---

[17] On Ricci and his methods, see Latourette, op. cit., pp. 92-98, including the references there given in the footnotes. See also Henri Bernard, La Père Matthieu Ricci et la Société Chinoise de Son Temps (1552-1610) (Tientsin, 2 vols., 1937), passim.

[18] Brucker, in The Catholic Encyclopedia, Vol. XIII, p. 520. On the development of mathematical and astronomical knowledge at Rome and the effect through the China mission, see Henri Bernard, L'Encyclopédie Astronomique du Père Schall, in Monumenta Serica, Vol. III, Fasc. 1, pp. 35 ff., Fasc. 2, pp. 441 ff.

[19] An excellent account of Schall, based upon careful research, is Alfons Väth, Johann Adam Schall von Bell, S.J., Missionar in China, Kaiserlichen Astronom und Ratgeber a Hofe von Peking 1592-1666 (Cologne, J. P. Bachem, 1933, pp. xx, 380).

[20] Schneller in Zeitschrift für Missionswissenschaft, Vol. IV, pp. 176-189.

[21] Moule in The New China Review, Vol. IV, pp. 450-456, translates an account of the trouble from the Ming Shih. See also Semedo, op. cit., pp. 205-226, and Huc, Christianity in China, Tartary, and Thibet, Vol. II, pp. 234-285.

sion. In Chengtu, in West China, the missionaries suffered great hardship.[22] In Fukien a local persecution broke out.[23] Yet the progress of Christianity did not seriously suffer. Jesuits ran with the hares and hunted with the hounds: they were found with both the Mings and the Manchus. They accompanied the Ming court on its wanderings. Two of them, Andrew Koffler (also called Andrew Xavier) and Michael Boym, were accorded official rank. The heir, the mother, and the first wife of Kuei Wang were baptized. Also among the Christians were the commander-in-chief of the Ming forces, the Ming Governor of Kwangsi, and two of the court eunuchs. Possibly back of at least some of these conversions was the hope of military aid from Europeans. Boym was sent to Europe with a message to the Pope and died in Tongking on the return journey. Koffler lost his life in the disasters which overtook the fleeing Kuei Wang.[24] On the other hand, Schall remained in Peking and shared in the dangers of two successive captures of that city by the contending armies. Partly by a prediction of an eclipse of the sun made with greater accuracy than the rival Chinese and Moslem astronomers were able to achieve, he won the confidence of the Manchu rulers, was given official rank, and was entrusted with the astronomical bureau.[25] He directed the casting of cannon to aid the Manchus.[26] The Emperor Shun Chih held him in high esteem, helped him with the erection of a church and a residence, and gave him a declaration praising Christianity which, displayed at the church, must have had something of the effect on the public mind that a formal edict of toleration would have made.[27]

During these years of civil strife the Christian communities seem to have increased in numerical strength. Even before the Manchu irruption missionaries were fairly widely spread. In 1624 six "colleges" were reported in the provinces.[28] Between 1620 and 1629 nineteen Jesuits joined the China mission.[29] It is said that in 1627 Christians numbered thirteen thousand in seven provinces

[22] Väth, op. cit., pp. 150-153.
[23] Servière, Les Anciennes Missions de la Compagnie de Jésus en Chine, p. 29.
[24] Thomas, Histoire de la Mission de Pékin, pp. 98-100; Girard de Rialle in T'oung Pao, Vol. I, pp. 99-117. On Boym see Paul Pelliot, Michel Boym, in T'oung Pao, Vol. XXXI, pp. 95-151, and Robert Chabrié, Michel Boym (Paris, Edit. Pierre Bossuet, 1933, pp. 283).
[25] Väth, op. cit., pp. 135 ff.
[26] Johann Adam Schall, Geschichte der chinesischen Mission unter der Leitung des Pater Johann Adam Schall, translated from the Latin by J. Schumann (Vienna, 1834), pp. 119-134.
[27] Schall, op. cit., p. 359; Väth, op. cit., pp. 166, 167, 171 ff.
[28] Histoire de ce qui s'est passe au royaume de la Chine en l'année 1624, extracts from letters to the General of the Society of Jesus, translated from the Italian (Paris, 1629), passim.
[29] Catalogus Patrum ac Fratrum e Societate Jesu qui . . . in Sinis adlaboraverunt, pp. 2-11.

and that in 1637 they had increased to forty thousand.[30] Shortly before the Manchu conquest, too, both Dominicans and Franciscans from the Philippines entered the Province of Fukien,[31] and the former established themselves so firmly that they have remained to the present day. During the time that the Manchus were making themselves masters of the Empire, from their occupation of Peking in 1644 to the death of Kuei Wang in 1662, the number of Christians continued to mount, perhaps in part because of the favour which the Manchu régime was showing to Schall. One account declares that before the Ming came to their end missions were to be found in all the provinces except Yünnan and Kweichow.[32] Another says that in 1650 there were 150,000 Christians in the realm and that in 1664 there were 254,980.[33] In 1650 a Franciscan established a mission at Tsinanfu, in Shantung, which enjoyed a long life.[34]

For a few years in the sixteen sixties persecution brought a reversal of fortune. The year 1661 saw the death of the Emperor Shun Chih. The succeeding reign, that of K'ang Hsi, one of the most brilliant in the entire annals of China, was ushered in with a regency. The Moslems whose astronomical calculations Schall had discredited obtained the ear of the regents and had the famous missionary, now aged, and several of his colleagues thrown into prison. The storm spread to the provinces and all the missionaries were ordered to be sent to Peking for trial. Numbers were exiled to Canton.[35]

In 1669 the Emperor K'ang Hsi deemed himself old enough to rule directly, and, falling out with the regents, dismissed them. Since the persecution had been the work of the regents, he was probably predisposed in favour of the missionaries. Schall had died in 1666, but through the foresight of the Jesuits a successor was at hand in Peking, Verbiest, who had had a thorough training in mathematics and astronomy. As Schall had done in the preceding reign, in a series of practical tests Verbiest demonstrated to K'ang Hsi his superiority over the Moslems, and the calendar was transferred to him and so was once more in the hands of his Society.[36] Although the prohibition against Chinese becoming

[30] Huc, op. cit., Vol. II, p. 290.

[31] Aduarte, Historia de la Provincia del Santo Rosario, translation in Blair and Robertson, The Philippine Islands, Vol. XXXII, pp. 13, 186 ff.; Biermann, Die Anfänge der neueren Dominikanermission in China, pp. 27-39; Maas, Die Wiederöffnung der Franziskanermission in China in der Neuzeit, pp. 47 ff.

[32] Servière, op. cit., pp. 22 ff.

[33] Brucker in The Catholic Encyclopedia, Vol. XIII, p. 522.

[34] Maas, op. cit., p. 143.

[35] Huc, op. cit., Vol. III, pp. 31-35.

[36] H. Josson and L. Willaert, Correspondence de Ferdinand Verbiest (Brussels, Palais des Académies, 1938, pp. xxiv, 591), passim; H. Bosmans, Ferdinand Verbiest, in Revue des Questions Scientifiques, 3d series, Vol. XXI, pp. 195-273, 375-461; H. Bosmans, Les Écrets Chinois de Verbiest, in Revue des Questions Scientifiques, 3d series, Vol. XXIV, pp. 272-298.

Christians was not removed, the missionaries were given back their churches, Chinese already Christian were allowed to retain their faith, Schall's titles were posthumously restored, and a mausoleum for him was sanctioned.[37] K'ang Hsi became increasingly cordial to Verbiest and, with his inquiring and versatile mind, studied mathematics under the latter's tuition. Verbiest, too, helped prepare cannon to assist in suppressing a rebellion which was taxing K'ang Hsi's resources.[38] K'ang Hsi used other Jesuits at court.[39] Since the Emperor was known to be friendly, the rule against Chinese becoming Christians became something of a dead letter and the Church had large accessions in both Peking and the provinces. A few even of the Manchus accepted the faith.[40]

The early portion of the reign of K'ang Hsi, and especially the two decades after the persecution of the sixteen sixties, witnessed a rapid augmentation of the missionary forces in China. In Europe France was growing in power. Louis XIV was a contemporary of K'ang Hsi and it was to be expected that the vigour of his reign would seek an outlet in missionary as well as in commercial activity in the South and East of Asia. The Société des Missions-Étrangères of Paris had China among its original objectives and in the territories assigned by the Propaganda to the initial vicars apostolic appointed from its members a large part of China Proper was included.[41] On his third trip to the Far East, Pallu, the leading figure in the early days of the Paris Society, reached China, and had with him Maigrot. Pallu died in China (October 29, 1684),[42] but Maigrot was aided by the arrival of additional colleagues.[43] In February, 1688, a party of French Jesuits reached Peking. They were trained in science, and especially in mathematics, and by their scholarly attainments obtained the interest and confidence of K'ang Hsi. In Peking they were given a house of their own and later erected their own church. Before long they constituted a group distinct from those of their Society who came out under Portuguese auspices. As time passed, although the Jesuits under the Portuguese padroado were not altogether happy over their coming,[44] they were strongly reinforced.[45]

---

[37] Tobar, *Kiao-ou Ki-lio*, pp. 1, 2; Huc, *op. cit.*, Vol. III, pp. 63, 64; Thomas, *op. cit.*, p. 107.

[38] Thomas, *op. cit.*, p. 109; Huc, *op. cit.*, Vol. III, pp. 78-80.

[39] Grimaldi's letter of 1686 from Peking, translation in *Bibliotheca Asiatica*, Vol. II, pp. 31, 32.

[40] Huc, *op. cit.*, Vol. III, p. 65; Le Comte, *Nouveaux Mémoires sur l'État Present de la Chine*, Vol. II, pp. 258, 259.

[41] Jann, *Die katholischen Missionen in Indien, China und Japan*, pp. 217, 218.

[42] *Nouvelles Lettres Édifiantes*, Vol. I, p. ix; Launay, *Histoire Générale de la Société des Missions-Étrangères*, Vol. I, p. 302.

[43] Launay, *op. cit.*, Vol. I, pp. 364, 365.

[44] Pinot, *La Chine et la Formation de l'Esprit Philosophique en France*, p. 86.

[45] Le Comte, *op. cit., passim;* Thomas, *op. cit.*, 113 ff.; Huc, *op. cit.*, Vol. III, pp. 107 ff.

From the Philippines came more Franciscans and Dominicans. The Dominicans were chiefly in the one province, Fukien, and mainly in its northern part.[46] The Spanish Franciscans were scattered in several of the provinces, all but one of them on the coast.[47] Brothers Minor also came from Italy, dispatched directly by the Propaganda. The first party arrived in 1684. They and their successors concentrated their efforts on the interior, especially on the Provinces of Shansi, Shensi, Honan, Hupeh, and Hunan.[48] Augustinians reached China by way of the Philippines, but were never so numerous as were the Jesuits, the Dominicans, or the Franciscans.[49] Jesuits other than French contined to come. Jesuit converts were the most numerous in and around Shanghai and Nanking.[50]

A beginning was made towards what it was hoped would become a native Chinese hierarchy. A Chinese whom we know best by his European name, Gregory Lopez, had been baptized by a Franciscan, had studied in Manila, had become a Dominican, and in 1656 had been ordained priest, the first of his race, so far as we know, to be accorded that position. In 1674, at the suggestion of Pallu, one of whose purposes in coming to the Far East had been the rearing up of an indigenous clergy, he was created Vicar Apostolic of Nanking. In 1690 he was appointed Bishop of Nanking.[51] However, although Lopez seems to have been worthy, Rome did not repeat the experiment, and not until the twentieth century were Chinese again raised to the episcopate.

An important complication in forming an episcopate for the Middle Kingdom was the attitude of the Portuguese. In China as in India the Portuguese Crown insisted that its padroado ran current outside as well as within the territories which it actually controlled. Lisbon greatly feared that its commerce in the Far East would be sacrificed to France and saw in the vicars apostolic a

---

[46] Biermann, *op. cit.*, pp. 129-136; André-Marie, *Missions Dominicaines dans l'Extrême Orient*, Vol. I, p. 207; Evaristo Fernández Arias, *El Beato Sanz y Compañeros Mártires del Orden de Predicatores*, map at end of the volume.

[47] Otto Maas, *Cartas de China. Documentos Inéditos sobre Misiones Franciscanas del Siglo XVII* (Seville, 1917), pp. 11, 12, 178; Moidrey, *La Hiérarchie Catholique en Chine, en Corée, et au Japon*, p. 181; Lorenzo Pérez, *Origen de las Misiones Franciscanas en la Provincia de Kwang-Tung (China)*, extracto del *Archivo Ibero-Americano*, Nos. 20-23 (Madrid, 1918), pp. 160 ff.

On the Franciscans in China in this period see also Anastasius van den Wijngaert, *Sinica Franciscana, Vol. II. Relationes et Epistolas Fratrum Minorum Saeculi XVI et XVII Collegit, ad fidem codicum redegit et adnotavit* (Quaracchi, Coll. S. Bonaventura, 1933, pp. xlvi, 662), reviewed by Paul Pelliot in *T'oung Pao*, Vol. xxxiv (1938), pp. 191-222.

[48] J. J. Heeren in *Journal of the North China Branch of the Royal Asiatic Society*, 1923, pp. 182-199; Moidrey, *op. cit.*, pp. 35, 182.

[49] Henri Cordier in *Revue de l'Extrême Orient*, Vol. II, pp. 58-71.

[50] Le Comte, *op. cit.*, Vol. II, p. 259.

[51] A. C. Moule in *The New China Review*, Vol. I, pp. 480-488, Vol. III, pp. 138, 139; Launay, *op. cit.*, Vol. I, p. 187; Moidrey, *op. cit.*, pp. 22-24.

French tool to this end. Rome was constrained to compromise. In 1690 it created the sees of Peking and Nanking, placed them, like the already existing bishopric of Macao, under the padroado, and granted to Portugal the privilege of delimiting the boundaries of these dioceses.[52] Since Portugal assigned most of China to the three sees, a conflict of jurisdiction arose with the vicars apostolic. The latter were not under Portugal, but directly under Rome. In spite of the oposition of the Portuguese, in 1696 the Pope cut down the areas allotted to the Bishops of Peking, Nanking, and Macao, and created eight vicariates apostolic, to which were apportioned nine provinces.[53] All but two of the nine, however, were in the interior, and most of them were relatively pioneer fields. The majority of the strongest existing Christian communities were in the sees of the padroado.

In 1692 the rising tide of imperial favour brought an edict of toleration. A local persecution in the Province of Chêkiang in 1691 and the enmity of some of the members of the influential Board of Rites made it clear that a more formal grant of freedom to Christians was necessary than had thus far been obtained. Two of the Jesuits in Peking had proved of service to the state in diplomatic negotiations with the Russians and had won the friendship of one of the Manchu princes. Through the good offices of this prince an imperial decree was obtained (March, 1692) which allowed Christian worship and assured protection to existing church buildings. The document contained no explicit permission to preach or to administer baptism, but it declared that Christianity held in it no danger of rebellion, and the general tenor made for full toleration.[54] The grounds for the act were expressly given as the service of the missionaries in the correction of the calendar, the casting of cannon, and assistance in diplomacy. K'ang Hsi contributed to the rebuilding of a church in Hangchow and sent a personal representative to worship there and in a church in Nanking.[55] In 1708 he entrusted to missionaries the mapping of the entire country.[56] The policy pursued by Ricci and his successors had borne the desired fruit.

It is not surprising that the succeeding decade and a half proved a time of

---

[52] Moidrey, op. cit., pp. 35, 36; Cordier in T'oung Pao, Vol. XVII, p. 275; Jann, op. cit., pp. 251-267.

[53] Jann, op. cit., pp. 251-267; Maas, Cartas de China, 2d series, pp. vi-viii, 185-187, 201, 260.

[54] The appropriate documents are in Tobar, op. cit., pp. 2-5. See also Charles le Gobien, Histoire de l'Édit de l'Empereur de la Chine en Faveur de la Religion Chrétienne (Paris, 1698).

[55] Letter of Bouvet, Nov. 30, 1699, in Lockman, Travels of the Jesuits into Various Parts of the World. Compiled from their Letters, Vol. I, p. 75.

[56] Mailla, Histoire Générale de la Chine, Vol. XI, pp. 313-315. Mailla himself had a share in fulfilling this assignment.

unprecedented prosperity for the Roman Catholic mission. A peaceful realm and a friendly monarch provided an unusually favourable environment. Compared with the nineteenth and twentieth centuries, the missionary staff was very small, but it was being augmented. Between 1694 and 1705 eighty-eight, including a few Chinese, joined the ranks of the Jesuits.[57] In 1697 the Propaganda sent out at least ten new recruits.[58] In 1700 four Brothers Minor arrived who had been dispatched by the Propaganda, and who, shunning the route by Lisbon, had come by the arduous way of Poland, Russia, Persia, and the sea.[59] In 1695 China is reported to have had seventy-five priests, of whom thirty-eight were Jesuits (thirty-two Europeans and six Chinese), nine Spanish Dominicans, five Spanish Augustinians, twelve Spanish Franciscans, four Italian Franciscans, and seven of the Missions-Étrangères of Paris.[60] It is said that in 1701 there were in China fifty-nine Jesuits, twenty-nine Franciscans, eight Dominicans, six Augustinians, and fifteen seculars (nearly all of the Paris Society).[61] At some time between 1692 and 1707 missionaries or Chinese Christians were to be found in all the provinces except Kansu.[62] In spite of the increase, the missionary staff was a pitiably small force with which to attempt the conversion of the largest fairly homogeneous group of mankind.

In view of the limited missionary staff, it is not surprising that the number of Christians was at best almost infinitesimal. How many Christians China had must be largely a matter of conjecture, but by 1705 the total was probably not more than three hundred thousand and it may have been much less.[63] Only a very few of the educated had become Christians, and, because of the proprieties which kept the exclusively male missionary staff from reaching them, women were in the decided minority.[64] In proportion to the population, the number of Christians was much less than in Japan at the height of the strength of the Church in that land. Unless the body of missionaries could be vastly augmented or unless some pressure from the outside could bring about the disintegration of Chinese culture with its resistance to Christianity, any hope of the conversion of a large proportion of the Chinese would be fantastic. Both these conditions came, but not until the very close of the nineteenth and the opening years of the twentieth century. In the meantime not even the zeal

[57] *Catalogus Patrum ac Fratrum e Societate Jesu qui . . . in Sinis adlaboraverunt*, pp. 20-33.
[58] Civezza, *Histoire Universelle des Missions Franciscaines*, Vol. II, pp. 262 ff.; Demimuid, *Vie du François-Regis Clet*, pp. 97-104.
[59] Civezza, *op. cit.*, Vol. II, p. 267.
[60] Maas, *Cartas de China*, 2d series, p. 120.
[61] Servière, *Les Missions Anciennes de la Compagnie de Jésus*, p. 55.
[62] Latourette, *A History of Christian Missions in China*, p. 128.
[63] Latourette, *op. cit.*, p. 129.
[64] Lockman, *op. cit.*, Vol. I, pp. 302-309, 449.

and heroism of the missionaries and the methods associated with the name of Ricci could ensure more than a precarious foothold.

The motives which led the small minority of Chinese who became Christians to embrace the faith of these strangers from the Occident we cannot certainly know. In the case of the very few who were associated with the astronomical bureau at Peking it may have been the desire for employment in a department of the government which was in charge of the missionaries. Upon occasional others the example of those of the scholars who had become Christians may have had some effect. Obviously some of the *literati* had first been impressed by the erudition of the missionaries in branches of learning in which the Chinese were deficient. The favours shown by the Emperors Shun Chih and K'ang Hsi must have broken down barriers in the minds of many. Taken alone, however, these would not lead many to the positive step of accepting Christianity, for the Emperors themselves still adhered to the non-Christian cults. Some of the influences leading to conversion which had been potent in other parts of the East were absent. The desire or the necessity of conformity to the wishes of European political masters which were so prominent in Portuguese India, in Ceylon, in some of the Dutch Indies, and in the Philippines could not be present, except in tiny Macao. Nor was the hope of encouraging contacts with a profitable European trade an object. Most of the converts were from humble folk far away from Macao and with not even indirect touch with European merchants. Presumably the impulse which brought to baptism the large majority of such converts as were made was the appeal of the faith presented by the missionaries and a religious hunger which was unsatisfied by the prevailing faiths.

To this growth of Christianity, encouraging but still slight, a series of untoward factors brought a prolonged and disheartening check.

First was the decline in the vigour of two of the lands from which many of the missionaries came, Spain and Portugal. Here as in so many other regions this contributed to a retardation in the spread of Christianity. In China, however, it was not so important as in some other countries, for Spaniards and Portuguese did not constitute so large a portion of the missionary staff as in such lands as the Philippines, Spanish America, and Brazil.

A second and more potent factor was a prolonged dissension over Chinese customs—usually termed the Rites Controversy. The issue was the attitude proper for Christians towards Chinese religious terms and practices. Was the policy adopted by Ricci and followed by many of his successors allowable? Were the words *T'ien* and *Shang Ti*, so familiar to the Chinese *literati*, sufficiently close to the Christian conception of God to be employed by the Church in the hope that there might be given to them such Christian content as they lacked? Could Christians consistently share in the traditional ceremonies in honour of the ancestors and of Confucius? Or if they could not share in them all, could they observe them in a modified form? Or did attempted accommodations to Chinese culture involve fatal compromises of fundamental Christian tenets? A number of associated questions were also involved, such as the propriety of Christians contributing to community festivals in honour of non-Christian divinities and of masses for the souls of the non-Christian ancestors of Chinese Christians. The discussion dragged on for over a century. It spread to Europe. It became complicated by rivalries between religious orders and the question of the Portuguese padroado. No other dispute over mission policy in the entire history of the spread of Christianity was so intense over so prolonged a period—unless it was the one concerning the Portuguese padroado in India. The comparable disagreement over the methods of Nobili and his successors, while at times acute, did not attain such proportions as did that over the Chinese rites.

A full story of the controversy would carry these pages far beyond any proper length. Here we must content ourselves with only the briefest of summaries. At the outset not all the Jesuits were agreed that Ricci's methods should be followed in their entirety.[65] In 1628 representatives of the two schools of thought in the Society, after an extended conference on the term to be used for God, failed to come to an agreement.[66] When they began establishing themselves in China, the Dominicans and Franciscans, at best none too cordial to the Jesuits, challenged the practices which they found many of their rivals pursuing. Since most of them had come by way of the Philippines, they carried the issue to those islands, and the Archbishop of Manila denounced to the Pope what was reported to him about the Jesuit methods in China—an indictment which was later withdrawn.[67] In 1643 one of the Dominicans, Morales, brought the case directly to Rome. He presented to the Propaganda a picture, in the form of questions, of Jesuit practices and inquired whether they could be allowed.[68] In 1645 the Propaganda replied, with the approval of the Pope, with a prohibition of the Jesuit methods as Morales described them.[69] The Jesuits were deeply disturbed and sent to Rome an agent who protested

---

[65] Henrion, *Histoire Générale des Missions Catholiques*, Vol. II, p. 374; Brucker in *The Catholic Encyclopedia*, Vol. XIII, p. 37.

[66] Henrion, *op. cit.*, Vol. II, p. 374; Joly, *Le Christianisme et l'Extrême Orient*, Vol. I, p. 120.

[67] Brucker in *The Catholic Encyclopedia*, Vol. XIII, p. 38; Couling, *The Encyclopaedia Sinica*, p. 485.

[68] Le Comte, *Des Cérémonies de la Chine*, pp. 122-128.

[69] Henrion, *op. cit.*, Vol. II, p. 377.

that his colleagues had been misrepresented and who set forth their version of their procedure. In due time (1656) a decree was issued which gave sanction to the practices as they were there portrayed.[70] When a Dominican asked whether the decree of 1645 was set aside by that of 1656 the Holy Office answered (1669) that both were to be obeyed "according to the questions, circumstances, and all things set forth in them."[71] The two accounts of what was being done in China were sufficiently at variance to save the two edicts from reciprocal inconsistency. Obviously, however, the issue was still far from being settled. Indeed, the controversy was intensified by what Rome had done. Each side could now claim Papal endorsement for its view.

In the closing years of the sixteenth century, the controversy, thus fanned by the indeterminate actions of the highest ecclesiastical authorities, blazed fiercely and spread to wider circles. To be sure, in a forty day conference which ended in January, 1668, representatives of the Jesuits, Franciscans, and Dominicans, brought together in the same house in Canton by the persecution which broke out during the minority of K'ang Hsi and confronted by the common danger of expulsion, seemed to come to a partial agreement which inclined towards the Jesuit position.[72] However, one of the group, a Dominican, Navarrete, went to Europe and there reopened the issue and endeavoured to obtain from Rome an unequivocal decision.[73] However, in 1693 Maigrot, the surviving pioneer of the Missions-Étrangères of Paris in China and Vicar Apostolic in Fukien, came out with a sharp order expressly forbidding in his vicariate what he deemed compromises with paganism. Two Jesuits within his jurisdiction refused acquiescence, were suspended by him, and carried their appeal to Rome. Maigrot also saw to it that Rome knew his side of the case.[74] The feeling was intensified by the fact that the complaining Jesuits were of the Portuguese padroado and were inclined to be restive under the authority of one of those vicars apostolic who had been appointed independently of Lisbon.

The debate now waxed strong in Europe. Writer after writer felt called upon to break out into print either for or against the Jesuits' practices.[75] Even the philosopher Leibnitz expressed himself—in favour of the Jesuits.[76] In China,

[70] Thomas, *Histoire de la Mission de Pékin*, p. 163.

[71] Thomas, *op. cit.*, p. 165.

[72] Brucker in *The Catholic Encyclopedia*, Vol. XIII, p. 38.

[73] *Ibid.;* Thomas, *op. cit.*, pp. 164, 165.

[74] Thomas, *op. cit.*, pp. 166-171; Launay, *Histoire Générale de la Société des Missions-Étrangères*, Vol. I, pp. 384 ff.

[75] See a long list of titles in Henri Cordier, *Bibliotheca Sinica* (Paris, E. Guilmoto, 4 vols., 1904-1908, supplement, 1924), cols. 870-926, 3579-3600.

[76] Franz Rudolf Merkel, *G. W. von Leibnitz und die China Mission* (Leipzig, J. C. Hinrichs'sche Buchhandlung, 1920, pp. vi, 254), pp. 98 ff.

the Emperor K'ang Hsi, asked by the Jesuits for an opinion, declared that the latter were right.[77]

Rome, thus pressed, could not but seek a definitive settlement. After prolonged deliberation, a decree was formulated (1704) which forbade the use of T'ien and Shang Ti in the translation for God and commanded the use of T'ien Chu, "Lord of Heaven," a term which Ricci had also employed. Christians were commanded not to participate in sacrifices to Confucius or to ancestors, and, while ancestral tablets bearing simply the name of the deceased were permitted, those having characters which designated them as the throne or seat of the spirit of the dead were proscribed.[78]

Clearly, if the growing but still fragile Christianity in China was not to suffer serious damage, the announcement and enforcement of this decision, so contrary to the methods of the majority of the missionaries and the Christians and to the express opinion of K'ang Hsi, required great discretion and tact.

This difficult task was assigned, as we have seen in the account of the somewhat similar controversy in India, to Charles Maillard de Tournon, to whom were given the titles Patriarch of Antioch and Legatus a Latere.[79] Both the choice and the method were unfortunate. Tournon proved to be maladroit and irascible and suffered from poor health. He was sent without Portuguese approval and made the journey on a French ship. Thus he inevitably encountered the jealous opposition of the Portuguese, who were already made sensitive by what they adjudged to be infringements of the padroado. In Peking, which he reached late in 1705, Tournon aroused the hostility of most of the Jesuits.[80] K'ang Hsi, at first courteous, was more and more antagonized by the Legate, and his ire was further aroused by the anti-Jesuit Maigrot, who was associated with Tournon.[81] The Emperor could not brook any one, particularly a Western "barbarian" who, like Maigrot, differed from him on an interpretation of Chinese customs and classical books. In the summer of 1706, after several months of rising irritation, K'ang Hsi commanded the Legate to leave Peking[82] and ordered the banishment of Maigrot and several others, missionaries and Chinese Christians, who had accentuated his wrath. Missionaries, if they were to remain in China, must have an imperial piao, or permit, and upon arrival from Europe all new missionaries were to be sent to the Court for examination to

[77] Mailla, Histoire Générale de la Chine, Vol. XI, pp. 300-304.
[78] Acta Causæ Rituum seu Ceremoniarum Sinensium Complectentia (Venice, 1709), pp. 50-60.
[79] Thomas, op. cit., p. 177.
[80] Jenkins, The Jesuits in China, pp. 59-74.
[81] Thomas, op. cit., pp. 181-193.
[82] Cordier, Histoire Générale de la Chine, Vol. III, pp. 327, 328.

determine whether a permit should be granted them.[83] Presumably the Chinese officials would see to it that *a piao* would be conditioned upon acceptance of K'ang Hsi's interpretation of the rites. Surviving Chinese documents, some of them in the Emperor's own handwriting, show how intense was the feeling of K'ang Hsi on the issue.[84] At Nanking, on January 25, 1707, on his way from Peking to the coast, Tournon explicitly commanded all missionaries, on pain of excommunication, that if they were asked their position they must declare that sacrifices to Confucius and the ancestors and the current honours to deceased parents were not permitted to Christians, that *T'ien* and *Shang Ti* are not the God of the Christians, and that they should give as their reason for this position the decision of the Holy See made in 1704.[85] Missionaries now had the unpleasant choice between obedience to the Pope and his Legate and acquiescence to the will of a non-Christian emperor. Missionaries who acknowledged the Portuguese padroado, and these included many of the Jesuits, could plead that the Legate's commands, since they did not have Portuguese approval, were not binding. Some, arguing that the Legate had acted on his own initiative, relied on a further appeal to Rome.[86] Franciscans in the Province of Shensi, although declining to sign the declaration required by the Chinese authorities, were permitted by K'ang Hsi to remain on the condition that they would not leave China without imperial permission.[87] Others, including Spanish Dominicans, who did not acknowledge the padroado, refused to sign a declaration in a form satisfactory to the officials, and were expelled from the country.[88] The Emperor ordered that Tournon be detained at Macao until a reply could be had from the appeal to Rome.[89] In Macao, Portuguese as it was, friction between Tournon and the local authorities was unavoidable. Acting under direction from the Archbishop of Goa, the Bishop of Macao forbade the recognition of the Legate's powers, for, unauthorized under the padroado, these were held not to be valid.[90] Tournon excommunicated the Bishop and some of the leading civil and military officials.[91] The wrangling was complicated and prolonged.[92] The Pope conferred on Tournon the Cardinal's hat, but the

---

[83] Thomas, *op. cit.*, pp. 196, 197.

[84] Fourteen documents on the Rites Controversy were published by the Palace Museum in Peiping in 1932 under the title *K'ang Hsi Yü Lo-ma shih-chi kuan-hsi wên-shu-ying-yin pên.*

[85] Thomas, *op. cit.*, pp. 202-205.

[86] Jann, *Die katholischen Missionen in Indien, China und Japan*, p. 430.

[87] Thomas, *op. cit.*, pp. 208, 209.

[88] Thomas, *op. cit.*, pp. 207, 208.

[89] Jenkins, *op. cit.*, p. 121.

[90] Montalto de Jesus, *Histoiric Macao* (Hongkong, 1902), p. 123.

[91] Jenkins, *op. cit.*, pp. 126-129.

[92] An account is given in Jann, *op. cit.*, pp. 434 ff.

bearers of the biretta did not reach Macao until early in 1710 and on June 8th of that year the unfortunate Legate died.[93] Rome had been unable to extricate him from his unhappy predicament.

In spite of the havoc in the China missions wrought by Tournon's embassy, Rome would not retreat from the position which it had taken in the decree of 1704. In reply to the Jesuit appeal, in 1710 the Inquisition supported Tournon's Nanking regulations and reaffirmed the Papal edict of 1704. It also prohibited further discussion of the question in the press.[94] In 1715, in the bull *Ex illa die*, Pope Clement XI again endorsed the decree of 1704 and Tournon's edict, and required all missionaries to take a written oath to abide by the bull. Yet a certain amount of uncertainty remained, for purely civil or political ceremonies were permitted and the decision as to the nature of a given custom was left to a bishop, a vicar apostolic, a visitor general, or a Papal commissioner.[95]

Tournon's mission had been so bungled that it was deemed advisable to send another legate to win K'ang Hsi to a more favourable attitude and to bring the missionaries to obedience. For this task, made almost impossible by the miscarriage of the Tournon effort, Jean Charles Mezzabarba was chosen. He was given the titles of Patriarch of Alexandria, Legate, and Visitor Apostolic. To avoid the debilitating conflict with the padroado the consent of Portugal was obtained, and the Legate went by way of Lisbon.[96] Mezzabarba arrived in Macao in September, 1720, and was received by K'ang Hsi on the last day of December of that year. Mezzabarba seems to have comported himself with dignity and tact, but the Emperor was somewhat contemptuous of him. K'ang Hsi had probably been led by the Jesuits to expect favourable action from Rome, and when, at his insistence, the bull *Ex illa die* was at last translated for him, he became highly incensed. He, the mightiest ruler of his generation, could not tolerate the efforts of a foreign ecclesiastic to alter, against his own expressed will, the customs of his subjects. To placate K'ang Hsi and to satisfy those missionaries who declared that the enforcement of the bull would wreck the Church in China, Mezzabarba issued eight "permissions" as interpretations of the section in the bull which allowed ceremonies of a purely civil or political character. These went far towards sanctioning modified forms of the debated rites. However, Mezzabarba failed to mollify K'ang Hsi.[97]

[93] Thomas, *op. cit.*, pp. 218-223.

[94] John Laurence von Mosheim, *Authentick Memoirs of the Christian Church in China . . . translated from the German*, p. 34.

[95] Thomas, *op. cit.*, pp. 243-251.

[96] Jann, *op. cit.*, pp. 500-505.

[97] On Mezzabarba see Mosheim, *op. cit.*, pp. 40-46; Huc, *Christianity in China, Tartary and Thibet*, Vol. III, pp. 289-320; Thomas, *op. cit.*, pp. 272 ff.; Mailla, *Histoire Générale de la Chine*, Vol. XI, pp. 337 ff.

Mezzarba's "permissions" left uncertainties as to the interpretation of the bull of 1715 and made further Papal action necessary. Rome again went into the whole dreary question, and in 1742 the bull *Ex quo singulari* annulled the "permissions," confirmed the bull of 1715, ordered disobedient missionaries to be returned to Europe for punishment, and prescribed a form of oath of sub-mission to the Papal decrees to be taken by all missionaries to China.[98] This ended the controversy, and while from time to time questions of interpretation and enforcement arose, the missionaries seem to have been loyal to their plighted word.[99]

The Rites Controversy, so prolonged and at times so bitter, could not fail to work damage to the Christian cause. By it the attention of missionaries had been at least partly diverted from the propagation of the faith. Because of it numbers of the already scanty missionary force had left China. The bitterness between missionaries and between those missionaries who obeyed Rome and their flocks, accustomed as the latter were to the tolerant ways associated with the name of Ricci, must have proved subversive to that love which is one of the cardinal tenets of Christianity. K'ang Hsi had been made suspicious and his hardly won friendship had cooled. The progress of the faith had been distinctly retarded.

Yet it is by no means certain that had Rome taken the opposite position and sanctioned the Jesuit accommodations to Chinese culture Christianity would have made much more headway. Christians might have become slightly more numerous, but the jealousies between the orders and between the padroado and the non-padroado missionaries would have remained. Moreover, the other hin-drances to the Christian cause—the decay of Spain and Portugal, the dissolution of the Society of Jesus, the increasing persecutions which punctuated the re-mainder of the eighteenth century, and the cutting off of support from Europe by the French Revolution and the wars of Napoleon—which were chiefly responsible for the evil days which overtook the nascent Church were quite independent of the controversy over the rites.

The third factor in checking the growth of Christianity in China in the eighteenth century was the abolition of the Society of Jesus, in 1773. In land after land, as we have seen, the action taken against the Jesuits by Spain, Portu-gal, and France, culminating in the Papal termination of the Society, brought to the progress of Christianity embarrassment and in extreme instances ruin. In China the effect was made serious by the fact that from the beginning the

---

[98] *Collectanea S. Congregatione de Propaganda Fide,* Vol. I, pp. 130-141; Grentrup in *Zeitschrift für Missionswissenschaft,* Vol. XV, pp. 100-110.

[99] For instances and the appropriate references, see Latourette, *A History of Christian Missions in China,* p. 151.

Jesuits had been the leaders in the propagation of the faith. The blow was not so disastrous as might at first have been expected. By no means all of the former Jesuits left the country. They were priests of the Church as well as members of the Society, and in the former capacity they continued their labours.[100] No reinforcements could come, however, and the last survivor died in 1814.[101] At the repeated request of the French ex-Jesuits that some other order be found to assume the burdens once borne by the Society, in 1783 the Lazarists, or, to give them their official name, the Congregation of the Priests of the Mission, were assigned by Rome to the China mission.[102] Some of them had already been in the Empire,[103] but the first to serve in this enlarged responsibility reached China in 1784. Before many years, one of them, Raux, was placed in charge of the bureau of astronomy,[104] so that the Roman Catholics still had an officially recognized foothold in Peking. Others, too, were employed by the Court as artists, mathematicians, and mechanics, and as interpreters in government correspondence with Europeans.[105] Yet the mission in Peking had been declining even before the dissolution of the Society of Jesus[106] and the Lazarists were unable to do more than to retard the course of the decay.

The most serious blow to the Roman Catholic missions in China (the fourth factor in retarding the spread of Christianity) was dealt by the persecutions which marked the eighteenth century. Of these persecutions, the Papal decisions on the rites seem to have been merely a minor cause which operated only in the reign of K'ang Hsi. We hear of persecutions under K'ang Hsi and even of an order that all Chinese Christians renounce their faith,[107] but this latter appears not to have been generally put into effect. While angered by the Papal decrees, K'ang Hsi continued his friendship for the Jesuits and presumably felt that the enforcement of the *piao* was a sufficient control and that no serious danger to the state was to be apprehended from the missionaries who remained.

Under the succeeding reign, that of Yung Chêng (1723-1726), persecutions became more intense. Why Yung Chêng was hostile we do not know, but

---

[100] Thomas, *Histoire de la Mission de Pékin depuis les Origines jusqu'a l'Arrivée des Lazaristes*, pp. 431 ff.

[101] Moidrey, *La Hiérarchie Catholique en Chine, en Corée et au Japon*, p. 187.

[102] Cordier in *The Catholic Encyclopedia*, Vol. III, pp. 675, 676; Demimuid, *Vie du François-Regis Clet*, pp. 74-90.

[103] Coste in *Revue d'Histoire des Missions*, Vol. III, pp. 328 ff.

[104] A. Thomas, *Histoire de la Mission de Pékin depuis l'Arrivée des Lazaristes jusqu'a la Revolte des Boxeurs* (Paris, Louis Michaud, 1925, pp. 758), pp. 19, 32, 33; Alphonse Favier, *Pékin, Histoire et Description* (Lille, 2 vols., 1900), Vol. I, p. 194.

[105] Richenet, letter of 1817, in *T'oung Pao*, Vol. XX, p. 121.

[106] Thomas, *Histoire de la Mission de Pékin depuis les Origines jusqu'à l'Arrivée des Lazaristes*, pp. 307 ff.

[107] Mailla from Peking, June 5, 1717, in *Lettres Édifiantes*, Vol. III, pp. 270-286.

apparently it was in part because of personal pique against a family of the imperial clan which counted some Christians in its circle. Whatever the cause, not many months after his accession, Yung Chêng commanded that all missionaries except those needed by the government in Peking be sent to Macao, that church buildings be confiscated, and that Chinese Christians give up their faith.[108] The edict was fairly vigorously carried out, with marked injury to the Christian cause.[109]

After Yung Chêng came Ch'ien Lung, with a reign which covered sixty years, 1736-1796. In it persecutions were frequent. Ch'ien Lung seems to have cherished no especial enmity against Christians. He continued to employ missionaries at his court. However, under his rule, although outwardly brilliant, the Ch'ing (Manchu) dynasty was showing indications of the slow decay which in 1912 brought it to an inglorious end. Various secret organizations were fomenting rebellion. The Emperor took strict measures to discover and destroy all books which he deemed seditious.[110] Under these circumstances, it is not strange that a tighter rein was held on Christians. Almost at the beginning of the reign, a fresh edict was issued commanding Christians to renounce their faith and expressly forbidding Bannermen, both Chinese and Manchu, to accept the foreign religion.[111] The decree was not uniformly enforced, but again and again, and in various parts of the Empire, persecutions harassed the Christian communities. They seem to have grown in intensity as the century proceeded, partly, perhaps, because of the rising threat of insurrection in the waning years of Ch'ien Lung.[112] The persecutions were the more trying because their increase roughly synchronized with the blow dealt by the abolition of the Society of Jesus.

To the end of the Jesuits and the mounting persecutions was added a fifth deleterious factor, the French Revolution and the wars of Napoleon. All Europe was thrown into turmoil. Income was cut off and the number of new recruits dwindled. Yet a few reinforcements arrived. Contact with the churches in Europe was not entirely severed.[113]

In spite of this rising tide of misfortunes, missions in China continued. The

[108] A translation of the text is in Cordier, Doc. pour servir à l'his. ecclés. de l'Extrême-Orient in Rev. de l'Extrême-Orient, Vol. II, pp. 54, 55.
[109] Mailla from Peking, Oct. 16, 1724, in Lettres Édifiantes, Vol. III, pp. 360 ff.; Mailla, Histoire Générale de la Chine, Vol. XI, pp. 446-470.
[110] L. C. Goodrich, The Literary Inquisition of Ch'ien-lung (Baltimore, Waverly Press, 1935, pp. xii, 275), passim.
[111] Parennin from Peking, Oct. 22, 1736, in Lettres Édifiantes, Vol. III, pp. 469-472; Mailla, Histoire Générale de la Chine, Vol. XI, pp. 512-517.
[112] Latourette, A History of Christian Missions in China, pp. 162-166, 171-175
[113] Latourette, op. cit., pp. 169-171.

Christian communities did not die out. In some areas they even increased. Just how many Christians were in China at the close of the eighteenth century we do not know. Estimates range from about two hundred thousand[114] to about three hundred thousand.[115] Apparently the number was not much if any less than at the height of the favour of K'ang Hsi and in what had seemed the era of greatest prosperity.

This persistence in the face of adversity was made possible largely by the heroism and devotion of missionaries. These were chiefly Jesuits, Dominicans, Franciscans, and members of the Missions-Étrangères of Paris. After 1784 the Lazarists were added. The Jesuits were strong in Peking, in the Provinces of Kiangnan and Chihli, and in Tartary (roughly Manchuria, Mongolia, and Sinkiang). The Spanish Dominicans were active in Fukien. Spanish Franciscans were in the Provinces of Shantung, Kwangtung, Kwangsi, and Fukien. Italian Franciscans were in Shansi. The Missions-Étrangères eventually were concentrated in the South-west and West, in the Provinces of Yünnan, Kweichow, and Szechwan. They had particularly strong communities in Szechwan. The Lazarists replaced the Jesuits and in addition gave some attention to Central China. Most of the provinces of China Proper contained some Christians. Care of these necessitated extensive journeys by the small missionary staff, and because of the chronic persecutions travel had usually to be unobtrusive and even in disguise.[116] The distressingly small foreign staff was augmented by Chinese priests. A few of these were educated at Naples in a college founded for that purpose in 1732 by a secular, Ripa.[117] True to their purpose, the missionaries of the Paris society trained Chinese for the priesthood, although in the face of great difficulties.[118] At least in 1817, the Lazarists had two seminaries in Peking conducted respectively by French and Portuguese members of the order.[119] The fidelity of the Chinese and foreign clergy repeatedly led to imprisonment and in more than one instance to martyrdom.[120] We hear, too, of Chinese lay Christians who were zealous in spreading their faith[121] or who went into death or exile rather than prove traitor to it.[122]

[114] L. E. Louvet, *Les Missions Catholiques au XIXe Siécle* (Lyon, Oeuvre de la Propagation de la Foi, c. 1895, pp. xvi, 543, 46), p. 234.

[115] Schmidlin-Braun, *Catholic Mission History*, p. 610.

[116] Latourette, *op. cit.*, pp. 160 ff.

[117] Matteo Ripa, *Storia della Fondazione della Congregazione e del Collegio de' Cinesi* (Naples, 3 vols., 1832), *passim*; *Memoirs of Father Ripa*, translated from the Italian by Fortunato Prandi (London, 1844), pp. 93-95, 131 ff.

[118] Launay, *Histoire Générale de la Société des Missions-Étrangères*, Vol. II, pp. 161-163.

[119] Richenet, letter of 1817, in *T'oung Pao*, Vol. XX, p. 121.

[120] Latourette, *op. cit.*, pp. 163-165, 172, 173.

[121] Letters of Saint-Simon, April 1 and May 29, 1782, in *Nouvelles Lettres Édifiantes*, Vol. I, pp. 298-301.

[122] Latourette, *op. cit.*, pp. 163, 171-173.

Roman Catholicism was the chief but not the only form of Christianity which entered China between A.D. 1500 and A.D. 1800. The Russian Orthodox Church was represented, and for a brief time Dutch Protestants had missions in Formosa, although then that island had not yet become a part of the Chinese Empire.

As we are to see in the following chapter, during these centuries the Russians were traversing Northern Asia. In that expansion they came into contact with China. In the sixteen-eighties in a border conflict K'ang Hsi's forces took several prisoners from Albazin, the chief Russian fort on the Amur River. These were brought to Peking, and were given a permanent residence in the north-east corner of the city. Presumably they were members of the Russian Orthodox Church. Certainly with them was a priest of that communion, Maxim Leontiev. Leontiev ministered to his small flock. A little later a priest and a deacon were sent by Metropolitan Ignatius of Tobolsk. Ignatius hoped that the colony might prepare the way for the conversion of China. In 1715 an archimandrite and other clergy were sent to Peking and were courteously received by K'ang Hsi. The Treaty of Kiakhta, made in 1727 between China and Russia, contained provision for an ecclesiastical mission in Peking. This was for the purpose of giving spiritual care to the descendants of the Albazinians and of assisting in the relations between the two countries by training Russians in the Chinese and Manchu languages. No effort seems to have been made to win Chinese to the Christian faith, but the Albazinian Christian community continued and in the nineteenth century became a radiating centre for missions among the Chinese.[123]

Before A.D. 1800 Protestant missions in the area eventually comprised in the Chinese Empire were limited to Formosa. In 1624 the Dutch built a fort, Zeelandia, on the island and held possession of it until the sixteen sixties. They were driven out by a picturesque and stubborn opponent of the Manchus, Chêng Ch'êng-kung, who is better known in the Occident under the name of Koxinga. Two decades later, in 1683, Formosa was brought by the Manchus into the Empire.

In the generation that the Dutch were in the island several of their clergy were active in attempts to spread the Christian faith. Among these we hear especially of G. Candidius and R. Junius. At least twenty-nine clergymen served in the island and several of them made progress in acquiring the local vernaculars. Within the area of Dutch commercial and political influence, hundreds of converts were won, schools were established, and catechists employed to instruct the neophytes and the children. Idols were destroyed, and

[123] See references in Latourette, op. cit., p. 200, note 1, and especially Archimandrite Innocent in The Chinese Recorder, Vol. XLVII, pp. 678 ff.; Cordier, Histoire Générale de la Chine, Vol. III, pp. 272-278, 340-342; Lübeck, Die russischen Missionen, pp. 8-10.

the missionaries reported that in more than one place Sunday was fairly strictly observed. The catechism and prayers were taught. A translation was made of at least the Gospel of Matthew. Sometimes an escort of troops was required to give protection to the missionary or teacher when a new village was entered. The complaint was made that while ability to repeat the catechism was a prerequisite to baptism, the lives of many of the new Christians left much to be desired. Chinese were to be found on the island and of these some seem to have become Christians. The large majority of the converts, however, appear to have been from the non-Chinese aborigines.[124] These latter were of a primitive culture which yielded fairly easily to pressure from the Dutch. So far as we know, the congregations did not long survive the collapse of Dutch rule. Presumably the Christianity which was so dependent upon Dutch prestige disappeared with the regime under whose ægis it had been initiated.

In two other areas more or less dependent politically on the Manchu Empire, Tibet and Korea, Christianity gained slight footholds before A.D. 1800. In both lands it was only Roman Catholic Christianity which effected an entrance.

It was not until the opening decades of the eighteenth century that Tibet became politically an apanage of China. More than two generations before that time the huge plateau, so difficult of access, had been penetrated by intrepid European missionaries. The urge to propagate the Christian faith sent hardy pioneers into areas not yet touched by those of their compatriots who were impelled only by the desire for trade, the lust of conquest, or the lure of exploration. Bento de Goes, the Jesuit who in 1603 left Lahore, crossed the Pamir, reached Yarkand, and in 1607 died in Suchow in the far North-west of China Proper, demonstrated that the Cathay of the Franciscan missionaries of the fourteenth century was the same as the China in which Ricci and his confreres were labouring, but almost certainly his route did not, as some have conjectured, take him across Tibet.[125] In 1624 another Jesuit, Antonio de Andrada, arrived at Tsaparang on the upper courses of the Sutlej, and there, on a second expedition, in 1626 began the building of a church. Reinforcements came and a few converts were made, but political conditions altered adversely, and by 1640 the region was closed to missionaries.[126] In 1631 another member of the

[124] This information is drawn from documentary records, largely contemporary letters and reports from Formosa, translated in Wm. Campbell, *Formosa under the Dutch Described from Contemporary Records* (London, Kegan Paul, Trench, Trübner & Co., 1903, pp. xiv, 629), more than half of which is concerned with missions. Volumes III and IV of *Archief voor de Geschiedenis der Oude Hollandsche Zending* (Utrecht, C. Van Bentum, 6 vols., 1884-1891) are also devoted to Formosa and much of their material has been translated in the above work by Campbell.

[125] Wessels, *Early Jesuit Travellers in Central Asia*, pp. 1 ff.

[126] Wessels, *op. cit.*, pp. 43 ff.; Filippi, editor, *An Account of Tibet. The Travels of Ippolito Desideri of Pistoia, S. J., 1712-1727*, pp. 3 ff.

Society, Francisco de Azevedo, made a journey which took him to Tsaparang and to Leh, on the upper part of the Indus.[127] From 1627 to 1632 through the efforts of two other Jesuits, Cacella and Cabral, a mission was temporarily established at Shigatse on the Tsangpo not so many days' journey from Lhasa.[128] In 1661 John Grueber and Albert d'Orville, also Jesuits, arrived in Lhasa *en route* to India and Rome from Peking by way of Kokonor and remained there for several weeks, presumably the first Europeans to see that capital of Tibet.[129] In 1716 Hippolyte Desideri, likewise of the Society, reached Lhasa by way of Leh. He spent several years in and near that city, studied Tibetan, and wrote a book to present the Christian faith as against Tibetan Lamaistic Buddhism. In 1721, since Rome had assigned the region to the Capuchins, he withdrew.[130]

The Capuchins had as a base the French settlement at Chandernagor, in Bengal, not far from Calcutta. The first group of missionaries left Rome in 1704. In 1707 a party reached Lhasa and there set themselves to acquire familiarity with the language and customs of the country. For a time after 1711 or 1712 hardship and poverty compelled the abandonment of Lhasa, but the Propaganda ordered that the mission be continued, and in 1716 a party of Capuchins once more arrived at the Dalai Lama's capital.[131] For several years the enterprise continued and baptisms were recorded. In 1745, however, persecution drove out the missionaries.[132] Converts were removed to two villages in Oudh and Nepal, but the Capuchin effort in Tibet was not renewed.[133] Not until the nineteenth century did missionaries again make their way into the great closed land.

Korea was within the cultural orbit of China and from time to time it had been politically subordinate to the Chinese Emperors. The Ch'ing (Manchu) Dynasty regarded it as a tributary state, but the Chinese administrative system was not extended to it. So far as we know, the first Christians in Korea came in connexion with the Japanese invasion under Hideyoshi, but we are not aware that any conversions were made among the Koreans. In 1619 and 1620 the famous Chinese Christian scholar, Hsü Kuang-ch'i, planned, unsuccessfully,

[127] Wessels, *op. cit.*, pp. 120 ff., 282 ff.
[128] Wessels, *op. cit.*, pp. 120 ff., 314 ff.; Filippi, *op. cit.*, pp. 19 ff.
[129] Wessels, *op. cit.*, pp. 164 ff., 337 ff.
[130] Wessels, *op. cit.*, pp. 205 ff.
[131] Filippi, *op. cit.*, pp. 112, 113; Adrien Launay, *Histoire de la Mission du Thibet*, Vol. I, p. 32; Jann, *Die katholischen Missionen in Indien, China und Japan*, pp. 385 ff.
[132] Launay, *op. cit.*, Vol. I, pp. 34 ff.
[133] Launay, in Piolet, *Les Missions Catholiques Françaises au XIXe Siècle* (Paris, Librairie Armand Colin, 5 vols., [no date] to 1902), Vol. III, p. 332.

a mission to Korea. Near the beginning of the seventeenth century one of Ricci's books on Christianity, written in Chinese, the language of Korean scholarship, was being read in the peninsula. About 1644 Schall came in touch at Peking with the ruler of Korea. The latter expressed himself as willing to take a missionary back with him, but in the troubled conditions accompanying the Manchu conquest Schall was unable to find one.[134]

It was not until 1784 that we hear of a Korean Christian. From then on the story of the faith in Korea had in it much of romance and even more of persecution. In that year there was baptized in Peking a Korean of a distinguished family by the name of Ri or Li who was in the train of the annual Korean embassy to the Manchu court. In Korea he had been in contact with a scholarly circle who for several years previously had been studying Christian books. On his return to Korea, Ri told his friends of his new faith. Conversions followed. Persecution by the state soon came. In 1785 Christianity was officially attacked, and at least one martyrdom is reported. The Christians had learned enough of the organization of the Church to desire bishops and clergy, and proceeded, without authorization from Rome or from Peking, to organize a hierarchy. One of their number was chosen bishop and several others were made priests. These clergymen preached, administered baptism and confirmation, and said mass. However, about 1789 from perusing Christian books some of them came to have doubts as to the validity of their procedure. A messenger was sent to Peking to seek advice. There he was given baptism, confirmation, and communion, and a letter from the Bishop which sought to encourage the Christians to spread their faith but informed them that the only sacrament which they could administer was that of baptism. The Christians assented and sent to Peking asking for priests. Instructions from the Bishop of Peking that the traditional honours to ancestors were incompatible with a Christian profession led to the defection of some of the converts, but by no means of all. Severe persecutions ensued, with martyrdoms. A European priest sent from Peking to Korea was halted on the frontier and reluctantly retraced his steps. Late in 1794 a Chinese priest succeeded in making his way into the country and there served the Christians. However, persecutions continued, and in 1801 he fell a victim to them. At that time Christians are said to have numbered ten thousand. Although left without a pastor, harried by the government, cut off from contacts with Christians on the outside, and deprived of its leaders from the upper classes, Korean Christianity did not die out. It persisted and had a continuous history until, in the latter part of the nineteenth century,

[134] Väth, *Johann Adam Schall von Bell*, p. 163.

more favourable days dawned.[135] Here, as in so many other regions, the Christian impulse displayed amazing vitality.

What effect did this Christianity, planted at so much cost and against such adverse conditions, have upon China? First it must be said that during this period China was not so violently disturbed by Christianity as was Japan. No such extreme measures were taken to stamp out the faith or to close the country against all foreign intercourse by which Christian ideas might filter in. Christians never constituted so large a proportion of the population as they did at the height of their prosperity in Japan.

Yet, as we have seen, Roman Catholic missions in China resulted in converts in most and perhaps all of the provinces, and in a total Christian community which even at the close of the eighteenth century, after a series of disheartening misfortunes, seems still to have been not far from two hundred thousand strong. How far the lives of these Christians were altered by their faith we do not know. A catechism was used, and a fairly good knowledge of it was required before baptism. The catechumen, too, was commanded to abstain from rites which the Church deemed superstitious and to destroy his idols.[136] Schools were provided for the children of Christians, both boys and girls, in which instruction was given in the Christian faith, and in which the boys were taught writing and the Chinese Classics.[137] Conversion often brought healing from the distressing affliction known as demon possession.[138] Provision was made for regular services in the absence of priests or catechists. The usual programme was to have a priest visit each Christian group at least once a year to preach, say mass, hear confessions, give instruction, and administer baptism.[139] An extensive Christian literature was prepared in Chinese, including translations of parts of the Scriptures and of prayers and hymns, and a large proportion of this was not so much for the purpose of winning non-Christians as for nourishing Christians in their faith.[140] Presumably, then, with all these requirements and aids, Christians must have showed lives which differed somewhat from those of their non-Christian fellows.

[135] Ch. Dallet, *Histoire de l'Église de Corée* (Paris, Librairie Victor Palmé, 2 vols., 1874), Vol. I, pp. 13 ff.
[136] *Nouvelles Lettres Édifiantes*, Vol. I, pp. 347-357.
[137] Letter of Dufresse, Oct. 26, 1800, in *Nouvelles Lettres Édifiantes*, Vol. III, pp. 446 ff.; the same, Oct. 28, 1803, in *op. cit.*, Vol. IV, pp. 62-71.
[138] *Nouvelles Lettres Édifiantes*, Vol. I, pp. 157-159.
[139] *Lettres Édifiantes*, Vol. III, pp. 187-195; *Nouvelles Lettres Édifiantes*, Vol. I, pp. 347-357.
[140] Latourette, *A History of Christian Missions in China*, p. 189.

Much was made of the baptism of infants *in articulo mortis*.[141] This, however, could have done little to augment the Christian community and by the fact that it was often administered surreptitiously and that death usually followed so promptly on the administration of the rite, it gave rise to evil tales and augmented popular hostility.

Upon the life of China outside of the infinitesimal Christian minority the effect of Christianity was not great. This is not surprising. It was scarcely to be expected that a mere handful 'of missionaries would work many changes in so massive and closely integrated a culture as that of China. The chief result was the introduction of Western European mathematics and astronomy and the improvement of the calendar.[142] The revision of the calendar made by the Jesuits remained in official use to the end of the Ch'ing (Manchu) Dynasty, in 1912.[143] The missionaries also contributed to the mapping of China. They brought in European forms of painting, of architecture, and of music.[144] They imported such mechanical appliances as clocks. They enlarged the Chinese knowledge of the map of the world. They were the channels for the most intimate contacts which China had yet had with the culture of Western Europe. These contacts proved a stimulus to the rather active intellectual life of the eighteenth century.[145] The effect was particularly marked upon a small minority of heterodox scholars, the forerunners of the intellectual revolution of the twentieth century.[146] Upon the non-Christian religions of the land Christianity made an impression, even though slight. In a Taoist collection, *Shên-hsien-kang-chien*, compiled in the time of K'ang Hsi and well known in Buddhist as well as Taoist circles, a brief account was included of the life of Jesus and of the Assumption of the Virgin Mary.[147]

An interesting and reverse effect was upon the Occident. Through their extensive writings, missionaries made China familiar to the upper classes of Europe. In consequence, something of a fad arose for things Chinese. Gardens, pavilions, and pagodas in Chinese style were numerous, the manufacture of

[141] Launay, *Histoire Générale de la Société des Missions-Étrangères*, Vol. II, p. 198; Entrecolles from Peking, Oct. 19, 1720, in *Lettres Édifiantes*, Vol. III, p. 292.
[142] Henri Bernard, *Matteo Ricci's Scientific Contributions to China*, translated by E. T. C. Werner (Peiping, Henri Vetch, 1935, pp. 108), *passim;* Henri Bernard, *L'Église Catholique des XVIIe-XVIIIe Siécles et Sa Place dans l'Evolution de la Civilisation Chinoise* (*Monumenta Serica*, Vol. I, Fasc. 1, pp. 155 ff.); Henri Bernard, *L'Encyclopédie Astronomique du Pére Schall* (*Monumenta Serica*, Vol. III, Fasc. 1, pp. 35 ff., Fasc. 2, pp. 441 ff.).
[143] Hu Shih, *The Chinese Renaissance*, pp. 29, 30.
[144] W. Devine, *The Four Churches of Peking* (London, Burns, Oates and Washbourne, 1930, pp. 225), pp. 41, 69-79.
[145] Liang Ch'i-ch'ao in *The Chinese Social and Political Science Review*, Vol. VIII, p. 38.
[146] L. Hodous in *The Chinese Recorder*, Vol. LVIII, pp. 422-425.
[147] K. L. Reichelt in *The Chinese Recorder*, Vol. LV, pp. 110 ff.

porcelain was begun, and lacquer, incense, tea, sedan chairs, the Chinese style of painting, and wall papers became fashionable.[148] European Deists believed that they saw in the Confucianism portrayed by the Jesuits a confirmation in their belief in "natural religion," the fruit of the effort of the human spirit to discover God, as against "revealed religion," the result of the active work of God, as described in Christian theology.[149] The liberal intellectuals of the Enlightenment cherished a warm admiration for Chinese culture. They regarded the China described by the missionaries as an example of what they deemed the ideal, a society governed by philosophers and controlled by reason.[150] In interpreting China to Europe the missionaries were making a greater immediate impression upon the latter than they were upon the former. It was a notable instance, of which there were many in the next century, of the sympathetic presentation by missionaries of non-European peoples and cultures to the Occident.

Upon the Christianity planted in China, the Chinese environment made a decided impression. Much of this was only temporary, for the refusal of Rome to accord its sanction to the adjustments associated with the name of Ricci eliminated most of the accommodations. In addition to the specific steps towards acclimatization which we have already noted, in 1615, at the request of the Jesuits, Rome granted permission to translate the missal and breviary into Chinese and to use Chinese in the administration of the sacraments, including the mass. However, before the decree could be fully carried out Rome felt it wise to rescind its action (1661).[151] Rome, too, as a concession to Chinese prejudice against the performance of dignified ritual bare-headed, allowed priests to wear in the mass a head-dress adapted from the cap of ancient Chinese scholars.[152] This was retained into the nineteenth century.[153] It is interesting, too, that the most eminent of the Chinese Christian scholars, Hsü Kuang-ch'i, presented Christianity to one of his friends as a force which would build "good and virtuous character, . . . elevate society to the high level of the best sages of classical antiquity, and . . . place the government and state upon the solid

[148] Henry Cordier, *La Chine en France au XVIIIe Siècle* (Paris, 1910), *passim*; A. Reichwein, translated by J. C. Powell, *China and Europe. Intellectual and Artistic Contacts in the Eighteenth Century* (New York, 1925), *passim*.

[149] N. Söderblom, *Das Werden des Gottesglaubens* (Leipzig, J. C. Hinrichs'sche Buchhandlung, 1916, pp. xii, 398), pp. 324-360; Virgile Pinot, *La Chine et la Formation de l'Ésprit Philosophique en France, passim.*

[150] For repercussions of this admiration in America, see *Writings of Thomas Jefferson,* Lipscomb ed., Vol. V, p. 183.

[151] Huonder, *Der einheimische Klerus in den Heidenländern,* pp. 158-160.

[152] *Ibid.*

[153] Devine, *op. cit.,* p. 164.

foundations of everlasting peace and order."[154] Here spoke a man steeped in the Confucian tradition. In his mind his new faith was already conforming in part to the patterns of his inherited philosophy.

To most of this penetration of Christianity by Chinese culture and ideals, Rome, in its decisions on the Rites Controversy, brought a sharp reversal. The major part of such adjustment as persisted took place almost unconsciously in the minds of Chinese Christians. Officially it was an uncompromising and uncompromised Christianity which was carried over into the China of the nineteenth century. It was a Christianity which adhered rigidly and tenaciously to the forms which it had developed in a quite different cultural background. It could have no hope of gaining many Chinese unless the structure of Chinese life to which it was so radically opposed should crumble. That under these conditions it survived at all must be attributed to the heroism of the priests, European and Chinese, who led it, and to a tough inward vitality in Christianity itself.

[154] Hu Shih, *op. cit.*, p. 30.

Chapter XV

RUSSIAN ASIA AND ALASKA

IN THE three centuries between A.D. 1500 and A.D. 1800 expanding Europe carried Christianity across Northern Asia and into North-western America. Here the agents were not, as elsewhere in this period, from Southern and Western Europe, but from Russia. The type of Christianity was not Roman Catholicism or Protestantism, but Russian Orthodoxy. The area was vast, but in most of it the population was sparse. A summary of what was accomplished can, therefore, he compressed into a very small space.

Before A.D. 1500 Russian fur traders had penetrated east of the Urals. However, it was not until the sixteenth century that the region began to be politically subject to Moscow. In the second half of the sixteenth century the conquest commenced. By A.D. 1600, through forces of Cossacks who had the advantage of firearms, the basin of the Irtysh had been seized. Small bands of adventurers—Cossacks, fur traders, trappers—made their way into the country. By the middle of the seventeenth century they had reached the eastern extremity of Asia, on Bering Straits. The Russian population of Siberia rose from about seventy thousand in 1662 to about one million in 1783. The Chinese Empire, in the latter part of the seventeenth and in the eighteenth century in the hands of the greatest of the Manchu rulers, blocked the way south-eastward along the Amur, but in the middle of the eighteenth century explorations were made in the Aleutian Islands and Alaska. Trading enterprises followed and a sprinkling of Russian settlements.[1]

It was to be expected that Russian Christianity would either accompany or closely pursue this eastward expansion with an attempt to hold the settlers to their hereditary faith and to win non-Christians. Here, as in European Russia, the support of the state was given. Here, too, most of the active missionaries were priests and monks. We read, moreover, that many of the fur traders, no matter how harshly they might deal with the natives, were, in their own fashion, religiously minded. Frequently fur-trading stations were named after churches in Russia or patron saints. As a rule, we are told, the first sables caught were donated to some church.[2]

[1] George Vernadsky, *The Expansion of Russia* (*Transactions of the Connecticut Academy of Arts and Sciences,* New Haven, Vol. XXXI, July, 1933, pp. 391-425), pp. 391-415.
[2] Bancroft, *History of Alaska,* p. 233.

The conquest of the Irtysh Valley was quickly followed by conversions. We hear of the baptism of several of the heads of local tribes—one of them as early as 1590.[3] In 1620, for the furthering of the work of the Church, Tobolsk was made the seat of an archbishop. The first incumbent, Cyprian, was given the active support of the Tsar. He built a number of monasteries and saw the baptism of a large number of pagans.[4]

By the close of the seventeenth century monasteries had been established as far eastward as Selenginsk and Nerchinsk, south-east of Lake Baikal, and at Albazin, on the Amur. At imperial command, priests were sent to settlements on the Lena. Conversions were registered among the non-Christian tribes of these regions.[5]

Early in the eighteenth century, under the energetic encouragement of Peter the Great, missionary activity among non-Christian peoples in Siberia, especially in Western Siberia, became marked. Presumably Peter the Great was interested in missions not for their religious significance, but as a means of assimilating non-Russian tribes and of extending his authority. However, in Filofei Leszczynski, Metropolitan of Tobolsk, the missions had a leader who brought to his office ardent religious zeal. Born in 1650 and educated in Kiev, it was not until 1702, when he was well along in middle life, that Filofei (Philotheus) took up the arduous frontier see. His diocese embraced the Russian possessions in Asia and the region west of the Urals included in the Governments of Perm and Orenburg. His vision ranged over all of this vast area. In 1705 he sent an archimandrite to Kamchatka. At the command of Peter he took over the missions to the Ostyaks and the Voguls, Finnish tribes on the Irtysh and the Ob. By imperial direction taxes were remitted for those who accepted baptism, and idols and pagan temples were destroyed and churches were erected in their stead. He obtained missionaries from Kiev. In 1709, ill and discouraged by failures, especially in Mongolia, Filofei laid down his office and retired to a monastery, but in 1711 he was back again in his difficult field. With military escort and with priests to assist him, he made journeys along the Irtysh and the Ob and baptized many among the Ostyaks and the Voguls. In 1715 he once more took up his diocese. He sent missionaries to various districts and tribes. In spite of his advanced years he himself made journeys which took him as far east as Lake Baikal. He was much interested in the Russian mission in Peking. In 1721, now past his three score years and ten, he finally resigned his diocese and sought retirement in a monastery.[6]

[3] Lübeck, *Die Christianisierung Russlands*, p. 37.
[4] Lübeck, *op. cit.*, pp. 37, 38.
[5] Lübeck, *op. cit.*, pp. 38, 39; Raeder in *Allgemeine Missionszeitschrift*, Vol. XXXII, pp. 403, 404.
[6] Lübeck, *op. cit.*, pp. 39-43; Raeder, in *op. cit.*, Vol. XXXII, pp. 404-406.

For a time after Filofei Leszczynski missions in the Tobolsk area marked time and reversions to paganism occurred. About the middle of the eighteenth century, however, conversions once more began. In 1748, for instance, a chief of the Ostyaks and a number of his tribe professed Christianity.[7]

In 1727 Irkutsk, in which in 1707 the Metropolitan of Tobolsk had consecrated a vicar, was erected into an independent diocese. Here a kind of missionary seminary was founded in which instruction was given in the Mongol and Chinese tongues. Converts were made among the Buryats, the Tunguses, and the Yakuts.[8] In the second half of the eighteenth century Cyril Suchanov laboured among the Tunguses. He learned their language, established churches and schools, and met with such success that for many years thereafter the descendants of those won by him were called "Suchanov Tunguses."[9]

In the first half of the seventeenth century some Kalmyks, a Mongol people, settled on the lower reaches of the Volga. Among them, beginning in the reign of Peter the Great, missions were systematically and vigorously undertaken. One of the Khans was baptized, with Peter as godfather, and his horde followed him. A special territory was assigned to the Christian Kalmyks, with the fortress at Stavropol, on the Volga, as a centre. The Gospels and prayers were put into the Kalmyk tongue. In 1737 the baptized were said to have been about three thousand, and the number later increased.[10]

In the first half of the eighteenth century active missions were conducted in Kamchatka. We hear of one which is said to have baptized five thousand of the natives and to have built four churches for them. Here, as in so many other parts of the Russian Empire, formal conversion was encouraged by the promise of exemption from tribute—in Kamchatka for ten years.[11] In 1742 the Holy Synod sent reinforcements and by 1744 two-thirds of the population are declared to have become Christian. By 1750 most of the population was reported as Christian. In the second half of the century a number of Olyuts, on the northern border of Kamchatka, were baptized by the priest Maxim Kasarev.[12]

Through much of Siberia were parish clergy. These came primarily to give spiritual care to the Russian colonists and government officials. In addition, some of them endeavoured to spread their faith among their non-Christian neighbours. Few of them, however, had a knowledge of the language of the non-Christian peoples among whom they worked or founded permanent missions.[13]

[7] Lübeck, *op. cit.*, pp. 74, 75; Raeder in *op. cit.*, Vol. XXXII, p. 411.
[8] Lübeck, *op. cit.*, pp. 63, 64; Raeder in *op. cit.*, Vol. XXXII, pp. 407, 408.
[9] Lübeck, *op. cit.*, p. 64.
[10] Lübeck, *op. cit.*, pp. 58-60.
[11] Bancroft, *History of Alaska*, p. 58.
[12] Lübeck, *op. cit.*, pp. 65, 66.
[13] Smirnoff, *A Short Account of the Historical Development and Present Position of Russian Orthodox Missions*, pp. 13, 14.

In America, in the Aleutian Islands and Alaska, missionaries were close on the heels of the explorers and traders. It is said, indeed, that one of the discovers of the Aleutians baptized the son of a chieftain.[14] Shelekhov, who did much to develop Russian commerce with America and who has been called the founder of the Russian colonies on that continent, had the spread of Christianity deeply at heart. He himself claimed to have won many of the natives to the faith, and it was at his request that the first missionaries were sent.[15] In 1794, in response to Shelekhov's expressed wish and by order of the Empress Catherine II, eighteen clergy and servitors, headed by an archimandrite, arrived at Kodiak Island.[16] Baranov, who was Shelekhov's representative and the most powerful man in the Russian enterprise in Alaska, was rough, uncultured, and hostile to the missionaries. The missionaries reciprocated his dislike and in his letters to Shelekhov the archimandrite complained bitterly of him and of his atrocities. It was another chapter in the long story of the opposition of representatives of the Christian faith to the exploitation of subject peoples and of the resulting antagonism between those whose motive in the expansion of Europe was economic and those whose purpose was religious. The Christian impulse was acting as a critic of ruthless cruelty. The missionaries were forced to make their own living by the labour of their hands. For years they received from the company which had the Russian monopoly of Alaska neither books, candles, or wine for the celebration of the sacraments. Yet within a few years nearly all the inhabitants of the Aleutian Islands were baptized. The archimandrite was recalled to Irkutsk to be consecrated bishop for Alaska, but on his way back to his distant diocese he was drowned and for many years the region was without a resident episcopate. Much of the Christianity was superficial, especially since few if any of the missionaries learned the native tongues. However, we know of one who strove earnestly to educate boys, to prevent polygamy, and to raise the level of morals of the neophytes, and who came to a martyr's end.[17] In the nineteenth century missions continued and had at least one missionary who learned the vernacular and prepared Christian literature in it.[18]

Russian Christianity made no effort to expand beyond the political boundaries of the Russian Empire. This is not surprising. We have seen that in this period, when in Roman Catholic and Protestant as well as in Russian Orthodox lands the Church was usually dominated by the state, generally missions were carried on in close conjunction with the economic or political programme of one

[14] Bancroft, *op. cit.*, p. 699.
[15] Bancroft, *op. cit.*, pp. 303, 304.
[16] Bancroft, *op. cit.*, p. 352.
[17] Bancroft, *op. cit.*, pp. 358 ff.
[18] Bancroft, *op. cit.*, pp. 703 ff.

or another of the European powers. However, both Roman Catholic and Protestant missions occasionally overpassed the boundaries of the secular enterprises of European governments and peoples. In this period Russian Orthodoxy seldom if ever did so. Even within the Russian Empire missions were never on the extensive scale that they were in Spanish, Portuguese, French, English, and Dutch colonial domains.

The reasons for the lesser missionary activity of the Russian Church are several. Some of them are to be found in the nature of Russian Christianity itself. The Russian Church was even more subordinate to the state than were the Roman Catholic and Protestant churches of the time. It was more quietistic. Its monks were more absorbed in the interior life and were less activistic than were the monks of Western Europe. Then, too, the territory occupied by Russia in Europe, Asia, and North America was so huge that there was little inducement to go outside it. Neither explorers nor merchants ventured far beyond what later became the Tsar's domains and it was hardly to be expected that missionaries would do so. Within these vast areas distances were great, travelling was difficult, and the population scanty and widely scattered. It was not surprising that the number of converts was not large. Yet in spite of these handicaps Russian Christianity displayed enough vitality to make itself felt throughout most of the Tsar's territories. Russian settlements were given churches and priests, and among non-Russian peoples missions were established from the Volga and the Urals to Alaska.

Chapter XVI

THE EFFECT OF CHRISTIANITY UPON ITS ENVIRONMENT: GENERAL: ON WESTERN EUROPE; RELIGION AND MORALS, POLITICAL LIFE AND GOVERNMENT, INTERNATIONAL RELATIONS, SOCIAL ORGANIZATION, SOCIAL REFORM AND POOR RELIEF, ECONOMIC ORGANIZATION, INTELLECTUAL LIFE, AESTHETIC LIFE: ON RUSSIA: ON THE EXPANSION OF EUROPE AND ON THE PEOPLES AND CULTURES AFFECTED BY THAT EXPANSION

WHAT effect did Christianity have upon human beings and human culture between A.D. 1500 and A.D. 1800? As compared with the two earlier periods of its expansion, was the influence of Christianity growing or declining? Was it a rising or a waning power in the life of mankind?

In its first five centuries Christianity, from most unpromising beginnings, from the apparent status of a small Jewish sect centring about one whose brief public career had been terminated by what to the casual observer must have seemed a somewhat pitiful and decidedly futile death, had evinced a phenomenal growth. In the most prominent and powerful cultural group of mankind, the Græco-Roman world, it had brought about the greatest religious revolution yet experienced by the human race. It had become the dominant faith and had either eliminated or had reduced to impotency all of its rivals except its parent, Judaism. In an empire which had seemingly lost the ability to create, it had brought into existence the Christian Church and Christian theology, both of them major and novel achievements, it had given rise to an extensive literature, and upon various phases of the culture in which it was immersed it had placed its stamp.

In the succeeding thousand years, from A.D. 500 to A.D. 1500, Christianity had been overtaken by a series of disasters which had slowed down its spread and repeatedly had seemed to make its future most dubious. The break-up of the Roman Empire, the state with which it had come to be closely associated, endangered its very existence. For most of the thousand years a succession of invasions of non-Christian peoples into Western Europe and the basin of the Mediterranean threatened to swamp it. A virile and younger religion, Islam, was enthusiastically espoused by some of the most successful of these invaders and in fully half of the littoral of the Mediterranean supplanted Christianity as the dominant faith and from Mesopotamia eastward all but stamped it out. Yet in this thousand years Christianity spread over a wider geographic area than in its first centuries, although in much of this territory it was represented only by minority groups and in large portions of Asia had died out before the fifteenth century had passed. Moreover, upon the culture of Western Europe it exerted more of an influence than it had upon that of the Roman Empire. Particularly in the latter half of the thousand years, it gave rise to a large number of fresh religious and cultural movements. In spite of the adversities which had overtaken it, in what we have called "the thousand years of uncertainty," Christianity made itself more widely and deeply felt than it had in its first five centuries.

We have repeatedly reminded ourselves that at the beginning of the three centuries between A.D. 1500 and A.D. 1800 the outlook for Christianity appeared unpromising. In Central Asia and in China the widely scattered Christian communities had either sadly shrunk or had completely disappeared. The Ottoman Turks, Moslems, had wiped out the Byzantine Empire, had transformed the central church building of Greek Christianity into a mosque, had made the Crescent dominant in Greece and the Balkans, and were threatening Western Europe. In the chief remaining stronghold of Christianity, Western Europe, the Renaissance had been accompanied by much of religious indifference and scepticism, the official structure of the Church was honeycombed with corruption, and the occupants of the throne of Peter seemed more intent upon collecting ancient manuscripts and examples of Greek and Roman art or upon promoting the worldly interests of the members of their families than they were upon extending the Kingdom of Christ. National states were appearing, ruled by absolute monarchs. Roman Catholic, Protestant, and Russian Orthodox princes were each intent upon dominating completely such sections of the Church as lay within their realms and making them subserve their personal or political ambitions. Education and the intellectual life were beginning to escape from the control of the clergy. Philanthropy was no longer so nearly exclusively an ecclesiastical function. In many respects, even in what remained of Christendom, Christianity seemed a diminishing force. Was Western Europe shedding its Christianity? Christianity, although driven out of much of the Mediterranean world, had been a tutor in civilization to the barbarian peoples of Northern Europe. Were these peoples outgrowing their teacher? Now that they were coming to manhood's estate, were these rude folk whom the Church had taught the rudiments of culture to regard Christianity as something outworn, as swaddling clothes which should now be cast aside? Were the thousand years of uncertainty to be followed by centuries of decisive and final decay? As the world had witnessed the decline and fall of the Roman Empire, was it now to see the decline and disappearance of the faith with which the Roman Empire in its later years had been so closely identified?

The facts proved to be quite opposite to this gloomy prognosis. Never had the influence of Christianity been so pronounced or so widespread as it was after A.D. 1500. Geographically that influence falls into two main divisions, Europe, where the faith had been the longest at work, and those peoples who were on the new frontiers of the faith. The first requires some elaboration and to it the major portion of this chapter must be devoted. The second has already been treated, region by region, in the preceding chapters. The conclusions there presented in discrete fashion must, however, be summarized and certain generalizations deducible from them must be stated.

We turn then, first of all, to the effect of Christianity upon Europe. As we have said in the earlier volumes, the impress of Christianity was more marked in the western part of the continent. In Western Europe, as we have pointed out,[1] in the preceding thousand years the faith had freer course and was less hampered than in the Eastern Mediterranean by the surviving structure of the Græco-Roman world, the pressure of Islam, and the recurring invasions of non-Christians.

At the outset we must note the religious results of Christianity. If new movements afford a correct gauge, between A.D. 1500 and A.D. 1800 Christianity stirred the religious life of Europe more profoundly than in any previous period of equal duration. The revivals which issued in Protestantism and the Catholic Reformation were more extensive and affected more peoples than any which Christianity had yet experienced. The many varieties of Protestantism gave evidence of the numbers of different individuals who had been quickened by the Christian impulse to creative thought and action. The many men and women who contributed to the raising of the level of spiritual life in the Roman Catholic Church, the succession of new orders and congregations which emerged, and the reforms carried through in existing orders are proof that the parent church was stimulated to a greater degree than ever before. In Russian Christianity for the first time several fresh quickenings of life began which gave rise to sects that separated from the state church.

The range of these revivals was not limited to the aristocracy, as had been most of those of the early part of the Middle Ages, when such movements as those of the Cistercians, the Carthusians, and the Premonstratensians drew their

[1] Vol. II, pp. 344, 345.

leadership chiefly from the nobility. The awakenings of this new age affected every class. Loyola and the founders of the Theatines were from the upper social strata. Luther was of peasant stock. Other leaders were from the middle classes. All levels of society were stirred. Christianity, having made its way first among the upper classes, had now become the conscious property of men and women drawn from all the different strata of the social hierarchy and was impelling to original action those of every degree of birth, the rich and the poor, the well-born and those from humble parentage.

This quickening of all ranks of society had been foreshadowed by movements in the latter part of the Middle Ages, notably in the thirteenth century. The rise and rapid spread of the Franciscans and Dominicans and the emergence of many groups, some of them deemed heretical by the official church, had been visible and at times tumultuous indications that a faith into which peoples had entered *en masse* and with no comprehension of its full import, of its exacting demands, and of its ability to transform individuals had now commenced to grip the imagination and to win the full allegiance of thousands who had begun to understand how revolutionary Jesus and the New Testament were.

In the sixteenth, seventeenth, and eighteenth centuries, after a partial pause in the fourteenth and fifteenth centuries, this movement had swelled to fresh and unprecedented dimensions. Religion of some kind, men seemingly must always have. In general the revivals of the sixteenth, seventeenth, and eighteenth centuries brought the religion of Europe to a closer approximation to what was set forth in the New Testament.

Moreover, this rising tide in the influence of Jesus and of the New Testament upon religion progressed in spite of the enhanced control of the Church by the state which marked these centuries. The ecclesiastical organizations of Protestantism, Roman Catholicism, and Russian Orthodox Christianity were dominated by the princes much more than the Church had been in Western Europe and in Russia during the Middle Ages. Yet, in general, the religious life of Europe was more vigorous than when the Church had been more nearly free from the control of secular princes. Moreover, at least in the case of Protestantism and Roman Catholicism, this increase in religious fervour and this growing approximation to the standards of Jesus did not issue in a retreat from the world to the interior life and the abandonment of human society to the secular state, but, as we are to try to show in this chapter, in an enlarged effect upon most of the phases of European culture. The rise of the absolute monarchies might modify but it could not halt the progressive permeation of the civilization of Europe by the faith to which nominal allegiance had been accorded in the mass conversions of the preceding twelve or thirteen centuries. Christianity proved to have a vitality which movements opposed to it might in some places repress but which, taken the world over, they could not permanently quench. The age-long tension between the impulse given by Jesus and the opposing features of human nature continued, unresolved and at times heightened, but Jesus was a growing factor in the life of Europe as well as of mankind as a whole.

We must not here take the space even to enumerate all the fresh religious bodies to which in these three hundred years the Christian impulse gave rise. In our accounts of the first five centuries and of the succeeding thousand years of uncertainty we could name and even briefly describe the chief new religious movements which stemmed from Christianity without overpassing the number of pages which could properly be allotted to them. In the centuries between A.D. 1500 and A.D. 1800 the number becomes legion. In these three centuries more appeared than in all the preceding fifteen hundred years. After A.D. 1800, as we are to see in later volumes, they multiplied still more rapidly. In general, while due in part to many other factors, personal, political, geographic, and racial, they are an indication of the growing effect of the impulse which had its rise in Jesus. The proliferation of the Christian movement into many new sects, orders, and congregations is an indication of a vitality whose manifestations have increased rather than diminished with time.

While we must not attempt a catalogue of the new branches of the Christian movement in the three centuries after A.D. 1500, we must call attention to the main groupings and to a few of the particular organizations. Fortunately these are so familiar even to amateurs in European history that no elaborate description of them is required.

What is usually denominated Protestantism was not, as we reminded ourselves in the initial chapter, one movement, but many. Of these, Lutheranism, in itself varied from country to country, Calvinism in its several forms, the Church of England as it eventually took shape, the protean Anabaptist wing with its many divisions, the Independents, the Socinians, the Quakers, Pietism, and the Wesleyans were only the more prominent. They had in common the fact that they arose out of Western Christianity and that they were denounced by the Roman Catholics as heretical. They interacted upon one another and had back of them a more or less thoroughgoing belief in the duty and the right of private judgment in matters religious and in the direct access of each Christian to God. Yet among themselves they differed widely. They were the result of the Christian impulse acting through many media, regional, national, and individual. None would have arisen except for that impulse, but each was coloured by the personal idiosyncrasies of its founder or by its particular environment.

In Roman Catholicism the growing life remained within one ecclesiastical fellowship, but it gave rise to many new orders and congregations. Of these the most notable was the Society of Jesus, but we have met others in our geographic pilgrimage—the Theatines, the Lazarists, the Foreign Missionary Society of Paris, and many more. Others we have not had occasion so much as to mention. Each had as a founder one who had been stirred profoundly and in fresh fashion by an impulse coming through the stream of historic Christianity.

In Russia the new movements took forms peculiar to that country. Some were protests against the alteration of the service books to which they had been accustomed. Others were ultra-ascetic, and still others were ecstatic. At least one arose out of contacts with Protestants from Western Europe.[2]

In Western Europe the new life was accompanied by an improvement in the education and morals of the clergy. The Catholic Reformation led to a greatly enhanced emphasis upon the training of parish priests. Seminaries for the education of the parochial ministry multiplied. The laxity of clerical morals which was so common in the Middle Ages and in the Renaissance decreased. While in the seventeenth and eighteenth centuries few men of outstanding genius occupied the Papal throne,[3] no such scandals and extreme worldliness attached to them as to the abler but largely secularly minded Popes of the fifteenth century. At the outset of the Protestant movement great difficulty was experienced in finding a sufficient number of ministers of good education and exemplary lives. At one time one-third of the parishes of England are said to have been vacant, the stipends were inadequate, and the social position of the clergy and their wives was inferior. In Germany less than one-half of the two thousand or so who were ordained at Wittenberg from 1537 to 1560 were university men.[4] Yet the quality of the clergy was probably not so poor as it had been on the eve of the Reformation. In the eighteenth century the average German Protestant pastor seems to have been a marked improvement over his sixteenth century predecessor. Educational standards for the clergy had risen and Pietism had led to more pastoral visitation and to a closer personal touch between the minister and the members of his flock. While under the influence of Frederick the Great the clergy became state functionaries, they were the agents of the

---

[2] See Frederick C. Conybeare, *Russian Dissenters* (Harvard University Press, 1921, pp. x, 370), *passim*.

[3] Eckhart, *The Papacy and World Affairs*, p. 157.

[4] Smith, *The Age of the Reformation*, p. 494. Lindsay, *A History of the Reformation*, Vol. II, p. 353, tells of the ignorance of the clergy as disclosed by a visitation of the Diocese of Gloucester by Bishop Hooker in 1551.

state in social service and often were the only persons of education in the villages.[5]

The centuries between A.D. 1500 and A.D. 1800 not only saw progress in the education and morals of the clergy. They also witnessed a rise in the level of the instruction of the laity and in the comprehension of the essentials of their faith by an increasing proportion of the general membership of the churches. Throughout the preceding fifteen hundred years efforts had been made to educate the laity and to bring their lives into conformity to the standards set forth by Jesus. The catechetical school of the Church of Alexandria and the office of catechist are evidence that in its early days the Church made provision for the instruction of its neophytes. Repeatedly in the Middle Ages we hear of commands by the ecclesiastical and secular authorities that the parish clergy instruct their flocks in such rudiments as the Ten Commandments, the Lord's Prayer, and the Creed.[6] The public confession of delinquencies early demanded of Christians, the penance imposed by the Church, the penitentials to which the Irish missionaries had given such an impulse, and the development of auricular confession were devices of pre-sixteenth century invention for the instruction and the discipline of the great body of Christians. However, so flooded had been the Church in Europe from Constantine on by mass conversions that these methods had never fully accomplished the task of assimilation. Now fresh efforts were made to lift the average lay Christian to a closer approximation to the demands of his professed faith. These were aided by the printing press, a recent invention which made possible the wider dissemination of literature, and by competition between the various branches of the Church in which each sought to combat the others' teachings and to remove all causes for the charge of laxity in morals.

In Protestantism the emphasis upon an intelligent faith and a correct life was marked. To be sure, Luther's interest was religious rather than moral[7] and the Reformation was often accompanied by the discrediting of traditional moral standards, by violence, brigandage, and murder, and by an emphasis on dogma rather than conduct.[8] Yet the direct access of every Christian to God without the intervention of the clergy and the priesthood of all believers were part of the essence of Protestantism,[9] and this freedom involved obligations. While, according to Luther, "a Christian man is perfectly free, lord of all, subject to

---

[5] Bruford, *Germany in the Eighteenth Century*, pp. 251-258.

[6] For a brief summary, see J. H. Maude in the *Encyclopedia of Religion and Ethics*, Vol. III, pp. 250 ff.

[7] McGiffert, *Protestant Thought before Kant*, p. 24.

[8] Smith, *The Age of the Reformation*, pp. 503-506.

[9] McGiffert, *op. cit.*, pp. 34, 44; Lindsay, *op. cit.*, p. 240.

none," he is also "a perfectly dutiful servant of all, subject to all."[10] Protestants early worked out catechisms, primarily for the instruction of the laity, and by means of the printing press these were widely distributed.[11] In pre-Reformation times it had been commonly assumed that to lead the perfect Christian life it was necessary to join a monastic order and that only thus could one completely forswear the world with its compromises of the Christian ethic. For the most part Protestantism denounced monasticism, but in theory it tended to require of all Christians the thoroughgoing commitment of life which had been the religious urge back of monasticism. Many Protestant groups endeavoured to put this principle into practice. This usually led to the separation of the Christian congregations from the communities about them. Except in communities constituted deliberately of those who had presumably entered upon this commitment, it was assumed that no city or state would be fully Christian. True churches, so the Protestant extremists held, are made up only of those who as individuals have had the Christian experience and have completely given themselves to the Christian way of life.[12]

While this ideal could not be fully carried out, the effect in many Protestant circles was to inculcate earnestness in understanding the Christian faith and in living up to its requirements. Thus in Scotland in the early part of the eighteenth century most country houses and even Edinburgh flats had closets for private devotions to which members of the household were supposed to retire daily for prayer and meditation, and for respectable families Sundays were observed by strict abstinence from labour and play and were filled with family prayers and attendance at church services.[13] In the early part of the eighteenth century, too, the ecclesiastical authorities in Scottish parishes took stern measures to punish transgressions of the moral code.[14] Not only in Scotland, but also in other circles where it prevailed, Calvinism tended to instil a deep conviction of personal vocation and responsibility and to stimulate men to high and strict moral endeavour.[15] Puritanism produced many a stalwart character among the laity.[16]

[10] Martin Luther, in *A Treatise on Christian Liberty*, translation in *Works of Martin Luther* (Philadelphia, A. J. Holman Co., 6 vols., 1915-1932), Vol. II, p. 312.

[11] *Encyclopedia of Religion and Ethics*, Vol. III, pp. 250 ff. For a number of these early catechisms see Ferdinand Cohrs, *Die Evangelischen Katechismusversuche vor Luthers Enchiridion* (in *Monumenta Germaniae Paedagogica*, Vols. XX-XXIII, XXXIX, Berlin, A. Hoffmann & Co., 1900-1902, 1907).

[12] Troeltsch, *The Social Teachings of the Christian Churches*, p. 695.

[13] Graham, *The Social Life of Scotland in the Eighteenth Century*, pp. 25, 26.

[14] Graham, *op. cit.*, pp. 321 ff.

[15] Osborne, *Christian Ideals in Political History*, p. 45.

[16] As an instance of this in one of the less well known laymen, see Roger Beadon, *Robert Blake, Sometime Commanding All the Fleets and Naval Forces of England* (London, Edward Arnold and Co., 1935, pp. 308), pp. 5, 141, 269.

In England it became the moral school of the middle classes.[17] In dissenting bodies in England, even in the low ebb of the latter part of the seventeenth and the early part of the eighteenth century, nonconforming congregations did much disciplining of their members for departures from their standards.[18] In England and Wales the opening years of the eighteenth century witnessed the formation of many societies by dissenters and members of the Established Church for the reformation of manners.[19] The enormous and persistent popularity of *The Pilgrim's Progress* must be attributed to its reflection of experiences and ideals which were widely prevalent among the Protestant laity. In Sweden the sixteenth century saw an extensive and rapid deepening of the religious and moral life. In Germany Protestant Christianity had such inward vitality and powers of recuperation that the wastage of the Thirty Years' War, far from crushing it, stimulated it to a greater emphasis upon righteous living and to practical helpfulness of the distressed.[20] Pietism, a form of this revival, led to a more personal and inward life among laity as well as clergy and placed emphasis upon "spiritual" religion.[21]

The widening and deepening stream of the influence of Christianity through Protestantism both gave rise to a flood of new hymns and was fed by it. The hymns of Luther, of Paul Gerhardt, of Tersteegen, of Zinzendorf, of Charles Wesley, of Isaac Watts, and of many another singer sprang from Christianity and nourished the Christian faith of both clergy and laity.

In the Roman Catholic Church the reform movement also led to an improvement in the religious instruction of the laity. Partly in competition with Protestants, catechisms were developed, particularly as one of the fruits of the Council of Trent.[22] To be sure, the attempt of the Council of Trent to revive something of the rigour of the penance of the early days of the Church largely failed, and sporadic attempts, such as those of Carlo Borromeo and the Jansenists, to tighten the discipline of that sacrament did not win the approval of the Papacy.[23] Yet such efforts, even though only by the minority of the clergy, must have had some effect. Moreover, the persistent endeavour was made to enforce the rule adopted the Lateran Council of 1215-1216 requiring of all the faithful confession at least once a year and communion at Easter.[24] The higher

[17] Troeltsch, *op. cit.*, p. 681.

[18] Bebb, *Nonconformity and Social and Economic Life, 1660-1800*, pp. 58-68.

[19] Allen and McClure, *Two Hundred Years: The History of the Society for Promoting Christian Knowledge*, pp. 61-107.

[20] Uhlhorn, *Die christliche Liebesthätigkeit*, Vol. III, p. 198.

[21] Troeltsch, *op. cit.*, pp. 682-686.

[22] A. J. Grieve, in *The Encyclopædia Britannica*, 14th ed., Vol. V, p. 26.

[23] Lea, *A History of Auricular Confession and Indulgences in the Latin Church*, Vol. II, pp. 184, 190 ff.

[24] Lea, *op. cit.*, Vol. I, pp. 250 ff.

standard for the education of the clergy, by raising the quality of those who heard confessions, must have resulted in a better use of the latter as a means of increasing the religious and moral knowledge and practice of the laity.[25] The labours of the Jesuits and of such men as Vincent de Paul[26] and Francis de Sales resulted in deepening the faith of thousands of laymen and laywomen.

In the Russian Orthodox Church, to resist the efforts of Jesuits to win adherence to Rome, a catechism was worked out and in 1672 was made standard by the Synod of Jerusalem.[27] Presumably this led to greater knowledge among the laity of the main tenets of the faith. In the seventeenth century Nikon revived the practice of preaching[28] and must have had an effect upon many among the great crowds which thronged to hear him.

It would be easy to exaggerate this rise in the quality of the Christianity of the masses. The majority of those who bore the Christian name still knew little of their faith and were far from an approximation to its ethics. Yet that the minority who showed an intelligent loyalty to the religion which they professed was increasing seems altogether probable.

That upon many outstanding individuals in Europe in this period Christianity had a profound effect is one of the most evident facts of European history. Men like Martin Luther, John Calvin, John Knox, Ignatius Loyola, Francis de Sales, George Fox, Oliver Cromwell, and hundreds of others who helped to mould the Europe of their day owed their prominence to the fact that something in Christianity had gripped them. Whether in proportion to the population the number of such men in each generation was greater than in earlier centuries would be impossible to determine. It is clear that none perfectly exemplified the faith which had so profoundly stirred them. Luther gave way to coarse vituperation. George Fox, who was the forerunner of one of the most magnanimous of Christian groups, was vindictive and rejoiced when misfortune overtook his enemies. Yet that the men and women whose Christian faith lifted them out of mediocrity to positions of outstanding influence mounted into the hundreds is indubitable. It is also certain that, with all of their failures completely to embody the ideals held up by Jesus, they bore something of a likeness to their master.

In spite of the activism of Western Christianity, both Protestant and Roman Catholic, the Christian impulse continued to give rise to great experts in medita-

[25] Lea, *op. cit.*, Vol. II, pp. 255 ff.
[26] On Vincent de Paul see Pierre Coste, *The Life and Works of Saint Vincent de Paul*, translated by Joseph Leonard (London, Burns, Oates and Washbourne, 3 vols., 1934-1935).
[27] A. J. Grieve, in *The Encyclopædia Britannica*, 14th ed., Vol. V, p. 26.
[28] Adeney, *The Greek and Eastern Churches*, p. 411.

tion and the inner life of the spirit. They appeared in both Protestantism and Roman Catholicism—men like William Law, Jeremy Taylor, and George Fox among the former, and among the latter such outstanding figures as Loyola, Theresa, Neri, Madame Guyon, and Fénelon.

Public worship, too, was improved. Roman Catholics celebrated the mass with new dignity and for it wrote some of the greatest music ever composed. Protestants developed many liturgies and forms of group adoration and prayer, some of them modifications of what had come to them from the old church, but several of them quite fresh.

Like the thousand years before them, these three centuries witnessed much scepticism. Christianity continued to be the official community faith of the states of the North and West of Europe, but, as earlier, many, while nominally conforming to it, privately and even publicly expressed their scorn for it or quietly ignored it. Whether scepticism was more or less widespread than in the preceding period it would be impossible to determine. It left more extensive records of its presence than in the Middle Ages, but presumably that was because of the dual reason that literacy had now spread outside the ranks of the clergy and that printing had made possible the wider dissemination of literature, whether that was for or against Christianity.

Scepticism developed in various forms. Some of it remained within organized Christianity. Some of it more or less openly abandoned that faith. What was known as rationalism was widely prevalent. It believed in the capacity of the human mind and sought by human intellectual effort to understand the universe. It held to "natural religion," developed by man's own efforts, and contrasted this with the "revealed religion" which taught that God is not to be found by man's unaided search but that in Jesus He took the initiative in making Himself known to man and in saving men from their sins. Deism arose, a trend of thought which in its most extreme forms maintained that God had indeed created the universe, but that having once set it in motion He had ceased to concern Himself actively with it. The beginnings of closer contact with other civilized peoples, especially those of India and China, brought some acquaintance with great religions hitherto almost unknown, and led a good many to question the claim that Christianity contained the only true revelation of God.[29] However, upon much of this sceptical thought Christianity exercised a profound influence. The larger proportion of the rationalists and deists continued to profess the Christian faith and found ways of reconciling their

---

[29] On the effect of these other faiths, see Nathan Söderblom, *Das Werden des Gottes-glaubens* (Leipzig, J. C. Hinrichs'she Buchhandlung, 1916, pp. xii, 398), pp. 324 ff.

conclusions with what had come to them through Christianity. Those who broke completely with Christianity were relatively few.[30] Religious toleration began to appear. It sprang from a number of sources. The humanism which preceded and accompanied the Protestant Reformation made for a moderation of intolerance. The multiplication of divisions in organized Christianity led numbers of thoughtful souls to distrust the reciprocal persecution with which many sought to crush their rivals. The growth of rationalism was paralleled by the demand that the human mind be allowed to search for truth without restraint by Church or state. Sometimes the secular authorities believed that the state was weakened by the persecution of religious minorities.[31] However, much of toleration and of the agitation for liberty of thought in matters secular as well as religious had its origin among groups of earnest Christians, chiefly Protestants, who were convinced that the attempt to constrain another to surrender an honestly held conviction was contrary to the New Testament. Anabaptists particularly taught that a true church is a voluntary congregation of believers and that he who has experienced the new birth which is his introduction into the Christian life is directly guided by the Spirit of God, is responsible to God for his own conduct, and must not be coerced.[32] It was a Baptist, Thomas Helwys, who gave what has been called the finest and fullest defence of religious toleration which up to his day had been written in English.[33] While Calvinism tended to intolerance, it was a Puritan, John Milton, who penned one of the classic pleas for the freedom of the press.[34] George Fox and the Quakers were notable as advocates of religious tolerance. It was in the New World with its greater room for experimentation, under the influence of the Quakers in Pennsylvania and of Roger Williams and the

[30] On rationalism and deism see Leslie Stephen, *History of English Thought in the Eighteenth Century* (New York, G. P. Putnam's Sons, 2 vols., 1876), especially Vol. I, pp. 91 ff.; Dawson, *Progress and Religion*, p. 190; McGiffert, *Protestant Thought before Kant*, pp. 186 ff.

[31] W. K. Jordan, *The Development of Religious Toleration in England from the Beginning of the English Reformation to the Death of Queen Elizabeth* (Harvard University Press, 1932, pp. 490), pp. 19 ff.; A. A. Seaton, *The Theory of Toleration under the Later Stuarts* (Cambridge University Press, 1911, pp. vii, 364), pp. 14 ff.; Francesco Ruffini, *Religious Liberty*, translated by J. P. Hayes (London, Williams and Norgate, 1912, pp. xxiv, 536), pp. 59 ff.; Figgis, *Studies of Political Thought from Gerson to Grotius*, pp. 94 ff.; McGiffert, *Protestant Thought before Kant*, p. 190.

[32] W. K. Jordan, *The Development of Religious Toleration in England from the Accession of James I to the Convention of the Long Parliament (1603-1640)* (London, George Allen and Unwin, 1936, pp. 542), pp. 258-261; Troeltsch, *The Social Teaching of the Christian Churches*, pp. 671-673.

[33] Jordan, *op. cit.*, pp. 274-284.

[34] John Milton, *Areopagitica. A Speech for the Liberty of Unlicensed Printing to the Parliament of England* (in *The Prose Works of John Milton*, edited by R. W. Griswold Philadelphia, J. W. Moore, 2 vols., 1853, Vol. I, pp. 166 ff.).

Baptists in Rhode Island, that these theories of religious liberty were first put into continuing operation. Religious toleration with its Christian roots came before political tolerance[35] and was one of the sources of the latter.

Did not the new burst of religious life by dividing Western Europe between Protestantism and Roman Catholicism fatally wound that spiritual unity which was a heritage from the Roman Empire and the Church of that empire? By reinforcing the disintegration of Europe into strong secular states did it not make for the political anarchy which has become, in the twentieth century, a major menace to civilization?

To a certain degree the answer must be yes. The new life was too potent and too particularistic to be confined to one ecclesiastical structure. The Christian vision of unity now as earlier was not so strong as the fissiparous results of a belief, also to be found in Christianity from the beginning, in the direct voice of God to the individual. One phase of the Christian impulse, a phase assisted by racial, national, and dynastic pride, disrupted the inclusive unity which was the result of another phase, a phase which had been supported by the Roman imperial tradition.

Yet we need also to remind ourselves of the bright as well as the sombre contributions of variety to European civilization, of the stimulus of one local culture upon another local culture. We must also remark that the Protestant revolt did not work such great destruction in the spiritual unity of Europe as is sometimes assumed. After all, there remained ethical principles and religious convictions common to all branches of Christianity which gave foundation to later European civilization. We are also to see, in a moment, that from the Christian impulse more mightily after than before the ecclesiastical division of Western Europe there arose movements which tended to regulate and reduce the frequency of the wars of Europe.

More boldly and frequently than the European thinkers of the Middle Ages, men of the three centuries after A.D. 1500 set forth plans for the realization of an ideal society. The most famous of the latter and the one which has given its name to all projects for a perfect social order was the *Utopia* of Thomas More. The *Utopia* had a large number of less distinguished fellows. The *Wolfaria* of Günzberg (who had once been a Franciscan and later was an ardent Lutheran),[36] the *Oceana* of James Harrington,[37] and the *Christianopolis* of the Protestant pastor Valentine Andreae, who tried to carry out

---

[35] Smith, *The Age of the Reformation*, pp. 641-651.

[36] McNeill, *Christian Hope for World Society*, p. 142.

[37] McNeill, *op. cit.*, p. 148; H. F. R. Smith, *Harrington and His Oceana* (Cambridge University Press, 1914, pp. xi, 222), *passim*.

in his parish the programme outlined in his book,[38] were well known in their day.[39] The eighteenth century *philosophes* had many projects for the reconstruction of society.

To claim an exclusive Christian origin for all of these designs would be to ignore the plain facts. More found the pattern for *Utopia* partly in Plato's *Republic* and in the *Timæus* and the *Critias*.[40] By no means all were modelled on the Kingdom of Heaven of the Gospels.

Yet in a large proportion of these designs the Christian impulse was strong. Thomas More was earnest in his Christian faith and fell a martyr to his loyalty to the Roman Catholic Church. The contrast between Machiavelli's *The Prince*, which practically eliminated Christianity, and More's *Utopia* discloses how much the latter owed to the Christian faith of the author. Even the *philosophes*, who had so important a share in laying the ideological basis for the French Revolution, were more largely indebted to Christian thinking than they quite realized. While they demolished the *Civitas Dei* of Augustine, they were impelled by the vision of a perfect society which had come to them largely through Christian channels to efforts to rebuild it with what they deemed more up-to-date materials.[41]

More extensively than in any preceding period, moreover, steps were taken to translate into actuality the plans for ideal societies which drew their inspiration largely or in part from Christianity.

In a preceding chapter[42] we have seen that in the New World with its opportunity for a fresh start, in several of the Thirteen Colonies of the British, efforts were made to build social structures which, better than anything in the Old World, would approximate to Christian standards.

In Europe itself there were many attempts, some of them on a large scale, to rebuild society on a more nearly ideal basis. Although by dominating the Church, the absolute monarchies of the period, in contrast with the Middle Ages when in Western Europe the Church as an organization was more nearly in control, seemed to have weakened the influence of Christianity upon the state, although some of the ecclesiastics who directed the affairs of state, men like Wolsey, Richelieu, Mazarin, and Alberoni, all of them cardinals, princes of

[38] McNeill, *op. cit.*, pp. 144-147; F. E. Held, *Christianopolis, An Ideal State of the Seventeenth Century, Translated from the Latin of Johann Valentin Andreae with an Historical Introduction* (Oxford University Press, 1916, pp. x, 287), *passim*.

[39] See a partial list of these plans in *The Encyclopædia Britannica*, 14th ed., Vol. XXV, p. 915. See also popular accounts of some of them in Lewis Mumford, *The Story of Utopias* (New York, Boni and Liveright, 1922, pp. xii, 315), Chaps. 1, 3-6.

[40] Sir Thomas More's *Utopia*, edited by J. C. Collins (Oxford, The Clarendon Press, 1904, pp. lii, 283), p. xxxvi.

[41] Becker, *The Heavenly City of the Eighteenth Century Philosophers*, pp. 29-31.

[42] Chapter VI.

the Church, in their public policies ran completely counter to the ethical principles of the faith which they professed, and although two of the latter, Richelieu and Mazarin, laboured to enhance the power of the state and did much
to secularize politics, Christianity was more potent in altering the political
structure and the political ideals of society than ever before. The straitjackets
imposed by the strong secular states could not entirely quench the vigour
displayed by the revived Christianity of the period. Some straitjackets were
broken by the irresistible ferment. Others showed in modifications which they
underwent the potency of the life which they sought to confine.

It is interesting and important to note the fashion in which the influence
of Christianity upon the state increased from period to period.

In the first five centuries Christianity did not appreciably change the policy
or structure of the Roman Empire, except that it brought about the substitution of itself for other faiths as the official religion, led to the elimination of
its rivals, and made slight alterations in some of the laws.

In the thousand years between A.D. 500 and A.D. 1500, in the Byzantine
Empire the coronation oaths reveal a modification in the theory of the monarchy. In Western Europe the theory, and in part the practice, was developed
of the supremacy of the Church, represented by the Pope, in Christendom
and the world, the Holy Roman Empire came into being, with its head
crowned by the Pope, and the principle was gradually clarified that kings
are responsible to God, and—a cognate belief—that there is a body of law
which the king must obey. Laws, too, were framed under Christian influences.
Christianity was far more potent in shaping political life than it had been in
the first period. Yet in the main the chief outlines of political organization
came into being from other than Christian causes.

Now, in the three hundred years between A.D. 1500 and A.D. 1800, the Christian impulse became more potent in working changes. Either as the major
factor or as a contributory cause, it brought about the political independence
of at least one people, the Dutch, strengthened the national feeling in some
other lands, and helped call into existence types of government with democratic tendencies which differed more markedly from their predecessors than
any in whose creation Christianity had thus far been a moulding influence.

The forms of Christianity grouped under Protestantism were particularly
powerful in working such changes. It is often said that Protestantism, in
breaking up the Medieval Church, furthered the control of society by the
secular state. Yet Protestantism increased the influence of Christianity in political life.

It is one of the commonplaces of history that Protestantism, by disrupting the Roman Catholic Church, was a contributory cause to civil strife and that it furthered the long disunity in Germany and was prominent in tearing the Netherlands from the empire of Philip II.

Moreover, with its emphasis upon the right and the duty of private judgment and of the direct access of each Christian to God, Protestantism made for the emphasis upon the individual and hence, in its more thoroughgoing forms, tended to democracy. Indeed, it is not too much to assert that modern democracy is the child of the Protestant Reformation.[43] Luther was inclined to give the state a distinct rôle as compared with the Church and to leave mundane matters to the former.[44] Indeed, Lutheranism became the ally of the absolute power of the state and of unconditional obedience to the government—although the latter was supposed to be responsible to God.[45] It is no accident that Germany, the home of Lutheranism, became increasingly, in the eighteenth and nineteenth centuries, the champion of this type of government and that in the twentieth century it became a leading exponent of the totalitarian state.[46] Yet Luther, with his famous declaration, *"Hier steh' ich; ich kann nichts anders,"* gave a powerful impetus to the movement in politics and in thought which led the individual to stand on his own feet against tradition and authority. Calvin was aristocratic in his outlook, distrusted the ordinary man, and lodged much of the control of Church in the hands of the clergy,[47] but he maintained that the state should be dominated by the religious ideal and governed according to the law of God as seen in the Bible.[48] Indeed it is said that through Calvinism there came into existence for the first time in history a Christian Church whose social influence was comprehensive and which moulded in a corporate fashion the entire life of state and society, both public and private.[49] As it operated in practice, moreover, Calvinism made for the power of the people as against the autocratic prince. French Calvinism produced the *Vindiciae contra Tyrannos*, in which it was argued that the sceptre of kings is from the people and that monarchs must not imagine that they are formed of material better than that of other men. This had marked influence in the Netherlands and in England was employed to justify the execution of Charles I and the Revolution of 1688.[50] The blunt

[43] Gooch and Laski, *English Democratic Ideas in the Seventeenth Century*, pp. 1, 2, 7.
[44] McGiffert, *Protestant Thought before Kant*, p. 59.
[45] Troeltsch, *The Social Teaching of the Christian Churches*, p. 553.
[46] Smith, *The Age of the Reformation*, p. 594. See a suggestive article by Martin Schroeder in *The Christian Century*, Vol. L, pp. 1466-1468.
[47] McGiffert, *op. cit.*, p. 95.
[48] H. T. Andrews in Paton, Bunting and Garvie, *Christ and Civilization*, p. 348.
[49] Troeltsch, *op. cit.*, p. 621.
[50] Gooch and Laski, *op. cit.*, pp. 12-17.

and fearless speaking of John Knox to Mary Queen of Scots is a striking instance of the clash between the power of the people and that of the monarch.[51] In Scotland Calvinism became a symbol of Scottish independence, added strength to Scottish nationalism, and brought a closer approach to popular government than the country had yet known.[52] When Queen Elizabeth demanded of the Scottish commissioners the grounds for their deposition of Mary they replied with a quotation from Calvin.[53] The Calvinistic provinces of the Netherlands in their revolt against Philip II and their formulation of a new government put into force the principle that princes exist for the sake of their subjects and not subjects for the sake of their rulers.[54] In the new university of Leiden, founded as an outcome of the struggle for independence, youths were instructed in the principles of democracy.[55] In England, Puritanism, in which Calvinism was a chief ingredient, impressed upon each the ideal of living for duty, and made for self-reliance, self-control, and a sense of worth which rendered some form of democracy possible and necessary.[56]

In Great Britain, through the Puritan Revolution and the Commonwealth, Calvinism and other forms of Protestantism brought about a political transformation which, in the sharpness and thoroughness of its change and in the size of the area and the number of people affected, was greater than any which Christianity had thus far effected. In this upheaval Calvinism was the dominant religious force, but it expressed itself not only through Presbyterians but also through Independents.[57] The latter favoured a congregational form of church government and tended towards democracy in each local church. This strain of Independency made for a stronger tincture of democracy in the Commonwealth than would have been there had Presbyterianism prevailed. Many minor Protestant groups were also present and added variety and colour to the political and social picture.[58] By the revolution Charles I was executed, the Stuarts ousted, and a republic substituted for the monarchy.

In this upheaval the dominant figure was Oliver Cromwell.[59] That Crom-

[51] Lindsay, *A History of the Reformation*, Vol. II, p. 313.

[52] Cunningham, *Christianity and Economic Science*, p. 66.

[53] Gooch and Laski, *op. cit.*, p. 39.

[54] Smith, *The Age of the Reformation*, p. 264.

[55] Gooch and Laski, *op. cit.*, p. 47.

[56] Troeltsch, *op. cit.*, p. 619; Smith, *op. cit.*, p. 345.

[57] See the relative strength of Presbyterianism and Independency discussed by J. H. Hexter in *The Problem of the Presbyterian Independents* in *The American Historical Review*, Vol. XLIV, pp. 29-49.

[58] Gooch and Laski, *op. cit., passim*.

[59] For an extensive bibliography on Cromwell, see W. C. Abbott, *A Bibliography of Oliver Cromwell. A List of Printed Materials relating to Oliver Cromwell, together with a List of Portraits and Caricatures* (Harvard University Press, 1929, pp. xxviii, 551).

well is one of the outstanding figures in European history is a commonplace. Here we must note, however, that he owed his position partly to the movement, so largely religious, out of which he arose, and partly to his own deep religious faith. Whether one likes or dislikes him, his prominence cannot be gainsaid. By some he is deemed the greatest of Englishmen. It was his complete commitment to the Christian faith as he understood it, and that largely as interpreted by John Calvin, which raised the country squire from mediocrity. In his young manhood he had a profound religious experience. Thereafter, in spite of periods of uncertainty and gloom, he believed himself committed to the will of God and to be an instrument of God. He was dependent upon prayer. When the remorseless logic of the course on which he had embarked led him to the execution of Charles I and brought him into all but absolute power in Great Britain, he strove to constrain the realm to conform to Christian ideals and to make it the champion throughout Europe of what he believed to be the true expressions of Christianity. His was a stormy course, for he came to his position through civil war, and he never had the hearty support of more than a minority of the population. On the one hand were the majority who were disturbed by the wrench from the accustomed patterns of government and society, and on the other hand were radicals who believed that he did not go far enough. Yet so long as he lived Cromwell retained his power and made England a force to be reckoned with on the Continent.

After death removed the great Protector, the effects of the revolution were by no means completely erased. The inevitable reaction brought the Stuarts back into power and in part restored the old regime, but the dreams awakened by the Puritans did not wholly die. Restraints on the royal power were permanently furthered. The experience of dissenters with democratic forms of church government in their local congregations had reflections, even though incomplete, in political ideas and institutions. The Revolution of 1688 and developments in the eighteenth century brought additional control of the royal power by Parliament. John Locke (1632-1704), whose opposition to absolute monarchy and whose insistence upon the right of the people to govern themselves had marked influence upon English constitutional law and polity and upon the formation of the ideas later embodied in the American and French Revolutions, came from a Puritan home and was educated in a Puritan atmos-

---

For Oliver Cromwell's own writings, see *The Writings and Speeches of Oliver Cromwell*, edited by W. C. Abbott (Harvard University Press, Vol. I, 1937). Good biographies are C. H. Firth, *Oliver Cromwell* (London, G. P. Putnam's Sons, 3d ed., 1924, pp. xiii, 496), and John Buchan, *Oliver Cromwell* (London, Hodder and Stoughton, 1934, pp. 554). Then, of course, there is the famous Thomas Carlyle, *Letters and Speeches of Oliver Cromwell* (first appeared 1846. The best edition, edited by S. C. Lomas, London, 1904).

phere. In his writings was the assertion, later made famous by the American Declaration of Independence, that men are, "by nature, all free, equal, and independent. No man can be put out of this estate without his full consent." While Locke departed from some of the religious teachings of his youth, he remained, in his own eyes, an earnest Christian, and to his Christian faith and rearing must be attributed much of his political and social philosophy.[60] Locke's older contemporary, Thomas Hobbes, who also did much to shape political thought, but who stressed the authority of the monarch more than did the former, had been influenced in part by Puritanism, but was more of a humanist and eventually gave up all belief in a knowledge of God through revelation.[61]

In the reaction from the Commonwealth religious dissent in England fell under a cloud, but it by no means disappeared. It stood for freedom of conscience and, while not being active in governmental matters, politically was inclined towards liberalism.[62] It had a recognized place in English society and as such provided a safety valve which helped to prevent a repetition of the violent revolution which had given birth to the Commonwealth.[63] Wesleyanism, which was so important in the life of England in the latter part of the eighteenth century, was loyal to the existing constitution. John Wesley believed that under it the people had sufficient liberty and in politics he was a mildly conservative force.[64] In the eighteenth century nonconformist Protestant Christianity in England made for moderate liberalism.[65]

It was not only those in the dissenting Puritan tradition whom the Christian impulse impelled to seek to restrain the power of absolute kings by law and the people's will. Richard Hooker (1553-1600), an Anglican clergyman, in his Laws of Ecclesiastical Polity, stressed a universal law which owes its origin to the loving will of God and which can be discovered by man, and made it

[60] Locke's political views are expounded in his Two Treatises on Government, which are in The Works of John Locke (London, 9 vols., 1794), Vol. IV, pp. 207 ff. The quotation is from the outset of Chap. 8. A good life of Locke is H. R. Fox Bourne, The Life of John Locke (London, Henry S. King and Co., 2 vols., 1876). See also Troeltsch, The Social Teaching of the Christian Churches, pp. 636, 637.

[61] Leo Strauss, The Political Philosophy of Hobbes, Its Basis and Genesis, translated from the German manuscripts by Elsa M. Sinclair (Oxford, The Clarendon Press, 1936, pp. xviii, 172), passim.

[62] Lincoln, Some Political and Social Ideas of English Dissent, 1763-1800, passim.

[63] E. R. Taylor, Methodism and Politics, 1791-1851 (Cambridge University Press, 1935, pp. xi, 227), p. 4.

[64] Maldwyn Edwards, John Wesley and the Eighteenth Century. A Study in His Social and Political Influence (Cincinnati, The Abingdon Press, 1933, pp. 220), pp. 13 ff.

[65] Warner, The Wesleyan Movement in the Industrial Revolution, pp. 271 ff., says that Methodism held that the institutions of society are the tools of the human will and are justifiable only to the degree that they are useful in promoting genuine happiness.

the basis of the state.[66] Somewhat similar principles were developed among Roman Catholics. Lainez, spokesman of the Jesuits at the Council of Trent, affirmed that all power springs from the people.[67] In opposing Henry of Navarre, Roman Catholics expressed the conviction that the king is subject to law.[68] Some of the great Jesuit writers early opposed the divine right of kings, held that the king is head of the state because the people have of their own accord transferred their authority to him, and maintained that subjects may resist their sovereigns.[69] It was the Jesuit Cardinal, Robert Bellarmine, who said, to the great irritation of James I of England[70] and royalists in the time of Charles I,[71] that "it depends on the consent of the people to decide whether kings, or consuls, or other magistrates are to be established in authority over them; and if there be legitimate cause, the people can change a kingdom into an aristocracy, or an aristocracy into a democracy."[72] Indeed, precedent for this opinion could be cited in the great Augustine, who declared that God "did not intend that His rational creature, who was made in His image, should have dominion except over the irrational creation, not man over man, but man over beasts."[73] Some Roman Catholics, like many Protestants, were inspired by their faith to challenge the autocratic power of the absolute monarchs of the day.

We need again to remind ourselves that when, near the end of these three centuries, the French Revolution broke out and altered the political structure of much of Europe, the ideas which underlay it had in part a Christian origin and that the hope which inspired them presumably had its roots to some degree in the Christian view of history which thinks of the human drama as culminating in an ideal society.[74] This does not mean that the pattern of the French Revolution corresponded fully to the Christian ideal, for of course it did not. It does mean, however, that the Christian impulse had a part in bringing about that political and social upheaval.

In Russia Christianity also had political effects. On the one hand, in bringing

---

[66] See the first four books in Richard Hooker, *The Laws of Ecclesiastical Polity, Books I-IV* (London, George Routledge and Sons, 1888, pp. 288).

[67] Gooch and Laski, *English Democratic Ideas in the Seventeenth Century*, p. 19.

[68] *Ibid.*

[69] Figgis, *Studies of Political Thought from Gerson to Grotius*, pp. 152-154.

[70] *The Political Works of James I Reprinted from the Edition of 1616 with an Introduction*, by C. H. McIlwain (Harvard University Press, 1918, pp. cxi, 354), p. 153.

[71] Robert Filmer in his *Patriarcha*, argued against Bellarmine's position, associating it with the Calvinist position (the *Patriarcha* is included in an edition of John Locke, *Two Treatises on Civil Government*, London, George Routledge and Sons, 1884, pp. 320).

[72] Robert Bellarmine, *De Laicis or The Treatise on Civil Government*, translated by Kathleen E. Murphy (New York, Fordham University Press, 1928, pp. 83), Chap. 6.

[73] Augustine, *The City of God*, Book XIX, Chap. 15.

[74] Becker, *The Heavenly City of the Eighteenth Century Philosophers*, pp. 29-31.

into existence the various dissenting groups, it weakened that structure of society in which the whole ecclesiastical organization was dominated by the monarch. On the other hand, it led the vast body of devout Christians to support the monarchy. They thought of Russia as the guardian and champion of true Christianity. Longing to see the Kingdom of God appear, they thought that they saw this hope about to be fulfilled in a "Holy Russia," a great body politic illuminated and crowned by the crosses on her myriad churches.[75]

Even though Christianity was able to alter the internal structure of the great monarchies of the sixteenth, seventeenth, and eighteenth centuries and to be a chief factor in destroying or weakening the absolutism of kings, was it potent enough to regulate the relations between states? Here were political machines built and dominated by ruthless men engaged in life and death struggles for power. War was chronic. To be sure, several of the outstanding monarchs, notably Philip II of Spain, were in their way profoundly religious, and some of their chief ministers, such as Richelieu and Mazarin, held high office in the Church, but their religious faith was either kept conveniently apart from their public policies or added the zeal of a fanatic to their diplomacy and their wars. In the Middle Ages the Christian conscience had developed the Peace of God and the Truce of God to soften the asperities of private warfare, and by placing its stamp on chivalry had modified the ethics of the military class. Great Popes, too, had successfully asserted the authority of the Church over temporal rulers. Christianity combined with the tradition of the Roman Empire to build the ideal of a supra-national society, Christendom, which sought to make actual in human life the ideals of Jesus and his Apostles. The final separation of the Greek from the Roman Church and the Protestant secession had weakened that unity and had dealt serious blows to that dream. The Popes were increasingly futile in the interrelations of the absolutist states. The Peace of Westphalia (1648) which terminated the titanic struggle of the Thirty Years' War also marked the end of the effective participation of the Papacy in the Western European states system.[76] Was not Christianity being ushered out of the international scene? Could it make itself at all felt in inter-state relations which in practice were so diametrically opposed to its ideals?

Moreover, Christianity was often given as an excuse for war and at times seemed to accentuate or even to cause the struggle. Differences between Roman Catholics and Protestants or between different schools of Protestantism con-

---

[75] Anton Kartashov, *Russian Christianity,* in *Theology,* Vol. XXX, p. 14.

[76] Carl Conrad Eckhardt, *The Papacy in World Affairs as Reflected in the Secularizing of Politics* (University of Chicago Press, 1937, pp. xiv, 310), devotes particular attention to this subject.

tributed to domestic and international strife. To be sure, no such prolonged series of wars as the Crusades took as their talisman the Christian symbol. In this some advance was registered, but in some ways it looked as though the Christian faith, far from bringing in the peace which it proclaimed, was still furthering the sword.

A closer examination discloses the fact that the picture is by no means so simple or so discouraging, and that the Christian impulse was giving rise to processes and ideals which were meeting the challenge of the new age. Indeed, although this would be hard to measure with accuracy, it is probable that Christianity was more nearly effective in regulating the relations between states and in placing their dealings with one another on the basis of law rather than of armed force than it had been in the Middle Ages. The Pope was no longer the arbiter of Western Europe. No more was his summons to war or to peace seriously heeded. However, just as in the inner life of the state the Christian conscience was successfully insisting that there is a law written into the nature of the universe which the rulers must obey, so it was leading outstanding thinkers to declare that this law must govern the relations between states. What is equally to the point, monarchs and peoples listened to them. International law was developed and served to restrain states, each of which claimed absolute sovereignty and to be a law to itself, and to bring some kind of order into the chaos of European international politics.

This is not the place to record even in brief summary the development of international law. We must, however, note the important part in it of the Christian impulse. Into international law many elements entered. Much came from pre-Christian Greece and Rome. Yet the concept of a family of nations was largely from Christianity, as the term used to designate it, Christendom, indicates. The foundations on which the later law of nations was built were in the work of Christian idealists of the Middle Ages and in the earlier writers of the Church. It was, however, a continuing and revived impulse from Christianity which was chiefly responsible for a further elaboration of old principles to control the lawlessness of the emerging absolute monarchies.

Both Roman Catholics and Protestants contributed to the growth of law as applied to the relations of these states with one another and with non-Christian peoples. It was in Spain, the first dominant monarchy of the new period, that the Christian conscience stirred up men to seek to place restraints on aggressions of the state against other peoples. It was there, through earnestly Christian Spanish churchmen and scholars, that what we think of as modern international law had its birth. A Dominican, a Basque, Francisco de Vitoria, Professor of Theology at the University of Salamanca, had much to do with its inception.[77] Born about 1483, his life spanned the discovery of America and the rapid growth of some of the absolute monarchies. Like his fellow Dominican, Las Casas, and some others of his order, he came out boldly in condemnation of the cruelty with which the conquest of the New World was being accomplished. He incurred the displeasure of Emperor and Pope by the limitations by which he sought to circumscribe the claims of both dignitaries to the Indies and to other lands across the sea. In his *De Indis Noviter Inventis* and his *De Jure Belli*, he set forth a conception of a community of nations which reached beyond Christendom and was co-extensive with the human race. He declared that no attempt to right a wrong to a particular state should be undertaken if it involved a greater injury to the entire world community and that neither a difference in religion, the extension of empire, nor the personal glory of a prince was a just cause for war. He also enunciated the startling doctrine that if the subjects of a prince were conscientiously of the conviction that a given war was unjust they must not serve in it. In all of this he was influenced somewhat by Aristotle, but also by the Christian Scriptures and by Augustine and Thomas Aquinas. The Jesuit Francisco Suarez (1548-1617), who was educated at Salamanca and was later the leading Professor of Theology at the University of Coimbra, helped further in the development of a philosophy of international law and of law in general.[78] The French churchman, Bonnor, in the sixteenth century laid down principles for the restraint of war.[79] Another important contribution to the growth of international law was by Alberico Gentili (1552-1608), who because of his Protestant convictions was forced to leave his native Italy and became Professor of Civil Law at Oxford. In his *De Jure Belli* Gentili gave the world a work which marked one more milestone in the regulation of international relations by law.[80]

What is usually esteemed the chief classic in the early formulation of international law is the *De Jure Belli et Pacis* of Hugo Grotius. In this the attempt was made to formulate rules, partly moral and partly juridical, by which a prince should guide his management of foreign affairs. The Peace of Westphalia seemed to give actuality to some of the ideals of Grotius, and the book

[77] On Vitoria see James Brown Scott, *The Spanish Origin of International Law. Francisco de Vitoria and His Law of Nations* (Oxford, The Clarendon Press, 1934, pp. 19a, 288, clviii), *passim*.

[78] Scott, *op. cit.*, p. 10a. See translation of Suarez's *De Bello* in Alfred Vanderpol, *La Doctrine Scolastique du Droit de Guerre* (Paris, A. Pedone, 1919, pp. xxviii, 534), pp. 362-412.

[79] Kennedy, *Influence of Christianity in International Law*, p. 78; Brace, *Gesta Christi*, p. 328.

[80] Alberico Gentili, *De Jure Belli Libri Tres*, text and translation (Oxford, The Clarendon Press, 2 vols., 1933); Osborne, *Christian Ideas in Political History*, p. 192.

was regarded as beginning a new era.[81] Grotius was a Dutch Protestant, was reared under strong religious influences, and from boyhood had marked religious interests. His keenest and most abiding concerns were either his theological enthusiasms and labours or were closely associated with them.[82] It is clear that his dominant motive in seeking to further the rule of law in the relations between states had a Christian origin. Indeed, he himself has told us that he was provoked to write his *De Jure Belli et Pacis* because he saw throughout the Christian world a license in making war of which even barbarous nations would be ashamed and because when arms were taken up all reverence for divine and human law was forgotten.[83] While he had respect for what he and his predecessors termed the law of nature, he esteemed the New Testament as the more holy law and desired to give it pre-eminence in his system.[84] It is significant that while the book was begun before the outbreak of the Thirty Years' War, it was completed and published (1625) after that struggle had been in progress for several years. Here, as at so many other times, the Christian impulse stimulated the human spirit to seek a cure for a vast social ill which threatened civilization. The Christian faith quickened the conscience and gave courage and hope to an individual to dedicate a brilliant mind to the task of bringing good out of a destructive convulsion of society.

Not so prominent as Grotius was a younger contemporary, Samuel von Pufendorf. The son of a Lutheran pastor, Pufendorf turned from theology to the study of law, but he continued to have a religious interest and presumably the Christian impulse was at least in part responsible for his contributions to international jurisprudence.[85] He insisted that the law of nations is not confined to Christendom but of right is a bond between all nations.

Many Christians were not content, as were most international lawyers, to count war as unavoidable and to rate some wars as being just. They denounced all war. Erasmus declared that war was un-Christian and wrong.[86]

---

[81] Walter Simons, *The Evolution of International Public Law in Europe since Grotius* (Yale University Press, 1931, pp. 146), p. 5.

[82] W. S. M. Knight, *The Life and Works of Hugo Grotius* (London, Sweet and Maxwell, 1925, pp. xiv, 304), pp. 29, 30.

[83] Hugonis Grotii, *De Jure Belli et Pacis* (Cambridge University Press, 3 vols., 1853), Prolegomena, sec. 28.

[84] Hugonis Grotii, *op. cit.,* Prolegomena, sec. 50.

[85] Samuel von Pufendorf, *De Officio Hominis et Civis Juxta Legem Naturalem Libri Duo.* Introduction by Walther Schücking (Carnegie Endowment for International Peace, 2 vols., 1927), *passim.*

[86] Desiderius Erasmus, *Querela Pacis* (see a translation published by the Open Court Publishing Co., 1917), *passim*; Erasmus, *The Education of a Christian Prince* (translation by L. K. Brown, New York, Columbia University Press, 1936), Chap. 11; Meulen, *Der Gedanke der Internationalen Organisation in seiner Entwicklung 1300-1800,* pp 124 ff.

Dean Colet boldly preached before Henry VIII that wars were seldom undertaken except from hatred and ambition and that a Christian prince had much
better imitate Christ than the Caesars or the Alexanders.[87] More than one
of the Protestant groups came out against all war. Among such movements as
those of the Anabaptists, the Mennonites, the Polish Socinians, the Friends,[88]
and, in Russia, the Doukhobors, there was a strong denunciation of all resort
to the sword and an insistence that the true Christian could never engage in
war. Something of this had been seen before A.D. 1500 among minorities
deemed heretical by the official Church.[89] But the conviction that Christians
should abstain from every war, while still held only by minorities, was now
asserted by a larger number and came into greater prominence than in the
preceding period.

Moved at least in part by their Christian faith, moreover, several daring
spirits put forward projects for the construction of a political order in Europe
that would eliminate the wars which so racked the Christendom of their day.
In 1623 a monk, Émeric Crucé, put forward a plan for establishing perpetual
peace and freedom of commerce throughout the world.[90] He suggested that
all the monarchs keep representatives in a given city there to adjust by the
judgment of all in a common assembly the differences which might lead to
war. Much less a product of the Christian conscience, but probably owing
something to it, was the famous Grand Design for the organization of Europe
which bore the name of King Henry IV of France but which seems to have
been the work of the vain and irascible but upright Protestant Sully and his
secretaries.[91] Moved by his Quaker principles, William Penn put forward an
Essay toward the Present and Future Peace of Europe,[92] in which he suggested
a diet or parliament for Europe to which disputes and complaints could be
brought for settlement by vote. A few years later, in 1710, John Bellers, a devout
Quaker and a friend of Penn, also came out with a suggested organization for
Europe to ensure peace and limit armaments.[93] Stirred by the War of the
Spanish Succession and by his connexion as a secretary with the negotiations
which brought it to a close, the French priest, Charles Irénée de Saint-Pierre,
worked out an elaborate plan for permanent peace and included in it not

---

[87] More's *Utopia*, Collins's edition, p. xxxvi.

[88] On the Friends see Hirst, *The Quakers in Peace and War, passim*. On some of the
other groups see Hirst, *op. cit.*, pp. 28 ff.

[89] On the Poor Men of Lyons see Hirst, *op. cit.*, p. 25.

[90] Meulen, *op. cit.*, pp. 143 ff.

[91] Meulen, *op. cit.*, pp. 160 ff.

[92] Meulen, *op. cit.*, pp. 171 ff.; Hirst, *op. cit.*, pp. 153 ff. See the text in *William Penn's
Plan for the Peace of Europe* (Old South Leaflets, Boston, No. 75, pp. 20).

[93] Meulen, *op. cit.*, pp. 177 ff.; Hirst, *op. cit.*, pp. 165 ff.

only Christendom but non-Christian states.[94] His ideas had an effect upon Rousseau in the latter's dreams of peace.[95]

None of these plans was put into operation, but they and others with a similar objective which multiplied as the eighteenth century progressed contributed to the growing peace movement of the nineteenth and twentieth centuries and came to partial even though disappointingly incomplete fruition in the League of Nations. While the projects for peace did not take institutional form before A.D. 1800, they were at least evidence that, largely because of the Christian impulse, Western Europe was being stirred as never before, and, indeed, as no other section of mankind had previously been, to hope for a day when war should be eliminated and to devise machinery by which that hope could be implemented throughout the earth.

These dreams of peace did not remain entirely on paper. Some of the Christian groups attempted to put them into effect. Minorities that they were, they could not expect to organize the entire world or even Europe according to their ideals. However, they could themselves abstain from military service and from paying taxes which were specifically designed as subsidies to armed forces. This many of them did, and at no small cost to themselves.[96] Moreover, in Pennsylvania, founded by one of their number, the Friends had an opportunity in a government largely controlled by themselves to carry out their pacific principles. This they endeavoured to do and for a time with some success. Their purpose brought them into embarrassing conflicts with royal governors. Moreover, as the population of the colony more and more became non-Quaker in composition the influence of the Friends diminished. Yet, even in the French and Indian War and the War of American Independence numbers of the Pennsylvania Friends consistently maintained their witness against the use of the sword.[97] Probably not in the early centuries of the Christian era, and certainly not since then, had so many Christians refused, even in the face of persecution, to share in war. The Christian impulse was increasing in momentum, even though slowly, in its struggle against war.

To a degree that had never been true of any other religion or of any philosophy Christianity was stirring men to resolute and hopeful action against war. In many another faith and philosophy were those who regretted and denounced war. Christianity, as did no other, impelled men to try to do something about it.

What was the influence of Christianity upon the social structure of society

[94] Meulen, op. cit., pp. 180 ff.
[95] Meulen, op. cit., p. 253.
[96] Hirst, op. cit., pp. 194 ff.
[97] Hirst, op. cit., pp. 353 ff.

in Europe in extra-political realms? In spite of the emergence of strong autocratic monarchies which subordinated the churches to the state, Christianity
evinced sufficient vitality to alter the political structure of much of Western
Europe more profoundly than it had been able to do anywhere at any previous
time. It was also potent in making for an international order whose basis
would be law and not brute force. Was it similarly powerful in other phases of
social organization?

Here, too, the effect of Christianity in this period was very marked. The
activism which had been so prominent a characteristic of Western Christianity
as opposed to the quietism of the Eastern forms of the faith continued to assert
itself. This tendency to be concerned with social problems and institutions and
to work for reforms which will bring human society more nearly in conformity
to the ideals which Christians believe that they see in the New Testament seems
inherent in Christianity. It is not only in the case of war that Christianity has
stirred men to hope and to action to uproot what they deem evil. It has done
so also in other realms of social relations. This social activity has been more in
evidence in Western than in Eastern Christianity partly because in the West it
was reinforced by the practical Roman temperament but chiefly because of the
fact that in the West, by reason of the more nearly complete collapse of Roman
political rule in the centuries after A.D. 500, this impulse within Christianity
was challenged by the need to re-establish order and was less trammelled than
in the East by institutions inherited from pre-Christian times. Once having
been given this impetus and having acquired momentum, the tendency to
mould society persisted and grew.

Within Western Europe the intensity of this activism varied with the type
of Christianity. In Lutheranism and in the Pietist outgrowths of Lutheranism
little of it existed. The Church was supposed to concern itself with purely
spiritual and inward matters and external secular affairs were left to the civil
authorities.[98] Yet it must be remembered that in the earlier days of his reforming activity Luther in his *Open Letter to the Christian Nobility of the
German Nation* summed up with great vigour all the German grievances which
had hitherto been stated separately,[99] and that the Peasants' Revolt which by
its excesses swung him over to the side of the princes and the social conserva-
tives,[100] while not due primarily to the Reformation, had a strong religious

[98] Troeltsch, *The Social Teaching of the Christian Churches*, pp. 561, 562, 718.

[99] Lindsay, *A History of the Reformation*, Vol. I, pp. 242, 243. See a translation of the
document in *Works of Martin Luther*, Vol. II (Philadelphia, A. J. Holman Co., 1916),
pp. 61 ff.

[100] See translations of his attacks on the Peasants' Revolt in *Works of Martin Luther*,
Vol. IV (Philadelphia, A. J. Holman Co., 1931), pp. 205 ff.

tinge.[101] Calvinism was more aggressive in transforming society. Calvin himself sought to regulate all phases of the life of Geneva.[102] In Scotland John Knox in his Book of Discipline endeavoured to inculcate the ideal that in every parish all unable to work should be supported out of public funds, that all able to work should be compelled to do so, that every child should be given an opportunity for an education, and that each youth of promise should have an open way to the universities. While this programme was not fully carried out, great strides were made in implementing it, as is shown by the stern measures taken to suppress vagrancy[103] and the emphasis placed on schools.

The religious and social ferment aroused by the Protestant movements brought into existence a number of radical groups. The communistic fellowships of the Anabaptists were numerous and some of them are famous.[104] The upheaval which led to the Commonwealth in England was accompanied by the Levellers, who wished a democratic organization, by the Fifth Monarchy men, some of whom were violent revolutionaries, and by the Diggers, whose stronghold was among the agricultural labourers and whose spokesman, Gerard Winstanley, influenced the Quaker Bellers, who in turn helped to shape the ideas of Richard Owen, and so formed a direct connexion between these seventeenth century Christian radicals and the socialism of the nineteenth century.[105] The Wesleyan movement was not out to work basic changes in society. However, John Wesley persistently contended against such evils as bribery and corruption in politics, smuggling, and the plundering of wrecked vessels.[106] Moreover, Wesley worked strenuously to relieve poverty and started missions to prisoners.[107] It was one of his warm friends and admirers, John Howard, who became an outstanding pioneer in prison reform.[108] Wesley, too, was a pioneer in the anti-slavery movement.[109] He did much to mould the English middle class and to inculcate in it steadiness, sobriety, and industry, and to teach it to regard wealth as a trust.[110] Wesley's followers worked against

[101] Lindsay, op. cit., Vol. I, pp. 95-113.

[102] Williston Walker, John Calvin (New York, G. P. Putnam's Sons, 1906, pp. xviii, 456), pp. 267 ff.

[103] H. I. Andrews in Paton, Bunting, and Garvie, Christ and Civilization, pp. 352, 353; Cunningham, Christianity and Economic Science, p. 66.

[104] Karl Kautsky, Communism in Central Europe in the Time of the Reformation, translated by J. L. and E. G. Mulliken (London, T. Fisher Unwin, 1897, pp. 293), pp. 155 ff.

[105] Troeltsch, op. cit., pp. 710-713.

[106] Edwards, John Wesley and the Eighteenth Century, pp. 158-164.

[107] Edwards, op. cit., pp. 148, 152.

[108] Edwards, op. cit., p. 150.

[109] Edwards, op. cit., pp. 113-128.

[110] Edwards, op. cit., pp. 52, 53.

the exploitation of one group for the benefit of another.[111] The Friends were pioneers in the advocacy of the equality of women with men, of the abolition of slavery, and of the humane treatment of the insane and the criminal.

The Peasants' Revolt in Germany, in which Protestant Christianity gave added incentive to an explosive attempt of the underprivileged to obtain better conditions for living and working, was paralleled by a slightly earlier revolt of peasants in Hungary which had as its leader and inspirer a priest who presumably owed at least in part to his Christian faith his rankling sense of the injustice meted out to the common people and his hope and resolution for betterment.[112] It must be added that both of these revolts were belated movements of the kind which were frequent in the Middle Ages. In making a permanent impression on political and economic conditions they were not nearly so potent as was the later Civil War in England which preceded the Commonwealth and the French Revolution. Since in initiating these two latter movements Christianity had a share, as it had in some of the earlier peasants' uprisings, it seems probable that in the realm of stimulating social change by violent revolution the Christian impulse was growing in effectiveness.

The Abbé de Saint-Pierre, in addition to his labours for universal peace, devoted his life to the formulation of programmes for increasing human happiness and for reforms in finance, economics, and education. Although sceptical as to certain features of Roman Catholic practice, he must have owed his incentive at least in part to his Christian faith.[113] Law, who had a marked influence among the devout in the English-speaking world, held up for admiration an unmarried woman who, with a modest private income, gave herself to helping the sick, the traveller, the unemployed, and the orphan,[114] and taught that since God had created all things for the common good of all men, each should use the share which had fallen to him for that same common good.[115]

The effects of these ideals were numerous and even to enumerate them would prolong these pages beyond any proper length. Some have been mentioned in the preceding paragraphs. There is room only for brief notice of a few others.

Added dignity was given to womanhood.[116] Such Protestant groups as the Baptists and the Quakers were concerned for the spiritual and social equality

---

[111] Warner, *The Wesleyan Movement in the Industrial Revolution*, pp. 279 ff.

[112] Stead, *The Story of Social Christianity*, Vol. II, p. 71.

[113] Bury, *The Idea of Progress*, pp. 129-143.

[114] William Law, *A Serious Call to a Devout and Holy Life* (the references are to the Everyman's Library edition, London, J. M. Dent and Sons, 1931, pp. viii, 355. The book was first published in 1728), pp. 73 ff.

[115] Law, *op. cit.*, p. 242.

[116] On the legal results, see Marianne Weber, *Ehefrau und Mutter in der Rechtsentwicklung* (Tübingen, J. C. B. Mohr, 1907, pp. xvi, 573), Chap. 4.

of men and women.[117] Through the Protestant movement marriage and romance were now combined. What had been in the Middle Ages the courtly tradition of unwedded love was united with the Christian standard of monogamy. Calvinism taught that husband and wife should join in the divine vocation of rearing children for eternal life and should be comrades in the religious pilgrimage.[118] The Roman Catholic Vincent de Paul led the way in developing the nursing profession for women and in 1616 founded the Daughters of Charity for the alleviation of misery.[119]

Consciences made sensitive and resolute by their Christian faith sought to eliminate amusements which they believed harmful. Thus Pope Pius V in 1567 issued a general prohibition of bull fights and ordered the excommunication of all who took part in them.[120] In Geneva, Calvin banned dancing, which in its current forms brought temptation to sexual irregularities, and playing cards, presumably because of the gambling entailed.[121]

In the latter part of seventeenth and in eighteenth century England the nonconforming Protestant churches gave the chief opportunity for the development of initiative and responsibility among the proletariat.[122]

The movements to abolish slavery among the natives of the New World which we have recorded in earlier chapters were coincident with efforts to end slavery in Europe. In Europe slavery was by no means so extensive as in America, but we read that in 1535 a Papal decree commanded that it be terminated in Rome.[123]

We hear much of the atrocities perpetrated on those accused of witchcraft, and sometimes by deeply religious people. It is important also to note that among both Protestants and Roman Catholics were those who had the courage to denounce the popular mania.[124]

Before A.D. 1500 few if any attempts had been made to reform prisons. Indeed, the tortures inflicted on prisoners in the Middle Ages and later, the nature of the cells in which prisoners were confined, the lack of proper food, drink, and sanitation, and the ingenious devices for giving excruciating pain to the human frame, are among the saddest pages in the annals of man's inhumanity to man.

[117] R. H. Bainton in *The Journal of Modern History*, Vol. VIII, p. 438; Troeltsch, *The Social Teaching of the Christian Churches*, p. 809.
[118] Bainton in *op. cit.*, Vol. VIII, p. 438.
[119] Stead, *op. cit.*, Vol. II, p. 205.
[120] Pastor, *History of the Popes*, Vol. XVIII, pp. 33, 34.
[121] Smith, *The Age of the Reformation*, p. 172.
[122] Bebb, *Nonconformity and Social and Economic Life 1660-1800*, pp. 163-173.
[123] Hoffmann, *Ursprung und Anfangstätigkeit des ersten päpstlichen Missionsinstituts*, p. 37.
[124] McNeill, *Christian Hope for World Society*, p. 179.

These evils were by no means eradicated after A.D. 1500. However, before A.D. 1800 a movement for prison reform had begun, given its initial impulse chiefly by those who had been stirred to the task by their Christian faith. Thus Olaus Petri, the foremost Swedish exponent of Lutheran ideas at the time of the Protestant Reformation, denounced the use of torture as a means of forcing a criminal to confess.[125] The Benedictine Mabillion, writing towards the close of the seventeenth century, gave incentive to the movement for a more humane treatment of criminals.[126] John Bellers, the Quaker, engaged in a ministry to prisoners.[127] As early as 1699 the Society for Promoting Christian Knowledge was discussing plans for the reform of the notorious Newgate and of other prisons about London.[128] James Oglethorpe, the Anglican, whose project for the settlement of Georgia had been in part for the purpose of enabling prisoners to make a new start in a different environment, took up in Parliament the cause of prison reform.[129] Raikes, the founder of the Sunday Schools, was active in the relief of prisoners.[130] John Howard, the most famous of all the pioneers in fighting the abuses of the prison system, seems to have owed to his Christian faith the incentive which drove him to extensive travels and herculean labours in behalf of his cause. Certainly he had been reared as a nonconforming Calvinist and continued as a devout member of nonconforming chapels.[131]

One of the most striking examples of the transforming effect of Christianity in a particular community centres around John Frederic Oberlin (1740-1826).[132] Born in Strasbourg, in his young manhood Oberlin became pastor of a poverty-stricken parish in the Vosges Mountains. Here through a long ministry he led in building roads, founded what are said to have been the first "infant schools," pioneered in the application of scientific agriculture, introduced seeds for his people from all over Europe, saw his parish through the trying years of the French Revolution, in a region of intolerance shielded Jews from persecution and so won the friendship of Roman Catholics that in his later years they

[125] Hallendorf and Schück, *History of Sweden*, pp. 130-152.
[126] Lallemand, *Histoire de la Charité*, Vol. IV, Part 2, pp. 115, 116.
[127] McNeill, *op. cit.*, p. 180.
[128] Allen and McClure, *Two Hundreds Years: The History of the Society for Promoting Christian Knowledge*, pp. 54-57.
[129] McNeill, *op. cit.*, p. 180.
[130] J. Field, *The Life of John Howard* (London, Longman, Brown, Green, and Longmans, 1850, pp. xvi, 495), p. 107.
[131] Field, *op. cit.*, *passim*; James Baldwin Brown, *Memoirs of the Public and Private Life of John Howard, the Philanthropist* (2d ed., London, Thomas and George Underwood, 1823, pp. xxxii, 657), *passim*.
[132] A biography written for a popular audience, but based upon earlier works and containing a useful bibliography, is Marshall Dawson, *Oberlin, A Protestant Saint* (Chicago, Willett, Clark and Co., 1934, pp. ix, 166).

worshipped in his church, and by education, preaching, and self-sacrificing giving made the community over until he became famous throughout Europe.

These many effects of Christianity in working basic alterations in social institutions and in directly attacking and uprooting widespread social ills were, in general, new, and marked an advance in the penetration of human society by the Christian leaven. Before these centuries Christians, while endeavouring, and successfully, to eliminate competing religions, had not usually striven to remove deep-seated customs and well-established institutions which were contrary to the Christian ethic. The more earnest Christians might seek to **withdraw** themselves from them by entering the monastic movement or by joining sects which were denounced by the Church as heretical, and they might even strive to check in Christendom some of the more palpable collective evils. Seldom, however, if at all, did they embark upon campaigns to rid the world at large or even Christendom of collective ills. Now reform movements, having their sources in large part in the Christian impulse, began attacks on large-scale ills and strove to eradicate them. It was not that they believed in the perfectibility of man. Some might do so. Indeed, the confidence in the perfectibility of man which played so large a part in eighteenth, nineteenth, and twentieth century social and political liberalism and reform may have had as one of its roots the belief of Francis of Assisi and Francis de Sales, inspired by their Christian faith, that the human heart is of such a nature that it can be won by love. However, the majority of thoughtful Christians cherished no easy optimism about the early eradication of all evil. Their faith had helped them to take too realistic a view of human nature to be led into that bypath. They did, however, believe that their faith called them to struggle to rid the world of practices which were in contradiction of Christian ideals, particularly those in which professed Christians were entangled. In the nineteenth century this movement for reform was to swell into a major stream.

Efforts to ameliorate the lot of individuals who had been maimed by the collective ills and sins of mankind had been prominent throughout the history of the Christian movement. Particularly in the Middle Ages under the Christian impulse institutions and organizations had multiplied to care for the sick, the orphan, the poor, the friendless, the traveller, and Christian captives in the hands of the Moslems. In the breakdown of society which followed the shrinking of the Roman Empire the Church had stepped into the breach and had become the protector of the weak.

In the three centuries between A.D. 1500 and A.D. 1800 new movements towards this end continued to spring from Christianity. States and cities took over some of the eleemosynary functions once performed by the Church.[133] This, however,

---

[133] Lallemand, *Histoire de la Charité*, Vol. IV, Part 1, *passim*.

did not necessarily mean that organized charities no longer arose from Christian roots. Often it merely indicated that Christians were implementing their humanitarian purposes through other than ecclesiastical instruments and that secular bodies were performing Christian functions and so were becoming more nearly Christianized. Moreover, the Christian conscience again and again led men and women to see and to seek to meet the needs of individuals and classes which were being neglected by existing agencies.

Here again a complete catalogue would prove too bulky, even if it could be compiled. Only a few somewhat random examples can be given. Religious orders continued to be the agents for the release of the thousands of Christians who were taken captive by the aggressive Moslem corsairs of North Africa.[134] We hear of at least one large gift for this purpose which made possible the ransom of several hundred through Franciscan tertiates.[135] As might have been expected, the Catholic Reformation was accompanied by many fresh philanthropic movements of the general types which had long had their place in the Church.[136] Ignatius Loyola, whose Society of Jesus became the greatest agency of that reform, had much of tender compassion and active love for children and fallen women and organized provision for the redemption of Christian captives held by Moslems.[137] The Council of Trent encouraged charity and formulated rules for its administration.[138] Many new orders and congregations came into existence for the care of the sick and the poor.[139] Numerous congregations of women were founded to minister to the sick and the destitute and to give religious instruction to the religiously neglected.[140] Among them were the Ursulines, the Daughters of the Cross, the Sisters of Christian Doctrine, and the Sisters of Charity.[141] We hear of a confraternity for visiting prisoners and for the burial of the destitute,[142] of a hospital for galley slaves founded at Marseilles by Vincent de Paul,[143] and of an organization for the relief of indigent students.[144] John of God, a spiritual son of the great preacher, John of Avila, ministered personally to the sick, instituted a hospital in Granada, and

[134] Lallemand, op. cit., Vol. IV, Part 2, pp. 164-176, 187-194; Goyau in Descamps, Histoire Générale Comparée des Missions, pp. 469-473.

[135] Lemmens, Geschichte der Franziskanermissionen, p. 344.

[136] Liese, Geschichte der Caritas, Vol. I, pp. 257-274.

[137] Stead, The Story of Social Christianity, Vol. II, pp. 75, 76; Lindsay, A History of the Reformation, Vol. II, p. 555.

[138] Lallemand, op. cit. Vol. IV, Part 1, p. 27.

[139] Lallemand, op. cit., Vol. IV, Part 1, pp. 45-52.

[140] Uhlhorn, Die christliche Liebesthätigkeit, Vol. III, p. 184.

[141] Uhlhorn, op. cit., Vol. III, pp. 210-214, 222, 227, 228.

[142] Pastor, History of the Popes, Vol. 10, p. 393.

[143] The Encyclopædia Britannica, 14th ed., Vol. XXIII, p. 168.

[144] Marie, Histoire des Instituts Religieux et Missionaires, pp. 238 ff.

organized a community for the care of the sick which spread to several lands.[145] Camille de Lellis after a severe illness devoted himself to the sick and by the time of his death (1614) several European lands had houses of his order.[146] Although in Germany the early part of the sixteenth century was one of mounting prices and destitution,[147] the first effect of the Protestant Reformation on charity was a decline in giving. Luther denounced the motives to which appeals for alms had been frequent in the Middle Ages—the gaining of entrance into heaven, the mitigation of suffering in purgatory, and penance—and substituted for them as a basis for almsgiving the voluntary and grateful response to the love of God.[148] This led for a time to a falling off in benefactions. Moreover, Protestantism, by its rejection of monasticism deprived itself of the organizations through which Christian philanthropy had long expressed itself and did not at once devise adequate substitutes. In time, however, Protestantism developed agencies for the care of the destitute. In Germany the Thirty Years' War destroyed many of the charitable institutions and dissipated a large proportion of the endowments which had supported them, but numbers of the Lutheran pastors remained with their flocks, sharing their sufferings and ministering to their distress.[149] Out of the Pietist movement came the famous orphanage in Halle.[150] The Friends were early deeply concerned over questions of poor relief.[151] In Scotland collections were taken in the churches Sunday by Sunday for the care of the destitute and the kirk session was the almoner and the money-lender of the poor.[152] Protestantism, while not giving rise to as many hospitals and charitable foundations directly controlled by ecclesiastical organizations as did Roman Catholicism, encouraged much active concern for the suffering. By stimulating thrift and industry it led many to escape from the ranks of those who required relief. As we have seen, moreover, from it issued many movements for social reform whose outcome was a struggle against the causes of destitution.

We must now inquire the effect of Christianity upon still another phase of the life of Europe, that of economic organization and ideas.

Here in the fifteen centuries which preceded A.D. 1500 the Christian impulse had already produced some changes. It had insisted that although individuals

[145] Pastor, op. cit., Vol. XI, p. 528; Lallemand, op. cit., Vol. IV, Part 1, pp. 35-39.
[146] Lallemand, op. cit., Vol. IV, Part 1, pp. 39-41.
[147] Uhlhorn, op. cit., Vol. III, pp. 8-14.
[148] Uhlhorn, op. cit., Vol. III, pp. 16-18; W. E. Chadwick, The Church, the State, and the Poor (London, Robert Scott, 1914, pp. viii, 223), pp. 91, 92.
[149] Uhlhorn, op. cit., Vol. II, pp. 195-198.
[150] Uhlhorn, op. cit., Vol. III, pp. 239-252.
[151] Bebb, Nonconformity and Social and Economic Life 1660-1800, p. 127.
[152] Graham, The Social Life of Scotland in the Eighteenth Century, p. 238.

have the use of what appears to be private property, ultimately the ownership is God's, and that they must utilize what they possess as a trust and for the good not only of themselves but also of their fellow creatures. Through the monastic rule which required work from those who embraced it, Christianity had helped to give dignity to labour and had made for clearing forests, draining swamps, and improving the methods of agriculture. The Church had placed a ban on charging or receiving interest on loans. There had been much talk of a just price.

In the three centuries after A.D. 1500 the effect upon economic life continued, but its manifestations were somewhat altered. Luther came out against the exaction of interest on loans,[153] but the protest against interest was weakened among both Protestants[154] and Roman Catholics[155]—perhaps because the rising prominence of capitalism made that practice seem less heinous. We hear of condemnations by the clergy, among them Luther in Germany[156] and the Calvinist pastors in Scotland,[157] of forestalling and monopolies which led to swollen prices at the expense of the common man, and of buying as cheaply and selling as dearly as possible, but after the straitjacket imposed on industry and trade by guilds in the Middle Ages, the swing of the pendulum was towards *laissez faire* and the Christian conscience raised no unanimous voice against it. Even the Levellers, a radical religious group in England at the time of the Commonwealth, who held that the enclosure of land robbed the common man of his rights and who advocated the cultivation of the disputed areas and the feeding of the populace from the crops thus raised,[158] did not endorse the general socialization of property. In general, the leading Protestant reformers condemned mendicancy and held that all Christians should work and should not depend upon another's wealth and labour.[159] The Wesleyan movement encouraged self-dependence and individual initiative and its adherents tended to rise in the economic scale.[160] Protestantism, particularly Calvinism and the dissenting minorities within Protestantism, made for industry and thrift.

[153] Martin Luther, *On Trading and Usury,* translated in *Works of Martin Luther,* Vol. IV (Philadelphia, A. J. Holman Co., 1931), pp. 12 ff.; *A Treatise on Usury,* translated in *Works of Martin Luther,* Vol. IV, pp. 37 ff.

[154] Stead, *The Story of Social Christianity,* Vol. II, p. 35; Cunningham, *Christianity and Economic Science,* pp. 64, 65; Troeltsch, *The Social Teaching of the Christian Churches,* p. 643.

[155] Robertson, *Aspects of the Rise of Economic Individualism,* pp. 133, 136-160; Brodrick, *The Economic Morals of the Jesuits,* p. 143.

[156] Stead, *op. cit.,* Vol. II, p. 35.

[157] Graham, *The Social Life of Scotland in the Eighteenth Century,* p. 150.

[158] Gooch and Laski, *English Democratic Ideas in the Seventeenth Century,* p. 181.

[159] Martin Luther, *On Trading and Usury,* translated in *Works of Martin Luther,* Vol. IV, p. 23.

[160] Edwards, *John Wesley and the Eighteenth Century,* p. 182.

It has been argued that Protestantism, particularly Calvinism, reinforced capitalism. The best known statement of that position has maintained that Protestantism tended to make a type of asceticism incumbent upon all Christians, the laity as well as the clergy, that Calvinism held up as an ideal unremitting industry in one's "calling" (for, according to Calvinism, and especially English Puritanism, God's Providence has prepared for everyone a calling in which he should labour), and that, while in principle the usefulness of this calling should be measured in terms of the value of the goods produced in it for the community as a whole, the theory led to the accumulation of private wealth. The very fact that it was taught that this wealth must not be allowed to induce its holder to live in idleness or extravagance favoured its further accumulation and its employment in commerce or industry. If property were obtained in this fashion and used for this purpose, its acquisition and possession, so it was held, became not a sin but a virtue. Thus was reinforced the prosperous *bourgeois* class with which capitalism was closely associated.[161] The hypothesis suggests that while capitalism was not necessarily the direct product of Calvinism, the two possessed an affinity for each other and that the growth of the former was assisted by the latter.[162] Calvinism, so it is suggested, produced courageous and enterprising *entrepreneurs* who aided largely in the growth of capitalism.[163] It is also said that the chief exponents of utilitarian liberalism, which was closely associated with the advocacy of *laissez faire* and so gave free rein to the development of capitalism in some of its phases, were nonconformist clergymen, Price and Priestley, and that the economic doctrines of the classic formulator of *laissez faire* economics, Adam Smith, rest on a foundation of religious optimism.[164]

This thesis has been vigorously attacked.[165] It is declared to misunderstand the Calvinist conception of calling, for the early Puritans used the latter in reproof of covetousness and of ambition and exhorted to the choice of a calling which would most conduce to the public good, and it is asserted that Roman

---

[161] The best known statement is Max Weber, *Die protestantische Ethik und der Geist der Kapitalismus*, translated by Talcott Parsons in *The Protestant Ethic and the Spirit of Capitalism* (London, George Allen and Unwin, 1930, pp. xi, 292). See also Richard Henry Tawney, *Religion and the Rise of Capitalism* (London, J. Murray, 1926, pp. xiii, 339), *passim*.

[162] Troeltsch, *The Social Teaching of the Christian Churches*, p. 915.

[163] Troeltsch, *op. cit.*, pp. 812, 813.

[164] Dawson, *Progress and Religion*, p. 192.

[165] See especially H. M. Robertson, *Aspects of the Rise of Economic Individualism. A Criticism of Max Weber and His School* (Cambridge University Press, 1933, pp. xvi, 223). A partial reply to Robertson is J. Brodrick, *The Economic Morals of the Jesuits* (Oxford University Press, 1934, pp. 158).

Catholic counterparts exist for most of the Puritan beliefs which are alleged to demonstrate the Calvinist origin of capitalism.[166] The discussion has given rise to an extensive literature. The impression gained by one who has nothing at stake in either answer is that Christianity, in both its Protestant and Roman Catholic forms, was opposed to much of the ethics associated with capitalism, but that many from both wings of the Christian movement were caught up in capitalism and twisted what had come to them from Christian theorists to justify practices and attitudes which were abhorrent to many of those who shaped the theologies and the organizations of the churches. It is probable that through Christian teachings, particularly those in the Calvinist-Puritan strain, thus misunderstood and twisted, came an added fillip to the growth of capitalism, a growth which was already in progress and which would have taken place without this stimulus.

It must also be said that by the time when, in the nineteenth and twentieth centuries, capitalism came to its full flowering, the Christian conscience had begun to contribute to movements which sought to mend the ills which capitalism brought or even to displace capitalism itself. Movements to protect the labourers and the underprivileged in a capitalistic economy and some of the various forms of socialism had their source partly in Christianity. Moreover, in the nineteenth and twentieth centuries the Christian conscience, particularly in Protestant circles, impelled many who accumulated fortunes under capitalism to give part of them to the public weal. A large proportion of the benefactions whose totals amounted to such huge sums derived their incentive in part from the Christian impulse. We must, however, postpone a fuller discussion of these effects to the volumes which deal with the later period.

From economics we pass to a very different realm, that of music.[167] Here some of the most marked developments were due either partially or chiefly to the Christian impulse. A special form of music, the oratorio, probably took its name from the Oratory of Philip Neri and the religious movement which he inaugurated.[168] Its themes were religious and in the hands of such masters as Bach and Handel it made lasting contributions to the aesthetic life of mankind. It seems almost a gratuitous banality to call attention to one of the most obvious facts in the history of music, the inspiration which Christian themes provided for those who laid the foundations for modern music. It was the Eucharist which so powerfully stirred Palestrina to create the great series of

[166] Robertson, *op. cit.*, pp. 1-32, 209-211.

[167] Standard works which cover the field are *The Oxford History of Music*, by various authors (Oxford, The Clarendon Press, 6 vols., 1901-1905), and Emil Naumann, *The History of Music*, translated by F. Praeger, edited by F. A. Gore Ouseley (London, Cassell and Co., 2 vols., no date).

[168] Pastor, *History of the Popes*, Vol. XIX, p. 187.

musical settings for the mass which helped to give expression to the new life of the Roman Catholic Reformation. It was the Church which accorded to Johann Sebastian Bach the opportunity to utilize his inherited talents and it was the Christian faith which provided him themes for many of his compositions—some of the greatest and most influential music ever written. Indeed Bach, although a sturdy Lutheran, at once represented the completion and perfection of a Christian musical development of almost a thousand years and became the awakener and father of modern music. He would have been impossible but for the music before him which was an outgrowth of the Christian impulse. A distinguished organist, he was also an unsurpassed composer. It was Biblical themes which educed the most notable music of Handel. Gluck, who did so much for the early stages of the opera, received a large proportion of his early musical instruction in a Jesuit seminary. Franz Joseph Haydn obtained in church choirs the initial training of his remarkable genius and some of his best remembered works have Biblical subjects. Mozart had for father a violinist in the service of the Archbishop of Salzburg and owed to the Church much of such scanty financial support as enabled him to give himself to the cultivation of his gifts. With its emphasis upon the laity and the priesthood of all believers, Protestantism made much of congregational singing. Luther expressed his faith in song and was a prolific writer of hymns. The Wesley revival stimulated one of the brothers, Charles, to poetic and musical expression and he became one of the most prominent and prolific writers of hymns in the English tongue. Samuel Wesley, the son of Charles, has been called the father of modern organ playing in England. Moreover, in these three centuries the nativity of Jesus, long an inspirer of song, gave rise to hundreds of Christmas carols. While not its only source, the remarkable musical development of this period had in the Christian impulse one of its chief creative inspirations. In this phase of European culture Christianity had more pronounced effects than in the preceding periods.

In painting, sculpture, and architecture, Christianity seems not to have been so dominant an influence in Western Europe as in the thousand years before A.D. 1500. Protestantism, indeed, brought something of a reverse to these arts. In their rage against what they deemed the idolatry of Roman Catholicism, Protestant iconoclasts destroyed many of the works of art, particularly the statues, in the churches which they took over. That was a temporary and sporadic phase of the early days of Protestantism, and its excesses were opposed by such outstanding leaders as Luther, Calvin, and Knox.[169] More serious

---

[169] Andrew Landale Drummond, *The Church Architecture of Protestantism. An Historical and Constructive Study* (Edinburgh, T. and T. Clark, 1934, pp. xviii, 342), p. 20.

was the permanent prejudice, particularly in congregations of Calvinist and Anabaptist traditions, against sculpture and painting of any kind in the churches. The rejection of the mass (even though something approaching it was retained by many of the Lutherans and Anglicans) deprived the Protestant portions of Europe of the inspiration around which the great cathedrals and the parish and monastic churches of the Middle Ages had been erected. Pre-Reformation church buildings might be retained by Protestantism, but the conceptions which had brought them into existence were altered and in them the Protestant forms of worship often seemed ill at ease and in perpetual contradiction to much of the spirit which had created them. Most of the great monastic buildings were allowed to crumble. Moreover, even in Roman Catholic lands the secular spirit in art became more prominent. In them the Church was no longer the only or even the chief patron of the arts. The Renaissance had brought admiration for pagan antiquity and a revival of the latter's artistic themes and styles. Even a casual excursion through the art galleries of Europe reveals how largely, in contrast with the Middle Ages, secular subjects had displaced religious themes in painting.

Yet in painting, sculpture, and architecture the Christian spirit continued to make itself felt. In England Christopher Wren, the son of a clergyman, used forms borrowed from the pre-Christian Græco-Roman world to create a type of church building which has enjoyed a wide vogue in Anglo-Saxon Protestant communities, not only in the British Isles but also elsewhere.[170] Albrecht Dürer, although many of his greatest paintings were completed before the outbreak of the Lutheran movement, was a warm friend and admirer of Luther.[171] Both Michelangelo and Raphael did much of their greatest work— some of the most notable sculpture and painting ever produced by the hand of man—under the inspiration of Christian themes and in the employ of the Church. The most famous achievement of the brilliant and versatile Leonardo da Vinci was the Last Supper. Although interspersed with secular themes, traditional Christian subjects were treated again and again by the artists of the period, even by the voluptuous Titian. Græco-Roman architectural forms were made by both Roman Catholics and Protestants to subserve Christian purposes. St. Peter's in Rome, St. Paul's in London, and many a New England meeting house are examples of the fashion in which styles created by classical antiquity were so successfully subordinated to Christian uses that their pagan origin was remembered only with an effort.

In the field of education the Christian impulse continued to be powerful.

A casual reading of the history of the period might lead one to believe that here Christianity had spent its force and had even become reactionary. After the collapse of the Roman Empire, the Church, impelled by its Christian purpose, had become the schoolmaster of Western Europe and the tutor of the barbarians of the North. Under its auspices most of the universities of the Middle Ages had arisen. Now some of these universities became static, the last citadels of an outworn and arid scholasticism, and more than one churchman invoked religion as authority for seeking to eradicate new ideas. However, a more careful perusal of the intellectual record of the three centuries between A.D. 1500 and A.D. 1800 leads to a quite different conclusion. The Christian impulse gave birth to effort after effort to provide schools for those who did not have them and to many a new pedagogical theory and procedure. Fully as much as previously and perhaps even more than ever, Christianity was a creative factor in stirring and educating the human spirit and intellect.

In general the educational results of Christianity in Western Europe in this period were seen in schools for the masses and the middle classes. In the Middle Ages the kind of formal training represented by the schools had been for the few. Parish schools there were, but the chief educational contributions of the early part of the Middle Ages had been through the monasteries and of the latter part of the Middle Ages through the creation and development of the universities. We have seen that religiously and politically after A.D. 155 Christianity stirred the masses and led them as never before to self-conscious activity. The Christian impulse also impelled men and women to provide schools for the masses and for the *bourgeoisie*. Christianity was taking formal education to the thousands who previously had known it little if at all. In religion the sixteenth, seventeenth, and eighteenth centuries saw the quickening of the great rank and file of Western Europe by the faith which had been adopted wholesale centuries before under the leadership of the upper classes. The masses had now consciously made Christianity their own and were being roused by it to independent action. So, also, the Christian impulse was giving rise to movements to open to all, the lowliest as well as the highest, the opportunity for at least elementary education.

It was to be expected that Protestantism, with its emphasis upon the responsibility and dignity of the individual Christian and upon the duty and right of private judgment, would stress education for the laity as well as for the clergy. In fostering schools, as it did, Protestantism was but running true to form. However, from within Roman Catholicism as well came movement after movement for education for the masses as well as for the aristocracy. The instances of this constructive effort of Christianity are so numerous that time can be taken merely to mention a few of the more outstanding examples. John Colet, Dean of St. Paul's in London, a reformer who remained within the Roman Catholic Church, regarded teaching as a religious duty and refounded the school connected with the cathedral.[172] Luther did much to stimulate popular education and declared that the civil authorities should compel parents to send their children to school.[173] Melanchthon, so prominent in the early Lutheran movement, was called the preceptor of Germany and is said to have done more than any one else to improve the educational methods of the country.[174] Together with another friend of Luther, John Bugenhagen, he brought the German *volksschule* into existence and reconstructed the university curriculum.[175] Out of Protestantism came compulsory elementary education for all children in some of the German states.[176] One of the most creative writers on educational method and anticipating some of the most progressive theories of later times was the deeply religious Moravian Bishop, John Amos Comenius (1592-1670).[177] From Pietism was born the University of Halle, which was a pioneer in including in its curriculum modern subjects taught in the vernacular.[178] In the city of Halle, moreover, the Pietist, August Hermann Francke, began schools whose methods had much to do with moulding later Prussian education.[179] It was a pupil of Francke, Hecker, who created the prototype of the *realschulen* which have had so large a part in German education.[180] In Holland in the early part of the seventeenth century the Dutch Reformed Church undertook, with the state, to establish elementary schools in every parish.[181] In Scotland the leaders in the Reformation, John Knox and his friend George Buchanan, had a plan for the endowment of a school in each parish and for high schools and colleges in all important towns.[182] This plan was not fully realized, and in

---

[172] J. H. Lupton, *A Life of John Colet* (London, George Bell and Sons, new edition, 1909, pp. xiv, 323), pp. 154 ff.

[173] Smith, *The Age of the Reformation*, pp. 664-666.

[174] Karl Hartfelder, *Philipp Melanchthon als Praeceptor Germaniae* (in *Monumenta Germaniae Paedagogica*, Vol. VII, Berlin, A. Hoffmann & Co., 1889, pp. xxviii, 687), *passim*; McGiffert, *Protestant Thought before Kant*, p. 71.

[175] McNeill, *Christian Hope for World Society*, pp. 212, 213.

[176] Monroe, *A Text-Book in the History of Education*, p. 433.

[177] Jvan Kvačak, *J. A. Comenius* (Berlin, Reuther und Reichard, 1914, pp. x, 192); S. S. Laurie, *John Amos Comenius, Bishop of the Moravians, his Life and Educational Works* (Cambridge University Press, 3d ed., 1887, pp. vi, 240); J. Kvačala, *Die pädagogische Reform des Comenius in Deutschland bis zum Ausgange des XVII Jahrhunderts* (in *Monumenta Germaniae Paedagogica*, Vols. XXVI, XXXII, Berlin, A. Hoffmann & Co., 1903-1904).

[178] Monroe, *op. cit.*, p. 501.

[179] McNeill, *op. cit.*, p. 220.

[180] Monroe, *op. cit.*, p. 498.

[181] Monroe, *op. cit.*, p. 436.

[182] Lindsay, *A History of the Reformation*, Vol. II, p. 307.

the eighteenth century popular education was at a low ebb, especially in the Highlands. However, the Christian conscience brought into existence the Society for the Propagation of Christian Knowledge, and this did much to improve conditions.[183] Moreover, the University of Edinburgh was founded as the direct result of action by the Protestant clergy and the municipal council.[184] In eighteenth century England, the universities, controlled by the state church, intellectually were in a bad way.[185] Yet Protestant nonconformists founded and maintained academies which gave the best and the most practical instruction to be had in the country.[186] Then, too, the Society for Promoting Christian Knowledge, begun in 1689 and supported by members of the Church of England, did much to found schools.[187] It was the charity schools, established by the devout for poor children, which were a chief means of popular education, religious and secular, in England, Scotland, and Wales,[188] and which in Wales, by teaching the Bible in the vernacular, in the eighteenth century gave rise to an intellectual and religious revival and helped to awaken national consciousness.[189] In 1783 Robert Raikes, a friend of Wesley and the Whitefields, opened the first Sunday School, the precursor of a vast, world-wide movement. John Wesley, by his circulation of literature in inexpensive form and through his advocacy of the Sunday School, gave a marked impetus to the education of the masses.[190] Towards the close of the eighteenth century the Anglican clergyman, Andrew Bell, and the Quaker, Joseph Lancaster, worked out independently of each other a system of inexpensive education by which instruction was relayed from the master through advanced pupils.[191] It was the devout Swiss Protestant, John Henry Pestalozzi, who put into practice Rousseau's theory of sympathy with the child as essential in the educative process.[192] In Roman Catholic lands, as we have suggested, the new tides of religious life

[183] Mackinnon, *The Social and Industrial History of Scotland*, p. 35; Graham, *The Social Life of Scotland in the Eighteenth Century*, p. 422.

[184] Stephen d'Irsay, *Histoire des Universités Françaises et Étrangères des Origines à nos Jours* (Paris, Auguste Picard, 2 vols., 1933, 1935), Vol. II, p. 21.

[185] See a description of Cambridge in H. M. Hyde, *The Rise of Castlereagh* (London, Macmillan and Co., 1933, pp. xii, 478), p. 46.

[186] Lincoln, *Some Political and Social Ideas of English Dissent, 1763-1800*, pp. 66, 67; Bebb, *Nonconformity and Social and Economic Life, 1660-1800*, pp. 163-173.

[187] Allen and McClure, *Two Hundred Years. History of the Society for Promoting Christian Knowledge*, pp. 135-165.

[188] M. G. Jones, *The Charity School Movement. A Study of Eighteenth Century Puritanism in Action* (Cambridge University Press, 1938, pp. xiii, 446), *passim*.

[189] Jones, *op. cit.*, p. 321.

[190] Edwards, *John Wesley in the Eighteenth Century*, pp. 135, 136.

[191] Monroe, *op. cit.*, p. 572; McNeill, *Christian Hope for World Society*, p. 222.

[192] McNeill, *op. cit.*, p. 221. See also August Israel, *Pestalozzi-Bibliographie. Die Schriften und Briefe Pestalozzis* (in *Monumenta Germaniae Pedagogica*, Vols. XXV, XXIX, XXXI, Berlin, A. Hoffmann & Co., 1903, 1904).

which gave rise to the Catholic Reformation led to new educational methods
and to extensive efforts for schools for the masses. The Jesuits gave much attention to the education of youth. Their schools and their *ratio studiorum* were
famous.[193] In the sixteenth century a Spanish Benedictine made what, so far
as we know, were the first successful efforts to teach deaf mutes to speak and
to write.[194] In the seventeenth and eighteenth centuries numerous congregations
of women sprang up which devoted themselves to popular education.[195] In the
latter part of the seventeenth century John Baptist de la Salle founded the
Brothers of Christian Schools largely for the purpose of instructing the children in the rural districts.[196] Nearly a century before the Piarists had been
brought into existence in Rome for the teaching, chiefly by the clergy, of poor
and ignorant children,[197] and the Fathers of Christian Doctrine, founded by
César de Bus, had been begun and had founded many schools, chiefly in
Southern France.[198] In 1702 the Brothers of St. Gabriel came into being, also
for the conduct of schools.[199] In the seventeenth century the Jansenist Gentle-
men of Port Royal undertook a project which planted "little schools" widely
in France. The outstanding educational thinker in the group, Antoine Arnauld,
rejected Jesuit methods, as might have been expected from the antagonism between the Jansenists and the Society of Jesus, gave attention to science, stressed
the use of the vernacular, and emphasized love for the child and close personal
contact between pupils and teachers.[200] In Ireland, "hedge schools," conducted
by lay teachers but encouraged by the Roman Catholic clergy, in the eighteenth
century were a force for popular education among a poverty-stricken and exploited peasantry and in the following century hastened the introduction of
a state system of education.[201]

Again it must be said that between A.D. 1500 and A.D. 1800 it was primarily
because of the Christian impulse that in Western Europe schools were provided
for the masses and that it was through the Christian impulse that new educational theories and procedures came into being and were put into effect. It
was from the Christian movement that the enthusiastic conviction arose which

[193] Robert Schwickerath, *Jesuit Education. Its History and Principles* (St. Louis, B.
Herder, 2d ed., 1904, pp. xv, 687), Chaps. 3, 4, 5.

[194] Lallemand, *Histoire de la Charité*, Vol. IV, Part, 2, pp. 55 ff.

[195] Schuetz, *The Origin of the Teaching Brotherhoods*, pp. 9 ff.

[196] Schuetz, *op. cit.*, pp. 19 ff.; Marie, *Histoire des Instituts Religieux et Missionaires*,
pp. 224-238.

[197] Schuetz, *op. cit.*, p. 20.

[198] *Ibid.*

[199] Schuetz, *op. cit.*, pp. 36 ff.

[200] McNeill, *op. cit.*, p. 218; Monroe, *op. cit.*, pp. 430-433.

[201] Patrick John Dowling, *The Hedge Schools of Ireland* (London, Longmans, Green
and Co., 1935, pp. xvii, 182), pp. 19-21.

sought for all the open door for at least the beginning of intellectual development, which enriched the course of study with new subjects that to the mind of the average man and woman the gamut of advancing human knowledge might be opened, and which inaugurated the trend that sought through formal education the development of the individual. From Christianity, although reinforced by other influences, came the ideal that education must be pupil-centred rather than for the purpose of regimenting the human mind and will into conformity with superimposed patterns.

In view of this effect upon education, it was to be expected that Christianity would exert a profound influence upon language and literature. Here again the results are seen not only among the upper classes and the highly educated few, but also among the masses. In Germany the Protestant Reformation, coming so soon after the invention of printing, increased enormously the output of books and has been said to have created the German book trade.[202] The Protestant Reformers sought to put their ideas into the minds of all and so created a literature in the vernacular. Through his translation of the Bible into German, a version which the movement that began with him made standard, and through his other writings, Luther did much to establish a common form of the German tongue for speech and writing.[203] Olaus Petri, whom we have already mentioned as one of the foremost early exponents of Lutheran ideas in Sweden, fostered among the Swedish people the use of books and transformed the written language, giving to it greater grace.[204] The profound effect upon the English language of the Authorized Version of the Bible is one of the commonplaces in the history of literature. Phrases from this "King James Version" have passed into the common speech, quotations from it have been frequent in writings dealing with secular as well as with religious subjects, and in diction it has made for simplicity, for the use of the concrete word, and for the preservation of words and constructions which were in use when it was made.[205]

Much of the great literature of the period bears indelibly the impress of Christianity. To be sure, many of the most famous writers, among them Voltaire, Gibbon, and Goethe, were rebellious against Europe's inherited faith. Yet all were in part shaped by it. Milton's *Paradise Lost* and Tasso's *Jerusalem Delivered* by their very titles bear witness to the Christian origin of their themes. The greatest humanist of the sixteenth century, Erasmus, owed the beginnings

[202] Lindsay, *A History of the Reformation*, Vol. I, pp. 300-302.
[203] *The Encyclopædia Britannica*, 14th ed., Vol. X, p. 216.
[204] Hallendorf and Schück, *History of Sweden*, pp. 130-152.
[205] See especially H. S. Cook, in *The Cambridge History of English Literature*, Vol. IV, pp. 54-58.

of his education to the Brethren of the Common Life and devoted much of his greatest writing to what he deemed Christian purposes. Spenser's *Faerie Queene* is an attempt to maintain through allegory the fight for the Christian virtues. It is asserted that Tudor prose is based in large part upon the style of devotional literature in English,[206] and that the moral purpose and the realism of Shakespeare's maturer plays have their roots in no small part in the preaching from the pulpits of medieval England.[207] As compared with the previous period it cannot be said that the influence of Christianity on literature had declined. A larger proportion of the writers were now from the laity and naturally were less absorbed in religion, but in the Middle Ages much of the current popular literature gave little evidence of the presence of Christianity and in these three centuries were many writings by laymen who were dominated by Christian themes.

In philosophy and science Christianity at first sight seemed a waning influence in these three centuries. Theology, the study of God, appeared no longer to hold the centre of the stage as it did for the great minds of the Middle Ages. The confidence in human reason associated with what is usually called rationalism, a movement especially strong in the eighteenth century, seemed to have weakened the belief in a divine revelation such as that around which historic Christianity had arisen and to which it had given pre-eminence. To be sure, theological discussion had penetrated to the masses and, through the differences between Protestants and Roman Catholics and within Protestantism, was probably even more widely current than in the preceding periods. Yet those intellects which were setting the pace and which were laying the foundations of that scientific outlook which was to attain such prominence in the nineteenth and twentieth centuries appeared to be relegating theology to a secondary place. Descartes might remain formally and even honestly a Roman Catholic, but with his *cogito ergo sum* he seemed to be ushering out of the centre of the intellectual process God and an objective revelation of God.

However, more careful observation and reflection disclose other facets. The basic assumption of the scientific approach, the possibility of an orderly, dependable universe, in which every occurrence has a definite correlation with what preceded it, a universe which can be understood by the human mind, is historically an outgrowth of the world view inherited from the theologians of the Middle Ages who declared that the universe is the product of the mind and

[206] G. R. Owst, *Literature and Pulpit in Medieval England* (Cambridge University Press, 1933, pp. xxi, 616), p. x.
[207] Owst, *op. cit.*, p. 591.

will of God. It was because God is the creator of both the universe and the human mind that man can understand at all the world about him and within him. To be sure, this view is also indebted to Greek philosophy and the Roman sense of law, but even these came to Western Europe largely through churchmen. Medieval theologians had established the tradition of logical, exact thinking.[208] The very rationalism which seemed to be dethroning God was based upon presuppositions which historically had come to Europe through Christianity. Protestantism, particularly in those forms, such as Congregationalism, Anabaptism, and Pietism, which emphasized a personal individual religious experience, may have contributed to the eighteenth century rationalism and the *Aufklärung*. Luther, with his famous *"hier steh' ich, ich kann nichts anders,"* was an example of the courageous and resolute reliance upon individual insight with which the Christian impulse inspired men. In an atmosphere in which such attitudes were abroad in religion, it was natural that a similar spirit should be manifested in other realms of life. It is conceivable that both may have been due in part to a common cause other than Christianity, but Christianity may have been the chief inciting factor and for many it undoubtedly afforded strong reinforcement.

Moreover, romanticism, that movement which had so marked a growth in the eighteenth century and was in part a reaction against the prevailing rationalism, owed much to Christianity. One of the contributing streams was Protestantism which with its teaching of the direct access of the individual soul to God became one of the sources of the romantic doctrine of inspiration.

Many of the outstanding intellectual achievements of these centuries were by men who had been nurtured in the Christian faith. Presumably they owed to that faith, even though in later life some departed from it, something of the impulse or the opportunity for intellectual growth. In several the causal connexion between their faith and their contributions to knowledge is obvious. In others it is not so clear or, possibly, may even not exist. It is evident that we owe to the religious awakening of the sixteenth century our modern calendar, for it was planned by the Council of Trent and was perfected under the direction of the reforming Pope Gregory XIII.[209] Copernicus, the formulator of the revolutionary interpretation of astronomy which bears his name, was educated by an uncle who was a bishop and through most of his life was in the service of the Church and was supported by it.[210] Although his system was opposed by

---

[208] On this point see Alfred North Whitehead, *Science and the Modern World* (New York, The Macmillan Co., 1935, pp. xii, 304), Chapter i, especially p. 18.

[209] Pastor, *History of the Popes*, Vol. XIX, pp. 283-296.

[210] J. G. Hagen, in *The Catholic Encyclopedia*, Vol. IV, p. 353.

many theologians, it was also espoused by others.[211] The struggle was one between Christians, not between Christians and non-Christians. It was not a battle
between science and religion, but arose from the opposition of some professing
Christians to ideas set forth by other professing Christians. It may well be that
the Christian impulse was more responsible for the daring venturesomeness of
the latter than for the alarmed conservatism of the former. Johann Kepler, distinguished for his further development of the Copernican ideas and for his
own additions to astronomy, was trained for the clerical profession and only
with great reluctance turned aside from it to the opportunities opened by his
genius for mathematics. Whether it was the Christian impulse which led him
to make such notable use of his remarkable native gifts we do not know, but it
was institutions founded by the Church which made possible for him, poverty-
stricken and of crippled physique, the education which he later put to such
eminent use.[212] Isaac Newton was reared in a religious atmosphere and went
to the university primarily with the purpose of entering the Christian ministry. While in some respects he later departed from what his contemporaries
esteemed as orthodoxy, throughout his life his chief interest continued to be
theology. It was his Christian purpose which led him to make use of his genius
for mathematics and science, and he seems to have regarded his labours in these
fields as dreary drudgery which had intrinsic value only as throwing light upon
the laws and attributes of God.[213] The discoverer of oxygen, Joseph Priestley,
had as his chief passion the pursuit of religious truth, and was impelled by it not
only to radical theological convictions but also into studies in physics and chem-
istry.[214] John Locke, who had so important an effect upon philosophy, especially through his *Essay on the Human Understanding*, was, as we have seen,
brought up in a Puritan atmosphere and through his life was earnestly religious.
Emmanuel Kant had his roots deep in the Pietist foundations which had under-
girt his youth and came into philosophy from theology. Berkeley, best remembered for his contributions to philosophy, was a bishop in the Anglican communion.[215] Presumably it was their initial religious interest, stimulated by
Christianity, which led both Kant and Berkeley into philosophy. Incontestably

---

[211] Smith, *The Age of the Reformation*, pp. 620, 621, tells of those who taught it as
well as those who opposed it at Wittenberg. The former Dominican Giordano Bruno,
who after a life of intellectual and physical wandering was excommunicated and burned
at the stake in Rome, was a protagonist of Copernicus.—*The Encyclopædia Britannica*,
14th ed., Vol. IV, p. 287.
[212] *The Encyclopædia Britannica*, 14th ed., Vol. XIII, p. 346.
[213] Louis Trenchard Moore, *Isaac Newton, A Biography* (New York, Charles Scribner's
Sons, 1934, pp. xii, 675), pp. 608-611, 622-649.
[214] Lincoln, *Some Political and Social Ideas of English Dissent, 1763-1800*, pp. 151 ff.
[215] John Wild, *George Berkeley. A Study of His Life and Philosophy* (Harvard University Press, 1936, pp. ix, 552), *passim*.

their philosophy was in part moulded by the religious convictions in which they had been reared. In some of the great minds which made substantial contributions to the science and philosophy of the period the Christian motive was not so strong as it had been among the most notable Western European thinkers of the Middle Ages. In a few it may have been lacking. Francis Bacon, for instance, spent most of his mature life in the service of the state and was secular in his outlook. Yet even a Francis Bacon had been educated in an atmosphere tinged with Christianity and could not but be affected by it. In the three centuries between A.D. 1500 and A.D. 1800 the Christian impulse had an important part in determining the intellectual climate of opinion and to at least some degree was responsible for the philosophy and for the advance in science and mathematics which the period witnessed.

Western Europe in the three centuries between A.D. 1500 and A.D. 1800 presented a contradictory picture—as it had done in the preceding thousand years. It was now nominally Christian. In some of its area Christianity had been adopted before A.D. 500. In other parts the formal conversion had been much more recent. Yet much of its life was in utter contrast to the faith which it presented. In its religion as popularly practised was a large amount that was contrary to Jesus. Its ethical conduct was even more in flagrant opposition to the New Testament. Wars of aggression, for power, and for national and dynastic prestige were chronic. In its economic activities greed and prudential selfishness appeared dominant. Much of its scholarship seemed to ignore God. However, in Western Europe Christianity had more freedom to make itself felt than in any other part of the Old World. From the Christian impulse came more new religious movements than ever before; through it ideals of marriage and of womanhood were being altered; because of it revolutionary changes in government, designed to give more opportunity and dignity to the common man, were in progress; idealists moved by it were seeking to curb war and to maintain the principle that wealth must be used as a trust for the public weal; and out of it were coming great music, great painting, sculpture, and architecture, better educational provisions for the masses, new educational theories and methods, and fresh discoveries in science. In several phases of the life of Western Europe Christianity was more potent than ever before.

In Eastern Europe and Western Asia Christianity did not have so marked an effect. In South-eastern Europe and on the east shores of the Mediterranean the Christian communities were politically subject to the Moslem. In them Christianity had its major effect in maintaining its own existence and in nourishing a group loyalty among its adherents. It was the Church which was the nucleus of communal feeling and from it later came movements for political independence which in the nineteenth century aided in the disintegration of the Ottoman Empire. Russia was the one land in Eastern Europe ruled by a professedly Christian state. In Russia Christianity, while making an impress upon the life of the nation, did not have such striking effects as in Western Europe.

The reasons why Christianity was less of an influence in Russia than in Western Europe were several. Because of the Byzantine tradition, the Church in Russia was less independent and more under the control of the state than in much of Western Europe. Even after A.D. 1500, when the absolute monarchies dominated the churches within their domains, in many a land in the West something of the earlier tradition of independence persisted and in Roman Catholic countries the Papacy remained a point of reference which could not be completely dominated even by a Charles V or a Philip II. Then, too, the tradition inherited from Greek Christianity was quietistic. Eastern monasticism was not as active in seeking to modify the life about it as was the monasticism of the West. Moreover, in A.D. 1500 much of Russia had been recently converted and its Christianity was not yet deeply rooted. Here and there, too, extensive enclaves of pagan peoples persisted. To the end of the sixteenth century the written sources of the Christian legends, brought to Russia in Bulgar and Serb translations, remained in the monasteries and not until the sixteenth century did they reach the masses.[216] At least until the sixteenth century many of the parish clergy were nearly or completely illiterate.[217] It is said that in the seventeenth century the popular indifference to religion was so great that many from the lower classes attended church only two or three times a year and that imperial ukases were required to drive the masses to church to receive the sacraments.[218] Some improvement came in the seventeenth century, but beginning with Peter the Great, at about the end of that century, the Tsar instituted an even closer control of the Church and virtually made it an arm of the state, a secularization of Russian civilization began, the Church ceased to be the chief source of cultural life, and many of the more deeply religious souls from the lower classes left the state church and joined one of the dissenting groups.[219]

This, however, is only one side of the picture. While not so potent as in Western Europe, Christianity was by no means without influence in Russia, and in some respects it made a deeper impression on Russian life than in earlier centuries. After 1550, as we have already noted, and as we shall see again in the

---

[216] Milukow, *Skizzen russischer Kulturgeschichte*, Vol. II, p. 197.
[217] Milukow, *op. cit.*, Vol. II, pp. 275-278.
[218] Conybeare, *Russian Dissenters*, p. 14.
[219] Vernadsky, *A History of Russia*, p. 115.

next chapter, Christianity became sufficiently rooted in the Russian soul to give rise to religious movements which departed from the official church and from the faith as it had come from the Byzantine Empire. We have seen, too, that this faith had become so deeply ingrained in the Russian spirit that Russians now thought of their land as the Third Rome, the champion of true Christianity against all heresies.[220] Occasionally a Metropolitan was impelled by his Christian convictions to stand out against the civil authorities. The Metropolitan Philip condemned the excesses of Ivan the Terrible and so championed the rights of the Church and of the people that his temerity won him deposition and death.[221] Nikon, one of the most famous of the Russian Patriarchs, while still only an archimandrite interceded with the Tsar on behalf of widows and orphans who were denied their rights in venal courts of justice.[222] The fact that Russia held to the Orthodox faith aided the growth of the Muscovite realms, for after the fall of Constantinople to the Turks the ruler at Moscow was the only independent Orthodox prince of importance and the Orthodox in adjoining realms, notably in Poland and Lithuania, were disposed to cast in their lot with him.[223] In the "Time of Trouble," the political confusion which began at the close of the sixteenth century, the Church remained the chief unifying institution and the Patriarch Hermogen called on his fellow-countrymen to rise against Polish domination and was imprisoned by the invaders. Many others of the leaders of the Church joined in the uprising which expelled the Poles.[224] Towards the end of the seventeenth and in the early part of the eighteenth century improvements were made in education, particularly that of the clergy and their children.[225] Higher schools of theology for training the clergy were established.[226] Church architecture introduced from the Byzantine Empire became so acclimatized that the Russians added to it elements of their own and developed a distinctive style.[227] In some respects, then, between A.D. 1500 and A.D. 1800, Christianity shaped Russian life more effectively than in the centuries before A.D. 1500.

It was not only in Europe, where it had long been present and had become the predominant faith that Christianity had marked effects upon its environ-

[220] Milukow, *op. cit.*, Vol. II, p. 19; Frere, *Some Links in Russian Church History*, p. 58.
[221] Frere, *op. cit.*, p. 78; Theophilus, *A Short History of the Christian Church*, p. 23.
[222] Conybeare, *Russian Dissenters*, p. 42.
[223] Frere, *op. cit.*, pp. 56, 57.
[224] Theophilus, *op. cit.*, p. 24.
[225] Milukow, *op. cit.*, Vol. II, pp. 279, 329-334.
[226] Milukow, *op. cit.*, Vol. II, pp. 181, 182, 283-294.
[227] Milukow, *op. cit.*, Vol. II, pp. 239, 240, 269-271.

ment. It was also outside Europe, on the new geographic frontiers of Occidental civilization, that the results of Christianity were seen. Indeed, in some respects these were more remarkable and spectacular than were those in regions where the faith had been longer established. In previous chapters we have already noted these effects area by area. However, if we are to obtain a comprehensive view of the entire picture, we must here endeavour to summarize what we have previously given in fragmentary fashion.

Christianity was a factor, and an important one, in bringing about the phenomenal geographic expansion of European peoples in these centuries. Prince Henry the Navigator, who was the directing mind and will of expeditions which eventually brought the Portuguese around the Cape of Good Hope to India, was an ardently religious man whose discoveries had back of them not only a desire for trade and for allies against the hereditary enemy, the Moor, but also a passion to spread the Christian faith.[228] Christopher Columbus was, in his way, an earnest Christian who desired to devote his wealth to the support of a crusade or to the assistance of the Pope in overcoming schism,[229] and he believed that it was his faith in God which enabled him to persevere on his first trip across the Atlantic when his men would have turned back and which on his return voyage gave him confidence in the face of a severe storm.[230] Magellan had a marked zeal for propagating Christianity,[231] and from this it seems a fair inference that from his faith he derived courage to go on in the face of difficulties. It would be absurd to claim that the Christian impulse was the sole or even the chief cause of the discoveries and conquests of the era, or that the explorers were models of Christian character. It is, however, clear that the Christian impulse was a factor, and it may well have been that it was decisive. Non-Christian peoples had been explorers and conquerors and had migrated to alien lands. None, however, had been so daring or had ranged so far afield. Is it too much to assume that this was because the Christian faith was added to the other motives—the desire for trade, for fame, and for adventure—which have moved all human migrants, and that even when a particular individual was not consciously impelled by it Christianity had entered into the cultural atmosphere in which he had been reared and so had provided the necessary additional stimulus?

[228] *Conquest and Discoveries of Henry the Navigator, being the Chronicles of Azurara* ... edited by Virginia de Castro e Almeida, translated by Bernard Maill (London, George Allen and Unwin, 1936, pp. 253), pp. 121-123, 130 ff.

[229] Pastor, *History of the Popes*, Vol. VI, p. 67.

[230] Columbus, *Journal of the First Voyage to America* (Van Wyck Brooks ed.), pp. 21, 190.

[231] See instances in Antonio Pigafetta, *Primo Viaggio intorno al Mondo*, by a companion of Magellan, translation in Blair and Robertson, *The Philippine Islands*. Vols. XXXIII, XXXIV.

The expansion of European peoples was by no means an unmixed blessing. If Christianity be at all responsible for it, this might conceivably be a count against that faith as a constructive force in the life of mankind.

However, that this expansion was in any way a benefit to mankind must be ascribed almost entirely to the manner in which the Christian impulse modified it. If, as seems probable, taken as a whole the expansion of Europe in these three centuries was a blessing and not a curse, it was chiefly because of Christianity. Christianity in its Roman Catholic and Protestant forms was the source of movements which endeavoured to protect the non-European peoples from ruthless exploitation. Christian priests appealed to the consciences of Spanish and Portuguese monarchs, made sensitive by their Christian faith, and obtained legislation, notably in the *Spanish Laws of the Indies*, which was remarkably humane. In the English possessions in the Americas scores of Protestant Christians sought to protect the Indian and to help him successfully to make his adjustment to the coming of the white man. On the frontiers of white settlements in the Americas, missionaries, both Protestant and Roman Catholic, induced large numbers of Indians to adopt a settled agricultural existence, founded schools for them, and taught them the white man's handicrafts. To be sure, no non-European peoples were stirred by the contacts to the creation of a fresh culture. This, however, was because, where any large numbers from these peoples became Christian, they were dominated by the white man and were in part assimilated to his culture. Yet in protecting subject peoples from exploitation by conquerors who bore the Christian name Christianity was far more effective than ever before. It had been unable to do much to soften the German conquest of the Wends or of the peoples on the Baltic. Now it proved remarkably influential in ameliorating the conquest of the American Indians and the Filipinos. Never before had any religion or any other set of ideas impelled conquerors over so extensive areas to regard their rule as being for the sake of the conquered. In the professions of high motives by European monarchs and their agents much of hypocrisy was present. However, there was also much of sincerity, and no small part of it was translated into action. By A.D. 1800 even the African slave trade and Negro slavery had been challenged in the name of the Christian faith.[232] In the following century the Christian conscience was to be the chief factor in bringing them both to an end. In other ways which we are to describe in succeeding volumes, in the nineteenth and twentieth centuries Christianity was to be increasingly potent in modifying in the direction

---

[232] See, for instance, Alonso de Sandoval, *De Instaurando Æthiopum Salute* (Madrid, 1647), which in Part I, Book I, denounces the evils of slavery and the slave trade. We have already seen (Chapter 6) the beginnings of the anti-slavery movement in the English colonies in America.

of the welfare of non-European peoples the impact of the Occident upon the rest of the world.

Another effect of the Christian faith upon the extra-European world of these centuries was the extensive spread of Christianity. Never before had any religion been propagated over so large a proportion of the earth's surface. In great sections of the Americas and the Philippines and among enclaves of the population in several lands of Southern and Eastern Asia Christianity supplanted its rivals. Moreover, never before had so many professional missionaries gone out over so wide an area for Christianity or for any other religion.

In many lands these missionaries and their converts displayed a remarkable heroism and persistence in the face of insistent persecution. Nothing quite equal to it had been witnessed in any other religion. Indeed, it is doubtful whether Christians themselves, except possibly in Moslem lands, had ever been called upon to face such prolonged unremitting persecution as was their lot in these centuries in China and in Japan. Even the attrition of Islam had not been accompanied by such unrelenting efforts to eradicate Christianity as were made by the Japanese under the Tokugawa, by the Manchu emperors who succeeded K'ang Hsi, and by the Korean persecutors of the latter part of the eighteenth and the first three-quarters of the nineteenth century.

Moreover, Christianity spread more widely through European settlements than any faith, including Christianity, had ever before been carried by migrations. In the Americas principally, but also in various parts of the fringes of Africa and of Asia and in small groups dotted across Siberia, Christianity was represented by new communities of European stock. For these white settlers, likewise principally in the Americas, the Christian impulse was almost the only source of schools, from those of primary grade up through the universities. Few of these communities displayed much vitality in giving rise to new religious movements. No new orders or congregations of any significance came into being in Spanish, Portuguese, or French America. Yet in the English colonies in North America a new type of Protestant Christianity was arising and the Great Awakening, largely indigenous, was evidence of a pulsing new life.

In the Thirteen Colonies of the English, moreover, the Christian impulse was an important factor in encouraging new experiments in government which looked towards greater opportunity for all. To be sure, neither Puritans, Quakers, Pilgrims, or the Baptist Roger Williams sought to establish utopias in America. They saw too deeply into human nature to believe that a fresh start in a new land with novel institutions would create perfect commonwealths or that men were wise enough and selfless enough to erect a flawless society.[233]

[233] Niebuhr, *The Kingdom of God in America,* pp. 46-58.

However, they did much to further democracy and to establish the idea of controlling through written constitutions the evil in men and the abuse of power.[234] They believed that God is sovereign in human society as in the rest of His universe, and that therefore all human exercise of power must needs be limited.[235] Christian ideas by way of Calvinism entered deeply into the soul of what later became the United States. In the seventeenth century, too, the influence of these ideals in the American colonies, particularly of New England, had repercussions in the mother country and aided in the movement which culminated in the Commonwealth.[236]

In view of all these facts it seems clear that between A.D. 1500 and A.D. 1800 the effect of Christianity upon the human race had increased. In Western Europe, where Christianity had long enjoyed freer course than elsewhere, more fresh religious movements were emerging from the Christian stream than ever before and both clergy and the masses of the laity were becoming better instructed in the tenets of their professed faith. In Western Europe, too, in spite of the rise of strong monarchical states which seemed to be strangling the Church, Christianity was moulding political institutions more than before and was the major factor in giving form to the ideal that above these states was a universal law which they must obey in their relations with one another and with the governments of non-Christian peoples. Christianity continued to be the source of fresh efforts to care for the sick, the broken, and the underprivileged. It was the largest single creative force in the remarkable development of music. It continued to furnish themes and inspiration for much of the greatest painting and sculpture. It was the major source of schools for the masses and of educational theories and procedures which in the succeeding nineteenth and twentieth centuries became revolutionary and formative in education the world around. Much of the great literature of the period was evoked by Christianity. The Christian impulse provided a large part of the undergirding for the conception of the universe out of which came the scientific approach and scientific discoveries. Theology was no longer so exclusively the centre of philosophy and scholarship, but the majority of the men who did most to mould the thought of these centuries were deeply indebted to an atmosphere in which Christianity was potent. Outside Europe, Christianity was an important cause of geographic discoveries, conquests, and settlements by Europeans. Even more

---

[234] Niebuhr, *op. cit.*, p. 79.
[235] Niebuhr, *op. cit.*, pp. 77, 78.
[236] Gooch and Laski, *English Democratic Ideas in the Seventeenth Century*, p. 79.

significantly, it softened the impact of Europeans upon non-Europeans and became the strongest constructive factor in the assimilation of non-Europeans to European culture. It spread more widely than ever any religion had spread before. It remained the faith of the European communities established outside of Europe and did much to mould the institutions of these settlements. After the thousand years of uncertainty when its future appeared most dubious, Christianity displayed augmented vigour and accomplished more than ever it or any other religion had previously done to shape the life of mankind.

Chapter XVII

THE EFFECT OF THE ENVIRONMENT ON CHRISTIANITY: IN
EUROPE; ON PROTESTANTISM, ON ROMAN CATHOLICISM,
ON RUSSIAN CHRISTIANITY: OUTSIDE OF EUROPE

HOW far and in what manner was Christianity moulded by its environment between A.D. 1500 and A.D. 1800? In these centuries, as we have
seen, Christianity had exerted a more widespread and a more profound influence upon the human race than in any preceding period. To what extent
was it itself modified by its setting?

In many ways the Christianity of A.D. 1800 differed more markedly from that
of A.D. 1500 than that of A.D. 1500 differed from that of A.D. 500. The three
centuries had witnessed more sweeping changes in the structure of Christianity
than had the preceding thousand years. During the thousand years between A.D.
500 and A.D. 1500 Christianity had so largely been on the defensive and its
energies had been so absorbed in winning the barbarians of Northern Europe
and in shaping their cultures that few alterations had taken place in its basic
structure. Most of the peoples whom it had gained had been of less complex
culture than that of the Mediterranean world with which Christianity was so
closely associated. They were inclined, therefore, to abandon their ancestral
cultures along with their ancestral faiths and to adopt that which came to
them with Christianity as its vehicle. With this attitude they were disposed
to accept as authoritative the forms in which Christianity was transmitted to
them. As time passed, to be sure, some movements arose which were ill content
with the authority of the Church which had come down to them from the
Græco-Roman era, but until A.D. 1500 that Church was powerful enough to
suppress them as heresies and to enforce uniformity. While this was taking
place in Northern Europe, where Christianity had made headway against a
backward paganism, on its southern and eastern frontiers—in Northern Africa
and Western, Central, and Eastern Asia—Christianity was either on the defensive against Islam or was represented by small minorities, largely with
foreign nuclei and foreign connexions, in the midst of high cultures. In both
cases Christians, to conserve their faith, tended to cling jealously to the forms in
which it had come down to them from the past. As a result, in A.D. 1500 the

creeds and the main outlines of the ecclesiastical structures adhered to by the majority of Christians were approximately what they had been in A.D. 500. Now, in A.D. 1500, the peoples of Northern Europe were culturally coming of age and were less bound by past tradition. In popular mass movements led, in Northern Europe, by those from the humbler ranks of society they were making their own the faith which had been given to them from abroad. As a result, due in part to the inward vigour of the faith which had so gripped these classes, modifications were made in that which had come from the older South. On what were then the southern and eastern frontiers of the faith, in the fourteenth, fifteenth, and sixteenth centuries Christianity suffered great numerical losses with the consequence that the churches there which had preserved so stubbornly what had been transmitted from earlier generations shrank rapidly and long before A.D. 1800 constituted a much smaller proportion of the total body of Christians than they had in the European Middle Ages. In addition, Christianity had accomplished a phenomenal growth on new frontiers in the Americas and Asia and while the large majority of its converts were politically and ecclesiastically subject to Europeans and accepted passively the forms in which the faith had been given them, in the Thirteen English Colonies in North America through emigrants from Europe a kind of Christianity was taking shape which in many respects was *sui generis* and which, in the nineteenth and twentieth centuries, was to become very prominent in world-wide Christianity.

Although the variations displayed by Christianity between A.D. 1500 and A.D. 1800 were in large part due to a vigour inherent in that faith which made itself felt in the peoples of Europe as they approached cultural maturity, the changes were due also to factors which were quite extraneous to the original Christian impulse. The emergence of strong monarchical states with autocratic rulers who insisted upon dominating all phases of life in their realms could not but have its effect. Now, too, as in other centuries, outstanding individuals who had had soul-shaking religious experiences attracted followers and left deeply embedded in the movements which arose from them the evidences of their struggles and their convictions. In each major land, moreover, something of the national spirit and history was reflected in the forms of Christianity within its borders.

In tracing the effect of the environment we must, as in the preceding chapter, first describe what occurred in Europe. Then, in briefer fashion, we must bring together in summary form what in earlier chapters has been said region by region of the results of the environment in lands outside of Europe.

In Western Europe the most obvious fact in the story of Christianity of these centuries is the disruption of the great church which had been dominant in the preceding thousand years. The movements embraced under the name Protestantism tore away from the Roman Catholic Church most of Northwestern Europe. Through the reaction from this experience as well as through the new tides of life which remained within it, Roman Catholicism itself was profoundly modified.

We must, then, turn first of all to Protestantism, to inquire as to the influence of the environment in giving it distinctive forms, and then look at the changes wrought in the Roman Catholic Church.

There seems to be significance in the fact that Protestantism became primarily the faith of peoples of Teutonic stock who dwelt outside what had once been the Roman Empire.[1] To this England at first sight seems an exception, for it coincides roughly with Roman Britain. Yet the variation from the generalization is explained when it is remembered that in the disorders preceding and accompanying the Anglo-Saxon invasions Roman culture disappeared from Britain to an extent that it did not in what later became France or in the Iberian and Italian Peninsulas and was supplanted by a Germanic culture. In a certain sense Protestantism seems to have been the outcome of the conscious appropriation by Teutonic folk of the Christianity which had come to them under Roman guise. Until the sixteenth century these peoples had more or less passively accepted what had been given them from the South. Then, as that faith really gripped them and particularly as it began to stir those who, like Luther, were of peasant stock and hence not so fully assimilated to Roman culture as were the aristocracy, they had religious experiences which made them ill at ease in the patterns which had been developed in the South and, as a consequence, revolted from the Roman Church. In a sense Protestantism was the result of Christianity becoming really at home among the Teutonic peoples. This interpretation can easily be pressed too far, for, as we are to go on to say, other factors entered into the shaping of Protestantism. Yet the fact remains that Protestantism has had its chief strongholds among peoples of Teutonic stock who dwell outside what were formerly the Roman *limes*. It is clear that Protestantism, while for a time having adherents in Italy and the Iberian Peninsula, never appealed to more than small minorities in these countries and was easily exterminated there. It is also obvious that it had a larger following in France, a region which had been longer and more continuously dominated by the Teutonic invaders and whose Romanization had been accomplished less thoroughly than in the case of Italy and the Iberian Peninsula, and yet in France, where Latin culture and modified Latin speech prevailed, Protestantism

[1] See this commented upon in Dawson, *Progress and Religion*, p. 178.

never won more than a minority. Moreover, in very few places was Protestantism permanently the majority faith among a non-Teutonic people. For a time it was strong in Poland and in Bohemia and it gained a continuing foothold in Hungary. It became dominant in Celtic Wales and in most of the Celtic parts of Scotland. Yet it was fairly early eliminated from Poland, it was all but stamped out from Bohemia, and its triumph in Wales and among the Celts of Scotland was due to the political and cultural domination of these areas by Protestant Anglo-Saxons. Even then Roman Catholicism retained enclaves among the Celts of the Scottish Highlands. Protestantism's chief strongholds were among peoples of Teutonic stock.

It had been suggested that the type of Protestantism most nearly congenial to the Latin soul is Calvinism, and that, accordingly, for the most part Calvinism is distributed, although somewhat irregularly, along the partially Romanized frontier between the old Roman Empire and the Germanic peoples.[2] Calvin himself was, of course, from France and was educated in France, and most of such Protestantism as was found within what was once the Roman Empire was either Calvinism or was strongly tinged with Calvinism.

Protestantism, even though it represented a revolt against Roman Catholicism, bore indelibly the marks of its Roman Catholic ancestry. Like the latter, it was more concrete, more activistic, more given to precise definitions and to organization, more austere and simple in its forms of worship than was the Christianity in which the Greek tradition was stronger.

Protestantism was not a purely religious movement.[3] But for men like Luther, Zwingli, and Calvin, with their profound religious convictions, it would not have come into existence, yet in various regions and countries it was coloured by non-religious elements, some of them in contradiction to the spirit of the New Testament.

In many respects Protestantism was as much political as religious. In few lands where it existed was it free from political complications. In several lands where it prevailed it did so because monarchs or princes saw in it a means of enhancing their authority. In a day when the power of monarchs was being increased, many rulers took advantage of Protestant ideas to obtain control of the church within their domains. The scholars of the Renaissance had revived the study of the old Roman civil codes. These codes encouraged the lawyers and statesmen of the sixteenth century to regard the Church as a department of the state[4] and to move further in the direction in which they were headed, towards the absolute power of the civil ruler over ecclesiastical

[2] Dawson, op. cit., p. 178.
[3] McGiffert, Protestant Thought before Kant, p. 9.
[4] Lindsay, A History of the Reformation, Vol. II, pp. 8, 9.

affairs. This became important both in Protestantism and in Roman Catholicism. National feeling, the aspirations of special classes, and the cultural characteristics of particular regions all entered into the shaping of Protestantism. These influences also existed in Roman Catholic as well as in Protestant regions. However, Protestantism, especially in its formative period, was more malleable than Roman Catholicism and so was more responsive to them and more moulded by them.

This mixed nature of the factors which made Protestantism and helped to determine its varied forms can be seen, even though necessarily briefly, by a rapid survey of the situation in each of the main Protestant countries.

In Germany, it need scarcely be said, the religious passion, the peculiar religious experience, and the convictions of Luther, had an important rôle in the shaping of Protestantism. Yet in Germany, too, Protestantism afforded the princes an opportunity for doing what the medieval Holy Roman Emperors had failed to do, obtaining complete control of the church within their domains. When the principle *cuius regio, eius religio* was written into the treaties which sanctioned the religious complexion of Germany, legal authority was given to every prince and princeling of the land to determine the form of faith of his subjects. In the case of Protestantism, this helped to clinch the hold which each civil lord had over the church in his possessions. Prominent, too, in the initial stage of the religious revolt of so much of Germany against Rome was the national resentment of Germans against Italians and the pride of the Elector of Saxony in his University of Wittenberg, of whose staff Luther was the chief glory.[5] In the imperial cities of Germany the burghers had long held the clergy in derision. German translations of the Bible had been read, and Hussite propaganda had had currency.[6] The tinder, therefore, was ready to burst into flame when touched by the spark of Luther's teaching. Moreover, treaties, which were in part artificial, helped not only to recognize but to determine the boundaries of Protestantism. Thus the so-called ecclesiastical reservation of the Peace of Augsburg by its provision that an ecclesiastical prince who turned Protestant should forfeit his principality became important in holding much of Germany to Roman Catholicism,[7] for it meant that the great ecclesiastical estates, which were particularly prominent along the Rhine and in the south of Germany, in those areas earliest won to the Christian faith, where the organization initiated by Boniface was potent, remained in the hands of the old church. The Thirty Years' War also modified the religious map of the Empire. Through the vicissitudes of the conflict Bohemia and Austria, in which

[5] Lindsay, *op. cit.*, Vol. I, p. 234.
[6] Lindsay, *op. cit.*, Vol. I, p. 308.
[7] Lindsay, *op. cit.*, Vol. II, p. 213.

at the outset of that struggle Protestantism was strong, became overwhelmingly Roman Catholic.[8]

In Transylvania the religions followed the racial divisions. The Saxons, who were the descendants of German settlers, became Lutherans, the majority of the Magyars Calvinists, and most of the Széklers (who were probably Magyars) Unitarians.[9] The absence of a powerful central government favoured the variety in religious organization which developed.

In Poland the Reformation for a time spread rapidly. At first it was welcomed by members of the lower classes who believed that through it they could obtain economic and social justice, and by nobles who saw in it a chance to gain control over the Church.[10] The lack of political cohesion which was one of the chronic weaknesses of Poland made for divisions within Protestantism. Many reciprocally hostile types of Protestantism gained followings—Lutherans, Calvinists, Socinians, Anabaptists, and Bohemian Brethren—and it was these divisions which weakened the opposition to Roman Catholicism and helped to facilitate the rewinning of the land to the old faith by Jesuit missionaries.[11]

In East Prussia it was the fact that the head of the Teutonic Knights, the body which had ruled the land since its conversion, turned Protestant, a step which he seems to have taken at least in part for the purpose of strengthening his own personal power, which brought about the triumph of the Reformation.[12]

In Scandinavia, as kings had been the leaders in the conversion of the region to Christianity and had used the new faith to strengthen their power, so the triumph of the Reformation was due chiefly to their successors and was likewise made to enhance the royal authority. Whether those monarchs who espoused the Reformation were consciously following the earlier tradition seems doubtful, but the parallel is at least interesting. At the time of the conversion of Scandinavia, however, the active missionaries were largely from England. This was because the Scandinavians, through their conquests, had close connexions with England and did not wish to be even ecclesiastically subservient to the strong Saxon Holy Roman Empire. In contrast, the Reformation came from Germany. Had Germany then been politically united and had the adoption of Lutheranism meant the suzerainty of that land, it may well have been that the Scandinavian monarchs would have pursued a different course. As

---

[8] Walker, The Reformation, pp. 443, 444.

[9] The Encyclopædia Britannica, 14th ed., Vol. XXII, p. 431.

[10] Smith, The Age of the Reformation, pp. 140-144; Pastor, History of the Popes, Vol. XVI, p. 141.

[11] Smith, op. cit., p. 143.

[12] Smith, op. cit., p. 113; Walker, op. cit., pp. 285, 286.

in the conversion of Scandinavia to Christianity, so in the triumph of Protestantism, the way had been prepared by earnestly religious men, in this instance some who had studied under Luther at Wittenberg or had been stirred by his writings.[13] Now, too, as in the initial adoption of Christianity, the religious change had its beginnings in the towns. Here as in Germany some of the strongest centres of the Reformation were in the cities.[14] In Sweden the man chiefly responsible for the victory of the Reformation was Gustavus Vasa. Gustavus Vasa led in the revolt of the Swedes against Danish rule and founded a new line of kings. The Swedish bishops favoured Denmark.[15] Gustavus Vasa by championing the Reformation not only scotched their power but also established the royal authority over the Church. In Denmark King Christian II used the Reformation to curb the landowning clergy and nobles and to elevate the urban middle class as a counterweight.[16] Although in 1523 he had to flee the country before a rebellion, his labours were continued by later monarchs.[17] In Iceland and Norway, then subject to the Danish crown, even more than in Sweden and Denmark the Reformation was the work of the king.[18] It is not surprising that, carried through so largely by royal action, the Reformation worked less immediate religious change in Scandinavia than in some other regions, and that much of the organization, including the episcopate, and of the forms of the pre-Reformation Church were continued and have persisted to the present. In Norway the real religious awakening which in theory Protestantism presupposed did not come until the eighteenth century. In Norrland, in Northern Sweden, where a sparse population, a stern environment, and long distances from church buildings made religious instruction and frequent church attendance difficult or impossible, church discipline was lax, non-Christian superstitions were rife, and warm religious life, when, towards the end of the eighteenth century, it had a tardy development, expressed itself largely through conventicles.[19]

In France a native son, Calvin, gave to Protestantism the form which prevailed. Calvin was a Picard, and it is said that to this fact Calvinism owes some of its characteristics. The independence of thought and the combination of fervent enthusiasm and deep tenacity of purpose which Calvin transmitted to his followers are declared to have been part of the Picard tradition. In Picardy,

[13] Lindsay, *A History of the Reformation*, Vol. I, p. 417.
[14] Smith, *The Age of the Reformation*, pp. 136-138.
[15] Walker, *The Reformation*, p. 279.
[16] *Ibid.*
[17] Lindsay, *op. cit.*, Vol. I, p. 418.
[18] Lindsay, *op. cit.*, Vol. I, p. 421.
[19] Stephenson, *The Religious Aspects of Swedish Immigration*, p. 27.

moreover, had been many sympathizers with Wyclif and Hus.[20] In France Protestantism early gained a foothold among all classes. Some of the great nobles and the middle classes in the cities employed it as an instrument against the royal power. Numbers of the lower clergy used it to denounce the existing order and the higher clergy.[21] Eventually Protestantism became strongest in the South and West where were memories of medieval dissent and where local independence and pride in Provençal culture seem to have prepared the ground.[22] Yet, as we have suggested, the strong impregnation of France with the Roman culture and the Latin spirit probably foredoomed Protestantism to a minority position.

In ecclesiastical as in political affairs the Swiss, remote in their mountain cantons, had been singularly independent. Episcopacy had sat lightly upon them.[23] Many of them welcomed the Reformation and they tended to a type of ecclesiastical government suited to their political and social life.

In Italy Protestantism never won a numerous following among the masses. Here and there among the educated it had strong exponents. As might have been expected, in these individualistic humanism was strong and they were predisposed to an intellectual approach towards religion. It is not surprising that the founders of the rationalistic, anti-Trinitarian strain or Protestantism, Socinianism, were Italians and that the movement took its name from them.[24]

The Netherlands tended to divide religiously according to their pre-Reformation groupings.[25] It was the Dutch in the North, where the permeation by the Roman spirit was least thorough, who became Protestant, rather than the Flemings in the Centre or the French in the South. It was natural that in a state, the United Provinces, whose political constitution took the form of a federation, the tendency was for each province to regulate its own ecclesiastical affairs[26] and that in the Calvinistic state church a good deal of theological variety was displayed and many small groups of Puritanical mystical tendencies came into existence.[27]

One of the commonplaces of history is that in England the wayward marital affections of Henry VIII were decisive in the separation of the Church from Rome,[28] and that it was the desire of the astute Elizabeth to bring to the

[20] Lindsay, op. cit., Vol. II, p. 92.
[21] Smith, op. cit., p. 207.
[22] Smith, op. cit., p. 216.
[23] Lindsay, op. cit., Vol. II, p. 23.
[24] Lindsay, op. cit., Vol. II, p. 426.
[25] Lindsay, op. cit., Vol. II, p. 227.
[26] Lindsay, op. cit., Vol. II, pp. 270-273.
[27] Troeltsch, The Social Teaching of the Christian Churches, pp. 682 ff.
[28] While it is true that before Henry VIII's decisive acts there had been talk of the Church in England being made a separate patriarchate and Henry VIII simply carried

support of the state a church which would include as many as possible of her subjects which contributed largely to the comprehensiveness of the Establishment. Yet it is also one of the commonplaces that Henry VIII's insistence upon a divorce from Catherine was by no means the only cause of the religious change, that the tendencies nourished by Lollardy had never fully disappeared, that secret Bible readings had long been held and services in the vernacular attended, that there had been those who desired the reform of the Church, and that Luther's writings had found entrance and readers.[29] In its liturgy and spirit the Church of England which came out of the separation from Rome was both an expression of the English temperament and helped shape that temperament. The conservatism and adherence to the past, the strong individualism, the marked emphasis on morality, the value placed upon order, the combination of sentimentalism and practicality, and the tendency towards the prophetic and Biblical are all features of the Church of England and seem also to be reflections of the English disposition.[30]

In Scotland Calvinism became the dominant form of Protestantism and entered from the Continent rather than from England in part because the cultural and political connexions of Scotland were with France and not with the feared and chronically hostile England, and partly because by the time Scotland was brought over to the Reformation Calvinism had succeeded Lutheranism as the more recent and aggressive form of Protestantism.[31] In Scotland Presbyterianism both moulded and was an expression of the Scotch temperament. Like Scotland itself, it was very distinct from the Anglicanism which prevailed south of the Border. It more nearly monopolized the religious life of Scotland than did the Church of England that of England. It is an interesting contrast, possibly reflecting differences in national qualities, that while in Scotland dissent from the Established Church usually resulted in the formation of another Presbyterian church, in England it never expressed itself in another episcopally governed body, but in groups whose polity and often whose creeds were quite different from those of the Church of England.

Political factors and national and regional cultural peculiarities were not the only non-religious elements in giving variety to Protestantism and in determining its forms.

---

further than his predecessors their desire to have some kind of control over the Church in their realms (Lindsay, op. cit., Vol. II, pp. 321, 332), it is also true that at the time of the separation there was no general dislike among Englishmen of the Papal jurisdiction (Gairdner, *Lollardy and the Reformation in England*, Vol. I, pp. 4, 5).

[29] Lindsay, op. cit., Vol. II, p. 316.

[30] Underhill, *Worship*, pp. 319-322; Inge, *The Platonic Tradition in English Religious Thought*, pp. 4, 5.

[31] Smith, *The Age of the Reformation*, p. 362.

Protestantism owed much to the Renaissance and to humanism. The fact has been frequently pointed out that whereas in Southern Europe humanism was in general accompanied by indifference to the inherited Christianity or by veiled or even open scepticism, in Northern Europe it was prevailingly religious and made for reform in the Church. The greatest humanist of his day, Erasmus, was from the Netherlands, was deeply religious, and most earnestly longed and worked for the purification of the official church. Zwingli was both a Protestant and a humanist. The humanistic strain was stronger in Socinianism than in any other major form of Protestantism[32]—although the roots of Socianianism go back before humanism into some of the intellectual currents of the Middle Ages[33]—but, while not dominant, it made itself felt in others, notably in Calvinism and such an offshoot from Calvinism as Arminianism, and in the Church of England.[34] Through Melanchthon it found entrance into Lutheranism.[35]

Also very important in giving to various types of Protestantism their peculiarities were the personal convictions, experiences, and characteristics of their leading founders. We have repeatedly called attention to the fact that several of the most influential of the founders, among them Luther, Zwingli, and Calvin, were of peasant stock, and that through them and other less prominent reformers the lower social groups of Northern Europe made Christianity their own and placed their stamp upon it. Luther particularly kept his close touch with the common man, in him much of the popular religion of his youth found expression, and this, with his experience of salvation through faith, his theology, his desire to perpetuate all in the medieval Church which was not expressly contrary to the Scriptures, and his convictions concerning the relation of Church and state have left their distinctive mark upon the type of Protestantism that bears his name. Zwingli and Calvin had no soul-shaking and cataclysmic religious experience such as that of Luther, and in the Reformed churches closely reasoned doctrines logically expressed have had a large place. Through his *Institutes* and his life of teaching at Geneva Calvin left as profound an impression of his mind and spirit upon the Reformed churches as did Luther upon the Lutheran bodies.

The Anabaptist wing of Protestantism took many forms and was not the prolonged shadow of any one or two great leaders. It traced its spiritual descent from some of the groups, usually of humble folk, of the Middle Ages, who, touched by the New Testament, attempted to reproduce what they be-

[32] McGiffert, *Protestant Thought before Kant*, pp. 107-109.
[33] Lindsay, *A History of the Reformation*, Vol. II, pp. 470-475.
[34] Lindsay, *op. cit.*, Vol. II, pp. 9-11.
[35] McGiffert, *op. cit.*, p. 71.

lieved to be the simplicity and the thoroughgoing commitment of life to the Christian ideal characteristic of Christians of Apostolic times. It seemed to spring spontaneously out of contact with the New Testament and broke out in many different places. It rejected the association between Church and state which was accepted and sanctioned by Lutherans, most Calvinists, and the Church of England. From its standpoint Christianity was not a religion to be adopted by a community as a whole because that community chanced to dwell in a given geographic locality or to represent a tribe or a nation or to be governed by a particular ruler or set of political institutions. It was a faith into which individuals entered one by one through a personal dedication and a personal experience of salvation. Anabaptists held that churches should be made up only of those who had had that experience, and that all Christians with that experience had direct access to God and should have equal rights in the Church. While rejecting celibate monasticism, they called for the same complete surrender that the monastery demanded. To the Anabaptist movements two streams contributed, the religious, which we have just attempted to summarize, and the social, the uprising of the common man, stirred and reinforced by the conviction born of the Chrisian impulse of the worth of all men, even the humblest.[36]

Somewhat akin in spirit to the Anabaptist movements were the Friends and the Pietists. All had this much in common: they held to the necessity for the true Christian of an unreserved dedication of life to the will of God and to the guidance of the individual by direct touch with the Spirit of God. Wesley, too, through his transforming contact with the Moravians, represented and propagated that kind of Christianity. The Quakers, the Pietists, the Moravians, and the Methodists each drew characteristic peculiarities from their great founders or leaders.

This, then, was the Protestantism which expanded during this period and which laid the foundations for the Protestant expressions of Christianity which were propagated in the nineteenth and twentieth centuries. It had varied forms, much of it was determined even more by political and social considerations than by the Christian impulse, and by the majority of its adherents it was accepted because it was the faith of the state into which they were born. Yet, as the missionaries of Roman Catholicism were mostly regular clergy, members of orders which were the means of expressing a single-minded adherence to the Christian faith, so the majority of those who were the active agents in the spread of Protestant Christianity among non-Christian peoples were either, like the Pietists and the Moravians, members of groups which emphasized a

---

[36] Lindsay, *op. cit.*, Vol. II, pp. 235-239, 421, 422, 432-448.

similar complete dedication to Christianity, or were individuals from within the state churches who were earnest in their faith. Those who were the channels for the transmission of Christianity of whatever kind to non-Christians were, as a rule, those who had taken their faith more seriously and had entered more fully into its spirit than had the majority.

Although Protestantism was probably more responsive to its environment than was the Roman Catholic Church, the Roman Catholicism of the sixteenth, seventeenth, and eighteenth centuries was also modified by its surroundings.

The territorial boundaries of Roman Catholicism, like those of Protestantism, were largely determined by social, cultural, and political factors. The Roman Catholic Church continued to have its stronghold in the area in which it had developed and whose culture had both shaped it and been shaped by it. It was primarily the faith of the Latin South, of what had once been the Latin-using sections of the Roman Empire. Where, as in portions of Germany, the Roman Catholic Church still held a considerable following among Teutonic peoples, it was largely in areas which were nearer what had once been the Roman Empire or had actually once been in that Empire and where the process of assimilation to Roman culture had gone further than in the North or in Anglo-Saxon Britain. It was also the faith of most of the Slavs of Western Europe and of the larger proportion of the Celts. The majority of the Celtic Irish held to it with passionate loyalty, partly because to them it symbolized their racial and cultural integrity as against their English overlords. The Roman Catholic Church was the one institution which was peculiarly theirs and which was not dominated by the hated Protestant masters from Great Britain.

The Roman Catholic Church was profoundly modified by the Protestant secession and by competition with Protestantism. It was also, as we have repeatedly seen in the preceding chapters, largely permeated by the Catholic Reformation. The Catholic Reformation was in part a Counter-Reformation— a conscious and deliberate attempt to remove some of the moral abuses to which Protestants pointed the finger of scorn, to define more clearly doctrines which were in dispute with Protestants, to organize for the conflict with Protestantism, and, if possible, to win back lost ground. The Catholic Reformation was also due to the rising tides of life which sought to purge Western Christianity of some of the failure to attain the New Testament ideal. As this among the Teutonic peoples gave rise to Protestantism, so in the Latin South it remained within the framework of the old Church, but wrought changes in it. In the sixteenth and seventeenth centuries alterations in Roman Catholicism it is, therefore, often difficult and sometimes impossible to distinguish between the effects of Protestantism and the outgrowths of the surge of life springing from the Christian impulse which was common to both wings of Western Christianity.

Some modifications in Roman Catholicism seem clearly the results of Protestantism. One arose from the obvious fact that Roman Catholicism ceased to be the faith universally accepted in Western Europe. While insisting even more earnestly that it was Catholic, and while, by its expansion in the Americas, Africa, and Asia extending over more territory than before the Protestant revolt, its leaders were now painfully conscious of the fact that it no longer commanded the allegiance of all Christian Europe.

These losses in European Christendom were accentuated by the fact that not far from the beginning of Protestantism the efforts for union with the Eastern Orthodox churches which had been in progress intermittently through the preceding centuries and which as late as the fifteenth century seemed crowned with success, finally broke down. Rome might win over individuals or groups from these churches, but any prospect of bringing them as entire bodies into communion with Rome had now become very remote.

An outstanding effect of this final division of European Christianity was to make of the Roman Catholic Church a sect and to develop within it the attitudes of a sect. The Roman Catholic Church was the largest of the Christian sects, but it was now unmistakably no longer Catholic in the sense that it embraced all Christians. As one result of its becoming a sect it now more emphatically than ever declared itself to be the only true and Catholic Church. It had less patience with variations within itself and was more zealous in rooting out what it termed heresies than in the days when it had included all Western European Christians and when it had from time to time been in union with the Church of the Byzantine Empire. To meet the competition with other types of Christianity, particularly Protestantism, it closed up its ranks and enforced stricter discipline among its adherents and particularly among its clergy. It became more controversial. It became more Roman and Italian. Whereas formerly it had occasionally had Popes from other countries and even from Northern Europe, the Dutch Adrian VI (reigned 1522-1523) was the last from the North to sit on the Fisherman's Throne, and, indeed, the last non-Italian to hold the post.

It may also have been a result of Protestantism, although more probably it was the outcome of forces which operated in both branches of Western Christianity, that Roman Catholicism tended more and more to a personal and individualistic type of piety which, as the centuries passed, centred increasingly upon the reserved sacrament.[37]

[37] Underhill, *Worship*, p. 261.

Partly because Protestantism led North-western Europe to withdraw the recognition accorded Rome during the Middle Ages, and partly because of the growing power of absolute, secular monarchs in the Europe which remained to Rome, the Papacy became a declining force in international affairs. No longer, as in much of the Middle Ages, was it an arbiter between monarchs and between peoples, the international tribunal and the supreme court of Europe. The Treaty of Westphalia (1648) registered the final ushering out of the Papal authority from the international negotiations of European states.[38] The change had begun long before 1648 and it was long after that date before Rome even tacitly acquiesced in its reduced status, but that Peace which ended the wars in which the religious differences between Protestants and Roman Catholics entered as a major factor and which largely fixed the religious map of Western Europe also marked the end of the power of the Pope as the head of the European states system.

More than once we have had occasion to notice the manner in which the Roman Catholic princes dominated the Church in their own domains. The most ardently and fanatically Catholic of them all, Philip II of Spain, was emphatic in his assertion of the royal authority over the Church in his realms. This growth in the control of the secular arm over the Church was both because of the distrust of the sincerity or the ability of the hierarchy to bring about the reforms demanded by the Christian conscience of the day[39] and an accompaniment of the general extension of the authority of the monarchs.

Partly as a result of the enhanced power of the monarchs and partly because of an increase in national consciousness, the Roman Catholic Church tended in various countries to reflect the peculiarities and the local cultural histories of those lands.

Thus the Christianity propagated by the Spaniards and Portuguese bore the imprint of the Iberian Peninsula. On it the long contact with the Moor had left traces. The Spanish peasant, like the Moslem of North Africa, had as the main tenet of his faith a belief in God, in the immortality of the soul, and in a heaven in which this earthly life is continued free from the misery which besets man here.[40] The Spanish dread was death, not sin.[41] The Iberian spirit was marked by individualism, an intense pride, loyalty to the Roman Catholic faith and a passion to spread it not because the faith was true but because

[38] Eckhardt, *The Papacy and World-Affairs*, p. vii.

[39] Lindsay, *A History of the Reformation*, Vol. IV, pp. 487-489.

[40] Mackay, *The Other Spanish Christ*, pp. 95, 96, citing Unamono's essay, *El Cristo Español in Mi Religión y Otros Ensayos* and Unamono's article in *The English Woman* (1909).

[41] Mackay, *op. cit.*, p. 99.

honour demanded it. Markedly characteristic of Iberian Roman Catholicism was the feeling that the church belonged to Spain or Portugal rather than Spain or Portugal to the Church, an emphasis upon deep emotion rather than reason or will, a strong abstract sense of justice and of right, an awareness of the tragedy of life which gave prominence to the passion of Christ, and much less of insistence upon personal ethics and upon conviction of personal sin than one finds in Anglo-Saxon Christianity.[42]

In France in the seventeenth and eighteenth centuries several tendencies shaped the Roman Catholicism of the land. The nationalism already nascent and encouraged by the union of the country under the Bourbons expressed itself in Gallicanism, a strong feeling of self-consciousness in the French Church. Louis XIV ruled the Church in his domains as autocratically as he did the state and at one time in a conflict with the Pope even threatened to separate the Church from Rome. In the French Church was a pronounced strain of religious humanism, one of whose outstanding exemplars was Francis de Sales. This displayed itself in a particular type of piety which believed in the possibilities of human nature, sought to reach the humble as well as the mighty with religious training, stressed scholarship,[43] and by its confidence in the nature of man and the freedom of the will helped prepare the way for the rationalism and the belief in the perfectibility of man which underlay the ideology of the French Revolution. French piety of the period also had a strong aristocratic strain.[44] Then, in part as a reaction against the religious humanism, came a movement which was in a minority and was eventually discredited, Jansenism, sternly Puritan in its morals, declaring man's nature corrupt, and stressing grace.[45]

In spite of the loss of the central place in the European states system which had once been his, and in the face of the tendency to assert the authority of the monarchs over the Church in the realms which curtailed his power, the Pope achieved an enhanced position within the Roman Catholic Church. The movement which sought to limit his power by means of general councils and which had been strong in the latter part of the thousand years before A.D. 1500 was now effectively curbed. In spite of the opposition of Spanish, French, and German bishops, the Council of Trent, which laid the legal foundations and gave the formal legislation for the Catholic Reformation, registered a victory for Papal supremacy. Pope Pius IV managed to keep in control of the Council

---

[42] Mackay, *op. cit.*, pp. 1-22.
[43] Brémond, *A Literary History of Religious Thought in France from the Wars of Religion down to Our Own Time*, Vol. I, pp. 105 ff., Vol. II, pp. 8-19.
[44] Brémond, *op. cit.*, Vol. I, pp. vi, 3-14.
[45] Brémond, *op. cit.*, Vol. I, pp. 305 ff.

Italian bishops whom he could direct, had the able support of the Jesuits, and so achieved the victory.[46] In a sense this development signalized the triumph of the Italians in the Church. It may also have been a reflection in ecclesiastical circles of the autocracy which at the time was so marked in the secular state.

Upon Roman Catholicism as upon Protestantism great individuals left the impress of their personal experiences and peculiarities. Thus the Society of Jesus witnessed to the military background of Ignatius Loyola. The discipline and obedience required of the soldier and the aggressiveness of the army were outstanding features of the Jesuits. It is from the military tradition that there seems to come the statement in the famous *Exercises* of Loyola that "we must be ready to renounce from our heart our private judgment, to obey in all things the Bride of Christ, and this bride is that Holy Catholic Church."[47] Indeed, so far was this obedience to go that the *Exercises* commanded that if the Church defines anything to be black which to our eyes appears to be white, we ought to believe it to be black.[48] Both Loyola and Theresa had been nourished on the chivalry and romanticism of the Middle Ages, and it is not surprising that these gave their tinge both to the Jesuits and to the Carmelites.[49]

In the new orders and congregations of the three centuries after A.D. 1500 the activism which seems typical of the West found increasing expression. Although the new life within the Roman Catholic Church largely followed the traditional forms and consented to wear the familiar garb of monasticism, this alleged monasticism was less and less kept apart from the world. Pursuing the tendency that had become prominent in the Franciscans and Dominicans, the new groups mixed actively in society and endeavoured to mould human affairs. This was notably true of the Jesuits, but it was also seen in the Theatines, the Lazarists, and the many teaching and hospital congregations. Even when, as later in the nineteenth and twentieth centuries, contemplative orders arose to give themselves primarily to prayer, their prayers were often designed to assist those who were engaged in work in the world outside the walls of the cloisters.

As before A.D. 1500, so afterwards, many attitudes and practices which were of non-Christian origin and some of which were directly opposed to the New Testament found their way into popular Roman Catholic Christianity. Thus

---

[46] Lindsay, *A History of the Reformation*, Vol. II, p. 591.

[47] Pastor, *History of the Popes*, Vol. XII, pp. 11, 12. The quotation from the *Spiritual Exercises* is from the first of the eighteen rules for thinking with the Church which conclude the *Exercises*.

[48] Ignatius Loyola, *Spiritual Exercises*, the thirteenth of the eighteen rules for thinking with the Church which conclude the *Exercises* (translation by C. Seager, London, Charles Dolman, 1847, p. 180).

[49] Kirk, *The Vision of God*, p. 397.

processions and public acts of penance were frequently employed in Italy as a means of curbing the pestilences which were so frequent in the sixteenth century and especial recourse against the plague was had to the Virgin and to St. Sebastian.[50] The notable artist Benvenuto Cellini, in his frank autobiography, recorded the manner in which even a presumably cultured man might look to the Roman Catholic faith for assistance in achieving the desires dictated by his enmity and in freeing the unrepentant from the guilt of homicide.[51]

The Eastern Churches, with the exception of that of Russia, showed the effects of their immersion in the Moslem world and of their political subjection to Moslem rulers. Their heads could usually be chosen only with the consent of the Moslem masters and the latter held them responsible for much of the civil administration of their flocks. That meant that bribery often entered into the appointments and that those elected owed their position not so much to their religious zeal as to their supposed willingness to co-operate with Moslem officials. It was to be expected that the body of the clergy would reflect the character of their leaders and that the tendency would be towards timidity, acquiescence, ignorance, and the formal repetition by rote of liturgies developed in freer days. New movements and creative life were all but impossible. The Christian communities, continued largely on the momentum of early centuries, slowly dwindled under the attrition of the encircling Islam.

Russian Orthodox Christianity was in a different situation. It was the faith of a growing empire whose rulers professed adherence to it. The fall of Constantinople to the Turk (1453) brought great changes in the Russian Church. Russia now became the chief champion of Orthodoxy. Moscow, in the eyes of the Russian Orthodox, became the "third Rome"—after the defection of Rome to the "heresies" of the Latins and the loss of the "second Rome," Constantinople, to the Moslem—the centre and champion of true Christianity. No longer was the Russian Church an apanage of the Œcumenical Patriarchate of Constantinople. Full autonomy was achieved and in 1589 an independent Russian patriarchate was created.[52] Moreover, the fact that Russia grew to imperial proportions and included many races and tribes under its sway and that among numbers of these diverse groups converts were made helped to give to the Russian Church a cosmopolitanism which the churches of the Balkans, constricted as they were within the Turkish domains, did not know.

Yet the fall of Constantinople furthered the subjection of the Russian Church

[30] Pastor, *op. cit.*, Vol. V, pp. 6, 7.
[51] *Autobiography of Benvenuto Cellini* (translation by J. A. Symonds, New York, The Modern Library, no date), Book I, Chaps. 33, 36, 38, Book II, Chap. 25.
[52] Eck, *Le Moyen Age Russe*, p. 124.

to the civil ruler, for the Metropolitan of Moscow no longer had a strong Œcumenical Patriarch to back him and the Tsar began to appoint to the office.[53]

As time passed the growth of the autocratic power of the Tsar brought the Russian Church into greater subordination to the civil authority and left it with less independent life of its own than was true of the Church in any major land in Western Europe. This development went back to the tradition inherited from the Byzantine Empire and this in turn was a continuation of the pre-Christian status of state religion in the Roman Empire as ancillary and subordinate to the civil rulers. It was accentuated by the outcome of a struggle in the sixteenth century between those on the one hand who opposed the ownership of land and those who on the other hand wished the Church to hold property and advocated a close connexion between Church and state and desired national status for the local saints. The latter school won and hastened the absolute control of the Church by the state.[54] Peter the Great, particularly by the measures which he took to extend the domination of the crown, accelerated the process which made of the Church chiefly an arm of the state. The Holy Synod, headed by a layman, was substituted for the Patriarch and was fully under the control of the Tsar.[55] The bishops became courtiers and functionaries of the state and stood for Tsarist absolutism.[56] In the eighteenth century the autonomy of the local parishes, long looked at askance by the government, declined and with its weakening the anæmia of religious life within the official Church was accentuated.[57]

After A.D. 1500 sects developed in Russian Christianity and were indications of vitality. They were much later in appearing than were sects in Western Europe, for in the latter region, as we saw in the previous volume, they had begun to emerge at least as early as the thirteenth century. Those in Russia were much more tardy in beginning and were neither as numerous nor as prominent as were those in the West. This may have been because the Mongol conquest slowed down and modified the normal course of development. It may also have been because Christianity in Russia had less inherent vigour than in Western Europe and did not so greatly stir the soul of the people.

When sects commenced in Russia they took forms which reflected the Russian environment. Prominent and fairly numerous were what were called the Old Believers. These finally separated from the state church in the second

[53] Frere, *Some Links in the Chain of Russian Church History*, pp. 62, 63.

[54] Milukow, *Skizzen russischer Kulturgeschichte*, Vol. II, pp. 16-31; Vernadsky, *History of Russia*, p. 61.

[55] Milukow, *op. cit.*, Vol. II, pp. 167-172.

[56] Conybeare, *Russian Dissenters*, p. 5.

[57] Conybeare, *op. cit.*, p. 72.

half of the seventeenth century. They arose as a protest against innovations. Some of these latter were changes in the service books and were enforced by the able and vigorous Patriarch Nikon. On comparison with the Greek originals, a study which was due in part to scholars from Kiev, the translations in use in Russia were found to have many errors. As early as the first half of the sixteenth century a learned Greek had pointed out at least some of these discrepancies and his corrections had caused a storm of protest.[58] Now about the middle of the seventeenth century Nikon brought about the adoption of versions made by the scholars from Kiev. Strong opposition arose. The dissidents claimed that Kiev was subject to Roman, unorthodox, and un-Russian influences, that the orthodoxy of the Greeks was suspect, partly because for a time the Greeks had assented to union with Rome, and partly because they were now under the Moslem and were, supposedly, partly Islamized.[59] There was indignation, too, at other Græcizing tendencies of Nikon and at the Patriarchate's attempts to bring the parishes, long governed locally, more closely under the control of the higher ecclesiastical authorities.[60] Opposition to Nikon's changes coalesced with that against the innovations of Peter the Great.[61] The result was schism. Only one bishop seceded with the Old Believers. After his death the latter, accordingly, could not ordain priests. One division of them obtained clergy from the state church, but one part managed without priests.[62] They flourished especially in the North, where under frontier conditions and the paucity of clergy the faithful had been accustomed to having laymen lead public worship.[63] It is significant that the main bone of contention with the state church was over the letter of the service books, for this reflects the emphasis placed by Russian Christians upon the formal service as the centre and the chief expression of their faith.[64] The movement was also evidence that many of the Russian lay folk were taking their religion seriously. Formerly, it is said, the large majority of Russians had thought little of religion and public worship was a dead form and was carelessly carried out. The Old Believers made religion primary and so stressed the meticulous performance of the ritual as they and their ancestors had known it that they were willing, because of it, to suffer obloquy and persecution.[65]

[58] Milukow, *op. cit.*, Vol. II, p. 36.
[59] Milukow, *op. cit.*, Vol. II, pp. 34, 38-44.
[60] Conybeare, *op. cit.*, pp. 18-20, 44-48.
[61] Frere, *op. cit.*, p. 143; Conybeare, *op. cit.*, pp. 91-94.
[62] Conybeare, *op. cit.*, pp. 101-105.
[63] Milukow, *op. cit.*, Vol. II, pp. 78-80; Conybeare, *op. cit.*, p. 107.
[64] Milukow, *op. cit.*, Vol. II, p. 34; Conybeare, *op. cit.*, p. 28; A. Kartashov in *Theology*, Vol. XXX, p. 12.
[65] Milukow, *op. cit.*, Vol. II, pp. 159, 160.

Other sects and movements there were in Russia. In the seventeenth century one had as its distinctive feature the voluntary death, by burning, of its adherents, on the belief that thus direct entrance into heaven would be assured.[66] The Doukhobors sprang up in the eighteenth century. They protested against all externals of religion, such as images, the sign of the Cross, and fasts, as powerless to achieve salvation, denounced the state church as a den of robbers, and insisted upon reciprocal love. They rejected private property, refrained so far as possible from taking life, and inculcated hospitality to strangers, the respect of children for parents and of youth for age, and industry in one's craft.[67] Their beginning is obscure, but it is said that contact with the Quakers may have assisted in it.[68] The Khlysty, possibly of sixteenth century origin, taught the reincarnation of Christ in individual Christians, said that a Christ could be recognized by his sufferings, practised the mortification of the flesh, and induced the reception of the Holy Spirit through ecstasies, trances, contortions, or convulsions. The initiated repudiated marriage.[69] The Skopsty, apparently an outgrowth of the Khlysty, practised emasculation and baptism by fire (a hot iron), and abstained from meat.[70] Some of these cults are reminiscent of Bogomilism and the Cathari, and may have been due to them or to some other movements of foreign origin.[71] On the other hand, they may have been purely indigenous. Until the nineteenth century Protestantism gained only a few converts in Russia.[72] Not until the nineteenth century, through contact with German Protestants, did the Stundists arise[73] and groups akin to the Anabaptists flourish.

The effect of the environment upon the Christianity which spread outside of Europe here requires only a summary, for in earlier chapters it has been described area by area.

First it must be said that most of this extra-European Christianity was an anæmic and imperfect reproduction of one or another of the forms of European Christianity. In the Spanish possessions it was chiefly Spanish Roman Catholicism. In Portuguese territories it was Portuguese Roman Catholicism. In Southern and Eastern Asia outside of the areas ruled by Portugal it was the more cosmopolitan Roman Catholicism of the type born of the Catholic Reformation and propagated by Frenchmen, Italians, Spaniards, Portuguese,

---

[66] Milukow, *op. cit.*, Vol. II, pp. 75-77.
[67] Conybeare, *op. cit.*, pp. 268-287.
[68] Milukow, *op. cit.*, Vol. II, p. 123.
[69] Conybeare, *op. cit.*, pp. 339-361.
[70] Conybeare, *op. cit.*, pp. 363 ff.
[71] Conybeare, *op. cit.*, pp. 261 ff.
[72] Milukow, *op. cit.*, Vol. II, pp. 104 ff.
[73] Conybeare, *op. cit.*, pp. 331 ff.

Flemings, or Germans. In French America there was French Roman Catholicism. In South India there was German and Scandinavian Pietism, in the East Indies and Ceylon Dutch Calvinism, in the Danish and British West Indies among the Negroes Moravian Pietism or Methodism, in Greenland Pietism, both Scandinavian and Moravian, and in the Thirteen Colonies various Protestant groups won followings which reflected the tenets and ecclesiastical practices of their teachers. In Siberia and Alaska it was Russian Orthodoxy which the new Christians reproduced.

Among non-European converts Christianity was accepted passively and only here and there were efforts put forth by non-European Christians to carry their faith to others or to give it local forms which accorded with indigenous cultural traditions. To be sure, some pre-Christian beliefs, attitudes, and practices persisted, but only seldom did these give rise to attempts at spontaneous new movements. In the West Indies a tendency in Negro Protestantism was to be seen—emotional, the product of what had been introduced, Moravianism and Methodism, and of the Negro temperament—but it had not yet become particularly creative. In India caste made itself felt, partly by the group acceptance of the Christian faith and the identification of Christianity with particular castes or sections of outcastes, and partly by the persistence of caste differences and customs within the Christian communities. In India and China attempts were made to adapt Christianity—in the one country to the Brahmin traditions, and in the other to the terminology, conventions, and cults inculcated by the ruling social class, the *literati*. In both lands, however, the initiative in the adaptations was by European missionaries.

Even among the communities of Europeans established by migration outside of Europe, with the exception of the English Thirteen Colonies, no new types of Christianity developed and while some missionaries went from them to non-Christians, most of the propagation of the faith was by European-born Christians.

Why this dearth of originality and this lack of zeal in spreading Christianity? It was in marked contrast to the record in Europe, both before A.D. 1500 and after A.D. 1500. Obviously the reason was not climate, for in some areas where Christianity had been planted among non-Europeans in these centuries the climate was as favourable for an advanced civilization as in Europe. Probably it was not race, for some of the races among whom Christianity was now found, notably the Chinese and Indians, had created high civilizations of their own. It was not even the disparity between European civilization and those cultures which the latter now overpowered, for in the thousand years after A.D. 500 the cultures of the peoples of North-western Europe had likewise given way before the culture of the Mediterranean Basin which came in association with Christianity, and yet in North-western Europe Christianity had developed distinctive forms and the peoples of Western Europe had become the most active of the propagators of Christianity among non-Christian peoples. Was it because Christianity lost its vigour when transplanted outside of Europe and because it had become so identified with European culture that it could spread only in connexion with it, and through long association with that culture had ceased to be flexible and had lost the power to adapt itself to another *milieu* or to take root in non-Occidental soil?

From the evidence afforded in the three hundred years between A.D. 1500 and A.D. 1800 no satisfactory answer can be given. It must be remembered that in no land to which it was propagated in this period was Christianity free to adapt itself or to stir the non-European Christians or, except in the English Thirteen Colonies, even the European settlers to independent movements. The state enforced conformity to European forms of Christianity. It must be recalled, too, that in all the lands politically subject to Europeans the aboriginal populations were under the political and economic domination of the white man and could not if they had wished have shown much cultural initiative. Moreover, practically all the communities of non-European Christians, whether Roman Catholic, Protestant, or Russian Orthodox, were ecclesiastically under the close control of the Europeans. The head clergy were practically all of European stock and the non-Europeans were kept in a state of tutelage. Even had non-European Christians desired to undertake adaptations of their faith to their old cultures they would have been sternly discouraged. Under such circumstances they were not likely to propagate the faith of which they had been such passive recipients. Yet the preceding pages have shown that in several countries, even in the face of these discouragements, converts were active in spreading their faith among their non-Christian fellows.

As to the communities of white settlers, it must be remembered that in the larger proportion of these, those under the Spanish and Portuguese flags, politically and commercially the mother country exercised meticulous and absolute control and allowed no variations. Ecclesiastically the mother land and European-born whites were dominant and the Inquisition saw to it that any deviation from standards set in Europe was quickly eliminated. Many of the Protestant churches in the colonies, too, were controlled from Europe.

The one exception both to this lack of initiative and to this dearth of new movements was the English Thirteen Colonies in North America. Here Christians of European stock were energetic in spreading their faith, here indigenous religious movements broke out, and here a new type of Christianity was emerging. Here, too, significantly, in the political and economic spheres the colonials enjoyed more liberty and experienced less interference and supervision from Europe than in any other of the overseas domains of European powers in this period. Here, in the nineteenth and twentieth centuries, developed a Christianity which was increasingly distinctive. Here, too, arose one of the greatest centres for the propagation of Christianity in other lands. Whether, had similar colonial policies been adopted, similar results would have followed in other overseas European settlements we may not know.

In Western Europe Christianity, partly because of the inward urge within it, and partly because of the forces playing on it from the outside, took on more original forms than at any time since its first five centuries. It reflected its environment, but not passively so. Like a growing plant, it gave evidence of the nature of the soil in which it was rooted, but its new growth was due to the vitality which coursed through it.

In Russia Christianity was more passive, but here, also, through new shoots it gave signs of inherent vigour. More than in the preceding period it showed variety, evidence that it had survived transplanting and had become acclimatized.

In these three centuries Christianity had been propagated more widely than ever before, and, indeed, than any faith had ever been. Yet, with the exception of the English Thirteen Colonies in North America, both among non-Europeans and Europeans the transplanted Christianity required continued nourishment from Europe and gave little indication by new and distinctive growth that it had taken firm root and would survive if its connexion with the parent plant were severed. The question still remained without the answer of unequivocal facts as to whether Christianity could exist apart from Europe and the Occidental cultural tradition. In its first five centuries Christianity through its triumph in the Mediterranean Basin had become so closely intertwined with Græco-Roman culture and its forms had been so largely determined by that association that it had henceforth been almost completely identified with civilizations and communities sprung from the Occidental stem. It was more and more profoundly altering Western civilization, but, although its adherents claimed for it universality and had propagated it among many races of many cultures and although it had shown its power to restrain the ruthlessness of the exploitation of non-Europeans by Europeans, it still retained its Western guise and flourished only when in continuous contact with Europe. It had not yet demonstrated that it could survive apart from that contact or that it could adapt itself to a totally different environment and live.

Chapter XVIII

RETROSPECT AND PROSPECT

IN A.D. 1500 the outlook for Christianity had not been encouraging. The thousand years of uncertainty which had followed the winning of the Græco-Roman world had closed on a minor note. In Central and Far Eastern Asia the extensive Christian communities which had sprung up after A.D. 500 had all but disappeared. The Moslem Turk had captured Constantinople, long a Christian bulwark against Islam, and had made the Crescent dominant in Asia Minor, Greece, and the Balkan Peninsula. In what remained to Christianity, Western and Northern Europe, the state of the faith was precarious. The Roman Catholic Church was honeycombed with corruption and was ruled by worldly Popes. Many earnest souls were outraged and discouraged. Moreover, a new Europe was appearing, and although Christianity had been a major factor in creating the culture of Medieval Europe, its very success threatened to be its undoing, for it was closely integrated with an order which was passing. The Renaissance had brought a new spirit of self-reliance which seemed to make dependence on the Christian God unnecessary and an admiration for pagan antiquity which appeared to discredit Christianity. The scientific age was dawning and man by his own efforts was discovering a new heaven and a new earth and so was seeming to demonstrate that truth of whatever nature is to be found by man's search rather than, as the Christian faith had claimed in the realms of religion and morals, through divine revelation. Strong secular states were emerging under absolute monarchs which insisted upon controlling the Church and making it serve their ends. The unprecedented geographic discoveries were being followed by a vast commercial and colonial expansion with ruthless exploitation of non-European peoples. It seemed preposterous to expect that the badly shaken and seemingly moribund Christianity of Europe could keep pace with this commercial and territorial activity, occupy the lands which it opened, win their peoples to the Christian faith, retain its hold on the European settlers, and turn the exploitation of non-Europeans by Europeans into a beneficent contact. Christianity was not inwardly at so low an ebb or outwardly so seriously threatened by destructive invasions as it had been about A.D. 1000, but it was badly shaken and seemed to be a declining force at the very time when it faced one of the greatest set of challenges and opportunities which it had known in its fifteen centuries of existence.

It is one of the amazing facts of history that this apparently dying religion experienced the greatest revival which it had yet known, moulded the new Europe more effectively than it had that of the Middle Ages, and, accompanying the explorers, merchants, and colonizers, spread over a larger proportion of the earth's surface than either it or any other religion had yet done and modified profoundly the new communities which Europeans established and the impact of Europeans upon non-Europeans.

The revival took two major forms—the emergence of the various new movements which are collectively known as Protestantism, and the inward reform and reinvigoration of the religious life and ecclesiastical structure which remained within the Roman Catholic Church. The various types of Lutheranism, Calvinism, Anabaptism, and Socianism were at once expressions and creators of a deepening and strengthening of the Christianity of North-western Europe. In the Roman Catholic fold new orders, notably the Society of Jesus, were brought into being by the new life and propagated it, old orders were reformed, the level of clerical morals and education was raised, and the laity were given improved religious instruction and supervision.

This revised Christianity had a larger part in shaping the Europe which succeeded A.D. 1500 than it had the Europe of the preceding thousand years and modified that Europe very much more than it had the culture of the Roman Empire. The nominal Christianity which was the community faith of Western Europe was brought much closer to an approximation to the standards of Jesus than had been that of the rank and file of medieval Europeans. The masses were stirred as never before to make their professed faith their own and to seek to embody it. In spite of the rise of absolute states which seemed to be secularizing political life, from the Christian impulse came forces which made for the insistence that there is a body of law which kings must obey, which contributed to the rise of democratic ideals and institutions, and which helped to create the ideology which at the end of the eighteenth century moulded the French Revolution. The frequent and recurring wars of the period were a contradiction of much which Jesus had taught, but out of the Christian impulse issued the inspiration of the outstanding creators of an international law which sought to curb and regulate war and to place the relations between states on the basis of law. From Christianity came projects for world peace, as yet not implemented, and minority groups which declined to participate in any war. Christianity, too, contributed incentive to many who endeavoured to uproot·deep-seated social ills, to improve the lot of the prisoners and the poor, to free the captives of the Moorish pirate, and to minister to the sick. Out of Christianity sprang great music, painting, sculpture, and architecture. Christianity inspired and shaped some of the best known and most widely read literature of the time. From men moved by a Christian motive came most of the innovations in education and the majority of the new schools which gave intellectual training to the masses and to the aristocracy. In spite of the seeming secularization of thought, several of the most creative minds of the three centuries after A.D. 1500 were profoundly influenced by Christianity and to Christianity some of them owed the stimulus which lifted them out of mediocrity.

From the revived Christianity a missionary movement of unprecedented proportions carried the faith to every continent and to many of the islands of the sea. In this movement Roman Catholics were predominant. That was chiefly because the powers which led overseas discovery and conquest, Spain and Portugal, were of that branch of the Church, but it was also because Roman Catholics already had at hand tradition, experience, and machinery for the propagation of their type of Christianity. Protestants were more tardy in developing missions to non-Christians, but wherever they were in contact with pagans they undertook the task of conversion and with each century their enterprises were augmented. Russian Orthodox Christianity spread northward and eastward among the pagans in European Russia and across Siberia into Alaska.

Through this missionary enterprise the majority of the Indians of Mexico, Central America, and South America became professedly Christian, the Spanish and Portuguese settlers in the New World were given spiritual care, hundreds of Indians in Canada, the Mississippi Valley, and the English Thirteen Colonies were baptized, strong churches arose among the white populations of these Colonies, the French in Canada were kept loyal to their ancestral faith, many of the Negroes who were transplanted to the Americas were led to adopt the religion of their masters, here and there along the fringes of Negro Africa Christian communities were brought into existence, several hundreds of thousands in India became Christian, a large minority in Ceylon took the Christian name, small Christian groups arose in Burma and Siam and larger ones in Indo-China and the East Indies, the majority of the Filipinos were induced to come to the baptismal font, promising beginnings, checked by persecution, were made in Japan and Korea, and Christianity was reintroduced into China and Christian communities totalling perhaps two hundred thousand were there founded.

It must be recalled, however, that few of these Christian communities gathered from among non-European peoples displayed much initiative in propagating their faith and that almost none of them developed new types of Christianity. They tended to acquiesce passively in the religious changes which the aggressive white man wished them to adopt. Moreover, among the settlements formed by those of European stock, only in the English Thirteen Colonies in North America did the transplanted Christianity show enough vigor to assume new forms and to give birth spontaneously to fresh religious movements.

In the remarkable explorations and widespread conquests and settlements by Europeans, Christianity was the source of some of the impelling motives and in several instances, as in the Philippines and the initial colonies in New England and Pennsylvania, was the most potent of the incentives.

Because of the Christian conscience, legislation was enacted by Spain and Portugal and measures taken to enforce it to protect the Indians in the American possessions of these powers from the rapacity of unscrupulous whites and to make of European rule a blessing rather than a curse. Through that conscience some laws were put on the statute books in behalf of Negro slaves in the Americas and the beginnings were made of the movement which in the next century resulted in the termination of the African slave trade and the abolition of slavery. In the Americas missionaries induced thousands of Indians to begin a settled existence and introduced among them new fruits, grains, and domestic animals, and taught them better methods of agriculture and simple industries. The Christian impulse was prominent in the founding and maintenance of the large majority of the pre-nineteenth century schools in the New World, whether those were of elementary, secondary, or university grade, and whether they were for those of Indian or of European stock. In the Philippines the Christian missionary was the major agent in obtaining action against the selfish exploitation of the Filipinos, in leading the latter to partial conformity to European culture, and in introducing new methods of husbandry. In China the missionary was a pioneer in making known to the Chinese the science and art of Europe. He also facilitated the diplomatic relations between China and Occidental Powers.

We are not here attempting to give a moral evaluation to these fruits of the Christian impulse in modifying the effects of the expansion of Europe. We are simply attempting to point out how important they were.

In the three centuries between A.D. 1500 and A.D. 1800, Christianity had become more widespread and had moulded more extensively and deeply than ever before the collective life of mankind. In its first five centuries its greatest achievements had been the winning of the peoples of the Roman Empire to at least a formal acceptance of the Christian name, the creation of the Christian Church, the Christian ministry, Christian literature, and Christian theology, and some modifications, few of them extensive, of the non-religious phases of Græco-Roman culture. In the succeeding thousand years, while the majority of the population on the southern and eastern shores of the Mediterranean were lost to Islam, the peoples of Northern Europe were won and scattered Christian communities were established which at their widest extent (in the thirteenth and fourteenth centuries) had their western limit in Greenland and their eastern limit on the shores of the China Sea. In these same centuries Christianity proved more of a moulding influence in the culture which arose in Northern and Western Europe than it ever had been in that of the Roman Empire. After facing a serious combination of crises in the fourteenth and fifteenth centuries, now, in the sixteenth, seventeenth, and eighteenth centuries Christianity had experienced a series of awakenings and revivals of greater magnitude than it had yet known, had deepened its impression upon most phases of the culture of Western Europe, had accompanied the expansion of European peoples to the Americas, Asia, and Africa, and had profoundly modified the effects of that expansion.

In the closing half of the eighteenth century a fresh set of disasters overtook Christianity. Again, as between the fifth and eleventh centuries and in the fourteenth and fifteenth centuries, the future of Christianity seemed insecure. Again it looked as though Christianity were a waning influence, about to be ushered out of the affairs of men.

The threat came not partly from without and partly from within, as in the preceding ebb-tides of Christian influence. Now it was almost entirely from within the areas touched by Christianity. In some respects this seemed more serious than the earlier crisis, for it might mean that Christianity was succumbing not from superior external pressure, but from internal weaknesses which were indications of a basic incapacity permanently to grip and hold the hearts of men or of an inability so to mould society that the forces inimical to all that Jesus stood for would be prevented from obtaining the upper hand. Indeed, some of the movements which menaced Christianity were in part an outgrowth of Christianity itself. It looked as though Christianity were working its own destruction.

The threats were cumulative and reached their height in the closing years of the eighteenth century.

First of all, since the last decades of the sixteenth or the opening decades of the seventeenth century, the countries chiefly responsible for the expansion of Christianity in this period, Spain and Portugal, had been losing their vigour.

They continued to hold large portions of the earth's surface, but they were less and less competent to utilize them or to spread the Christian message and nourish the Christian communities within them. The increasing somnolence and stagnation affected the Church along with other phases of life in Spain and Portugal and the Spanish and Portuguese overseas possessions. They were at their worst in the latter half of the eighteenth century when the Iberian Peninsula fell victim to Napoleon's forces and was devastated by the wars which finally expelled the French.

In the second place, the organization which had had so large a part in the propagation of Christianity in the sixteenth, seventeenth, and eighteenth centuries, the Society of Jesus, was expelled from Portuguese, Spanish, and French territories, and then was dissolved by the Pope. Thus in a time of increasing difficulties Christianity was deprived of one of its most active missionary agencies.

A third adverse circumstance was a growing religious apathy and scepticism. In the eighteenth century the prevailing temper in intellectual circles was a rationalism which seemed to be antipathetic to Christianity. In part it was the product of the humanism and the intellectual self-respect which were to no slight degree the fruit of the Christianity of the Middle Ages. Yet, in the direction which it took in the eighteenth century, rationalism was antagonistic to Christianity. It held that truth is to be reached on man's initiative through the use of the human intellect, whereas Christianity declared that man's salvation from ignorance and sin was wrought by the divine initiative and by a revelation which was the act of God and not of man. With rationalism went a confidence in the native goodness and capacity of man and a belief that if only the shackles imposed by priests, rulers, and ignorance could be removed, by his own unaided efforts man would develop to perfection. This, too, was in part the fruit of the Christian teaching of the infinite possibilities within man, but it ignored or denied the Christian conviction that man can attain these possibilities only when, through the grace and act of God, he is freed from the fatal taint inherent in his nature which, unremoved, for ever nullifies his highest endeavours and drags him towards the mire. Sometimes the exponents of this rationalistic humanism openly attacked Christianity and the Church. At other times they poured ridicule on them. To a certain extent rationalism penetrated the leaders and membership of the churches and numbed conviction and cooled enthusiasm.

A fourth threat to Christianity came through the social and political upheavals which in the latter half of the eighteenth century and the first quarter of the nineteenth century either overturned or badly shook the existing order in

Europe and the overseas possessions of European powers. The Seven Years' War transferred Canada and part of the Mississippi Valley from France to England and thereby brought to an end French missions in this vast area and put French Roman Catholic communities on the defensive. The American Revolution wrought the separation of the Thirteen Colonies from the British Empire and during the quarter of a century of confusion which accompanied and followed the war religious life declined and the new fire which only a few years before had given such promise in the Great Awakening seemed quenched. The French Revolution upset not only France but most of Western Europe. Much of it was anti-clerical and even anti-Christian and from it the churches suffered severely. Both the American Revolution and the French Revolution were in part due to ideals which had Christianity as one of their chief sources. Yet one of the immediate results of both of them, and particularly of the more widespread of the two, the French Revolution, was reverses to Christianity. Out of the French Revolution came the Napoleonic Wars. These, combined with the French Revolution, wiped out or weakened much of the pre-nineteenth century social, economic, and political structure of Europe. Inevitably the religion and the churches which had been closely intertwined with that structure were injured. The Wars of Napoleon, too, brought transfers of territory and with them the interruption or termination of existing ecclesiastical conditions. Thus Ceylon passed to the British and by that cession Dutch Calvinism in the island was dealt a blow from which it never recovered. To a large extent as an outgrowth of the French Revolution and the Napoleonic Wars the vast regions held by Spain and Portugal on the mainland of the Americas broke away from the mother countries and in the upheaval most missions paused or ceased and in areas long professedly Christian the Church was badly weakened.

Added to these events in Europe and in overseas European possessions were severe and insistent persecutions of Christians in Eastern Asia. In Japan persecution had driven Christianity into hiding and had cut off communication between the Japanese Christians and their fellow-believers in the Occident. In Korea it was devastating the nascent Church. In China it was increasing and was slowly strangling the feeble Christian groups. To be sure, these attacks from outside Europe were not bringing losses anywhere nearly so huge as those of the earlier periods of major decline, but they were threatening to extinguish Christianity in some of the most populous sections of the globe.

These reverses, it will be noted, affected the Roman Catholic Church more than they did the Protestant communions, and it had been chiefly through the former, rather than the latter, that in the three centuries after A.D. 1500 Christianity had been spread among non-Christian peoples. It was, indeed, through Roman Catholicism that Christianity had had most of its expansion since at least the third century. The blow, then, to the spread of Christianity seemed peculiarly serious.

Yet, dark though the prospect for Christianity was at the close of the eighteenth century, it was not nearly so sombre as in the eighth, ninth, and tenth centuries or as in the fifteenth century. The ebb in the influence and apparent vitality of the faith was much less than at the preceding low-water marks. In contrast with the other two, almost no territory had been actually lost. Moreover, the sag that had followed the decline of Spain and Portugal and the apathy that had accompanied the eighteenth century rationalism had not brought nearly the moral corruption which had poisoned the internal life of the churches in the preceding two major periods of crisis. Then, too, much more than in the tenth century and even more than in the fifteenth century indications of rising tides of life within the churches were becoming apparent. These were especially marked in Protestantism. In the British Isles the Evangelical Awakening which had been begun by the Wesleys was continuing. In the very years when the French Revolution and the Napoleonic Wars were shaking Europe to its foundations new societies were coming into existence in Great Britain for the spread of the Christian Gospel throughout the earth. In the United States the period of the Napoleonic Wars saw the outbreak of a revival which was fully as extensive as the Great Awakening and witnessed the beginnings of American Protestant missions to peoples outside the Americas.

When Waterloo brought the Napoleonic Wars to their close and the Congress of Vienna fixed the new political map of Europe, the new tides of life swelled to a flood. Protestant Christianity became more vigorous than ever before. The Roman Catholic Church experienced an unprecedented revival. The expansion of Europe continued at a quickened pace and paralleling it, out of this aboundingly vital Protestantism and Roman Catholicism, Christianity spread more rapidly and over a wider area than ever before. Upon the culture of Occidental peoples Christianity continued to have a profound effect, in some phases more pronounced than at any previous time. Among non-Occidental peoples Christianity became more potent as a transformer and moulder of individuals, of groups, and of cultures than at any time in its history. Christianity entered upon the century of its greatest influence. To this story we must devote our next three volumes.

BIBLIOGRAPHY

THE bibliography of the present volume is on a different principle from those of the two preceding ones. In them every title was listed chapter by chapter and approximately in the order in which the first reference to a given title was made. In the current volume works are listed alphabetically according to authors. Only those works are included to which reference is made more than once in the footnotes. For those to which reference is made only once the needed bibliographical information of date, publisher, and length, is given with the reference. This procedure, it is hoped, will make for a somewhat briefer and more usable list of books.

Acosta, Joseph, *De Natura Novi Orbis Libri Duo et De Promulgatione Evangelii apud Barbaros, sive, de Procuranda Indorum Salute, Libri sex* (Coloniae Agrippinae in Officina Birckmannica Sumptibus Arnoldi Mylii, 1596, pp. 581).

Acta Sanctorum Quotquot toto orbe coluntur, vel a catholicis scriptoribus celebrantur, quae ex Latinis et Graecis, aliarumque gentium antiquis monumentis collegit, digessit, notis illustravit Joannes Bollandus Societatis Jesu Theologus, etc. (Brussels, 1863, Vols. 68—).

Adeney, Walter F., *The Greek and Eastern Churches* (New York, Charles Scribner's Sons, 1928. [Preface, 1908.] Pp. xiv, 634). Scholarly.

Alenconiensis, Eduardus, *Collegii S. Fidelis Pro Missionibus Ordinis Fratrum Minorum Capuccinorum Conspectus Historicus* (Rome, Apud Curiam Generalitam O. M. Cap., 1926, pp. xvi, 156).

Allen, W. O. B. and McClure, Edmund, *Two Hundred Years: The History of The Society for Promoting Christian Knowledge, 1698-1898* (London, Society for Promoting Christian Knowledge, 1898, pp. vi, 551). The standard history, based upon records, letter-books, reports, and minutes.

Allgemeine Missions-Zeitschrift (Berlin, 1874-1923). A standard Protestant periodical on missions, founded by Gustav Warneck.

Alzona, Encarnacion, *A History of Education in the Philippines 1565-1930* (Manila, University of the Philippines Press, 1932, pp. xi, 390). Fairly scholarly, based upon a variety of printed sources.

The American Historical Review (New York, The Macmillan Co., 1894 ff.). The official publication of the American Historical Association.

Anderson, James S. M., *The History of the Church of England in the Colonies and the Foreign Dependencies of the British Empire* (London, Rivington's, 2d edition, 1856, 3 vols.). Based partly on manuscript sources. By a clergyman of the Church of England.

André-Marie, *Missions Dominicaines dans l'Extrême Orient* (Paris, 2 vols., 1865).

Andrews, Charles M., *The Colonial Period of American History* (Yale University Press, 3 vols. [thus far], 1934-1937). By an eminent authority and careful scholar. Fully documented.

Anesaki, Masaharu, *A Concordance to the History of Kirishitan Missions (Catholic Missions in Japan in the Sixteenth and Seventeenth Centuries)* (Proceedings of the Imperial Academy, Tokyo, 1930, pp. 225).

Anesaki, Masaharu, *History of Japanese Religion with Special Reference to the Social and Moral Life of the Nation* (London, Kegan Paul, Trench, Trubner and Co., 1930, pp. xxii, 423). A work by a thoroughly competent and distinguished scholar in the field of religion. Himself a Buddhist, he is very fair to Christianity.

Arias, Evaristo Fernández, *El Beato Sanz y Compañeros Mártires del Orden de Predicatores* (Manila, 1893).

Arnold, T. W., *The Preaching of Islam. A History of the Propagation of the Muslim Faith* (New York, Charles Scribner's Sons, 1913, pp. xvi, 467). Scholarly, based on primary sources, sympathetic with Islam, having as one of its purposes the refutation of the popular belief that Islam was spread almost entirely by force.

Arnold, W. E., *A History of Methodism in Kentucky* (Vol. I, From 1782 to 1820, Vol. II, 1820-1846. Louisville, Herald Press, 1935, 1936). Based upon extensive research, by a Methodist clergyman.

Attwater, Donald. *The Catholic Eastern Churches* (Milwaukee, Wis., The Bruce Publishing Co., 1935, pp. xx, 308). By a Roman Catholic. Contains excellent bibliographies.

Aurelius, *De Kapucijnen en de Missie* (Brasschaat, A de Bièvre [1927?], pp. 151). By a Capuchin.

Bancroft, Hubert Howe, *History of Alaska, 1730-1885* (San Francisco, A. L. Bancroft and Co., 1886, pp. xxxviii, 775). Well documented. Most of the histories of Hubert Howe Bancroft are said to have been largely written by one or more members of the staff which he assembled. He himself planned the enterprise and financed it and wrote widely scattered portions of the histories. See *The Dictionary of American Biography*, Vol. I, pp. 570, 571, with the bibliography on p. 571. They are all valuable for their extensive use of the sources.

Bancroft, Hubert Howe, *California Pastoral, 1769-1848* (San Francisco, The History Co., 1888, pp. vi, 808).

Bancroft, Hubert Howe, *History of Arizona and New Mexico, 1530-1888* (San Francisco, The History Co., 1889, pp. xxxviii, 829).

Bancroft, Hubert Howe, *History of Central America* (San Francisco, A. L. Bancroft and Co., 3 vols., 1882-1887).

Bancroft, Hubert Howe, *History of Mexico* (San Francisco, A. L. Bancroft and Co., 6 vols., 1883-1888).

Bancroft, Hubert Howe, *North Mexican States*, Vol. I, 1531-1800 (San Francisco, A. L. Bancroft and Co., 1883, pp. xlviii, 751).

Banks, Charles Edward, *The History of Martha's Vineyard, Dukes County, Massachusetts* (Boston, George H. Dean, 3 vols., 1911-1925). Based upon extensive research.

Baron, Salo Wittmayer, *A Social and Religious History of the Jews* (New York, Columbia University Press, 3 vols., 1937). Objective, scholarly.

Bebb, E. D., *Nonconformity and Social and Economic Life 1660-1800. Some Problems of the Present as They Appeared in the Past* (London, The Epworth Press, 1935, pp. 198). Carefully done.

Bechler, Theodor, *August Gottlieb Spangenberg und die Mission* (Herrnhut, Missionsbuchhandlung, 1933, pp. 138).

Becker, Carl L., *The Heavenly City of the Eighteenth-Century Philosophers* (Yale University Press, 1932, pp. 168). Semi-popular lectures by a thoughtful and original historian.

Bennett, Wendell C., and Zingg, Robert M., *The Tarahumara. An Indian Tribe of Northern Mexico* (The University of Chicago Press, 1935, pp. xix, 412). An objective study of contemporary culture based upon residence and careful investigation.

Berg, Ludwig, *Die katholischen Heidenmission als Kulturträger* (Second edition, Aachen, Aachener Missionsdruckerei, 3 vols., 1927). Carefully supported by references to authorities, which as a rule are standard German experts and missionary periodicals. Warmly pro-Catholic and critical of Protestants.

Bernard, Henri, *Aux Portes de la Chine. Les Missionaires du Seizième Siècle 1514-1588* (Tientsin, Procure de la Mission de Sienhsien, 1933, pp. xxvii, 283). Well documented.

Bernstein, A., *Some Jewish Witnesses for Christ* (London, Cooperative Jewish Converts' Institution, 1909, pp. 535). Pro-Christian, pro-Protestant, with few precise references to sources.

Bertrand, J., *La Mission du Maduré d'apres des Documents Inédits* (Paris, Librairie de Poussielgue-Rusand, 4 vols., 1847-1854). Made up largely of documents.

Bibliotheca Asiatica. Part II. The Catholic Missions in India, China, Japan, Siam, and the Far East, in a Series of Autograph Letters of the Seventeenth Century (London, Maggs Brothers, 1924). A catalogue giving translations of many of the letters.

Biermann, Benno M., *Die Anfänge der neueren Dominikanermission in China* (Münster i. W., Verlag der Aschendorffschen Verlagsbuchhandlung, 1927, pp. xxii, 236).

Bishop, Morris, *The Odyssey of Cabezo de Vaca* (New York, The Century Co., 1933, pp. vii, 306). A well written, scholarly account.

Bittinger, Lucy Forney, *The Germans in Colonial Times* (Philadelphia, J. B. Lippincott Co., 1901, pp. 314). Contains an excellent bibliography.

Blair, Emma Helen, and Robertson, James Alexander, *The Philippine Islands 1493-1803. Explorations of Early Navigators, Descriptions of the Islands and their Peoples, their History and Records of the Catholic Missions, as Related in Contemporaneous Books and Manuscripts, Showing the Political, Economic, Commercial and Religious Conditions of those Islands from their Earliest Relations with European Nations to the Beginning of the Nineteenth Century* (Cleveland, The Arthur H. Clark Co., 55 vols., 1903-1907). A standard collection.

Blanco, Matiás Ruiz, *Conversión en Pirítú (Colombia) de Indios Cumanagotos y Palenques* (Madrid, Librería de Victoriano Suarez, 1892, pp. xiii, 228). By a Franciscan who was for several years a missionary in the region. In Vol. 7 of *Colección de Libros Raros ó Curiosos que Tratan de América*.

van Boetzelaer van Dubbeldam, Carel Wessel Theodorus, *De Gereformeerde Kerken in Nederland en de Zending in Oost-Indië in de dagen der Oost-Indische Compagnié* (Utrecht, P. Den Boer, 1906, pp. viii, 358). The doctoral dissertation of a distinguished expert on missions.

Bolton, Herbert Eugene, *Kino's Historical Memoir of Pimería Alta . . . 1683-1711* (Cleveland, The Arthur H. Clark Co., 2 vols., 1919). By an outstanding scholar.

Bolton, Herbert Eugene, *Rim of Christendom. A Biography of Eusebio Francisco Kino, Pacific Coast Pioneer* (New York, The Macmillan Co., 1936, pp. xiv, 644). Well written, based upon extensive research.

Bolton, Herbert Eugene, *Spanish Exploration in the Southwest, 1542-1706* (New York, Charles Scribner's Sons, 1916, pp. xii, 487). Translations of original narratives, with notes.

Bolton, Herbert Eugene, *Texas in the Middle Eighteenth Century. Studies in Spanish Colonial History and Administration* (Berkeley, University of California Press, 1915, pp. x, 501). Based upon original manuscript sources and extensive research and travel, by a well-known specialist.

Bourne, Edward Gaylord, *Spain in America, 1450-1580* (New York, Harper & Brothers, 1906, pp. xx, 350). Scholarly, critical, well written.

Brace, C. Loring, *Gesta Christi: or a History of Humane Progress under Christianity* (London, Hodder and Stoughton, 1889, pp. xxiii, 520. The first edition was in 1882). Well written; taking a frankly pro-Christian position; based largely on the sources; not always critical in scrutinizing its data.

Braden, Charles S., *Religious Aspects of the Conquest of Mexico* (Durham, N. C., Duke University Press, 1930, pp. xi, 344). Well documented, in large part from first-hand sources, but only those in print. By a Protestant, written with historical fairness and appreciation of the work of Roman Catholics.

Bradford's History of Plymouth Plantation 1606-1646, William T. Davis, editor (New York, Charles Scribner's Sons, 1908, pp. xv, 437).

Braga, Erasmo, and Grubb, Kenneth G., *The Republic of Brazil. A Survey of the Religious Situation* (London and New York, World Dominion Press, 1932, pp. 184). Braga was Executive Secretary of the Committee on Co-operation in Brazil and probably at the time of his death the leading Protestant in the country. Grubb spent a good deal of time there to collect information.

Brasseur de Bourbourg, *Histoire du Canada de son Église et de ses Missions* (Paris, Sagnier et Bray, 2 vols., 1852). By a Vicar-General of Boston, formerly Professor of Ecclesiastical History at the Seminary of Quebec.

Bremond, Henri, *A Literary History of Religious Thought in France from the Wars of Religion down to Our Own Times,* translated by K. L. Montgomery (London, Society for Promoting Christian Knowledge, 2 vols., 1928). Scholarly, in a delightful style, from a warmly pro-Roman Catholic viewpoint.

Brion, Marcel, *Bartholomé de las Casas, "Father of the Indians,"* translated from the French by Coley B. Taylor. With an Introduction by Ernesto Montenegro (New York, E. P. Dutton and Co., 1929, pp. xvii, 314). A popularly written account, favourable to Las Casas, based partly upon Las Casas's writings.

Brodrick, J., *The Economic Morals of the Jesuits: An Answer to Dr. H. M. Robertson* (Oxford University Press, 1934, pp. 158).

Brookes, George S., *Friend Anthony Benezet* (Philadelphia, University of Pennsylvania Press, 1937, pp. 516). Sympathetic, based upon exhaustive research.

Brou, A., *Saint François Xavier* (Paris, Gabriel Beauchesne et Cie., 2 vols., 1912). Sympathetic.

Brown, William, *History of the Propagation of Christianity among the Heathen since the Reformation* (William Blackwood and Sons, 3d ed., 3 vols., 1854). Based upon the sources.

Bruford, W. H., *Germany in the Eighteenth Century: The Social Background of the Literary Revival* (Cambridge University Press, 1935, pp. x, 354). Scholarly and well written.

Brumbaugh, Martin Grove, *A History of the German Baptist Brethren in Europe and America* (Mount Morris, Ill., Brethren Publishing House, 1899, pp. xxii, 559). Largely on the colonial period. Based upon extensive research.

Bury, J. B., *The Idea of Progress: An Inquiry into its Origin and Growth* (London, Macmillan and Co., 1920, pp. xv, 377).

De Bussierre, Le Vicomte M.—Th., *Histoire du Schisme Portugais dans les Indes* (Paris, Jacques Lecoffre, 1854, pp. 363). An anti-Portuguese treatise. Several pertinent documents are included, some in French translation only and some in the original as well.

Byington, Ezra Hoyt, *The Puritan as a Colonist and Reformer* (Boston, Little, Brown and Co., 1899, pp. xxvi, 375). Semi-popular in method and purpose.

Calder, Isabel MacBeath, *The New Haven Colony* (Yale University Press, 1934, pp. vi, 301). Based upon extensive and careful research.

Camargo, G. Baez, and Grubb, Kenneth G., *Religion in the Republic of Mexico* (London, World Dominion Press, 1935, pp. 166). Pro-Protestant.

Capuchins Missionaires. Missions Françaises. Notes Historiques et Statistiques (Paris, Société et Librairie Coopératives St. François, 1926, pp. iv, 86). No author given. A popular summary.

Cary, Otis, *A History of Christianity in Japan* (New York, Fleming H. Revell Co., 2 vols., 1909). The standard account in English, especially of Protestant missions. The first volume deals with Roman Catholic and Greek Orthodox missions, and the second with Protestant missions. The work contains much excellent information, but is not always critical and is defective in the scantiness of its bibliography and of references in footnotes to the sources of its information. The author is a Protestant, but his attitude towards non-Protestant missions is irenic. He was long a missionary in Japan.

Catalogus Patrum ac Fratrum e Societate Jesu qui a Morte S. Fr. Xaverii ad annum MDCCCLXXII Evangelio Christi Propagando in Sinis Adlaboraverunt (Shanghai, Pars Prima, 1873).

The Catholic Encyclopedia (New York, 16 vols., 1907-1913). Written for informative and apologetic purposes.

Catholic Negombo. A Brief Sketch of the History of the Catholic Church in Negombo under the Portuguese and the Dutch (Colombo, The "Catholic Messenger" Press, 1924, pp. 33). A popular account based on good authorities.

Caulin, Antonio, *Historia Coro-Graphica Natural y Evangelica de la Nueva Andalucia Provincias de Cumaná, Guayana y Vertientes del Río Orinoco* (1779, pp. 482). By an Observant Franciscan, a missionary.

Cesinale, Rocco da, *Storia delle Missioni dei Cappuccini* (Paris, P. Lethielleux, 1867, Rome, Tipografia Barbèra, 1872, 1873, 3 vols.). Verbose, laudatory, confined largely to the period before 1700, based upon extensive research in the printed and manuscript sources. A standard work.

Charlevoix, P. de, *Histoire du Christianisme au Japon* (new edition, Liege, H. Dessain, 2 vols., 1855). By a Jesuit.

Chase, Stuart, in collaboration with Marian Tyler, *Mexico, A Study of Two Americas* (New York, The Macmillan Co., 1931, pp. vii, 338). The authors were in Mexico about five months and have based their book partly upon their observations there and partly upon about thirty books and a few magazine articles.

Chatterton, Eyre, *A History of the Church of England in India since the Early Days of the East India Company* (London, Society for Promoting Christian Knowledge, 1924, pp. xxiv, 353). Based upon the sources.

Chinard, Gilbert, *Les Réfugiés Huguenots en Amérique* (Paris, Société d'Édition "Les Belles-Lettres," 1925, pp. xxxvii, 245). Contains an extensive bibliography.

The Chinese Recorder, published at Foochow, 1867, as *The Missionary Recorder,* at Foochow, 1868-1872, as *The Chinese Recorder and Missionary Journal,* and at Shanghai, 1874, et seq. Beginning about 1911 the name was shortened to *The Chinese Recorder.*

The Chinese Social and Political Science Review (Peking, The Chinese Social and Political Science Association, 1917 ff.).

The Christian Century (Chicago, 1894 ff.).

Church History (Published by the American Society of Church History, Chicago, 1932 ff.).

Da Civezza, Marcellino, *Storia Universale delle Missioni Francescane* (Vols. I-V, Rome, Tipografia Tiberina, 1857-1861; Vol. VI, Prato, Tipografia di R. Quasti, 1881-1883; Vol. VII, Parts 1 and 2, Prato, Tipografia Giachetti Figlio e C., 1891; Vol. VII, Parts 3 and 4, Vols. VIII-XI, Florence, Tipografia di Ariani, 1894, 1895). A monumental work, emphasizing the romantic, adventurous side of the story, somewhat diffuse and not always critical. It brings the history down to about the end of the eighteenth century.

de Civezza, Marcellin, *Histoire Universelle des Missions Franciscaines. Ouvrage traduit de l'Italien et disposé sur un plan nouveau par le P. Victor-Bernardin de Rouen, O. F. M.* (*Tome II, Asie,* Paris, 1898).

Clavigero, Francisco Javier, *The History of [Lower] California translated from the Italian and edited by Sara E. Lake and A.A. Gray* (Stanford University Press, pp. xxvii, 413). By a Mexican Jesuit of the eighteenth century.

Clemen, Carl, *Der Einfluss des Christentums auf andere Religionen* (Leipzig, A. Deichertsche Verlagsbuchhandlung D. Werner Schall, 1933, pp. 122). A brief treatment of a large subject, well documented, by a professor at the University of Bonn.

Coke, Thomas, *A History of the West Indies, Containing the Natural, Civil, and Ecclesiastical History of each Island: with an Account of the Missions Instituted on those Islands from the Commencement of their Civilization; but more especially of the Missions which have been established in that Archipelago by the Society Late in Connexion with the Rev. John Wesley* (Liverpool, Nuttall, Fisler and Dixon, 3 vols., 1808). By the first organizer of Methodist missions in the West Indies.

Colección de Documentos Inéditos Relativos al Descubrimiento, Conquista y Organización de las Antiguas Posesiones Españolas de América y Oceanía Sacados de los Archivos del Reino y muy Especialmente del de Indias (Madrid, 1864 ff.).

Coleridge, Henry James, *The Life and Letters of St. Francis Xavier* (London, Burns and Oates, 2 vols., 1872). By a Jesuit.

Collectanea S. Congregationis de Propaganda Fide seu Decreta Instructiones Rescripta pro Apostolicis Missionibus (Rome, 2 vols., 1907).

Columbus, Christopher, *Journal of First Voyage to America with an Introduction by Van Wyck Brooks* (New York, Albert and Charles Boni, 1924, pp. viii, 251). From the abstract by Las Casas.

le Comte, Louis, *Des Cérémonies de la Chine* (Liege, 1700).

le Comte, Louis, *Nouveaux Mémoires sur l'État Present de la Chine* (Amsterdam, 2 vols., 1697). Made up of letters of the author, a Jesuit, from China.

Conybeare, Frederick C., *Russian Dissenters* (*Harvard Theological Studies, X.* Harvard University Press, 1921, pp. x, 370). Based upon standard Russian secondary accounts, not on the sources. Somewhat biased in favour of the dissenters.

Corwin, Edward Tanjore, *A Manual of the Reformed Church in America* (New York, Board of Publication of the Reformed Church in America, 1902, pp. viii, 1082).

Coste, Pierre, *La Congrégation de la Mission Dite de Saint-Lazare* (Paris, Librairie Lecoffre, J. Gabalda et Fils, 1927, pp. viii, 231). By a Lazarist, based upon standard authorities.

Coste, Pierre, *The Life and Works of Saint Vincent de Paul. Translated from the French by Joseph Leonard* (London, Burns, Oates and Washbourne, 1934, 1935). A standard work.

Couling, Samuel, *The Encyclopædia Sinica* (Oxford University Press, 1917, pp. viii, 633). Carefully done, but with the short-comings of a pioneer work.

Crantz, David, *The History of Greenland* (London, The Brethren's Society for the Furtherance of the Gospel among the Heathen, 2 vols., 1767).

Crétineau-Joly, J., *Histoire, Religieuse, Politique et Littéraire de la Compagnie de Jésus. Composée sur les Documents Inédits et Authentiques* (Third edition, Paris, Jacques Lecoffre et Cie, 6 vols., 1859). Well written; not always critical; some documents given, at least in part; laudatory of the Jesuits.

Cuevas, Mariano, *Historia de la Iglesia en Mexico* (Vol. I, Tlalpam, D. F. [Mexico], Imprenta del Asilo "Patricio Sanz," 1921).

Cunningham, W., *Christianity and Economic Science* (New York, Longmans, Green and Co., 1914, pp. viii, 111). A careful and stimulating essay.

Dahmen, Peter, *Robert de Nobili, S. J. Ein Beitrag zur Geschichte der Missionsmethode und der Indologie* (Münster i.w., Verlag der Aschendorffschen Verlagsbuchhandlung, 1924, pp. xii, 82).

Dahmen, Pierre, *Robert de Nobili, l'Apôtre des Brahmes, Première Apologie, 1610. Texte inédit latin traduit et annoté par le P. Pierre Dahmen, S. J. de la Mission du Maduré. Bibliothèque des Missions Mémoires et Documents,* Volume III (Paris, Editions Spes, 1931, pp. 205). By an earnest defender of Nobili.

Dawson, Christopher, *Progress and Religion: An Historical Enquiry* (London, Longmans, Green and Co., 1929, pp. xvii, 254).

Delanglez, Jean, *The French Jesuits in Lower Louisiana (1700-1763)* (Washington, D. C., The Catholic University of America, 1935, pp. xxvi, 547). A doctoral dissertation, by a Jesuit.

Delany, Francis X., *A History of the Catholic Church in Jamaica, B. W. I., 1494 to 1929* (New York, Jesuit Mission Press, 1930, pp. xi, 292). By a Jesuit. Chiefly a collection of documents and notes.

Delplace, L., *Le Catholicisme au Japon* (Brussells, Albert Dewit, 2 vols., 1909, 1910). By a Jesuit.

Demimuid, M., *Vie du Bienheureux François-Régis Clet. Prêtre de la Congregation de la Mission Martyrisé en Chine le 18 Février, 1820* (Paris, 1900).

Descamps, Baron, *Histoire Générale Comparée des Missions* (Paris, Librairie Plon, 1932, pp. viii, 760). Seven other writers have contributed. A standard survey by Roman Catholic scholars, of Catholic mission history from the beginning, together with chapters on the spread of Protestantism and of some other religions.

De Schweinitz, Edmund, *The Life and Times of David Zeisberger* (Philadelphia, J. B. Lippincott and Co., 1871, pp. 747).

Diaz del Castillo, Bernal, *Historia Verdadera de la Conquista de la Nueva España* (Paris, Librería de Rosa, 4 vols., 1837).

Dictionary of American Biography (New York, Charles Scribner's Sons, 21 vols., 1928-1937).

Los Dominicos en el Extremo Oriente. Provincia del Santísimo Rosario de Filipinas. Relaciones publicadas con motivo del Séptimo Centenario de la Confirmación de la Sagrada Orden de Predicadores (no date or place of publication. Pp. 391. Date c. 1916). Done by a commission; no names of authors given.

Douglass, H. Paul, *Church Unity Movements in the United States* (New York, Institute of Social and Religious Research, 1934, pp. xxxviii, 576). Shares the scholarly, objective qualities of the work of this Institute.

Drummond, Andrew Landale, *The Church Architecture of Protestantism: An Historical and Constructive Study* (Edinburgh, T. and T. Clark, 1934, pp. xviii, 342).

Dubbs, Joseph Henry, *History of the Reformed Church, German* in *The American Church History Series,* Vol. VIII (New York, The Christian Literature Society, 1895), pp. 213-423.

Dubnow, S. M., *History of the Jews in Russia and Poland from the Earliest Times until the Present Day.* Translated from the Russian by I. Friedländer (Philadelphia, The Jewish Publication Society of America, 3 vols., 1916-1920). By a Jewish author.

Du Plessis, J., *A History of Christian Missions in South Africa* (London, Longmans, Green and Co., 1911, pp. xx, 494). A standard work, by a South African scholar.

Du Plessis, J., *The Life of Andrew Murray of South Africa* (London, Marshall Brothers, 1919, pp. xvi, 553). Not only the standard biography, but also virtually a history of the Dutch Reformed Church in South Africa in the nineteenth and the early part of the twentieth century.

Ecclesiastical Records State of New York (Albany, James B. Lyon, State Printer, and University of the State of New York, 7 vols., 1901-1916).

Eck, Alexandre, *Le Moyen Age Russe* (Paris, Maison du Livre Etranger, 1933, pp. xiv, 570).

Eckhardt, Carl Conrad, *The Papacy and World-Affairs as Reflected in the Secularization of Politics* (University of Chicago Press, 1937, pp. xiv, 310).

Edwards, Maldwyn, *John Wesley and the Eighteenth Century: A Study of His Social and Political Influence* (Cincinnati, The Abingdon Press, 1933, pp. 220).

Elsner, Salesius, *Die deutschen Franziskaner in Brasilien* (Trier, Paulinus-Druckerei, 1912, pp. 136). Chiefly on the nineteenth and twentieth centuries.

The Encyclopædia Britannica (London, The Encyclopædia Britannica, 14th ed., 24 vols., 1929).

Engelhardt, Zephyrin, *The Missions and Missionaries of California* (Santa Barbara, Mission Santa Barbara, 2d ed., 2 vols., 1929, 1930). By a Franciscan, pro-missionary; expressing positive views on controversial subjects; based upon extensive and careful research.

Ettinger, Amos Aschbach, *James Edward Oglethorpe, Imperial Idealist* (Oxford, The Clarendon Press, 1936, pp. xi, 348). A careful piece of work, based upon extensive research.

Faust, Albert Bernhardt, *The German Element in the United States with Special Reference to its Political, Moral, Social, and Educational Influence* (New York, The Steuben Society of America, 2 vols., 1927, copyrighted 1909). A standard work.

Fenger, H. M., *Bidrag til Hans Egedes og den Grønlanddske Missions Historie 1721-1760* (Copenhagen, G. E. C. Gad, 1879, pp. xv, 348). Carefully done, from printed and unprinted sources.

Fenger, J. Ferd., *Den Trankebarske Missions Historie* (Copenhagen, C. A. Reitzel, 1843, pp. 371). An English translation has been published (Tranquebar, Evangelical Lutheran Mission Press, 1863, pp. iv, 324).

Ferro, Bartolomeo, *Istoria delle Missioni de' Chierici Regolari, Teatini con la descrizione de' Regni, Provincie, Città, Luoghi, Fede, Riti, e Costumi delle Genti, ove andarono, e passarono li Missionarii, con li viaggi pericolosi, fatiche fattevi, e frutto raccoltovi per la Cattolica Religione* (Rome, Gio. Francesco Buagni, 2 vols., 1704). Very verbose and detailed and concerned chiefly with the missions to Georgia (in the Caucasus) and India.

Fides News Service (Rome, c. 1926 ff.). A mimeographed set of news release notes on current happenings in Roman Catholic missions. Compiled in close co-operation with the Association for the Propagation of the Faith.

Figgis, John Neville, *Studies of Political Thought from Gerson to Grotius 1414-1625* (Cambridge University Press, 2d ed., 1931, pp. vii, 224).

Figueroa, Francisco de, *Relación de las Misiones de la Compañia de Jésus en el Pais de los Maynas* (Madrid, Librería General de Victoriano Suaréz, 1904, pp. xv, 420 [original date 1661]). In *Colección de Libros y Documentos Referentes á la Historia de América,* Vol. I.

de Filippi, Filippo (editor), *An Account of Tibet. The Travels of Ippolito Desideri of Pistoia, S. J., 1712-1727.* Introduction by S. Wessels, S. J. (London, George Routledge and Sons, 1932, pp. xviii, 475).

Findlay, G. G., and Holdsworth, W. W., *The History of the Wesleyan Methodist Missionary Society* (London, The Epworth Press, 5 vols., 1921-1924). An official history, based largely upon the manuscript records of the society.

Fortescue, Adrian, *The Orthodox Eastern Church* (London, Catholic Truth Society, 1929, pp. xxxiii, 451). By a Roman Catholic, based upon wide reading. Has good bibliographies.

Fortescue, Adrian, *The Uniate Eastern Churches. The Byzantine Rite in Italy, Sicily, Syria, and Egypt* (London, Burns, Oates and Washbourne, 1923, pp. xiii, 244). A posthumous work, by a Roman Catholic.

Fosdick, Lucian J., *The French Blood in America* (New York, Fleming H. Revell Co., 1906, pp. 448). Popular in style, with admiration for the Huguenots.

Fox, George, *The Journal of George Fox* (Everyman's Library edition. New York, E. P. Dutton and Co., 1924, pp. xxii, 359). The tercentenary text, by Norman Penney, with numerous excisions from the Ellwood text.

Frere, W. H., *Some Links in the Chain of Russian Church History* (London, Faith Press, 1918, pp. xvii, 200). Scholarly, based upon extensive reading, well written, sympathetic.

Froylán de Rionegro, *Relaciones de las Misiones de los PP. Capuchinos en las Antiguas Provincias Españolas hoy Republica de Venezuela 1650-1817* (Seville, La Exposición, 2 vols., 1918). Unpublished documents of the seventeenth and eighteenth centuries.

Gairdner, James, *Lollardy and the Reformation in England. An Historical Survey* (London, Macmillan and Co. Ltd., 3 vols., 1908-1911). A standard work.

Gallo, Luigi, *Storia del Christianesimo nell' Impero Barmano Preceduta dalle Notizie del Paese* (Milan, Boniardi-Pogliani di Ermen, 3 vols., 1862).

García, Genaro, *Documentos Inéditos ó muy Raros Para la Historia de México* (Mexico, 36 vols., 1905 ff.).

Gewehr, Wesley M., *The Great Awakening in Virginia, 1740-1790* (Durham, N. C., Duke University Press, 1930, pp. viii, 292). Scholarly, fully documented. See review, very favourable, by W. W. Sweet, in *American Historical Review,* July, 1930 (Vol. XXXV), pp. 887, 888.

Gledstone, James Paterson, *The Life and Travels of George Whitefield* (London, Longmans, Green and Co., 1871, pp. lx, 533).

Godwyn, Morgan, *The Negro's and Indian's Advocate, Suing for their Admission into the Church, or a Persuasive to the Instructing and Baptizing of the Negroes and Indians in our Plantations. Shewing, that as the Compliance therewith can prejudice no man's just interest, so the wilful Neglecting and Opposing of it, is no less than a manifest Apostacy from the Christian Faith. To which is added, A brief Account of Religion in Virginia* (London, printed for the author, 1680, pp. 174).

Gonzalez Davila, Gil, *Teatro Eclesiastico de la Primitiva Iglesia de las Indias Occidentales Vidas de svs Arzobispos, Obispos, y Cosas Memorables de svs Sedes* (Madrid, Diego Diaz de la Carrera, 2 vols., 1649, 1655).

Gooch, G. P., *English Democratic Ideas in the Seventeenth Century. Second Edition, with Supplementary Notes and Appendices by Professor H. J. Laski* (Cambridge University Press, 1927, pp. x, 315).

Goodman, Fred S., *Glimpses of the Story of the Waldensians* (New York, The American Waldensian Society, 1928, pp. 20). A popular pamphlet.

Goodwin, Edward Lewis, *The Colonial Church in Virginia with Biographical Sketches of the First Six Bishops of the Diocese of Virginia and Other Historical Papers together with Brief Biographical Sketches of the Colonial Clergy of Virginia* (Milwaukee, Morehouse Publishing Co., 1927, pp. xxiv, 342). A posthumous work by the historiographer of the (Episcopal) Diocese of Virginia, completed by his daughter.

Graham, Henry Grey, *The Social Life of Scotland in the Eighteenth Century* (London, A. and C. Black, 1937, pp. xi, 545). Well documented; full of detailed information.

Griffin, Joseph A., *The Contribution of Belgium to the Catholic Church in America (1523-1857)* (Washington, D. C., The Catholic University of America, 1932, pp. xvi, 234).

Griffini, Michelangelo, *Della Vita di Monsignor Gio: Maria Percoto della Congregazione di S. Paolo Missionario ne' Regni di Ava e di Pegu' Vicario Apostolico e Vescovo Massulense* (Udine, Fratelli Gallici, 1781, pp. x, 220). By a Barnabite.

Grössel, Wolfgang, *Die Mission und die evangelische Kirche im 17 Jahrhundert* (Gotha, Friedrich Andreas Perthes, 1897, pp. x, 235).

Guilday, Peter, editor, *The Catholic Church in Contemporary Europe, 1919-1931. Papers of the American Catholic Historical Association*, Vol. II (New York, P. J. Kenedy and Sons, 1932, pp. xiv, 354).

Haas, Hans, *Geschichte des Christentums in Japan* (Tokyo, 2 vols., 1902-1904). Carefully done, but carries the story down only to 1570.

Hallendorff, Carl, and Schück, Adolf, *History of Sweden* (London, Cassell and Co., 1929, pp. xxiv, 446). By two eminent Swedish historians; translated from the Swedish by Mrs. Lajla Yapp.

Hamilton, J. Taylor, *A History of the Unitas Fratrum, or Moravian Church, in the United States of America. The American Church History Series*, Vol. VIII (New York, The Christian Literature Society, 1895, pp. 425-508).

Hare, Lloyd C., *Thomas Mayhew, Patriarch to the Indians (1593-1682)* (New York, D. Appleton and Co., 1932, pp. xii, 231). Based upon careful research.

Harvard Journal of Asiatic Studies (Cambridge, Mass., Harvard-Yenching Institute, 1936 ff.).

The Harvard Theological Review (issued quarterly by the Faculty of Theology in Harvard University, Cambridge, Mass., Harvard University Press, 1908 ff.).

Hasluck, F. W., edited by Hasluck, Margaret M., *Christianity and Islam under the Sultans* (Oxford, Clarendon Press, 2 vols., 1929). Well documented.

Hawks, Francis L., *Contributions to the Ecclesiastical History of the United States of America* (New York, Harper & Brothers, Vol. I, 1836, pp. 286, 332). This volume is entitled *A Narrative of Events Connected with the Rise and Progress of the Protestant Episcopal Church in Virginia.*

Hazard, Ebenezer, *Historical Collections, Consisting of State Papers, and other authentic documents, intending for materials for an History of the United States of America* (Philadelphia, T. Dobson, 2 vols., 1792, 1794).

Heimbucher, Max, *Die Orden und Kongregationen der katholischen Kirche* (Paderborn, Ferdinand Schöningh, 2d ed., 3 vols., 1907, 1908). Well documented, with excellent selected bibliographies.

Henrion, le Baron, *Histoire Générale des Missions Catholiques depuis le XIII siècle jusqu'a nos jours* (Paris, Gaume Frères, 2 vols., 1846, 1847). Laudatory, not always critical.

Heusinger, Edward W., *Early Explorations and Mission Establishments in Texas* (San Antonio, Texas, The Naylor Co., 1936, pp. xvi, 222). Based upon careful research.

Hirst, Margaret E., *The Quakers in Peace and War: An Account of Their Peace Principles and Practice* (London, The Swarthmore House, pp. 560). Well documented.

History-Album of St. Joseph's Apostolic Central-Seminary Verapoly—Puthenpally—Alwaye South India (1932, pp. 72).

Hoffmann, Karl, *Ursprung und Anfangstätigkeit des ersten päpstlichen Missionsinstituts: ein Beitrag zur Geschichte der katholischen Juden und Mohammedanermission im sechzehnten Jahrhundert* (Münster in W., Verlag der Aschendorffschen Verlagsbuchhandlung, 1923, pp. xi, 234). Well documented.

Hole, Charles, *The Early History of the Church Missionary Society for Africa and the East to the end of* A.D. *1814* (London, Church Missionary Society, 1896, pp. xxxviii, 677).

Hu Shih, *The Chinese Renaissance.* The Haskell Lectures, 1933 (Chicago, The University of Chicago Press, 1934, pp. viii, 110).

Huc, Évariste Régis, *Le Christianisme en Chine, en Tartarie et au Thibet* (Paris, 4 vols., 1857, 1858. The first three volumes are translated into English (London, Longman, Brown, Green, Longmans, and Roberts, 1857, 1858).

Hull, Ernest R., *Bombay Mission-History with a Special Study of the Padroado Question* (Bombay, Examiner Press. No date. Vol. I, 1534-1858, pp. vii, 493, x; Vol. II, 1858-1929, pp. xiv, 521). By a Jesuit, with the express purpose of objectivity on the padroado question, and incorporating many documents, given in English translation.

Hull, William I., *William Penn and the Dutch Quaker Migration to Pennsylvania* (Swarthmore College Monographs of Quaker History, No. 2, 1935, pp. xiii, 445). Based largely upon manuscript sources.

Humbert, Jules, *Les Origines Vénézuéliennes. Essai sur la Colonization Espagnole au Vénézuéla* (Bordeaux, Feret et Fils, 1905, pp. xx, 340). A doctoral dissertation.

Humboldt, Alexander de, *Personal Narrative of Travels to the Equinoctial Regions of the New Continent during the Years 1799-1804.* Translated into English by

Helen Maria Williams (London, Longman, Rees, Orme, Brown and Quen, 1822-1829).

Humphreys, David, *Historical Account of the Incorporated Society for the Propagation of the Gospel in Foreign Parts. Containing their Foundation, Proceedings, and the Success of their Missionaries in the British Colonies, to the Year 1728* (London, Joseph Downing, 1730, pp. xxxi, 356). By the secretary of the Society.

Huonder, Anton, *Der einheimische Klerus in den Heidenländern* (Freiburg im Breisgau, Herdersche Verlagshandlung, 1909, pp. x, 312). Based upon fairly wide reading.

Huonder, Anton, *Der hl. Ignatius von Loyola und der Missionsberuf der Gesellschaft Jesu. Zum 300 jährigen Gedächtnis seiner Heiligsprechung* (Aachen, Xaverius Buchhandlung, 1922, pp. 122). Scholarly, by a Jesuit.

Hutton, J. E., *A History of Moravian Missions* (London, Moravian Publication Office, 1923, pp. 550).

Hyamson, Albert M., *A History of the Jews in England* (London, Methuen and Co., 2d ed., revised, 1928, pp. xxi, 327). Excellent bibliographies.

Icazbalceta, Joaquin García, *Colección de Documentos para la Historia de México,* Vol. I (Mexico, 1858), contains Toribio Motolinia, *Historia de los Indios de Nueva España,* a contemporary account by a Franciscan.

Icazbalceta, Joaquin García, *Nueva Colleción de Documentos para la Historia de México* (Mexico, Antiqua Librería de Andrade y Morales, Sucesores, 5 vols., 1886-1892).

Inge, William Ralph, *The Platonic Tradition in English Religious Thought* (New York, Longmans, Green and Co., 1926, pp. vii, 117). The Hulsean Lectures at Cambridge, 1925-1926.

Izaguirre, Bernardino, *Historia de las Misiones Franciscanas y Narracion de los Progresos de la Geografia en el Oriente del Peru* (Lima, Talleres Tipográficos de la Penitenciaría, 12 vols., 1922-1926). Based upon a careful use of sources.

Jaboatam, Antonio de Santa Maria, *Novo Orbe Serafico Brasilico ou Chronica dos Frades Menores da Provincia do Brasil* (printed at Lisbon in 1761 and reprinted by order of Instituto Historico e Geografico Brasileiro, Rio de Janeiro, Typ. Brasiliense de Maximiano Gomes Ribeiro, 2 parts, 1858, 1859).

Jacobs, Henry Eyster, *A History of the Evangelical Lutheran Church in the United States* (New York, The Christian Literature Co., 1893, pp. xvi, 539). In *The American Church History Series.*

Jann, Adelhelm, *Die katholischen Missionen in Indien, China und Japan. Ihre Organization und das portugiesische Patronat vom 15 bis ins 18 Jahrhundert* (Paderborn, Ferdinand Schöningh, 1915, pp. xxviii, 540). Scholarly, by a Capuchin.

Jenkins, Robert C., *The Jesuits in China and the Legation of Cardinal de Tournon. An Examination of Conflicting Evidence and an Attempt at an Impartial Judgment* (London, David Nutt, 1894, pp. 165). An attempt to be impartial. Favours the Jesuits. Uses as chief authority the collection of original documents, most of them never before published, which came out in Venice in 1761, 1762, printed by Giuseppe Bettinelli.

Jenks, David, *Six Great Missionaries of the Sixteenth and Seventeenth Centuries* (London, A. R. Mowbray and Co., 1930, pp. vii, 252). Popular, sympathetic account of Roman Catholic missionaries by an Anglican.

Johnson, Guion Griffis, *Ante-Bellum North Carolina. A Social History* (Chapel Hill, N. C., The University of North Carolina Press, 1937, pp. xv, 935). Based upon exhaustive research in sources, manuscript and printed.

Joly, Léon, *Le Christianisme et l'Extrême Orient* (Paris, P. Lethielleux, 2 vols., 1907). A book more for purposes of edification than based upon sound scholarship. The author pleads for more native clergy.

Jones, Rufus M., *The Quakers in the American Colonies* (London, Macmillan and Co., 1923, pp. xxxii, 603). Scholarly, well documented, by a Quaker.

Jordan, W. K., *The Development of Religious Toleration in England from the Accession of James I to the Convention of the Long Parliament (1603-1640)* (London, George Allen and Unwin, 1936, pp. 542).

Josson, H., *La Mission du Bengale Occidental ou Archidiocèse de Calcutta, Province Belge de la Compagnie de Jésus* (Bruges, Imprimerie Sainte-Catherine, 2 vols., 1921). Based upon careful research, by a Jesuit.

The Journal of Modern History (Chicago, 1929 ff.).

The Journal of Negro History (Washington, D. C., 1926 ff.).

Journal of the American Oriental Society (New Haven, Conn., 1881 ff.).

Journal of the North-China Branch of the Royal Asiatic Society (Shanghai, 1858 ff.).

Juan, Jorge, and Ulloa, Antonio de, *Noticias Secretas de America* (London, R. Taylor, Part I, 1826).

Kagawa, Toyohiko, *Christ and Japan* (New York, Friendship Press, 1934, pp. vi, 150).

Kalkar, Chr. H., *Geschichte der christlichen Mission unter den Heiden* (Gütersloh, C. Bertelsmann, 2 vols., 1879, 1880).

Keesing, Felix M., and Keesing, Marie, *Taming Philippine Headhunters. A Study of Government and of Cultural Change in Northern Luzon* (London, George Allen and Unwin, 1934, pp. 288). The result of six months' intensive study in the Philippines.

Keleman, Pál, *Battlefield of the Gods. Aspects of Mexican History, Art and Exploration* (London, George Allen and Unwin, 1937, pp. 212). Semi-popular.

Kelsey, Rayner Wickersham, *Friends and the Indians 1655-1917* (Philadelphia, The Associated Executive Committee of Friends on Indian Affairs, 1917, pp. xi, 291).

Kennedy, C. M., *The Influence of Christianity upon International Law* (Cambridge, Macmillan and Co., 1856, pp. xvi, 158). The Hulsean Prize Essay in the University of Cambridge for the year 1854.

Kirk, Kenneth E., *The Vision of God. The Christian Doctrine of the Summum Bonum* (London, Longmans, Green and Co., 1931, pp. xxviii, 583). The Bampton Lectures for 1928.

Klett, Guy Soulliard, *Presbyterians in Colonial Pennsylvania* (Philadelphia, University of Pennsylvania Press, 1937, pp. xi, 297). Carefully done.

Knittle, Walter Allen, *Early Eighteenth Century Palatine Emigration* (Philadelphia, Dorrance and Co., 1937, pp. xix, 320). Scholarly.

Kölbing, Friedrich Ludwig, *Die Missionen der evangelischen Brüder in Grönland und Labrador* (Gnadau, Hans Franz Burkhard, 1831, pp. viii, 254, 180). Compiled largely from reports of missionaries.

Koenen, H. J., *Geschiedenis der Joden in Nederland* (Utrecht, C. Van der Post, Jr., 1843, pp. xvii, 519). Scholarly.

Kuruppu, D. J. B., *The Right Rev. Dr. Jules Andrew Brault, O. M. I., Bishop of Jaffna* (Colombo, The "Messenger Press," 1923, pp. ii, 33).

Lallemand, Léon, *Histoire de la Charité* (Paris, Alphonse Picard et Fils, 4 vols., [the 4th vol. in 2 parts], 1902-1912). A standard work, well documented, favourable to the Church; especially valuable for its many concrete illustrations and citations of sources.

Lanning, John Tate, *The Spanish Missions of Georgia* (Chapel Hill, N. C., University of North Carolina Press, 1935, pp. xiii, 321). Based upon careful research.

Las Casas, Bartolomé de, *Colecion de Las Obras*. Juan Antonio Llorente, editor (Paris, 2 vols., 1822).

Latourette, Kenneth Scott, *A History of Christian Missions in China* (New York, The Macmillan Co., 1929, pp. xii, 930).

Launay, Adrien, *Histoire de la Mission du Thibet* (Lille, Desclée, De Brouwer et Cie, 2 vols., no date).

Launay, Adrien, *Histoire des Missions de l'Inde Pondichéry, Maïssour, Coïmbatour* (Paris, Charles Douniol, 5 vols., 1898).

Launay, Adrien, *Histoire Générale de la Société des Missions-Étrangères* (Paris, Pierre Téqui, 3 vols., 1894). By a member of the Society. Based upon the archives.

Lea, Henry Charles, *A History of Auricular Confession and Indulgences in the Latin Church* (Philadelphia, Lea Brothers and Co., 3 vols., 1896). A standard work, based upon wide reading in the sources.

Lea, Henry Charles, *History of Sacerdotal Celibacy in the Christian Church* (New York, The Macmillan Co., 3d ed., revised, 2 vols., 1907). A standard work, based largely upon the original sources, with a bias against sacerdotal celibacy and the Roman Catholic Church.

Lea, Henry Charles, *The Inquisition in the Spanish Dependencies* (New York, The Macmillan Co., 1908, pp. xvi, 564).

Lea, Henry Charles, *The Moriscos of Spain: Their Conversion and Expulsion* (Philadelphia, Lea Brothers and Co., 1901, pp. xii, 463). Somewhat anti-Roman Catholic.

Le Clercq, Christian, *First Establishment of the Faith in New France,* translated by John Gilmary Shea (New York, John G. Shea, 2 vols., 1881). By a Recollect missionary in Canada in the seventeenth century.

Leger, Mary Celeste, *The Catholic Indian Missions in Maine (1611-1820)*. (Washington, D. C., The Catholic University of America, 1929, pp. x, 184). A doctoral dissertation, based partly upon unpublished manuscript material.

Lemmens, Leonhard, *Geschichte der Franziskanermissionen* (Münster i. W., Aschendorffschen Verlagsbuchhandlung, 1929, pp. xx, 376). Carefully done, by a Franciscan.

Lescarbot, Marc, *Histoire de la Nouvelle-France* (Paris, Librairie Tross, new edition, 3 vols., 1866). First published in 1609.

Lettres Édifiantes et Curieuses, Concernant l'Asie, l'Afrique et l'Amerique, avec quelques Relations Nouvelles des Missions, et des Notes Geographiques et Historiques. (Published under the direction of M. L. Himemartin, Paris, 1843). The editing is said sometimes to have been in the interests of edification.

Liese, Wilh., *Geschichte der Caritas* (Freiburg i. Br., Caritasverlag, 2 vols., 1922). From a Roman Catholic standpoint, with a warm appreciation of the part of the Church in charity.

Lincoln, Anthony, *Some Political and Social Ideas of English Dissent 1763-1800* (Cambridge University Press, 1938, pp. 292). Well documented.

Lindsay, Thomas M., *A History of the Reformation* (New York, Charles Scribner's Sons, 2 vols., preface 1906, 1907). A standard summary from a Protestant viewpoint.

Lindsey, Charles, *Rome in Canada. The Ultramontane Struggle for Supremacy over the Civil Authority* (Toronto, Lovell Brothers, 1877, pp. 398). Anti-Roman Catholic and especially against ultramontanism in Canada.

Lockman, *Travels of the Jesuits into Various Parts of the World: Compiled from their Letters. Now First Attempted in English Intermix'd with an Account of the Manners, Government, Religion, &c. of the Several Nations Visited by those Fathers. With Extracts from other Travellers, and Miscellaneous Notes* (London, 2 vols., 1743). Chiefly a translation from *Lettres Édifiantes et Curieuses.*

Lockwood, Frank C., *Story of the Spanish Missions of the Middle Southwest. Being a Complete Survey of the Missions founded by Padre Eusebio Francisco Kino in the Seventeenth Century and later Enlarged and Beautified by the Franciscan Fathers during the Last Part of the Eighteenth Century* (Santa Ana, Calif., The Fine Arts Press, 1934, pp. vi, 78). Specializes on the sites where Kino erected churches.

Loskiel, Georg Heinrich, *Geschichte der Mission der evangelischen Brüder unter den Indianern in Nordamerika* (Barby, 1789, pp. 783).

Louvet, L.-E., *La Cochinchine Religieuse* (Paris, Challamel Aine, 2 vols., 1885).

Lucas, Samuel, *Charters of the Old English Colonies in America* (London, John W. Parker, 1850, pp. xx, 123).

Luccock, Halford E., and Hutchinson, Paul, *The Story of Methodism* (New York, The Methodist Book Concern, 1926, pp. 508). Competent, written in popular style.

Lübeck, Konrad, *Die Christianisierung Russlands* (Aachen, Xaveriusverlagsbuchhandlung, 1922, pp. 118). By a Roman Catholic scholar, using a good deal of Russian material, as well as that in Western European languages. Objective, scholarly.

Lübeck, Konrad, *Die russischen Missionen* (Aachen, Xaveriusverlagsbuchhandlung, 1922, pp. 68). Careful and objective, by a Roman Catholic scholar.

Maas, Otto, *Cartas de China. Documentos Ineditos Sobre Misiones Franciscanas del Siglo XVII* (Seville, 1917).

Maas, Otto, *Misiones de Nuevo Méjico* (Madrid, Hijos de T. Minuesa de los Ríos, 1929, pp. lvi, 272). Made up largely of documents.

Maas, Otto, *Las Órdenes Religiosas de España y la Colonización de América en la Segunda Parte del Siglo XVIII. Estadísticas y Otros Documentos* (Barcelona, A. G. Belart, Vol. II, 1929). Documents, collected by a Franciscan.

Maas, Otto, *Die Wiederöffnung der Franziskanermission in China in der Neuzeit* (Münster i. W., 1926, pp. xxix, 183).

McCarter, John, *The Dutch Reformed Church in South Africa with Notices of Other Denominations* (Edinburgh, W. and C. Inglis, 1869, pp. vi, 147). The author was for several years a pastor among the Dutch.

McConnell, S. D., *History of the American Episcopal Church from the Planting of the Colonies to the End of the Civil War* (New York, Thomas Whittaker, 1890, pp. xiv, 392). Excellent.

McGiffert, Arthur Cushman, *Protestant Thought before Kant* (New York, Charles Scribner's Sons, 1911, pp. 261).

Mackay, John A., *The Other Spanish Christ. A Study in the Spiritual History of Spain and South America* (London, Student Movement Press, 1932, pp. xv, 288). By a scholarly Protestant missionary executive, long a missionary in Peru.

Mackichan, D., *The Missionary Ideal in the Scottish Churches* (London, Hodder and Stoughton, 1927, pp. 238). A semi-popular series of lectures.

Mackinnon, James, *The Social and Industrial History of Scotland from the Union to the Present Time* (London, Longmans, Green and Co., 1921, pp. viii, 298). An objective survey.

Maclagan, Edward, *The Jesuits and the Great Mogul* (London, Burns, Oates and Washbourne, 1932, pp. xxi, 434). A scholarly study based upon the sources.

McNeill, John T., *Christian Hope for World Society* (Chicago, Willett, Clark and Co., 1937, pp. vii, 278). A thoughtful series of lectures by a church historian.

MacNutt, Francis Augustus, *Bartholomew de Las Casas, his Life, Apostolate, and Writings* (Cleveland, The Arthur H. Clark Co., 1909, pp. xxxviii, 472).

Maghalhães de Gandavo, Pero de, *The Histories of Brazil,* translated into English by John B. Stetson, Jr., with a facsimile of the Portuguese original (New York, The Cortes Society, 2 vols., 1922). A sixteenth century account by one who had spent some time in Brazil.

Mailla, Joseph-Anne-Marie de Moyriac de, *Histoire Générale de la Chine* (Paris, 13 vols., 1777-1785).

Manross, William Wilson, *A History of the American Episcopal Church* (New York, Morehouse Publishing Co., 1935, pp. xvi, 404). By a member of the faculty of General Theological Seminary. Except for Chapters 1, 2, and 8, based upon the original sources.

Margolis, Max L., and Marx, Alexander, *A History of the Jewish People* (Philadelphia, The Jewish Publication Society of America, 1927, pp. xxii, 823). Excellent, comprehensive history, by Jews. Selected bibliographies.

Marie, Élie, *Aux Avant-postes de la Chrétienté. Histoire des Instituts Religieux et Missionnaires* (Paris, P. Lethielleux, 1930, pp. xii, 343). Covers many but not all of the religious orders and societies, missionary and otherwise, from ancient times into the present, and in each instance gives a selected bibliography of monographs and periodical articles.

Mascarenhas, Fabian J., *A Brief History of the Catholic Community of Mangalore. A Tribute to Their Excellencies Sir Arthur and Lady Lawley on the Occasion of Their Visit to South Canara, in Nov., 1907* (pp. 12).

Mather, Cotton, *Magnalia Christi Americana or the Ecclesiastical History of New-England from its First Planting in the Year 1620 unto the Year of Our Lord, 1698* (Hartford, Silas Andrus, 2 vols., 1820).

Maurer, Charles Lewis, *Early Lutheran Education in Pennsylvania* (Philadelphia, Dorrance and Co., 1932, pp. xii, 284). Especially good on details of schools in particular regions.

Maxson, Charles Hartshorn, *The Great Awakening in the Middle Colonies* (The University of Chicago Press, 1920, pp. vii, 158). Carefully done and based upon the sources.

Means, Philip Ainsworth, *Fall of the Inca Empire and the Spanish Rule in Peru: 1530-1780* (New York, Charles Scribner's Sons, 1932, pp. xii, 351). Based upon extensive research.

Mecham, J. Lloyd, *Church and State in Latin America* (Chapel Hill, N. C., University of North Carolina Press, 1934, pp. viii, 550). Objective. Based largely upon printed sources.

Meigs, Peveril, 3d, *The Dominican Mission Frontier of Lower California* (Berkeley, University of California Press, 1935, pp. vi, 192). Excellent.

Mendieta, Gerónimo de, *Historia Eclesiástica Indiana* (Mexico, Antigua Libreria, 1870, pp. xlv, 790). By a Franciscan who served in Mexico in the second half of the sixteenth century; based largely upon primary sources.

Meulen, Jacob ter, *Der Dedanke der Internationalen Organization in seiner Entwicklung* (Haag, Martinus Nijhoff, 2 vols., 1917-1929). Well documented.

Miller, Perry, *Orthodoxy in Massachusetts 1630-1650. A Genetic Study* (Harvard University Press, 1933, pp. xvi, 353). Carefully done.

Milukow, Paul, *Skizzen russischer Kulturgeschichte,* translated into German by E. Davidson (Leipzig, Otto Wigand, Vol. II, 1901, pp. ix, 447).

Minutes and Letters of the Coetus of the German Reformed Congregations in Pennsylvania 1747-1792 together with Three Preliminary Reports of Rev. John Philip Boehm, 1734-1744 (Philadelphia, Reformed Church Publication Board, 1903, pp. xxii, 463).

Mode, Peter G., *The Frontier Spirit in American Christianity* (New York, The Macmillan Co., 1923, pp. x, 196). A suggestive and scholarly essay.

Moidrey, Joseph de, *La Hiérarchie Catholique en Chine, en Corée et au Japon (1307-1914)* (Zi-ka-wei, Imprimerie de l'Orphelinat de T'ou-sè-wè, 1914, pp. 2, 301). (*Variétés Sinologiques,* No. 38.)

Monroe, Paul, *A Text-Book in the History of Education* (New York, The Macmillan Co., 1914, pp. xxiii, 772).

Montalbán, Francisco J., *Das spanische Patronat und die Eroberung der Philippinen. Nach den Akten des Archivs von Indien in Sevilla* (Freiburg im Breisgau, Herder and Co., 1930, pp. xi, 131). Well documented.

Monumenta Nipponica (Tokyo, 1938 ff.). Issued from (the Roman Catholic) Sophia University. Rich in studies of sixteenth century Roman Catholic missions in Japan.

Monumenta Serica (The Catholic University Press, Peking, 1935 ff.).

More, Thomas, *Sir Thomas More's Utopia Edited with Introduction and Notes by J. Churton Collins* (Oxford, The Clarendon Press, 1904, pp. lii, 283).

Moses, Bernard, *South America on the Eve of Emancipation. The Southern Spanish Colonies in the Last Half-Century of Their Dependence* (New York, G. P. Putnam's Sons, 1908, pp, v, 356). By an authority.

Moses, Bernard, *The Spanish Dependencies in South America. An Introduction to the History of Their Civilization* (New York, Harper & Brothers, 2 vols., 1914). A standard work, thoroughly documented.

Mosheim, John Laurence de, *Authentick Memoirs of the Christian Church in China. . . . Translated from the German* (London, J. and J. Tonson, and S. Draper, 1750, pp. 60). Anti-Roman Catholic, and especially anti-Jesuit. Principally on the Rites Controversy.

Müllbauer, Maximilian, *Geschichte der katholischen Missionen in Ostindien von der Zeit Vasco da Gama's bis zur Mitte des achtzehnten Jahrhunderts* (Freiburg im Breisgau, Herder'sche Verlagshandlung, 1852, pp. xii, 372). The result of diligent research. The chief emphasis is on Jesuit missions. A standard work, but not always critical.

Müller, Karl, *200 Jahre Brüdermission. 1 Band. Das erste Missionsjahrhundert* (Herrnhut, Missionsbuchhandlung, 1931, pp. viii, 380).

Mulvey, Mary Doris, *French Catholic Missionaries in the Present United States (1604-1791)* (Washington, D. C., The Catholic University of America, 1936, pp. ix, 158). A doctoral dissertation.

Néez, Mgr., Evêque de Céomanie Vicaire Apostolique du Tonkin Occidental, *Documents sur le Clergé Tonkinois aux XVIIᵉ et XVIIIᵉ Siècles* (Paris, P. Téqui, 1925, pp. ix, 273). Néez was vicar apostolic of Western Tongking in the eighteenth century and his manuscript, prepared 1754-1761, contains the biographies of fifty-three native priests of the Tongking mission of the Société des Missions Étrangères.

The New China Review. Edited by Samuel Couling. (Shanghai, 1919-1922.)

Newman, A. H., *A History of the Baptist Churches in the United States* (New York, The Christian Literature Co., 1894, pp. xv, 513). In *The American Church History Series.*

Niebuhr, H. Richard, *The Kingdom of God in America* (Chicago, Willett, Clark and Co., 1937, pp. xvii, 215). A brilliant interpretation of the religious history of the United States.

Nouvelles Lettres Édifiantes des Missions de la Chine et des Indes Orientales (Paris, 8 vols., 1818-1823).

Oliver, Edmund H., *The Winning of the Frontier* (Toronto, The United Church Publishing Co., 1930).

O'Rourke, Thomas P., *The Franciscan Missions in Texas (1690-1793). The Catholic University of America Studies in American Church History,* Vol. V (Washington, 1927, pp. iv, 107). A doctoral dissertation, ardently Roman Catholic.

Osborne, C. E., *Christian Ideas in Political History.* Holland Memorial Lectures, 1925 (London, John Murray, 1929, pp. xiv, 319).

Pagés, Léon, *Histoire de la Religion Chrétienne au Japon depuis 1598 jusqu'a 1651* (Paris, Charles Douniol, 2 vols., 1869, 1870). Vol. II is made up of documents.

Palou, Francisco, *Historical Memoirs of New California Translated into English from the Manuscript in the Archives of Mexico.* Edited by Herbert Eugene Bolton (Berkeley, University of California Press, 4 vols., 1926). By a participant and eyewitness of Franciscan missions in California.

Pannier, Jacques, and Mondain, Gustave, *L'Expansion Française Outre-Mer et Les Protestants Français* (Paris, Société des Missions Évangéliques, 1931, pp. 179). Contains excellent bibliographical notes.

Parkman, Francis, *A Half-Century of Conflict* (Boston, Little, Brown and Co., 2 vols., 1892).

Parkman, Francis, *The Jesuits in North America in the Seventeenth Century* (Boston, Little, Brown and Co., 1903, pp. xvii, 586). Based chiefly on the Jesuit *Relations.*

Parkman, Francis, *La Salle and the Discovery of the Great West* (Boston, Little, Brown and Co., 11th ed., revised, 1879, pp. xxv, 483).

Parkman, Francis, *The Old Régime in Canada* (Boston, Little, Brown and Co., 14th ed., 1885, pp. xvi, 448).

Parsons, Elsie Clews, *Mitla Town of the Souls and Other Zapoteco-Speaking Pueblos of Oaxaca, Mexico* (The University of Chicago Press, 1936, pp. xix, 590). Based upon personal investigation.

Pascoe, C. F., *Classified Digest of the Records of the Society for the Propagation of the Gospel in Foreign Parts, 1701-1892* (London, at the Society's Office, 1893, pp. xvi, 980).

Pascoe, C. F., *Two Hundred Years of the S.P.G. An Historical Account of the Society for the Propagation of the Gospel in Foreign Parts, 1701-1900* (London, at the Society's Office, 1901, pp. xli, 1429). Very detailed, by an assistant secretary of the Society.

Paske-Smith, M., *Western Barbarians in Japan and Formosa in Tokugawa Days 1603-1868* (Kobe, J. L. Thompson and Co., preface 1930, pp. xiii, 431). A scholarly piece of work by the British Consul at Osaka. A good many documents are included.

Pastor, Ludwig, *The History of the Popes from the Close of the Middle Ages,* edited by Frederick Ignatius Antrobus (St. Louis, B. Herder, 2d ed., 20 vols., 1902-1930). Based on archives. Begins the story with 1305.

Paton, John Brown, Bunting, Percy William, and Garvie, Alfred Ernest, editors, *Christ and Civilization: A Survey of the Influence of the Christian Religion upon the Course of Civilization* (London, National Council of Evangelical Free Churches, 1910, pp. xi, 546). Semi-popular, by twelve scholars, warmly appreciative of Christianity.

Paul, R. C., *History of the Telugu Christians* (Madras, "Good Pastor" Press, 1929, pp. ix, 120). By a local Roman Catholic priest, based upon Kroot's *History of the Telugu Christians, Histoire des Missions Étrangères de l'Inde, The Catholic Expositor of Madras, The Catholic Directory,* and personal knowledge.

The Pennsylvania German Society's Proceedings (Lancaster, Pennsylvania, 1891 ff.).

Penny, Frank, *The Church in Madras. Being the History of the Ecclesiastical and Missionary Action of the East India Company in the Presidency of Madras in the Seventeenth and Eighteenth Centuries* (London, Smith, Elder and Co., 1904, pp. xii, 702). Based upon the documents, chiefly official despatches and replies of the East India Company.

Pérez, Rafael, *La Compañía de Jesus en Colombia y Centro-América despues de su Restauración. Parte Primera desde el llamamiento de los PP. de la Compañía de Jesus á la Nueva Granada en 1842, hasta su expulsión y dispersión en 1850* (Valladolid, Luis n.de Gaviria, 1896, pp. xx, 453). By a Jesuit.

Perry, William Stevens, *The History of the American Episcopal Church, 1587-1883* (Boston, James R. Osgood and Co., 2 vols., 1885). Old, but standard. By a bishop.

Pieris, P. E., *Ceylon and the Hollanders 1658-1796* (Tellippalai, Ceylon, American Ceylon Mission Press, 1916, pp. xvi, 181).

Pieris, P. E., *Ceylon: The Portuguese Era. Being a History of the Island for the Period 1505-1658* (Colombo, The Colombo Apothecaries Co., 2 vols., 1913). By a member of the Ceylon Civil Service who drew his information chiefly from an unpublished history by a Jesuit of the seventeenth century, later Provincial of his Order in India, Fernão de Queyroz. The history is chiefly of political events.

Pieris, P. E., and Fitzler, M. A. H., *Ceylon and Portugal. Part I, Kings and Christians 1539-1552. From the Original Documents at Lisbon* (Leipzig, Asia Major, 1927, pp. 408). The documents are given in English translation, without reproducing the originals, with an excellent brief introduction summarizing the historical background.

Pierling, P., *La Russie et la Saint-Siège* (Paris, E. Plon, Nourrit et Cie, 3 vols., 1896-1901). By a Jesuit.

Pinot, Virgile, *La Chine et la Formation de l'Esprit Philosophique en France (1640-1740)* (Paris, Paul Geuthner, 1932, pp. 480). Scholarly and well written.

Prakasar, S. Gnana, *A History of the Catholic Church in Ceylon. I. Period of Beginnings, 1505-1602* (Colombo, Literature Committee for the Catholic Union of Ceylon, 1924, pp. xiv, 283). Written by an Oblate, based upon wide reading. In general it is objective.

Prescott, William H., *History of the Conquest of Mexico* (Paris, Baudry's European Library, 3 vols., 1844).

Prescott, William H., *History of the Conquest of Peru* (New York, American Publishers Corporation, 2 vols., no date). The preface is dated 1847.

Priestley, Herbert Ingram, *Tristán de Luna, Conquistador of the Old South. A Study of Spanish Imperial Strategy* (Glendale, Calif., The Arthur H. Clark Co., 1936, pp. 215). Based upon original documents.

Proceedings of the American Antiquarian Society (Boston, latterly Worcester, 1813 ff.).

Queyroz, Fernão de, *The Temporal and Spiritual Conquest of Ceylon.* Translated by S. G. Perera (Colombo, A. C. Richards, Acting Government Printer, Ceylon, 1930, pp. 28, xxviii, 1274). Fernão de Queyroz was born in Portugal, 1617, went o India as a Jesuit, 1635, for a time (1677-1680) was Provincial of his Society, and died in Goa 1688. The book was written 1671-1686. It was based upon existing histories, some of them in manuscript, and upon reminiscences of those who had served in Ceylon. Its purpose was to animate Portugal to recover Ceylon from the Dutch.

Raucaz, L. M., *In the Savage South Solomons. The Story of a Mission* (The Society for the Propagation of the Faith, 1928, pp. 270). The author is Vicar Apostolic of the South Solomon Islands.

Rauws, Joh., Kraemer, H., Van Hasselt, F. J. F., and Slotemaker de Brüine, N. A. C., *The Netherlands Indies* (London, World Dominion Press, 1935, pp. 186).

Recopilacion de Leyes de los Reinos de las Indias, mandudas imprimir y publicar por la Magestad Católica del Rey Don Carlos II (Madrid, Boix, 4 vols., 1841).

Redfield, Robert, *Tepoztlán; a Mexican Village; a Study in Folk Life* (University of Chicago Press, 1930, pp. xi, 247). Objective. Based partly upon a study of pertinent books and partly upon a residence of eight months in the village in 1926 and 1927.

Do Rego, Sebastião, *L'Apostolo di Ceylan P. Giuseppe Vaz della Congregazione dell' Oratorio di S. Filippo Neri dall' edizione di Venezia 1753* (Mangalore, Codialboil Press, 1897, pp. xxiii, 391). The old standard biography.

Revista de la Exposición Misional Española, Barcelona, 1929 (Barcelona, 1928-1930). A periodical published in connexion with the missionary exposition which formed part of a general exposition at Barcelona.

Revue d'Histoire des Missions (Paris, 1924 ff.).

Revue de l'Extrême Orient (Paris, 1882 ff.).

Revue des Questions Scientifiques (Louvain, la Société Scientifique de Bruxelles, 1877 ff.).

Richardson, Leon Burr, editor, *An Indian Preacher in England: Being Letters and Diaries Relating to the Mission of the Reverend Samson Occom and the Reverend Nathaniel Whitaker to Collect Funds in England for the Benefit of Eleazer Wheelock's Indian Charity School, from which grew Dartmouth College* (Hanover, N. H., Dartmouth College Publications, 1933, pp. 376).

Richter, Julius, *Die evangelische Mission in Niederländisch-Indien* (Gütersloh, C. Bertelsmann, 1931, pp. 167). The only general history, except in Dutch, of missions in the Netherlands East Indies. Somewhat lacking in footnote references to the sources.

Richter, Julius, *Indische Missionsgeschichte* (Gütersloh, C. Bertelsmann, 2d ed., 1924, pp. vi, 570). The standard history of Protestant missions in India. There is an English translation of an earlier edition.

Richter, Julius, *Mission und Evangelisation im Orient* (Gütersloh, C. Bertelsmann, 2d ed., 1930, pp. 294). The standard account of Protestant missions in the Near East. There is an English translation of the first edition. Few footnote references to authorities are given and the book is somewhat scanty in bibliography.

Rippy, J. Fred, and Nelson, Jean Thomas, *Crusaders of the Jungle* (Chapel Hill, N. C., The University of North Carolina Press, 1936, pp. x, 401). The story of missions in tropical South America during the colonial period. Semi-popular in style, scholarly.

Rivero, Juan, *Historia de las Misiones de los Llanos de Casanare y los Rios Orinoco y Meta* (Bogota, Silvestre y Compañia, 1883, pp. xiv, 443). Written in 1736 by a Jesuit.

Robertson, H. M., *Aspects of the Rise of Economic Individualism: A Criticism of Max Weber and his School* (Cambridge University Press, 1933, pp. xvi, 223).

Rochemonteix, Camille de, *Les Jésuites et la Nouvelle-France au XVIIIe Siècle d'après des Documents Inédits* (Paris, Alphonse Picard et Fils, 2 vols., 1906).

de la Roi, J. F. A., *Die evangelische Christenheit und die Juden unter dem Gesichtspunkte der Mission geschichtlich betrachtet* (Karlsruhe and Berlin, H. Reuther, 3 vols., 1884-1892). Although lacking in many precise references to the sources, it contains excellent bibliographies.

Rojas y Arrieta, Guillermo, *History of the Bishops of Panama* (Panama, Imprenta de la Academia, 1929, pp. xvi, 255). The author, an Archbishop of Panama, has written a somewhat critical work, in many ways a chronicle, based upon fragments of information and confessedly incomplete.

Rommerskirchen, Joh., *Die Oblatenmissionen auf der Insel Ceylon im 19. Jahrhundert 1847-1893* (Hünfeld, Verlag der Oblaten, 1931, pp. xi, 247). By an Oblate; in its original form a doctoral dissertation (Fulda, Fuldner Actiendruckerei, 1930, pp. ix, 81).

Roth, Cecil, *A History of the Marranos* (Philadelphia, The Jewish Publication Society of America, 1932, pp. 422). Apparently based upon wide reading and research, but with few explicit references to the sources.

Roth, Cecil, *Venice and Her Last Persecution of the Jews: a Study from Hebrew Sources. Extract from Mélanges offerts a M. Israel Lévi par ses élèves et ses amis a l'occasion de son 70e anniversaire* (Paris, Librairie Durlacher, 1926, pp. 411-424).

Ryan, Edwin, *The Church in the South American Republics* (New York, The Bruce Publishing Co., 1932, pp. viii, 119). By a Roman Catholic priest; popular in style, but scholarly.

D'Sa, M., *History of the Catholic Church in India* (Bombay, The Lalka Printing and Litho Works, 2 vols., 1910, 1922). Not very well articulated; more like a series of notes; taken from various books and put roughly in chronological order.

D'Sa, M., *The History of the Diocese of Damaun* (Bombay, Presidency Printing Press, 1924, pp. 276, iv). The author, a priest, is not always critical, but uses old authorities which he seems to follow fairly closely, and often gives the documents or selections from them.

Saco, José Antonio, *Historiade la Esclavitud de la Raza Africana en el Nuevo Mundo y en especial en los Paises Américo-Hispanos* (Barcelona, Imprenta de Jaime Jepús, 1879, pp. 442). Based upon fairly extensive research.

Saldanha, Joseph L., *The Christian Puranna of Father Thomas Stephens of the Society of Jesus* (Bolar, Mangalore, Simon Alvares, 1907, pp. xciv, 597). A work of the seventeenth century reproduced from manuscript copies and edited with a biographical note, an introduction, an English synopsis of the contents, and a vocabulary.

Schilling, P. Dorotheus, *Das Schulwesen der Jesuiten in Japan (1551-1614)* (Münster i.W., Regensbergschen Buchdruckerei, 1931, pp. xxviii, 86). A scholarly, well documented study by a Franciscan, much of it based upon unpublished documents.

Schlund, Erhard, *St. Franziskus und sein Orden in der Heidenmission. Zum 700 jährigen Jubiläum der Missionstätigkeit des Franziskanerordens 1219-1919* (Düsseldorf, Missionsverwaltung der Franziskaner, pp. 63). A brief popular account, by a Franciscan.

Schmidlin, Joseph, *Katholische Missionsgeschichte* (Steyl, Missionsdruckerei, 1924, pp. xi, 598). A standard work by a distinguished Roman Catholic specialist on missions, with extensive bibliographical notes.
There is an English translation by Matthias Braun (Mission Press, Techny, Ill., 1933, pp. xiv, 862) which makes additions to the bibliographies, especially of more recent works and works in English, and here and there adds to the text and footnotes. In some portions, therefore, it is fuller and better than the German original.

Schmidlin, Joseph, *Catholic Mission Theory (Katholische Missionslehre im Grundniss)*. A translation (Techny, Ill., Mission Press, S.V.D., 1931, pp. xii, 544). The author (Roman Catholic), Professor of Missiology at the University of Münster, has avowedly leaned heavily on Gustav Warneck in outline and material, partly because available Roman Catholic material on many points is lacking. The translation, Matthias Braun, editor, has made a certain amount of revision in the original to fit it for English-speaking countries. The citations from English works draw largely upon Protestant writings.

Schuetz, John J., *The Origin of the Teaching Brotherhoods* (Washington, D. C., The Catholic University of America, 1918, pp. 104). A doctoral dissertation.

Schurhammer, G., and Voretzsch, E. A., *Ceylon zur Zeit des Königs Bhuvaneka Bāhu und Franz Xavers, 1539-1552. Quellen zur Geschichte der Portugiesen, sowie der Franziskaner—und Jesuitenmission auf Ceylon im Urtext herausgegeben und erklärt* (Leipzig, Asia Major, 2 vols., 1928). Thorough, scholarly.

Schwager, Friedrich, *Die katholische Heidenmission der Gegenwart im Zusammenhang mit ihrer grossen Vergangenheit* (Steyl, Missionsdruckerei, 1907, pp. 446). A standard work.

Scott, James Brown, *The Spanish Origin of International Law. Francisco de Vitoria and His Law of Nations* (Oxford, The Clarendon Press, 1934, pp. 19a, 288, clviii). By the Secretary of the Carnegie Endowment for International Peace. Scholarly.

Semedo, Alvarez, *The History of the Great and Renowned Monarchy of China. . . . Lately written in Italian by F. Alvarez Semedo, a Portughess, after he had resided twenty two yeares at the Court, and other famous Cities of that Kingdom. Now put into English by a Person of quality and illustrated with several Mapps and Figures to satisfie the curious, and advance the Trade of Great Brittain. To which is added the History of the later invasion and Conquest of that flourishing Kingdom by the Tartars. . . .* (London, John Crook, 1655, pp. 308).

Servière, J.de la, *Les Anciennes Missions de la Compagnie de Jésus en Chine (1552-1814)* (Shanghai, Imprimerie de la Mission, 1924, pp. iv, 82).

Shea, John Gilmary, *History of the Catholic Missions among the Indian Tribes of the United States, 1529-1854* (New York, P. J. Kenedy, 1899, pp. 514). By a Roman Catholic, favourable to missions.

Smirnoff, Eugene, *A Short Account of the Historical Development and Present Position of Russian Orthodox Missions* (London, Rivingtons, 1903, pp. xii, 83). By the chaplain to the Russian Embassy in London; based upon careful study of reports of the Chief Procurator of the Holy Synod and of the various missions.

Smirnov, Jean N., *Les Populations Finnoises des Bassins de la Volga et de la Kama. Études d'Ethnographie Historique. Traduites du Russe et Revues par Paul Boyer. Première partie. Groupe de la Volga ou Groupe Bulgare. I. Les Tchérémisses. II. Les Mordves* (Paris, Ernest Leroux, 1898, pp. viii, 486).

Smith, Preserved, *The Age of the Reformation* (New York, Henry Holt and Co., 1920, pp. xii, 861). A standard summary.

Some Correspondence between the Governors and Treasurers of the New England Company in London and the Commissioners of the United Colonies in America the Missionaries of the Colony and Others between the Years 1657 and 1712 to which are added the Journals of the Rev. Experience Mayhew in 1713 and 1714 (London, Spottiswoode and Co., 1896, pp. xxxii, 127).

Southey, Robert, *History of Brazil* (London, Longman, Hurst, Rees, Orme, and Brown, 3 vols., Vol. I, 2d ed., 1822; Vol. II, 1817; Vol. III, 1819). Based largely upon manuscripts.

Starr, Frederick, *In Indian Mexico. A Narrative of Travel and Labor* (Chicago, Forbes and Co., 1908, pp. xi, 425).

Stead, Francis Herbert, *The Story of Social Christianity* (London, James Clarke and Co., 2 vols., no date). Laudatory of the social changes wrought in the world by Christianity throughout the course of its history.

Steichen, M., *The Christian Daimyos. A Century of Religious and Political History in Japan (1549-1650)* (Tokyo, Rikkyo Gakuin Press, no date, pp. xi, 369). Based partly upon letters and other first-hand material.

Stephenson, George M., *The Religious Aspects of Swedish Immigration. A Study of Immigrant Churches* (Minneapolis, University of Minnesota Press, 1932, pp. viii, 542). Carefully done and based upon sources and an extensive literature.

Stock, Eugene, *The History of the Church Missionary Society: Its Environment, Its Men, and Its Work* (London, Church Missionary Society, 4 vols., 1899-1916). The standard history, by a secretary of the Society.

Strassburger, Ralph Beaver, edited by William John Hinke, *Pennsylvania German Pioneers. A Publication of the Original Lists of Arrivals in the Port of Philadelphia from 1727 to 1808* (Norristown, Penn., Pennsylvania German Society, 3 vols., 1934).

Streit, Rob., and Dindinger, Johannes, *Bibliotheca Missionum* (Münster i.W., Aschendorffsche Buchhandlung, and Aachen, Xaverius Missionsverein, 9 vols., 1916-1937, to be continued). Vols. I-V by Streit, Vols. V-IX by Dindinger. The standard bibliography of Roman Catholic missions.

Sweet, William Warren, *Methodism in American History* (Cincinnati, American Book Concern, 1933, pp. 434).

Sweet, William Warren, *The Story of Religions in America* (New York, Harper & Brothers, 1930, pp. vii, 571). An historical survey confined to the United States.

Tacchi Venturi, Pietro, *Opere Storiche del P. Matteo Ricci, S.I., edite a cura del comitato per le onoranze nazionali con prolegomeni note e tavole* (Macerata, 2 vols., 1911).

Tennent, James Emerson, *Christianity in Ceylon: Its Introduction and Progress under the Portuguese, the Dutch, the British, and American Missions: with an Historical Sketch of the Brahmanical and Buddhist Superstitions* (London, John Murray, 1850, pp. xv, 345).

da Terzorio, Clemente, *Le Missioni dei Minori Cappuccini Sunto Storico* (Rome, various printers, 1913 ff.). By an officer of the Capuchins; based upon published books and unpublished manuscripts, and arranged by the regions in which the Capuchins have worked.

Terzorio, Clemen a, *Manuale Historicum Missionum Ordinis Minorum Capuccinorum* (Isola del Liri, Soc. Tip. A. Macioce & Pisani, 1926, pp. 516.) A succinct historical summary with an excellent bibliography.

Theology. A Monthly Journal of Historic Christianity (London, Society for Promoting Christian Knowledge, 1920 ff.).

Theophilus (Bishop), *A Short History of the Christian Church and The Ritual of the Eastern Orthodox Church, Its History and Meaning* (San Francisco, Douglass Brothers, 1934, pp. 46). An official statement for a popular audience.

Thomas, A., *Histoire de la Mission de Pékin depuis les Origines jusqu'a l'Arrivée des Lazaristes* (Paris, Louis-Michaud, 1923, pp. 463). Uses edicts, letters, memoirs, some of them unpublished, as well as secondary works; anti-Jesuit in the Rites Controversy.

Thompson, Robert Ellis, *A History of the Presbyterian Churches in the United States* (New York, The Christian Literature Co., 1895, pp. xxxi, 424). One of *The American Church History Series.*

Thwaites, Reuben Gold, *France in America 1497-1763* (New York, Harper & Brothers, 1905, pp. xxi, 320). Well written, by an outstanding expert.

Thwaites, Reuben Gold, *The Jesuit Relations and Allied Documents: Travels and Explorations of the Jesuit Missionaries in New France 1610-1791. The Original French, Latin, and Italian Texts, with English Translations and Notes; Illustrated by Portraits, Maps, and Facsimiles* (Cleveland, The Burrows Brothers, 73 vols., 1896-1901).

Tobar, Jérôme, translator and commentator, *Kiao-ou Ki-lio "Résumé des Affaires Religieuses" Publié par Ordre de S. Exc. Tcheou Fou* (Shanghai, Imprimerie de la Mission Catholique, 1917, *Variétés Sinologiques* No. 47, pp. ix, 252).

Torquemada, Juan de, *Monarchia Indiana* (Madrid, Nicolas Rodriguez Franco, 3 vols., 1723). Long a standard secondary account; by a Franciscan in New Spain.

T'oung Pao (Leyden, 1890 ff.).

Townsend, Leah, *South Carolina Baptists 1670-1805* (Florence, S. C., The Florence Printing Co., 1935, pp. 391). A doctoral dissertation based upon extensive research.

Transactions of the Asiatic Society of Japan (Yokohama and Tokyo, 1874 ff.).

Troeltsch, Ernst, *The Social Teaching of the Christian Churches,* translated by Olive Wyon (New York, The Macmillan Co., 1931, pp. 1019). A translation of *Die Soziallehren der christlichen Kirchen und Gruppen,* first published in 1911.

Uhlhorn, G., *Die christliche Liebesthätigkeit* (Stuttgart, D. Gundert, 3 vols., 1882-1890). The period covered is from the beginning through the Reformation. An English translation of the first volume has been made under the title *Christian Charity in the Ancient Church* (by Sophia Taylor, Edinburgh, T. and T. Clark, 1883, pp. 424).

Underhill, Evelyn, *Worship* (New York, Harper & Brothers, 2d ed., 1937, pp. xxi, 350).

Väth, Alfons, *Johann Adam Schall von Bell, S.J.* (Cologne, J. P. Bachem, 1933, pp. xx, 380).

Vandenbosch, Amry, *The Dutch East Indies: Its Government, Problems, and Politics* (Grand Rapids, Mich., Wm. B. Eerdmans Publishing Co., 1933, pp. 385). Scholarly, based upon wide reading and upon travel in The Netherlands and the East Indies.

Vanderpol, Alfred, *La Doctrine Scolastique du Droit de Guerre* (Paris, A. Pedone, 1919, pp. xxviii, 534).

Vasconcellos, Simão de, *Chronica da Companhia de Jesu do Estado do Brasil* (No city given. A. J. Fernandes Lopes, 2 vols., 1865). By a provincial of the Brazilian Jesuits, partly a contemporary of the events he relates. The story is carried to 1570.

Vedder, Henry C., *A Short History of the Baptists* (Philadelphia, American Baptist Publication Society, new edition, 1907, pp. xvi, 431). By a competent scholar.

Vernadsky, George, *A History of Russia* (Yale University Press, Revised edition, 1930, pp. xix, 413). An excellent summary by a thoroughly competent scholar. The major portion is devoted to the nineteenth and twentieth centuries.

Villaneuva, Francisco Alvarez de, *Relación Histórica de Todas las Misiones de los PP. Franciscanos en las Indias y Proyecto para Nuevas Conversiones en las Riberas de Afamado Río Marañón. Memorial dirigido á S.M. el rey D.Carlos III en 28 de Mayo de 1781* (Madrid, 1892, pp. 76). In *Colección de Libros Ráros ó Curiosos que Tratan de América,* Vol. VII.

Visser, B. J. J., *Onder Portugeesch-Spaansche Vlag. De katholieke Missie Van Indonesië 1511-1605* (Amsterdam, N.V. de R.K. Boek-Centrale, 1925, pp. 337).

Walker, F. Deaville, *The Call of the West Indies: The Romance of Methodist Work and Opportunity in the West Indies and Adjacent Regions* (London, The Cargate Press, no date, pp. 190).

Walker, Williston, *A History of the Congregational Churches in the United States* (New York, The Christian Literature Society, 1894, pp. xii, 451). By a competent scholar.

Walker, Williston, *The Reformation* (New York, Charles Scribner's Sons, 1902, pp. xii, 478). A standard text book.

Walsh, James J., *American Jesuits* (New York, The Macmillan Co., 1934, pp. ix, 336). Warmly sympathetic with the Jesuits.

Warneck, Gustav, *Abriss einer Geschichte der protestantischen Missionen von der Reformation bis auf die Gegenwart, mit einem Anhang über die katholischen Missionen* (Berlin, Martin Warneck, 10th ed., 1913, pp. x, 624). There is a translation of the seventh German edition, by George Robson (New York, Fleming H. Revell Co., 1901, pp. xiii, 364).

Warner, Wellman J., *The Wesleyan Movement in the Industrial Revolution* (London, Longmans, Green and Co., 1930, pp. x, 299).

Watters, Mary, *A History of the Church in Venezuela 1810-1930* (Chapel Hill, N. C., The University of North Carolina Press, 1933, pp. ix, 260). Carefully done, based upon the sources.

Weber, Eugen, *Die portugiesische Reichsmission im Königreich Kongo von ihren Anfängen 1491 bis zum Eintritt der Jesuiten in die Kongomission 1548* (Aachen, Xaveriusverlagsbuchhandlung, 1924, pp. 186). Based upon the sources.

Weigle, Luther A., *American Idealism* (Yale University Press, 1928, pp. 356). A competent survey of the religious history of the United States.

Wenger, John C., *History of the Mennonites of the Franconia Conference* (Telford, Penn., The Franconia Mennonite Historical Society, 1937, pp. xvi, 523). Based upon careful and extensive research.

Wentz, Abdel Ross, *The Lutheran Church in American History* (Philadelphia, The United Lutheran Publication House, 2d ed., 1933, pp. 465). By an outstanding Church historian.

Wesley, John, *The Journal of the Rev. John Wesley* (Everyman's Library Edition, New York, E. P. Dutton and Co., 4 vols., 1921).

Wessels, C., *Early Jesuit Travellers in Central Asia 1603-1721* (The Hague, Martinus Nijhoff, 1924, pp. xvi, 344). Fully documented, with some of the original sources printed *in extenso*.

Wheelock, Eleazer, *A Plain and Faithful Narrative of the Original Design, Rise, Progress and Present State of the Indian Charity-School at Lebanon, in Connecticut* (Boston, Richard and Samuel Draper, 1763, pp. 55).

White, Charles L., *A Century of Faith: with an Introduction by President Arsten Kennedy de Blois. Centenary Volume Published for the American Baptist Home Mission Society* (Philadelphia, The Judson Press, 1932, pp. 320). A memorial volume by a past executive secretary of the Society.

Wiggers, Julius, *Geschichte der evangelischen Mission* (Hamburg and Gotha, Friedrich und Andreas Perthes, 2 vols., 1845, 1846).

Wilgus, A. Curtis, *Colonial Hispanic America* (Washington, D. C., The George Washington University Press, 1936, pp. ix, 690). By several authors; contains excellent bibliographies.

Zaleski, L. M., *The Martyrs of India* (Mangalore, The Codialbail Press, 1913, pp. 263). By the Delegate Apostolic of the East Indies; takes traditional views; written for purposes of edification.

[Zaleski, L. M.] *Les Martyrs de l'Inde: Constance des Indiens dans la Foi* (Calcutta, Catholic Orphan Press, 1896, pp. vii, 256).

Zeitschrift für Missionswissenschaft (Münster i.W., 1911 ff.). Under the editorship of Professor Schmidlin; the best of the scholarly Roman Catholic periodicals devoted to missions.

INDEX

Abenaki, 177, 178
Abyssinia, 46, 73, 77, 79, 81
Acadia, 173, 174
Activism, 231, 381, 398
Adams, Will, 331
Adrian VI, 439
Æquum Reputamus, bull, 40
Africa, 240-246
Africa, North, 3, 23, 75
Agra, 258
Agriculture, in Venezuela, 138; in the Philippines, 318
Aiguillon, Duchess d', 175
Akbar, 257
Alaska, 370
Albania, 72, 73
Albany, New York, 195, 221
Albazin, 359, 368
Alberoni, 385
Aldeas, 160
Aleutian Islands, 370
Alexander VI, 6, 8, 19, 40, 90
Alexander VII, 91
Alexandria, Patriarch of, 79
Alfonso, King of Congo, 242, 243
Algiers, 75
Algonquins, 175, 177
Alibamons, 181
Allouez, 180
Altar River, 123
Amazon, 149, 151, 152, 166
Amboina, 300-303, 305, 306
America, 194
America, 88 ff.; discovery and conquest of, 7
American Board of Commissioners for Foreign Missions, 281
Amsterdam, 303; Classis of, 189, 202, 245
Amur River, 367, 368
Amusements, 401
Anabaptists, 13, 383, 399, 436, 437
Ancestors, ceremonies in honour of, 350
Anchieta, Joseph de, 163
Andalusia, Apostle of, 19
Andrada, Antonio de, 360
Andreae, Valentine, 384, 385
Angelicalas, 19
Angleri, Peter Martyr, 44
Angola, 243, 244

Anjiro, 323, 324
Anjou, hospital sisters of, 173
Antigua, 234, 235
Antioch, Patriarch of, 79
Anti-slavery movement, in Thirteen Colonies, 225, 226
Apaches, 123, 127
Apurimac, 150
Aquaviva, 257
Aquinas, Thomas, 394
Arabs, 249
Arakan, 293, 294
Araucanians, 152
Arawaks, 237
Archangel, 66
Arequipo, 150
Arima, 325, 327, 332
Aristotle, 394
Arizona, 123
Arkansas, 181
Armenians, 3, 80, 276
Arnauld, Antoine, 414
Art, 5; influence of Christianity upon, 409, 410
Asbury, Francis, 214
Ashikaga, 322
Asia, Central, 3
Astronomy, 417, 418
Asunción, 153, 154
Atahuallpa, 145, 150
Ataide, Alvaro de, 338
Aufklärung, 49
Augustine, 394
Augustinian Recollects, in the Philippines, 310
Augustinians, 20; in Mexico, 110; in Venezuela, 141; in New Granada, 143; in Peru, 146; in Africa, 242; in India, 273; in Ceylon, 287; in Indo-China, 298; in the East Indies, 302; in the Philippines, 309-318; in China, 339, 344, 346, 348
Aurangzeb, 258
Ava, 293, 294
Aveiro de Arcos y Maqueda, Duchess de, 39
Avignon, 7
Avila, John of, 19, 404
Avitabile, 263
Ayuthia, 295

Azevedo, Francisco de, 361
Azevedo, Ignacio de, 163
Azores, 242

Babylonian Exile, 7
Bach, Johann Sebastian, 408, 409
Bacon, Francis, 419
Bahamas, 233
Bahia, 161, 162, 165, 236
Baikal, Lake, 368
Baji, 243
Balboa, 133
Balkan Peninsula, 3
Baltimore, 205
Banda Islands, 300, 306
Bannermen, 357
Baptism of infants in articulo mortis, 364
Baptist Missionary Society, 50
Baptists, 193, 195, 203, 204, 208, 210, 211, 213, 215, 231, 234, 383
Baranov, 370
Barbados, 233, 234
Barclay, Henry, 221
Barnabites, 16, 18; in Burma, 294
Bassein, 251, 263, 293
Batan Islands, 314
Batavia, 305, 306
Bavaria, Duke of, 342
Baxter, John, 235
Behaine, Pigneau de, 299
Bell, Andrew, 413
Bellamy, 231
Bellarmine, Robert, 259, 261, 391
Bellers, John, 396, 399, 402
Bellomont, Earl of, 221
Beltrán, Luis, 143
Benedictines, 20, 22; in Mexico, 111; in Brazil, 162
Bengal, 258, 263, 273
Benin, 242
Berkeley, George, 232, 418
Bermuda, 232, 233
Bertrand, Louis, 143
Beschi, Joseph-Constant, 261, 275
Bethlehem, Pennsylvania, 203, 223
Beza, 59
Bhaktamala, the, 276
Biard, 171
Bible, translations of, 9, 280; translation of, by Eliot, 219; translation of into Malay, 304, 305; translated into Chinese, 363; and literature, 415
Bicholim, 268
Bienvenida, Lorenzo de, 120
Bijapur, 263, 267, 268
Bio-Bio, 152

Bishoprics, in Spanish America, 99
Blair, James, 208
Bobadilla, 92
Boehm, John Philip, 201
Böhme, Anton Wilhelm, 279
Bogomilism, 72
Bogotá, 139, 142, 143
Bohemia, 13, 33
Boil, Nernal, 107
Bolivia, 150, 153
Bombay, 256, 266, 268, 269
Bonnor, 394
Book of Common Prayer, 191, 192
Borneo, 302
Borromeo, Carlo, 19, 380
Bosnia, 72
Boston, 192, 218
Bourbon, island, 245
Boyle, Robert, 45, 277
Braganza, House of, 268
Brahmins, 255, 260-263, 265, 267, 268
Brainerd, David, 220
Brainerd, John, 220
Brant, Joseph, 221
Bray, Thomas, 48, 189, 206, 212
Brazil, 43, 160-167; Protestantism in, 236
Brébeuf, Jean de, 176
Brest, 78
Brethren, Church of the, 199
Brethren of the Common Life, 9, 416
Britto, Giovanni Éttore de, 261
Britto, Philip de, 293
Brothers of Christian Schools, 414
Brothers of St. Gabriel, 414
Brown, David, 281
Bucer, Martin, 59
Buchanan, Claudius, 281
Buchanan, John, 412
Buddhism, 9, 290, 292, 323-331, 341
Buenos Aires, 153
Bugenhagen, John, 412
Bull fights, 401
Bungo, 324
Burma, 293, 294
Buryats, 369
Bus, César de, 414
Bush Negroes, 237
Byzantine Empire, conquered by Turks, 3, 10
Byzantine Rite, 79

Cabeza de Vaca, 97
Cabral, 161, 251, 361
Cacao, 138, 318
Cacella, 361
Cadillac, 182

Cajamarquilla, 150
Calchi, 294
Calcutta, 273, 280, 281
Calendar, Chinese, 342-344, 349, 364; Gregorian, 417
Cali, 143
Calicut, 251
California, 128-130; Lower, 122-124
Callenberg, John Henry, 61, 76
Calverts, 205
Calvin, John, 13, 16, 25, 433, 436
Calvinism and society, 399; and the state, 387-389; effect on laity, 379, 380; and capitalism, 407, 408; and the Latin spirit, 430
Camaldolese, 18
Camaldulians, 18
Cambodia, 296, 298
Campanius, John, 222
Canada, 168-185
Cancer, Luis de Barbastro, 132
Candelarians, 141
Candidius, G., 359
Cannon, cast by Jesuits, 343
Canons, of St. John the Evangelist, 242
Canton, 337, 340, 351
Cape Coast Castle, 246
Capetown, 245
Cape Verde Islands, 242
Capitalism, and Calvinism, 407, 408
Capuchins, 16, 20, 32, 33; in Russia, 78; in Egypt, 79; in Syria, 80; in the Caucasus, 81; in Darien, 135, 139; in Venezuela, 137-139; of Catalonia, 140; in Brazil, 162, 166; in French America, 173, 182, 184; in Africa, 242, 244; French, in India, 269, 270; in India, 272; in Tibet, 361
Caquetá, 152
Carácas, 138
Caraffa, Giovanni Pietro, 16
Cards, playing, 401
Careas, 287
Carey, William, 281
Caribs, 141, 235
Carmelites, in Brazil, 162; in French America, 182; in the Congo, 243; in India, 266, 268, 269
Carmelites, Discalced, 20; in Mexico, 111; in Lower California, 124
Caroline Islands, 314
Carols, Christmas, 409
Caron, Joseph le, 173
Cartagena, 144
Cartier, Jacques, 171
Casanare River, 139, 140

Caste, 270, 281
Castro, Matthaeus de, 267, 268
Castro, Thomas de, 265, 268
Catechisms, 17, 37; Protestant, 379; Roman Catholic, 380; Russian Orthodox, 381
Catechists, 297
Catherine II, 77, 370
Caughnawaga, 179
Cayugas, 178, 179, 181
Celebes, 300-302
Cellini, Benvenuto, 443
Central America, 133-136
Ceram, 306
Ceuta, 75
Ceylon, 254, 255, 285-292
Champlain, 172, 176
Chandernagor, 361
Chaoch'ing, 340
Ch'aochou, 341
Chapetones, 101
Charcas, 150
Charity, 403-405; Brethren of, 19; Daughters of, 23
Charity schools, 413
Charles I, execution of, 387-389
Charles V, 6, 74, 88, 93, 98, 100, 108
Charles VII of France, 6
Charleston, 211
Charleston Association of Baptist Churches, 211
Chartres, Sisters of Saint Paul of, 245
Chêng Ch'êng-kung, 359
Chengtu, 343
Chequamegon, 180
Cheremis, 68, 69
Chesapeake Bay, 132
Chiapa, 96
Chiapas, 135
Ch'ien Lung, 336, 357
Chihuahua, 121, 122
Chihli, 358
Chile, 150, 152
Chillán, 150, 152, 153
Chiloé, 153
China, 3, 4, 255, 311, 336-366
Chinese, in the Philippines, 313
Ch'ing Dynasty, 357, 361
Chiquitos, 153
Chiriguanos, 151
Christian II, of Denmark, 433
Christian Faith Society, 45
Christianity, state in 1500, 1-9; awakening in the sixteenth century, 8 ff; cause of new life in Europe and expansion of Europe, 10, 11; effect on environment,

372-426; effect of environment upon, 427-449; decline of, near end of eighteenth century, 453-457; revival of in nineteenth century, 457
Christianopolis, 384, 385
Christian Schools, Brothers of, 23
Christian Science, 193
Christ, Order of, 38, 40
Church Missionary Society, 50, 281
Church of England, in West Indies, 232-234
Cistercians, 20, 22
Civitas Dei, of Augustine, 385
Classis of Amsterdam, 189, 202, 245, 303
Claver, Pedro, 98, 144
Clavius, Christopher, 340
Clement VII, 74
Clement VIII, 329
Clergy, improvement in, in Europe, 377, 378; native, 38, 39; native, in India, 274; native, in Indo-China, 297; native, in Japan, 330; native, in the Philippines, 315, 316, 320; native, in China, 346, 358
Clerks Regular of the Mother of God, 19
Clerks Regular of St. Paul, 18
Clocks, 5, 340, 364
Cochin, 249, 255, 263, 266
Cochin, Bishop of, 287
Cochin China, 296-299
Coddington, William, 192
Codrington, Christopher, 233
Coetus, 202
Coetus correspondentium, 303
Coffee, 138
Coimbra, 22, 255
Coke, Thomas, 235
Colegio de Santa Cruz en Tlatelulco, 116
Colet, John, 396, 412
College of New Jersey, 215
College of St. Paul, Goa, 257, 324
Collegium de cursu evangelico promovendo, 64
Collegium Urbanum de Propaganda Fide, 34
Colombia, 142-144
Colombo, 285-291
Colorado River, 123
Columbus, Christopher, 4, 86, 422
Comenius, John Amos, 412
Commissary of the Bishop of London, 189, 206, 208, 211
Commonwealth, in England, 14, 388-390, 399
Communion, in East Indies, 305
Communion. Roman Catholic, 380

Company for the Propagation of the Gospel in New England and Parts Adjacent to America, 45, 189, 221
Compass, 5
Concepción, 152, 153
Conciliar movement, 7
Confession, 380; in Spanish America, 105, 116
Confucianism, 9, 365
Confucius, 350
Congo, Kingdom of, 242, 243
Congregation for the Propagation of the Faith. See Propaganda
Congregation of the Mission. See Lazarists
Congregation of the Priests of the Mission. See Lazarists
Congregationalism, 188, 193, 195, 213, 215
Connecticut, 192, 219
Constantinople, 71
Contented of the God-loving Soul, 231
Copenhagen, 64
Copernicus, 15, 417
Copts, 3, 79
Cordoba, Pedro de, 107
Cordova, Pedro de, 136
Corn, 318
Cortés, Hernando, 108-110, 124
Cossacks, 367
Costa Rica, 134
Cotton, 116
Cotton, John, 192
Cozumel, 109
Cranganore, Archbishop of, 265
Cranmer, 60
Creoles, 39; admitted to episcopate, 102
Critias, 385
Cromwell, Oliver, 388, 389
Crucé, Émeric, 396
Cuba, 108
Cuddalore, 280
Cuius regio, eius religio, 431
Cuzco, 96, 146, 149
Cyprian, 368

Daimyo, 324-333
Dale's Laws, 207
Damaun, 263
Dances, pagan, persistence in Mexico, 119
Dancing, 401
Danes, in India, 277-281
Danish West Indies, 236
Darien, 135, 139
Darmstadt, 62
Dartmouth College, 220
Daughters of the Cross, 404
Davies, Samuel, 209

Deaf mutes, 414
De Indis Noviter Inventis, 394
Deism, 23, 365, 382
De Jure Belli, 394
De Jure Belli et Pacis, 394, 395
Delaware, 196, 197, 221
Delawares, 220, 223
Delhi, 258
Democracy, in Thirteen Colonies, 228; and Christianity, 387-391
Demon possession, 363
Denmark, and the Lapps, 64, 65
Deputati ad res Indicas, 303
Descartes, 416
Desideri, Hippolyte, 361
Detroit, 182
Diamper, Synod of, 264
Diaz da Costa, Donna Juliana, 258
Dimitri, 78
Discoveries, geographic, of fifteenth and sixteenth centuries, 4, 7
Diu, 263
Dolores, Nuestra Señora, 123
Dominicans, arrive in America, 93; in Spanish America, 100; on Hispaniola, 95, 107; in Mexico, 110, 113, 120; in Lower California, 129; in Central America, 134; in Venezuela, 137, 139; in New Granada, 142, 143; in Peru, 145, 146; in Africa, 242, 244; in India, 251, 263, 264; in Ceylon, 287; in Burma, 293; in Siam, 295; in Tongking, 298; in East Indies, 302; in the Philippines, 310-319; in Japan, 327-329; in China, 339, 346, 348, 350, 351, 353, 358
Donnés, 176
Doukhobors, 396, 446
Doutrinas, 160
Druillette, 178
Dürer, Albrecht, 410
Dunkers, 199
Durand, Nicholas, 43
Durango, 121, 122
Dutch, in Brazil, 161, 166, 236; in America, 177, 194-199, 201, 202; in South Africa, 245; in India, 266, 277; in Ceylon, 288-292; in East Indies, 301-306; in Japan, 333, 334; in Formosa, 359, 360
Dutchess County, New York, 222, 223
Dutch West India Company, 189
Dvina, 63

East India Company, Dutch, 245, 246, 301-306
East India Company, English, 269, 277, 281
East Indies, 300-306

Economic effects of Christianity, 405-408
Ecuador, 146, 147
Edinburgh, University of, 413
Edmundson, William, 210
Education, in Peru, 148; in Thirteen Colonies, 227; in the Philippines, 319; religious, in Europe, 378-381; effect of Christianity upon, 410-415
Edwards, Jonathan, 215, 220, 231
Edzard, Esdras, 60
Egede, Hans, 237, 238
Egede, Paul, 238
Egypt, 3, 46, 77, 78
Eliot, John, 44, 218-220
Elizabeth, of England, 14, 32, 387, 434
Elizabeth, of Russia, 69, 76
Elizabeth Islands, 217
El Paso, 125
Emerson, Ralph Waldo, 194
Encomenderos, 87, 92
Encomienda, 92, 109
England, Church of, 14, 48, 49
England, Church of, in Thirteen Colonies, 187, 188, 193, 205, 213
England, nonconformity in, 380; Puritan Revolution in, 388, 389; and Protestantism, 434
English, in India, 266, 268, 269
Enlightenment, 49, 68
Ephrata Society, 231
Erasmus, 13, 21, 395, 415
Eskimos, 237, 238
Essay on the Human Understanding, 418
Ethiopia, 4
Eudists, 23
Europe, spread of Christianity in, 55-77; effect of Christianity upon, 373-421
Europe, Western, Christianity in, 4
Evangelical movement, 49
Exercises, of Loyola, 442
Ex illa die, bull, 354
Ex quo singulari, bull, 298, 355

Fabricius, Philip, 280
Faerie Queene, 416
Fathers of Christian Doctrine, 414
Fénelon, 382
Fenicio, 275
Ferdinand, 6, 74
Ferreira, 332
Ferrer, Rafael, 151
Fifth Monarchy Men, 399
Filipinos, 309-321
Finney, Charles G., 193
Fisher Coast, 253-256, 261, 273, 274
Fjellstroem, 65

Flax, 149
Flores, 302
Florida, 132, 133
Foreign Missionary Society of Paris. See Société des Missions Étrangères of Paris
Formosa, 359, 360
Fort Christina, 196
Fox, George, 45, 196, 208, 210, 221, 234, 381-383
France, power of King over Church, 6; reform of the Church in, 22; and missions, 41; Roman Catholic Church in, 441; and Protestantism, 433
Francis I of France, 6
Franciscans, Conventual, 20; Discalced, 20; Observant, 20; colleges for preparation of missionaries, 37; in Egypt, 79; in Spanish America, 100; in West Indies, 107; in Mexico, 110, 113, 120, 121; in Yucatan, 120; in New Mexico, 125, 126; in Texas, 126, 127; in California, 128-130; in Florida and Georgia, 132, 133; in Central America, 135; in Venezuela, 137-139; in New Granada, 142, 143; in Peru, 146-153; in Paraguay, 155; in Brazil, 161, 166; in Africa, 242-244; in India, 251, 262, 264, 266, 274; Goanese, 268; in Ceylon, 285-288; in Burma, 293; in Siam, 295; in Indo-China, 298; in the East Indies, 302; in the Philippines, 309-318; in Japan, 327-329; in China, 339, 344, 346, 348, 350, 351, 353, 358
Frank, Jacob, 58
Francke, August Hermann, 46, 48, 412
Francke, G. A., 200
Frankfurt, 199
Frederick the Great, 377
Frederick IV, of Denmark, 278
Freeman, Bernardus, 221
Frelinghuysen, Theodore Jacobus, 214
French, in Brazil, 161; in North America, 168-185; in India, 270, 272, 273; in Indo-China, 297-299; in China, 345, 346
French Revolution, 357, 391, 441
French West Indies, 169, 184
Fresenius, John Philip, 62
Friends. See Quakers
Frontenac, Fort, 182
Fukien, 343, 344, 346, 358
Fur-trade, French, 170; in Siberia, 367

Galileo, 5
Galle, 289, 290
Gallicanism, 441
Galvão, Antonio, 300
Gante, Pedro de, 112-114

Garcés, Juan, 136
Garcés, Julian, 113
Garhwal, 258
Garrison, William Lloyd, 194
General Court of Massachusetts, 217, 219
Geneva, 399, 401
Gentili, Alberico, 394
Gentilismus Reseratus, 277
George, Archdeacon, 265
Georgia (in the Caucasus), 73, 81, 263
Georgia (North America), 132, 133, 212
Gerhardt, Paul, 380
Gericke, 280
German, Archbishop of Kazan, 68
Germanía, 74
Germans, in America, 198-203; and Roman Catholic missions, 42
Germantown, 199, 226
Germany, 14; missions from, 46; effect on Protestantism, 431
Ghent, Peter of, 112-114
Gibbon, 415
Gila River, 123
Gilbert, Nathaniel, 234
Glasgow Missionary Society, 50
Gluck, 409
Gnadenhütten, 223
Goa, 249, 251, 253, 255-257, 262, 263, 272, 274, 324
Goa, Archbishop of, 250, 261, 267, 268
Goes, Bento de, 360
Goethe, 415
Golden Horde, 67
Gorton, Samuel, 192
Goto Islands, 325, 334
Granada (in Spain), 73, 75
Gran Chaco, 148, 151
Grand Design, of Henry IV, 396
Great Awakening, 14, 29, 30, 49, 190, 193, 214-216, 220, 227, 230, 232
Great Mogul, 256-259
Green Bay, 180
Greenland, 237, 238
Gregory XIII, 340
Gregory XIV, 318
Grenada (in West Indies), 233
Grotius, Hugo, 304, 394, 395
Grueber, John, 361
Gründler, 279
Guadeloupe, 184
Guadelupe, Virgin of, 118
Guatemala, 95, 133, 134
Günzberg, 384
Guiana, French, 168, 184; Spanish, 140
Guinea Coast, 242, 246
Gurius, 68

Guru, 260
Gustavus Adolphus, 196
Gustavus Vasa, 43, 64, 433
Guyon, Madame, 382

Haiti. See Hispaniola
Hakluyt, 43
Half-way Covenant, 193
Halle, 47, 61, 200, 201, 212, 278-282; orphanage of, 405; University of, 412
Halmahera, 300
Hamilton College, 221
Handel, 408, 409
Hangchow, 347
Hanover, New Hampshire, 220
Hariot, 44
Harrington, James, 384
Harvard College, 218
Haven, Jens, 238
Haydn, Franz Joseph, 409
Hecker, 412
Hedge schools, 414
Helwys, Thomas, 383
Henrico, 44, 207, 223
Henriquez, 257
Henry IV, of France, 22
Henry VIII, of England, 14, 434, 435
Henry the Navigator, 38, 241, 422
Henry, Negro bishop, 243
Hermogen, 421
Herrara, Diego de, 317
Herrnhut, 47
Hesselius, Andrew, 222
Heurnius, Justus, 43, 304, 305
Heyling, Peter, 46, 77
Hidetada, 331, 332
Hideyori, 328, 331
Hideyoshi, Toyotomi, 323-328
Hieronymites, 33, 94, 100, 107
Highlanders, Scotch, 213
Hinduism, 9, 11
Hindustani, 280
Hirado, 324
Hispaniola, 93, 95, 99, 107
Hobbes, Thomas, 390
Holy Roman Empire, 4
Holy Synod, 444
Honan, 346
Honduras, 135
Hooker, Richard, 390
Hooker, Thomas, 192, 218
Hopkins, Samuel, 226, 231
Hospitallers of St. John of God, 19, 100, 111, 310
Hospitals, 404; in Philippines, 319
Hottentots, 245, 246

Howard, John, 399, 402
Hsianfu, 342
Hsü Kuang-ch'i, 341, 342, 361, 365
Hsü, Paul, 341, 342, 361, 365
Huallaga River, 149
Huánuco, 150
Hudson Bay, 180
Hugli, 273, 293
Huguenots, 33, 193, 195, 196, 208, 211, 245
Humanism, 9, 436
Humiliati, 20
Hunan, 346
Hupeh, 346
Huron Indians, 172, 175-177
Hus, John, 9, 11
Hyder Ali, 271
Hymns, Protestant, 380

Iceland, 433
Île de France, 245
Illinois, 180
Inca, 145
Independents, 388
India, 3, 4, 247 ff
Indians, in Spanish America, 86 ff; exploited by Spaniards, 89, 90; admitted to clergy, 101, 102; Protestant missions to, 216-225
Inquisition, 56, 74; in America, 99, 116; in India, 269
Institutum Judaicum, 61
Interest, attitudes towards, 406
International law, 393-395
International relations, effect of Christianity upon, 392-398
Introduction to the Devout Life, 17
Ireland, 414
Irkutsk, 369
Iroquois, 176-179, 181, 221, 223
Irtysh Valley, 368
Isabella, 6, 21, 74, 88, 92
Islam, 1, 3, 4, 9, 11, 247, 248; conversion of Christians to, 71-73; in East Indies, 302-304; in the Philippines, 307
Italy, and missions, 41; and Protestantism, 434
Ivan IV. See Ivan the Terrible
Ivan the Terrible, 63, 66-68, 421
Iyemitsu, 331
Iyeyasu, Tokugawa, 323-331

Jacobites, 80, 265
Jaffna, 286, 287, 289, 290
Jaipur, 259
Jamaica, 108, 233-235
James I, of England, 44, 224, 391

Janizaries, 71
Jansenism, 23
Jansenists, 380, 414
Japan, 322-335
Japanese, in Cochin China, 296; in the Philippines, 313
Jauja, 150
Jehangir, 258
Jerome de Royer de la Dauversière, 173
Jerusalem Delivered, 415
Jerusalem, Synod of, 381
Jesuits, 17, 19, 22, 27, 32, 33; dissolution of, 42; missions for Jews, 57; in Abyssinia, 79, 80; in Russia, 78; in Spanish America, 100; in Mexico, 110, 120-125; in Lower California, 124, 125; in Florida and Georgia, 132; in Nicaragua, 134; in Venezuela, 139; in New Granada, 143; in Peru, 147; in the Maynas, 151, 152; in Bolivia, 153; in Paraguay, 154-156; in Brazil, 161-166; in French America, 171-185; in New York, 195; in Maryland, 223; in Africa, 243-245; in India, 251-265, 269, 270, 272, 273, 274, 276; in Ceylon, 287, 288; in Burma, 293; in Siam, 295; in Indo-China, 296, 297; in East Indies, 301, 302; in the Philippines, 310-319; in Japan, 323-332; in China, 338-356, 358; in Tibet, 360, 361; and education, 413, 414
Jesus, impulse from, 3, 4, 11
Jesus, Society of. See Jesuits
Jews, missions of Roman Catholic among, 55-59; missions of Protestants among, 59-63; in Russia, 63
Jiménez, Francisco, 149, 150
Jogues, Isaac, 176
John III, of Portugal, 22, 161, 252, 263
John of the Cross, 20, 21
John of God, 404
Juan, Prince, 86
Juan Santos, 150
Judaism, conversion of Christians, to, 63; in America, 99
Julius III, 80, 161
Junius, R., 359

Kabul, 258
Kagoshima, 324
Kalmyks, 70, 369
Kama, 68
Kamchatka, 368, 369
Kandy, 287, 289, 291
K'ang Hsi, 336, 344, 345, 347, 352-356
Kansu, 348
Kant, Emmanuel, 418

Karaiyar, 287
Karawa, 287
Karawola, 287
Kasarev, Maxim, 369
Kazan, 68, 69, 77
Kennebec River, 177, 178
Kentucky, 213
Kepler, Johann, 418
Khlysty, 446
Kiakhta, Treaty of, 359
Kiangnan, 358
Kiangsi, 341
Kiernander, 280
Kiev, 24, 368, 445
King James Version, 415
King Philip's War, 219
King's College, 190
Kingston, Jamaica, 236
Kino, Eusebio Francisco, 122, 123
Kirkland, Samuel, 221
Knox, John, 388, 399, 412
Kodiak Island, 370
Koffler, Andrew, 343
Kokonor, 361
Kola Peninsula, 66
Kola River, 66
Korea, 327, 361, 362
Kotte, 287, 288
Koxinga, 359
Kuei Wang, 342, 343
Kwangsi, 358
Kwangtung, 340, 358
Kweichow, 358
Kyoto, 324, 327
Kyushu, 324-331, 334

Labrador, 238
Ladrones, 314
La Fontaine, 261
Lahore, 258, 360
Lainez, 391
Laissez faire, 406, 407
Laity, improvement in, in Europe, 378-381
Lake of the Woods, 180
Lake of Two Mountains, 181
Lambert, La Motte, 295, 297
Lancaster, Joseph, 413
Landa, Diego de, 120
Language, effect of Christianity upon, 415
Laos, 298
La Paz, 150
Lapps, 43, 64-67
Laramans, 72
La Salle, 126, 181, 182
La Salle, John Baptist de, 414

Las Casas, Bartolomé de, 93 ff, 132, 134, 137, 146
Lateran Council, 380
Laval-Montmorency, François Xavier de, 36, 174, 180
Law, international, 393-395
Law, William, 382, 400
Laws of Ecclesiastical Polity, 390
Laws of the Indies, 91, 92, 96, 97, 99, 107
Laynez, 57
Lazarists, 23, 245, 272, 356, 358
League of Nations, 397
Lebanon, Connecticut, 220
Legaspi, 309
Leh, 361
Leibnitz, 46, 351
Le Jeune, 175
Lellis, Camille de, 405
Leo X, 6
Leontiev, Maxim, 359
Leszczynski, Filofie, 368
Levellers, 399, 406
Leyden, 43, 303
Lhasa, 361
Liele, George, 235
Light in the West, 61
Lima, 148; University of, 148
Linen, 116
Lisbon, 252; missionaries to go by, 269
Litchfield County, 223
Literati, 336, 341, 349
Literature, effect of Christianity upon, 415-417
Liturgies, 382
Livonia, 63
Loanda, 244
Loango, 244
Locke, John, 389, 418
Log College, 215
Lollardy, 435
London, Bishop of, 189, 213, 225
London Missionary Society, 50
Long Island, 220
Lopez, Gregory, 346
Loreto, 124
Louis XIV, 345
Louisiana, 182
Loyola, Ignatius, 16, 17, 19, 27, 33, 252, 404, 442
Lucaris, Cyril, 77
Lucca, 19
Lübeck, 46
Lütkens, Franz Julius, 278
Luther, Martin, 13, 14, 16, 25, 381, 436; and Jews, 59; and the state, 387; hymns of, 380, 409; *Open Letter to the Christian*

Nobility of the German Nation, 398; and charity, 405; and education, 412; translation of the Bible, 415; Lutherans, 195, 200-203, 209, 210, 211; in India, 278-282
Luzon, 314
Lyons, Poor Men of, 9

Mabillion, 402
Macao, 327, 333, 337, 339, 342, 347, 353, 354
Macassar, 301
Macerata, 339
Machiavelli, 5, 385
Madagascar, 23, 245
Madeiras, 242
Madras, 251, 280
Madura, 256, 259-262, 273
Magdalena River, 123, 142-144
Magellan, 308, 309, 317
Magyars, 432
Maigrot, 345, 351, 352
Maine, 172, 177, 178
Makemie, Francis, 204, 209
Malabar, 263-265
Malabar Christians. See Syrian Christians
Malabar Rites, 269-271
Malacca, 249, 255, 294, 295, 338
Malay Archipelago, 300-306
Malay language, 304
Malay Peninsula, 294, 295
Malindi, 244
Manar, 286-288
Manchus, 342, 343
Manila, 296, 311-320, 327, 332; Archbishop of, 350
Manuale Lapponicum, 64
Maps, in China, 340, 364
Maracaibo, 139
Maranhão, 165, 166
Marañon River, 149, 151
Marathas, 271
Marathi, 275
Marawa, Prince of, 261
Mariana, 314
Marie de l'Incarnation, 175
Marii, 68
Maronites, 80
Marquette, 180
Marranos, 56
Marriage, 401; in Mexico, 115, 119
Marroquin, Francisco, 133
Martaban, 294
Martha's Vineyard, 217, 218
Martín de Valencia, 112
Martinique, 184

Martyn, Henry, 281
Mary, Queen of England, 32
Mary, Queen of Scots, 388
Maryland, 205, 206, 225
Mass, 382; the first said in America, 86
Massachusetts, 191, 217-219; first charter of, 44
Masse, 171
Mathematics, 5
Matthew of St. Joseph, 266
Mauretania, 40
Mauritius, 45, 245
Maya cult, 118
Maya, writing, 120
Mayhew, Experience, 218
Mayhew, John, 218
Mayhew, Thomas, 217, 218
Maynas, the, 151, 152
Mazarin, 385, 386, 392
Medicine, 116; in Japan, 330
Meditation, 381, 382
Melanchthon, 16, 25, 412, 436
Melchites, 79
Mem de Sá, 163
Mendelssohn, Moses, 62
Mendoza, Juan de, 137
Mendoza, Viceroy of Mexico, 124
Menendez, Pedro de Avila, 132
Mennonites, 199, 226
Menstruation, 270
Mercedarians, 33, 134, 135, 141, 146, 166
Merici, Angela of Brescia, 19
Mesopotamia, 3
Mestizos, admitted to clergy, 101
Meta River, 139
Methodists, 195, 206, 213, 214, 234, 235
Methods, in Mexico, 114, 115; in Spanish America, 102-107
Mexico, 308, 310, 311; missions in, 108-123; Las Casas in, 95, 96; University of, 116
Mexico City, 110
Mezzabarba, Jean Charles, 271, 294, 354, 355
Michelangelo, 410
Michoacán, 121
Microscopes, 5
Middle Ages, 4, 5, 8
Milton, John, 383, 415
Minaya, Bernardino de, 93
Mindanao, 313, 314
Ming Dynasty, 4, 342, 343
Mission, Spanish, as a frontier institution, 103-107
Missions-Étrangères of Paris. See Société des Missions-Étrangères

Mississippi River, 126, 180, 181
Mitla, 118
Miyako, 324
Mocorito, 121
Mogul, Vicariate Apostolic of the Great, 268
Moguls, 256-259
Mohammedanism. See Islam
Mohawks, 177-179, 221, 223
Mojos, 153
Moluccas, 255, 301, 302
Mombasa, 244
Monarchies, control of the Church, 375, 376
Mongols, 67
Monserrate, 257
Montauks, 220
Monterey, 128
Montreal, 173, 179, 182
Moody, Dwight L., 193
Moors, 73, 74
Moplas, 251
Moquegua, 150
Morales, 350
Moravia, 13
Moravians, 14, 47, 48, 60, 61, 66, 202, 203, 210-212, 222-225, 234-239, 246, 281, 437
More, Thomas, 384, 385
Moriscos, 74, 75
Mormons, 193
Moscow, 24, 67
Moslems, converted, 73-75; in Ceylon, 289; in Malay Peninsula, 294. Also see Islam
Mosques, 256
Mozambique, 244, 253
Mozart, 409
Mt. Desert Island, 172
Muhlenberg, Henry Melchior, 200, 201
Muhlenberg, Peter, 209
Music, in Philippines, 319; effect of Christianity upon, 408, 409
Mysore, 261, 271

Nabhadas, 276
Nagasaki, 325, 327-331
Namur, Sisters of Charity of, 23
Nanch'ang, 341
Nanking, 341, 346, 347
Nantes, Edict of, 195; revocation of the edict of, 32
Nantucket, 217, 218
Naples, 358
Narragansetts, 217
Narváez, 97
Natick, 219
Natural religion, 382

Navarre, 74, 252
Navarrete, 351
Nayarit Indians, 123
Nazareth, Pennsylvania, 203
Near East, 3, 76, 77
Neches River, 126
Negombo, 287, 289
Negroes, in Spanish America, 90, 98, 106, 107, 108, 144; in Brazil, 164; in Thirteen Colonies, 224-226; in English and Danish West Indies, 233-236; in Africa, 240-246
Nepal, 361
Nerchinsk, 368
Neri, Philip, 19, 57, 255, 263, 408
Nestorianism, 3, 80, 264, 276
Netherlands, 388, 434
New Amsterdam, 194
New Brunswick, 178, 214
New England, 191-194, 217-219
New England Company, 45, 221
New England Theology, 231
Newfoundland, 171
New France, 168-185
Newgate, 402
New Granada, 142-144
New Haven, 192, 196
New Herrnhut, 238
New Jersey, 196, 214, 225; College of, 190
New Laws, 95, 96
New Lights, 231
New London, 219, 220
New Mexico, 125, 126
New Netherland, 194, 195
New Orleans, 181, 182
Newport, 192, 226
New Rochelle, 195
New Spain. See Mexico
Newton, Isaac, 418
New York, 194-196, 221
New York City, 194, 195
Nicaragua, 95, 134
Nicholson, Francis, 206
Nicobar Islands, 281
Nijni Novgorod, 70
Nikon, 24, 68, 421, 445
Nilakandam-Pullay, 273
Nobili, Robert di, 259-262, 269, 270, 276
Nobrega, Manoel de, 162
Nobunaga, Oda, 322-325
Nonantum, 219
Norfolk County, 208
Norrland, 433
Northampton, 215
North Carolina, 209, 210, 221, 224, 225
North-west Coast (of North America), 124

Norway, 433
Norwich, 219
Notre-Dame de Montreal, Society of, 173
Nova Scotia, 171
Nueva Guatemala de la Asuncion, College of, 135
Nuevas Leyes, 95
Nursing, 401

Oaths, coronation, 386
Ob, 368
Oberconsistorium of the Palatinate, 201
Oberlin, John Frederic, 402, 403
Oblates of St. Ambrose, 19
Ocapa, 314; College of Santa Rosa de, 149, 150, 152, 153
Occom, Samson, 220
Oceana, 384
Ogdensburg, 181
Oglethorpe, James Edward, 212, 402
Old Believers, 68, 444, 445
Old Mohawk Church, 221
Olier, Jean Jacques, 173
Olmedo, 109
Olyuts, 369
Omura, 325
Oñate, Juan de, 125
Oneidas, 178, 179, 221
Onondagas, 178, 179, 181
Oratorians, 263, 291
Oratorians of Olinda, 166
Oratorio, 408
Oratory, Congregation of the, 19
Oratory of Divine Love, 18
Order of Christ, 38, 40, 241, 250
Order of St. John of God, 263
Orinoco, 137, 139, 141
Ormuz, 249
Ortiz, Tomás, 110
d'Orville, Albert, 361
Osaka, 327
Osorio, Diego Alvarez, 134
Ostyaks, 368
Ottawas, 180
Ottoman Empire, 4
Ottoman Turks. See Turks, Ottoman
Oudh, 361
Owen, Richard, 399
Oxygen, 418
Oyomei, 334

Padroado, Portuguese, 241, 250, 263, 266, 267; in India, 266-269; in China, 345, 346, 350, 353
Palæologi, 71

Palatinate, 199, 201
Palatinates, 211
Palestrina, 408
Pallu, François, 35, 295, 297, 345, 346
Paloú, 128
Pamir, 360
Pamlico Sound, 44
Pampas del Sacramento, 150
Pamplona, Francisco de, 137
Panama, 133-135
Panatahuas, 149
Papacy. See Popes
Pará, 151, 166
Paradise Lost, 415
Paraguay, 97; Jesuits in, 154-156
Paraná, 149, 155
Paravas, 253, 254, 256, 259, 260, 274, 282, 286, 287
Pariahs, 260, 262, 270, 271, 280
Paris Foreign Missionary Society. See Société des Missions-Étrangères
Paris, Treaty of, 183
Passionists, 24
Patna, 281
Patriarchate, Œcumenical, 71
Paul III, 90, 93, 113
Paul IV, 16
Paul, Vincent de, 23, 381, 401, 404
Paulines, 18
Payva, Antonio de, 301
Peasants' Revolt, 14, 398, 400
Pedro de Gante, 112
Pegu, 293, 294
Peking, 341-343, 358, 359, 362, 368
Peltrie, Madame de la, 175
Penance, 380
Penn, William, 188, 197, 198, 396
Pennsylvania, 197-205, 222, 225, 397
Persecutions, in Japan, 328-334; in China, 356-358; in Korea, 362
Pereira, Julian, 257
Pernambuco, 161, 165, 166, 236
Persia, 3, 73
Peru, 145-153
Peshawar, 258
Pestalozzi, John Henry, 413
Peter the Great, 68, 78, 368, 369, 444
Petri, Olaus, 402, 415
Phanariots, 71
Philadelphia, 198-205
Philadelphia Association (Baptist), 203, 210
Philanthropy, 403-405
Philip, Metropolitan, 421
Philip II, 6, 21, 28, 74, 88, 93, 285, 308, 392
Philippine Islands, 307-321, 327-332
Philosophes, 385

Philosophy, 418
Piarists, 414
Piazza di Spagna, 34
Picardy, 433
Pietism, 14, 46-48, 60, 61, 437
Pigneau de Behaine, 299
Pilgrims, 191
Pilgrim's Progress, The, 380
Pious Fund, 39, 125, 130
Piquet, 181
Pisco, 150
Pius IV, 441
Pius V, 21, 57, 93, 401
Pizarro, Francisco, 145, 146
Plütschau, 278
Plymouth, 191, 217
Pocahontas, 224
Podcarpathian Rutherians, 79
Poland, 32, 33, 432; Jews in, 57, 58
Polotzk, 63
Pondicherry, 270, 271
Popes; attempts to rally Western Christendom against the Turks, 3; corruption of in fifteenth and sixteenth centuries, 8; reform, 20, 21; power in Spanish America, 87, 88; decline of influence of in international affairs, 392, 393, 440; changes in position of, 440-442
Popoyan, College of, 152
Porto Rico, 108
Port Royal, 171
Portsmouth, 192
Portugal, power of King over Church, 6; reform of the Church in, 22; and missions, 40
Portuguese, as discoverers, 4, 7; in America, 160-167; in Africa, 241-246; in India, 247 ff., 277, 278; in Ceylon, 285-292; in Malacca, 295; in East Indies, 300-303; in Japan, 322-333
Post, Christian Frederick, 223
Pragmatic Sanction of Bourges, 6
Prangui, 260
Preparation of missionaries, 37
Presbyterians, 204, 209, 211-213, 215
President and Society for the Propagation of the Gospel in New England, 45
Priestley, Joseph, 418
Primería Alta, 122
Prince, The, of Machiavelli, 385
Princeton University, 215
Printing, 5
Prison reform, 399, 401, 402
Propaganda, 345, 346, 348; organization of, 33-35; and preparation of missionaries, 37; and native clergy, 38

Protestantism, rise of, 12-15; losses to
Roman Catholicism, 31-33; in America,
186 ff; in India, 276-282; in Ceylon,
289-291; in East Indies, 303-306; in Formosa, 359, 360; in Africa, 245, 246; in
general, 376; effect upon the state, 386-
390; and education, 410-415; moulded by
Teutonic peoples, 429, 430; in part prod-
uct of political conditions, 430-433
Protestant missionary methods, 50, 51
Protestant missions, reasons for lesser
prominence than Roman Catholic mis-
sions, 25-27; in general, 29, 30; increase
of, 42; beginning and development of,
42-50; to the Indians, 216-225
Provençal, 434
Providence, 192
Prussia, East, 432
Prussian Society for Philosophical Knowl-
edge, 46
Pufendorf, Samuel von, 395
Pulicat, 277
Pulo Condor, 299
Purana, Christian, 275
Puritanism, 14; effect on state, 388-390; on
economics, 407, 408
Puritans, 191-193, 195, 206, 208
Putumayo, 152

Quakers, 14, 45, 193-210, 212, 221, 222, 226,
396, 397, 400, 437
Quebec, 36, 172-178, 182
Quebec Act, 183
Quechua, 147
Querétaro, Franciscan college in, 121, 127,
128, 150
Quesada, Jimenez de, 142
Quetsalcoatl, 112
Quevedo, Juan de, 90, 133
Quilon, 251, 264
Quinte Bay, 181
Quito, 151
Quixos, 152

Rada, Martin de, 317
Raikes, Robert, 402, 413
Raleigh, 44
Ransom of captives, 404
Raphael, 410
Raritan Valley, 214
Rationalism, 23, 382
Ratio studiorum, 414
Rauch, Henry, 222
Realschulen, 412
Recollects (Franciscans), 23, 172, 173, 182
Redemptionists, 23

Reformation, Catholic, 15-17
Reformation, Protestant, 12-15
Reformed Church (Dutch), 194, 195, 214,
215
Reformed Church (German), 200-204, 211
Religion in Europe, effect of Christianity
upon, 374-384
Renaissance, 4, 11; and Protestantism, 436
Repartimientos, 92, 109
Republic, of Plato, 385
Retezi, Donna di, 149
Réunion, 245
Revealed religion, 382
Revivals, 216, 230
Revolution of 1688, 389
Rhode Island, 192, 193, 219
Rhode Island College, 190
Rhodes, Alexander of, 297
Ri, 362
Ricci, Matteo (Matthew), 339-342, 362
Richelieu, 385, 386, 392
Rio de Janeiro, 43, 161, 165, 236
Rio de la Plata, 153
Rio Grande, 126, 127, 128
Ripa, 358
Rites Controversy, in China, 349-355
Rites, Malabar, 269-271
Roanoke Island, 44
Roger, Michael, 339, 340
Rogerius, Abraham, 277
Romanæ sedis antistes, bull, 261
Roman Catholic missions, reasons for
greater prominence of as against Protest-
ant and Russian, 24-29; methods, 36-40;
decline in eighteenth century, 42
Roman Catholicism, gains at expense of
Protestantism, 31-33; revival in, in gen-
eral, 377; influenced by Protestantism,
438, 439; becomes a sect, 439
Roman Catholics, in New York, 195; in
Pennsylvania, 204; in Maryland, 205
Romanticism, 417
Rome, Jews in, 56, 57
Roti, 306
Rouen, Archbishop of, 174
Rousseau, 397, 413
Roxbury, 218
Royer de la Dauversière, Jerome de, 173
Ruggerius, Michael, 339, 340
Russia, Christianity in, 24, 443-446; politi-
cal effects of Christianity in, 391, 392;
effect of Christianity upon, 420-421
Russian missions among pagans, 66-70;
among Moslems, 76
Russian Orthodox Church, in China, 359;
in Siberia, 367-369; in Alaska, 370

Russians, and the Lapps, 66, 67
Ruthenian Uniates, 78

Sá, Men de, 163
Saco River, 178
Sacrifices, human, 119
Saint-Pierre, Charles Irénée de, 396, 400
Salazar, Domingo de, 310-312, 318
Salem, North Carolina, 211
Sales, Francis de, 17, 22, 381, 441
Salsette, 251, 256, 275
Salt, in baptism, 270
Salvatierra, Juan Maria, 124
Salzburgers, 212
Samoiedes, 66
San Antonio River, 127
San Carlos, College of, 155
San Diego, 128, 130
San Domingo, 108
Sandoval, Alfonso de, 98, 144
San Fernando, College of, 121, 127, 128
San Francisco, 130
Sangi Islands, 306
San Ignacio University, 319
San Jose, Francisco de, 149, 150
San Luis, seminary of at Quito, 151
Sannyasi, 260, 261
San Salvador, Congo, 243
San Salvador, island, 86
Sanskrit, 260, 275
Santa Cruz, 161
Santa Fé, Seminary of, in Goa, 274
Santa Maria de la Concepción, 86
Santa Marta, 142, 143
Santa Misericordia, 319
Santo Tomás, University of, 319
São Paulo, 163
São Salvador, 161, 162, 165
São Thomé, 243
Satsuma, 325
Sault Ste. Marie, 180
Savaria, Adrianus, 43
Scandinavia, 432
Scepticism, 382
Schall, Johann Adam, von Bell, 342-345, 362
Schenectady, 221
Schism, in Papacy, 7
Schlatter, Michael, 202
Schmidt, George, 246
Schultz, Stephan, 61
Schultze, 280
Schwartz, Christian Friedrich, 280
Schwenkfelders, 200, 202
Scientific approach, 416
Scotch-Irish, 204, 209

Scotland, religious life in eighteenth century, 379; and Presbyterianism, 435
Scottish Missionary Society, 50
Sebastian, St., 443
Secular clergy, in Spanish America, 100, 105, 106, 117; on the Rio Grande, 128; in New Granada, 142; in French America, 182; in India, 251, 274; in Philippines, 315, 316
Segura, 132
Selenginsk, 368
Seminaries, 17
Seminarium missionis Indicæ, 255
Sendai, 329
Senecas, 178, 179
Senegambia, 242
Separation of Church and state, 230
Sepúlveda, 96
Serampore, 281
Sergeant, John, 220
Serra, Junípero, 128-130
Seven Years' War, 169
Shah Jehan, 258
Shakespeare, William, 416
Shang Ch'uan, 338
Shanghai, 342, 346
Shang Ti, 341, 349, 352, 353
Shansi, 346, 358
Shantung, 344, 358
Shelekhov, 370
Shên-hsien-kang-chien, 364
Shensi, 346
Shigatse, 361
Shimabara Rebellion, 332, 333
Shinto, 326
Shun Chih, 343
Siam, 295, 298
Siau, 302
Siberia, 367-369
Sicily, 4
Sierra Gorda, 128
Sierra Leone, 242, 246
Sierra Madre, 121
Silk, 116
Sillery, 175, 177, 178
Sinaloa, 121, 122
Singhalese, 290
Sinodos, 104
Sioux, 180
Sisters of Charity, 404
Sisters of Christian Doctrine, 404
Skopsty, 446
Slavery, movement to abolish, 401. See also Indians, Negroes
Slavonic, 78

Société des Missions-Étrangères of Paris, 35, 36, 174, 181, 182; in India, 272; in Siam, 295; in Indo-China, 297-299; in China, 345, 348, 358

Society, effect of Christianity upon, in Europe, 398-403

Society for the Furtherance of the Gospel, 238

Society for Promoting Christian Knowledge, 48, 189, 210, 212, 279, 280, 402, 412

Society for Propagating Christian Knowledge (Scotch), 49, 220

Society for the Propagation of the Gospel in Foreign Parts, 49, 189, 193-196, 206, 208, 210, 211, 212, 224, 225, 233, 246, 279

Society for the Propagation of the Gospel in New England, 218-221

Society for the Promotion of the Knowledge of God among the Germans, 202

Society of Jesus. See Jesuits

Socinianism, 13

Socotra, 253

Solanus, Francis, 147, 148, 153

Solomon Islands, 310

Solor, 302

Somaschi, 19

Sonora, 121-123

Sotelo, 329

Sousa, Thomé de, 161

South America, Spanish, 136-156

South Carolina, 211, 224, 225

Spain, power of King over Church, 6; reform of the Church in, 21; and missions, 40, 41

Spangenberg, Augustus Gottlieb, 203, 223

Spaniards, in East Indies, 300-303; in the Philippines, 307-321; in Japan, 327-331

Spanish America, 83 ff.

Spener, Philip Jacob, 46, 60

Spenser, 416

Spice Islands, 4

Spiritual Exercises, 17

Spittle, in baptism, 270

Srinagar, 258

Standing Order, 188

State, influence of Christianity upon, 386-392

St. Augustine, Florida, 132

Stavropol, 369

St. Christopher, 184

Stephens, Thomas, 275

St. Eustatius, 235

St. Ignace, 180

Stiles, Ezra, 226

St. John of God, Order of, 100, 111

St. John River, 178

St. Kitts, 234

St. Lawrence River, 171

Stockbridge, 220

Stoddard, 215

Strawbridge, Robert, 206

St. Sophia, 71

St. Sulpice, Society of, 173

St. Thomas Christians. See Syrian Christians

St. Thomas, West Indies, 236

Student Volunteer Movement for Foreign Missions, 193

Stundists, 446

Stuyvesant, Peter, 194

St. Vincent, 235

Suarez, Francisco, 394

Suchanov, Cyril, 369

Sudan, 3

Sudras, 262, 280, 281

Sully, 396

Sulpicians, 23, 173, 181

Sulu Archipelago, 314

Sumitada, Omura, 325

Sunday Schools, 413

Supa, 301

Surgery, 116

Surinam, 236, 237

Synod of Philadelphia, 209

Syriam, 293

Syrian Christians in India, 3, 248, 263, 265

Sweden, Church of, 197

Swedes, and the Lapps, 64; in America, 196, 197, 222

Szechwan, 358

Széklers, 432

Tahiti, 314

Takayama, Justus, Ukon, 324

Talamanca, 135

Talaur, 306

Tamil, 260, 261, 275, 278, 280, 290, 291

Tampa Bay, 132

Tangier, 75

Tanjore, 261, 280

Taoism, 364

Tappan, Arthur and Benjamin, 194

Tarahumara, 131

Tarata, 151

Tarija, 150, 151

Tarma, 150

Tasso, 415

Taylor, Jeremy, 382

Tcheremis, 68

Telescopes, 5

Telugu, 260, 280

Tendai, 325
Tennent, Gilbert, 214
Tennent, William, Junior, 214
Tennent, William, Senior, 214, 215
Tepoztlán, 118
Ternate, 300, 302, 304
Terra de Guerra, 134
Terreros, Don Pedro de, 127
Tersteegen, 380
Teutonic peoples and Protestantism, 429, 430
Texas, 126-128
Theatines, 16, 18, 81, 263-265, 294, 302
Theologia Germanica, 9
Theology, 416
Theresa, 20, 21, 442
Thirteen Colonies, the, 49, 50, 186 ff.
Thirty Years' War, 14, 32, 395, 405, 431
Thomas, S., 224
Thompson, Thomas, 246
Thorpe, George, 44
Tibet, 360, 361
Tiburcio de Redin, 137
Tieffentaller, 275
T'ien, 341, 349, 352, 353
T'ien Chu, 352
Tiene, Gaetano di, 16
Tilaran, 135
Timaeus, 385
"Time of Trouble," 421
Timor, 302, 306
Tinnevelly, 280
Tipu Sultan, 271
Titian, 410
Tlatelulco, Colegio de Santa Cruz en, 116
Tlaxcala, 113
Tobago, 234
Tobolsk, 368, 369
Toju Nakae, 334
Tokugawa, 323-332
Tokyo, 329
Toledo, Francisco de, 148
Toleration, religious, 229, 230, 383; in China, 347
Tongking, 296-298
Torelli, Countess Louise of Guastalla, 19
Toribio Alfonso de Mogrovejo y Robles, 147
Torres, Tomas de, 154
Tournon, Charles Maillard de, 270, 271, 352-354
Tranquebar, 277-281
Transylvania, 432
Travancore, 254, 256
Trejo i Sanabria, Fernando de, 154
Tremellius, 59

Trent, Council of, 21, 380, 441
Trichinopoly, 280
Trincomalee, 287
Trinidad, 108, 137, 139, 140
Trinitarians, 250
Trondhjem, 65
Tryphon, 66
Tsaparang, 360, 361
Tsars, and the Church, 444
Tsinanfu, 344
Tucumán, 148, 150, 154
Tulasi Dasa, 276
Tulsi Das, 276
Tunguses, 369
Tunis, 75
Tunja, 142
Tunkers, 199
Turks, Ottoman, 3, 71, 72
Tuscarawas Valley, 223
Tuticorin, 256

Ucayali River, 149, 150
Ukraine, 78
Uniate Churches, 78-81
Unitas Fratrum. See Moravians
Urban VIII, 34
Ursulines, 19, 175, 272, 404
Utopia, 384, 385
Utrecht, Treaty of, 179

Vaca, Cabeza de, 97
Valdivia, 152
Valencia, 74
Valencia, Martín de, 110, 112
Valignani, Allessandro, 339, 340
Valverde, Vincente de, 145, 146
Vasco da Gama, 250
Vaz, Joseph, 274, 291, 292
Venezuela, 136-142
Venice, 6
Ventimiglia, Antonio, 302
Verbiest, 344, 345
Vicars apostolic, institution of, 38; in India, 267, 268; in Indo-China, 297; in China, 346, 347
Vicente, 285
Vicenza, 18
Vieira, Antonio, 164, 165
Villalobos, 309
Villalobos, Francisco, Marques de, 108
Villalpando, Luis de, 120
Villegagnon, 43, 236
Villemarie de Montreal, 173
Vincent de Paul, 23
Vinci, Leonardo da, 410
Vindiciae contra Tyrannos, 387

Virampatnam, 296
Virgin, 118, 119, 131; of Guadelupe, 118; image of, in Ceylon, 289
Virginia, 44, 190, 206-209, 223, 224
Vitoria, Francisco de, 90, 393, 394
Vives, 34
Vizcaino, 124
Voguls, 368
Volga, 68, 369
Volksschule, 412
Vologda, 67
Voltaire, 415
Voluntaryism, 230
Votyaks, 70

Walæus, 304
Waldensians, 195, 208
Waldo, Peter, 9, 11
Wang Yang-ming, 334
War, Christianity and, 392-398
Warwick, 192
Watts, Isaac, 380
Welsers, in Venezuela, 137
Weltz, Justinianus von, 46, 236
Wesley, Charles, 380, 409
Wesley, John, 48, 49, 212, 234; influence on politics, 390, 399; on social reform, 399
Wesley, Samuel, 409
Wesleyan revival, 14
Westen, Thomas von, 65
West Indies, 45; French, 169, 184; Protestantism in, 232-236
Westphalia, Peace of, 392, 394, 440
Wheelock, Eleazer, 220
Whitaker, Alexander, 207, 223, 224
Whitefield, 29, 49, 212, 213, 220
White Sea, 66
William and Mary College, 45, 224
Williams, Roger, 192, 217, 383
Wilmington, 196, 222
Windsor, Connecticut, 215
Winstanley, Gerard, 399
Wisconsin, 180

Witchcraft, 401
Wittenberg, 13
Wolfaria, 384
Wolsey, 385
Women, missionaries in Spanish America, 100; equality with men, 400
Woolman, John, 196, 226
Worship, public, 382
Wren, Christopher, 410
Wyoming Valley, 223

Xavier, Andrew, 343
Xavier, Francis, 22, 251-255, 274, 286, 301, 302, 323, 324, 338
Xavier, Jerome, 258
Ximenez de Cisneros, 20, 21, 73, 94
Xumilla, Mateo de, 146

Yajiro, 323, 324
Yakuts, 369
Yamaguchi, 324
Yarkand, 360
Yazoos, 181
Yedo, 329
Yenicheri, 71
Yoshishige, Otomo, 324
Young People's Society for Christian Endeavour, 193
Yucatan, 109, 120
Yung Chêng, 356, 357
Yünnan, 358

Zacatecas, Franciscan college in, 121, 127
Zambesi, 244
Zapotec Indians, 118
Zeisberger, David, 223
Zen Buddhism, 324, 326
Ziegenbalg, Bartholomäus, 278, 279
Ziegenhagen, 200
Zikawei, 342
Zinzendorf, Nicolaus Ludwig, 47, 61, 200, 203, 223, 236, 237
Zumárraga, 112, 113, 115-117
Zwingli, 13, 16, 436

EUROPE

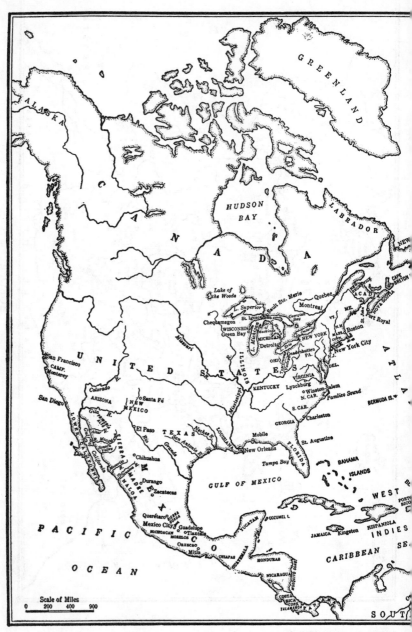

NORTH AND CENTRAL A

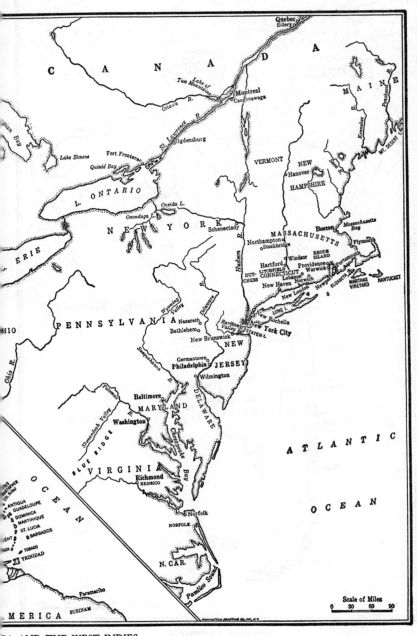

CA AND THE WEST INDIES

SOUTH AMERICA

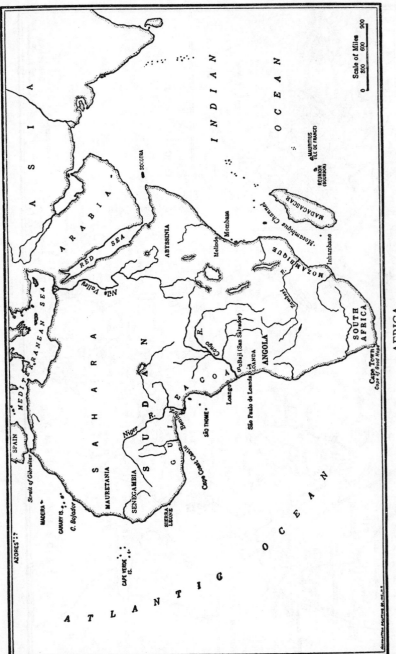

AFRICA

ASIA AND ADJACENT ISLANDS